12 FREE Gifts Inside Just For You

1. From Chains to Change Success Kit (Action Assignments) from Profit Attraction Coach, Ari Squires: Page 8
2. Forgive Yourself After Heartbreak (Video Course) from America's Forgiveness Coach, Stephanie McNeal-Brown: Page 21
3. Check Your Shame Meter (Assessment) from International Speaker, Lorna Blake: Page 32
4. Change Journey Travel Log (Online Workbook) from Life Coach, Edward E. Mosley Jr.: Page 41
5. Self-Mastery Workbook (Workbook) from Coach to High Achieving Women, Nicole S. Mason: Page 52
6. Five Minute Face Course (Video Training) from Beauty Educator, Shavon Dotson: Page 64
7. 4 Step Guide to Shampoo and Prep Natural Hair (Audio Course) from Natural Hair Educator, Alisha Davis: Page 74
8. Maximizing Independence for Quality of Life (Resource Guide) from Healthcare Professional, Ronita Boullt: Page 84
9. Daddy-Daughter Forgiveness (Audio Course) from Marriage Planner, Tameishia Pigford: Page 96
10. 7 Major Pursuit of Talent Pitfalls to Avoid (Resource Guide) from Talent Manager, Rondale Alexander: Page 106
11. Rewrite Your Story (Action Guide) from Self-Love Coach, Cathy Staton: Page 118
12. 11 Ways Youth Can Become Agents of Change (Resource Guide) from Police Officer, Sherrie Johnson: Page 126

Empowered by Ari Squires

NO MORE CHAINS – IT'S TIME FOR CHANGE

Copyright © 2018 by Ari Squires
All Rights Reserved.
Scripture quotations marked (NIV) are taken from the Holy Bible, New International Version®, NIV®. Copyright © 1973, 1978, 1984 by Biblica, Inc.™Used by permission of Zondervan. All rights reserved worldwide.
No part of this book may be reproduced or transmitted in any form or by any means, electronic or mechanical including photography, recording or any information storage and retrieval system without written permission from the author or publisher.

DISCLAIMER: The purpose of this book is to educate and entertain. The author and publisher shall have neither liability nor responsibility for anyone with respect to any loss or damage caused, directly or indirectly, by the information contained in this book.
We cannot and do not make results guarantees or give legal advice.
Cover Design: Visual Conceptionz Interior Design: SheEO Publishing
ISBN-13: 978-1732570757
ISBN-10: 1732570752

For general information or other products and services, contact Ari Squires at www.AriSquires.com, info@arisquires.com

Published in the United States by
SheEO Publishing Company
526 Wolfe Street
Suite 1
Fredericksburg, VA 22401
www.SheEOPublishing.com

Printed in the United States of America

Visit www.NoMoreChainsFilm.com
to watch these transformative stories come to life.
No More Chains: Succeeding Against the Odds – Available Now
No More Chains 2: It's Time for Change – January 1, 2019 Release
Contact Orders@SheEOPublishing.com to book a screening

Dedication

In memory of my mother and father, and to those very special people who are helping me empower minds and change lives.

Table of Contents

Acknowledgements	1
About the Visionary	3
Introduction - *Ari Squires*	5
Emotional Chains	
Fifty Percent of the Problem - *Stephanie McNeal-Brown*	11
Fatherless Daughter Breaks Chain of Shame - *Lorna Blake*	23
A Broken Man - *Edward E. Mosley Jr.*	33
You Were Born to Be Great - *Nicole S. Mason*	43
Mental Chains	
Mindset Over Matter - *Shavon Dotson*	55
A New Love Story - *Alisha Davis*	65
Environmental Change Leads to Mindshift Changes - *Ronita Boullt*	75
Generational Chains	
Daddy – Daughter Issues - *Tameishia Pigford*	87
Chasing a Ghost - *Rondale Alexander*	97
When Love Hurts - *Cathy Staton*	107
A Product of the Projects - *Sherrie Johnson*	119
Conclusion	
Action Step 1	127
Action Step 2	129
Action Step 3	130
Action Step 4	131
Action Step 5	132
It's Time for Change	134

Acknowledgments

I am deeply indebted to those individuals who over the centuries stood up for change. I am also indebted to black writers and film producers and directors who courageously share our stories to bring awareness to our history and reawaken the souls of black and brown people.

Director John Singleton encouraged me not to create with the hope that people will like it. Instead he taught me to create from the depths of my soul because that is where true art lives. His words brought new life to my creative process and have freed me from doubt, fear, and rejection.

I am a product of the great Harriet Tubman who reportedly said, "But I could have saved thousands if they knew they were slaves." These two champions have inspired me deeply.

I also want to thank and acknowledge several other people in my life who worked directly with me to make this book possible. First, this book could not have been completed without the loving support of my husband, Darryl Squires. I thank him for his support in many ways. He made this book possible by keeping my life calm, peaceful, and happy.

I thank each contributor for openly sharing their stories in humility. Without your willingness to release your own chains by sharing your past and present pains, we could not assist in freeing others from theirs.

I thank Cynthia Dixon for going above and beyond the call of duty as project manager for this book series. You were part of the first *No More Chains* book anthology, and you left a powerful impression. You will always be a part of this family. Your grace, faithfulness to me and the authors, and patience are worth more than gold. Your support was needed and greatly appreciated.

K.A. Tracy for your forgiveness and coming onboard to help me see this project through from beginning to the end with editing and professional guidance and support.

I want to thank my brother Darrin Dewitt Henson for his genuine love for me and support for this movement. Your words encourage me, and your passion for seeing growth in others propels me to keep on keeping on.

I want to acknowledge Louis Penn for the book covers and Sachi for the design. Your creativity was like magic to bring the vision to life.

A special thank you to my son, Amare Squires. You inspire me just by your presence alone in this process. You always pushed me when I didn't feel like being pushed.

A huge acknowledgment to my daughter, Avanti Squires, whose soul and spirit speaks peace. You are and will always be my breath of fresh air.

About the Visionary

Ari Squires is the founder of SheEO Publishing Company, an innovative and forward thinking publishing, design, and ghostwriting company committed to creating polished and rich content books, planners, and journals by dedicated editorial and creative design teams that bring great ideas and stories to life. SheEO Publishing Company teaches authors how to market and leverage their stories and expertise for life-long profits, media exposure, and success across all genres including educational, reference, fiction, devotionals, self-help, memoirs, and autobiographies. SheEO Publishing Company also offers its signature business PUSH Planner.

Ari coaches her clients to have their work seen well beyond their local reach into media outlets. Her premier clients have been booked for local and international television appearances on Trinity Broadcast Network, FOX News Channel, the Food Network, and other broadcast outlets as well as national publications reaching millions to promote their expertise and launch their businesses. Ari's clients have reached #1 bookselling success on Amazon, and their books are available in local bookstores throughout the country.

As an accomplished business mogul, author, speaker, film, and event producer, Ari found her literary voice by writing and speaking about her personal story and how ultimate success is simply a matter of releasing one's chains to see all the possibilities. Ari's audience and readers gain valuable insight on how to create winning habits while acquiring the tools needed to stand out. Celebrated as a change agent and master motivator with an awe-inspiring voice, Ari turned her mess into the No More Chains movement through her book *No More Chains: A Woman's Roadmap to Finding the Strength to Reclaim Her Destiny*. She also produced an inspirational documentary series, *No More Chains*. She has been featured on the *MadameNoire* webzine, the *Black Business Journal*, *Huffington Post,* Radio One and more, to showcase her passion for and expertise in business strategy, live event success, book leverage, and marketing.

Ari challenges aspiring and new authors to live their lives with purpose, bold action, and courage. She focuses on areas of personal development, mindset mastery, business coaching, heart-driven living, and success strategies and training. Ari's literary work gives her audiences with a sense of empowerment and leaves a call to action that encourages them to reach their full potential. She believes that everyone is equipped; people can do and become anything that they put their minds to. Success and money come with discipline and one decision: to live life on your own terms.

Ari is also the author of *All I See Is Possibility: Wisdom and Inspiration on Getting What YOU Want, The Mindset of a SheEO: Seven Core Principles of Creating and Sustaining Profitable Success as a Woman in Business,* and *The PUSH Planner: The Daily Strategic Business Planner Pushing Your Toward Success.*

Introduction

When I think about No More Chains and what this movement means to me, I think about when I was a slave to my chains, holding myself back from giving all I had to offer to this world because I did not believe in myself. When you are mentally stuck, lacking action when action is necessary, it manifests in becoming physically stuck. When I was mentally enslaved, naturally this "stuck-ness" created financial chains that stunted my growth and caused me to do things I had no business doing. As I vibrated at such low frequencies, my chains grew into emotional pain, and I found myself doing damage to myself and others. It took reading and educating myself—exactly what you're doing now—for the chains to fall off.

I learned that the effects of being mentally, physically, financially, and emotionally free would allow me to live the life of my dreams. I started to change the way I thought about myself and began to believe in my inner powers to take control of my life, take matters into my own hands, and realize that I was the one responsible for overcoming anything in my life. I realized the possibilities of me making a huge difference in my life and in the lives of other people. Releasing those chains and letting those strongholds go has led me to where I am now, which is mentally strong. There's nothing that I can't do! I am physically strong because I now take actions on every single thing that I know is going to make a difference in my life and others. I am financially stable, debt-free, and money just comes to me. I attract it.

I'm also emotionally stable now. I have emotional intelligence. I know when—and when not to—shut off my emotions. Being a witness to the effects of change is something that I want for everybody. It's my life's purpose. I believe it is possible for all of us to live a life with no chains, barriers, or limitations, and if we do have them, and they do come our way, it's important that we know how to overcome them and push through them. No matter what.

What I've discovered by working with people, by helping them develop and build businesses and write books and share their stories, I realize what holds us back. My friends, we are in our own way because we are stuck in our own stories. We are stuck in our fears or those childhood experiences that scared us. Or stuck in not having the right information.

I was raised by a Baptist mother who was raised by Baptist father who was raised by Baptist mother and father. For me I know their way of thinking was different from the way I saw the world as a child. I had to unlearn some things, so I could relearn what was right for me and felt good to me. In releasing my chains and stepping into my own power, I had to be okay with not being accepted by my peers—and possibly being ridiculed because of my differences—because I didn't follow the norm.

Even when it comes to my marriage, it is not typical. I don't have a marriage that most would subscribe to. Some people say that in order for a marriage to work it has to be a certain way, and that's not true. I feel like my marriage is the opposite of what they say a marriage is supposed to be, yet ours works for us.

Just because we're taught something as a child or we've been brought up to believe something, those handed-down beliefs do not necessarily have to be the same ones we carry in our personal journey. Those too are chains that we don't realize or want to believe or accept because we've been so programmed by society, the media, family, our upbringing, or in school that we forget we can question something if it doesn't feel right to our soul.

Generally, we are hesitant to do something different and don't appreciate the concept that we are the co-creators of our own lives. That doesn't take anything away from one's Creator; it just adds more substance to the decisions we make that help us better understand our power within, that help us break free from our self-prescribed chains, that help us change our lives.

Personally, I didn't get fully free until I released those chains of wanting to be accepted, following what society says is the norm. Because of that I no longer participate in holidays or celebrations that have historical socioeconomic and racial trauma to humans that I'm not comfortable with. I have vowed to dig deeper than the surface and get down to the *why?* My curiosity has caused me to do a lot of research to find out what was hidden from history textbooks. I notice that we as individuals are not questioning what's happening and why we make certain mistakes and decisions, and why we get in our own way. No, not anymore. It's time for change!

With the No More Chains movement, it is my hope that you see yourself in each of these individuals. Their stories are not going to be your stories, but they are definitely going to be similarities. In those similarities I want you to ask yourself: *How can I change too?*

I decided to do this series again because I felt that while the first series was phenomenal—we shared stories and people were inspired—we just scratched the surface of what we need to heal, collectively. So with this series we're digging deeper. We're giving you action steps on how to attract abundance to you, how to heal from your mental, emotional, and generational wounds so that whatever it looks like for you, you can release your chains.

Enjoy the stories, but please don't forget to take the steps. There's a huge difference between inspiration and aspiration. Inspiration is a feeling but doesn't do much. But aspiration can move mountains because when we aspire to do something, we make plans, set goals, and move! In order for you to change, you have to change. If you want to see change, you have to change. In order to see different results, you have to do things differently. That's what this movement is about.

Get ready to smile, laugh, cry, go down memory lane, and get angry because that's what it takes to get out of our own way, heal, and release the chains.

Ari Squires

**Please visit www.nomorechainssuccesskit.com
to receive your free No More Chains Success Kit**

To grow we must recognize the many faces of emotional chains and how they hold us back. The lethal misconception that something is wrong with us keeps us roaming in a trance of unworthiness, which saps joy, self-love and freedom right from under us.

~Ari Squires

Fifty Percent of the Problem

We were the picture-perfect family: Tall, dark, and handsome husband. Educated, powerful, petite wife. Four beautiful children—two boys, two girls—and a Chocolate Labrador retriever to boot.

Picture perfect: lacking in defects or flaws; ideal.

However, inside the home behind closed doors, it was another story. In some ways and on some days, life was good; things were perfect. But in other ways and on other days, it was a real-life horror show.

Five days a week things ran pretty smoothly, but, oh, the weekends. Most people live for the weekend. But for us, the atmosphere between my husband and me on weekends resembled a battleground in Afghanistan. Sadly, the children were the collateral damage.

It wasn't as if we were putting on a mask or being fake; we were doing what people do when there's no intervention: making due with the broken pieces. We were just surviving and doing the best we could in spite of the constant battlefield atmosphere. It seemed like we were in recovery five days a week and for two days a week, everything blew up.

I remember it just like it was yesterday. It was very early in our marriage, and we were in an argument regarding his beeper and suspicious numbers. It was very heated because this was not the first time I suspected improprieties. I was so angry that I grabbed his beeper and threw it across the neighbor's lawn.

He was so furious that he started grabbing the crystal, taking it outside, and dropping it on the sidewalk. All of my beautiful crystal was being destroyed, and he wouldn't stop. Out of desperation I called the cops. Still enraged, I picked up our biggest knife, held it in my hand, and demanded he tell me the truth.

After the cops came I told them exactly what had happened. He told his side. The cops approached me and to my surprise told me that since I was the aggressor, they had to take me in. There I was—my entrepreneur, beautiful, college-educated self from a good family—handcuffed in the backseat of a police car headed to jail!

It was surreal; I could not believe it.

After I was fingerprinted and booked, I was put in a holding cell and held overnight. Thankfully, my husband showed up the next morning, and I was released on my own recognizance. I was ordered to check in once a week. This went on for months then suddenly the charges were dropped, and I was free. But I was arrested two more times before I decided to do something about my rage. I finally submitted to God and got therapy.

My therapist was able to downgrade me from rage to anger because we change little by little. I stayed in the marriage despite the heartbreaking constant weekly dance of suspected infidelity, his denials, and me swallowing the lies.

And poof, twenty years had passed!

There was a husband trapped in a web of infidelity and a wife trapped in rage, strife, and discord. A husband who'd been beaten down and a wife who'd become bitter behind the destruction. Surprisingly, despite this crazy-making cycle, we both wanted the same thing, but we had no idea of how to achieve it. A happy, healthy, thriving marriage and family seemed impossible.

This story, however, is not about him. It is so tempting to make this issue all about him because that is what is expected in a cheating husband situation. No, I want to talk about something that is rarely talked about. Because in society, the cheated-on wife—the victim—is heralded and celebrated for her right to be angry. She is held in the highest regard for her bitterness because she is entitled to be that way. I was held in the utmost respect in my community because few knew of my secret rage and arrest record.

Even the Bible says in Proverbs 18:17 that the one who states his case first seems right until the other comes and examines him. I was continually stating my case to my friends and anyone else who would listen, and I would justify my actions with my anger, but no one was cross-examining me.

For those reasons I want to talk about the part that women play in the breakdown of their marriage. The 50 percent that no one talks about. And if you are a woman caught in the crossfire of infidelity, I want to tear down the victim in your story, so you can be victorious in your life. I want to shine the light of truth, so you can be healed.

I believe it is high time that you stop giving away your power to your husband and the people who have hurt you in your past. It's time for you to take responsibility for your part in the breakdown of your marriage because it takes two people to ruin a marriage.

You, my dear, may be 50 percent of the problem.

Take a moment and sit in that. Consider that you may have some responsibility in your relationship problems. You may not be so angry to go to jail; however, if you want to move forward with your life, if you want to be free, it is time for you to release the chains of anger, bitterness, and unforgiveness. And trust me; if I can do it, anyone can.

If I can break the chains of three generations of bitterness, you can too. When I made the decision to change my life, I became aware of things about my heritage that I had not noticed before. I took inventory of the relationship influences in my life. Did you know you can inherit more than money and possessions from your ancestors?

One of the first and primary influences in a girl's life is her mother. I evaluated my mother's life and relationship with my father. I surmised that although they loved each other and stayed married for forty-eight years until my father's death, my mother was bitter behind years of his infidelity.

Next I examined my grandmother's life. Same conclusion. She lived a life of bitterness and never recovered. I did not want my children to inherit bitterness, so I made a decision to do differently. I made a conscious choice to change my life and deal with my 50 percent.

As Dr. Phil says, I experienced *a changing day in my life* after attending the funeral of my college sweetheart. Afterward I had a conversation with my high school sweetheart. Those two occurrences were pivotal in my life and reminded me of who I am. It was a wake-up call from my former self to remember I am worthy of love. I realized how far I had fallen and allowed infidelity to change me.

I had gone from a confident, self-assured woman full of love, life, and light—I was voted most likely to succeed by my high school peers—to a shrunken, unsure, negative, complaining, town crier. Instead of taking responsibility for myself and my actions and setting boundaries, I was playing the victim in a major, debilitating way.

In the aftermath of infidelity, I'd strayed away from my sense of self. I realized that my life was not where I wanted it to be, and I was not the person I knew was trapped deep inside. I knew there was more and different for my life.

From the time I was a little girl, I always had a sense of something extraordinary inside me. I perceived greatness and importance emanating from deep within. I did not consciously hold it back, but it faded. I had allowed the cares of life to dissipate and dim my light.

In my quest for change, I conducted a painful evaluation of my life and how far I'd depreciated myself. I realized that if I did not address my self-defeat and bitterness, I'd continue to poison everything and everyone around me.

I sought God. I cried. I prayed. I mourned. I went to therapy, conferences, workshops, and Church. I went through programs and hired coaches. I read books. I listened to YouTube and podcasts. I changed my circle. I started to walk in my purpose. I discovered that the antidote for bitterness, hurt, anger, depression, and self-pity is a simple but complex solution: forgiveness.

It was time to stop licking my wounds and drowning in my continuous pity party. It was time to put on my big girl panties and live! It was time to go from heartbreak to the abundant, prosperous, and happy life that I knew was destined for and promised by God. Once I made that decision, I was able to bit-by-bit, piece-by-piece, pull myself out of that dark place. Because we change little by little.

You can make a decision too. Begin to take notice of what was is in your hands and all the broken pieces of your life puzzle. I believe that from all those shattered pieces, God can create a beautiful mosaic. Attain the energy and motivation to seek out the picture of what He wants to create. There is more for you and your life. I know for me, at times, the only motivation and strength I had to keep moving forward was faith.

At the time I had no consciousness of what was taking place, but as I reflected back it was crystal clear to me. Three things helped me heal and can work for you: a process, accountability, and community—or simply, PAC. All the components of PAC led to my transformation. I literally went from heartbreak to happy.

Now that I've received a deeper level of healing, I help women go from heartbreak to happy with my Passport to Freedom: Forgiveness Action Plan. You don't have to merely survive and live a life of misery! I say that because healing is a process, and there are levels of healing and forgiveness. But you do have to take the first step by deciding.

Just like many others I've paid a costly tuition for the knowledge I gained in my journey. It has cost some of us our marriages, delayed by years the fulfilling of our destinies, hurt some of us dearly financially, and resulted in lost opportunities and relationships.

But don't despair because you can gain much more than you've lost. You can gain a deep, amazing, and real relationship with God. You have the opportunity for teachable moments by being transparent and humble before your children. You can learn what true friendship is. And most importantly learn to accept yourself, flaws and all. All of this is priceless, and more is priceless!

Maybe your relationship is not currently in survival mode, but you sense a downward spiral, and you want to prevent it. Maybe you are in the middle of a crisis, and you want solutions. Maybe you want to ensure that your next relationship does not end the way the last one did. Or just maybe you want to cover your 50 percent. Whatever your goals, here are seven questions to help protect you from the dark hole of bitterness.

Do you recognize who you are and who you want to be? It is so surprising how many women enter relationships without really knowing who they are. Maybe it's not so much of a surprise because there is no class in school and few people are taught this in church.

And why not because to know and be known is one of our deepest desires. The few people that really know frequently arrive there via a crisis. Think about it; if you know who you are and are firm in your knowledge, you are unstoppable.

Do you take responsibility for yourself and your actions (or non-actions) in your relationship, or do you blame others for all your challenges? Creating boundaries and realizing that you are only and solely responsible for taking your power back is how you are able to reclaim your time and regain your dignity. You have to stand firm in your decisions in order to get your strength, confidence, and self-worth back. You have to own you!

What do you want in a relationship? Many times we grow up with a fantasy of what we want and how things are supposed to be. That can be a blessing and a curse. Of course we all have a type; however, you need to be mindful of what you want. As you live, learn, and grow so will your desires and choices.

Have you identified your boundaries? A boundary is a line that marks the limits of an area; a dividing line. Do you know what your limit is and what is off limits for you? Do you know where your responsibility starts and ends in a relationship? Do you have a tendency to get out of your lane? Do you allow others to get in your lane?

These are all boundary matters. Establish yours and live like you have.

What are your non-negotiables in a relationship? Are they on-point or unrealistic? If so, have you communicated them to your significant other? One of the key differentiators is your ability (or inability) to articulate, identify, and stick to your relationship non-negotiables. What are your non-negotiables?

Since relationship skills are rarely taught, most of us determine our partners simply by attraction and/or chemistry. It is a huge mistake for that to be the sole determinant. These attractions may not all be physical but can be materialistic and idealistic as well.

Are you willing and able to make responsible, hard choices if your boundaries and non-negotiables are crossed? By establishing boundaries and non-negotiables, it makes it easier to recognize a problem. Although in order to love a person rightly, you need to keep no records of wrongs; however, crossed boundaries and non-negotiables are measuring sticks. Otherwise, there could be disorder, perpetually hurt feelings, and worse—abuse.

Know your limits. Be able to decipher your needs and wants and your mate's needs and wants. If your boundaries and non-negotiables are compromised, learn to say no when you want to say yes. Stand firm.

Have you forgiven? This is the area where there is much confusion. People don't forgive for many reasons. Some are seemingly justifiable, and you may have a right to be unforgiving. However, you are hurting yourself and the people around you by living in unforgiveness. Sometimes the effects are subtle, and sometimes everyone and everything you come in contact knows: *She's bitter!*

You may have heard the saying: *Unforgiveness is like swallowing poison and expecting the other person to die.* It's so true! Your unforgiveness is a cancer, and it rots you from the inside out. It changes everything about you. Does any of this describe you? If so, is this what you want?

Forgiveness is a choice, and then the journey begins. That's the reason I developed Passport to Freedom: Forgiveness Action Plan because heartbreak-to-happy is a destination, and sometimes you need help along the journey. It's a marathon and not a sprint.

Few women fully realize the huge impact the ability to forgive can have on your happiness. Forgiving people tend to be happier, healthier, and more empathetic. On the other hand, the inability to forgive tends to make you into a woman who can't seem to stop plotting revenge or ruminating about how you've been wronged. Unforgiving people tend to be hateful, angry, and hostile, which also makes you anxious, depressed, and neurotic.

Do you want your personal and professional aspirations to reach their ultimate potential? It requires you to forgive and release yourself from anything and everything that consistently drags you down. It's not an easy task but a crucial one.

I want that for you and every living creature on the planet. Every dream that you have, I want it to come true. Every hurt, I want it healed. I want you to do and be and have everything you are destined to. Forgiveness, I believe, is the master key to unlock freedom.

It begins with you making a choice. Are you ready? Let's go!

About the Author

When a woman's partner is unfaithful, it's not uncommon for their entire life to unravel. Stephanie McNeal-Brown's passion and pleasure is to see women bounce back from this stressful experience, forgive everyone who hurt them, and live out their God-given purpose. She helps women go from heartbreak to happy after infidelity, so they ultimately have the power to live their best life.

Through her six-year forgiveness coaching journey, Stephanie discovered that it takes three things for a woman to recover from infidelity—process, accountability, and community—and a three-cord braid is not easily broken.

Her education and training include an MBA in marketing and certification in PREP, a science-based, empirically-tested method of teaching relationship education sponsored by the National Institutes of Health. Stephanie is also a licensed facilitator of Identity and Destiny, a step-by-step guide to help you find, know, and live your God-given purpose, and is certified to teach entrepreneurship to adults and children. She had previously served as a women's ministry leader and is a member of the Alpha Kappa Alpha sorority.

The mother of four—Leah, 14; Nyah, 15; Solomon, 17; and recent college graduate Harry, 23—Stephanie loves reading, writing, learning, and the adventure of travel. She is currently separated from her husband of twenty-three years and is a full-time caregiver to her mama living with Alzheimer's.

**Please visit www.forgiveyourselfafterheartbreak.com
to receive your free Forgive Yourself after Heart Break video course**

Fatherless Daughter Breaks Chain of Shame

"Mom, it's time for you to address this. Are you gonna let him do you like that? This man needs to take responsibility for his actions no matter what age he was at the time. If you don't do it, I will because it should have been addressed already. I'm going to get in touch with him and ask: *Did you have sex with my grandmother? If you did, then you're my mom's father and my grandfather.*"

And my heart ached for my twenty-one-year-old son having to feel like he needed to step in and do something to clear the air about a situation that was more than a half-century old.

It had been coming for years. After my mom's passing in 2006, I meant to do a DNA test. I got in touch with my uncle to ask if he would help me prove the man my mother said was my father—his brother—was in fact my father. He said he would.

He called me January 1, 2016, to wish me a Happy New Year and said: "You'd better do that thing quickly because I don't know how much longer I'm going to be around."

He passed suddenly almost a year later in early December 2016. I had never gotten the DNA test done.

My father's ex-wife has been in touch over the past five years to say she has a deep knowing that I am my father's child. She encouraged me to do a DNA test to prove it.

The last straw for me is my younger son getting involved. My sons deserve to know for sure who their grandfather is. I owe it to them, to myself, to the generations before and those to come to get this handled. When I dug deep to find out what was underneath the delay, you know what I found? Shame.

One of my mom's favorite sayings was: *Shame is not a load, but it could break your neck.* She would also back it up by saying: *There are some things that it's better to take to the grave with you than to talk about.*

I have an intuition that this heavy load of shame, while it didn't break her neck literally, it seeped into her bones over time causing cancer of the bone marrow resulting in her early death at sixty years old, leaving our family completely devastated from a void that can never be filled— I'm tearing up just writing about her.

I feel moved to change things. I am breaking the chain of family secrets and lies that hide scandalous things in place never to be resolved. I'm emphatically breaking the generational curse of shame that sits in bones, organs, and body parts creating disease and cutting lives short. I am breaking the chains of embarrassment and guilt that rob us of our power as I reclaim my freedom to stand as a beacon for others who want to break free.

I'm breaking the chain of shame and embarrassment locked in place for decades surrounding my paternity as if I had done something wrong to cause this. It's time to change this long-standing dysfunction that exists within families across cultural, ethnic, and socio-economic backgrounds where some people never take responsibility for their actions. It's time to change the way many families bury their heads in the sand ignoring what happened as if doing so makes it go away. I'm stepping up and inviting people to step forward and take responsibility for their actions regardless of how many decades later an incident occurred.

It's time to stop shrinking myself to fit this situation. It's time to stop playing small about it. I love Marianne Williamson's quote that I had on my website for eons:

"Your playing small does not serve the world. There is nothing enlightened about shrinking so that other people will not feel insecure around you. We are all meant to shine, as children do. We were born to make manifest the glory of God that is within us. It is not just in some of us; it is in everyone, and as we let our own light shine, we unconsciously give others permission to do the same. As we are liberated from our own fear, our presence automatically liberates others."

An ugly rift had developed between my mom and my mom's niece. My paternal uncle had endeared himself to the maternal side of my family and was long-time friends with Mom's niece. My uncle called her and said he was convinced he was my father.

Mom had been battling cancer. After it had come back full force and she was given a few months to live, her niece chastised her for not knowing who the father of her child was and for giving me the wrong brother's name when my father was someone else. My mother and her niece had a falling out which was never resolved before Mom's death because the one thing my mom couldn't stand was being shamed. Mom was disappointed in her relative, but the person she was most angry with was my paternal uncle. How could he spread such lies? And how could her relative take sides with a stranger over her aunt? How could this be happening to her when she had acted from integrity and done the right thing?

She had told me many times ever since my childhood that after she had become pregnant, she wrote a letter to my father telling him.

He responded, "Please say it's somebody else's. Say it's one of your cousins, anybody but me. I can't be part of this."

What she did was keep the pregnancy secret.

My maternal grandmother eventually found out and helped her through the pregnancy. I was lucky to have been born into my grandma's arms, but I came through with a broken heart, a defeated spirit, and a feeling of disappointment that I was somehow not good enough for my father to want me.

I wallowed in the shame of being illegitimate from as early as I could remember. Why did I have to be a bastard child who wasn't allowed to carry the name of her father because he was too young? I remembered feeling embarrassed to say who my father was when I was asked by strangers who saw my resemblance to my paternal relatives. I wanted to disappear. I used to hang my head in shame.

Many were the times when my maternal grandmother would tell me to hold my head high as if she was echoing Helen Keller, who said: "Never bend your head. Always hold it high. Look the world straight in the eye."

My mother said that shortly after I was born, my father's older brother approached her about adopted me, saying he wanted me to know him as my father. She told my uncle that she could not and would not say he was my father to protect his brother. Plus letting him adopt me didn't feel right to her. Mom said she would allow him to be involved as the uncle he is. And so my earliest and most vivid memories of having a connection to my father's family came through this uncle who stayed present in my life throughout my growing up and through many of my life events.

Having this shameful encounter with her niece and my uncle while she was ill made Mom vulnerable. She never allowed herself to cry about anything, yet she broke down and cried about it to me. I could tell she felt robbed of her dignity and integrity. I wanted to do something to resolve it. I knew there had to be a way. My mother came from an era when people had no way to prove their story. So they would pray and ask God that one day they would be vindicated.

I believe she is cheering me on from the other side to bring a resolution to this and to clear her name.

I'd had very minimal contact with my father until I arrived in Canada when I was nineteen. I had received an invitation from friends of the family to visit Canada. I had been feeling very unsafe because of the political turmoil and ongoing gun violence in the inner-city community where I lived in Jamaica. After arriving in Canada and staying with the family friends, I felt safe and wanted to make Canada my home.

I had been in touch with an immigration lawyer who explained that Canadian immigration laws would allow it if I had a close family member who was a permanent resident or citizen. I called my paternal uncle who was living in New York to let him know what I had found out. He suggested it should be fairly easy as my father was living in Canada. He shared the phone number to reach him.

When I reached my father at his office where he worked as a manager, I asked him if he would help me stay in Canada. He was hesitant and uncomfortable with my request. He said he would think about it, explaining that it would be best for me to get in touch with him at work only. He also said he couldn't invite me home as he had a wife and kids. I explained I wasn't looking for that kind of help. I wasn't even asking for money or a place to stay. What I needed was for him to fill out forms, go to the immigration office with me, and help me apply for my permanent resident status by acknowledging that he was my father.

It took repeated phone calls, weeks of frustrating moments, and months of convincing him. But he did show up with me at the immigration office when it mattered, to swear that he was my father. I remember it very well because I felt like a fly on the wall bearing witness to this.

It was extremely awkward and uncomfortable to be in the same room with him when the immigration officials asked him several times. "Are you saying you fathered this young woman when you were fourteen years old"?

And his response each time was, "Yes."

By the end of that appointment, I received my permanent resident status in Canada as if by magic. I remember shaking inside during that immigration appointment. When we got outside, it felt weird talking to him, yet I was extremely grateful. I thanked him profusely for his help in allowing me to stay in Canada. I was planning to send him a gift to express my thanks. He gave me the work address and told me to keep contact with him at his office only. I did exactly as he asked. And over the next several years I bumped into him a few times at church events.

It came as a complete shock to me when I found out that we shared the same faith and at the time he was a church leader.

That was many years ago now, and my uncle, my father's older brother, recently passed away. It felt awkward attending his funeral with all the other relatives including my father. It had been a couple of years since we had seen each other. When we said good-bye he promised to be in touch to have a meal together. He didn't keep his word which was nothing new.

I learned from one of my aunts that she recently had a conversation with my father, telling him: "It's time for you to own up that you are Lorna's father."

According to her, he's now saying he isn't my dad because his older brother took responsibility before he died.

I've called my father several times recently asking for his participation in a paternity DNA test, and he still has not said yes.

How am I taking this? Like a champion. This is what I tell myself, and I'm sharing it with you. No matter what circumstances you may have come from; no matter the pain you may have endured; no matter the shame, embarrassment, or humiliation you may have experienced, I am here to bear witness that you are nothing short of a miracle. You are not here by chance or by accident but by Divine design. Nothing about you is by accident even if the circumstances appear suspect. That was how you've chosen and were chosen to show up on the world stage in this lifetime, and the world needs you. The world needs your gift. The world needs you exactly as you are with your challenges, the pain of your past, and all that you bring to this life.

As I take a look at my life, I am who I am and can share my unique gifts with the world because of the pain I've endured. Who would I be without my story? Where would I be without the pain of my past? What would I be without the shameful, embarrassing, humiliating circumstances I have faced and continue to face but pushing through it all? These battle scars have been gifted to me to help me serve the world with dignity, humility, and a deep sense of empathy.

I'm someone who is now living my dreams after living my nightmares. I've been helping facilitate breakthroughs, empowerment, and transformation for other people for over fifteen years. I want to help you experience healing in your own life.

I've received tremendous benefit from Louise Hay's mirror exercise and have incorporated some of my own mantras and affirmations into it.

Magical Mirror Mantras

Get in front of a mirror and repeat this first thing in the morning and the last thing at night for ninety days.

To release shame

I no longer allow my past and the shame of my past to control me. I no longer allow the opinions of others to keep me playing small. I no longer allow my limiting thoughts to keep me in a box.

To release pain surrounding your birth, your paternity

I recognize that I am not the mistakes my parents made. I may have come into this world as a result of what seems to be accidental, but I am no accident. I am miraculous and phenomenal!

To play a bigger game in life

The very thing that has been keeping me playing small has been designed to raise me up bigger and more powerfully than I could ever imagine. Everything about me including my past is perfect for the work I am here to do on the planet.

To feel more confident

This is a new season, and it's got my name written on it.

Meditation to Release Pain of the Past

This meditation can provide a sense of peace and help you let go the pain of your past without struggle.

Sit in a comfortable position with your back fully supported, and allow yourself to feel your feet flat on the floor or ground. Close your eyes and take a couple deep breaths in. Slowly release the breath out. Feel the weight of your body being completely supported by the surface you're sitting on. Know that you are supported.

As you breathe in bring in wisdom, insight, and awareness. As you breathe out let go fear, worry, self-doubt. Once again breathe in and allow yourself to receive insight, new understanding, healing. As you breathe out release all distractions, stress, tension. Be fully present to this moment.

Become aware of the place in your body where you're feeling the pain/shame of your past. Notice where exactly in your body this shows up. Thank this pain for showing up so it can be released. Bring a blue light or whatever color you choose from the heavens or infinity into your crown and then direct this laser light to the exact place of your pain/shame and see/feel/sense the light dissolving this pain completely.

Observe the place where that pain was. Give thanks for its removal. Take a couple of more deep breaths and give thanks for the powerful being that you are. When you're ready, open your eyes and come back to the space/time/room where you are.

#

As someone who has gained tremendous help from counselors, coaches, and women's circles, I believe in the power of these resources to bring tremendous value to our lives. I'd like to make myself available to help you break through.

About the Author

Lorna Blake is an international speaker, award-winning author, leadership, and prosperity mindset coach, empowering thousands globally.

Please visit https://bit.ly/2MmGoUh to receive your Check Your Shame Meter

A Broken Man

Has something ever held you hostage so strongly you knew it was bad for you, but it was the answer to all of your problems? Well, meet my friend, Mr. Alcohol. He was the chain that held me in bondage for many years.

Things were finally starting to look good for me and the family. We had just purchased our dream home, I received some awesome news of being offered a government position, I was halfway done with my coursework for my PhD, and I was so happy to be retiring from the Marine Corps after twenty-one years of honorable service. And then it all started slipping away when we received the news that my mother-in-law had been diagnosed with cancer.

For years I dealt with all of my issues by using alcohol because it allowed me to forget about everything going crazy in my life.

My mother-in-law became so ill that we eventually had to find a caregiver for her during the day while we went to work. During that same time, Raquel told me she wasn't feeling well herself and was going to go to the doctor. I asked her if she was okay and she replied yes and that she would wait to schedule her appointment until later because she wanted to make sure that her mom was okay first before dealing with anything personal.

Not long after that conversation, my mother-in-law passed on March

13, 2010. In April Raquel finally went to the doctor, and the preliminary results were not good at all. She was diagnosed with a very aggressive type of cancer. The news just tore my heart completely apart. How was I supposed to tell our kids that they were losing their mom not even thirty days after their grandmother had died?

To deal with it I started drinking my problems away because I wasn't ready to accept everything that was about to happen. What was the purpose? Why was I being used, and what message was I supposed to receive from going through these horrible things all at once? I was a walking time bomb ready to explode, a broken man experiencing things that many people will never experience in their life—sudden deaths, financial stress, losing a job, and major alcohol issues. And I kept everything on the inside.

Raquel's doctor sent the biopsy off to the University of Maryland in Baltimore for analysis. After a week went by, the results came back, and we got the call to come in and discuss the results. We arrived at the doctor's office, and when he began to explain the results, my body and mind went weak as if I was outside of myself.

What do you mean she has appendix cancer? What is that?

I couldn't even move. I felt as heavy as concrete and shook my head in disbelief. I wondered how this could be happening not even a month after my mother-in-law passed away; how had this living, breathing disease showed his head in my house again?

As the doctor started rattling off the statistics I became breathless; there was only a 32 percent survival rate.

This cannot be happening.

I'm sitting there wondering what the hell this was all about. How do I bury a mother and a daughter in less than six months? We left the appointment in disbelief and returned home in complete silence, not uttering a word to each other because neither of us had the words to speak as we were both thinking about what the hell just happened.

Raquel started becoming sicker each day, and every time we went to the doctor something else was going wrong. Her feet were swollen, breathing problems, she couldn't retain any foods, collapsed lungs, unable to urinate, etc. These issues started happening so consistently that I started missing work and couldn't leave the house because of the amount of pain she was in.

I eventually got approval from my supervisor to telework so I could take care of my wife. Raquel's health diminished rapidly, and soon she couldn't even walk up and down the stairs at home. So I carried her up and down the same stairs just as I did my mother-in-law a few months before. As things progressed with Raquel, I slowly started to disengage from friends and started drinking more to avoid the reality of what was going on around me. I began to form another persona of myself that could handle everything; he smiled, he laughed, and he never cried because he couldn't show any weakness. He was like Superman.

I remember going to work one day, and it felt like I was not really present because I had so much on my mind, without any answers. When I finally gathered my thoughts enough to try and work, I got a call from Raquel's nurse saying my wife was in tremendous pain and should go to the emergency room. Speeding down the highway, I asked the Lord to heal my wife.

When we checked into the hospital, the doctor immediately informed me that Raquel's kidneys were failing, and they needed to admit her asap. During the time she was in the hospital, I started getting up at 4:00 a.m. so I could go to the hospital and spend a couple of hours with her before going back home to get the kids ready for school then head to work. I kept this routine up for about a month because it was the only way I could take care of everything and free my mind a little during the day. But I would drink to get through the tough nights and lonely moments.

One day we got a call from a doctor at the University of Maryland in Baltimore to ask if Raquel would consider heated intraperitoneal chemoperfusion (HIPEC), a procedure used to treat advanced abdominal cancers. We decided that we would try it. My wife was getting sicker by the day, and after several visits to the ER, it was time for her scheduled surgery and away we went to Baltimore. We checked in and completed all the paperwork for the surgery and were directed to the waiting room until they were ready to prep her for surgery. We talked, we prayed, we exchanged kisses, then they took her away for a fourteen-hour procedure.

Since she would be in surgery, I left to grab something to eat, take a shower, and maybe try to get some rest. But to my surprise I got a phone call about two hours later from the hospital saying that I needed to come back as soon as possible. When I arrived at her unit, the doctor was waiting for me. He explained that he had to stop the procedure because the cancer had spread throughout her body, and the only way that he could move forward would be to remove some of her major organs. I didn't understand. I thought the HIPEC procedure was a way to burn all the cancer away, so why would it not burn the cancer off her organs? Then he hit me with the most devastating news ever.

"Mr. Mosley, the problem is that the cancer has now penetrated her organs."

I was completely speechless.

Once Raquel was released from the hospital, we again drove home in almost complete silence, both thinking about our kids. How badly would the news hurt them, or would they even understand?

In the days that followed, her pain increased, and she required more visits to the ER. Trying to remain normal, we agreed that I would go to work as if nothing had happened. But as I was attending a class on October 7, 2010, my cell phone rang; it was the nurse at home. I walked out of the classroom to listen to the message that stated: I needed to come right away because Raquel wasn't responsive.

Again my heart dropped, and I raced home. I ran upstairs and found Raquel rapidly gasping for air, unresponsive. We immediately called 911 then I made some calls to ensure the kids had somewhere to go because I knew in my spirit that Raquel was leaving us that day. And she did.

As the days and months passed after Raquel's death, I withdrew and drank even more to take my pain away. The first holidays were the hardest for me and the family; we felt like we didn't have anything to celebrate. The kids asked wasn't Thanksgiving a time to give thanks and Christmas was a time for life and happiness?

So things were not going well at all. And with the loss of my wife's income, I had to make some hard decisions. And to make things worse, I had issues at work to deal with. Less than three months after burying my wife, I was terminated seven days before I would have concluded my one-year probationary period. Our new chief of staff told me that it was based on me not completing my work assignments during the time I was out from work caring for my dying wife. He further said that some important projects that were not accomplished were my fault.

I asked myself: *How can a man go from two incomes to one income to no income after being approved in writing to telework?* To top it off I started getting letters that my house was going into foreclosure.

My life was spiraling out of control. While I was trying to deal with my other issues, I received multiple DUIs within a two years' time. So now I am dealing with the DUI charges, lawyers, court fees, state requirements, and a host of other legal issues that included losing my security clearance. I was literally tired of my life; I didn't even have the energy or the will to get out of the deepening hole that I was sinking in day by day.

I remember my oldest daughter came and thanked me for not leaving; she told me that most men would have left and not cared. Those words from my daughter touched me in such a way and was a pivotal point in my life because I had just received my second DUI. At that moment I knew I was tired of all the lying and drinking. When the police asked me that night if I had been drinking, I simply replied yes and didn't even try to get out of the charges. It was time for me to change what I was doing to my family because I was all that they had. I needed to stop being selfish and change my thought process because I was about to lose everything that I loved so dearly.

Before my court date for the second DUI, I understood all the legal issues I was facing. Because it was my second offense within five years,

I was potentially looking at three to five years in prison. I prepared my family, had a guardian in place, and appeared in court. Then something happened that I had no control over: my lawyer found an error in the first DUI proceeding that violated a Supreme Court ruling and it was thrown out. So the second DUI became a firstoffense with a much shorter jail time. At that exact moment I knew my life was about to change.

I accepted the ruling from the judge, and he allowed me to report to jail after I had gotten my kids situated. Once I was placed in my cell, I chose my rack, and before I closed my eyes I noticed a cross had been drawn on the wall directly by my head. And I immediately felt the presence of God over me. By that point my drinking over the past several years had become out of control; I was about to lose everything I had worked so hard for. My parents had taught me better than that, and I shouldn't have allowed alcohol to take over my life. But drinking was my way to cope with stress and everything that was going on in my life.

I closed my eyes and started to silently cry because I knew that I was saved, and God's grace allowed me to change my way of thinking and my way of life. I knew at that exact moment that I was ready and committed to changing my life. I finally admitted that post-traumatic stress and the feeling of loss and loneliness had brought me to this point in my life. I stopped thinking of me and started thinking of everyone I had let down and hurt and what I needed to do in order to fix my situation. That's when I changed my way of thinking, and it has drastically changed my life.

In order to fix my thinking, I sat down and wrote my daily routine for about a week because I wanted to see exactly what I did and when my alcohol triggers were the highest. Once I knew what environment would cause me to desire alcohol, I was able to adjust that pattern. For instance, I knew that I desired a drink immediately after work because it had become a daily habit, so I decided to go get a smoothie immediately after work. It took about a month to change the habit.

I want to leave you with this thought: when you change your way of thinking, you will change your life forever. Everything that I went through had a reason, and the more I shared my story with others of how I made it through, the more it helped them to heal. I was able to make it through by my faith and by using some simple approaches I developed. I sat down one day and started writing a plan of action in regard to my life and was able to identify steps that allowed me to find myself, which helped me to develop my CHANGE model.

If you are ready and want to make a CHANGE in your life, I invite you to allow my company, Limitless Bounds, to support you. Even though my story may be different from yours, I'm sure you are struggling with difficult issues. You may have tried to change a bad habit, to stop drinking or being an abuser, but nothing is working. Or you may be having issues in school, a marriage, or relationships. By using my six-step CHANGE model, you'll be able to release the chain that is holding you back in order to live a happy, healthy life.

During my darkest moments when I was broken, sad, hurting, and I had no money to pay my bills after losing my job; I knew that my children needed me. They had already lost their mom and grandmother, so I needed to be strong and take care of my family. The song "My Testimony" by Marvin Sapp speaks directly to my brokenness because I made it. I didn't give up, and through my faith *I made it!*

About the Author

Edward E. Mosley Jr. is an author, inspirational speaker, life coach, change facilitator, and a Marine veteran with twenty-one years of faithful service. Having lost his wife in October 2010 to appendix cancer, Edward has developed a special approach for connecting with men of any age trying to excel in life while dealing with difficult issues of existence. He is a youth football coach, a volunteer with the Aspire mentoring program, and a guest speaker with the nonprofit Change in Action. Edward has a BA in business, an MS in human resource management and development, an MS in entrepreneurial management, and an MBA. He currently lives in Virginia and is the founder and chief executive officer of Limitless Bounds.

Please visit http://bit.ly/LBJourneyTravelLog to receive your Change Journey Travel Log

You Were Born to Be Great

"Nicky, you're not like the people you are hanging with."

Those were words that my grandmother spoke to me repeatedly throughout the course of my life. She would tell me about any person I introduced her to in a split second. Her words were always the same: *I can read a book by its cover any day!*

My response would always be the same: *Grandma, those are my friends. Everybody is not like you say they are.*

After many years and experiences, Grandma, you were right.

It is important for me to unpack this story in a way that will provide the depth of what my grandmother was trying to convey to me. I was an only child and an only grandchild. Although my parents were divorced, I was indeed a daddy's girl. Being an only child, I naturally wanted to connect with other kids. But that didn't always work out the way that I hoped it would.

I ran into lots of problems early on in life trying to get in where I didn't fit. Being an only child gave me ample opportunity to read and study more, so books became my siblings. This studious behavior only added to my problems because I was then placed in the talented and gifted class. As much as I tried to fit in and be average, it just didn't work. It would take me to almost lose my life to realize the truth of what my grandmother had been trying to tell me all those years.

I grew up assisting my grandmother with her business and was running it by the age of ten or so—ordering supplies, waiting on customers, counting the money, etc. I was my grandmother's trusted employee. Looking back, I can see clearly now that right from the start my life was set up differently from those I grew up with.

We didn't live in the community where my grandmother's business was located. She was one of two women business owners in the community. I could speak business lingo because I was exposed to business conversations and negotiations early on in life. Those unique experiences set me up for the greatness I would later embrace in my life, but I was hell-bent on hanging with average people and being accepted by them. It is amazing to have conversations with people who you grew up with and hear their perspective of you. Most of the time people see greatness in you before you see it in yourself.

When I became a teenager, I started dating hustlers. I was so naïve because I didn't even know what a hustler was. I shake my head at myself even as I type these words. So many people have walked this same road that I have been on, and it's my hope and desire that my story will cause some young person, particularly some young girl, to take a deep inventory of herself and understand that she is great and make a conscious decision to walk away from people and a lifestyle that is worlds apart from how she is being raised by parents and people who love her and have her best interests at heart. Young people, please listen to those that are in your life because everybody's story does not have a happy ending.

I continued to date hustlers for no other reason than the fact that everybody else was doing it. I don't think this was even a conscious decision as much as it was a subconscious decision because of the company I chose to keep. My grandmother was also correct in her assessment that birds of a feather flock together. It is true that we begin to pick up the habits and behaviors of those we choose to spend time with on a regular and consistent basis.

Going down that path led to being date-raped by the first hustler I decided to go out with. The funny thing is your mind can make you believe all sorts of things if you aren't careful. That is exactly why we all need wise people in our lives to guide and direct us. The reality of the situation really didn't hit me until many years later when I was in college and listening to someone else at a forum talk about being date-raped. I knew that the guy forced himself on me, but I somehow made it less of what it really was because I had agreed to go to his house. But that was how my thirteen-year-old mind processed the violation.

Sometimes it takes more than one event for people to become aware of who they really are. That is why we can't give up on people when they make mistakes consistently during their youth while trying to figure life out in a way that makes sense to them. However, there will come a time when ignoring signs and warnings lands you in big trouble. That is exactly what happened to me on June 7, 1992.

Yet again I was entertaining a hustler, knowing and understanding that we were living in two different worlds. I had graduated from college, was on my way to law school, and prided myself on being a college girl who knew how to navigate the hood in which she grew up in. Wrong thinking, wrong perspective, just wrong!

At approximately 2:00 a.m. in the morning on June 7, 1992, I was sitting in the car when two men walked up. As they approached, I looked out the rear window to see the barrel of a gun right before they opened fire, gunshots piercing the calm of the early morning. I later found out it was a hit on the guy I was with that night. Unfortunately, I just happened to be at the wrong place at the wrong time. Things certainly could have ended very differently for me, but God had another plan for my life!

As the bullets rang out, I started screaming and hollering the name of Jesus, and it felt like some force literally picked me up and pushed me down the street. I don't remember opening my driver's side car door. It felt like an out-of-body experience. When I came to myself, I was running down the lonely, dark street. There weren't any other cars in sight. No one was out there to help me as I ran for my life, still hearing the gunshots behind me. I never looked back to see if anyone was chasing me. I just kept running for as long as I could and as far as I could. That turned out to be only two blocks away from where my car was parked. The gunshots were still going when I suddenly began to feel like I had been shot. My heart was racing at an unbelievable speed, my legs got weak, and I could barely breathe.

I was walking alongside the front porches along the street feeling faint when I looked up and saw two people on their front porch. The only words I could get out were, "They shot him. They shot him."

They didn't ask me any questions. They just told me to come inside and lie down on the floor. I didn't get their names, but I provided a description to my mom. My stepsister verified the address and the description of the people who helped me that morning.

I told them I was trying to make it back to my stepsister's house, but

I just couldn't run any longer. The man called 911 and my stepsister, and the woman kept talking to me in a calm voice, assuring me that everything was going to be alright. In a matter of minutes, my stepsister was at their front door watching me come out of the house.

I desperately wanted to go back to the scene to let the police know that it was my car my friend and I had been sitting in. When the police and paramedics arrived, they didn't find me, but they found my purse in the car, the keys in the ignition, and one shoe on the floor in front of the driver's seat.

Everyone in the neighborhood knew that was my car, and someone called my mother to tell her that they didn't know if I was dead or not, but my car was shot up, and the guy in the car was dead. My mother never fully recovered from that telephone call, but that's another story for another time. That was a day that changed the very course of my life and the lives of those who loved me the most.

For many years after this life-altering event, which took place less than a month after I had graduated, my life seemed to be one big blur. What was once normal became foreign. The people I called friends were nowhere to be found. My grandmother was correct, and my life as I knew it was totally shut down! Soon thereafter, I found myself living on the run because I wasn't sure if the people who shot my friend were going to be looking for me.

I also wasn't sure whether my friend's family members were going to come looking for me, especially since he died in the car and I did not. I was faced with rumors that I set him up and that was the reason I didn't die. Of course that was a complete lie. I wouldn't know where to begin to have someone murdered. I was a law-abiding citizen with a dream in my heart to go to law school to help people who were victims of crime. This was indeed a huge twist of events in my life that I did not count on and was not prepared to handle.

I suffered a great deal emotionally, physically, and mentally. I couldn't sleep for months. I was barely eating, so I dropped a tremendous amount of weight. I couldn't concentrate, so my four-year-old son bore the brunt of that aspect of the ordeal the most. He and I had just walked across the stage together when I graduated from Howard University. Then he encountered and experienced a despondent, depressed, and detached mom. Everyone who loved me the most suffered too. When I did finally make it back to work, I would show up with my hair in shambles, looking disheveled, and feeling lost and uncertain. Detectives were coming to my job and my home trying to speak with me. I was mentally exhausted, embarrassed, and just downright in shock. It took me years to get my life back on track.

I was a witness at the murder trial. I knew the person who was arrested for my friend's murder. We all grew up in the same neighborhood—sort of. Even though we didn't live where my grandmother's business was located, since I spent most of my time there I considered myself from that particular neighborhood. Wrong thinking, wrong perspective, just wrong!

It was apparent that I was not considered a member of the neighborhood, at least from my vantage point, since the perpetrators chose to shoot my car up. It would be one year and several months before the prosecution was ready to bring the case against the perpetrator. They only apprehended one shooter. During that time, I was the recipient of a scholarship to a paralegal program. My dreams of starting law school were shattered, so I had to do a slow climb back to the point of applying again. As I look on it now, the fact that I was rejected nine times before being admitted was God's grace, because I wasn't mentally stable enough to focus on a rigorous law school program, trying to raise my son, and trying to put the pieces of my life back together.

While attending the paralegal program, I met an attorney teaching one of the courses. I asked her if I could serve as her intern, and she said yes. We were working at the courthouse one day, and I noticed a family member of my murdered friend. I hadn't told the attorney about what was going on in my life, so I did not want the cousin embarrassing me in front of my teacher and the many people in the courthouse that day.

So as the cousin was walking towards me, I am literally spilling my guts about everything that had transpired in my life the previous year. The attorney was overwhelmed and so was I. By the time the cousin was close enough to speak to me, my teacher and I were both looking shell shocked. The cousin smiled widely and told me how glad she was that I was alive and fine and doing okay. Her words left me speechless and weak at the knees because my adrenaline was preparing for a battle. She hugged me and walked away. I had to run to the restroom because I could not stop the torrential rain of tears flowing down my face. I wept and wept in the bathroom until I felt like there wasn't any water left inside of me.

After I gathered myself my teacher and I were able to discuss the matter. I told her that I was scheduled to go before the grand jury the next day.

It's Time for Change

She immediately offered to serve as my lawyer. She represented me without a fee. I had not even thought about retaining counsel because in my twenty-three-year-old mind I wasn't guilty, and I hadn't done anything wrong.

Again, wrong thinking, wrong perspective, just wrong.

You never go to court without representation! I went through the grand jury proceeding, which was very stressful for me. The prosecution indicted the perpetrator. The day the trial was scheduled to start, he pled guilty. This meant that I would not have to offer my testimony again. The stress of the grand jury proceeding was enough for me!

As the years went by, I slowly put my life back together. I gave my heart to the Lord. I began serving in my local church. I eventually was accepted into law school on the tenth time that I applied. I passed the bar exam and became a practicing attorney. I accepted my call to preach. I started a ministry to empower and encourage women. I started a business. I have written books. I have traveled internationally to preach and conduct leadership training.

The perpetrator served his time in prison. Nineteen years later, I saw him at my youngest son's school. His sons attended the same school unbeknownst to me. When he saw me, he made a quick move toward me, and I wasn't sure what to do. I guess he could see the look on my face because before he got very close, he started apologizing to me. He said that he wanted to ask my forgiveness for what he did that fateful morning that our paths had crossed. He explained that he took advantage that I happened to be there that morning with my friend in the car, vulnerable to attack.

You see, when there is greatness in your life, God will do whatever is necessary to ensure that you accomplish what you were sent to the earth to do. A few years after that life-altering event, my mom shared with me that she went back to the house of the people who helped me that morning. She wanted to say thank you. The person who answered the door told my mom that no one by those descriptions ever lived there. Well, those people were angels assigned to my life. I am sure of it, and no one can make me doubt it.

Your greatness will cause miracles to happen in your life to get you to the place that you were destined to be from the beginning. You were born to be great; show up great!

About the Author

Nicole S. Mason is known as the leader's leader and is sought after for her wise counsel and effective leadership strategies. She serves as coach and confidante to high-achieving women in the marketplace and in ministry. Aligning her leadership acumen and her faith creates a powerful combination for those who retain Nicole to help them to make strategic decisions and power moves.

Nicole is a licensed attorney in the State of Maryland and is the founder and chief executive officer of Strategies for Success, a speaking and leadership coaching company. In this capacity she works with female leaders and executives to pull out what is already inside of them through the powerful practice of coaching and speaks professionally on the topics of confidence, how to show up great, and the power of you, to name a few.

She is also the host of her own radio program, the *Nicole Mason Show,* on the Radio One Network that can be heard around the world. The show highlights powerful women sharing their stories of trials to triumph as encouragement to other women that trouble really does not last.

Nicole has also served on nonprofit boards and has been the recipient of many awards for her ground-breaking and trailblazing work as the only female African-American leader to serve in her position in the organization where she is currently employed. She has been featured in numerous magazines and newspapers and on more than twelve media outlets. Nicole serves as an ambassador for the American Heart Association, bringing awareness to heart disease and its impact on women. She is an example to women that you can do whatever you set your mind to do. Nicole is a natural-born encourager, and if ever in her presence, you will definitely feel the impact of her encouraging spirit!

**Please visit www.selfmasterywithnicole.com
to receive your Self-Mastery Workbook**

You start living the moment you decide your life is your own with no apologies or excuses. No one to lean on, rely on, or blame. The gift is yours to make up your mind and decide that you are responsible for the quality of your life. This is when you break the chains to become free. Many of us are just one decision away from the most amazing journey of our lives.

~Ari Squires

Mindset Over Matter

At a very young age, I knew that the world was much bigger than my hometown, Milwaukee, WI. Even though I grew up in a very rough neighborhood, one where dreams often died with the dreamer on those cold, mean inner-city streets, I knew that I had to find a way out; both my dreams and my life depended on it.

Have you ever wondered *Why me?* especially when it seems like one thing after another, with no end in sight to the pain, the suffering, the depression, and the guilt? I've asked God the *why me?* question more times than I care to share, and if I'm honest, there was one point in my life where I just figured I was paying for every bad word, action, or thought that had ever entered my mind. I grew up in a household where the Holy Bible was the law, and for years my religion told me that when God was angry with me, He would take out His wrath on me, so I just chalked up my circumstances to a God who was in constant fury with me.

As a little girl, whenever I would do something bad, I would get my mind set and prepped for the bad thing that was going to inevitably happen to me as a result of my disobedience. That mindset plagued my life for years, and it wasn't until my thirties that I was able to break the chain that bound me to believe I would always be a product of my circumstance, that I did not have the power to change the path that my life was going down.

When chains are broken and mindsets are changed, you start to realize that the sky really is the limit for what you can do, the life you can live, and the impact that you can have on this world. Now that I'm able to look back over the things that bound me and almost broke me, I understand that it wasn't God taking out His wrath on me; instead, I was making deliberate choices to keep myself in the sunken place. The shift for me happened when I decided to stop living my life according to what others believed I could or should be, and I started to believe that my dreams were simply goals waiting to be accomplished.

Born and raised on the northside of Milwaukee, Wisconsin—yes, there are black people in Wisconsin—I grew up believing that gun violence, drugs, and poverty were normal since that was my reality every day. As the youngest of five children, I always felt like a unicorn in my family; I never quite felt like I fit all the way. I was the ugly duckling, the one with the smartest mouth, and the one with the biggest dreams. Growing up, I didn't quite realize that we were living in poverty because I had never met anyone who was living above and beyond how we were living. It was common to see street corner drug deals, police raids of the neighbors' homes, and RIP T-shirts adorned with the faces of the latest victims of gun violence plastered on them.

My first real understanding of death happened when I learned that my eleven-year-old next-door neighbor was gunned down by a stray bullet in a drive-by shooting. It was a shock to my system because my young mind couldn't comprehend how someone my age and so innocent could be gone so tragically.

Unfortunately, that wasn't the last time I would have to cope with a violent death. It became so common that it was numbing; it became just another T-shirt to rock—well, until it happened on my front porch. Watching my eldest brother laying on our front porch desperately and unsuccessfully trying to hold onto life was the final straw for me. I couldn't numb that pain. It wasn't fair, and I wondered what bad thing my family had done to receive such wrath from God.

That was the moment I knew God was watching, and He wasn't pleased, so I vowed to get my life together and do whatever was necessary to stay in His good graces. I turned my life around. I was going to church faithfully, praying every chance I had, and working hard to keep temptation away. And being a freshman in college, there was temptation surrounding me daily. My method worked for a while, at least until I ended up eighteen years old and pregnant six months after my brother had died.

I knew that God was punishing me for *one* reckless night I had. For a fleeting moment I thought I had made it. There I was, a black girl from the inner-city of Milwaukee, attending one of the best universities Wisconsin had to offer—for free. But it was clear to me that it wasn't in the cards for me to get away from the 'hood. I had a victimization mindset at the time, and I was blaming everything around me for the things happening to me.

I spent the remainder of that summer packing up my belongings and saying my goodbyes to the city that had given me my first dose of adulthood. During my last night on campus, I took a long walk on the silent streets of Madison. I kept trying to convince myself that leaving the university and moving back home was for the better. Although the argument was compelling in my head, my heart wasn't so convinced. I hated home and everything that it stood for. I felt like I was settling for second best when I had a chance to experience the absolute best.

Once again I figured God must have been mad at me. I knew that I would go home and work some second-rate job, go to a second-rate school, and live a second-rate life. I was better than that—at least I thought I was. I had no one to help guide me in making the best decision for my life. My family had convinced me that moving back home would allow them to support me more, and I needed all the support that I could get. So I guessed it just made logical sense. I went home and hoping to relieve some of the anxiety I was experiencing, I picked up my pen and allowed my heart to guide me.

Dear daughter,

It's going to be just you and me from here on out, and that's okay. You've made me realize that I am worth so much more than I've been settling for. Yes, I'm eighteen, a college dropout, and pregnant, but I refuse to feel ashamed anymore. I'm ready to step into my greatness because now I understand that my greatness is tied to your future.

Love always,

Mommy

Maybe it was the breakthrough I needed, and with a newfound sense of purpose, things were about to get better. I was no longer living just for me, and I knew that every decision I ever made needed to be done for the sake of my unborn child. My mother told me that my life was not my own anymore, that I needed to grow up and be the mother this little girl deserved. I internalized those words and lived by them.

I went back to Milwaukee with more than just purpose; I went back with a plan. I lived at home with my parents until my daughter was seven months old. Determined that I would not let her grow up the same way I did, we packed up the few items I owned, and I went back to college. It was hard but not impossible. I slept when I could, studied while she was in daycare, gave up everything that made college fun, and dedicated myself to finishing school within the next four years so I could make something of myself for my daughter.

I finally got it right, and in December 2007 I walked across the stage with my three-year-old by my side and received my degree. I believed the hard part was finally over, and I was ready to step into the good job I knew would finally come since I had done right by my daughter, beat the odds, and got that degree.

Three years later I was working for a little more than minimum wage, on welfare, and on the brink of eviction for the millionth time. My depression had gotten the best of me, my insomnia was at an all-time high, and I was fresh out of motivation.

After living my life the right way—being the good mother and sacrificing it all for the sake of my daughter—I was ready to give up. I was spending my nights sitting in the bathroom on the floor, crying in the dark. I couldn't let my daughter see how broken her mother was and how much of a failure I had turned out to be. I was tired of hearing what mothers are supposed to do and how much mothers are supposed to sacrifice for their kids. I was all out of energy to give; motherhood was literally sucking the life out of me.

It was the moment I found myself contemplating the value of my own existence and realized that I was over trying to fit into everyone's perfect idea of what I should be. I was fed up with believing that God was constantly punishing me for my transgressions. I was tired of finding myself broke and almost evicted month after month. I had finally gotten to the point where I said: *I quit trying to be the perfect daughter, the perfect mother, the perfect idea of success.* It wasn't working, so I was ready to try a new mindset. The moment I decided that I no longer wanted to live my life afraid of disappointing my parents, my daughter, and God, is when I finally found the freedom I had been searching for my whole life.

I was tired of being bound to the mindset telling me to give more of myself to everyone other than me. I was ready to start discovering my own truth and figure out what my purpose really was because it had to be more than just being a mother. I stepped out on faith in a major way and quit my minimum wage job, moved to one of the most expensive places in America, and prayed that interviews turned into steady employment.

I always had an affinity for makeup; it was my therapy when I was battling depression. With a $100 investment, I decided to launch my own beauty career as a freelance makeup artist. I didn't know the first thing about running a business, but it didn't matter. It was something that was in my heart ever since my first makeup job at the Chanel counter when I was in college, and I was ready to turn this hobby into a hustle.

I was finally doing the things that served me, and it scared me, but I didn't care. I was a businessowner, something that no one else in my family could say, and I was proud but not because I was the first to do it. No; I was proud because it was the first step in building a new legacy.

Determined to overcome fear and self-doubt, I took the little money I had and invested it back into my business every chance I got. I invested in business coaches, personal development mentors, makeup workshops, beauty books, classes, and webinars. In an industry full of beauty professionals, I was determined to figure out my niche—the one thing that could help me stand out—and serve the clientele I really wanted to serve.

While I loved makeup and providing beauty services to my clients, I also knew there was a higher calling to my life. I knew there was a way I could take my pain, hurt, depression, anxiety, tribulations, and triumphs to impact the masses. I began to focus on teaching my clients the importance of taking time for themselves. I knew that there were women out there who were facing some of the same struggles I had once faced: giving too much of myself to others and never taking time to maintain myself. I began sharing my mediation tips, my podcast suggestions, my book list, and my fifteen-minute beauty routine with anyone who was willing to listen.

On this journey to being my best self, I've learned that the mind is one of the most powerful tools a person can have. Your thoughts turn into actions, decisions that are responsible for growth or your demise. Everything starts with just a thought. If you think you don't have enough time, then you will never have enough time. If you believe that you have no value, then others won't believe you have value either.

I've determined that my goal in this life is to educate, empower, and inspire women, and through my business I help women heal from their past hurt and traumas by teaching them how to tap into their full feminine power and live their best life through daily self-care and self-love. It's time to stop putting everyone else first and to stop trying to fit into other people's expectations of what your life should look like. Own your power, your creativity, your uniqueness, and your dreams. Someone else's breakthrough is tied to freedom. If you're unsure of where to start, use these three tips to help start releasing your own chains that are holding you down

Protect your energy and your space. For you to really start shifting your mindset, you will need to learn how to protect your energy and the thoughts that you allow yourself to think. Start to monitor the content you are consuming because that content will influence how you think and how you feel.

This may sound simple and petty, but one of the first things I cut out of my life was anyone's social media pages that made me feel horrible about myself. That change had nothing to do with those people, but it had everything to do with where my mind went when I would run across those social media pages. I cut out the content that was leading me to compare my life with theirs. I started to only tap into social media pages that were empowering, uplifting, connecting, and encouraging. That minor change made an enormous difference in my life.

Take time for yourself every morning. I truly believe that if you look good, you will feel good and vice versa. I believe in starting every morning with a morning meditation or morning mantra while I spend fifteen minutes implementing my beauty routine. Even on days when I may not have fifteen full minutes, I spend at least five minutes affirming my beauty, my intelligence, my worth, and my goals as I take the time to practice some self-maintenance. I love to show up fully for myself every day, and that means making sure that I put my game face on every day. A little concealer and some lip gloss makes a world of difference to my confidence.

Start small and celebrate your wins. Set goals for yourself daily, and remember to celebrate the progress you've made towards those goals. If you have a goal to spend fifteen minutes on your beauty routine in the morning but could only carve out five minutes, celebrate that you took five minutes for yourself today. We get so caught up in winning the war that we forget to celebrate the little battles we overcome daily.

Start your business, write your book, take that trip, and remember to congratulate yourself every time you get one step closer to those goals. Don't focus on how long it takes you to get to the goal; be proud of yourself for being willing to work towards it.

About the Author

Shavon Dotson is a professional makeup artist and beauty educator who specializes in creating a natural beauty look by focusing on glowing skin that doesn't feel heavy or greasy. She believes in the healing power of makeup and the power of touch. She uses her talents to create a serene and calming environment for her clients that allows them to get into a positive space, so they feel like they can conquer the world. But makeup isn't all she's made of; she's always had a passion for empowering and inspiring women through her beauty education courses.

Shavon combines her love for makeup and her expertise in program development to create content with tangible outcomes customized to fit the need of the client. Through her understanding of the importance of both mindset and skill set in her business, she has been working tirelessly at creating the life of her dreams and is dedicated to educating, empowering, and inspiring other women to do the same.

**Please visit http://bit.ly/fiveminutebeauty
to receive your Five Minute Face course**

A New Love Story

Every adversity is a blessing in disguise, provided it teaches some lesson we would not have learned without it.
— *Napoleon Hill*

I grew up in Little Rock, Arkansas. My life started out as what some might seem a fairytale because in the black community at that time there weren't too many homes where both parents were college graduates. My parents, like those of many of my friends, were married and worked together to raise their children. I had two sisters, and we lived in a lovely home.

Then things started to unravel.

When I was an adolescent, I noticed my parents' idyllic relationship developing cracks. They started having disagreements, which advanced to arguments. Soon they were shouting at each other, and our household became full of tension. As the eldest I used to comfort my two sisters although I was just as upset as they were at the sound of our parents' raised voices.

Eventually my mom decided she couldn't take it anymore, and she left—by herself. Even nowadays it's not too often that fathers get custody of their kids, but back then it was really rare. In a reversal of the usual situation, it was my mom who paid child support to my dad and he who made all the decisions regarding our day-to-day lives: what clothes we wore, what movies we got to see, etc. Although Mama didn't live far away, we rarely got to visit her; it was as if she'd lost interest in us.

At twelve years old—my sisters were just eight and six when Mama left us—it was hard to cope with not having her around. I'll never forget the day my period started, and I had to tell my daddy. It was embarrassing for both of us. My daddy loved us in his own way, and he provided for us. But he wasn't an affectionate man and didn't give the hugs and kisses I craved.

Starved for both attention and affection, I started acting out. My grades dropped, and I got into fights at school, especially whenever I heard somebody talking about my mama having left us. At that point in my life, I just didn't care about anything. My sisters had a hard time too. Nobody likes being the odd man out, and *everybody* had a mama—everybody except us.

My uncaring attitude wasn't helped by my heavy workload. Daddy needed help keeping the house and us looking nice, and as the eldest sibling it fell on me to help with cooking, cleaning, laundry, even braiding my sisters' hair. I resented the work I had to do and sometimes lost my patience with them.

Eventually we adapted to the absence of our mother, at least on the outside. But inside all three of us were angry at her for leaving us. Maybe it wouldn't have been such a big deal if we'd been boys, but as girls we really needed her. My dad, perhaps recognizing our need for feminine influence, began seeing another woman and married her shortly after the divorce came through. My stepmother was a good woman who took over running the household and made life more pleasant for us, but having a mother figure in the house isn't necessarily a substitute for a mother's love—at least for me it wasn't.

Being younger, my sisters listened to our stepmother better than I did. I never stopped longing for my mother's attention, and I decided that when I turned eighteen, I would seek her out and try to build a relationship with her. It took me many years to forgive her for not being there emotionally through my teenage years when like most girls, I had worries and doubts about my appearance and my attractiveness to boys. Eventually I did forgive her, and I was able to get my sisters to do the same.

Once I had children of my own, I was determined to always be there for them. I understand that kids don't come with instruction manuals; parents have to use their best judgment. I always felt my mother made a serious mistake by leaving us behind, but I came to the conclusion that just because I didn't understand my parents' behavior doesn't mean I love them any less. I also felt that I would learn from their mistakes and be a better parent to my own children.

Eventually I took control of my emotions and got my life back on track and not a moment too soon because major challenges lay ahead. I went to a trade school and studied cosmetology, but during my last few months there, I began losing my hearing, a terrifying experience for a twenty-one-year-old. Then just before cosmetology graduation I learned I was pregnant.

Right before graduation my best friend and I shared an apartment in a rental property my father and stepmother owned. In a crazy coincidence she got pregnant about the same time I did. I kept my pregnancy secret as long as I could, but eventually my father found out and evicted us. My best friend moved back in with her parents, but my father wouldn't let me do that; he said I was a bad influence on my sisters. I moved in with my baby's father, but after we fell behind on the rent, we got evicted. After graduating cosmetology school, my boyfriend's hours got cut from full- to part-time, we didn't have much money. We ended up moving in with his family.

My hearing was getting worse, and after my baby was born, I became completely deaf in both ears due to otosclerosis, a condition where bone grows in the inner ear. Fortunately, Arkansas Rehabilitation paid for the surgery on one of my ears, so I only wear one hearing aid instead of two.

I once read that the ears are our intake valves. The sounds they absorb feed our minds and can be converted into creative power. We learn nothing from talking, but there is no limit to what we can learn by listening. I thank God for allowing me to go through this challenge at such an early age because it gave me the awareness to keep my mouth closed and be a better listener.

You can't respond to negativity if you can't hear it. Not being able to hear rumors and gossip freed me up to concentrate on being the best person I could be. A hearing loss, at least to me, is not as devastating as the loss of eyesight or a limb. With my hearing aid I'm able to be fully functional and don't consider myself disabled.

Losing my hearing is just another example of some things being out of my control. Those who learn to adapt to life's curveballs are the ones who will succeed. Living with hearing loss has both challenges and advantages. And that is pretty much how life is. You always want to find the advantages in any situation and focus on the positive side of the issue, and most of the time the negative will reverse itself. Don't let your disadvantages control the way you want your story to end.

Your only limitation is the one which you set up in your own mind.

— Napoleon Hill

Looking back on my younger adulthood, I spent a lot of time being angry, and I made some terrible decisions. In hindsight I believe there's a direct correlation between the two. I was angry about blossoming into womanhood. I was angry about my father's lack of affection and his refusal to let me come home when I was in trouble. I allowed my anger at my mother to prevent me from fully accepting the love my stepmother offered me. And I was angry about suffering hearing loss at such a young age. I believe that I made the subconscious decision to just let life happen and not do anything to steer it in a positive direction.

I married my children's father after our second child was born, knowing he was hooked on drugs and alcohol. Now I see the futility in trying to improve the life of someone who has no interest in making things better. I realize I should have put the energy I invested trying to get him clean and sober into improving life for my children and me. In the wake of my failure to stop my husband's substance abuse, I found myself getting angry then feeling nothing at all as if I was dead inside.

My internal battle was obvious to others; my family and friends would tell me I was a mean person who said hurtful things. That behavior stemmed from my feelings of hopelessness, of being stuck in a life that would never improve. One day I just broke down, asking myself what was wrong with me; there was no answer, just a raging desire to improve my life. I truly feared for my sanity, and I decided to utilize the resources at the public library to get help. That's where I discovered the book *Transform Your Thinking and Transform Your Life* by Dr. Bill Winston.

> *God wants to bring a radical transformation in your mind and heart so that you can have supernatural courage in the face of insurmountable odds.*
> — Dr. Bill Winston

I discovered that the good thing about our brain is that it willingly adopts any changes we bring about in our thought patterns. Our actions are the manifestations of our thoughts. How we think shows through in how we act. Attitudes are mirrors of the mind.

In other words, it's up to you to change the direction of your life. *You* have to stand up for your own sanity. *You* have to break free from past hurts and disappointments. *You* have to believe your life can be better then take action to *make* it better.

That knowledge has changed the way I am raising my children and how I communicate with them. I've made more time to talk with them. I often ask how they feel about current situations. I ask about what challenges them, what they're concerned about. I encourage them to share their opinions in a respectful manner. Most of all I find myself hugging them and telling them I love them nearly every day, giving them the affection missing from my own childhood. My newfound knowledge has taught me to seek happiness and contentment in the present.

> *How simple it is to see that we can only be happy now, and there will never be a time when it is not now.*
> — Gerald Jampolsky

When we are under pressure, we find out how strong our resolve is, how much we can withstand. We learn what we can push through and what empowers us. My life-changing experience has empowered me to push through any challenge and to work toward my goals, knowing it is possible to attain them.

My professional goal is to empower black women through teaching them techniques to make their natural, textured hair more manageable, to give them knowledge about the needs of their hair. Many women aren't aware of how to get their hair healthy again and keep it that way. As a salon owner and hairstylist with seventeen years' experience, I help women get control of their hair, learn to love its kinky texture, and to nurture it. My love of hair gift has empowered me to help women discover ways to enjoy a new, natural lifestyle, so they don't have to panic if it suddenly begins to rain. My transformational hair programs will release old behaviors and beliefs black women have held for years pertaining to themselves and their hair. Once this happens they will find a new love and create a new hair story.

Start creating *your* new love story.

> *To activate others, you must activate yourself; to be enthusiastic, you must first be enthusiastic yourself.*
> *— David J. Schwartz, Ph.D.*

Self-Empowerment Tools

Try my hair-love affirmations:
I love my hair.
I love the texture of my hair.

I love the behavior of my hair.
I love the color of my hair.
I love the style of my hair.
I love myself.
I am beautiful…………………………….

Quotations that help me release my emotional chains

Don't wish it was easier, wish you were better. Don't wish for less problems, wish for more skills. Don't wish for less challenges, wish for more wisdom.
— Jim Rohn

Principle: Knock a challenge down with positive wishes.

What daily discipline can keep you strong?

We are not going to succeed in everything we attempt in life. That's a guarantee. In fact, the more we do in life, the more chance there is not to succeed in some things. But what a rich life we are having! Win or lose, we just keep winning.
— Susan Jeffers

Principle: Practice asking and listening.
What motivates you? How can you be a better listener?
Principle: The magic of thinking big.
What is your biggest magical desire?
Principle: Stretch your vision.
How can you add value to your life?
Principle: Don't let old traditions paralyze your mind.
What new ideas can you create for self-improvement?

The above tools can be used to think creatively and improve the quality of your goals. These tools will recondition your thinking and prepare you for success. I hope that sharing my story will free someone from being paralyzed, chained to unwanted circumstances. Fall in love with yourself again; make a habit of turning every defeat into a victory, learning from your mistakes, and moving on. It is possible to salvage something from every setback. Change your story to create a new love story!

About the Author

Owner of Real Natural Salon, Alisha Davis has been dubbed the Naturalogist due to her passion to teach women and children easy solutions to achieving and maintaining natural, healthy hair. She discovered her vocation as a child braiding her little sisters' hair and helping them feel confident about their natural tresses.

Her innate talent soon grew into a fifteen-year cosmetology career and natural hair care line, Real Natural Solutions, which has propelled Alisha to the top of her field with clients, bloggers, and media outlets alike clamoring for her expertise on how to maintain her natural hair techniques in between salon visits.

Alisha's simple yet modern approach has made her a key stylist and trainer in the natural hair industry. Her ability to create moisturized, shiny hair and beautiful, soft waves empower women to love their hair and keep her training classes filled and in demand.

And the mindset she shares helps clients not only love their hair but have the confidence to love who they are from the inside out, the first step toward personal and professional success. Alisha resides in Little Rock,

Arkansas, when she is not traveling the country doing salon makeovers, natural hair technique classes, and one-on-one hair assessments.

Please visit www.freegiftfromalisha.com to receive your 4 Step Guide to Shampoo and Prep Natural Hair

Environmental Change Leads to Mindshift Changes

When I was fifteen, my parents moved us from the projects of the inner city to the suburbs. For the first time I would attend public school. In our old neighborhood my brother and I were the only ones who went to Catholic school. My classmates there had broader experiences and easier access to engage in typical teenager activities because they had transportation. My classmates also got to do things like go on vacation to visit relatives in other states during the summer. My brother and I were limited to where we could go because my parents didn't have a car. My dad was legally blind, and my mother didn't learn to drive until later in life. So we got around on public transportation or depended on family and friends who had transportation.

I did have friends at school, and they liked hanging out with me in my neighborhood just sitting out on the porch or in the courtyard engaging in people-watching and sharing idle neighborhood gossip. It was exciting for my friends who were not used to living in a busy urban area where something was going on at all hours of the day and night such as spontaneous block parties, random fighting, and occasional gunshots.

On the other hand I preferred going to my friends' neighborhoods because it was much quieter. Plus their parents had cars and took us all over the city to shopping centers and movie theaters. For them these were short drives, but for me to get there, I'd have to take two buses and plan on more than an hour's travel time each way. Those same transportation issues prevented me from participating in after-school activities, and I felt a little jealous of my friends in the projects who lived much closer to the public high school and were able to join athletic teams and clubs.

I'd been born with a port wine birthmark that covered one side of my face that I'd been relentlessly teased about as a child, which left me almost painfully shy. When my parents told my brother and me that we'd be moving and going to a new public school, we were both crushed; we'd dreamed of going to the local high school with our friends from the neighborhood, me in particular because I already knew the kids, and they knew me (and my birthmark). We received a happy surprise when the kids at our new high school considered us hip because we were from the city. I was so busy socializing with my new friends, trying to keep in contact with my old ones from the projects, and finally getting to attend school functions that I had little time for studying.

By my junior year I had cut down on all that socializing and hung mostly with three new friends: a girl I had several classes with, her sister who was one year behind us, and her sister's friend, also a year younger. The four of us ate lunch together every day. All three of them were honor students, and as I hung out with them, my mindset began to change. I started paying more attention in my classes, turning in higher quality homework assignments, and my grades started to improve. My initial motivation was not wanting my new friends to think I was stupid, but their excitement about the new things they learned became as infectious as the flu.

Before I knew it I also became eager to do well in school and for the first time found myself thinking about my life after graduation. My friends all planned to attend college and pursue good-paying careers. I began to see possibilities I had never thought of or discussed with friends from my old neighborhood. Their only interests seemed to be scoring alcohol, going clubbing, and being in the know about the latest gossip—generally trying to act grown. A few of them were even having babies. None of them had long-term plans to secure a stable future and live independently; instead, they all talked about finding a good man to take care of them, getting married, and settling down. When I was with them, I spoke wistfully of the same things, but after my exposure to a different mindset, those sentiments became less sincere. I didn't fully recognize it at the time, but changing neighborhoods and high schools was my introduction to a new way of thinking, from settling for a stagnant, unsatisfactory life to pursuing one of ambition and unlimited potential and possibilities.

Mindset Shifts and Growth Transitioning to Adulthood Realities

This shift in mindset meant I had to overcome resistance and opposition to reach my highest potential as I transitioned from teenager to full-fledged adult. As we began our final semester senior year, my friend who was in my grade and graduating with me, informed me she had applied to a historically black college and university (HBCU), and I started thinking about what college I would apply to.

Despite buckling down in class, I was pretty much an average student in the C+ range, and I wasn't sure about my chances for acceptance. Even though my parents didn't pressure my brother and me about attending college, they wanted to make sure we learned skills so we could earn a better living than they had. I know if I wanted to attend an HBCU or another college, my parents would help me arrange financing for my tuition because my parents wanted us to have experiences they were unable to have.

After graduation I enrolled in the local community college to determine if college was for me. To my embarrassment I was required to take remedial courses in English and math. I thought the math classes were a joke because it was basic arithmetic, which I passed within the first two semesters before advancing to college math. But the remedial English classes opened my mind to the fundamentals of various writing styles I hadn't grasped in my earlier academic education because of distractions—both external and internal—that posed barriers to my learning. As I recognized my potential for learning, my mindset shifted, and I swiftly moved through the remedial courses, pushing past the stigma of having to take them while in college.

Even though I was doing well in community college, I still had challenges to face. After completing my third semester, I began working a full-time job at the post office to reduce my student loan obligation and to not burden my parents with taking care of me. So I was working a midnight shift then attending classes during the day, balancing a full load of four courses.

I also helped out at my dad's vending stand. I understood that was a family obligation; I didn't expect to be fully paid. I chose to work at the post office and not the family business because I wanted to be independent and earn my own money. Based on my experiences up to then, I considered myself a success and felt I was making it. I had graduated high school and was attending college. I would earn a degree, begin a career, save my money, and perhaps be able to buy a home right after I got married for my kids to grow up in. I'd be an honorable citizen who contributed positively to society. I thought if I stayed on the path and focused on my goals, I would beat the odds and fulfill my parents' dream of achieving more than they had, making them proud.

What I didn't factor in was the reality of life: biases, judgments, corruption, injustices. I was somewhat naïve in thinking the world was a fair place where everyone had good intentions. I had a wake-up call when I realized that was not the case, that despite my hard work to make good grades by studying, other students cheated or, it was rumored, slept with the professors. I also learned that it's not possible to do it all, i.e., carry a full course load, earn good grades, work full-time, and help out at the family business.

I also tried to maintain friendships with the girls I'd grown up with in my childhood school and old neighborhood, even though we had chosen different paths. It all became too much, and I suffered a nervous breakdown. My struggle for success had left me mentally and physically exhausted. At just nineteen years old, I learned the hard way that doing it all is a myth.

I didn't really process what had happened to me, but the counseling I received during my five days as an inpatient at a psychiatric facility helped me understand. I remember my mom and dad coming to get me and my mom praying over me after they brought me home. I also had difficulty accepting the fact that I needed to take medication to help control my moods and anxiety. I wanted to be normal like everyone else, to function without pills. And the medication made me gain weight, beginning a battle that went on for many months.

Faith to Faith: A Journey

After my release from the mental health facility, I had regular appointments at the clinic there for medication management reviews and follow-ups with a psychiatrist. I would get frustrated because the psychiatrist was not able to tell me when I would be able to stop taking the prescribed medication, saying "It's up to you to determine when that will be."

I had always been healthy and wasn't familiar with the concept of taking long-term medication. I thought of it being like an antibiotic: take it twice a day for ten days, and then you're done. I had not yet returned to school and had given up my job at the post office, so I settled into an empty daily routine of sleeping, eating, and watching TV. I slowly began to accept that I'd have to take the medication indefinitely. I also accepted that I might not ever finish college.

Then on one visit to the psychiatrist, I announced I was dissatisfied with doing so little, having so many follow-up appointments, and him not being able to tell me when I could stop taking the medication that was making me fat. The psychiatrist pointed out that the majority of my weight gain wasn't due to the pills but to inactivity, sitting around eating and watching TV. He suggested we end my regular visits and asked me to come back in three months, and I agreed.

A few weeks later I went with my mom to the local Walmart, where I encountered the two sisters I'd been friendly with in high school. We had lost contact after graduation. They couldn't conceal their surprise at the change in my appearance; I'd gained nearly one hundred pounds since they'd last seen me. I was still kind of out of it, and my mom told them I'd been ill. They invited me to have lunch with them the next day.

During our lunch they updated me about their lives. They both were working part-time and attending college, and one of them had a summer internship lined up at a good company, where she hoped to work full-time after earning her degree. As I listened to them, my mind shifted to the old days when we would discuss our goals and dreams for our lives after high school, and I became depressed because they were on track, and I'd fallen by the wayside.

The next day while lying in front the TV, I suddenly began sobbing uncontrollably, so much that I feared I was having another breakdown. I begged God for help, to allow me to function without my medication and confessed to Him that I was afraid I wouldn't be able to do it. I instantly felt a warmth spreading throughout my body. I didn't take my medication that day or any day since, and that was over twenty years ago. I believe that was the moment my spiritual chains were released. I began reflecting on the lunch with my old friends, remembering the goals I had set for myself after graduating. I started talking with God, asking Him how I could get back on track. I didn't want to live with my parents for the rest of their lives, but how could I live on $475 of monthly social security disability insurance benefits? Then the Holy Spirit started giving me instructions, directing me to contact the psychiatrist and ask him for help getting a job. A few days later I kept my appointment with the psychiatrist and asked him for resources in finding employment. I could see his eyes light up as if thinking: *She's finally got it,* and he handed me the business card of an employment specialist and told me to contact them.

I did contact that person, and we met a few days later. She connected me to the state's Vocational Rehabilitation Services, which paid the tuition for me to return to school. I became a student peer/mentor at the mental health clinic. After graduating with a bachelor's degree in rehabilitation services, I began working for the mental health clinic as an employment specialist.

My life was forever transformed when I experienced the power of God in a spiritual encounter. My faith increased, challenging me to see past my limitations and to trust God more with my life's journey. I learned how to surrender, to seek God's wisdom and understanding, to lay my will down, to discover what I wanted, and figure out how to make it happen. I prayed for God's direction and trusted His process, timing, and infinite wisdom.

I learned my life experiences had led me to a greater purpose: to serve humanity. I developed patience and greater compassion, especially for the most vulnerable among us. I created my brand, Caring with Compassion, as a call to action, promoting disability awareness, education, and compassion toward others. I create online education courses, training, workshops, digital content about disability awareness, and recently published my first e-book, *A Guide to Accessing Services and Resources in the Healthcare Social Services for Persons with Chronic Healthcare and Disabilities Quality of Life*. I also wrote the book *Caring with Compassion: A Legacy of Love,* honoring my parents' legacy. What a caregiver and healthcare professional has taught me about having a servant's heart, unconditional love, and compassion as I serve others.

I hope that by sharing my story and experiences, you are inspired and encouraged to live your best life on purpose, for purpose, in purpose.

Recognizing the need for having the right mindset moving forward to live your best life, here are three things I'd like you to consider on your journey.

Environmental change. A change in your environment can lead to significant changes that shift your mindset, allowing you to experience something different than what has become familiar and stagnant, hindering your growth. Evaluate your current environment on purpose.

Growth transitioning. As you evaluate and make changes in your environment, it will lead to transitions from the familiar to the unknown, and this is where you will recognize your growth for your purpose.

Faith to faith: A journey. Experiencing internal and external growth on the journey will challenge your faith as you move in your purpose you were created for.

About the Author

As a disability advocate, consultant, and educator, Ronita Boullt promotes disability awareness using thirty-plus years of experience in healthcare social services systems, supporting individuals with chronic healthcare conditions and disabilities. She educates many individuals with and without disabilities who need to understand how to navigate an integrated healthcare system by bringing awareness to healthcare professionals and medical providers in accessing services for consumers' quality of life, allowing individuals with disabilities to remain at home maximizing independence cost effectively.

Ronita hold a BS in rehabilitation services and counseling, she's a certified patient advocate and has worked as a case manager serving the most vulnerable populations: individuals with intellectual developmental disabilities, the elderly, disabled veterans, and those diagnosed with chronic health conditions.

Her most personal experiences have come from being a caregiver to her mom for fourteen years and her own health issues that placed her on the path of healthcare. Having navigated the healthcare systems for both herself and her mom, she has learned to use her voice to ensure that quality services are provided. She has advocated and worked in collaboration with various health care teams, maximizing appropriate services to accomplish rehabilitation, health goals, and quality care.

These personal experiences awakened her passion for educating the general population about disability awareness: how to serve persons with chronic health conditions and disabilities with more compassion, recognizing their abilities, taking a holistic person-centered planning approach, and becoming knowledgeable about appropriate resources to better serve them and maximize their independence and quality of life.

Please visit www.ronitaboullt.com to receive your Maximizing Independence for Quality of Life resource guide

Some chains that have kept you bound and enslaved are not your fault. Thay are your family history's fault. Now it's your responsibility to heal first, then break the cycle.

~Ari Squires

Daddy-Daughter Issues

Hurt. Broken. Confused. Angry. Frustrated. Disappointed. Resentful. Rejected.

These eight words sum up the emotions I held onto for over thirty years toward my biological father. Yet I decided to do what many hurt daughters would consider insane and chose to honor him. For you ladies who suffer from daddy-daughter issues, keep reading. This chapter will help you identify your truth through my personal truth in realizing it's not about the pain of what happened but the purpose of why it happened. By knowing my truth, I can own my dysfunctional experience as it was the very thing that unlocked my destiny.

To give you the landscape, my mother and father were high school sweethearts. They were together for twenty years, married for seventeen. Within that timeframe, my dad had five children of which I am the eldest daughter. Although he did live with us, I considered him present but absent. I witnessed my mom experience a lot of lonely nights crying. Eventually my mother had enough, and now they have been divorced for over twenty years.

From watching the hurt he caused my mother and not receiving the personal affection I was longing for, my desire to grow and foster a relationship with my dad faded. My naïve twelve-year-old-self thought the divorce would mean that now my sister and I would get two of everything, one from mom and one from dad. In my 20/20 hindsight vision, I realize how wrong it was to think that. I don't want to leave the impression he did nothing; however, I just wished he had done more. It bothered me to think that my dad was willing to watch my sister and me struggle financially. It just didn't seem fair to me that my mom was the only one who made sacrifices to take care of us.

Besides dealing with that as a youth, I was also broken. I always desired to be daddy's little girl, but after tattling on my dad to my mom that we were at another woman's house, I was cut off at four years old. I was on an everlasting quest for my dad to give me another chance to hang out with him and not tell. I worked so hard to be seen by him, but I received praises, kisses, and pats on the back from everyone but my dad. This broke me because although I had the attention of everyone else, it felt like I was seen by no one because the one person I wanted to see me did not. As his eldest daughter, I couldn't understand why he didn't see me the way others saw me: ambitious, charismatic, and diligent. I witnessed my mother's dedication, faithfulness, and tear-filled eyes only to realize that it wasn't just me he didn't see.

I was also confused that despite my efforts, I never heard him say: *Good job, Meisha. You made Daddy proud.* I worked hard to graduate in the top 5 percent of my class for middle school and high school. I went on to become the first in my family to graduate from college and study abroad in two different countries and afterward landed Fortune 100 corporate jobs. None of this appeared to be enough as it always came across as an expectation and not a congratulation.

All this together made me angry, frustrated, and disappointed to the point I thought I could just suppress the pain and move on without ever having to deal with it. Not dealing with it caused me to build so much resentment that when I did meet the love of my life, I struggled with not bringing that emotional baggage into the relationship.

Fast forward a couple of years. I met a man named Brian who changed my life. The reality is he was everything I had prayed for. When he proposed to me, my one stipulation was for us to attend premarital counseling. I knew the effect of not preparing for marriage, so in an effort to break the generational curse, I recognized we needed to start off building our foundation with God in the center of it. God was the one who designed marriage in the first place.

As we went through the premarital courses, our pastor asked me who was giving me away, and I said I didn't know yet. He looked surprised.

"Do you have a living father?"

I replied yes.

"Well, he should be giving you away."

Our pastor emphasized what the Bible said, which was to honor thy father and thy mother. Interestingly enough, the Bible does not list any exceptions, which means God expects us to do our part by honoring our parents.

This was a tough pill to swallow, and it got tougher when my fiancé told me I needed to have a talk with my dad prior to us getting married. He provided me with the hard truth that it was necessary to forgive my dad to avoid bringing the baggage of rejection into our marriage. He also went a step further and told me not to call him until I had spoken with my dad. Scared of the outcome but knowing how much I wanted us to be in the best position to have a strong marriage, I decided to write out my pain in a four-page letter to my dad. I will spare you the details of that letter, but just for a second imagine what you would say as a hurt, broken, confused, angry, frustrated, disappointed, resentful, rejected twenty-five-year-old girl.

As I approached the end of my expression, I felt somewhat relieved but nervous at the same time; I wasn't sure how he would take my truth. I pressed send and messaged my dad on his two-way pager to check his email. My heart pounded, and my hands trembled. Crazy thoughts were going through my head about what his reaction could be. Then the wait was over. He replied to my email saying he didn't know I felt that way and if I really didn't want him to give me away, then he wouldn't. But he would still pay his part for the wedding.

I felt bad because deep inside I did want my father to give me away, just not under the current circumstances. I recall getting so angry when he took credit for doing things he wasn't responsible for. We had each other's phone number and address, just not a true relationship. I did not want to walk down the aisle that way. After my father and I had a heart-to-heart conversation, I pushed the reset button and proudly accepted him to be the man to give me away.

If you are a father reading this, please note that your daughter needs your love and reassurance. You should be quick to ask for forgiveness and be willing to express things you may have dealt with growing up. She needs to hear your reasons for not being there.

On the day before my wedding and the entire day of my wedding, I was able to be daddy's little girl. I finally had his attention. I had forgiven my dad and was looking forward to a bright, lasting future with my husband.

My dysfunctional experience was the exact journey that propelled me into my destiny. My pain had purpose. In 2014 I opened a wedding planning and design company called Dream Celebrations, Inc. During wedding consultations I would ask the bride who was giving her away. Most times her response was the look of hurt I knew so well and could easily see she was a product of daddy-daughter issues.

Her body language would get tense with eye-rolling, a distorted facial expression, and head swirling as she would say, "I'm not letting my dad give me away. For what? He hasn't done anything for me."

I would then become a vessel, sharing experiences that brought me to my clarity point and in turn helping the bride to see the importance of honoring her father. I personally feel that the act of not honoring your father allows for generational curses to keep you chained to a reality that you do not have to take on.

After two years of working as a wedding planner, I realized so many couples were preparing for their one wedding day, but I didn't see the same effort and commitment preparing for their marriage. And without preparation, they could end up in a tough place costing them their marriage. I did some research and found that the national divorce rate is well over 50 percent, and it is at 70 percent for African-American couples. The role of father and the role of husband have some similarities, so if the bride does not respect or honor her father, she will find it difficult—whether consciously or unconsciously—to display that level of honor toward her husband. That leads to conflict and far too often, divorce.

It made me take a leap of faith to get aligned with my truth and rebrand myself because being a wedding planner wasn't my desire. It did not allow me the type of impact I was trying to achieve, which was helping women overcome within (WOW). I wanted to WOW my couples and their guests, not just through the beauty of planning, coordinating, and decorating but to show them the beauty of forgiveness and love. I settled on the title marriage planner and WOW expert. We help couples best prepare for their *marriage* all while transforming their venue into a magical space that makes them and their guests say, WOW! when their room is revealed.

Our couples complete an assessment that identifies their strengths and growth areas. We then pair them with a licensed professional counselor to help them develop in the areas of communication, conflict resolution, financial management, affection and sexuality, and relationship roles to name a few. We understand issues come up and differences occur; therefore, we just want to make sure our couples have the tools to help them sustain their marriages.

You may be thinking: *Okay, happy ending,* but I can't leave you thinking that the struggle of forgiveness is easy. Years have gone by since the original conversation with my dad where I thought I had totally forgiven him. Within the past few years, I've noticed that some of those old feelings had reemerged. I didn't know or couldn't understand how that could happen after I had forgiven him. By then I knew my soul's purpose was to help brides forgive their dads so they could fully love their husbands. However, knowing I still struggled with the relationship between myself and my dad, made me feel like a hypocrite, so I shied away from my calling. I stopped telling couples about the special, unique service our company was offering.

I took a different approach. I decided to pray to understand why those feelings were recurring so I could really help brides fully forgive their dads. Once you forgive someone that should settle it. But those eight words kept coming back to me when I thought about my dad. I had to get honest and assess why it was so hard to simply let go. People tell you to do this all the time, but I haven't heard anyone tell us how to let go. After undergoing my own healing process, I was able to dissect the how-to into a five-step healing program with an emphasis on showing hurt people how to LETGO, so they can live their best life. I especially teach this to brides because I want what God wants for their union, which is for it to prosper.

Carrying unforgiveness was my chain that needed to be broken. I used to feel like I was hurting my dad by not forgiving him because I wanted him to feel the same pain and rejection I felt. But unforgiveness only causes grief and additional hurt. It allows you to continually relive and replay all that happened, and then you get stuck there. I caught myself saying it is hard to forgive but American gospel singer and Grammy award winner Tina Campbell elevated my perspective with, "It's too hard not to."

People need to understand it's the weight you can't see that causes you not to soar in various areas of your life. Think about it; planes have weight requirements. If the luggage or the passengers weigh too much, the plane will not take off. Something or someone will have to be removed. That's how it is in life. If we walk around with too much baggage, we will be weighted down and not able to soar.

My weight represented bitterness and unforgiveness. Once I was finally able to LETGO, I became free. I began not looking at myself as a victim. So many people tell you: *Things happen for a reason.* You've possibly even told someone that yourself. But when it applies to your own life, it's a harder pill to swallow. I've had to learn to embrace my journey, my trials, and tribulations because things really *do* happen for a reason.

Because of the pain and hurt I've gone through, I now help women forgive their fathers faster than the thirty years it took me. I help impact the lives of women, their marriages, and families. We go through things so that we can be a blessing to others and meet them where they are and not judge them. I am helping to reduce the divorce rate and putting couples in the best position to have a strong marriage. I am breaking generational curses and helping women see the value and importance of protecting their marriages and families.

Even though I did not have the type of relationship I thought was ideal with my earthly father, I've been able to have that plus so much more with my Heavenly Father. God makes me think I am his most precious daughter. No offense to anyone reading this, but I am Daddy's little girl. He provides for me during times of lack. He gives me shortcuts and shows me favor. He is always present. He gives me money, sometimes even in the form of an anonymous check. He even gave me a car. I am totally spoiled by Him.

I want readers to know God is real, and you can have a real relationship with Him. You can be Daddy's little girl too, even if you weren't that with your earthly father. But you have to LETGO of those eight negative adjectives. Oddly enough, eight represents a new beginning and the start of a new era. This is your time to take back control of your life. There are thousands of people who are not being helped by you because you are weighted down.

Isaiah 61:7 (NIV) says: "Instead of your shame you will receive a double portion, and instead of disgrace you will rejoice in your inheritance. And so you will inherit a double portion in your land, and everlasting joy will be yours."

I interpret this to mean we will receive double for our trouble. Then why must we hold so many grudges and ill-will toward the person who caused us grief? Have you ever considered that person might have been used to allow you to unlock your purpose? Did it occur to you that person may have done the best job they knew how to do at the time? When we think about parenthood, we must take notice that it doesn't come with a book, and the baby isn't born with a manual. Did you ever stop to consider how that person was raised, what life experiences caused them to act the way they do? No, most times we do not. I know I didn't. I was so focused on me and what happened to me that I never considered thinking about him and the generational curses he was dealing with.

Hopefully you see how honoring my father after the pain and through purpose wasn't insane. But it is insane for you to not LETGO, so let's stop the insane behavior and start doing what will change generations. There is a legacy inside of you. Let's reveal it to the world.

About the Author

Tameishia Pigford, affectionately known as Meisha, is a certified wedding planner and event designer who creates over-the-top, premium experiences for her clients that leave them saying wow! After working in human resources where she developed her people skills and helped organize corporate events, Meisha designed her own wedding, sparking her love of event planning.

Meisha now owns an award-winning planning and design firm, Dream Celebrations, Inc., and through her work as a marriage planner and WOW expert, she assists couples with not only preparing for their big day but also for their marriage. Her goal is to help lower the divorce rate in this country one couple at a time.

**Please Visit http://letgothepast.com
to receive your Daddy-Daughter Forgiveness audio**

Chasing a Ghost

I was a young boy between the age of five and seven years old when I last saw my father. I remember being so ecstatic spending time with him. He gave me $20, bought me a brand-new JanSport backpack, and got me a kid's cheeseburger meal to go at Burger King. My last memory of him was telling me to sit at the bus stop and wait for him to come back.

In my young mind I figured he just had a quick errand to run and would surely be back to get me. Hours passed, and I sat, swinging my feet, patiently awaiting his return. Finally a woman came up to me and asked why I was sitting at the bus stop all alone. She somehow contacted my mother, and I was taken home. Looking back, it was then that my childhood resentment morphed into hatred for the man I called my father.

My mother told me many stories about my dad that often made me feel worthless. She told me that my father did not want me because he was too young to be a father. She told me that he actively encouraged her to abort me, or he would leave. I am of course thankful to my mother for keeping and caring for me until adulthood.

However, like many children with an absentee parent, I held a high level of resentment toward my mother and father. I've heard many stories of how children were angry at their mothers because they just knew that there was something that she did to make the father leave. We often believe that the absent parent is perfect and can do no wrong. Though it's difficult to admit, I felt that way for a long time. After all the hurtful things about my father were relayed to me, I found myself becoming emotionless, and my heart was as cold as an icebox.

Though I could not stand my father, my mother wanted me to have a relationship with his side of the family. She would take me over to my paternal grandma's house, and all my aunts and uncles would be there. My favorites were Auntie Bonnie, Auntie Faye, and Uncle Fly, who always gave me money and ensured that I was taken care of.

During one visit to my grandmother's house, I was greeted by my Uncle Fly, who was on the porch with all these half-naked women. As a child I could not understand why so many women were hanging out at my grandmother's house and how my uncle seemed to have control over all of them. He would point to each woman and direct her to do some task—*You, you, and you, go to the store; you go cook me some food, etc.*

I asked him, "Are these all your girlfriends?"

To which he replied, "Yeah, they all love me and will do whatever I tell them to do."

I looked at Uncle Fly as somewhat of a father figure. From that point on I figured that was the way of life: for a man to have multiple women to fulfill all sexual requests and have all of them love you unconditionally with zero drama. To this day I think my Uncle Fly was a pimp, but I cannot confirm or deny. During my early teenage years, I did not believe in relationships, but I wanted to have sex. Like most boys who are raised without a positive father in the home, I got most of my sex education from my boys in the streets. My mother sat down with me and gave a quick and generalized lecture about sex, which went in one ear and out the other. I never had a man give me a mature and detailed conversation about sex, namely the consequences of having unprotected sex. As a result I became a father at fifteen.

I was in denial at first and refused to believe that I was a having a child. Over time I came to accept it and followed my mother's advice on looking for jobs to provide for my baby. Those jobs did not pay enough, and I felt I was working more than spending time with my child. Working a nine to five was not feasible, so I began to get more involved with the streets. I idolized basketball players and drug dealers. I looked at the basketball players as what I wanted to be in the distant future. I viewed the drug dealers as role models/father figures in the here and now because like many young men in the hood, I saw the fast money with little effort.

I was so fascinated by the fast life and making easy money that I began selling drugs for the big-time drug dealers in my neighborhood. Selling drugs for them was my way of giving back to them for teaching me life lessons, buying new school clothes, and shielding me from harm in the streets like a father would have done. They tried to keep me in line and always told me to stay my a** in school, stop skipping class, and to make a difference in the world one day by doing more good than bad.

Later I became affiliated with the Gangster Disciples and began learning from the old heads we called original gangsters. These guys were well-respected in the neighborhood and had done everything from drug dealing to murder. They instantly took me under their wing because I was in the streets more than I was at home. During my junior year of high school, I was shot two times and nearly died from my wounds and severe blood loss. I went through several months of rehab and almost lost my leg to infection. The doctor told me that I might never be able to have more kids because the bullet had ruptured veins close to my private area. I went through months of depression and became enraged. I went from feeling like a victim and turned into a perpetrator. I felt like Tupac; it was *me against the world.* After about six months of therapy, I went back to selling drugs and gangbanging like the tragic event never even happened, and I was crazier than ever.

It was times like that when I truly longed for my biological father. As a father myself I could never fathom abandoning my children. I cannot imagine missing all the milestones and achievements. Over the years I have found myself attempting to "earn" his love, something no child should have to do. Much of my motivation and drive to be great was to gain his approval. I have spent many years thinking if only I could achieve this or accomplish that my father would surely be proud of me and want to be in my life. It's been forty-four years, and that day has not come.

I have moments where I think that maybe he was never taught how to be a father and that this is a generational chain I believe I am finally breaking. Like many in the black community, I unfortunately do not know much about my family history beyond my parents' generation. I knew my grandmother, but never heard anything about my grandfather.

I gave up on ever having a relationship with him though that has always been my strongest desire. When I turned forty, with my mother's and paternal aunt's encouragement, I attempted to connect with him. I spoke with him on the phone, and we decided that it would be good for me to visit him. I bought the plane ticket, bought gifts for him, told all my family and friends. I was beyond thrilled to finally be face-to-face with my dad again; I just knew that once he got to know me, he would love me! But unfortunately, just like many times before, he stood me up. This moment took me right back to that day at the bus stop; I felt alone, afraid, angry, and embarrassed.

So as one would expect, this is still a chain that has kept me stagnant. I find it difficult to trust people, and I still battle with abandonment issues. In personal relationships I find myself never fully committing. I never want to lose control and give my all to anyone for fear of being discarded. One good thing that came out of this experience with my father is that I have learned what I do not want to be. I have vowed never to make my children feel unloved. I take pride in being there for my children, through the good and the bad.

I have released putting the responsibility for my father leaving on my mother. For a long time I believed that my mom did something to cause my father to abandon me. She raised me to be the man I am today. The pain from not having my father around made me act out a lot as a child and continually disobey my mother. I finally realized the reason I did this was because I was mad at her for not convincing him to stay. As a man he made the decision to leave, not my mother. My father holds total responsibility for walking out my life as a child.

For me, *it's time for change* means releasing the hurt and moving on, living life without regrets. I must make peace with knowing that I may never have the relationship with my father that I have always desired. I must live my life to the fullest and not allow anything to hold me back. It means using my experience to mentor other young men with absentee

It's Time for Change

fathers and giving them the coaching and guidance that we as black men so desperately need.

I realized it was time for a change in November 1995 when my mom kicked me out of the house. Chicago police officers raided our home because they suspected drugs were on the premises. They broke down the back door and came into the house with guns drawn. They found nothing, but I was forcibly removed because of disorderly conduct. My mom told the police officers that I could never come back to her home again and if I did she wanted me arrested. I was now homeless, in the middle of a Chicago winter with nowhere to go. The streets became my new home. I slept on the trains during the night and caught a few hours of rest at my friend's house during the day. That's when I learned the real value of a dollar and ate breakfast, lunch, and dinner off $10 a day. Now a new chain was created; I did not just have hatred for my father, I had an extreme dislike for my mother as well.

Three months later God finally answered my prayers, and I was accepted into the United States Air Force. My mother had no knowledge that I had joined the military, and I knew she would blow a gasket when she found out. I called her three months later after boot camp and told her I had joined. She instantly hung up on me. Before I knew it months had passed without us talking, and now I was leaving the States and off to Germany for four years.

During my military tour in Germany, I began to mature more after the birth of my second child. I was still struggling with showing any kind of emotion or getting totally committed to a relationship. Those emotional chains were still pulling me down even as an adult. Seven years later I got married and had my third child. I wanted to do things differently this time around and not have any more kids out of wedlock. In the military I never really had the opportunity to raise my previous children, so I wanted to make sure I did this time. I always tell my kids they have three different daddies, and they look crazy at me. I explain to them I was at three different points in my life when they were born. Loving and caring for my children helped in my healing process from growing up as a fatherless child. I was learning how to love unconditionally by pouring all my love into children and getting it all back in return.

Learning how to love others no matter how you might have been treated helped me to love harder. I can willingly express my emotions more now. Since releasing the pain of the past, I have become a better man and father to my children. I have learned from my past experiences how to take a negative situation and turn it around into something positive.

Despite years of trauma and difficulties, I am proud of the man I am and the man I am becoming. I have accomplished so much more than anyone ever expected, and you can too. I have defied the odds and broken many chains in my life. Today I can say that I'm a God-fearing man, retired military veteran, excellent father, business owner, and community leader. I'm a man who lives life to the fullest and strives to be better every day while giving back to the youth in my community. I found out a few years ago that my father was an entrepreneur as well. I had always wondered where the desire to own my business originated. It was already in my blood. As much as I never wanted to be like that man, we shared the passion of being our own boss.

My greatest hope is to one day finally have a healthy relationship with my biological father. I have spent so many years chasing the idea of having a relationship with him that it changed me as a man. I have always worked through whatever shortfalls or obstacles that came my way to prove something to him. I wanted him to know that he made a mistake walking out of my life as a child. The pain I felt of not being wanted by my father, carried on in adulthood and affected every relationship whether professional or personal.

I appreciate my father for providing me with a blueprint on how to not to be as a dad. I have broken the generational chain. My kids receive everything from me a father should provide because I know what I missed as a child. Once I released those chains of feeling never being good enough to be loved, it enabled me to express my love more freely. I have finally found inner peace with the situation that had me chained down my entire life. Even if I never get the opportunity to have a relationship with my father, I will continue to love others and take what I have learned to grow more as a man.

I hope my story and experiences can be useful to someone else. It took the OGs in the neighborhood to tell me old stories about what they had been through when they were young to guide me to do better. My story and the stories of others can be useful in preventing you from making the same mistakes, and you can be a better man.

My purpose in life is to love my children unconditionally and pay forward to someone else the information that helped me. I feel I have been through the fire but still made it through by the grace of God and a praying mother.

Here are a few tips I can give you that can be useful for your personal and professional success:

First, always be honest because people will respect you more and want to do business with you. Be respectful of others' time, money, and ideas.

Second, have a *never give up* attitude. Always believe in yourself even when others do not. You can be your own worst enemy in your personal life and professional career. My struggles and setbacks in life could have defeated me. I have always believed that the sun comes after the storm, and I knew one day I would make it through. Never give up on yourself, and keep pressing through no matter the disadvantages against you. Defy the odds and become successful.

Third, release all chains and allow nothing to hold you back from chasing your destiny and fulfilling your dreams. Always keep in mind that there are people in far worse situations than you who have overcome their obstacles. Everything starts with believing in yourself and waking up every morning with a purpose to do something great in life. Break whatever chains might hold you back—whether physical, emotional, or spiritual—and embrace the opportunity to live free.

A favorite quote of mine comes from the rapper Drake. He said, "Never let success get to your head, and never let failure get to your heart."

Don't forget the people who assisted you along the way. There are several individuals I know who've had great success in life but never give back. People are drawn to a person that is genuine, trustworthy, and unwilling to let success change them in a negative manner. You cannot let failure be the reason you give up and never try again.

About the Author

Rondale Alexander, who grew up on the South Side of Chicago, Illinois, is the CEO of Rondavu, LLC. During his six-year tenure, Rondale has overseen operations and strategic planning for Rondavu Talent Management, which represents several celebrity clients. He has helped shape his clients' careers and guided them toward new opportunities. He has set up public appearances, offered advice on contract negotiation, and helped to build his clients' overall brand.

Prior to this role, Rondale spent twenty years in the United States Air Force, with deployments including Qatar, South Korea, and Kosovo. Before retiring with an honorable discharge, Rondale rescued two men from a major car accident, rendering immediate first-aid that helped save their lives. For his act of heroism, Rondale received Air Force-wide recognition.

Rondale holds a BA in organizational management and is currently pursuing an MBA at the University of the Incarnate Word in San Antonio, Texas. In his spare time Rondale enjoys traveling, caring for his children, and mentoring at-risk youth.

Please visit http://bit.ly/Rondavu7MajorPitfallsToAvoid
to receive your guide on 7 Major PitfallstoAvoid While Trying to
Pursue Your Talent

When Love Hurts

I was born into a family that did not know how to express love and with a generational curse of domestic violence. The odds were stacked against me from the time I left my mother's womb.

As far back as I can remember, I was always looking for love from men and things. When I say *things* I mean clothes. Shopping made me feel good. When I was sixteen my mother took me down to the health clinic to get birth control pills. She didn't talk about it to me; she didn't explain why she was doing it or anything about sex. My mother was mean and strict. We couldn't hang out or do things like normal teenagers, which is why I couldn't understand why she put me on the pill in the first place.

That was right around the time my mother and father split, which didn't affect me at all because my father was never around. He was an alcoholic, and my mother never really seemed to care. My parents never displayed love for us. I knew this was not a regular home; it always seemed cold, broken, and depressing. I just wanted to get out of there. I expected more from my parents. I wanted to be held and told that they loved me. I wanted them to take us places and do things that other families did. I wanted to be encouraged or for one of them to help me with my homework. I expected them to act like they cared for the children they brought into this world.

I would not say that I was a bad teenager growing up. I did sneak out some and talk back, but I didn't think I did anything so bad to be beaten with wooden sticks, brooms, and extension cords, but that was her form of discipline.

After my father left my mom got a boyfriend. That was the first time I was exposed to domestic violence, but back then I didn't know what it was. My mom's boyfriend would beat her then tell her that he loved her. The more this happened it planted a picture in my mind that a man can show his affection and love by beating you. This same boyfriend came into our room and tried to touch us. When I told my mom, she didn't believe me. It took a neighbor that I shared the information with to convince her I was telling the truth. She kicked him out afterward.

I was about seventeen years old when I shared with a guidance counselor at school about the abuse I was receiving at home. She told me about the emancipation process: you could file papers with the juvenile court stating why you wanted to divorce your parents and if they agreed, all they had to do was sign a document, and you were free to leave and would no longer be under their supervision.

Emancipation could set me free from the house of hell, so I took the necessary steps. The day I was preparing to leave my heart ripped apart as I packed. I imagined my mother would come over and ask: *Why are you leaving?* But she didn't, and my thought was: *Why isn't she trying to stop me? She must not love me. If she did love me, she wouldn't let me leave. She doesn't care about me.*

I left, and we didn't speak for about a year. I went to stay with a friend and eventually at nineteen got my own apartment, setting in motion a chain of events that would alter my life forever. I left home broken, unloved, and unwanted, when all I really wanted was my parents to love me. But how could they? They didn't understand emotions.

My search for love took off with a bang. I started looking for love in all the wrong places. I was living the fast life of clubbing, drinking, and doing things I had no business doing. One of my best friends was seeing a guy who was friends with her cousin. She told me her cousin wanted to meet me. He had come by my job a couple of times, and we all decided to watch a movie at my place. I was kind of hesitant because I had heard he was a drug dealer. But I was a little naïve and trusted my best friend.

Movie night came, and we were all sitting in my living room, which was dark except for the light from the television. I was on one side of the living room with my date, and my best friend was on the other side. As we sat and watched the movie my date began to whisper in my ear: *Let's go into the bedroom.* He did that on and on, and I continued to say no. Even though I was sleeping with men, I didn't sleep with anyone on the first date or let them into my bedroom.

He became frustrated and grabbed a chunk of my hair in the middle of my head and pulled it hard. The pain I felt was unexplainable. He did this very discretely and insisted that I go to the bedroom, or he would pull my hair out. I convinced myself: *Cathy, just go with him to the room, he just wants to talk and chill.*

As we walked into the room, he still had a grip on my hair. He shut the door and motioned me to the bed still gripping my hair. He put me on the bed and got on top of me and whispered in my ear that if I screamed or said anything, he would kill me. I had no reason to not take him seriously because he was a drug dealer, and I truly believed he would kill me. As he tried to penetrate me, I begged him to not do it. He pulled my hair with one hand and forced himself inside of me with the other.

While I was sexually assaulted, I did not fight back or try to flee. My body froze, and I was paralyzed in a state of incredible fear. I asked God: *Why are you letting this happen? Why don't you love me? Please make him stop.*

Once he was done he reminded me of what he would do if I said anything. We walked out of the room as if nothing had happened. I would remain silent for years before sharing it with my best friend and many more years before I would break my silence and share it with the world. I felt guilty and ashamed because I didn't fight back. I was afraid that people would blame me for what happened. The burden at times was overwhelming. I went from being a talkative person to having a flat affect, quiet, reserved, and I had difficulties expressing myself.

The rape, my broken home, childhood abuse, being unloved, not loving myself, not knowing my worth, low self-esteem, and years of physical, mental, verbal, and psychological abuse, at the hands of different men held me captive in chains. Wallowing in the pain made me unable to forgive and love someone else. I didn't trust anyone, and if I could not get what I was looking for out of one man, I would move to the next. It was like I was looking for my next fix. There were times when all I could do was to sit, cry, and try to survive. Even with all the people I knew, I still felt alone. I felt as if my life didn't matter. There was even a time when I thought about killing myself. It was just a thought, no plan of how.

One-day God spoke to me through all this pain. He had not deserted me, and He did love me. He showed me that He did care about everything that was happening to me and that there was purpose in my pain. God never wastes hurt. He showed me what love is in scripture. I would read 1 Corinthians 13:4–8 every day.

> Love is patient, love is kind. It does not envy, it does not boast, it is not proud. It does not dishonor others, it is not self-seeking, it is not easily angered, it keeps no record of wrongs. Love does not delight in evil but rejoices with the truth. It always protects, always trusts, always hopes, always perseveres. Love never fails.

Prayer and strengthening my relationship with Him help me see that I really did have a life to live. I started seeing things I didn't know were in me. I woke up one day and got all my hair cut off and a tattoo. My friends thought I was crazy. But I was a changed woman. After I got more into scripture, I found out that tattooing the body was wrong as a Christian, so I said I would never get another tattoo. Reading scripture also showed me that I was beautifully and wonderfully made. It showed me that I was not the names I was called like ugly and fat. God showed me that He wanted me to help other people going through that same hurt. He wanted me to share my story. He used all the pain and gave me the gift of speaking to be able to help others. He embraced me and showed me how to embrace myself. Reading scripture, prayer, and meditation got me through and still gets me through. In order for me to embrace my journey, I had to do it unbothered by what people would think about me being raped and abused. All the pain I experienced had to happen to bring me healing and to prevent greater suffering.

I needed healing and closure, or I would remain lost and unfulfilled my whole life. I didn't want that. I felt there must be more out there for me than depression and lack. I realized that the first step in my healing transformation was learning how to love myself. This process would not be easy. There were things I had done and said that I was ashamed of. One of the hardest things I had to let go of was thinking that no one would want me if they knew I had been raped. This was one of the reasons I stayed silent for so long. The embarrassment was eating away inside of me.

For me to start loving me, I first had to forgive myself for all the wrong I had done in the past. That meant I had to walk in my truth. I had to accept me for who I was and allow God to come into my heart and help me be fully transparent. Then I had to forgive those who I thought played a part in hurting me. That wasn't easy for me, but forgiveness is not for others; forgiveness is for you. It set me free from feeling like they held me hostage.

I forgave my parents because I think they did their best with what they had. I am not making excuses for what my parents did. I am not saying that they couldn't have done things differently. The abuse was a generational curse. My great grandmother was abused, my grandmother, my mom, and aunts. My mom abusing me was a choice, but she might not have realized what she was doing was wrong. Because she wasn't loved she did not know how to love me. I realized later that I could not fix my parents. But I could show them how to love, and I did just that. I started telling them that I loved them. I would hug and embrace them, call them, take them places, and do family things. I had to rewrite my story so that they and my child could see something different. It was up to me to break the generational curse and chains that held me and my family back for far too many years and show them something different.

If we just keep sweeping our chains under the rug, more children will be hurt. We will never get to a better place. The cycle will never end. If the cycle continues, we remain lost, broken, and never become free.

Seeing my mom get abused by her boyfriends, sent me into the world thinking that if a man hit you, he loved you. Therefore I allowed this to happen in my relationships. My biggest challenge was asking myself why? Why did I allow these things to happen? What was it about me? The search deep inside would be another life-changing realization.

When you make the decision to start loving yourself, you won't allow anyone to treat you badly or put you in an uncomfortable situation. One of my favorite Bible verses that I read every day while healing was Psalm 139:14: "I praise you because I am fearfully and wonderfully made; your works are wonderful, I know that full well." God helped me realize there was nothing wrong with me and that He made me in His image. I learned what true love was by loving myself. I also learned I could accept and give the right kind of love.

Experiencing any kind of trauma can affect you for years and destroy your life if you let it. It happens to too many of us. That's why the *no more chains* movement is so needed. When it comes to domestic violence and sexual assault, know that it's not your fault. You can't blame yourself.

In addition to forgiveness and self-love, there is a process you must go through anytime the devil comes after you. First, realize exactly who the enemy is. Our battle is spiritual. The devil will use people and your past to make you think badly about yourself. Negative self-talk is high on the devil's list for seeking and destroying who God says you are. The devil is a liar. Don't believe anything that he tells you negative about yourself. Don't allow him to let your past destroy you.

I have helped so many people by sharing about my sexual assault and domestic violence. Using my voice landed me a chance to go before millions on national television. I learned that it is okay to speak up and speak out.

Second, replace any lie you're told with the truth. Silence everything in your mind that is negative or hurtful and says that you are not enough. No matter what you are going through, God loves you and will help you turn pain into gain. Everyone has a past and goes through something. We cannot let our past define us.

I was supposed to be a statistic. I wasn't supposed to survive what had happened to me. But I chose to not allow it to destroy me. It's hard to overcome being raped because of the trauma associated with it, but with God's help I did it. The childhood abuse I suffered could have very well sent me in the direction of violence and crime. I could have let low self-esteem, feeling unworthy, and hopelessness from being abused in my adult years take a toll on the rest of my development. There are so many little girls who grow into adult women walking around hurting. I could have been one of those women. I chose to do something about it. You can too. I believe if we acknowledge the problem and seek help, there is healing and hope.

Realizing my self-worth saved my life, and it can do the same for you no matter where you are in your journey to healing. Understand that our self-worth should never depend on others. Yes, compliments and appreciation are nice and powerful, but accepting yourself and your own uniqueness is liberating. When you love yourself, there is no need to pretend or wish you were someone else.

Learning to love myself allowed me to celebrate the woman that God created, and it helped me live out my primary purpose. Think about how your restoration can help change your family dynamics. Removing your mask of *I'm not hurting* allows for the authentic person to come out. Doing this will take some time. Peeling back the layers of lies the enemy told you to define yourself by won't be easy. In doing this realize what is unique about you and celebrate your uniqueness. Remember you are not like anyone else. He set you apart.

I have learned to live my life unapologetically. Learn to be okay with saying no, set boundaries, and balance family and work. Your journey will also require you to regularly examine your circle of influence. Not having the right people in your circle could hurt your journey to self-love. On your journey to self-love, it is important to stay in your lane. Know the role you play. Yield to God; not everything will go your way.

Unconditional love is another step on the journey to self-love. Learning to love people unconditionally is a commitment. Loving someone unconditionally does not mean that we must agree with them; it means we accept them as they are in their growth. That was hard for me. What helped me was thinking about how Christ loves me unconditionally despite the things I've done.

God used my story for His glory. In my healing and transformation, I realized that I did not want anyone else to go through what I had. In praying for a way to help, God gave me a vision for the nonprofit MyHelpMyHope Foundation, which brings awareness to domestic violence, sexual assault, and human sex trafficking. My organization helps women and their children fleeing these types of trauma situations. We provide resources, education, training, goal coaching, shelter, food, school uniforms, and Christmas for children in local domestic violence and homeless shelters. We believe that everyone has the right to a healthy relationship.

As an advocate for these causes, I discovered my gift for speaking and helping those affected by these traumas to heal and walk in their purpose. I do not heal anyone. God heals. He uses me to help. I have written self-help books, I speak, and I have started a life coaching consulting business to help those who are hurting and having a hard time to push past their pain. I consider myself a stepping stone as one journeys to self-discovery. I have a gift to help people learn how beautiful and wonderful they are by teaching them how to love themselves inside and out.

Self-love is what breaks generational chains. Learning how to love myself changed my life. I learned to focus on the things I was doing right instead of obsessing over the things I was doing wrong. I learned to focus on all the great things about me instead of on what I didn't like about myself. Self-love is not being selfish. Self-love is necessary for your journey. Learning to love yourself leads to happiness. You light up the world with your gifts, and you inspire others to do the same. We cannot love anyone else or give love until we first learn to love ourselves. Self-love means growing and making healthier choices. One outlet I used was journaling my feelings and emotions. This will help you learn what is working for you and what is not working for you. Ask for help. It is okay to do this. We cannot do everything by ourselves.

God is love, and love starts at home. Displaying love to our children creates healthy relationships, healthy families, healthy communities, and a healthy world. When we learn the art of self-love, we create a world full of happiness and joy and release ourselves from emotional heartache and pain.

My journey to self-love has baffled many. People wonder how I got through all the pain, the abuse, sexual assault, church hurt, and so much more. They wonder how I went from hating high school with low grades because I was bullied, to graduating with three bachelor's degrees at one time, founding a nonprofit, and starting my own business. I decided that enough was enough. I wanted something different out of my life. After all I went through, God had to have a purpose for my life. On my journey to self-love, I found out how strong I was. I discovered I was smart, intelligent, resilient, beautiful, empowering, inspiring, a leader, a teacher, a winner, and people needed what I had to offer. Self-love will give you peace and freedom.

Nothing can hold you back when you love yourself. Step into your greatness. Be yourself and let your light shine in the world. I thank God for redemption and deliverance. I am no longer ashamed.

> *God whispers to us in our pleasures, speaks in our conscience, but shouts in our pains.*
> *—C.S. Lewis*

About the Author

Cathy Staton brings with her over twenty years of leadership development experience as a self-published author, Christian counselor, motivational speaker, philanthropist, and life and business coach. Cathy has received leadership training from dynamic coaches such as Latrece Williams McKnight and Ari Squires. Her cutting-edge life skill strategies and uncompromising integrity are the hallmarks of her services to help women find their voice and use life's stumbling blocks to rebuild their lives.

Cathy serves as a domestic violence and sexual assault advocate providing a message of hope, encouragement, empowerment and inspiration. She is the founder of MyHelpMyHope Foundation, a 501(c)(3) nonprofit organization that assists women and children in crisis situations. She is also the CEO of Cathy Staton Coaching & Consulting, a company that provides affordable life coaching to those who want to reach their maximum potential in life and business. Through one-on-one coaching, group coaching, and custom presentations, she uses proven techniques to help people find fulfillment doing what they love.

Cathy is the recipient of numerous awards including the Wavy TV Channel 10 Who Care award, the Zeta Phi Beta Sorority Finer Woman award, Hampton Roads Gazeti Exemplar award, ACHI Magazine Woman of the Year award, ACHI Magazine Philanthropist award, Genieve Shelter Hero award, and the Garden of Hope Unity award from Gethsemane Community Fellowship Church. Cathy's work has been featured on the nationally syndicated Dr. Oz Show, Wavy 10 News, 13 News Now, and WTKR Channel 3. Cathy has also been featured in publications such as the Virginian-Pilot, the New Journal and Guide, the Hampton Roads Gazeti, and Tidewater Women. In 2017 the Obama Administration, Michelle Obama, and Oprah Winfrey selected The MyHelpMyHope Foundation as a change maker. Cathy has earned an AS in psychology, a BS in Christian counseling, a BS in life coaching, a BS in addiction and recovery from Liberty University, and is currently earning her Master's Degree in Professional Counseling.

Please visit www.cathystatonfreebie.com to receive your Rewrite Your Story step-by-step action guide

A Product of the Projects

My early childhood was spent growing up in the Butler Housing Project in Fort Worth, Texas, where my brother and I were raised by our mother and grandmother. Nineteen years old and single, my mother had to drop out of school and stop attending church because she was an unwed mother. However, my grandmother made sure we attended church regularly which seemed like every day. I learned how to read by reading Bible scriptures. My mother constantly stressed the importance of an education, so I have always excelled academically. Then my mother met someone that would change our lives forever.

Prior to meeting *him*, my mother always took us with her wherever she went. No matter if it was to the store, to a friend's house, or to the park where she spent time with her friends, we were right there with her. The three of us were inseparable. Shortly after my mother introduced us to *him*, the four of us moved out of the projects, taking me and my brother away from a home filled with so much love and affection. Instead we found ourselves in a place where we felt isolated and alone. If she wasn't yelling at us, she was ignoring us. We couldn't talk to her like we used to. She would wake us up to go to school, feed us dinner, then we went to bed. If we asked her for help with our homework, she would yell, "Go figure it out!"

I remember when *he* lost his job after getting hurt on a construction site. We felt like servants getting his beer and cigarettes, attending to his every need. Worst of all he would tell my mother to beat us. When we lived with my grandmother, my mother didn't hit us if we did something wrong. She would talk to us and explain why we shouldn't do what we did. Now she had turned into a strict disciplinarian. We received beatings all the time, even though we usually did not deserve them. If she was having a bad day, she would beat us. If she was mad at *him*, she would beat us.

My brother received a beating I'll never forget. *He* told my mother to beat my brother with an extension cord, and she did. At one point my brother accidentally hit her while grabbing for the cord. My mother started pounding him with her fist, fighting like he was a man. My brother was bleeding and screaming. I jumped in between them, pushing my mother away from him. When she tried to hit me, I ran outside to the pay phone and called my grandmother, who came to get us. My mother was crying as we packed up our things. She told us if we left, not to come back. My brother and I were crying. We didn't want to leave our mother, but we didn't like the way she treated us either.

For more than a year, we lived in the Butler Housing Projects with my grandmother in her one-bedroom apartment. I slept on a piece of foam on a foldout bed behind her bedroom door, and my brother slept on the floor in the living room. My mother never called. I was angry at her for treating us that way. She had changed because of him.

Although I remained on the honor roll at school, my attitude was terrible. I was so angry with my mother, and I took it out on others. For example, if someone at school was being picked on, I would speak up for them. Most of the time it turned into fights. That day I was forced to protect my brother from my mother had changed me. I took on the role of protector and defender. If someone said something I didn't like, I would fight back verbally or physically. That was the total opposite of how my grandmother raised me.

Words can't harm you.

Don't let people control you.

You can't control what others do to you, but you can control your response to it.

My mind was so messed up I ignored her loving words and great wisdom. I mean, what else was I supposed to do? I was hurting. My mom, the first woman I'd ever loved, gave up on me for some man and left me to grow up without a mom.

Eventually my grandmother could no longer afford to take care of us on her fixed income, so we had to move back in with my mother. She didn't talk to us, just at us. She totally isolated herself from us. We had to talk to her through her closed bedroom door.

We didn't eat dinner together. She would feed us then she ate dinner with him. We couldn't get seconds, so if my brother was still hungry, I would give him my food when my mother wasn't looking.

I longed for her love and affection. When continuously making the honor roll didn't get her attention, I got involved in other extracurricular activities. She once told me she had played softball. So I began playing basketball, volleyball, and running track. And I was good at all of them. But she never saw her baby girl play in even one game. I finished fourth

It's Time for Change

overall in my middle school, but I couldn't tell if she was proud or not. The beatings started again. There were times I didn't want to dress out in physical education because of the bruises left behind by the belt or extension cord.

By the time I started high school, my attitude was: *If my mother doesn't care about me, why should I care about myself?* During my freshman year I got into multiple fights and failed algebra and Spanish. I was fourteen the last time my mother beat me. I stood there and took every hit from the extension cord, each cutting the skin on my arms, on my legs. I thought: *Really? A beating?* I would not give her the satisfaction of seeing me cry. Lord knows it was painful. I had goosebumps, and my breathing was hurried. I just stared her in the face and took every hit. I had my fists balled up by my side, wanting to hit her. When it was over, I left home and went to live with a relative who was like a mother to me.

During that time I made all of my own decisions, good or bad. I was angry all the time. I got suspended for fighting and skipped school to be with my boyfriend since eighth grade. My aunt would sign me back into school because my mother stopped talking to me after I had moved out.

By my sophomore year, I came to the realization that self-afflicted pain and self-destruction was not the solution to my problems. My grandmother had always told us that in order to succeed in life, we needed an education. I enrolled in business classes and had plans of becoming a certified public accountant. I excelled in my accounting classes, receiving all As. I was amazed at how compiling receipts and other documents and making sense out of them reminded me of how I grew up: taking adversity and making sense out of it.

But then during my senior year I became pregnant by my boyfriend. I was seventeen and still angry much of the time. I almost had a fight when I was pregnant! But I thought about my unborn child and walked away. My dreams of playing on the varsity basketball team and receiving an advanced honors diploma with a concentration in business were replaced with going to night school, graduating a semester early with a general diploma and getting a job when my son was only a month old. I was determined not to end up like my mother and go on welfare.

The following September my grandmother died unexpectedly from a heart attack. Without my biggest fan, I didn't know where to turn. I tried to keep working and started dating someone new. When we broke up, I stopped working and found myself following the same path as my mother; I ended up on welfare and living back in the Butler Housing Projects. Some would say I was living a generational curse: living day-to-day without a plan.

I tried going to junior college but couldn't focus. My grandmother would have turned over in her grave if she knew I was living like a projects chick. Even though I was raised in the projects, my grandmother didn't raise us with a projects mentality.

She would say, "It's not where you live; it's how you live."

She raised us to be independent and make a way out of no way, not to depend on a check from the government.

After being shot at by a jealous baby momma, and almost shooting her with a 12 gauge shotgun, I decided I didn't want to die in the streets or let someone else dictate my behavior. I remembered how my grandmother

It's Time for Change

advised my eldest cousin to join the military. Grateful that she had planted that seed, I took my grandmother's advice and joined the military to make a better life for me and my son. I did have a few fights in basic training. But receiving a dishonorable discharge was not an option, so I learned how to control my anger. I focused on being a better person and, most importantly, being a better role model for my son.

While in the military I got married to give my son the childhood I never had; a mother and a father. At first I was very protective of my son because of all that I had seen as a child. It's hard to erase our past, but I knew I had to at least move past it and accept it as a part of my journey.

I had reservations when my husband wanted to discipline him or told me how to discipline him. I never wanted my son to talk to me through a door. I didn't make the same mistake in choosing a partner that my mother had. Not only did my husband show my son how a father should treat a son, he also showed me how a man should treat a woman with a child. I needed that.

I worked full-time as a soldier, mother, and wife. I earned my associate degree and started on my bachelor's. Shortly after receiving an honorable discharge from the Army, I became a law enforcement officer, which is my greatest accomplishment.

As a law enforcement officer, I work directly with the community I serve. I'm not just an enforcer of the law; I am a mentor and a role model to the youth in my community. Having a similar background to the youth I come in contact with, I can relate to their generational scars and provide guidance and assistance to steer them away from the criminal justice system.

I consider myself an example of how to not be a product of your environment. As an officer assigned to public housing, I tell them what my grandmother told me: *It's not where you live; it's how you live.*

As a school resource officer, I stress the importance of getting an education and getting along with your peers. As a basketball coach for our Police Athletic League, I work with the forgotten youth in our community who are at-risk from lack of parenting and other socioeconomic factors.

I know my passion and love for education helped me build character, so seeing the youth I work with graduate from high school and turn their lives around makes me proud. Even angry parents of juveniles I have arrested, thank me for caring enough to follow up with their child when I see them in the community.

Having a job that I love and being appreciated is my greatest accomplishment. Despite working ten-to twelve-hour days, I still find time to volunteer with the PTA and as a youth advisor at church. My life experiences have without a doubt molded me into a compassionate person willing to advocate for others. I have made an impact in my community as an intelligent, capable, dedicate, personable professional. As the executive director of the Police Athletic League, I learned a lot about running a nonprofit. I used this knowledge and skill to start my own business, Jada's Prints, a custom apparel business. My long-term goal is to partner with a school or technical center and teach youth how to make an honest living decorating apparel, instilling the same work ethic and character I have acquired while preparing them for the workplace or to become entrepreneurs themselves.

More than anything, I want to be a living example that troubled beginnings don't always lead to tragedy; life is about choices and self-accountability. Abuse can become achievements. Poverty can become power. It's time to change!

About the Author

Sherrie L Johnson is a dedicated mother of three biological children—Nickolaus, Kori, and Layla-Simone—and a mother figure to several others. As a member of Third Baptist Church, she has served on the Youth Ministry and the Women's Ministry. Sherrie is a US Army veteran and a seventeen-year law enforcement officer with the local police department where she was recently promoted to a Patrol Sergeant in the Uniform Field Operations Division becoming the first black female to attain this position. She earned an associatedegree from Saint Leo University, a bachelor's degree from Virginia State University, and has completed her firstyear at Concord Law School.

She was voted class president of the Fifty-Seventh Basic Police Academy, executive director of the Petersburg Police Athletic League, president of the Fraternal Order of Police, Lodge No. 16, and served on the Virginia PTA board of managers as the James River District Director.

Please visit bit.ly/nmc2freebie to receive your 11 Ways Youth Can Become Agents of Change guide

Conclusion

No matter how your life has unfolded so far, every single thing you have experienced has been valuable and necessary for shaping you into the person you are destined to become.

No matter how challenging. How hard. How tough. Life wants to you expand. And sometimes that expansion comes through challenge, or heartache, or loss, or struggle.

Know that it all has been divinely orchestrated because life loves you. So take a moment to give thanks and appreciation for everything your pain has brought you so far, no matter how tough.

Acknowledge all the beautiful inner growth and transformation you have experienced and remember that is way more important than what it looks like from the outside. And then take a deep breath and release whatever you no longer want to carry so you can get ready to enjoy what the rest of your life has to offer.

The thing about change is that in order for things around you to change, you have to change.

Action Step #1: Recognize That the Problem Is Not Outside of You; It's Inside of You.

Perception is projection. We don't see things as they are; we see them as *we* are.

It's Time for Change

The way we perceive the world determines the world we project around us. This means we have the ability to change the reality we are projecting simply by changing how we see it.

Every thing, event, and person is neutral. It just is. And then we come along and place a label on it—good or bad, right or wrong, positive or negative. We also make it mean something.

Your true power lies in not necessarily changing your reality but in changing the way you are experiencing your reality. Change the way you are labeling the events, people, or circumstances in your life. And most importantly, changing what you are making these events mean about *you*.

The way we perceive the world is based on how our beliefs, our memories, our thoughts, and our emotions combine together to create our stories, the chain of thoughts that typically play through our minds about the different areas of our lives.

The problem is that many of us have come to believe that our stories are true. We have spent our entire life accruing evidence from our world to support them. Because we have perceived the world through our stories, we have in turn created a world that reflects our stories.

Once you realize that everything you're telling yourself is just a story, you now have a choice.

You can choose how you perceive your world. You can choose to perceive your world in a way that supports and empowers you rather than in a way that limits and disempowers you.

Action Step #2: Heal Your Relationship with Yourself; Heal Your Relationship with Others.

It's time to take a deep look inwards.

We all have a nasty inner critic who not only attacks us but also attacks others. I encourage you to change your relationship with your inner critic and start transforming it into your inner cheerleader.

The inner critic judges, blames, compares, shames, and criticizes. Whereas the inner cheerleader just loves unconditionally and freely, and this type of love does not need to be earned.

Our inner critic is driven by fear, while our inner cheerleader is the voice of love. Fear cannot dim the light of love, yet the light of love will completely outshine the darkness of fear.

We heal all fears and shame through love, embracing them and opening up to them. Every time we push against our fear-driven inner critic, we actually strengthen that voice within us.

This step is about beginning to see your inner critic not as your enemy but rather as a part of you crying for love. The fear voice is simply a light that shows you an area of yourself not being loved.

The areas of yourself and your life that the inner critic attacks the most are the areas that require the most love from you.

This is not about eliminating your inner critic but rather changing your relationship with it. You have the ability to change how you respond to it.

Action Step #3: Master the Art of Manifestation.

The key to mastering manifestation is to understand that everything is energy.

Everything that you see in your world—whether it is a piece of furniture, money, or your body—is simply a mass of vibrating energy that has come together to form matter. If you put any of these things under a very strong microscope, all you will see is a mass of atoms and molecules buzzing together.

Yes, this concept can mess with your head a little initially; however, once grasped it will support you in the process of manifesting what you desire.

The next thing for you to understand is that energy can vibrate at different rates: a high/fast vibration or a low/slow vibration.

To explain this let's use water as an example. When you heat water, you cause the atoms that comprise water to vibrate at a faster rate. This changes the form of the water, and it turns to steam.

But when you freeze water, you slow down the vibration of the atom's energy within the water, which makes it denser and creates ice.

The most powerful way to apply this principle is understanding that you can hold your body in a high and light vibration or in a low and slow vibration.

Thinking positive, happy thoughts raises your vibration and makes the energy in your body vibrate at a higher rate that creates more positive emotions. This in turn attracts more positive and good things to you.

Thinking negative, sad thoughts makes the energy in your body vibrate at a lower rate, creating more negative emotion. This in turn attracts more negative things to you.

Action Step #4: Script a New Story for Your Life.

Mindset is everything. It's easy to say change your mindset, but how do we do that? Do we snap our fingers then *boom*, our mindset is instantly changed? Not really. You have to constantly focus on keeping yourself in a positive, receptive energy to allow what you want to come to you. You also have to focus on how you want things to be instead of how they are now.

Get two pieces of lined paper to write about what you desire for your life. Write this in the present tense as if it's true. Describe each area of your life as you want it to be. Describe how you will feel when you are living this.

This is your new story. This is the story you are going to begin to tell yourself about your life. Next, try this exercise that I have recently incorporated into my own life, and I love it. I highly recommend you try it and commit to it.

Desire Creation Audio Track

Record an audio track describing your dream life and telling yourself that you can have it. This will be something that you can listen to everyday.

1) Choose a method to record your audio. Options include:
    Garage Band software (on a mac)
    Download Audacity http://audacity.sourceforge.net/
    Voice memo app on your iPhone.

2) Take your desire script from worksheet 1 and read it out loud. You can either read it like: *I am living my dream life. Every day I wake up and...* etc. Or you can read it as though you are talking to yourself: *Self, you are living your dream life. Every day you wake up and ...* etc. It's up to you.

3) Personalize this audio. You can say positive and empowering affirmations to yourself. You can paint a picture of how it will feel when you have these desires. You can even tell yourself all of the reasons why this is possible. Include whatever you like!

4) This is about you creating something where every day you can hear your own voice affirming that everything you desire is coming to you. You will hear your own voice telling you what it's like to live your dream life.

5) Once you have recorded the audio, put it on your iPod and set aside time each day to listen to it. If you cannot set aside dedicated, listen to it on your way to work or while making dinner.

6) Update your track as often as you want to. Add in more details or as your desires manifest you may want to record new ones to reflect the new dreams you are dreaming.

Action Step #5: Heal with Love

Tune into your heart and ask yourself: *What would it look like if I loved and accepted myself just as I am? What would be different? What actions would I be taking?*

Describe it and journal it.

This is a really powerful practice to turn down the voice of your inner critic and help you start redeveloping a loving and beautiful relationship with yourself.

I want you to imagine what you looked like as a little four-year-old. If you cannot remember, find an old photograph.

1. Close your eyes. Create a clear picture on the screen of your mind of what you looked like. What was your hair like? Your skin? Your eyes? What are you wearing?

2. Imagine yourself at the age you are now. You can see the little four-year-old. What is she doing? Where is she? Is she at school or at home? How is she feeling?

3. Approach her. As you move closer to her, notice her reaction. Does she want to come and talk to you or play with you? Or does she run away? Whatever she wants to do, just allow her to do it.

4. When she is ready, ask her to come and sit on your lap so that you can talk to her. Take some time to see how she is. Ask her questions to find out how she is feeling, or if there is anything she needs. If she is not happy, ask her what she needs from you in order to feel happy.

5. Now give her love. Show her love in whatever way you want whether it is by cuddling her, kissing her, singing to her, or playing with her. Notice the feeling that comes up in you as you give her love.

6. Stay with this. Keep giving her love. Feel the feeling of love inside you.

7. Now allow her to guide you through the rest of the exercise. She may

want you to stay with her and play. She may want to say goodbye, so she can do her own thing. Or she may want to stay cuddling you. Allow her to show you what she wants and needs.

8. When you're finished stay sitting with your eyes closed and notice the emotions that are inside of you. Notice the feeling of love inside of you. This is what it feels like to love yourself. You do not need to do anything or be anything. You are already deserving of love just as you are.

Anytime you want to reconnect with love for yourself, imagine you are with your child self. Send her love. Send yourself love.

It's Time for Change

There are no limits to what you can create and experience in this lifetime. When you tap into your true power and release all of the limiting beliefs holding you back, you will be invincible.

Now it is time to live big. It is time to live your dreams. Use the space below to write down everything you can do to transform that dream into a reality. Write down everything you can think of.

If you had unlimited confidence, unlimited self-love, and believed in yourself 100 percent, what steps would you be taking? What brave, bold action steps could you follow through on that would lead you to your grand five-year vision? Declare them on paper.

Where to from here?

It's time to shine your light and show the world who you are. Take on board everything you have learned or discovered and step forward into the world with a brave heart and bold ambitions.

Revisit these worksheets, action steps, and stories whenever you need support. Use the exercises and practices you have learned whenever you need a boost.

Stay connected with our tribe through the My Story Has Purpose Facebook community and keep sharing yourself with the people who are here to support you.

If you have some feedback on your experiences, or if you would like to share with me what you achieved, I would love to hear from you. Please email me at info@arisquires.com.

You Are Amazing!

www.ingramcontent.com/pod-product-compliance
Lightning Source LLC
Chambersburg PA
CBHW052053070526
44584CB00017B/2161

The Moderate Bolshevik

Mikhail Tomsky from the Factory to the Kremlin, 1880–1936

Charters Wynn

Haymarket Books
Chicago, IL

First published in 2022 by Brill Academic Publishers, The Netherlands
© 2022 Koninklijke Brill NV, Leiden, The Netherlands

Published in paperback in 2023 by
Haymarket Books
P.O. Box 180165
Chicago, IL 60618
773-583-7884
www.haymarketbooks.org

ISBN: 978-1-64259-916-9

Distributed to the trade in the US through Consortium Book Sales and Distribution (www.cbsd.com) and internationally through Ingram Publisher Services International (www.ingramcontent.com).

This book was published with the generous support of Lannan Foundation and Wallace Action Fund.

Special discounts are available for bulk purchases by organizations and institutions. Please call 773-583-7884 or email info@haymarketbooks.org for more information.

Cover art and design by David Mabb. Cover art is a detail of *Construct 34, Morris, Daisy, / Popova, untitled textile design*, wallpaper mounted on linen (2006).

Printed in the United States.

10 9 8 7 6 5 4 3 2 1

Library of Congress Cataloging-in-Publication data is available.

Contents

Acknowledgements VII
List of Illustrations IX

Introduction 1
   1   Note on Transliteration 9

1 The Making of a Moderate Working-Class Bolshevik Leader 10

2 Balancing Act: Tomsky during War Communism and the Trade-Union Debate 59

3 Detour East: From Disgraced Exile in Tashkent to Redemption inside the Kremlin 116

4 Getting Together then Falling Apart: Tomsky and British Trade Unionists 170

5 Tomsky during NEP: Trade Unions and the Intra-Party Struggle 214

6 NEP's Last Stand: The Eighth Trade-Union Congress 280

7 Tomsky Outcast: Tormenting a 'Right Deviationist' 314

Conclusion 381

Bibliography 391
Index 433

Acknowledgements

Many years have passed since I first began to study Tomsky. It is a pleasure to thank the sources of funding for the research and writing of this book I received along the way. From outside the University of Texas at Austin I received a grant from the International Research and Exchanges Board (IREX), a Kennan Institute for Advanced Russian Studies Research Scholarship, and a National Council for Soviet and East European Research Award. Sources of support from within the university included a University Research Institute Grant, a Dean's Fellowship, and an Institute of Historical Studies Fellowship.

My research took me to various archives and libraries a number of times. In particular, I appreciate all the archivists and staff members who assisted me at the Russian State Archive of Social-Political History (RGASPI), the State Archive of the Russian Federation (GARF), and the Hoover Institution Archives. I am also particularly indebted to the Inter-Library Loan staff at the University of Texas Libraries who tracked down nearly everything I requested, no matter how rare or obscure.

All the chapters of this project have benefitted from helpful questions and comments from colleagues at innumerable conferences, including the one I hosted at the University of Texas. I thank Alexis Pogorelskin for turning the papers at that conference into a special issue of *Canadian-American Slavic Studies*. Barbara Allen, Clayton Black, and William Chase, among others, offered useful suggestions as commentators on panels at the Association for Slavic, East European & Eurasian Studies. I have also received helpful feedback on all the various parts of this book at the wonderfully collegial conferences of the Study Group on Revolutionary Russia. In addition, Judith Coffin and Leone Musgrave provided useful feedback on individual chapters, while Lars Lih caught an error in one of my articles on Tomsky. Barbara Allen generously shared some of the notes she took in the Federal Security Service (FSB) archives.

Earlier drafts of parts of this book have been previously published as articles. I am grateful for their editors' permission to include them here. Part of Chapter 1 appeared in 'Young Tomsky: The Making of a Working-Class Bolshevik Leader', *Revolutionary Russia*, 25, 2: 119–40. Part of Chapter 4 appeared in 'Getting Together and then Falling Apart: Tomsky and British Trade Unionism during NEP', *Russian Review*, 73, 4: 571–95. Part of Chapter 6 appeared in 'NEP's Last Stand: Mikhail Tomsky and the Eighth Trade Union Congress', *Canadian-American Slavic Studies*, 53, 1–2: 149–75. And a part of Chapter 7 appeared in 'The "Right Opposition" and the "Smirnov-Eismont-Tolmachev Affair"' in *The 'Lost' Politburo Stenograms: From Collective Rule to Stalin's Dictatorship*, edited by Paul Gregory and Norman Naimark, New Haven: Yale University Press, pp. 97–117. I am grateful to all the 'anonymous' reviewers who provided editorial suggestions on these earlier drafts, especially Barbara Allen. Two reviewers of the entire manuscript for the Historical Materialism Book Series, one of whom was Clayton Black, also provided helpful comments.

I have been fortunate in the Department of History at the University of Texas to have worked with helpful colleagues and dear friends, especially Judith Coffin, David Crew, Tatjana Lichtenstein, and Michael Stoff. My deepest thanks go to Joan Neuberger, always my first reader and always full of valuable suggestions. She has been my best friend, a wise colleague, and an endless source of encouragement. Together we share a love for our wonderful sons, Max and Joel. It is to them I dedicate this book.

Illustrations

1. Mikhail Tomsky 46
2. Tomsky and Zinoviev en route to meeting 64
3. Tomsky with Delegates of the Eighth Party Congress 80
4. Alexander Shlyapnikov 82
5. Tomsky, on the far right, behind Stalin and Lenin, with Trotsky 88
6. Tomsky, seated fourth from the left, at the Presidium of the Ninth Party Congress 90
7. David Ryazanov 109
8. Yan Rudzutak 118
9. Negotiations with Basmachi 131
10. Grigory Safarov 137
11. Settlers' homestead in Turkestan 141
12. Tomsky wearing Turkish sheepskin hat 152
13. Tomsky in the Kremlin 162
14. Alexander Lozovsky 174
15. Tomsky at British Trades Union Congress in Hull 182
16. Tomsky with Alf Purcell 189
17. Walter Citrine 191
18. Composite Poster of Soviet Officials in 1924 with Tomsky in top row, far right 217
19. Leon Trotsky in 1925 227
20. Stalin, Rykov, Zinoviev, and Bukharin relaxing together 230
21. Tomsky with Nadezhda Krupskaya at Lenin's funeral 234
22. Nikolai Bukharin 241
23. Stalin with Tomsky and Kalinin in 1926 247
24. Tomsky with Rykov at the Seventh Trade-Union Congress 249
25. United Opposition leaders Trotsky, Kamenev, and Zinoviev 254
26. Tomsky on the Lenin Mausoleum in November 1927 260
27. Interrogation protocols for the Shakhty Trial 276
28. Tomsky and Tomskaya socialising with Gorky and Yagoda 291
29. Stalin with Kaganovich 303
30. Tomsky and Kalinin with party functionaries 335
31. Same photo with Tomsky's face blacked out 336
32. Tomsky in 1936 360

Introduction

'I can't live without the party', Mikhail Tomsky told his 15-year-old son before deciding to grab one of his guns and shoot himself.[1] A devoted member of the party since its inception, and one of the three party leaders who had desperately tried at the end of the 1920s to block the Stalinists' lurch into the draconian industrialisation and forcible collectivisation of agriculture that would cost millions their lives, Tomsky's suicide in the summer of 1936 shocked members of the Bolshevik Party. It served as one of the first deaths in the Great Purges and mass repression that violently unfolded over the next two and a half years. Tomsky was determined to decide his own fate once it became clear that Stalin, his former friend and political ally, had patiently and methodically put him in his deadly sights. He was not going to provide one last service to the party and confess in a Moscow show trial as an 'enemy of the people' to such ludicrously fantastic crimes as being a terrorist and fascist spy.[2] Nor was he going to denounce the Bolshevik Party, which would have meant denouncing virtually his entire adult life. Many in the West with reason viewed Tomsky as a tragic hero.

While Lenin, Stalin, Trotsky, and Bukharin have been the subject of innumerable biographical studies, little has been written about Tomsky outside Russia other than to link his name with Nikolai Bukharin and Alexei Rykov as the leaders of what the Stalinists labelled the Right Deviation and later the Right Opposition.[3] He still remains, in the words of Jerry Hough, 'a shadowy figure in most histories of the period'.[4] Yet appreciating Tomsky's role is central to understanding early Soviet history, since as the head of the trade unions and one of the members of the Politburo, the Orgburo, the Central Committee of the Party, the Central Executive Committee of the Soviets, and the Executive Committee of the Comintern, he had a seat on all the most important policymaking bodies in the early Soviet state. Catherine Merridale, in her rousing defence of the value of writing biographies of early Soviet leaders, while noting

---

1 Gorelov and Shapovalova (eds) 2001, p. 150.
2 Arthur Koestler in his fictional classic *Darkness at Noon* suggests that the idea of providing 'a last service' was what led 'Old Bolsheviks' at show trials to confess to crimes they had not committed: Koestler 1941, p. 190.
3 During the Gorbachev era, with the 'rehabilitation' of Tomsky, he attracted the attention of some Russian scholars, particularly Oleg Gorelov: Gorelov 2000. Gorelov generously shared his manuscript with me when it looked like it could no longer be published in Russia.
4 Hough and Fainsod 1979, p. 118. Zinoviev and Kamenev still await their biographers, though Clayton Black and Alexis Pogorelskin are working toward filling that gap.

that political biography is often considered an unworthy subject for serious historians, argues that 'biography is not merely a matter of satisfying our curiosity about individuals. It also offers a glimpse of the collective mentality of one of the most remarkable groups of people in twentieth-century politics'.[5]

Tomsky played a key role in the most important developments during the transition from tsarist to Stalinist Russia. The sole proletarian in the very top echelon of the party throughout the 1920s, he was at the centre of many of the thorniest issues facing the new Soviet regime.[6] Most notably, Tomsky was in the middle of the debates over what should be the role of trade unions in the self-proclaimed workers' state. As we will see, his attempts to mediate between the extremes of the party were not always successful. Lenin even banished him for a short time to Central Asia during the first years after the Bolshevik seizure of power, where his experiences defending so-called kulaks against horrible abuses by party fanatics helped shape many of the moderate positions he later favoured. Tomsky's widely respected abilities quickly brought him back to Moscow and to even more political prominence.

To the extent that Tomsky is mentioned in studies of the 1920s, historians have cursorily and unfairly dismissed him as an ineffectual loser or a dupe in the political manoeuvring following Lenin's death – a naïve, uneducated worker amid intellectually superior and politically ruthless party leaders. While historians have argued, from various perspectives, that the Stalinist outcome was all but inevitable, Stalin's victory over those he labelled 'Rightists' was far more contingent than that. It was hardly a foregone conclusion to contemporary participants and observers, who thought there were alternative paths open to the Soviet leadership at the end of the 1920s.[7] Many expected the more moderate members of the Politburo to prevail. Leon Trotsky, for one, predicted they would soon 'hunt down Stalin'.[8] It was even widely rumoured that Tomsky might replace Stalin as general secretary, which would have made him de facto head of the Bolshevik Party.[9] While Bukharin primarily articulated the theoretical defence of NEP, Tomsky in his dual roles as a member of the

---

5 Merridale 1995, p. 37.
6 Mikhail Kalinin and Yan Rudzutak, who both became full members of the Politburo in 1926, had been workers before the revolution, but unlike Tomsky they were of peasant origin. The Central Committee elected Tomsky to the Politburo in April 1922.
7 Stephen Cohen's biography of Bukharin remains the most important challenge to the dominant historiography: Cohen 1973. E.A. Rees, in agreeing that Stalin's victory was not inevitable, argues that 'in the Central Committee and the Politburo itself the prevailing mood favoured unity' (Rees 2012, p. 5).
8 Quoted in Deutscher 1959, p. 428.
9 Reiman 1987, p. 28; RGASPI, f. 17, op. 2, d. 35, ll. 3–8.

Politburo and as head of the huge trade-union bureaucracy played a central part in the desperate attempt to preserve the class-conciliatory policies of NEP and prevent the predictably catastrophic policies of forced collectivisation and de-kulakisation. The politically savvy Tomsky rallied supporters and undercut opponents over the course of nearly a decade. Stalin's ultimate victory required five years of concerted effort after Lenin's death before he accumulated enough power to oust Tomsky and the other moderate leaders. It is fair to conclude, as has been suggested, that Tomsky was tough, but in the end outmatched politically by Stalin.[10] That of course was not some unique failing on Tomsky's part. Stalin, the master political infighter, outmatched every member of the party leadership during the 1920s, to more or less the same extent.

Who was this man, Tomsky? It is not easy to uncover the man behind the public image. Like other Soviet leaders, Tomsky was generally unwilling to share information about his personal life.[11] In addition, memoirs, diaries, letters, and other such sources, which could provide some insights into his private life and thoughts are missing from his skimpy personal file in the former central party archive in Moscow.[12] Fortunately, despite the lack of substantial personal papers, there is a rich cache of material available on Tomsky's career. His distinctive voice comes through in his administrative decisions and disputes with other leaders at party and trade-union congresses and conferences, Central Committee plenums, Politburo and the Presidium of the Central Control Commission sessions, and articles for party and trade-union journals. This is especially true in his attempts to defend himself during the 1930s from the Stalinist regime's attacks. A particularly rich source is the stenogram of Tomsky's multi-day purge testimony, behind closed doors in 1933, where he was called upon to describe his life, from his youth, entry into the revolutionary underground, leadership of the trade unions, and role in various policy disputes on the Politburo. The memories in late life of his youngest son, who was arrested following Tomsky's suicide and suffered for years in Siberia, as well as the candid impressions of foreign trade-union leaders with whom he worked, also proved valuable. In addition, the tsarist political police kept close tabs on him

---

10 Kotkin 2014, p. 717.
11 The major exception among the Old Bolsheviks is Trotsky, who survived long enough to write an autobiography. Another notable autobiography is by the worker-*intelligent* Semen Kanatchikov.
12 Tomsky's personal archive had been confiscated from his apartment when his family was arrested in 1937: Gorelov 2000, p. 268. I can no longer wait for them to be released from the APRF, the archives of the President of the Russian Federation. Also, since Tomsky has no living heirs, gaining access to his political police files, access such as Barbara Allen gained for her biography of Alexander Shlyapnikov (Allen 2015), has not been possible.

and his wife while he was in the revolutionary underground. That is all supplemented by the publication of a great amount of archival material since the collapse of the Soviet Union. In addition to contemporary Russian and non-Russian newspapers, I also draw on the voluminous secondary literature on Revolutionary and Stalinist Russia.

Tomsky, who is often described as one of the most appealing and charismatic of the Bolshevik leaders, enjoyed widespread personal popularity and was held in high regard across the Bolshevik political spectrum.[13] His appeal did not spring from his outward appearance. Far from physically imposing, Tomsky was short and stocky (less than five feet, three inches tall), with bad teeth and deafness in one ear later in life.[14] Relatively dark-skinned, many Russians pejoratively thought he looked like a Tatar. Yet virtually the entire trade-union leadership as well as much of the political leadership were utterly devoted to him throughout the 1920s. They made him the focus of a minor cult of personality. Though he was the most modest of the Bolshevik leaders, numerous factories, a sports stadium, a ship, as well as the Higher Trade Union School in Moscow were named after him. The trade-union leadership under Tomsky also honoured him by publishing four volumes of his articles and speeches before he fell out of favour.[15] Lenin, who was a poor speaker outside the confines of party meetings, highly valued Tomsky's rapport with workers as well as his administrative skills. Vyacheslav Molotov agreed that 'Tomsky was good at leading the masses. He could talk with workers'.[16] His long-time adversary Trotsky praised Tomsky's 'character and caustic, sarcastic mind'.[17] Tomsky put to good use his irrepressible sense of humour. A skilled if sometimes longwinded orator, Tomsky loved to litter his speeches with jokes. The stenographic reports of his speeches to a wide variety of audiences were always punctuated with many bracketed insertions of 'laughter'. Even the hardcore Stalinist Lazar Kaganovich conceded he 'loved to listen to Tomsky's interesting and witty speeches'.[18] Unlike other party leaders, Tomsky also could charm foreign

---

13 Bukharin and Rykov also enjoyed great personal popularity. But it seems that Tomsky was the most popular of the three with the party rank and file. Trotsky and Zinoviev, in contrast, were not popular.
14 Tomsky's height is perhaps not as short as it seems. Many of the Old Bolsheviks were short. Bukharin was even shorter at just above five feet tall. Lenin was five feet, five inches. Even the relatively tall Stalin's height was only five feet, six inches.
15 The publication of three additional volumes was abruptly cancelled following Tomsky's defeat at the Eighth Trade-Union Congress in December 1928.
16 Molotov 1993, p. 119.
17 Trotsky 1988, p. 228.
18 Vatlin et al. (eds) 2000d, p. 113.

non-communists. The Menshevik émigré newspaper, *Sotsialisticheskii vestnik* (Socialist Herald), described him in its obituary as 'the most colourful and admirable figure among the Bolshevik leaders'.[19] The British 'reformist' trade-union leaders, with whom he worked for many years in pursuit of international trade-union unity, likewise widely admired Tomsky and were charmed by his biting wit and down-to-earth character. Despite their acrimonious disagreements during the latter half of the 1920s, the British trade unionists were so distressed when Tomsky fell out of favour that they were determined to overcome official resistance to renew their friendship with him when they visited Moscow in the mid-1930s.[20] Tomsky likewise quickly won the devoted support of his administrative assistants shortly after he became head of the Soviet publishing industry in 1932, a position he held until the day of his death in 1936.

Tomsky was moderate in temperament as well as policy, but could be forceful if necessary, even exploding in anger during some of the most bitter debates. His colleagues generally viewed him as a level-headed politician and administrator. Tomsky had 'horse sense', in the words of one contemporary observer.[21] Although he proved to be shrewd and far more diplomatic than his politically inept 'Right Deviationist' colleague Bukharin, observers were also struck by how straightforward and blunt he usually was in political discussions and debates. Tomsky was not inclined by nature to bow to authority. Both in his rise from an impoverished youth up the party ranks, and then on the Politburo and as head of the trade unions, Tomsky did not shy away from a fight, even with Lenin, who described him as 'subtle, firm, and stubborn'.[22] Alexander Shlyapnikov, the leader of the 'Workers' Opposition', was more critical. Because of Tomsky's willingness to pursue compromises once it became clear the party leadership would deny the trade unions the primary role in economic management, Shlyapnikov characterised him as spineless on a number of occasions. But most of his colleagues strongly disagreed. Trotsky thought his 'years of hard labour, and various other trials, had produced in him a tremendous amount of physical and moral strength'.[23] One foreign interviewer noted that when provoked, the face of the usually genial Tomsky was 'full of fire' as he launched into a blistering speech.[24] During the fight with the Stalinists at the end of the 1920s, Molotov thought Tomsky was 'venomous'.[25]

---

19 *Sotsialisticheskii vestnik*, 30 August 1936, p. 11.
20 Citrine 1936, p. 81.
21 Dunn 1928, p. 164.
22 Lenin 1960–70, vol. 45, p. 297.
23 Trotsky 1988, p. 228.
24 Lee 1928, p. 128.
25 Molotov 1993, p. 182.

Tomsky, who generally put in long, exhausting hours, had an enormous capacity for work, which often left little time for his wife and children. He commonly could not endure the strain. Like seemingly all the other 'Old Bolsheviks', especially those who did not spend the years before the Bolshevik seizure of power in European exile, Tomsky suffered from frequent bouts of debilitating illness. Years inhaling toxic fumes as a lithographer, and nine years in prison and frigid Siberian exile caused him to suffer throughout his later life from seriously debilitating illnesses that sometimes meant he not only needed to take time off from work, but needed to seek treatment abroad. Given that the worst physical breakdowns came when he was under particularly nasty political fire, it is tempting to characterise his ailments as psychosomatic; not that this made the symptoms any less incapacitating. In any case, the once incurably upbeat Tomsky, even in prison, became increasingly despondent and even deeply depressed following his ouster from power. He repeatedly suffered from what doctors diagnosed as nervous breakdowns.

By all accounts, including by fellow party members with radically different views, Tomsky was the most moderate of Bolsheviks. But what does it mean to be a moderate Bolshevik? It has been suggested that the very notion of moderate Bolshevism is an oxymoron.[26] But Bolshevik politics during 1917, the Civil War, and NEP were obviously far less monolithic and homogeneous than they were to become during the 1930s. Although all shared a commitment to advancing the revolutionary cause, Bolshevik Party leaders embraced a diversity of views and favoured a range of policy positions. As a pragmatic leader in his particular domain, Tomsky tried to find a sustainable middle ground between defending the trade unions' autonomy from the government, while as one of the handful of top party officials, also supporting the party's general oversight of the unions. His opposition to rash economic policies would ultimately prove to be central to his moderate views. Tomsky, who had struggled unsuccessfully along with other party leaders to reverse the suffering and deprivations of the Civil War years, afterwards strongly favoured a gradual, evolutionary approach to industrialisation and collectivisation. He proved to be one of the fiercest defenders of the moderate economic policies of NEP, which were unfurled in 1921. The cautious pragmatism he embodied, which was shared by most of his fellow Soviet trade unionists, stood in stark contrast to the romantic adventurism of others in the party leadership. Tomsky did not think the party should run after utopian dreams or rely on radical enthusiasm, the so-called

---

26   Denial of the existence of a conflict between radicals and moderates is applicable to the 1930s, but not the 1920s.

revolutionary-heroic tradition in the party. As one contemporary, the 'ultra-leftist' German Comintern member Arthur Rosenberg, observed about this highly skilled former lithographer:

> Tomsky represented the views of a minority of skilled and better-paid Russia workmen who had grown weary of revolution and refused to listen any longer to the socialist fables. Their desire was to defend and improve their living conditions with the assistance of the trade unions. If the Soviet state were to take on a semi-middle-class character that would not cause them any anxiety, since the skilled workmen as a professional class would not be likely to suffer from the change.[27]

While there is an underlying truth in this overstatement of Tomsky's identification with skilled workers, once economic conditions stabilised under NEP, Tomsky as head of the trade unions fought on behalf of unskilled workers, particularly in his efforts to reduce the enormous wage gap between them and skilled workers. He also fought to improve employment opportunities for women and young workers, although arguably not as hard as he might have.

In contrast to all these elements of moderation, Tomsky proved to be a zealous participant in the intra-party power struggle and could be far from moderate during this political infighting toward those with whom he most strongly disagreed; especially those he thought threatened to abandon the moderate economic policies of NEP. No European-style social democrat, he supported the banning of dissident factions within the Bolshevik Party who opposed his moderate policies. He worked arm-in-arm with Stalin, Bukharin, and Rykov to crush, in turn, the Left, Zinovievite, and United Opposition. In addition to sharing the Bolsheviks' unwillingness to tolerate any dissent within their ranks, it was Tomsky's condemnation of Trotsky's policies, and his dislike of Trotsky's haughty personality, that would largely explain his role during the intra-party power struggle, including his alliance with Stalin.

Tomsky and Trotsky were the polar opposites in the party leadership. In contrast to Tomsky's relative moderation in his defence of NEP and the trade unions, Trotsky was the quintessential party radical during the first years of the Soviet regime with his advocacy for militarising labour, creating 'labour armies', and 'shaking up' the trade unions. Likewise, Tomsky clashed with Trotsky over international affairs. After initially sharing the Bolsheviks' intoxicating belief that revolution in Russia would spark revolution in Europe and Asia, Tomsky

---

27 Rosenberg 1934, p. 206.

sought to create an alliance between Soviet workers and the non-communist trade unions in Europe. This would again put him at loggerheads with Trotsky, the firebrand of international revolution. But Tomsky, like so many others, completely failed to appreciate how Stalin, who had seemed to share his moderate views, would ultimately elbow him aside and essentially adopt Trotsky's platform. Tomsky is said to have complained to his friends, 'We thought that after we finished with Trotsky we would be able to work peacefully; but now it appears that the same methods of struggle are to be applied against us'.[28]

The last major battle in defence of the moderate policies of NEP took place in December 1928 on Tomsky's home turf within the trade-union leadership, where he had enjoyed virtually unchallenged personal authority. The other moderates in the party leadership had hoped Tomsky, the only member of the Politburo to head a mass non-party organisation, might be able to mobilise the trade-union functionaries to push back against Stalinist intrigues. The failure of Tomsky and his allies to undertake a public struggle against Stalin, while their prestige was still great, has been seen as their major blunder.[29] But Tomsky's loyalty to the party [*partiinost'*] was such that he feared any division within it could fatally undermine it. Indeed, he and his fellow moderates, while conducting a determined, yearlong fight behind the scenes, never considered appealing over Stalin's head to the party rank and file as the United Opposition had unsuccessfully done the year before. Even though they now considered Stalin an existential threat to the revolution, the moderates refused to entertain doing anything that might threaten the Bolshevik Party's monopoly on political power.

Tomsky recanted for his political 'mistakes' during the last six plus years of his life, but the Stalinists had good reason to question his sincerity. Tomsky would privately condemn Stalin's leadership during the early 1930s and fantasise with other former oppositionists about removing him from power. Nothing ever came of that other than increased persecution at the hands of the Stalinist leadership. Despite all the torment the Stalinists inflicted on him, Tomsky remained committed to the Bolshevik cause and took pride in his leadership of the book publishing industry, where he courageously came to the aid of at least one former colleague who found himself under even darker clouds than Tomsky. As head of Soviet publishing, Tomsky refurbished the industry, implemented the Stalinist doctrine on socialist realism, and under intense pressure, published truly stupendous numbers of textbooks, all while enduring

---

28   Quoted in Trotsky 1981, p. 309.
29   Daniels 1960, p. 363.

unrelenting political harassment from Stalinists, including being hauled before multiple purge commissions and Central Committee Plenums and Party Congresses.

Tomsky, like others, never imagined Stalin would pursue former party opponents to the grave. But once he realised that Stalin was determined to put him and other remnants of defunct opposition groups within the party through what became known as the Great Purges, Tomsky, unlike others, took matters into his own hands.

1 Note on Transliteration

I have deliberately mixed two systems of transliteration. The names of authors and titles in the footnotes and bibliography follow the Library of Congress transliteration system. That system is modified in the text, where the names of people appear in forms easier for those unfamiliar with the Russian language. The Library of Congress's final 'ii' in male names is replaced by 'y', as for example, Tomsky, instead of Tomskii. The female version of Russian last names has also been used, such as Tomskaya instead of Tomskaia. The extra 'i' in names like Mariia is dropped and 'y' is used instead of 'i' in front of vowels in names like Vyacheslav. The Russian soft signs are also dropped in the text, so it is Sokolnikov not Sokol'nikov. Where possible, first names have been used instead of initials.

CHAPTER 1

The Making of a Moderate Working-Class Bolshevik Leader

> Tomsky was undoubtedly the most outstanding worker within the Bolshevik Party and perhaps in the Russian Revolution as a whole.
> LEON TROTSKY

∵

This chapter focuses on Tomsky's youth and years in the revolutionary movement up to the Bolshevik seizure of power in 1917.[1] It will account for Tomsky's rise into the top ranks of the Bolshevik Party even though he had no more than an elementary-school education. Tomsky's formative experiences before the revolution marked him as a typical worker-*intelligent*, but unlike other such workers, Tomsky became a member of the Bolshevik leadership.[2] His prudent caution in the 1905 Revolution and during 1917 demonstrates that, more so than other so-called Right Bolsheviks in the party leadership, Tomsky fairly consistently advocated moderate positions before as well as after the Bolshevik seizure of power.[3] Once at the top, Tomsky did not shy away from challenging other party leaders. His ambition, remarkable self-confidence, and gift for public speaking, as well as his political skills and relatively moderate inclinations, distinguished him from the thousands of fellow Bolsheviks from working-class backgrounds. While his suffering at the hands of the tsarist political police was all too typical, Tomsky spent nearly double the time in tsarist prison and Siberian exile of the average Bolshevik activist.[4] It was following his first stint in Siberia, as we shall see, that Tomsky, who was born Mikhail Pavlovich

---

1 Part of Chapter 1 has been previously published in 'Young Tomsky: The Making of a Working-Class Bolshevik Leader', *Revolutionary Russia*, 25, 2: 119–40.
2 The most notable exception is Alexander Shlyapnikov, a skilled worker who for one year was Commissar of Labour before becoming a leader of the Workers' Opposition.
3 The most obvious example of that is Nikolai Bukharin, who was on the far left of Bolshevism in 1918.
4 Figes 1996, p. 124.

Efremov, adopted his revolutionary pseudonym. Although he shared the Bolshevik leadership's general aversion to sharing aspects of their personal lives, in this chapter we will begin to flesh out this side of Tomsky.

Tomsky's early life experiences help us understand why he would rise to the heights of political power following the Bolshevik Revolution. To address issues concerning his youth and political career it will be useful to compare his experiences with those of Semen Kanatchikov, a fellow worker-*intelligent* in the Bolshevik movement who, unlike Tomsky and virtually all former workers, wrote a book-length autobiography. Kanatchikov's memoirs, which allow us to accompany him from his first frightened step into a factory through his subsequent evolution into a skilled radicalised worker, gives voice to many of the experiences Tomsky shared with Kanatchikov. They both stood out from the mass of fellow workers by becoming highly skilled and by entering the revolutionary movement, which entailed various privileges and hardships. Their paths diverged when Tomsky rose into the top echelon of the Bolshevik Party and early Soviet regime, but their trajectories converged again during the 1930s when they both suffered for their oppositional pasts.

Tomsky and Kanatchikov shared similar early-life experiences. Born into poverty within a year of each other – Kanatchikov in 1879 and Tomsky in 1880 – they came of age during Russia's late nineteenth-century industrial boom. Raised within households struggling to survive, both entered the industrial labour force in their teens. Where their backgrounds significantly diverge is the different social milieus within which they spent their childhood years. Kanatchikov grew up in a poor peasant household in Moscow's rural hinterland, the monotony of which he itched to escape. Tomsky, in contrast, spent his earliest years in a squalid factory town on the outskirts of St. Petersburg, Kolpino, which marks him as an atypical worker, since most workers in the 1890s, like Kanatchikov, started life as peasants in the countryside.[5] His father worked as a metal worker and his mother a seamstress. Tomsky was among the relatively few workers who were what Soviet historians called hereditary proletarians.[6]

Yet many aspects of lower-class culture crossed the rural-urban divide. The drinking binges common in Russia among male peasants and workers, and

---

5   RGASPI, f. 593, op. 1, d. 1, l. 1. Large state-owned armaments and shipbuilding complexes, as well as a metalworking plant, operated in Kolpino, which is located a few miles southeast of the St. Petersburg's city limits. According to Andrei Bely, 'nothing could be gloomier' than Kolpino: quoted in Bater 1976, p. 300.
6   In 1902, St. Petersburg industrial enterprises, surprisingly, had the lowest proportion of hereditary workers in Russian industry: Economakis 1998, pp. 7–8.

the domestic violence connected with it, shaped both Kanatchikov's and Tomsky's childhoods, though in quite different ways. Beatings followed whenever Kanatchikov's despotic father returned home from drinking, keeping the young Semen, his siblings, and especially his mother in 'mortal fright', and provoking what Kanatchikov described as feelings of 'animal hatred' toward his father.[7] Tomsky, who never knew his father, might be the lucky one. With a strength, or perhaps a foolhardiness Kanatchikov's mother lacked, Tomsky's mother chose to become a single parent shortly before Tomsky's birth, refusing to accept any longer the continual beatings and insults her drunkard of a husband inflicted on her. But while Tomsky was never exposed to the drunken scenes his sister and older brother had endured, that benefit might have been more than offset by losing the income his father had earned as a metal craftsman. Tomsky also later recalled that the stigma associated with illegitimacy caused him much childhood grief and shame.[8]

Tomsky endured a childhood of, in his own words, 'utter destitution'.[9] Kanatchikov's family also knew need, but they benefitted from the off-farm earnings the adult males brought into the household, thereby escaping the plight of the poorest peasants. Tomsky's earliest years would have been far worse if not for the generosity of his grandfather, with whom Tomsky often lived until he was six years old, along with his sister and brother. But his childhood was not free of family violence. Tomsky's grandfather could not protect him from his much older brother, who suffered from tuberculosis and often could not find employment. Tomsky later bitterly recalled how his brother commonly took out his frustration by brutally mistreating 'little Misha'.[10] After his grandfather's death, the family of four lived from hand to mouth on the pittance Tomsky's mother earned as a washerwoman and occasional seamstress. Tomsky's difficult childhood shares much with Joseph Stalin's, whose mother, following the death of her abusive, alcoholic husband also struggled to raise her son on what she could earn as a washerwomen and seamstress.[11]

A striking similarity between Tomsky and Kanatchikov was their life-long eagerness to learn. In a country where 79 percent of the population was still illiterate as late as 1897, and compulsory primary schooling was not yet instituted,

---

7   Kanatchikov 1986, p. 5.
8   Kozelev 1927, p. 9.
9   TsGAODM, f. 2870, op. 1, d. 296, reprinted in Karpachev and Minaeva (eds) 1992b, p. 100.
10 Gambarov et al. (eds) 1989, part 3, p. 146.
11 McDermott 2006, p. 18. Stalin's mother Ekaterina eventually earned more since she learned the craft of dressmaking and got a steady job in a dressmaking shop. She was also literate, perhaps unlike Tomsky's mother. As in the case of Tomsky, Ekaterina's relatives contributed financially to Stalin's upbringing: Khlevnuik 2015, p. 12.

neither Tomsky nor Kanatchikov had an opportunity for much education (only a tiny percentage of lower-class children equalled Kanatchikov's four years of formal education). For Kanatchikov to attend school required travelling to a larger village, where the teachers relied on rote memorisation and harsh discipline, the norm in village schools. Tomsky also had only a few years of formal education. He claimed he learned to read by age five at a private boarding school that he and his sister were able to attend for a year because his aunt worked as a servant there. Here again assistance from a relative made a major difference in Tomsky's childhood. At age nine, Tomsky began the first of three years at a publicly funded elementary school. Tomsky remembered that 'studying came easily' and that his mother had 'ambitious dreams' for her talented son. He graduated at the top of his class and earned high scores on the entrance exam to a vocational school. But Tomsky's hopes of continuing his education were crushed because his family's straits made the 50-ruble tuition prohibitively expensive. He later bitterly described the tuition as a 'bribe'.[12] This future Soviet leader never had the opportunity to enter a secondary school, much less a university, which continued to rankle decades later.[13]

Tomsky grew up fast as his education shifted from the classroom to the factory floor. Tomsky entered the labour force at a younger age than most of his counterparts. At the tender age of 12, before his social betters even entered secondary school, he successfully sought factory employment, though it was illegal to do so.[14] He first became an apprentice box maker in the Theodore Kibbel box factory, which paid him a measly five kopeks a day. The firm's treatment of its workers played no small part in putting Tomsky on the revolutionary path. The Kibbel factory, in tune with the brutal labour-management practices of the time, fired the young Tomsky after he injured a finger in a factory accident.[15] The move into industry was also traumatic for Kanatchikov, even though he was older when he moved from the countryside into a factory apprenticeship in Moscow. The 16-year-old Kanatchikov was first dazzled and then overwhelmed. 'My delight', he recalled, 'turned into depression, into some kind of inexplicable terror before the grandiose appearance and cold indifference of

---

12   TsGAODM, f. 2870, op. 1, d. 296, reprinted in Karpachev and Minaeva (eds) 1992b, pp. 100–1.
13   Both parents of Alexei Rykov, with whom Tomsky would later be closely associated as fellow leaders of the 'Right Deviation', died before he was eight years old. Rykov, like Tomsky, relied on a relative for material support. But in Rykov's case, his aunt helped him get into the local gymnasium. Rykov subsequently studied law at Kazan University: Oppenheim 1977, pp. 420–1.
14   The tsarist regime in 1882 outlawed child labour under the age of 16.
15   Gorelov 2000, p. 7.

my surroundings … I felt like a small insignificant grain of sand … it was only with great effort that I could keep from crying'.[16]

Tomsky moved from job to job during his first years as one of St. Petersburg's 100,000 industrial workers – from the Laferm tobacco factory, to the metal shops of the Burno Hofmark engineering works, to the Rouss-Smirnov engineering factory. These experiences acquainted him with the increasingly militant mood of a growing number of workers, at a time when a workday of 16 or more hours was still common.[17] In 1894, the just 14-year-old Tomsky participated in the birth of the St. Petersburg labour movement when he answered the call of his fellow Rouss-Smirnov workers to go on strike.[18] The strike's failure cost him his job and left him unemployed for months. Kanatchikov, as a worker in Moscow, lacked a comparable experience since workers there remained more quiescent than workers in other parts of the empire.[19]

Tomsky and Kanatchikov, while enduring hardships, took advantage of the opportunities Russia's booming late nineteenth-century urban economy afforded. Fifteen years old and jobless, with dreams of gaining a skill (if no longer further education), Tomsky jumped at an opportunity to become an apprentice lithographer at V. Nessler's, a well-known St. Petersburg firm.[20] Likewise, Kanatchikov became an apprentice patternmaker at the Gustav List machine-building factory in Moscow. They both survived years of abuse. Adolescents like Tomsky, who hoped their apprenticeship would be a 'temple of learning', were thrust into a traumatic, oppressive environment where beatings were pervasive and they were 'compelled to spend most of their waking hours for six or seven days a week labouring in the company of unrelated but demanding adults', as Mark Steinberg noted in his study of workers in the printing industry.[21] By the time he was 20 years old, Kanatchikov was a respected patternmaker, while Tomsky achieved the rank of master lithographer at age 21. Tomsky, who worked at a variety of the capital's chromolithographic factories, achieved such prominence that his portrait appeared in 1903 on one of the posters advertising the profession.[22] They had both achieved the status

---

16   Kanatchikov 1986, pp. 7–8.
17   An 1896 textile strike in St. Petersburg led to the introduction of national legislation in 1897 limiting the workday to 11 and a half hours.
18   Gambarov et al. (eds) 1989, part 3, p. 147. Tomsky's authorised biography in this volume by P. Kashin absurdly characterised him as one of the leaders of the strike.
19   Kanatchikov moved from Moscow to St. Petersburg in late 1898 partly because he thought more workers there had political 'consciousness': Zelnik 1976a, p. 282.
20   Lithography is a fairly complicated method of printing an illustration.
21   Steinberg 1992, pp. 68–71.
22   Kun 1992, p. 273; Gorelov 2000, p. 6. Andrei Karelin, a well-known St. Petersburg photographer and graphic artist, created the poster.

of a so-call worker aristocrat, with wages far higher than that of the average worker, in challenging professions that allowed for an uncommon degree of on-the-job independence and responsibility. Unlike in England and elsewhere, the 'labour aristocracy' in Russia did not play a politically conservative role.

The acquisition of a skill was of great psychological significance. It provided an empowering sense of self-worth and dignity. Both Tomsky and Kanatchikov felt proud of what they had made of themselves. It is worth emphasising the enormous gap between the horrendous conditions of the mass of poorly paid, unskilled workers fresh from the countryside, living crowded together in barracks or 'corners' of apartment rooms, and the 'respectability' and relative comfort enjoyed by the still small but growing number of young, skilled workers. When Kanatchikov first arrived in Moscow, for example, he had shared an apartment with about 15 other men from his native region.[23] Now he shared a room with just one other fellow worker and 'no longer experienced any financial needs. I had bought myself a holiday "outfit", a watch, and for the summer, a wide belt, gray trousers, a straw hat, and a pair of fancy shoes'.[24] Tomsky could afford to rent a small apartment of his own on the outskirts of St. Petersburg and to dress as a typical proletarian dandy. He could also afford go to the theatre and dances.

While Kanatchikov remained single, Tomsky successfully courted a local beauty from a more prosperous family, Maria Ivanova Shvaiko, whose long brown braids seem to have particularly caught his fancy. Her family and neighbours were anything but pleased. They strongly objected that he was not good enough for her. To scare him off, they jumped him and beat him up once, including knocking out some teeth. But Tomsky remained undeterred, and a smitten Maria Ivanovna continued to meet with him despite her family's persistent refusal to give her their blessing.[25] She would later become his wife and the mother of their children.[26]

Though both Tomsky and Kanatchikov still worked long days in dangerous conditions – as a lithographer Tomsky breathed a considerable amount of stone dust and chemical fumes – they continued to share a love of reading and began to acquire an appreciation of some of 'the finer things in life'. Tomsky developed

---

23   Kanatchikov 1986, p. 9.
24   Kanatchikov 1986, p. 71.
25   Gorelov 2000, p. 270. Kanatchikov turned his awkwardness around women into a doctrinaire defence of proletarian bachelorhood as necessary for the fully committed, 'conscious' worker: Zelnik 1976a, pp. 277–8.
26   Gorelov and Shapovalova (eds) 2001, pp. 152–3.

a love of photography.²⁷ This proved to be a godsend, as we will see, when the authorities exiled Tomsky to eastern Siberia in 1916. And despite their lack of much formal education, both Tomsky and Kanatchikov developed a strong interest in the world of ideas, exposure to which produced profound effects. Tomsky, the quintessential autodidact, never abandoned his passion for studying, though he did find time to relax and hone his skills in billiard halls.²⁸

Such 'advanced' or 'conscious' workers as Tomsky and Kanatchikov often spent most of their free time in small, close-knit groups [*kruzhki*], which sometimes played an agitational role, with or without support from members of the radical intelligentsia. Kanatchikov recalled in his memoir how he responded to one of the first illegal pamphlets he read – a propaganda tract distributed by the Social Democrats entitled *What Should Every Worker Know and Remember?* 'This book produced a total transformation in my ideas ... For an entire week I was in a state of virtual ecstasy ... My past life seemed completely boring, dull, uninteresting'.²⁹ Tomsky's exposure to radical literature also had a profound effect. He found his first contact in 1903 with illegal literature exhilarating. Almost from that very moment, Tomsky tells us, he decided to devote his life to the revolutionary cause. So, despite his relatively comfortable place in tsarist society, in 1904, at the relatively old age of 24, Tomsky joined a Social-Democratic study circle and began to study the party's programme with a Bolshevik acquaintance, Ivan Teodorovich.³⁰ The gap between Tomsky's first participation in a strike at age 14 and his introduction to radical literature a decade later was unusually long. In addition, at Tomsky's age workers generally were unwilling to take the risks, for the first time, of joining the revolutionary underground, especially if like Tomsky, they had a family. But his delay in joining a radical study circle can also be explained by the destruction of the Social-Democratic movement in St. Petersburg after the 1896 textile

---

27 Gorelov 2000, pp. 7, 97n1. On the fumes: Steinberg 1992, p. 28.
28 At age 40, for example, he began learning English: Kun 1992, p. 273. Tomsky's devotion to intellectual self-improvement had its limits though. Tomsky professed to love art, but decades later confessed, to laughter at a party conference, that 'I don't like to go to museums. They're boring. I'd rather go hunting': RKP(b) 1927c, p. 293.
29 Kanatchikov 1986, p. 34. As Nikita Khrushchev's biographer noted, 'the theme of the first encounter with banned books is a classic trope of Russian revolutionary memoirs': Taubman 2003, p. 26.
30 Bukharin, in contrast, joined when he was only 17 years old. But he was eight years younger than Tomsky, so he did not join the Bolshevik Party until two years after Tomsky, in 1906: Cohen 1973, p. 11. RGASPI, f. 593, op. 1, d. 1, l. 34; Shapovalova 1989, p. 82. In the words of Pierre Broué, 'At [Tomsky's] age, the majority of the others [who would form the leadership of the party] had behind them years of political militancy': Broué 1963, p. 61.

workers' strike. Following crippling mass arrests, no citywide workers' organisation existed in the capital during the following four years to reach out to potential recruits like Tomsky.[31]

Although most workers had at most a rudimentary understanding of why the leaders of the Russian Social-Democratic Labour Party (RSDRP) split into two factions at the party's Second Congress in 1903, it is not surprising that when Tomsky decided to become a Marxist, he identified himself with the more dynamic Bolsheviks rather than the more passive Mensheviks, especially given that the person who introduced Tomsky to Marxism happened to be a Bolshevik. John Keep suggested, 'Such workers responded most eagerly to [the Bolsheviks] who spoke with assurance and who offered a program of actions that was simple, clear, and convincing'.[32] In the only quantitative study of the composition of the Bolshevik and Menshevik factions, David Lane demonstrated that Russian workers in Tomsky's and Kanatchikov's age cohort overwhelmingly aligned themselves with the Bolsheviks.[33] But it is important to note that these labels typically meant little to workers just recently drawn into the revolutionary movement.

Although at this time Tomsky was only beginning to understand Marxist doctrine and the political goals of the Social-Democratic movement, he and his family soon paid a high price for his radicalisation. In July 1904, the same month he officially became a Bolshevik Party member and his first son was born, Tomsky was fired when his employer caught him reading the Social Democrats' underground paper *Iskra* (The Spark). After spending several fruitless months looking for another job, the 25-year-old Tomsky concluded he was being blackballed in St. Petersburg. He had indeed been placed on the unreliable list [*spiski neblagondezhnykh*]. Tomsky's search for work took him and his family to the Estonian industrial city of Revel (later Tallinn), a city whose employers often sent recruiters to St. Petersburg in search of skilled workers. Tomsky quickly landed a job as a lithographer at the Zvezda plant in the spring of 1905.[34] He entered a city seething with discontent. Before Tomsky's arrival, news of 'Bloody Sunday' reached the city – the massacre of unarmed workers and their families in St. Petersburg on 9 January 1905. It took some time before Tomsky was able to make contact with local Bolsheviks since most of the city's radicals were Mensheviks.[35]

---

31 Wildman 1967, pp. 112–13.
32 Keep 1963 p. 148. Robert Tucker makes a similar case for the appeal of Lenin's writings to the 'practical workers' in the movement: Tucker 1973, p. 30.
33 Lane 1969, pp. 50–1, 71.
34 Shapovalova 1989, p. 82.
35 TsGAODM, f. 2870, op. 1, d. 296, reprinted in Karpachev and Minaeva (eds) 1992b, p. 101.

During the 1905 Revolution both Kanatchikov and Tomsky became devoted revolutionaries. Kanatchikov's role was more prominent since he was in the capital. Soon after joining the Bolshevik-controlled Moscow Committee of the RSDRP, the party sent him to serve on the Bolsheviks' Petersburg Committee, which entrusted Kanatchikov with agitating workers in the Narva district, an important industrial area of the city. He also composed his first leaflet, written for some underground newspapers, and gave talks at various workers' clubs on 'political economy' and the trade-union movement in the West.[36] His efforts produced fruit. The Bolsheviks made significant inroads in the Narva district. On 6 October, for example, Kanatchikov and fellow activists organised a meeting of some 600 workers. When the Central Bureau of St. Petersburg trade unions was created in November, he became one of the 10 members in its secretariat.[37]

It was in Revel, away from the more dramatic events in St. Petersburg, that it was first apparent that Tomsky had what it took to gain the respect of fellow radical activists, even though his easy-going, witty disposition also let them feel free to kid him. Estonian activists gave him the nickname of the Canary [*Kanareika*]. Tomsky lacked a winter coat, so even in the midst of winter he wore a yellow-streaked summer coat that reminded his fellow activists of a canary's plumage.[38] Tomsky quickly made a name for himself among his fellow 150 employees in the Zvezda factory, and in the city's taverns, and not just for his skill at billiards.[39] At the Social-Democratic meetings in the forest outside the city, which consisted primarily of Mensheviks, Tomsky discovered he had a talent for clear, forceful public speaking. He was able to speak the 'masses language' and was good at leading them, as Leon Trotsky and Vyacheslav Molotov would attest years later.[40] Elected to the government-sanctioned Council of Factory Elders (*Starostas*), Tomsky's fellow members on the Council, who were almost all Estonian, viewed him as an 'ideas man' who could reach out to the Russian workers in the city as well as to the Russian soldiers and sailors stationed there.[41]

---

36 Zelnik 1995, pp. 5, 14–15, 18.
37 Nosach 2001, pp. 50–1.
38 Kozelev 1927, p. 16.
39 Rudnev 1989, p. 97.
40 Trotsky 1988, p. 228; Molotov 1993, p. 119.
41 Kozelev 1927, pp. 12–13; Rudnev 1989, p. 98. *Starostas* (factory elders) were elected worker representatives in a system the tsarist government established in June 1903, with the goal of pushing workers to express their discontents through official channels. It was the only form of legal factory representation before the October Manifesto in 1905. For the Bolshevik Tomsky to stand for election as a *starosta*, and then be approved by factory man-

Tomsky's leadership skills and relatively moderate inclinations were also first apparent in Revel. He helped orchestrate the city's October 1905 general strike, which lasted 10 days, and was also instrumental in the Revel Council's decision to send a delegate to the St. Petersburg Soviet of Workers' Delegates so they could coordinate their actions. He was also among the *starostas* who met with the governor and City Duma in an attempt, unsuccessful as it turned out, to avoid bloodshed.[42] Though the City Duma on 16 October accepted some of the strikers' demands, including the release of political prisoners, the meeting was cut short on news that crowds had begun looting gun shops and liquor stores. Before long, soldiers fired five volleys into the crowd, killing 60 and wounding nearly 200. The massacre outraged the entire city. In the funeral procession on 20 October, which had a cortege of over 20,000 mourners and stretched for over three miles, even city leaders took part.[43] Tomsky helped organise the elaborately staged affair, which in the words of one historian, was 'meant not only to convey sympathy for the victims of arbitrary violence but also to demonstrate popular hostility toward the old order'.[44]

Tomsky assumed his first administrative position in November when he was elected by his fellow workers at the Zvezda plant to the Presidium of the Revel Soviet of Workers' Deputies, which was modelled after the one in St. Petersburg.[45] Tomsky and his fellow radicals in Revel achieved remarkable success. In the entire empire, only St. Petersburg workers responded in greater numbers to the calls for a general political strike in November.[46] To promote awareness of the general strike in Revel, Tomsky and some comrades, with guns, broke into Tomsky's place of employment, the Zvezda plant, in order to print leaflets announcing the general strike.[47] It was also during these final months of 1905 that Tomsky, taking advantage of the October Manifesto's promise to legalise trade unions, helped to organise the Revel Metal Workers' Union and became

---

agement, which the law required, was unusual. As Carmen Sirianni writes, 'most workers, not to mention the Social-Democratic Party, rejected this form of paternalistic representation': Sirianni 1982, p. 18.

42   Kozelev 1927, pp. 16–17. The Council of Factory *Starostas* in Revel was created in the spring of 1905. With Tomsky's participation, it went far beyond its legal mandate and fulfilled some of the functions of the Soviet of Workers' Deputies, which was created at the end of November, such as presenting workers' demands, organising meetings, and leading strikes. These councils rarely played such a significant role elsewhere in the empire during the 1905 Revolution.
43   Pal'vadre 1928, p. 46; Rudnev 1989, p. 99.
44   Ascher 1988, p. 262.
45   GARF, f. 5451, op. 41, d. 614, l. 418; Kulikova and Khazanov 1988, p. 65.
46   Ascher 1998, p. 281.
47   Gorelov 1989, p. 5.

its chair.[48] This was his first step on the path of becoming a leader in the country's trade-union movement.[49] That Tomsky, a lithographer who just recently arrived in the city, organised metal workers is testimony to his organisational skill as well as his central role in the city's labour movement.[50] Tomsky's final act in the 1905 Revolution was as one of the three organisers of the December political strike, which closed down the railroad line running through the city.[51]

As the autocracy regained the upper hand in January 1906, tsarist authorities carried out mass arrests of radicals who had come out into the open during 1905. The secret police arrested Tomsky along with the rest of the Revel Soviet on 13 January 1906.[52] Kanatchikov, who the RSDRP's Central Committee had sent from St. Petersburg to the Urals in January, was also arrested in 1906.[53] While Kanatchikov sat in prison for two months, Tomsky did so for twice as long.[54] The authorities' failed to intimidate Tomsky, who later remembered he productively used the time in prison to deepen his knowledge of Marxism, after a cellmate, August Rei, offered to tutor him.[55] In the prison chapel, Tomsky also finally married Maria Ivanovna. Given Tomsky's shame at his own illegitimate birth, it is perhaps surprising he waited so long to marry the mother of his own child. But their decision to marry might have been made for a simple, pragmatic reason. It gave Tomskaya (Efremova) the right to visit him in prison.[56]

Without a trial, the authorities decided to march the 26-year-old Tomsky out of prison and put him on an arrest wagon bound for western Siberia.[57] Tomsky's administrative exile was in the village of Parabel.[58] Tomsky like other radicals continued to devote his free time to his self-education.[59] In these 'universities' hours went by in lively debates over one radical idea or another, with Tomsky

---

48 Kozelev 1927, pp. 18–20; Nosach 2005, p. 102.
49 It also meant Tomsky was one of the first Social Democrats to devote himself to trade-union work.
50 As noted above, Tomsky did work in metal shops as a young teen.
51 Kar'iakhiam, Krastyn, and Tila (eds) 1981, p. 65. The strike began on 8 December.
52 Rudnev 1989, p. 99; Karpachev and Minaeva (eds) 1992b, pp. 101, 115.
53 Zelnik 1995, p. 5.
54 Kozelev 1927, p. 21.
55 Rei was one of the most prominent Estonian Mensheviks: Kozelev 1927, p. 21; Rudnev 1989, p. 99.
56 Gorelov 2000, p. 269.
57 Unlike earlier, prisoners no longer had to make the trip on foot and in chains.
58 Exiles were not denied any civil liberties and privileges: Babcock 2016, p. 13.
59 Kanatchikov was able to read both classic Russian fiction and works of history and political economy while in prison, including even Lenin's *The Development of Capitalism in Russia*. Rykov's sister Faina, posing as his fiancée, was able to provide Kanatchikov with many if these books: Kanatchikov 1986, pp. 125–6, 249–50.

generally siding with the other Bolsheviks.[60] But Tomsky's Siberian exile did not last long since tsarist exile could be astonishingly lax. Tomsky escaped from this 'open air prison without bars' with a few of his comrades, two months after arriving.[61] Sadly, unbeknownst to him, his wife, with little money and under a false name, to be with him had travelled across the empire with their two-year-old son Mikhail, only to learn he had escaped. At a meeting of political exiles, they managed to raise enough money for her return trip.[62] Tomsky, on the way back to St. Petersburg, made use of the Social Democrats' underground network. In Tomsk he was hidden by the party for the first time. It was then that he adopted his revolutionary pseudonym.

From a nationwide perspective, despite his considerable successes in Revel, Tomsky's role in the 1905 Revolution had not been an especially prominent one. But once back in St. Petersburg in August 1906, the Social Democrats, on the lookout for workers with leadership qualities, welcomed Tomsky with open arms, especially since so many members of the intelligentsia, as well as workers, had become demoralised by the post-1905 crackdown and began to abandon Social-Democratic organisations. Others decided to go into emigration in order to escape future arrests.[63] Tomsky's administrative talents, the party's desire to promote workers, and the Okhrana's success in decimating Social-Democratic ranks led to his growing stature within both the Bolshevik Party and the emerging trade-union movement.

Tomsky and Kanatchikov were the relatively rare Bolsheviks who at this time began to devote their energies to trade unionism, which the tsar's 1905 October Manifesto promised to legalise for the first time.[64] After Lenin in *What Is To Be Done?* criticised what he called workers' 'trade-union consciousness', the Bolsheviks were reluctant to come to terms with workers' interest in trade unions. Many party members strongly opposed any Bolshevik involvement in them, while the Mensheviks urged their 'practical' workers (as the underground activists were called) to actively participate in trade unions to strengthen their members' 'class solidarity and class consciousness'.[65] The Menshevik efforts in

---

60 Kozelev 1927, pp. 21–2; Dunaev 1926, p. 14.
61 Kozelev 1927, p. 24.
62 Gorelov and Shapovalova 2001, p. 152.
63 GARF, f. 102, op. 238, d. 5, ll. 143–8. While other leading worker-Bolsheviks emigrated to Europe, such as Shlyapnikov and Shmidt, Tomsky remained in Russia. Leaders of the RSDRP from the intelligentsia, such as Plekhanov, Lenin, Martov, Trotsky, Zinoviev, and Kamenev spent little time, if any, in Russia after 1900.
64 Trade unions were not formally legalised until 4 March 1906.
65 Egorov and Bogoliubov (eds) 1983–84, vol. 1, pp. 188–9. The *praktiki* stood in contrast to the émigré thinkers and litterateurs.

1905 to organise and expand trade unions paid off. By December, 74 unions had formed in St. Petersburg and 91 in Moscow with tens of thousands of members. Despite the Bolshevik leadership's relative disinterest in trade-union organising, Tomsky could look back with pride at his success in getting a collective agreement signed between the St. Petersburg Printers' Union and city enterprises in 1906. In 1907 he became the chair of the Engravers' and Chromolithographers' Union, which he helped to form, and then merged the lithographers and printers into one union.[66] In these roles, although Mensheviks generally remained dominant, Tomsky worked to establish closer ties between the unions and the Bolsheviks.[67]

Party members engaged in trade-union affairs were considered 'second-grade communists' [*kommunisty vtorogo sorta*], as Tomsky recalled decades later. It obviously annoyed him that true Bolsheviks were supposed to be engaged in writing articles and giving speeches, not organising workers.[68] Yet it is also clear that members of the party leadership, such as Grigory Zinoviev, increasingly valued Tomsky's contributions.[69] He was appointed in early 1907 to the St. Petersburg Committee. The Petersburg Committee was by then encouraging Bolsheviks to work in the unions, clearly alarmed that, in its words, the Mensheviks were using the trade unions 'to win over the masses'. Lenin himself, in 1907, reappraised his attitude towards unions.[70] The satisfaction and increased self-confidence Tomsky derived from the party leadership's recognition that he had been correct to emphasise the importance of trade-union activism is easy to imagine. His focus on trade-union organising would place him on the moderate wing of the Bolshevik Party. Work in trade unions then and in the future generally attracted the more moderate Bolsheviks. Tomsky and Kanatchikov, these two, rising worker-*intelligents*, must have crossed paths and at times probably worked together after Tomsky's return to the capital. Kanatchikov was in and out of St. Petersburg during these years as he also fulfilled various party and trade-union assignments.

While Tomsky was in prison in 1906, Kanatchikov was chosen to be a delegate to the RSDRP's 'Unity Congress' in Stockholm.[71] Kanatchikov was star struck.

---

66   Gambarov et al. (eds) 1989, part 3, p. 148.
67   Kulikova and Khazanov 1988, p. 65.
68   TsGAODM, f. 2870, op. 1, d. 296, reprinted in Karpachev and Minaeva (eds) 1992b, p. 101; Gorelov and Shapovalova (eds) 2001, p. 25.
69   Gorelov and Shapovalova (eds) 2001, p. 21.
70   Swain 1983, pp. 18–19. Tomsky also was assigned to do underground party organising in the Vasilevsky Island district: Gorelov 2000, p. 10.
71   The RSDRP congress attempted to reunite the Bolshevik and Menshevik factions. The attempt was ostensibly successful, but that success proved short-lived.

He later would write, 'for the second time I was able to see Vladimir Lenin in all his grandeur, locked in single combat with Menshevik leaders'.⁷² Kanatchikov never again left Russia to attend a party gathering after his attendance in Stockholm. Perhaps he missed attending the London conference because he spent two months in prison in 1907. In any case, Kanatchikov chose to switch his activities from the revolutionary underground to engage in 'legal work', particularly in the Leather Workers' and Woodworkers' Union. He did so with the party's approval. Kanatchikov was elected executive secretary of both unions and became a member of the Central Bureau of Petersburg Trade Unions. He also served on the editorial board of the Menshevik-dominated journal *Vestnik profsoiuzov* (Trade Union Herald), while working with Zinoviev to create a Bolshevik counterweight to it, the short-lived *Vestnik professional'nogo dvizheniia* (Herald of the Trade-Union Movement). He also continued to be a speaker in workers' self-education 'clubs'.⁷³

Though Kanatchikov was gaining some self-confidence and prominence in the Bolshevik movement, it was Tomsky whose career as a professional revolutionary took off. In 1907 he was appointed not only to the St. Petersburg Committee, which rivalled in importance the émigré Bolshevik Central Committee. He was also named St. Petersburg's sole representative on the editorial board of the Bolsheviks' central mouthpiece, *Proletarii* (The Proletarian), on which he served with three prominent Bolsheviks: Zinoviev, Mikhail Kalinin, and Alexander Bogdanov.⁷⁴ Tomsky assumed the responsibility of covering trade-union issues for the newspaper, while remaining active in the party and trade-union work throughout the city. Kanatchikov also wrote for *Proletarii*.⁷⁵ Tomsky, who had to support himself and his family with the job he found at the Haimovich tin works, also served on the editorial commission of the Bolshevik newspapers *Vpered* (Forward) and *Sotsial-Demokrat* (The Social Democrat); the latter newspaper was intended to be the central organ of the RSDRP, but unlike *Proletarii*, it appeared only fitfully because of the Bolshevik-Menshevik infighting.⁷⁶ Tomsky's party and trade-union work, and his tireless organisational activity,

---

72   Zelnik 1995, p. 15.
73   Zelnik 1995, pp. 5, 17–18; Swain 1983, pp. 35, 38, 62. These clubs and the unions shared a close relationship. The Central Bureau was an illegal organisation that worked to coordinate the actions of the legal unions.
74   Shapovalova 1989, p. 83. *Proletarii*, nominally the central organ of the RSDRP, became the Bolshevik house newspaper and its editorial board served as a cover for the central, secret organisation of Bolsheviks, the 'Bolshevik Centre'. During the years 1907 to 1909, Bogdanov and Lenin competed for control of the paper.
75   Zelnik 1995, p. 18.
76   Kozelev 1927, p. 30; Karpachev and Minaeva (eds) 1992b, p. 115; Service 1985, p. 176.

clearly brought him considerable renown and respect within Bolshevik ranks.

It is no surprise then that Tomsky – even though his health often failed to withstand the rigors of immediately resuming long days of factory work and radical activities – was chosen to be one of the 17 delegates from St. Petersburg to the Fifth Congress of the RSDRP. The delegates met crowded together in a shabby little church in a run-down working-class suburb of London in the spring of 1907.[77] Not only was Tomsky making a name for himself; he was also making important personal connections with party leaders. For example, as Kanatchikov had earlier, Tomsky became friends with Kalinin, one of Lenin's first supporters in Russia.[78] Theirs would be a long-lasting friendship until, as a Stalinist, Kalinin turned against Tomsky.[79] Tomsky's growing prominence is evident in the fact that he had taken Kalinin's spot in the St. Petersburg delegation, though the party still sent Kalinin to the congress as a non-voting delegate.[80] Especially given his impoverished childhood and teenage years as an unskilled worker in St. Petersburg's labour force, one can imagine the 27-year-old Tomsky's excitement at the opportunity to see life beyond Russia's borders. But he may have seen little of London after his long journey, although delegates recalled gathering around Lenin on the grass in Hyde Park and watching the debates at the Speakers' Corner there, perhaps on the days and evenings the congress had to close in order to let the congregation hold services.[81] With the party nearly bankrupt, despite various 'expropriations', most of the delegates during the three weeks of the congress were lodged in cheap boarding houses or overnight shelters in London's East End, and given such a pittance for living expenses that Lenin instructed Maria Andreeva, Maksim Gorky's actress-mistress, and Natalia Bogdanova Korsak, Alexander Bogdanov's wife, to provide them with sandwiches and beer during the breaks.[82]

---

77 Gorky 1933, p. 5. Other members of the St. Petersburg delegation included Zinoviev and Emelyan Yaroslavsky, but not Alexander Shlyapnikov, who like Tomsky was a Bolshevik member of the Petersburg Committee. Four of the Petersburg representatives aligned themselves with the Mensheviks: RKP(b) 1963a, pp. 225, 622.

78 Kalinin, who like Kanatchikov was born a peasant, also became a worker. He joined the RSDRP at its inception in 1898.

79 Kitaeff, 1954, p. 57. The congress was originally scheduled to convene in Copenhagen. That plan was blocked at the last minute by the Danish Social Democrats, under pressure from the king. Tomsky and the other delegates had already illegally arrived when they were told they had 12 days to leave or face deportation and certain arrest: Rappaport 2010, p. 152; Zelnik 1995, p. 4.

80 Kitaeff 1954, p. 57.

81 Muravyova and Sivolap-Kaftanova 1983, p. 179; Balabanoff 1973, p. 72; Rappaport 2010, pp. 153, 162.

82 Muravyova and Sivolap-Kaftanova 1983, pp. 169–70; Rappaport 2010, p. 155. It is not clear

Tomsky's appearance at the congress, which was to focus on improving relations between the party and trade unions, among other issues, attracted the attention of Lenin and other Bolshevik leaders.[83] Although a third of the 303 delegates with voting privileges were workers, only 38 of those identified themselves as part of the Bolshevik faction.[84] With so relatively few true proletarians among the Bolshevik delegates, Tomsky found himself, as Kanatchikov had a year earlier, surrounded during the recesses by members of the intelligentsia, especially those émigrés who had been living in Western Europe. Anatoly Lunacharsky later remembered, 'When the occasional worker or autodidact of humble origins worked his way into the upper ranks of the Bolshevik Party, he was made a fuss of as evidence that this was a real workers' party'.[85] Cut off from direct contact with Russian workers and dismayed at the revolutionary underground's falling fortunes, numerous delegates overwhelmed Tomsky with questions about the mood of Russian workers.[86]

Lenin, in particular, spent quite a bit of time with Tomsky. During some of the congress's sessions Lenin had Tomsky sit next to him and was seen occasionally whispering into his ear.[87] Delegates also noticed that during breaks in the proceedings Lenin and Tomsky often chatted with one another, although Tomsky also enjoyed getting together with fellow worker delegates during the breaks at the congress.[88] What especially attracted Lenin's attention was Tomsky's eagerness to engage in the party infighting and doctrinal disputes that

---

if Tomsky was one of the few lucky delegates who stayed with either Russo-Polish Jewish émigrés or British socialist families in London. Lenin and Krupskaya joined Gorky and Maria Andreevna in the comfort of the Hotel Imperial in Russell Square, a five-minute walk from the British Museum. The most sensational of the 'expropriations' was organised shortly after the congress in June 1907, a dramatic bank heist in Tiflis masterminded by Stalin, which brought in a haul of US $3.4 million in today's money: Montefiore 2007, pp. 14, 170.

83   The congress adopted a resolution on trade unions that called for party members to push them to recognise 'the ideological leadership of the Social-Democratic Party and also to establish organisational links with the party': RKP(b) 1963a, p. 616. This resolution was the product of a commission established to debate trade-union issues that included four Bolsheviks, but it is unclear whether Tomsky was one of them: Williams 1986, p. 20.

84   There was a total of 105 Bolsheviks at the congress. Thirty of the workers at the congress identified themselves as Mensheviks, of whom there were 97 at the Congress: RKP(b) 1963a, pp. 656–7.

85   Lunacharsky 1968, p. 146. Yan Rudzutak, with whom Tomsky would work closely together in the years to come, was another worker in attendance: Nosach 2005, p. 192.

86   Trotsky 1941, p. 91.

87   Gorky 1933, p. 12.

88   One of these workers was Kliment Voroshilov: Kozelev 1927, p. 29.

so preoccupied the party's émigré leaders. Lenin had jokingly promised Gorky that 'there's going to be a fine old free-for-all here'.[89] In the tense debates between Bolsheviks and Mensheviks on tactics and strategy, one delegate recalled that 'the congress was dominated from its opening session by an all-absorbing, almost fanatical, spirit of factionalism'.[90] While Stalin did not speak during the entire congress, relegated with most of the delegates to cheering and jeering, Tomsky with gusto joined the attacks on the leading Menshevik 'Liquidators', Yuly Martov and Pavel Axelrod.[91] The Bolsheviks characterised as Liquidators those who were prepared to give up clandestine, illegal political activity, including liquidating the party underground organisation, to concentrate instead on legal work among trade unions and in the Duma. Whatever the lack of polish in Tomsky's speech from the rostrum, he more than made up for that through blunt force. In sharply opposing the Menshevik support for the 'neutrality' of trade unions, he defended the Bolsheviks' support for Social-Democratic Party leadership of the trade-union movement. Maksim Gorky remembers Tomsky taunting Martov for his opposition to discussing an armed uprising: 'Have we got to cut our arms off for Comrade Martov's peace of mind'?[92] Nor was Tomsky shy about abusively attacking Axelrod, another of the founders of Russian Social Democracy. 'Comrade Axelrod,' Tomsky declared, 'you've clearly lost touch with life in Russia during your long sojourn abroad. You're looking at Russia through Genevese glasses; you've not noticed the growth of our party. Your conception of it is characteristic of a Genevese high-school student'. Tomsky did not stop there. Denying there was friction between workers and intellectuals in the party, he sharply criticised Axelrod's and his fellow Mensheviks' proposal to call for a 'workers' congress' as a 'purely *intelligent* enterprise', and denounced in a similar vein the 'syndicalist' views of the Menshevik Grigory Khrustalev-Nosar, who had been the chair of the St. Petersburg Soviet in 1905.[93] Tomsky declared, at the end of his insulting speech, 'You have fallen into a ditch, Comrade Mensheviks. But is this the fault of the cart? When the worker Mensheviks here talk about the bourgeois intelligentsia, it is

---

89 Quoted in Rappaport 2010, p. 159.
90 Balabanoff 1973, p. 72; Montefiore 2007, p. 172.
91 Stalin was there as one of the 39 unofficial delegates with no voting rights.
92 Gorky 1933, p. 14.
93 RKP(b) 1963a, pp. 526–8. The Mensheviks since July 1906 had been advocating for the convocation of a workers' congress, which they hoped would lead to the establishment of a mass workers' party. It attracted considerable working-class support in St. Petersburg and elsewhere: Ascher 1972, pp. 254–65. Syndicalism is a radical philosophy that advocated for workers' control of the economy and the destruction of the centralised state. The tern syndicalism comes from the French word for trade unionism (*syndicalisme*).

clear to me that they are speaking about their own leaders'.[94] Tomsky's attack, which received applause, played a central role in the congress's rejection of a resolution supporting the notion of a separate, non-party 'workers' congress'.[95] The congress instead adopted a Bolshevik resolution that argued that a workers' congress would inevitably lead to 'the subordination of the broad working masses to the influence of bourgeois democracy'.[96] Their fear, in fact, was that it would lead to the establishment of an English-style Labour Party.[97] The conference also adopted the Leninist proposal, which Tomsky had defended, that called on the party to lead the trade-union movement.[98] 'Amid the most remarkable galaxy of talent ever assembled at a Social Democrat congress', as one historian put it, Tomsky's performance so impressed Gorky that he ended his discussion of the congress by linking him with the most prominent Marxist revolutionaries in Europe: 'Next to Lenin, I was moved most of all by the eloquent, vigorous speech of Rosa Luxemburg against the Mensheviks and the crushing, sledge-hammer blows of M.P. Tomsky's speech against the idea of a Labour Congress'.[99]

Tomsky's partisan attack, downplaying intelligentsia domination within the Bolshevik faction, flies in the face of much of the literature on worker-*intelligent* relations within the Russian Social-Democratic movement, beginning with Allan Wildman's classic 1967 study.[100] Kanatchikov's memoir highlights both worker activists' discontent with their usually subordinate position within the party as well as their social unease and sense of inadequacy in the presence of the radical intelligentsia.[101] When a trembling Kanatchikov spoke at a 'liberal banquet' in 1904, he remembered how 'all my ideas suddenly fled from my head, and I was unable to utter a single word ... I spoke haltingly, stammeringly – I stopped, resumed, paused ... After this unsuccessful

---

94   RKP(b) 1963a, pp. 527–8.
95   The vote was 143 against, 117 for, with 17 abstentions: RKP(b) 1963a, pp. 557–8.
96   RKP(b) 1963a, pp. 612–13. This vote was 165 to 94, with 21 abstentions: Ascher 1972, p. 265.
97   Souvarine 1939, p. 109.
98   RKP(b) 1963a, p. 616.
99   Gorky 1933, p. 17; Woods 1999, p. 304. The Bolsheviks did suffer a serious defeat on the issue of expropriations, with the overwhelming majority of the delegates, 170 voters, denouncing expropriations with only 35 voters voting for them, one of whom was Tomsky: RKP(b) 1963a, pp. 582–3. The fiery Polish Jew Luxemburg attended the congress as a delegate of both the Polish and German Social-Democratic Parties. She supported Lenin while expressing misgivings about some of Lenin's ideas and tactics. Most significantly, in her speech at the congress she argued against Lenin's support for an armed uprising rather than reliance on mass actions by workers: Nettl 1969, p. 332.
100 Wildman 1967.
101 Zelnik 1976b, p. 433.

performance, I was unable to make myself speak before a large audience for a long time to come'.[102] To the extent Tomsky was not disingenuous when he downplayed tensions between worker and intelligentsia activists, it may be that because of his urban origins as well as the fact that as a printer he frequently interacted with members of the intelligentsia, he did not suffer the sort of acute psychological discomfort that workers from the countryside felt when thrust together with members of the intelligentsia.[103] Tomsky in fact seemed to feel completely at ease. Encouraged by Lenin's attention, this gifted worker seemed in his element in these party debates, clearly enjoying his attacks on the intellectual émigrés clustered in European cities, particularly Geneva.

Following the Fifth Party Congress in London, Tomsky actively participated in Bolshevik tactical debates. He joined other St. Petersburg party leaders at a conference later in 1907 near Lenin's safe house outside Kuokkala, Finland.[104] Their purpose was to prepare for the tactical debates at the upcoming Fourth Conference of the RSDRP in Helsinki, where the Bolsheviks would be in the minority. Agreeing on how to respond to Stolypin's dissolution of the Second Duma proved especially difficult. Delegates strongly disagreed with one another over whether they should boycott or participate in the elections to the Third Duma. The so-called Boycotters in the party occupied the opposite position from the 'Liquidators'. They favoured boycotting all legal organisations, from the Duma to the trade unions, to concentrate on fomenting another revolutionary upsurge. Lenin's desire for the party to participate in the Duma elections carried the day and Tomsky was placed on a three-person commission charged with organising the electoral campaign. He was also chosen to be one of the two St. Petersburg delegates to attend the Helsinki Conference, where the issue of party work in the trade unions was a major topic of discussion.[105] But the party leaders failed to supply him with the necessary funds for the trip. Tomsky remembered arriving in this unfamiliar city hungry, tired, and without money for lodging. After walking the streets, he ventured into a hotel bar where

---

102   Kanatchikov 1986, p. 384.
103   Kanatchikov's extraordinary level of social awkwardness, it should be noted, arguably had as much to do with his personality as the rural-urban divide. Urban skilled workers, such as Nikolai Yezhov, who grew up in St. Petersburg, could be equally poor public speakers: Getty and Naumov 2008, p. 23.
104   Shapovalova 1988, p. 62. Tomsky met with Lenin before the September meeting, along with Nikolai Poletaev, who had been a member of the Petersburg Soviet in 1905. Poletaev would be a successful Bolshevik candidate in the elections to the Third Duma: Kulikova and Khazanov 1988, p. 67.
105   Nosach 2005, p. 104.

his skill at billiards again came in handy – he won enough at the tables to pay for his room and board.[106]

Tomsky suffered another arrest shortly after the Helsinki Conference. After returning to St. Petersburg, he had organised a meeting to share the deliberations with the city's RSDRP Party Committee, which must have been infiltrated by an Okhrana informer. The police arrested all 14 attendees at this 1908 meeting. Charged with belonging to the St. Petersburg Party Committee, after four months in jail, the Regional Court (*Sudebnaya palata*) convicted Tomsky and sentenced him to one year in in the notorious Kresty prison.[107] Released from prison on bail, an undeterred Tomsky immediately returned to trade-union work, which before long would result in another spell in prison.[108]

The Bolsheviks began to consider a variety of ways to reach workers after the urban revolution subsided. Lenin, as noted above, now supported the trade unionists' focus on the new legal opportunities that had been achieved in 1905. Tomsky later recalled an amusing interaction with Lenin regarding the cultural programmes some mutual aid societies sponsored. Tomsky, like many others, did not think they were 'worth our attention', while Lenin now increasingly thought the Bolsheviks should seize whatever opportunities arose.[109] Tomsky remembers jokingly asking Lenin, do you really recommend that we join worker balalaika circles? Lenin responded positively, 'even if these circles attract only three-to-five workers. And if they play "God Save the Tsar", teach them how to play the "Marseillaise"'.[110] What was increasingly clear to Tomsky was that, despite his denunciation at the Fifth Party Congress of party 'neutrality' in the trade unions, that is what most workers wanted. They, moreover, wanted the trade unions to focus on bread-and-butter improvements in their lives, even if it was just a five-kopeck increase in their wages.[111]

---

106 From Gorelov's interview with Tomsky's son Yury, reprinted in Gorelov 2000, pp. 13–14.
107 The police knew that Tomsky was then using the alias of Alexander Fedor Artamonov: Nosach 2005, p. 104. Tomsky, before his arrest, also helped organise a demonstration in support of St. Petersburg's unemployed and presented demands on their behalf to the city duma: Gorelov 2000, pp. 15–16.
108 TsGAODM, f. 2870, op. 1, d. 296, reprinted in Karpachev and Minaeva (eds) 1992b, p. 102. The Bolshevik deputy to the Third Duma Poletaev, with whom Tomsky travelled to Finland in 1907, managed to get him released on a 100-ruble bail: TsGAODM, f. 2870, op. 1, d. 296, reprinted in Karpachev and Minaeva (eds) 1992b, p. 102; Gorelov 1989, p. 11.
109 Whether to participate in mutual aid societies was hotly debated during the years 1908–12, especially in 1909: Swain 1983, pp. 58–9.
110 Tomskii 1926b, pp. 18–19. Mutual aid societies focused primarily on delivering material benefits to their members who became sick or injured.
111 Tomskii 1926b, p. 17.

In addition to his ability to speak publicly, either to crowds of workers during 1905 or to the *intelligenty* leadership at party congresses, Tomsky also began to assert himself on the written page. *Proletarii* on 13 November 1908 published a long article by Tomsky. Using Lenin's title, he called on the party to again confront the issue of 'What Is to Be Done'?[112] As radical fortunes continued to wane, Tomsky addressed the sad state of local party organisations. He described party activists' morale in St. Petersburg as one of 'complete confusion and demoralisation', with the number of organised workers just a small fraction of the 'tens of thousands' of a few years before.[113] As for those members of the intelligentsia who hadn't abandoned the party, Tomsky complained, they went to their dachas in the summers, or in the case of students retreated to their 'bourgeois' parents' homes. Others of course were in prison or exile or had emigrated. In any case, to Tomsky this highlighted the party's failure to focus on recruiting cadres from among workers rather than members of the intelligentsia. Increasingly dispirited, workers felt abandoned, he argued, 'not knowing what to do'![114] Tomsky argued if the party finally reoriented itself and succeeded in creating more party leaders from among the workers themselves, it could build on a much more solid foundation.

In the mostly complimentary commentary by Lenin that accompanied the publication of Tomsky's letter in *Proletarii*, Lenin particularly chose to praise Tomsky's implicit criticism of those ultra-left Bolsheviks labeled 'Recallists' (*Otzovists*) because they demanded in 1908–09 that the depleted party recall members from the trade unions and deputies from the Duma in order to concentrate on illegal activities, including preparing for and organising an armed insurrection. Lenin wrote, 'Mikhail Tomsky is absolutely right when he strongly objects to the "invention of slogans" in general and such slogans as "Down with the Duma" in particular. He is a thousand times right when he contrasts this "confused floundering" with sustained social-democratic work of organisation, propaganda, and agitation'.[115]

---

112   Lenin had taken the title from Nikolai Chernyshevsky's novel.
113   Gorelov and Shapovalova (eds) 2001, p. 28. RSDRP membership in St. Petersburg had fallen to only 1,000 in early 1909: Williams 1986, p. 83. At the beginning of 1907, there were 52 unions with 52,000 members. By the middle of 1908, largely as a result of police suppression of any unions connected with the Mensheviks or Bolsheviks, there were only 28 unions, with just 22,300 members. And only 7,418 of those members paid their dues: Nosach 2005, p. 104.
114   Gorelov and Shapovalova (eds) 2001, pp. 28–9. While some skilled, literate workers like Tomsky had suffered from arrests, others, like many of the remaining members of the intelligentsia, simply quit the movement: GARF, f. 102, op. 238, 1908, ed. khr. 5, t. 1, l. 148.
115   Lenin 1958–65, vol. 17, p. 295.

Tomsky's eagerness to participate in factional disputes gave him additional opportunities to glimpse life inside Western Europe, where his moderate inclinations were increasingly on display.[116] Tomsky travelled to France in June 1909, a month after being freed from a seven-month stint in prison, to attend a conference conducted in a Parisian café, of the 'Bolshevik Centre'.[117] Tomsky, as the, sole representative of the St. Petersburg branch of the party, was one of just three representatives from the underground movement inside Russia (and the only 'proletarian from the bench') who met with nine émigré party leaders to discuss various issues over the course of nine days, particularly the feud between Lenin and Bogdanov, arguably the number-two Bolshevik and for a time the leader of its ultra-left wing.[118] Tomsky, who was an extremely active participant in the various debates, along with Zinoviev, Rykov, and Lev Kamenev, predictably sided with Lenin against the 'Recallists', as the Bogdanovists were labelled. But while Tomsky forcefully criticised the physician-philosopher Bogdanov's views as 'deviations from the path of revolutionary Marxism', he and Rykov refused to support resolutions by Lenin that most harshly condemned the Bogdanovists.[119] The meeting, on Tomsky's suggestion, reformulated its condemnation of Bogdanov. Rather than formally expelling Bogdanov from Bolshevik ranks, he was just expelled from the editorial board of *Proletarii*. The increasingly self-confident Tomsky was the only Lenin supporter to vote against a related resolution.[120] And he pointedly expressed his dismay over the impact these intra-Bolshevik factional squabbles would have on rank-and-file supporters.[121] Tomsky, as the historian Paul Le Blanc argues in his discussion of the meeting, proved himself to be a 'talented, capable, and independent-

---

116 Kanatchikov, in contrast, was organising trade unions and workers' clubs for participation in the First All-Russian Congress for the Struggle against Drunkenness. He was chosen as a delegate to the congress. Kanatchikov was among those 'conscious' workers who distinguished themselves from their 'backward' cohorts by not drinking vodka: Zelnik 1995, p. 19; Kanatchikov 1986, p. 168; Phillips 2000, pp. 12–7, 133. In Allan Wildman's words, they were 'almost as alienated from average workers as the intelligentsia': Wildman 1967, p. 37.
117 The Bolshevik Centre was disguised as usual as the editorial board of *Proletarii*. Lenin had created the secret Bolshevik Centre after the London congress to organise revolutionary activity: Williams 1986, p. 83.
118 The St. Petersburg Committee unanimously elected Tomsky as their representative: RKP(b) 1934b, pp. 3, 6. Bogdanov, who had supported Lenin during the 1903 Bolshevik-Menshevik schism, had previously been close to Lenin. Gorky's efforts to mediate between Lenin and Bogdanov were to no avail: Sochor 1988, p. 7.
119 RKP(b) 1934b, p. vii; Shapovalova 1989, p. 84.
120 Kamenev abstained.
121 RKP(b) 1934b, pp. 14–15.

minded' revolutionary leader, who was 'fully prepared to disagree with Lenin on a variety of issues'. He cannot be dismissed as simply some sort of Lenin yes-man.[122]

Tomsky continued his rise in the Bolshevik ranks. After attending the Paris conference, as a Central Committee representative, he went off to Moscow, Odessa, and the Urals to try to help revitalise their devastated Bolshevik organisations.[123] He also established an underground printing press that produced thousands of party proclamations.[124] Tomsky, in addition, as noted above, was appointed to the editorial board of Lenin's newspaper, *Vpered*, and became editor-in-chief in Moscow of an illegal party newspaper, *Rabochee znamia* (The Worker's Banner), which managed to reach party activists some distance from Moscow.[125] In the Moscow party organisation Tomsky worked together with Bukharin and Rykov. But while Bukharin and Rykov focused on student and intellectual circles, Tomsky devoted his energies to recruiting workers into the party organisation.[126] A fellow party and trade-union activist in Moscow at the time remembered that Tomsky, with his 'special comradely qualities' and ability to relate to workers and they to him, played the central role in restoring the Moscow organisation soon after his arrival there.[127] Lenin, and other leading party figures, in appreciation, decided to provide him with regular income, making him a full-time 'professional revolutionary'. But the 50-ruble stipends often failed to arrive, and as a letter intercepted by the police in 1908 reveals, he and his wife, and now two children, were in desperate straits, including often going hungry.[128] They certainly would have lived better on the wages he could earn as a lithographer. But his wife, Maria Tomskaya, it should be noted, did not begrudge him for their hardships. She had come to share his commitment to the cause and joined the RSDRP. Since Tomsky was one of just two or three activists in all of Moscow on the party payroll, the demands on him from local party and trade-union circles proved extremely taxing. As a result, Tomsky's health was increasingly problematic.

---

122   Le Blanc 1990, p. 153.
123   TsGAODM, f. 2870, op. 1, d. 296, reprinted in Karpachev and Minaeva (eds) 1992b, p. 102. Bolshevik membership, after growing to around 40,000, had fallen below 10,000 by 1910: Lane 1969, p. 13; Schapiro 1959, p. 101.
124   GARF, f. 102, OO, 1909, d. 5, ch. 34, l. 107.
125   Vasily Smirnov read a copy of the paper in Yaroslavl: Kitaeff 1954, p. 122.
126   Shapovalov 1988, p. 63. As has been noted, Tomsky would join together with Bukharin and Rykov to oppose Stalin in 1928.
127   Gorelov 1989, p. 12.
128   GARF, f. 102, op. 265, d. 267, l. 75.

Tomsky's and Kanatchikov's deep involvement in the revolutionary underground and attendance at party gatherings outside the country, unsurprisingly led to their repeated arrests. Unlike the Bolsheviks who had fled abroad, including such prominent worker-*intelligents* as Shlyapnikov and Vasily Shmidt, Tomsky and Kanatchikov suffered numerous arrests between 1906 and 1917 and spent years in prison and Siberian exile. Kanatchikov, who had been previously arrested and spent time in prison and exile numerous times, beginning in 1900, was betrayed and re-arrested for the final time in early 1910. The prosecutor described Kanatchikov as a 'prominent party member'. Kanatchikov was held in solitary confinement at the Petersburg House of Preliminary Detention for two years while the case was under investigation, where he took the opportunity to expand his self-education. In his words, 'as far as intellectual nourishment was concerned, my set-up in the prison was not bad at all'.[129] In Tomsky's case, by late 1909 the police were determined to put him away for good. His fourth and final arrest proved difficult for the police. Okhrana files, for months, are full of reports on Tomsky, the target of a full-scale manhunt after the arrest of most of the Moscow committee and the discovery of its printing press.[130] In their attempts to arrest him, Tomskaya was put under surveillance. She was arrested and briefly detained when the police carried out a search of their apartment and found some radical literature, but Tomsky continued to elude them.[131] Tsarist agents, who were instructed to be on the lookout for 'a short man with a moustache, prominent jaw, and a mouth missing many teeth', finally arrested Tomsky upon his arrival from Odessa at a St. Petersburg railroad station. The Paris Okhrana congratulated the Moscow authorities for having arrested a 'notable SD', informing them that though 'a worker by occupation, Tomsky is highly educated and advanced'.[132]

Tomsky spent two years in Moscow's notorious Butyrka prison complex before his December 1911 trial, the last of the big trials of Social Democrats following the 1905 Revolution. Butyrka, like Kresty where Tomsky had been previously imprisoned, was widely considered to be among the absolute worst of

---

129 Kanatchikov tried to teach himself German while studying mathematics and the history of philosophy: Zelnik 1995, pp. 20.
130 GARF, f. 102. op. 2. d. 5. ch. 34 (3), ll. 122, 127, 206; f. 102, op. 239, d. 5, ch. 34 (4), ll. 210, 220, 244.
131 GARF, f. 102, 1909, op. 231, d. 5, ll. 125, 244. Yury Fignater's speech at the Sixth Trade-Union Congress: VTsSPS 1925, p. 431.
132 GARF, f, 102, OO, op. 238, ed. kh. 474, l. 141. Whereas members of the 'privileged classes' had previously been the primary target of political arrests, after the 1905 Revolution political prisoners consisted mainly of workers, peasants, and soldiers: Babcock 2016, p. 4.

the tsarist prisons.[133] As we saw with Kanatchikov's time in prison, Tomsky's confinement contributed to his political education, but it also did further damage to his health. The Butyrka prison, Russia's largest, had long held political prisoners, and would do so again during Stalin's Great Purges.[134] The majority of the prison cells were in big barrack-like blocs, which were extremely hot in the summer. Its overcrowding and filth led to disease epidemics. After 1906, conditions in Butyrka became dramatically worse as the numbers in prisons nearly doubled. Medical and dental care were rarely available.[135] On the positive side, Butyrka did have an excellent library containing Russian classics, thanks to the liberal publishing houses that donated free copies of their books to it.[136] If Butyrka was like other tsarist prisons, inmates could check out books to read in their cells twice a week.[137]

The decision to transfer Tomsky from St. Petersburg to conduct his trial inside Moscow's Kremlin highlighted its importance. Of the 33 Social Democrats to be tried, the prosecutors in their bill of indictment treated Tomsky as the central figure, primarily because of his role as editor of *Rabochee znamia*.[138] Tomsky, who chose to defend himself, was the sole defendant to address the court at length. He clearly enjoyed being in the limelight. Tomsky calmly and firmly presented the Bolsheviks' programme in simple, clear language.[139] One of Tomsky's co-defendants later recalled how Tomsky's cheerful, lively, witty demeanour, including his love for cracking jokes, lifted their spirits during the trial.[140] When asked by the court whether he was guilty of belonging to the RSDRP, Tomsky defiantly replied that he felt 'honoured' to be a party member.[141] After the 11-day trial, the court sentenced him to five years of hard labour in the Butyrka penal colony, to be followed by banishment to eastern Siberia.[142] In

133   Tomsky had also earlier spent a little time in Butyrka while he was on his way to Siberian exile in 1906: Kozelev 1927, p. 22.
134   Yemelyan Pugachev, the leader of a major eighteenth-century peasant rebellion, was its most notable former inmate.
135   Gorelov 2000, pp. 34–5.
136   Conquest 1990, pp. 266, 269.
137   Babcock 2016, p. 43.
138   TsGAODM, f. 2870, op. 1, d. 296, reprinted in Karpachev and Minaeva (eds) 1992b, p. 102. Nikolai Bukharin, Yury Fignater, Mikhail Rykunov, and N.S. Petrova were among those on trial. One of the defendants was only 17 years old: Dunaev 1926, p. 27. Some sources refer to 35 instead of 33 defendants.
139   Dunaev 1926, p. 29.
140   Yury Fignater's speech to the Sixth Trade-Union Congress: VTsSPS 1925, p. 432.
141   Gorelov 2000, pp. 38–9.
142   TsGAODM, f. 2870, op. 1, d. 296, reprinted in Karpachev and Minaeva (eds) 1992b, p. 102; Kozelev 1927, p. 64; Gorelov, 2000, pp. 32–40. Although the court acquitted none of the

1911 Kanatchikov suffered a somewhat similar fate: he was exiled to a village in eastern Siberia, but he did not have to endure time in a prison penal colony first.[143]

In the Butyrka penal prison Tomsky managed to maintain his upbeat personality despite the horrible conditions there. Fellow prisoners remarked on his cheerfulness and wit, even in the bleakest of times. 'It was necessary to have a colossal will in order to endure the heavy prison regime', one prisoner later recalled, 'and in this regard Tomsky deserved enormous credit for lessening with some encouraging words the despondency, the blues, each of us experienced. He raised, if only slightly, our mood and belief in the cause'.[144] Regarding conditions in Butyrka, the quality and quantity of the food ranked highest among the prisoners' complaints. It was tolerable at best, but usually disgustingly oily buckwheat gruel and rotten, smelly cabbage soup. The food was difficult on the stomachs of long-term prisoners such as Tomsky, who suffered from gastritis. His conditions were lightened somewhat by the efforts of his wife, Maria Tomskaya. She joined a circle of nearly forty wives of Moscow Social Democrats who sought to provide each of the political prisoners with five rubles of monthly spending money. Tomskaya contributed to this mutual aid fund through her earnings as a skilled seamstress.[145] Prisoners, through such outside help, along with their own pitiful prison earnings, could improve their diet and state of mind by buying overpriced food from the prison store such as sugar, sausage, tea, milk, cheese, and cigarettes.[146]

Tomskaya herself was placed under increased surveillance following Tomsky's arrest and conviction. For more than two years, beginning on 20 November 1909, they monitored her every move. We get a picture of Tomskaya's physical appearance from the first page of her police dossier, which described her as 28–30 years old with two children, a height of four foot, eight inches, brown hair, a normal physique, pale white face, a thin, straight nose, and an ordinary

---

defendants, Bukharin was released after a few months since this was his first arrest: Cohen 1973, p. 12. When Bukharin was arrested again the following year, he was sent into administrative exile to Arkhangelsk Province: Turton 2010, p. 87.

143   Zelnik 1995, pp. 5, 20–1.
144   Shapovalova 1989, pp. 85–6.
145   GARF, f. 533, op. 1, d. 417, l. 11.
146   Gorelov 2000, p. 41. When Kanatchikov was imprisoned in St. Petersburg in 1900, the Russian 'Red Cross' provided him with food packages once a week, which included a pound of butter, cheese, coffee, a lemon, and sometimes a little sausage. It led Kanatchikov to state, hyperbolically, that 'materially, we workers were generally better off in prion than we were in our regular lives, when we worked in factories': Kanatchikov 1986, pp. 126–7, 423n11.

gait.[147] The Okhrana ultimately decided to arrest Tomskaya on 14 April 1912 as a member of the Moscow organisation of the RSDRP. Charged with being 'a threat to public order and tranquility', she was thrown in jail and forcibly separated from her children.[148] The authorities almost immediately moved Tomskaya from a local police station to the same prison as Tomsky. Her brother Vladimir Shvaiko managed to visit her numerous times in the Butyrka prison, perhaps to criticise her for marrying Tomsky and getting involved in radical activity as much as to offer comfort and support. In any case, her brother evidently did not offer to take under his wing the Tomskys' two boys, Mikhail and Victor, now seven and three years old. Frantically concerned about her children's wellbeing, Tomskaya vigorously demanded that her children be reunited with her. She sent a petition to the head of the prison. 'I humbly ask you to bring my children to me', she wrote, 'since they are suffering greatly from staying with strangers and are forced to go from one to the other'.[149] Such pleas could be successful. Some women revolutionaries were even released from prison if their children had no one to care for them.[150] But rather than eliciting sympathy, the warden flatly rejected Tomskaya's pleas. She was even punished for them, including being thrown into solitary confinement. A month later, on 21 June 1912, the prison's so-called Special Board informed her of its verdict. Tomskaya was released, but for two years she was banned from the capitals and their provinces. Allowed to go to a place of her choosing, Tomskaya chose the city of Tula as her place of exile.[151]

Tomsky continued to work long hours in the Butyrka penal colony before he was eventually sent into Siberian exile. For 'good behaviour', on 12 December 1912, the authorities finally removed his shackles.[152] But Tomsky apparently never lost his fighting spirit. He even helped organise in October 1915 a strike protesting against the pittance the prisoners received for their labour.[153] This

---

147 Gorelov 2000, p. 42.
148 The Russian Criminal Code gave the government the right to sentence anyone simply suspected of seditious activity. The punishment could be as severe as administrative exile to Siberia.
149 Gorelov 2000, p. 42.
150 Turton 2010, pp. 82, 85.
151 Gorelov 2000, p. 44. This was a common sort of practice. Rykov, for example, was barred from attending universities in the capitals but could attend Kazan University: Oppenheim 1977, p. 421.
152 In addition to the obvious physical relief, removing the shackles allowed Tomsky to work in workshops that didn't allow prisoners in shackles. Tomsky went to work in the military-uniform workshop, one of the largest in the Butyrka prison, with nearly fifteen hundred prisoners: Gorelov 2000, p. 45.
153 While the owners of the privately-owned workshops paid the Butyrka prison a ruble a day

once again landed him in an isolation cell. Although his role in this strike ran the risk of lengthening his sentence of hard labour, Tomsky was released on schedule on 10 April 1916.[154]

Even exile to a Siberian village outside Kirensk, a small town of 3,000 residents on the Lena River, apparently did not alter his disposition.[155] Given his repeated arrests and previous escape from administrative exile, Tomsky was sent to a distant and isolated town in eastern Siberian, where escaping and returning to European Russia was extremely difficult.[156] N. Starikov, a Socialist Revolutionary Party fellow political exile, who met Tomsky at the waystation, remembered that this 'small convict, dressed in a worn penal battalion jacket and grey pants, with a penal battalion beret on his head, was always distinguished by his animated cheerfulness and joi de vivre ... [by his] positive energy and indomitable will ... [and] the liveliness of his mind and character'.[157]

With renewed hope for a revolutionary upsurge, as discontent with the war grew, but obviously without foreknowledge of what the future might bring, the now 36-year-old Tomsky had to go about making a life for himself in the godforsaken boondocks of Kirensk. Tomsky's arrival there might have been met by 'political' members of the exile colony, who would have provided him with a room and some provisions, which seems to have been customary.[158] Tomsky's wife and children, after their long, forced separation, before long joined him in Kirensk.[159] Tomsky was fortunate since it was rare for families to voluntarily join their husbands and fathers in Kirensk like Tomskaya and the children did.[160] One of the scourges of life in Kirensk was the loneliness and lack of

---

for each prisoner's labour, the prisoners themselves received only three kopecks: Dunaev 1926, p. 31.

154 The 'Italian strike' was over the pay the prisoners received in the sewing workshop, where Tomsky and his fellow prisoners sewed military greatcoats, shirts, and pants. One of the antics Tomsky and his fellow prisoners who were opposed to the war engaged in was to sew inside the greatcoats anti-war notes: Gorelov 2000, pp. 45–7; GARF f. 533, op. d. 1121, ll. 13–14, 20, 24–7.

155 Of those 3,000 inhabitants, every tenth one had been exiled there as a 'state criminal': Ivanova 1992, p. 139. Kirensk was located about 1,000 kilometres northeast of Irkutsk.

156 Over 40 percent of the exiles 'escaped' from eastern Siberia, but few, if any, made it back to European Russia: Babcock 2016, pp. 130–5.

157 Quoted in Kozelev 1927, p. 69.

158 Tucker 1973, p. 157; Kanatchikov 1986, p. 363.

159 Gorelov 2000, p. 49. Wives had long been allowed to join their husbands in exile. The Tsarist authorities thought they would have a pacifying effect on the exile communities: Beer 2017, pp. 26, 239. It might have been a more complicated issue in Tomskaya's case since she too was a member of the RSDRP.

160 Babcock 2016, p. 95. Kanatchikov's fiancée, Bliuma Landau, also joined him in his place of exile in eastern Siberia in 1912, where they got married. Kanatchikov had met the

intimacy so many exiles experienced. Tomskaya's willingness to make the long trip, with their two children, to such a desolate place, is testimony to the strong bond between Tomsky and Tomskaya. But whether it was good parenting for Tomskaya, who could have stayed put in European Russia, to take the boys, now aged 12 and seven respectively, across Russia to live in the extremely inhospitable climate of Kirensk is open to question. Glimpsing into the future, the older boy's education was forever stunted. Mikhail never gained more than an elementary-school education and never became more than a machinist in later life, unlike other children of the privileged elite when Tomsky became a top party official.

Political exiles such as Tomsky, once they settled into the place where they had been sent, were required to support themselves. Tomsky ironically, and very fortunately, initially worked in the tsarist bureaucracy, as a statistician on the agricultural census. He collected statistical information on peasants' property in 42 villages along the Lena River. The Siberian peasants viewed Tomsky as a government representative, including one old peasant who thought Tomsky was the governor.[161] Once he finished with the census, Tomsky opened with a fellow exile, Alexander Borovsky, a photography business in which they took photographs primarily of fellow exiles, soldiers, and local residents.[162] This was extremely enterprising on their parts since it was difficult to find work during the long, dark, and bitterly cold winters, although the government did provide political exiles with some minimal support.[163] In his free time, given his later love of hunting, Tomsky almost certainly devoted some of it to hunting in the thick coniferous forests of the taiga outside Kirensk. If Maria Tomskaya had time away from childrearing, there were opportunities for private tutoring in town and selling some of her needle work.[164] In addition, Kirensk had an amateur theatre, which put on productions such as Chekhov's 'Seagull'. Given Tomskaya's later choice to become employed in the Soviet Commissariat of Enlightenment's Worker-Peasant Theatre Administration, she probably took a keen interest in these local productions, or maybe even performed in them.[165]

Jewish Menshevik in 1905. Landau had saved him from arrest in 1909 and brought him books when he was arrested and imprisoned in 2010: Zelnik 1995, pp. 4, 18, 20, 23, 26.

161 GARF, f. 533, op. 1, d. 1020, l. 17. All the commercial shops and artisanal workshops in town were in the hands of the political exiles or they were their exclusive employees, including the chief accountants for the two largest enterprises in town.

162 Dunaev 1926, p. 32; Kozelev 1927, p. 70.

163 Babcock 2016, pp. 79, 117.

164 Both Kanatchikov and his wife tutored. As a result, he remembered, 'we lived not too badly': Zelnik 1995, p. 23. They, at the time, did not have any children.

165 Gorelov 2000, pp. 49, 272.

THE MAKING OF A MODERATE WORKING-CLASS BOLSHEVIK LEADER 39

Kirensk was one Russia's largest centres for deportees. Tomsky could keep up his spirits by socialising with some of the over one thousand fellow political exiles from the town or one of its neighbouring villages, since they lived under only nominal police surveillance.[166] He enjoyed cooking, telling witty anecdotes, or getting into heated arguments with his fellow exiles.[167] But for all their camaraderie, they were also distrustful, wondering who among them might be working for the Okhrana.[168] Trying to put that out of their minds, the exiles as a group, like Tomsky individually, proved to be extraordinarily enterprising. The exiles established an illegal mutual aid society, toward which all political exiles paid one percent of their wages. The mutual aid society provided loans and grants, medical assistance, and popular education. It was also where they got together and engaged in fierce debates.[169] The enterprising political exiles also ran their own cafeteria, bakery, pastry shop, and grocery store. They also established a community garden. In the memoirs of contemporaries, Tomsky was one of the most respected and influential people in this exile community. As evidence of that, his fellow exiles entrusted him, shortly after his arrival, with managing the cafeteria and bakery.[170] All in all, given their plight, the colony of political exiles managed to create a reasonably good life in Kirensk. Although Siberian exile is commonly regarded as one of the most terrible abuses of tsarist tyranny, Tomsky's time in Kirensk, difficult as it was because of climatic conditions, was an improvement over the mistreatment and malnourishment in the Butyrka prison.

Tomsky's increasingly poor health makes his positive outlook during his years in prison and exile all the more impressive. Tomsky's childhood poverty, years of work as a lithographer and in a hard-labour prison, followed by the bone-chillingly cold winter he spent in Kirensk (where the average January temperature is minus 27 degrees centigrade) did irreparable damage to his health. Tomsky became anaemic and suffered from serious stomach pains,

---

166 Revolutionaries often paradoxically found greater freedom in Siberia than elsewhere in the empire. In the words of the writer Anton Chekhov, 'Out here nobody worries about saying what he thinks ... there's no one to arrest you and nowhere to exile you to': quoted in Beer 2017, p. 298. On the number of political exiles: Babcock 2016, p. 76.
167 GARF, f. 533, op. 1, d. 1020, l. 1; Kozelev 1927, p. 69.
168 GARF, f. 533, op. 1, d. 1020, l. 24. Personal animosities often commonly undercut the commonalities in these exile colonies as well: Beer 2017, p. 350. Tomsky did learn after the collapse of the autocracy, and their occupation of the police station, that one of the exiles with whom he had socialised had ties with the police: GARF, f. 533, op. 1, d. 1020, l. 19.
169 Babcock 2016, pp. 82, 86.
170 Gorelov 2000, p. 51.

asthma attacks, rheumatism, and problems with his nerves.[171] One can only wonder how long Tomsky could have fought off depression if events far from Siberia had not suddenly intervened.

Tomsky and Kanatchikov were caught by surprise when news arrived in March 1917 of the tsar's abdication and the Provisional Government's sweeping amnesty of all political prisoners.[172] Once they got over their disbelief and shock, political exiles felt overjoyed that all their suffering had evidently been worthwhile. Kanatchikov chose to remain in Siberia, moving with his wife and son to the western Siberian town of Novonikolaevsk, where he had time to read and write, edit a newspaper, and be a husband and father to his two children, Vladimir and Evgenii (although he did spend a brief time in Petrograd as Novonikolaevsk's Social Democratic representative at the meetings following Lenin's arrival in April).[173] Kanatchikov's decision to remain in Siberia helps account for why he never rose to a top position in the Bolshevik Party. As Zelnik states, 'It is interesting to speculate about the role [Kanatchikov] might have played in 1917 had he chosen, as did so many other exiled revolutionaries, to return to the familiar territory of Petrograd or Moscow'.[174]

Tomsky initially engaged in some local actions with fellow political exiles in Kirensk. They disarmed the local police and gendarmes and organised a solemn one-day strike in honour of the victims of the February Revolution. They also formed a Kirensk Executive Committee in which he served as its spokesman and the editor of two issues of a new newspaper, which in dramatic fashion informed local residents about the historic events in Petrograd. They printed the newspaper in the local police station, which they occupied.[175] At the same time, with the criminal justice system in complete disarray, Tomsky characteristically was determined to maintain order and prevent any 'excesses', which he feared might be committed by the non-political, criminal exiles.[176] The political exiles generally had viewed the 'criminal' exiles with extreme disdain. In

---

171 GARF, f. 533, op. 1, d. 1034, ll. 1, 3; Gorelov 2000, p. 35. Kanatchikov, for his part, suffered from typhoid fever in another remote eastern Siberian village not far from Tomsky's place of exile: Zelnik 1995, p. 18. Kanatchikov had caught typhoid fever earlier, in the spring of 1909.
172 News of the abdication arrived by the telegraph. Daily newspapers, when they managed to reach Kirensk, arrived from Irkutsk 14–15 days after they had been published: GARF, f. 533, op. 1, d. 1020, ll. 3, 21.
173 Zelnik 1995, p. 6. Kanatchikov had been allowed to move from eastern to western Siberia in 1916.
174 Kanatchikov 1986, p. 388; Zelnik 1995, p. 6.
175 GARF, f. 533, op. 1, d. 1020, ll. 15–6, 23; Kozelev 1927, pp. 72–3.
176 GARF, f. 533, op. 1, d. 1020, l. 19.

Kanatchikov's words, 'we had to expand a great deal of energy in order to draw a sharp and distinct line between ourselves – political people who were struggling for an idea and suffering for our convictions – and the ordinary criminal offenders'.[177] Tomsky then focused on facilitating his and fellow political exiles' return home, joining with the other leaders of the Social Democrats and Socialist Revolutionaries to create a fund from the city's coffers that granted each political exile 100 rubles.[178] In addition, the Provisional Government provided political exiles with 245 rubles for a family of four to return to European Russia.[179]

Tomsky did not wait to leave with his family. He quickly became impatient at being stuck in this remote corner of Russian at this revolutionary moment in history and was one of the first exiles to leave. The ambitious Tomsky's return to Moscow proved to be hazardous as well as extremely difficult. Tomsky was unwilling to wait two months for the Lena River to fully thaw, when he could have taken the steamboat to Irkutsk, as his family did on their way back to Moscow.[180] Despite all of his serious ailments, in a testimony to his almost unbelievable self-discipline and determination, Tomsky traversed 350 kilometers to the nearest railroad station on horseback![181] It would be nice if the documentary evidence provided some detail about how he managed to do that. In any case, after arriving in Moscow at the end of March, Tomsky caught the train to Petrograd when he heard the news of Lenin's imminent return to the capital.[182] Tomsky might well have been greeted in the capitals as a celebrity and a 'martyr for the cause', like other arriving political exiles.[183]

Tomsky's confidence in his own political judgment had continued to grow during his years in exile. Free of the insecurities that plagued Kanatchikov, so typical of workers in the intelligentsia-dominated Bolshevik Party, Tomsky now felt emboldened enough to spar with Lenin himself. His political positions in 1917 reveal a man no longer content to be the party's favourite son from workers' ranks. In doing so, he carved out a distinct persona during the various debates. Tomsky proved to be the voice of caution in 1917, defending the notion of an independent newspaper for the Petersburg Bolsheviks, questioning calls for

177 Kanatchikov 1986, p. 367.
178 Gorelov 2000, p. 53.
179 Babcock 2016, p. 170.
180 Most of the exiles left Kirensk at the end of May and the beginning of June: Babcock 2016, p. 170.
181 Kozelev 1927, p. 73.
182 Shapovalova 1989, p. 86.
183 Babcock 2016, p. 171.

street demonstrations in June and July, as well as the decision to unilaterally seize power in October.

Tomsky managed to get to Petrograd in time to attend the party meetings that followed Lenin's arrival from Switzerland at the Finland Station, although he did not (despite evidence to the contrary) participate in the debate over what almost immediately became known as the 'April Theses', Lenin's appraisal of the political moment entitled 'The Report on the Current Situation'.[184] At the All-Russian Seventh Party Conference, held from 24–29 April, Tomsky was present, but he kept his opposition largely to himself.[185] Lenin in the end succeeded in winning over a majority of the party leaders to his position opposing the Provisional government.[186]

Tomsky's off-the-record opposition to Lenin's April Theses did not hurt his standing in the party, where he earned respect for his vigour and businesslike attitude. On the recommendation of Vasily Shmidt, a fellow Bolshevik heavily involved in trade-union affairs, Tomsky immediately put his organisational talents to work as a party activist in Petrograd's outlying Porokhovsky district, a Right SR and Menshevik stronghold with a negligible Bolshevik presence. Tomsky distinguished himself there as one of the party's better orators at workers' and soldiers' meetings.[187] But his impressions of the anti-Bolshevik sentiment in the Porokhovsky Soviet of Workers' and Soldiers' Deputies confirmed his relatively pessimistic views about the prospects for Lenin's radical

---

184 According to both Trotsky and the Russian historian Galina Ivanova, Tomsky played a significant role in the debate within Bolshevik ranks over the 'April Theses': Trotsky 1932a, pp. 319–21, 327; Trotsky 1941, p. 200; Ivanova 1992, pp. 142–3. Other sources seem to corroborate their accounts: such as Volobuev 1993, p. 317 and Lazitch and Drachkovitch 1972, p. 23. I am extremely grateful to Lars T. Lih, who shared his doubts about how I portrayed Tomsky's role in April in a 2012 article, before demonstrating it was a matter of mistaken identity by Ivanova, coupled with Trotsky's desire to distort the role of various Bolsheviks to serve his own polemical purposes. Ivanova assumed the Mikhail in the stenographic report was Tomsky, but it was actually Shutko. Trotsky, for his part, was obviously relying on second-hand accounts since he did not arrive in Petrograd until 4 May 1917.

185 The official stenographic report of the April All-Russian Conference listed Tomsky as present but does not show any comments by him: RKP(b) 1958, p. 330. Smirnov remembers Tomsky supporting Rykov's opposition to Lenin's thesis at the Central Committee Plenum on 20 April, but not speaking on the record against it: Kitaeff 1954, p. 122.

186 Those critics included 'the rightists' Stalin and Kamenev, who had formulated a moderate agenda for the Bolsheviks in Petrograd, including conditional support for the Provisional Government, prior to Lenin's arrival from exile: Khlevniuk 2015, pp. 43–7. In the end, in the voice vote by the 152 delegates at the conference, only three voted against the resolution while eight abstained: RKP(b) 1958, p. 245. How individual delegates voted is not identified in the stenographic report.

187 RGASPI, f. 593, op. 1, d. 1, l. 4; Ivanova 1992, pp. 144–6.

agenda.[188] Yet Tomsky no doubt deserves at least some of the credit for the rapid growth of Bolshevik membership in this partly industrial rural suburb (there were two large factories), from 70 members in March to 1,035 members in early July.[189] Tomsky during the following couple months also actively participated in the often-heated debates at the meetings held in the Kshesinskaya mansion, the Bolshevik Party headquarters.[190] But it was increasingly apparent that what physical and emotional strength Tomsky could muster after his gruelling return from Siberia and years of imprisonment and exile was gradually sapped by his feverish participation in party, trade-union, and soviet politics. For the moment, at least, Tomsky refused to slow down.

The respect Tomsky quickly garnered was evident in the elections on 10 May to the Petersburg Committee's nine-member Executive Commission, where he received the second largest number of votes.[191] This was the foremost body of the Bolshevik organisation in Petrograd. The members of this Executive Commission, which met every other day, entrusted Tomsky with deciding numerous issues facing various districts of the city as well as within the Petersburg Committee itself.[192] According to Tomsky, the heavy-handed and tactless manner of many Bolshevik trade unionists was largely responsible for the Menshevik domination of the trade unions in Petrograd.[193]

The Petersburg Committee, the largest single Bolshevik organisation in the country, often demonstrated considerable independence from Lenin and the Central Committee. It relied on Tomsky to carry out negotiations concerning any disagreements between the two bodies.[194] Most significantly, Tomsky successfully pushed for a resolution from the Executive Commission to create a party newspaper for the city because he felt the Central Committee's newspaper, *Pravda* (The Truth), insufficiently addressed local issues.[195] In his speech

---

188 RKP(b) 1927a, p. 110.
189 Ivanova 1992, p. 144. This was of course part of a rapid upsurge in Bolshevik members across the city. The membership of the Petrograd Bolshevik Party, which was 3,000 in March, rose to 16,000 in May and 49,500 in October: Abrosimova 1998, p. 37.
190 Zinoviev 1925, pp. 129, 139. The Bolsheviks had taken over the large and elegant mansion of Nicholas II's first love, the famous ballerina Mathilda Kshesinskaya, with the permission of the soldiers who had seized it after she fled the mansion during the February Revolution: Rabinowitch 1976, p. 8.
191 Stanislav Kosior received 23 of the 27 votes, while Tomsky received 22, as did V.B. Vinokurov: RKP(b) 1927a, pp. 99–100, 103.
192 Abrosimova 1998, pp. 37–8; Ivanova 1992, pp. 145–6.
193 Sirianni 1982, p. 48.
194 RGASPI, f. 593, op. 1. d. 1, l. 6.
195 Tomsky added that the Central Committee focused 'exclusively on principled political points and did not devote attention to practical work': RKP(b) 1927a, pp. 120–1; RGASPI, f. 593, op. 1, d. 1, l. 10.

on the issue, Tomsky could not suppress the tension he felt with intellectual members of the party now flooding into the capital after spending more than a decade in exile. 'You don't write in comprehensible Russian', Tomsky admonished them, 'not everyone can understand your articles'. Workers want 'a popular newspaper'.[196] But he did not anticipate how Lenin strongly opposed the Petersburg Committee's decision to have their own newspaper.

Tomsky proved to be Lenin's main opponent in the ensuing heated debate over this issue on 30 May.[197] Tomsky argued the Central Committee's organ *Pravda* focused on issues of international and national significance, neglecting issues of a more local character. Tomsky, who insisted the issue is not that we want to conduct 'our own particular line', refused to back down. Addressing Lenin's criticism, he argued, 'Disagreements with you on questions of principle are possible. We want to have our own voice and influence and not play the role of a poor relative to the Central Committee ... Not separatism, but life itself pushes us to the publication of an independent paper'.[198] Tomsky's position carried the day. In the vote that followed, the Petersburg Committee rejected Lenin's resolution 15–12, with two abstentions.[199] A month later, Tomsky reported on the Petersburg Committee's newspaper to the Bolsheviks' Second City Conference. Here an even more sizable majority of the delegates voted in support of Tomsky's position despite Lenin's continued opposition.[200]

Tomsky also continued to devote much of his energy to the burgeoning trade-union and factory-committee movements. Tomsky would push factory committees to carry out close oversight of management. Convinced that the Provisional Government was incapable of establishing 'any form of law and order in the economic life of the country', Tomsky called on workers 'to finally take control of industry'.[201] In his attempt to increase Bolshevik influence in the unions, Tomsky fervently participated in polemical attacks on the Mensheviks and the SRs on the pages of the trade-unions' newspaper *Professional'nyi vestnik* (The Trade-Union Herald) as well as at the First All-Russian Congress of Soviets of Workers' and Soldiers' Deputies, 3–5 June. All the same, at other

---

196   RKP(b) 1927a, p. 121.
197   Lenin argued, 'Petersburg, as a separate locality, does not exist. Petersburg is the geographic, political, and revolutionary centre of all of Russia. The life of Petersburg is being followed by all of Russia. Petersburg's every step is a guiding example for all of Russia. Based on this the life of the Petersburg Committee cannot be considered a local affair': Abrosimova et al. (eds) 2003, p. 233.
198   RKP(b) 1927a, pp. 120–1.
199   Abrosimova et al. (eds) 2003, pp. 240–1.
200   RKP(b) 1927b, pp. 43–4, 46–7. The vote took place on 3 July.
201   Quoted in International Labour Office 1927, p. 52.

times during 1917, Tomsky felt he was wasting his time by constantly engaging in theoretical disputes with Mensheviks and SRs.[202] Tomsky was also a Bolshevik delegate at the Third Conference of Trade Unions, 20–28 June. The conference debated various key issues, on some of which the majority Mensheviks and minority Bolsheviks could not agree despite the conference's theme of unity. The conference concluded by electing for the first time an All-Russian Central Council of Trade Unions (VTsSPS) to oversee the trade-union movement.[203] Tomsky's participation in the conference played a key role in determining his life's future course. Though Tomsky was not elected to the Menshevik-dominated VTsSPS in 1917, this was the institution he was to head during the 1920s.

Tomsky, as a leading figure in the Petersburg Committee, also distinguished himself in the debates raging inside the Bolshevik party in mid-1917. Along with Zinoviev, Kamenev, Kalinin, Victor Nogin, and others, he was part of what was labelled the right wing in the Bolshevik leadership.[204] Tomsky, in particular, injected realism and foresight into the Bolsheviks' debate over whether to organise a mass anti-government, anti-war street demonstration in early June, which Lenin initially strongly supported.[205] At a joint meeting of the Bolshevik's Party's Central Committee, All-Russian Military Organisation, and the Executive Commission of the Petersburg Committee on 6 June, in the face of enthusiastic worker, soldier, and sailor support for organising a demonstration against the Provisional Government, Tomsky called for further deliberations. Arguing the party needed to thoroughly investigate potential pitfalls before making a final decision, he called on his comrades to stop and recognise they were deliberating in the dark, given how little they knew about how the 'broad working masses' would respond if called to pour out into the streets, some of them armed with guns. Tomsky predicted the First Congress of Soviets (which was then in session) would vigorously oppose the march.[206]

---

202 Ivanova 1992, pp. 162–3.
203 Kulikova and Khazanov 1988, pp. 68–9; Acton, Cherniaev, and Rosenberg (eds) 1997, p. 448. VTsSPS is an acronym of Vserossiiskii Tsentral'nyi Sovet Professional'nykh Soiuzov (The All-Russian Central Council of Trade Unions).
204 Abramovitch 1962, p. 54.
205 Rabinowitch 1968, pp. 56–7.
206 The All-Russian Congress of Soviets met 3–24 June. The party composition of its Executive Committee was proportionate to the political alignment of the delegates to the congress. Tomsky was selected as a candidate member: Shelestov 1990, p. 98.

FIGURE 1 Mikhail Tomsky
WIKIMEDIA COMMONS

It is to be expected that the Executive Committee of the Petrograd Soviet of Workers' and Soldiers' Deputies will do everything it can to prevent the demonstration and will first of all try to exert their influence on the soldiers ... The mood of class antagonism is so high ... that it cannot be expected the demonstration will take place peacefully. Imagine what could happen in a clash of hundreds, perhaps thousands of people. This might turn out to be more than a demonstration. We need to be especially careful in taking this step.[207]

---

207 RKP(b) 1927a, p. 140.

The cautionary words of the 'prudent Tomsky', as Leon Trotsky characterised him, helped to convince the rest of the Petersburg Committee to delay a final decision until after consulting with rank-and-file activists from the garrison, trade unions, and factory committees to see whether Petrograd's soldiers and workers were willing to follow the Bolsheviks' lead.[208] After further deliberations on 8 June, at a conference of about 150 Bolshevik activists, with Tomsky's ultimate support, the delegates finally decided to proceed with the demonstration on the third round of votes.[209]

Tomsky, following the vote, threw himself into helping prepare the worker-soldier demonstration. Bolshevik appeals generally seemed to be embraced, with thousands of workers and soldiers making plans to demonstrate. But the next day, 9 June, the Soviet Congress of Workers' and Soldiers' Deputies, alarmed at the escalating support for the Bolshevik demonstration against the coalition Provisional Government and rumours that many planned to come heavily armed, at what was almost the last minute – the demonstration was scheduled for the afternoon of the following day – prohibited the demonstration from going forward. Later that day, the Bolshevik Central Committee, the Petersburg Executive Commission, and the Military Organisation called an emergency meeting to consider cancelling the demonstration. Tomsky and others vehemently opposed calling off the demonstration, arguing that it was too late to back down to the Soviet. Fourteen of the 16 participants agreed and voted in favour of proceeding with the demonstration. But the five members of the Bolshevik Central Committee met later, after midnight, and on Lenin's recommendation, at 2 a.m., called off the demonstration that was scheduled to begin just 11 hours later. Lenin argued it was premature for the party to risk everything by taking a stand at this time against the Soviet.[210]

The fiery side of Tomsky's personality now came to the fore. Tomsky and other representatives of the Petersburg Committee expressed outrage at both the Central Committee's decision and its failure to consult with them. The historian Alexander Rabinowitch argues 'the differences which developed between the Petersburg and Central Committees over the cancellation issue were the most serious of the whole February to October period'.[211] When Lenin and

---

208 Trotsky 1932a, p. 442.
209 The final vote was 131 in favour, six opposed, and 22 abstentions, but in the two preceding votes only 58 and 47 had voted in favour of demonstrating: RKP(b) 1927a, pp. 273–4. The stenographic record does not indicate how individual delegates voted, but Tomsky later revealed he had in the end voted to support the resolution.
210 Rabinowitch 1968, pp. 70–7, 86.
211 Rabinowitch 1968, p. 86.

others on the Central Committee defended the 'strategic retreat' at an emergency meeting on 11 June, Tomsky pointed out that when he had voted to support the demonstration, he had not 'closed his eyes' to the prospect that the Soviet would take the most drastic measures against us, including firing machine guns at us. He ridiculed Lenin's assertion that previously unknown factors necessitated the last-minute cancellation. 'We considered the question very seriously ... and foresaw everything'. Tomsky boldly proclaimed, 'it was infantile' for the Central Committee 'to think the demonstration would be peaceful'.[212] To support his proposal to convene a citywide party conference to discuss the intra-party problems, which was adopted, Tomsky argued 'The Central Committee not only committed a political mistake – it was guilty of intolerable wavering ... faith in the [Central Committee] leadership by those of us who are [Petersburg Committee] executives has been undermined'.[213] In these and other blunt criticisms of Lenin and various members of the Central Committee, Tomsky demonstrated once again his remarkable self-assurance and assertiveness vis-à-vis the party's *intelligent* leaders. It took extraordinarily strenuous efforts by Tomsky and other Bolshevik agitators, going from one factory and barrack to another that day, to restrain the workers and soldiers from going out on to the streets as previously planned.

The moderate socialist leadership of the Congress of Soviets, in an attempt to appease the capital's increasingly angry workers and soldiers, voted on 12 June to call for its own demonstration on 18 June. The Petersburg Committee responded unenthusiastically to the Bolshevik Central Committee's decision to participate. The Central Committee sought to turn it, contrary to the wishes of the Soviet leaders, 'into an expression of support for the transfer of all power to the Soviet'. Tomsky expressed the scepticism shared by other members of the Petersburg Committee when he questioned whether the party could turn the demonstration away from supporting the Soviet leadership. He also bitterly added that if the 10 June demonstration had not been cancelled, 'the Bolsheviks would have hegemony in Petrograd and would not now have to follow behind the Soviet'.[214] Tomsky and fellow members of the Petersburg Committee decided in the end to actively support the demonstration. In doing so it adopted Tomsky's amendment that obligated all party members to march under banners with Bolshevik slogans, even if their fellow factory workers refused to do so.[215]

---

212   RKP(b) 1927a, pp. 159–60.
213   RKP(b) 1927a, pp. 159–61, 196.
214   RKP(b) 1927a, p. 180.
215   RKP(b) 1927a, pp. 182–3.

Tomsky's cutting speeches at Petersburg Committee meetings in June, and frequent arguments with Lenin and other members of the Central Committee, as earlier, did not stop the growth of his authority and influence within the party.[216] On 16 June he became a member of the Executive Committee of the First All-Russian Congress of Soviets, along with such other notable Bolsheviks as Bukharin, Felix Dzerzhinsky, and Alexandra Kollontai.[217]

The 18 June demonstration, the Soviet's demonstration, proved to be an enormous success for the Bolsheviks, contrary to Tomsky's expectations. Most of the 400,000 workers and soldiers, who poured out into the streets from virtually all of the city's factories and military regiments, eschewed the official slogans, choosing instead to carry, as Tomsky had encouraged them to do, the forbidden banners of the Bolsheviks – 'All Power to the Soviets'! and 'Down with the Ten Capitalist Ministers'!'[218] In the words of one historian, 'The urban lower classes in Petrograd proved to be far more susceptible to the ideas of the Bolsheviks and the Anarchists than anyone had suspected'.[219]

The Anarchists, who were prominent among those who supported the massive pro-Bolshevik demonstration, attracted Tomsky's attention. Their black flags stood out among the endless red ones and they carried banners embroidered with the slogan, 'Down with Authority and Capitalism'!'[220] They were clearly enjoying increasing support from Petrograd workers, particularly in the militant working-class district of Vyborg, and among the sailors and workers at the Kronstadt naval base as well as in many trade unions.[221] Tomsky, although alarmed by the Anarchists' growing influence, warned the Bolshevik Party against breaking with them, stating that 'by fencing ourselves off from the Anarchists, we may fence ourselves off from the masses'.[222] But even as the Bolsheviks and Anarchists increasingly worked together arm-in-arm, Tomsky called on *Pravda* to immediately publish articles focused on weaning workers away from the Anarchists.[223] The Petersburg Committee advocated supporting more radical positions such as overthrowing and arresting the members

---

216 This independent streak did have negative political affects later – first, in 1921, when the Central Committee temporarily exiled Tomsky to Central Asia for not enforcing the party line on trade unions.
217 Shelestov 1990, p. 98; Ivanova 1992, p. 157. Tomsky was a non-voting member.
218 Rabinowitch 1968, p. 106.
219 Thomspson 1989, p. 83.
220 Sukhanov 1984, p. 418; Avrich 1967, p. 124.
221 Avrich 1967, p. 167n60.
222 Quoted in Sirianni 1982, p. 52.
223 RKP(b) 1927b, p. 173; Rabinowitch 1968, pp. 62–3.

of the Provisional Government.[224] Even so, the Anarchists, for their part, criticised the Bolsheviks as being too moderate. As it would turn out, the Anarchists' support and influence appears to have reached its peak during the summer of 1917.

Following this massive, peaceful demonstration, Tomsky became alarmed when rank-and-file Bolsheviks began to call for an armed march against the Provisional Government. On 20 June, Tomsky again urged those itching to take more militant action to be more cautious. The Petersburg Committee adopted his resolution calling on Bolsheviks to restrain workers and soldiers from trying to start an armed uprising, by a vote of 19–2.[225] Tomsky would reiterate the need for caution at the Bolsheviks' Second All-City Petrograd Conference on 1 July, by which time Lenin had furtively fled to Finland.[226] Lenin would briefly sneak back into the city, but he continued to be, in Zinoviev's words, 'hopelessly paralyzed by indecision'.[227] Tomsky shared Lenin's fear that if workers and soldiers now went out onto the streets it might 'fatally' undermine the further development of the revolution.[228] Tomsky was speaking in particular about the increasingly explosive unrest among unskilled workers at the Putilov and other factories in the city.[229]

Encouraged by the Anarchists and Left Bolsheviks, on 3 July columns of angry and unruly workers, soldiers, and sailors marched either to the Kshesinskaya mansion in search of Bolshevik leaders or to the Tauride Palace in search of leaders of the Soviet.[230] When two strongly pro-Bolshevik machine-gun regiments burst into the Kshesinskaya mansion, the Bolsheviks' Second Petrograd Conference's Presidium gave Tomsky the job of presenting the Central Committee's position that a revolution at this time was premature. Tomsky lectured them, stating 'The regiments should not have gone out into the streets without first asking the party Central Committee to consider the ques-

---

224 Rabinowitch 1976, p. xxii. The Anarchists were the only movement on the left besides the Bolsheviks to favour the destruction of the Provisional Government: Avrich 1967, p. 129.
225 Rabinowitch 1968, pp. 126–7. Volodarsky co-sponsored the resolution.
226 Tomsky had just been elected to the Bolsheviks' Presidium of the Second All-City Conference of the Petrograd Organisation, along with Latsis, Volodarsky, Boky, and M.M. Kharitonov: RKP(b) 1927b, pp. 8, 12. Robert Service states that an exhausted Lenin, suffering from severe headaches, left for Finland to convalesce: Service 1991, p. 192.
227 Quoted in Figes 1996, p. 427.
228 RKP(b) 1927b, pp. 27–8.
229 They were threatening to go into the streets if their demand for a minimum wage was not met: Smith 1983, p. 124.
230 The Anarchists fanned the flames of unrest that had been sparked by the Provisional Government's decision to ship units of the Petrograd garrison, in particular the First Machine Gun Regiment, to the front: Rabinowitch 1968, pp. 135–40.

tion of a demonstration. You have not acted in a comradely manner'.[231] After the rebuffed machine gunners angrily left, Tomsky called on party members and sympathisers 'to restrain the masses from further demonstrations ... We are not able to determine all the "ifs" of the present situation. But to take the initiative in our own hands would be risky' and could do grave damage to the party.[232] He called instead for the Executive Committee of the Petrograd Soviet of Workers' and Soldiers' Deputies to take it upon themselves to seize power.[233]

This policy of restraint enjoyed the overwhelming support of delegates of the Bolshevik Petrograd Second City Conference.[234] A disapproving Trotsky characterised Tomsky as a 'compromiser' who was 'more inclined by character to restrain the masses from action than summon them to it', but he conceded that 'an overwhelming majority of the conference was at one with Tomsky'.[235] They too thought that the timing was premature. Later in the day, Tomsky and other party leaders went to the Tauride Palace with their words of restraint, after learning tens of thousands of armed soldiers and workers were marching there.[236] Their pleas for the crowd to disperse peacefully were met with hoots and catcalls.[237]

Tomsky's efforts went for naught as the demonstrators seized control of the streets on 4 July. During the so-called July Days, the party leadership in the end felt it had no choice but to come out in half-hearted support of the demonstrators. This time Tomsky's fears proved all too correct. With the tens of thousands of demonstrators confused about what to do, and with the release of slanderous documents alleging that Lenin was a German agent, the Provisional Government was able to call in reliable military units willing to disarm and scatter the insurgents. Within a few days, the Provisional Government arrested several prominent Bolsheviks, including Trotsky and Kamenev, along with several hundred rank-and-file party members. Troops seized the Bolshevik party headquarters, the Kshesinskaya mansion, destroyed the printing press of *Trud* (Labour), shut down the Bolsheviks' mass-circulation newspapers *Pravda* and *Soldatskaya pravda* (The Soldiers' Truth), and raided many of the party's district and factory committee offices. Hundreds of demonstrators were killed or wounded. It was a total disaster for the Bolsheviks. Most contemporary

---

231 RGASPI, f. 593, op. 1, d. 1, l. 11; Ivanova 1992, p. 167.
232 RKP(b) 1927b, p. 50.
233 Ibid.
234 Service 1991, p. 193. Zinoviev and Kamenev also tried to restrain local activists.
235 Trotsky 1932b, p. 20.
236 RGASPI, f. 593, op. 1, d. 1, l. 12.
237 Deutscher 1967, pp. 148–9.

observers agreed that the July Days had inflicted a fatal blow to the Bolsheviks' chances of ever coming to power. Tomsky wrote at the time in *Spartak* (Spartacus), a theoretical journal intended for a popular audience, that the success of the 'counter-revolution', in his opinion, was 'the direct result of the conciliations, vacillations, and indecision' of Lenin and other Bolshevik leaders.[238] But he regarded the July uprising as nonetheless a laudable attempt 'to expand and deepen the revolution'. He considered the call for 'All Power to the Soviet' as calling not for 'a dictatorship of the proletariat, but a dictatorship of a true labour democracy, including the peasantry as well as the working class'.[239]

After playing such a prominent role in the Bolshevik leadership during June and early July, Tomsky seemingly disappeared. He was physically spent. With Bolshevik support on the wane following the July uprising, and the party's leaders hiding or under arrest, Tomsky slacked off enough to feel the effects of years of inhaling toxic fumes, exhausting hard labour, prison, and exile to the brutal winter conditions in eastern Siberia. His gruelling return from Siberia and his feverish participation in trade-union, soviet, and party politics had also taken their toll. Finally, heeding his doctor's warning to slow down, on 20 July Tomsky moved to Moscow, where he rejoined his family.[240] At the first meeting of the Petersburg Committee's Executive Committee without Tomsky, on 16 July, Moisei Volodarsky lamented that the strength of the committee had been seriously diminished by Tomsky's absence.[241] As he would do in later years, including at such crucial junctures in Soviet history as the Stalinist challenge to his leadership at the Eighth Trade-Union Congress in 1928, Tomsky took to bed. Molotov, who obviously had an axe to grind, later criticised Tomsky's departure harshly. 'Tomsky disappeared when the going was toughest ... Here is a prominent leader for you! What steadfastness'![242] But July and August, prior to the Kornilov Affair, were of course quiet months for the Bolsheviks after the July debacle, with Lenin in hiding in Finland and Trotsky, Kamenev, and other key leaders in prison. Even Lenin became pessimistic about the party's prospects.[243]

---

238   *Spartak* 1917, no. 7, p. 27: quoted in Ivanova 1992, p. 170. Tomsky wrote his article, entitled 'About the Petrograd Events, 3–5 July', after he moved to Moscow. It was published in September. *Spartak* regularly published articles by Bukharin, Osinsky (Obolensky), and other Bolshevik Party leaders.
239   Quoted in Ivanova 1992, p. 170.
240   TsGAODM, f. 2870, op. 1, d. 296, reprinted in Karpachev and Minaeva (eds) 1992b, p. 103; Kozelev 1927, p. 75.
241   Ivanova 1992, p. 170.
242   Molotov 1993, p. 283.
243   Rabinowitch 1976, p. 37.

Tomsky threw himself back into the fray in August as he regained some strength, despite his doctor's order forbidding him from assuming any major responsibilities.[244] Although this prohibited an appointment to the Moscow Soviet of Workers' and Soldiers' Deputies, which was working long hours, seven days a week, Tomsky energetically carried out the various tasks assigned to him by the Soviet, which was chaired by the Bolshevik moderate Victor Nogin.[245] Working-class leaders with Tomsky's administrative and oratorical skills were in exceedingly short supply in Moscow. The Soviet, for example, put Tomsky to work in the commission supervising elections to the Moscow Municipal Dumas. Under the new electoral law based on 'universal and equal suffrage', the Bolsheviks received over 51 percent of the votes in the 24 September municipal elections, which was a major increase from the 11 percent the Bolsheviks received in June.[246] Tomsky was elected a member of the Rogozhsky-Simonovsky district (raion) duma, where he engaged in lively debates with Kadet and SR representatives.[247] He also served as an editor for the Moscow Metalworkers' Union's journal, *Moskovskii metallist* (The Moscow Metalworker), and wrote a number of articles on such issues as the Constituent Assembly and the role of trade unions in the revolution.[248] Tomsky's moderate predisposition meshed well with the other moderate leaders of the Metalworkers' Union, one of the two Bolshevik trade-union strongholds in Moscow, who declared in October they were for soviet power, but against one-party power.[249] Tomsky was also elected chair of the executive committee of the Moscow Council of Trade Unions (MGSPS) and became editor of its journal, *Professional'nyi vestnik*.[250] Diane Koenker, the preeminent historian of Moscow in 1917, argues that the soviet and the trade unions commanded workers' institutional allegiance far more than the political parties at the time when Tomsky arrived in the city. In that

244 Shapovalova 1989, p. 86; TsGAODM, f. 2870, op. 1, d. 296, reprinted in Karpachev and Minaeva (eds) 1992b, pp. 103; Volobuev (ed.) 1993, p. 318.
245 RGASPI, f. 593, op. 1, d. 1. l. 15.
246 TsGAODM, f. 2870, op. 1, d. 296, reprinted in Karpachev and Minaeva (eds) 1992b, pp. 103, 116; Bowman 1973, pp. 112–13. The turnout, however, was fairly low, which Koenker interpreted as evidence of Moscow workers' low political consciousness: Koenker 1981, p. 227.
247 Kozelev 1927, p. 77.
248 RGASPI, f. 593, op. 1, d. 11, ll. 14–16; Kozelev 1927, p. 75. Vladimir Polonsky and Gregory Melnichansky served with Tomsky on the journal's editorial board. Tomsky became editor-in-chief with the publication of the journal's fourth edition in November.
249 Koenker 1981, p. 227. The Textile Workers' Union was the other Bolshevik union stronghold.
250 Tomsky published a number of his own articles, in simple language, for his working-class readers, on contemporary political events and the trade unions' role in them. Tomsky was elected chair of the MGSPS a little later, on 4 December 1917.

context, she argues the Bolsheviks represented workers more effectively than any of the other socialist parties.[251]

Moscow was not the revolutionary hotbed that was Petrograd. There was nothing in Moscow comparable to Petrograd's mass demonstrations in June or July. In fact, when a couple hundred Moscow demonstrators took to the streets on 4 July they were outnumbered by hostile crowds of anti-Bolshevik hecklers. The Bolshevik leaders, for their part, were generally moderate and willing to work with the Mensheviks and SRs, with whom they substantially agreed on local issues in the June elections to the municipal duma. Likewise, the three socialist parties in August agitated together in factories and barracks during the Kornilov Affair. Even so, worker and soldier outrage at the Kornilov Affair gave the Bolsheviks a major boost in Moscow. But most Moscow party leaders remained extremely cautious. They even proved reluctant to support strikes for fear they would lead to what they considered a premature, uncontrollable general strike. When some Moscow workers joined the October fighting, according to Koenker, they did so not 'in order to seize power for the soviets, but to defend the soviets from the counter-revolution'.[252]

Tomsky actively participated in the Bolsheviks' intra-party debates on the eve of their seizure of power. Upon learning of the plans for an armed insurrection, Tomsky voiced his opposition.[253] Moderates such as Tomsky feared that an attempt to seize power would either end in failure, like the July Days fiasco, or if successful, would provoke a civil war. Tomsky favoured instead a broad, all-socialist coalition government, as did other moderate Bolsheviks as well as Left Mensheviks and Left SRs.[254] But Tomsky confined his criticism to party gatherings, unlike Kamenev and Zinoviev, who on 18 October expressed their opposition publicly in Gorky's non-party, leftist newspaper *Novaia zhizn'* (The New Life).[255] After Lenin persuaded the Central Committee to support an

---

251   Koenker 1981, pp. 186, 190.
252   Koenker 1981, pp. 121, 123, 197, 227, 267, 327, 335.
253   Trotsky 1932c, p. 192.
254   The willingness of Moscow Bolsheviks in August to work together with Mensheviks and SRs enraged Lenin, although in early September he too briefly adopted a similarly moderate stance: Rabinowitch 1976, pp. 133, 169–74. The blame for the failure to create a coalition socialist government might rest as much on the Mensheviks and SRs as on the Bolsheviks. If the moderate socialists' leaders had come out for a Soviet government following the Kornilov Affair, instead of forming a third Provisional Government coalition with the Kadets, it arguably would have won the support of most Bolshevik leaders despite Lenin's objections: Sirianni 1982, pp. 82–3.
255   Unlike Tomsky, Rykov and Nogin openly voiced their support for Zinoviev's and Kamenev's opposition to the seizure of power: Daniels 1960, p. 65.

uprising, Tomsky unenthusiastically followed Lenin's instructions to start preparing for the seizure of power in Moscow. He knew opposition to an armed insurrection was strong within both the city's party committee and among the Bolshevik rank and file in the city.[256] Younger, more militant Bolsheviks, such as Bukharin, however, dismissed such cautionary voices as Tomsky's and enthusiastically embraced preparations for the Bolshevik seizure of power in Moscow.[257]

Tomsky and other moderate Bolshevik leaders in Moscow acted only because events in Petrograd forced their hand. Nogin, the Bolshevik chair of the Soviet, desperately did all he could to avoid an armed confrontation.[258] The Moscow Soviet elected a Military-Revolutionary Committee to organise an insurrection only on 25 October after receiving news of the overthrow of the Provisional Government in Petrograd.[259] Most Moscow workers were unwilling to risk their lives to achieve soviet power and seemed content to sit on the side-lines.[260] Tomsky noted as late as 26 October that the trade-union leaders in the city were not even aware of the Military-Revolutionary Committee's plan to call for workers to go into the streets to defend the soviet from counter-revolution.[261]

In the swirl of events in Moscow's October, Tomsky proved willing, albeit reluctantly, to go against his own belief that it was premature for the Bolsheviks to try to seize power. He helped convince the other members of the Moscow Trade-Union Council, crowded together in its bureau's small one-room office, to rally behind the Bolsheviks' call for a general strike.[262] But as he had in the 1905 Revolution, Tomsky wanted to do what he could to avoid any bloodshed. In his proposal supporting the general strike he emphasised that workers needed to conduct themselves in 'an orderly and peaceful manner'.[263] Tomsky's fellow moderate members on the Moscow party committee shared his concerns, and like most Moscow workers, had little enthusiasm for an armed insurrection.[264] But with power hanging in the balance, at the meeting of the

---

256 Shapovalova 1989, p. 86.
257 Cohen 1973, pp. 52–3. The celebrated, left-wing journalist John Reed described Bukharin as 'more left than Lenin': Reed 1977, p. 223.
258 Koenker 1981, p. 342.
259 Colton 1995, p. 85.
260 Koenker 1981, pp. 335, 340.
261 Istprof MGSPS 1927, p. 122.
262 Tomsky was a delegate of Moscow's Metalworkers' Union.
263 Istprof MGSPS 1927, p. 122.
264 Koenker 1981, p. 342. Others on the Moscow Committee included Yan Rudzutak, David Ryazanov, Boris Kozelev, Mikhail Rykunov, and F.D. Denisov.

Moscow Soviet of Trade Unions on 26 October, primarily for defensive purposes, Tomsky proposed that the city's 17 unions join together to support the Military-Revolutionary Committee and the transfer of power to the Soviet.[265] But rather than succumbing entirely to the revolutionary mood, he focused on practical concerns. He continued to caution that 'concrete steps' needed to be taken to ensure that essential city services, particularly food distribution, would not be disrupted. To achieve that, Tomsky called, for example, for bakers, grocery store employees, and other workers in food enterprises to remain on the job.[266] The trade-union soviet supported Tomsky's proposal.[267]

In the face of fierce, if sporadic, house-to-house fighting and the reversal of the Bolsheviks initial seizure of the Kremlin on 27 October, Tomsky travelled with Ilya Veger to Petrograd on 28 October, at the request of Moscow's Military-Revolutionary Committee.[268] Tomsky and Verger met with Lenin at the Bolshevik headquarters at Smolny the following day, where Tomsky argued that workers and soldiers in Moscow needed reinforcements.[269] Despite the obstacles that remained in Petrograd, they prevailed and on 30 October a squad of 500 sailors from the Baltic fleet arrived in Moscow in an armoured train, followed on 1 November by a second squadron of sailors and Red Guards.[270] Further reinforcements arrived during the following days. With this added support, at dawn on 2 November the Bolshevik forces captured once and for all

---

265 Istprof MGSPS 1927, p. 122. Alexander Arosev, a leading member of the Military-Revolutionary Committee during the Bolshevik seizure of power in Moscow, ended his memoir, *October 1917*, with a mention of Tomsky's role. He was taken to task for this as the Great Purges got underway following Tomsky's suicide. On 19 December 1936 *Pravda* published a short notice about the recently published memoir (written in 1920), which asked, 'Why such touching "concern" for a man who fought against the party in the ranks of its most vicious enemies'?: Slezkine 2017, pp. 793, 983. Arosev, a close friend of Molotov since childhood, was arrested on 3 July 1937 and shot on 8 February 1938: Fitzpatrick 2015, pp. 135, 317.
266 Istprof MGSPS 1927, pp. 121, 123. Tomsky's proposal authorised workers in other stores to go on strike.
267 Istprof MGSPS 1927, p. 124.
268 Victor Serge, the former Left Oppositionist, argued that humanitarian 'wavering' by Right Bolsheviks allowed the counter-revolutionaries to regroup, which directly led to the bloodshed Tomsky so wanted to avoid in the Kremlin fighting: Serge 1992, pp. 76–7.
269 Gorelov 1989, p. 24. Veger met with Lenin on 29 October, the following morning. The lack of appreciation of Tomsky's role in 1917 is at least partly due to how he disappeared from history, even during the Khrushchev era. For example, in a major textbook, the author wrote that Lenin met only with Veger: Belykh (ed.) 1969, p. 253. This removal of Tomsky from the historical record is especially curious since the roles of other leading oppositionists such as Rykov, Kamenev, and Zinoviev were not similarly erased in this text.
270 Nosach 2005, pp. 107–8.

the Kremlin, the old fortress and religious and governmental centre in the heart of the city. The Moscow city government's Committee for Public Safety surrendered to the Military-Revolutionary Committee later that day. It was Tomsky who announced to the meeting of the Military-Revolutionary Committee that the soldiers and officers of the Moscow garrison had gone over to the side of the revolution and victory was theirs.[271] In the words of the historian Yuri Slezkine, it was 'in Moscow where the fate of the revolution was decided'.[272]

During the fighting Tomsky remained concerned with maintaining civil order and preserving Moscow's cultural heritage.[273] But he did not go as far as the litterateur Lunacharsky, who resigned from the party in protest on 2 November because he could not 'bear the monstrous destruction of beauty and tradition' after hearing rumours of the shelling of the Kremlin.[274] The heaviest fighting during the 10-day battle had taken place around the Kremlin. The bombardment caused damage to many buildings, including the massive Cathedral of the Assumption, the most important church in Moscow. But the damage was not as bad as Lunacharsky initially feared and he quickly returned to his post as Commissar of Enlightenment. Tomsky's hopes to avoid bloodshed were not realised, however, with approximately 500 people killed on each side. The Bolshevik seizure of power in Moscow proved to be more violent than anywhere else in the country.

Most Bolshevik leaders in Moscow initially proved to be at least as moderate and conciliatory as Tomsky, if not more so. Rykov expressed his opposition to repression and terror and promised that the elections to the Constituent Assembly would proceed as scheduled, and once it was convened, 'power will be transferred to it'.[275] But well before those elections, just days after the seizure of power, Rykov quit the Central Committee to protest the Sovnarkom's 'temporary' decree to suppress the anti-Bolshevik press, announced just two days after the Bolshevik seizure of power.[276] Tomsky did not follow Rykov's lead.

---

271 Gorelov 1989, pp. 24–5.
272 Slezkine 2017, p. 138.
273 That extended to Tomsky's decision, without consulting other members of the Military-Revolutionary Committee, to allow the Patriarch and other clerics inside the Kremlin to have their own armed guards: Ivanova 1992, p. 176.
274 Reed, 1977, pp. 220–1. Lenin laughed at Lunacharsky's distress and unsuccessfully called for his removal from the party: Stites 1989, p. 77; Daniels 1960, p. 65.
275 Koenker 1981, pp. 240, 345. Many Moscow workers shared Rykov's views.
276 Zinoviev, Kamenev, Nogin, and Vladimir Milyutin also resigned from the Central Committee. They returned to the fold within a matter of weeks. Widespread resistance to the censorship decree led to its suspension.

As the newly elected chair of the Moscow Soviet of Trade Unions, he defended closing the newspaper *Russkoe slovo* (The Russian Word) as necessary to protect the revolution.[277] The opposition to the Bolshevik seizure of power by *Russkoe slovo*, one of the major 'bourgeois' newspapers, was particularly inflammatory. But Tomsky was concerned about how this closing would affect the workers employed there.[278] A week later, on 15 December, Tomsky called for providing all workers in enterprises that were forced to close with at least two-thirds pay.[279]

In sum, Tomsky as a party and trade-union activist in the revolutionary underground demonstrated considerable initiative and administrative skill despite his minimal education and the hardships of his youth. His eagerness to throw himself into political debates at the party's highest level was most unusual. The contrast with Kanatchikov's inability 'to face a crowd of sophisticated intellectuals', highlights Tomsky's remarkable self-confidence.[280] His public speaking skills set him apart from other Bolshevik working-class *praktiki*, few of whom were natural orators. Tomsky also made a name for himself by attacking such Social-Democratic luminaries as Martov and Axelrod just a couple years after joining the party. Uncommonly ambitious, Tomsky worked hard to rise within the party's ranks. Whereas Kanatchikov chose to remain in Siberia following the collapse of the autocracy, Tomsky literally galloped across the frozen Siberian steppe to return to the centre of the political fray. By 1917 he was increasingly willing to question Lenin himself, calling his tactics in June 'infantile'. Few Bolshevik worker-*intelligents* had such nerve. During this rise to power, he also displayed the political pragmatism that would make him a so-called Right Deviationist a decade later. The prudent scepticism and caution that led Tomsky to initially oppose Lenin's armed insurrection in 1917 would be evident in 1928 when he joined with Bukharin and Rykov to oppose Stalin's tragically reckless plunge into forced collectivisation and breakneck industrialisation.

---

277 Istprof MGSPS 1927, p. 148. Tomsky was elected on 1 December 1917.
278 Under the autocracy *Russkoe slovo* had been the leading paper of the moderate opposition. The Moscow Printers' Union's leaders worked out a temporary solution by persuading the Moscow Soviet to employ the workers to print the Soviet's newspaper, *Izvestiia* (The News), but that fell apart two weeks later when they were not paid: Koenker 2005, p. 50.
279 Istprof MGSPS 1927, p. 163.
280 Kanatchikov 1986, p. x.

CHAPTER 2

Balancing Act: Tomsky during War Communism and the Trade-Union Debate

> The Russian worker is a bad worker compared with people in advanced countries.
> VLADIMIR LENIN

∴

> The political content of the [trade-union] debate has had so much refuse heaped upon it that I do not envy the historian of the future who tries to get to the truth of the matter.
> LEON TROTSKY

∴

Tomsky emerged as one of the leading figures in the Soviet state following the Bolsheviks' seizure of power. After playing a central role in the First Trade-Union Congress in January 1918, he would become the chair of the VTsSPS (All-Union Central Council of Trade Unions) in October.[1] Then, in March 1919, Tomsky also became one of the 19 members of the Communist Party's Central Committee. This dual responsibility as a key member of the party leadership and as the head of the organisation that was supposed to protect workers' interests put Tomsky at the centre of the debates over the function of trade unions in the self-proclaimed 'workers' state'. Tomsky was a skilled politician and he generally succeeded in balancing these two responsibilities. But his willingness to compromise with other members of the political leadership outraged militant trade unionists, in particular Alexander Shlyapnikov and other supporters of the Workers' Opposition. Likewise, Tomsky's efforts to placate those trade unionists outraged members of the political leadership. Not only did it

---

1 The VTsSPS was an executive body charged with administering trade-union affairs between trade-union congresses. The First Trade-Union Congress approved the establishment of the VTsSPS as a permanent body.

prove impossible to reconcile their mutually exclusive views, Tomsky's attempt to occupy a middle position provoked an intense backlash. Lenin stripped him of his chairmanship of the VTsSPS in May 1921. Tomsky's removal came on the heels of the so-called trade-union debate, an extraordinary, unprecedented debate about the role of trade unions in the revolutionary state, and by extension, the relationship between workers, the state, and the party. In the words of one historian, it threw the party into the 'severest crisis of its history'.[2]

Historians often view Tomsky's leadership of the unions during the Civil War, particularly in the intense debates over the role of trade unions, unfavourably in comparison with the positions taken by the Workers' Opposition and Mensheviks. If compared instead with mainstream Bolsheviks, Tomsky clearly led the party's moderate wing and vehemently opposed Trotsky's attempts to eviscerate the trade unions. He fought, within limits, to defend workers' interests. But Tomsky was a Bolshevik Party member first and foremost. When evaluating the decisions he made during the first years of Soviet trade unionism, Tomsky thus should not be evaluated as if he were a long-time trade unionist like David Ryazanov, who had joined the party primarily in order to advance the interests of the trade unions. It was quite the opposite; although Tomsky did take his trade-union responsibilities very seriously and they would become his primary focus during the 1920s. That he and Lenin sometimes agreed during key moments of the 'trade-union debate' also should not be interpreted as based on some sort of blind 'loyalty' to Lenin and other party leaders, as the historian Jay Sorenson repeatedly stated in his major, if dated, study of the trade unions. During these years, Tomsky, who enjoyed considerable power and autonomy, often fought for positions diametrically opposed to Lenin's. Tomsky, in particular, developed a deep antipathy toward Trotsky for his repeated denigrations of the trade unions. That antipathy would later play a key role in the power struggle following Lenin's incapacitation in 1922.

The Bolsheviks came to power with no blueprints on how to address various major issues or how to contend with the collapse of the economy. While they shared core aspirations, virtually everything had to be improvised, as Tomsky realised at the First Trade-Union Congress in January 1918, when he stated, 'In the period when everything stored up by the centuries was literally turned upside down by the proletarian revolution, to take into account and to foresee not only the general direction of this advance, but to foresee exactly all its details beforehand would have been hopelessly pedantic'.[3] Or

---

2 Sorenson 1969, p. 103.
3 Quoted in Kaplan 1968, p. 183.

in the words of the historian Jeremy Azrael, 'Anyone who approaches pre-revolutionary Marxist-Leninist theory in search of a comprehensive and systematic doctrine of industrial organisation and management is foredoomed to disappointment'.[4] One of the Bolshevik leaders on economic policy, N. Osinsky, bluntly stated, 'If one asks oneself how our party before 25 October conceived the system of workers' control as a whole and on the basis of what economic order we meant to construct it, we shall nowhere find a clear answer'.[5] This lack of a clear programme, and party leaders' naïve underestimation of the challenges awaiting them, led to lots of acrimonious disagreements and makeshift solutions. Tomsky would stand at the centre of these debates and decisions.

All Bolsheviks initially expressed their support for workers' control.[6] Tomsky, for example, published an article in *Moskovskii Metallist* (Moscow Metalworker) on 29 October 1917 in which he stated that workers, through the Bolshevik seizure of power, had achieved 'workers' control and the regulation of industry'. He called on workers to immediately participate in the management of production in each and every enterprise.[7] Two weeks later, on 14 November, in one of the new regime's first decrees, workers' control became official policy.[8] Lenin embraced the notion of workers playing a central role in the economy and government, going so far as to proclaim that 'the illusion that only the bourgeoisie can run the state must be fought against. The proletariat must take the rule of the state upon itself' and 'set about the organisation of control and production on a countrywide scale'.[9] But it quickly became apparent that for many party leaders, including Lenin, workers' control sadly became little more than a slogan. The horrible state of the economy, including the general breakdown in transportation, the shortage in cities of food and other supplies, and the loss of raw materials due to German occupation, undermined their desire to implement this and various other long-sought goals.[10]

The enormity of the economic challenges the regime inherited, and the party's tenuous hold on power, would shape the initial decisions of nearly

---

[4] Azrael 1966, p. 12.
[5] Quoted in Carr 1952, p. 60. N. Osinsky (Valerian Obolsensky) headed the Supreme Council of the National Economy (VSNKh) from December 1917 until March 1918.
[6] The Russian word *kontrol'* is weaker than the English word control. It means worker supervision of management, rather than actually running the factories.
[7] Quoted in Gorelov 2000, p. 100.
[8] Dewar 1979, pp. 160–1.
[9] Lenin proclaimed this in December 1917: Lenin 1960–70, vol. 26, pp. 365–6.
[10] The economic decline that began with the outbreak of the world war in August 1914 had become far worse by the time the Bolsheviks seized power from the Provisional Government in October 1917.

all Bolshevik leaders, including Tomsky. Tomsky recognised that his desire to champion workers' interests had to be balanced with the need to accelerate the recovery of industrial production and overcome various other economic challenges. In the words of the historian Robert Daniels, the Bolsheviks 'came to power in the wrong place and ultimately had to recast their goals in conformance with the actual problems' they faced.[11] Tomsky wrote a number of articles immediately after the Bolshevik seizure of power in which he described these challenges for his working-class readers in *Professional'nyi vestnik*. In one, published in December 1917, Tomsky decried the grave shortages of raw materials and fuel, the increasing unemployment with demobilised soldiers flooding back into cities, and the fall in real wages. He denounced attempts by the owners of enterprises to withhold wages and, in his words, 'sabotage production'. To address these issues Tomsky, who had just been elected to the three-person Secretariat (Executive Committee) of the newly formed Moscow Soviet of Trade Unions, suggested that the trade unions create commissions to carry out workers' control in individual enterprises.[12] Most workers shared Tomsky's initial view that the economic chaos was largely the result of 'willful sabotage' by employers.[13]

The First All-Russian Congress of Trade Unions opened in Petrograd on 7 January 1918 in a celebratory mood, even though Bolshevik authorities just days before had authorised, for the first time, firing on an unarmed crowd, which was marching in the tens of thousands toward the Tauride Palace under the slogan of 'All Power to the Constituent Assembly'.[14] Red Guards and soldiers killed or wounded dozens of these demonstrators before forcibly dissolving the popularly elected body because it refused to rubber stamp the Bolsheviks' seizure of power.[15] The Central Committee entrusted Alexander Shlyapnikov, the Commissar of Labour and future leader of the Workers' Opposition, with

---

11   Daniels 1960, p. 408. The historian E.H. Carr suggests that Lenin during 1917 never thought workers would actually assume control over manufacturing or factory organisation but would instead focus on financial and commercial decisions: Carr 1952, pp. 58–9.
12   Tomskii 1928a, pp. 10–13. The other two members of the Moscow Secretariat were Andrei Andreev and Grigory Melnichansky: Nosach 2005, p. 57.
13   Smith 1983, p. 167. It is difficult to know to what extent the closing of factories was due to the shortages of fuel and materials, as the owners argued, or to their opposition to the trade unions' and factory committees' demands for workers' control: Husband 1985, pp. 19–20.
14   Perhaps intentionally, the trade-union congress met quite a distance away from the Tauride Palace. It was held in the Nicholas Cavalry Academy, which was across town along the Obvodny Canal.
15   Rabinowitch 2007, pp. 104–27; Krausz 2015, p. 215.

organising the closing down of the Constituent Assembly.[16] For all of Tomsky's initial reservations about the Bolshevik seizure of power, like virtually all Bolshevik leaders, he apparently did not voice opposition to the closing of the Constituent Assembly, even though he had been one of the 19 members of Moscow's Bolshevik ticket in the elections to the assembly.[17] Tomsky had devoted part of November to actively campaigning in Moscow where, like in Petrograd, the Bolsheviks received a large plurality of the votes.[18] Tomsky's acceptance of the closing down of the Constituent Assembly was in stark contrast to the large minority of non-Bolshevik delegates at the trade-union congress, who expressed their utter outrage. The trade unions were an unusual institution in Soviet Russia in that they were still a multi-party organisation (and would remain so for a number of years). Of the 428 delegates with voting rights at the congress, there were in addition to the 281 Bolsheviks, 67 Mensheviks, 21 Left SRs, 10 Right SRs, six Anarcho-Syndicalists, six Maximalists, and 37 non-party delegates.[19]

Tomsky, as head of the Moscow trade unions and one of the party leaders entrusted with the preparatory work for the First Trade-Union Congress, met with Lenin a number of times on the eve of the congress in January 1918 to see what he and other party leaders had in mind for the unions.[20] During these meetings Tomsky urged Lenin to support the trade unions, and certainly not move to have them absorbed into the government.[21] Tomsky feared that Lenin had come to share Grigory Zinoviev's position that trade unions were essen-

---

16 Allen 2015, p. 106.
17 Lenin, in his 'April Theses', had criticised the Provisional Government for not announcing when the elections to the Constituent Assembly would be held, so he later felt he had to allow the elections to go forward even though the Bolsheviks had already seized power: Lenin 1960–70, vol, 24, p. 25.
18 Radkey 1989, p. 36. Although none of the Bolsheviks were devotees of 'bourgeois democracy', many favoured direct labour self-government through the soviets, not a Bolshevik one-party government: Krausz 2015, pp. 221–2. That was most likely Tomsky's position. Only Alexander Lozovsky and David Ryazanov voted against the Central Executive Committee's decision to permanently close the Constituent Assembly. In addition, prior to the vote, Nogin, Zinoviev, and Rykov resigned from the Central Committee in protest: Daniels 1960, p. 68; Engelstein 2018, p. 199. Surprisingly, the forcible closing of the Assembly initially provoked little public protest among the population at large.
19 VTsSPS 1918, p. 134. The Bolsheviks' preponderance of delegates was the result of various manoeuvres on their part. The Mensheviks had dominated many of the various trade-union executive committees during 1917. Only the Metalworkers' and the Textile Workers' Unions strongly supported the Bolsheviks.
20 Tomsky edited many of the resolutions that were presented to the delegates of the congress: Nosach 2005, p. 108.
21 Rokitianskii 2009, p. 290.

FIGURE 2   Tomsky and Zinoviev en route to meeting
NATIONAL ARCHIVES

tially superfluous, no longer necessary because in the self-proclaimed workers' state, trade unions would have no need to struggle against their own government.[22] Tomsky unsuccessfully tried to convince Lenin of the fallacy of many of the positions in Zinoviev's draft of his report to the congress, particularly his argument for the immediate 'statification' [*ogosudarstvlenie*] of the trade unions. Zinoviev's draft resolution did not even touch on the need to protect workers' economic interests. Tomsky, as we will see, ultimately managed to get Lenin to compromise.

Tomsky was the Bolsheviks' second main spokesperson after Zinoviev at the congress. He provoked outrage from many when he vehemently defended the close relationship between the Bolshevik Party and the trade unions. The trade-union congress proved so highly contentious that sessions were repeatedly interrupted and speakers were often heckled, with Tomsky often serving as the provocateur. He characterised the Menshevik position that it was necessary for the trade unions to be politically 'neutral' (non-party), in order to fight

---

22   Nosach 2005, p. 43.

for workers' economic rights, as a 'bourgeois idea' and insisted there was no middle ground on this issue.[23] Tomsky declared, 'either you are with us or you are against us'.[24] And indeed the resolution adopted at the congress resolutely denounced the idea of trade-union neutrality. According to the resolution, 'Those who, in the course of speeches, make themselves out to be neutral, are, generally when it comes to actions, a source of strength to the bourgeoisie and traitors to the working classes. All revolutionary socialists must definitely break with the idea of trade-union neutrality'.[25]

On the related question of the relationship between the Soviet government and the trade unions, Tomsky's position was more nuanced than what he expressed on the floor of the congress, where he had seemed to agree with Zinoviev that trade-union independence was unnecessary since the exploitation or oppression of workers by their own government was impossible.[26] But behind the closed doors of the communist caucus meeting, while holding firm to his position on the 'non-neutrality' of the unions, Tomsky vehemently opposed Zinoviev's talk of subordinating the unions to the government or incorporating them into the government.[27] All Bolshevik Party delegates belonged to its party 'fraction' [*fraktsiia*], which is translated in this work as caucus, like the party caucuses within the United States Congress.[28] It met outside the regular proceedings of the trade-union congress, with the express purpose of excluding non-Bolshevik Party delegates. Tomsky had chosen not to make his opposition to Zinoviev an issue on the floor of the congress in the interest of maintaining an image of party unity in front of the Menshevik and SR delegates. He also may have done this as the price for Lenin's verbal agreement that 'statification' would be put off to the indefinite future. In any case, Tomsky enjoyed the support of other leading Bolshevik trade unionists, such as the chair of the congress Shlyapnikov and the head of the Petrograd trade unions David Ryazanov, in speaking out against Zinoviev's posi-

---

23 Tomskii 1928a, pp. 20–2. Lenin had initially supported trade-union neutrality, but reversed himself in 1907, when he called for 'the close drawing together of the union with the party': quoted in Hammond 1957, p. 67.
24 Tomskii 1928a, p. 22.
25 VTsSPS 1918, pp. 119–20. Tomsky made similar arguments at another meeting that was occurring at the same time as the trade-union congress, the Third Congress of Workers' and Soldiers' Soviets. Many of the delegates, like Lenin and Tomsky, went back and forth between the two congresses: Gorelov 1998, p. 31.
26 Shapovalova 1989, p. 87.
27 Kozelev 1927, p. 81. Kozelev was, like Tomsky, a member of Moscow's Bolshevik delegation at the congress.
28 It could also be translated as a party 'cell'.

tion.²⁹ Tomsky made it clear he did not equate trade-union work towards fulfilling the goals of the party with subordination to the government. The trade unions, Tomsky argued, needed to maintain a separate identity. He so strongly opposed Zinoviev and other Bolsheviks who continued to call for the immediate 'statification' of trade unions that he and the entire Moscow delegation temporarily walked out of the caucus.³⁰ The congress adopted Zinoviev's resolution although a large contingent voted against it.³¹ Following that vote, Tomsky arranged to have another meeting with Lenin. Tomsky convinced Lenin to 'soften' the resolution. While retaining the resolution's focus on the ultimate statification of the trade unions, Lenin agreed to put off any decision to implement that into some unspecified future.³² This revised resolution, which the congress adopted, simply declared that the trade unions would 'inevitably' become part of the state at some undetermined later date.³³ In the meantime the Commissariat of Labour (Narkomtrud), which the fellow former worker Shlyapnikov headed, was to play that role in collaboration with the trade unions. The adopted compromise thus successfully papered over the differences. In the words of the historian Isaac Deutscher, the VTsSPS 'accepted the subordination to the government as a matter of high policy [but] the Bolshevik trade unionists jealously guarded the prerogatives of their organisation'.³⁴ But Tomsky, normally even tempered, remained so upset that he refused to stand for election to the VTsSPS Presidium when the vote was held at the end of the congress. He agreed to enter only as a candidate member.³⁵ Tomsky nevertheless gave the concluding speech of the congress.³⁶

29 Nosach 2001, p. 166.
30 VTsSPS 1918, pp. 138–9; Shapovalova 1989, p. 87. Georgy Melnichansky, Boris Kozelev, and Yan Rudzutak were among the Moscow delegates: Gorelev 1989, p. 31.
31 The vote was 108 in favour, 48 against, and 12 abstentions: Nosach 2005, p. 43. Obviously, if the whole congress had been allowed to vote, the negative vote would have been far higher.
32 Nosach 2005, pp. 44, 108.
33 Gorelov 2000, p. 61; Nosach 2005, p. 108; International Labour Office 1927, p. 31.
34 Deutscher 1950, p. 21. Or in the words of Jay Sorenson, 'who would rule, the unions or the Soviet apparatus? It was an issue that would plague the Bolsheviks for years to come': Sorenson 1969, p. 31.
35 Shapovalova 1989, p. 87; Kozelev 1927, p. 82. The Presidium of the VTsSPS, a smaller body, would meet more frequently than the entire VTsSPS. In addition, leading trade unionists were allotted seats on all the newly formed governmental bodies, including one-third of the seats on the Executive Committee of the Soviets (VTsIK), which constituted the government's highest executive and legislative body between meetings of the All-Russian Congress of Soviets: Deutscher 1950, p. 22.
36 Zinoviev had left the congress to focus on other issues.

This First Trade-Union Congress did not tackle other fundamental issues such as wages, labour protection, and social insurance, but did address the highly contentious issue of whether workers would be allowed to strike. As noted above, the trade unions were not a one-party organisation, unlike other institutions in the one-party state. The Menshevik delegates, frustrated that key issues were being resolved at the congress's Communist Party caucus, succeeded in having this and other contentious issues brought to the floor even though they were not on the agenda. Their chief spokesmen, the major Menshevik leaders Yuly Martov, Ivan Maisky, and Vasily Cherkin maintained that unions, to defend workers' interests, needed to have the power to sanction strikes.[37] While many Bolshevik delegates supported the Mensheviks' position, most supported Tomsky's view that strikes, by hurting the economy, 'would play into the hands of counter-revolutionaries and capitalists'.[38] Tomsky believed that the interests of individual groups of workers had to be 'subordinated to the interests of the working class as a whole'.[39] He shared such a view with the visiting British labour delegation a little later, stating, 'Our tactics differ entirely from those adopted in England or the United States. In those countries the unions are trying to improve conditions for their own members only. Here we are trying to improve conditions for the entire working class'.[40] For Tomsky this obviously meant that trade unions needed to transform themselves into organisations that devoted much of their energies to trying to restore the shattered economy.[41]

Tomsky also played a key role in drafting a resolution that undermined the factory committees, which during 1917 had spontaneously seized control of many factories and their managements, and naturally enough focused only on their own particular factory.[42] Tomsky criticised the simultaneous existence of two forms of economic organisation of the working class with overlapping functions.[43] Amid the heated debates at this first congress, the proposal to incorporate the factory committees into the trade unions by making them the

---

37   VTsSPS 1918, p. 117; Gorelov 1989, p. 30.
38   VTsSPS 1918, p. 118; Kaplan 1968, p. 251. Tomsky adopted this view that to strike against the workers' state amounted to an act of treason immediately after the Bolshevik seizure of power: Sorenson 1969, p. 36.
39   Tomskii 1928a, p. 36.
40   British Labour Delegation 1920, p. 118. Tomsky, in his long speech to the British delegation, pleaded with them to come to the aid of their 'Russian brothers': Berkman 1925, p. 138.
41   VTsSPS 1918, pp. 116–20, 374.
42   For the most part factory committees only seized control of factories in immediate danger of cutbacks or closure: Mandel 1984, p. 366.
43   Quoted in Shkliarevsky 1993, pp. 167–8.

local, subordinate branches of the corresponding trade unions enjoyed a general consensus.[44] Even the maverick Ryazanov, a trade-union organiser since 1905, who only joined the Bolsheviks in the summer of 1917, enthusiastically supported it.[45] It should be noted, however, that it would be some time before this absorption became a reality. It was no easy feat to persuade workers to relinquish control of the enterprises they had seized.

Tomsky, following the congress, became the leading figure in the trade unions. Zinoviev, now preoccupied with other responsibilities, was no longer even a member of the VTsSPS when its Executive Committee moved with the government from Petrograd to Moscow, as the Red Army's fortunes deteriorated.[46] Tomsky would remain head of the Soviet trade-union movement for all but a few months over the next ten years. His position was formalised at the Fourth Trade-Union Conference in May 1918, when Tomsky became the VTsSPS chair [*predsedatel'*].[47] As a hereditary proletarian from St. Petersburg and a talented organiser with a large amount of day-to-day experience interacting with workers, he seemed to many party and trade-union officials to be the obvious choice to head the trade unions.

Tomsky was skilled at party infighting for resources. He outmanoeuvred the heads of other institutions in the fierce scramble for office space when the government moved to Moscow. He obtained arguably the most desirable building in the city for the trade unions' headquarters. The less successful commissariats and other institutions, in contrast, found themselves scattered around Moscow in commandeered mansions, offices, and hotels.[48] The VTsSPS managed to get an enormous, yet elegant eighteenth-century building, which was renamed the 'House of Unions' (*Dom Soiuzov*).[49] This jewel of classic Russian architecture, with its four-columned portico, had been the Club of the Nobility before the revolution, where members of the high nobility and their guests ate, drank,

---

44   Factory committees became the basic unit of the trade unions and all workers, from skilled to unskilled, would be part of the same trade union, such as the Textile Workers' Union as opposed to belonging to craft unions.
45   Dewar 1979, p. 33.
46   Well-known Mensheviks such as Maisky, Chirkin, and I. Volkov also were made members of the VTsSPS's Presidium: Nosach 2005, p. 70.
47   Nosach 2001, p. 209.
48   Stalin, for example, unsuccessfully tried to seize, in the dead of night, the Hotel Siberia, to be the headquarters for the Commissariat of Nationalities but it had already been grabbed by VSNKh: Trotskii 1941, pp. 256–7; McNeal 1988, p. 51.
49   The trade unions had a leg up for over other institutions interested in the building because Tomsky along with his fellow Moscow trade unionists had forcibly taken the building during the October seizure of power. The Moscow Central Trade-Union Council (MGSPS) had made it their headquarters: Tomskii 1928a, p. 434.

and gambled into the wee hours of the night.⁵⁰ It also had the advantage of being near the Kremlin. Tomsky's office was large, with an outer office with two secretaries, and an inner room for private conversations.⁵¹ The VTsSPS held its meetings in the room where the nobles had held theirs, while receptions, conferences, and congresses took place in what had been the nobility's magnificent ballroom known as the Hall of Columns.⁵² Its 28 marble Corinthian columns extended three stories to the ceiling, where huge crystal chandeliers lit up the room. But conditions in the building during the Civil War were nothing like they had been previously.⁵³ They had become extremely austere. An employee remembered 'there was no luxury at all, no trace of luxury of any kind. It was extreme poverty, just the very minimum requirements for work. Little heating or none at all, and above all, a terrible smell of fish soup that filled the whole building'.⁵⁴ There was even a lack of such basic items as tables and chairs. Those sorts of problems would end following the introduction of NEP in 1921.

Tomsky did not spare himself as he threw himself wholeheartedly into the demanding work of heading the trade unions. With little apparent concern for his health, he worked long, exhausting days together with his associates to prepare all sorts of instructional materials and establish wage scales.⁵⁵ Tomsky also would regularly travel outside Moscow, especially after the VTsSPS came under criticism for its lack of contact with provincial trade-union councils.⁵⁶ Sometimes he could not endure the strain and would ask the Central Committee for some time off, as for example in July 1919.⁵⁷

---

50   The 23 national unions also had their headquarters in the House of Unions. Likewise, in Petrograd the trade-union leadership secured a spacious, three-storied palace built by a grand duke for its Palace of Labour [*Dvorets Truda*], as the headquarters for the city's trade unions. Like Smolny, the Bolshevik Party headquarters, the Palace of Labour had also been a school for daughters of the aristocracy before 1917.
51   Citrine 1936, p. 127. The VTsSPS set up additional trade-union offices in the eighteenth-century, former Foundling Home nearby on the Moscow River: Colton 1995, pp. 98–9.
52   Harrison 1921, p. 77. It was here that Tsar Alexander II told the nobility in 1856 that it was necessary to abolish serfdom.
53   Leo Tolstoy set several scenes in *War and Peace* in the club: Pevear and Volokonsky 2007, pp. 303–15; Rubenstein 2016, p. 104. It was also known as the English Club because it was modelled on similar clubs in England.
54   Rosmer 1971, p. 93.
55   Kulikova and Khazanov 1988, p. 69.
56   Tsuji 1989, p. 38.
57   Adibekov et al. (eds) 1990, p. 145. The Politburo in this instance appointed Rudzutak as his temporary replacement: GARF, f. 5451, op. 42, d. 12, l. 23. It should be noted that Rudzutak himself was often ill as well, with relapses of tuberculosis, since, like Tomsky, he had spent years in prison for his revolutionary activities: Nosach 2005, pp. 192–3, 199.

After the decree by the Sovnarkom (Council of People's Commissars) nationalising all large-scale factories and medium-size enterprises in June 1918, the trade unions required all workers in state enterprises to become union members.[58] In addition, in April 1920, Tomsky announced that dues would be deducted from wages when workers were paid.[59] With these funds and governmental subsidies, the trade unions undertook the task of supplying provisions to workers. They provided housing as well as food ration cards, although the scarcity of food meant they would be either worthless or require standing in long queues during the bleak years of the Civil War. Sometimes they also provided clothing and many other basic necessities.[60]

Tomsky became increasingly alarmed at the steep decline in labour productivity, which he thought, already by the spring of 1918, had reached 'catastrophic proportions', threatening the complete collapse of industrial production. Desperate to bolster labour discipline, which in addition to the scarcity of fuel, raw materials, and the increasing disrepair of factories, was a significant factor in the collapse of production. As most skilled and radical workers began to volunteer for the Red Army or were appointed to various posts in the party, state, and economic bureaucracies, inexperienced and undisciplined workers increasingly constituted an ever-larger proportion of the industrial labour force. When these often-absent workers actually showed up for work, in the words of the historian of Moscow workers, William Chase, they commonly 'preferred card games, revelry, and drinking to production, and consciously and unconsciously damaged machines'.[61] Tomsky declared that unions needed to incentivise workers, and if that was not effective, to pressure workers. Having been given the power to set production norms and wages, after deliberations with Narkomtrud and the Supreme Council of the Economy (VSNKh), the VTsSPS on 3 April 1918 called on every trade union to fix norms of productivity for every category of workers and to issue bonuses for workers who exceeded

---

58 Soviet authorities in the preceding months had been nationalising individual factories, in an ad hoc manner, to prevent them from closing: Read 1996, p. 242. The June decree stipulated that the former owners were to continue managing their firms until VSNKh sent them specific orders: Sirianni 1982, pp. 209–10. Some historians, such as Richard Pipes, argue that the nationalisation of industry was part of the initial Bolshevik programme rather than a response to such circumstances as the refusal of private enterprises to submit to workers' control, but that does not appear to be the case: Pipes 1990, p. 671.
59 Tomskii 1925b, p. 69.
60 By the end of 1920 trade-union membership had expanded to some seven million members and trade unions were playing a role in all aspects of the Soviet regime's economic and political life.
61 Chase 1987, p. 36.

their norms.⁶² During the rest of the Civil War the VTsSPS retained the right to administer these bonuses despite the efforts to wrest it away from them by industrial managers, soviets, and the Food-Supply Commissariat (Narkomprod).⁶³ The 1918 Labour Code codified the use of disincentives. Workers who failed to meet their norms were to have their wages reduced proportionally, down to two-thirds of their full wage.⁶⁴

Tomsky's determination to increase productivity and raise labour discipline extended to his grudging support for the introduction of piece-rates, even though 'piece-rates are exactly the kind of wage norm to which we always objected' and which workers greatly resented. Shlyapnikov, the Labour Commissar, likewise supported the revival of piece-rates.⁶⁵ By July they were being widely introduced in determining wage rates.⁶⁶ In practice, as rubles were becoming completely worthless given the runaway inflation, these wages increasingly became payments in kind. At this same time, given the urgency of reversing the worsening conditions, Tomsky called for punishing those workers who did not fulfil the norms set by the trade unions. For 'dealing with drunkards, those who negligently carry out their obligations at work, those who are not punctual at work', Tomsky stated, 'the [comradely] courts must pass sentences, even going so far as removing the guilty ones from the factory and excluding them from the union'.⁶⁷ Such actions no doubt angered many workers and undermined the trade unionists' links with workers on the shop floor, although the historian Simon Pirani suggests many workers supported Tomsky's measures to improve labour discipline, with some calling for even harsher measures.⁶⁸ These 'comradely courts', it should be noted, were also charged with protecting workers from mistreatment by foremen and other factory authorities. Factory management, the trade union, and the factory committee each provided one of the three judges and the local trade-union organisation oversaw the deliberations.⁶⁹ The targets of these hearings were almost

---

62 Brinton 1970, p. 38; Sirianni 1982, p. 156.
63 Pirani 2008, p. 29.
64 Dewar 1979, p. 195.
65 Allen 2015, p. 104. But David Ryazanov did not: Smith 1983, p. 249.
66 Carr 1952, p. 110. Tomsky argued there should be a maximum limit on how much workers could earn in bonuses because he feared that workers, given their inadequate diet, would overexert themselves. 'The worker who does more than one-third or one-fourth above the norm should not receive extra wages for doing so': quoted in Kaplan 1968, pp. 337–8.
67 Quoted in Kaplan 1968, p. 340.
68 Chase 1987, p. 51; Pirani 2008, p. 6. These 'comradely courts', however, had no jurisdiction over criminal matters: Sorenson 1969, p. 147.
69 Chase 1987, p. 45; Husband 1990, p. 62.

always unskilled rather than skilled workers.[70] Whether the 'comradely courts' made much impact on improving labour discipline is open to question. In any case, they were gradually phased out.

Tomsky called on the unions and VSNKh to coordinate their efforts to restore the production destroyed by war and civil war. The new Soviet government, in cooperation with the trade unions, had established VSNKh in December 1917 with the mission of working out a plan 'for regulating the economic life of the country'.[71] In May 1918, Tomsky would be a VTsSPS delegate to VSNKh's first congress, where he declared that 'VSNKh and the trade unions are organisations so completely akin, so closely interwoven with each other, that independent tactics of the part of these two organisations are impossible'.[72] The congress resolved that, rather than simply 'workers' control', the management of nationalised enterprises should use what was called the 'collegial managerial principle' [*kollegial'nost'*], which would include some trade-union representatives, along with the so-called bourgeois specialists and former administrators, on managerial boards. These boards would elect a director accountable to VSNKh.[73] As we will see, this hardly settled the matter.

Tomsky also continued to engage in turf battles. The Fourth Trade-Union Conference in March 1918 focused on the relationship between the trade unions and the government's Commissariat of Labour. The government had mandated close collaboration between the Commissar of Labour and the top trade-union officials. Not unlike his position toward the factory committees, Tomsky argued that the coexistence of the VTsSPS with Narkomtrud introduced an undesirable dualism in economic policy as well as a useless duplication of work. All decisions of trade-union congresses and conferences, Tomsky argued, should be 'binding' on Narkomtrud.[74] The conference adopted Tomsky's resolution, which recognised trade unions as 'the single authoritative representative of

---

70 Sirianni 1982, p. 225.
71 Nove 1969, pp. 50–1; Deutscher 1950, p. 28.
72 Quoted in Cliff 1987, p. 121. Tomsky also declared at the congress that 'all the tasks of the trade unions at the present time are closely interwoven with the tasks of restoring production destroyed by the war': quoted in Carr 1952, p. 114. VTsSPS members constituted 30 of the 69 members of the VSNKh's first policy-making plenum, although power quickly became concentrated in the VSNKh's Presidium, from which VTsSPS members were excluded. But a large percentage of the administrators in the VSNKh's various branches were former workers elected at trade-union conferences: Sirianni 1982, p. 220.
73 Malle 1985, pp. 113, 116; Priestland 2007, p. 88. This term, 'bourgeois specialist', was attached to any educated professional trained before the revolution who was not a member of the party.
74 Dewar 1979, pp. 27–9.

the organised, industrial proletariat'.[75] Likewise, the VTsSPS sought to preclude Narkomtrud from going behind its back by responding to the requests of individual unions. In his closing argument, Tomsky quite simply declared, 'I want to subordinate Narkomtrud to the trade unions'. His resolution passed overwhelmingly.[76] But it should be noted that Narkomtrud, at its conference that same month, explicitly rejected the notion that it was mandatory for it to accept all VTsSPS decisions.[77]

Tomsky also weighed in on central issues outside the purview of the trade unions. He addressed, for example, the controversial Brest-Litovsk treaty, which had been signed with Imperial Germany on 3 March. When the Mensheviks and some Bolshevik delegates at the Fourth Trade-Union Conference in May denounced the signing of the treaty, Tomsky defended Lenin's view that the new regime had no choice but to get out of the war, although he agreed with fellow Bolsheviks, including Lenin, that it was 'a shameful peace'. Tomsky rationalised the signing of the humiliating treaty with the belief that this was just a 'truce', since revolution in the West was about to happen. Tomsky argued that 'the exact day and hour we don't predict, not wanting to be charlatans', but he was sure it was imminent.[78] For some time Tomsky, like all members of the party leadership genuinely expected the Bolshevik seizure of power to spark a world socialist revolution. But as we will see in chapter four, he would face the reality that revolution in the West had become increasingly unlikely more quickly than others.

Especially troubling to Tomsky was that the party increasingly and blatantly interfered in trade-union affairs. By the end of 1918, Tomsky and his cohorts on the VTsSPS Presidium urgently sought a way to stop this interference, which was provoking considerable protests by non-party workers. Tomsky convened a meeting of the party caucus of the VTsSPS at the end of November to share his concerns. Tomsky, who was a moderating force when it came to the treatment of non-party trade unionists, in his report to the congress insisted on the immediate ending of such actions as the dispersal of the Menshevik-dominated

---

75   VTsSPS 1923, p. 27.
76   VTsSPS 1923, p. 41. Tomsky also proposed that soviets and dumas did not have any independent jurisdiction over the trade unions and Narkomtrud. Tomsky's Paragraph Nine of the 'Resolution on the Relationship between the Trade Unions and the Commissariat of Labour' declared the soviets, dumas and other governing bodies can decide economic problems 'only when, for the given problem, there exists a definite decision of the directing trade-union organisation and the Commissariat of Labour'. The conference delegates adopted this resolution: Kaplan 1968, pp. 217–18.
77   Sirianni 1982, p. 126.
78   Gorelov 2000, p. 67; Garvy 1958, p. 44.

Petrograd Printers Union in the fall of 1918 and the creation of the so-called Red Printers' Union.[79] Similar efforts had occurred in other cities.[80] Tomsky argued that 'red workers' who sought to dissolve the existing trade unions were engaging in unauthorised actions and should be excluded from working in trade unions, and in some cases, even be arrested.[81] The overwhelming majority of the delegates at the November VTsSPS party caucus supported this and other proposals by Tomsky criticising party interference in trade-union affairs.

It was in this context of party interference that Tomsky worked with the Politburo in preparation for the Second Congress of Trade Unions, which convened on 16 January 1919. Politburo members at the preceding 17 December 1918 meeting had demanded that the VTsSPS present their resolutions for the upcoming congress to the Central Committee. Tomsky told the Politburo he strongly opposed this party 'order' [*diktat*], but under pressure submitted. Only on 16 January 1919, the day of the opening of the congress, did the Central Committee give its final approval, with amendments, to the proposed resolutions. The Politburo instructed Bukharin to lead the congress's communist caucus and for Lenin to speak at the plenary session. Thus, already in the run-up to the congress, the Central Committee was putting serious pressure on the VTsSPS against any displays of independence during the congress.[82]

At the congress, which opened in the Hall of Columns of the House of Unions, Tomsky was re-elected chair of the VTsSPS Presidium. In his opening report Tomsky looked back at the year since the first congress. He defended his decision, 'for better or worse', of making supporting the Soviet government the trade unions' primary task.[83] With the Civil War now in full swing and the survival of the regime increasingly in question, Tomsky argued the trade unions needed to do whatever they could to protect the revolution and defeat the White Armies, which enjoyed the support of several Western nations. That included, he stated, mobilising 'hundreds of our best agitators to help raise discipline in the Red Army'.[84] In addition to the large number of trade-union officials who left their positions to assume leadership posts in the Red Army,

---

79 This had been carried out by Nikolai Gordon, the head of the Petrograd Printers' Union and one of Zinoviev's protégés: Koenker 2005, pp. 39, 53–4.
80 The move was unpopular with the overwhelming majority of printers: Garvy 1958, p. 50.
81 Nosach 2005, p. 111; Koenker 2005, pp. 54–5. As late as 1920 the Bolsheviks still faced organised political opposition by the Mensheviks in the Chemical Workers' Union as well as the Printers' Union and by the Left SRs in the Bakers' Union: Pirani 2008, p. 32.
82 Nosach 2005, p. 13.
83 VTsSPS 1919, p. 13.
84 VTsSPS 1919, p. 12.

the trade unions became the main body responsible for recruiting troops. In Moscow, for example nearly three-quarters of all workers between the ages of 20 and 24 joined the Red Army, as did over half of workers between 25 and 30.[85] Ultimately perhaps as many as half of all their 3.5 million trade-union members were mobilised as rank-and-file soldiers in the Red Army.[86] In addition, large numbers of trade-union functionaries had been reassigned to new positions in the rapidly expanding Soviet bureaucracy. Tomsky acknowledged that as a result of this massive outflow, the unions were seriously depleted and woefully lacking in competent functionaries, from bookkeepers to political instructors. Regarding the trade unions' bookkeepers, he found their work so poor it looked like sabotage, but concluded, 'I do not think it is sabotage, only Russian illiteracy'.[87] Tomsky lamented, 'it is our misfortune and the misfortune of all the working class that it suffers, at present, from a lack of trained conscious workers'. The union instructors, for their part, were themselves often politically illiterate and needed instruction.[88] But despite the siphoning off of their talent and these shortcomings, Tomsky argued the trade unions were working tirelessly and their work was improving. Tomsky summarised the trade unions' range of activities during these critical months of the Civil War as we 'fought against hunger, organised food detachments, removed valuable workers from the factories to send them to the front, fought epidemics, organised commissariats, administered production, and continued organisational work within the working class'.[89] It was not for naught. The Red Army's superiority in numbers, manned by peasant conscripts as well as the trade-union recruits and conscripts, would play a key role in its ultimate victory.[90] And to provide food for its members, when that became in desperately short supply, the Military Rations Bureau (Voenprodbiuro) of the VTsSPS oversaw the food detachments that factory committees sent into the countryside to exchange manufactured and industrial products for grain, and when that proved insufficient, to simply requisition (that is, steal) grain from 'kulaks'.[91] In fact, these detachments often could not distinguish 'kulaks' from other peasants and simply took any avail-

---

85 Chase 1987, p. 32. Thirty percent between the ages of 30 and 35 also served.
86 Tomskii 1928a, pp. 130–1; Deutscher 1950, p. 25. The unions sometimes granted deferments [*otsrochki*] to their most valued functionaries.
87 Quoted in Kaplan 1968, p. 238.
88 VTsSPS 1919, pp. 14, 20.
89 Tomskii 1928, p. 448. Typhoid, influenza, smallpox, and cholera epidemics killed large numbers of workers during the Civil War years.
90 Mawdsley 1987, p. 276.
91 Chase 1987, pp. 22–4.

able grain. Rather than distribute rations to individual workers, workers generally received their rations in the form of meals in public and factory cafeterias.[92]

Tomsky's report on the challenges facing the trade unions did not placate the Mensheviks at this January 1918 Second Trade-Union Congress.[93] They characterised workers as atomised and demoralised and denounced the trade unions' work as unresponsive, undemocratic, and brutal. Chirkin reported that in the many industrial districts he visited, either no one elected the trade-union leaders, or if there were genuine elections, they were annulled if 'objectionable' people were elected. Others more subservient to the central trade-union administration would be appointed to replace them.[94] The Mensheviks claimed that workers voicing their discontent with such conditions were denounced as 'saboteurs' and 'put up against the wall'. Tomsky agreed relations between the trade-union leadership and the rank and file needed to be more democratic, conceding that because of the crisis conditions, 'we took some administrative measures'.[95] Mark Kefali, the Printers' Union leader, who described the trade-union leaders as generally 'not bad people and not badly disposed towards the trade-union movement', expressed the Menshevik argument that the trade union's guilt went back to their decision to essentially subordinate the trade-union movement to the Soviet state and Bolshevik Party.[96] Tomsky's counter-attack received loud applause from the assembled delegates. 'When comrade Kefali accuses us of supporting Soviet power he doesn't understand that for us this is high praise – we are proud of this'.[97]

For all his relative moderation, compared to other Bolshevik leaders, Tomsky did not shy away from supporting strong measures if he thought they were necessary to safeguard Soviet power. The Tomsky-led VTsSPS increasingly restricted the ability of non-Bolsheviks to agitate in the unions and organise strikes. Worried about the course of the Civil War, Tomsky increasingly defended the use of such tactics against Mensheviks. At the congress, he stated:

> We do not insist that these [non-Bolshevik] unionists obey us blindly, but merely that they follow the general plan. When we ask them to work in the

---

92   Chase 1987, p. 25.
93   As at the First Trade-Union Congress, at the Second Congress there was also a large number of non-Bolshevik delegates. At the first congress 33 percent were non-Bolsheviks, while 29 percent were non-Bolsheviks at the second congress. But the VTsSPS Presidium consisted of eight Bolsheviks: Garvy 1958, p. 68.
94   VTsSPS 1919, p. 19.
95   VTsSPS 1919, p. 24; Koenker 2005, p. 62.
96   VTsSPS 1919, p. 16.
97   VTsSPS 1919, p. 23.

interests of the dictatorship of the proletariat and to promote proletarian discipline, it is not that we have any personal spite against the Mensheviks as such. But we must root out all those who, having recognised at the First Congress the necessity of collaborating with the Soviet government, still persist in organising strikes against the government. The unions that foment strikes must suffer for it.[98]

When the Soviets' All-Russian Central Executive Committee (VTsIK), the Moscow Soviet, and the Red Army, at a joint session in June 1919, declared that only 'iron discipline' could save the revolution, Tomsky wholeheartedly agreed.[99] He supported the use of state violence against perceived opponents of the regime. Tomsky declared at the Second Trade-Union Congress, 'It would be ludicrous if we refrained from using violence for the purpose of strengthening the new society we are building'.[100] With such statements and positions Tomsky obviously was far from a consistently moderating force among the Bolsheviks. But to his credit, he would later recall with shame some of his most extreme positions during this period.

The 'statification' of the trade unions was contested at the Second Trade-Union Congress just as it had been a year before at the first congress. For Lenin, who gave a long speech at the congress, this meant striving 'to educate the working and exploited people, to enlist them in the work of governing the state and administering industry without officials, without the bourgeoisie, and without capitalists.' Lenin called for the trade unions to become 'the chief builders of the new society'.[101] Although Tomsky, along with the majority of the delegates supported Lenin's formulation of statification, he reiterated that, just as at the First Trade-Union Congress, the resolution was not calling for the trade unions to take on 'the functions of organs of state power' anytime soon. While that would be 'the inevitable result' of close cooperation between the state and the unions, he emphasised that 'if you look at our proposed resolution, you will see that not a word is said about the immediate statification of the trade unions'.[102] In fact the adopted resolution explicitly stated that, 'in view of the actual state of development of the trade-union movement, it would be a great mistake

---

98 VTsSPS 1919, p. 96.
99 Dewar 1979, p. 44.
100 VTsSPS 1919, p. 84. Tomsky also took other illiberal positions. He did not support, for example, freedom of the press. The congress passed his proposal not to allow any 'bourgeois' newspapers except *Russkie vedomosti* (Russian News) to attend congress sessions.
101 Lenin 1960–70, vol. 28, pp. 419–26.
102 VTsSPS 1919, p. 82.

to immediately transform the unprepared unions into state organs or to allow the unions to have arbitrary control over state institutions'.[103] Ryazanov voiced the views of the minority of the delegates opposed to the resolution, who supported syndicalist ideas and argued that de-statification should be the goal.[104]

The trade unions clearly controlled at least one branch of the government, not vice versa, as the Commissar of Labour, Vasily Shmidt, recognised. Shmidt had replaced Shlyapnikov after the Central Committee had ousted him from his position as Labour Commissar in early September 1918.[105] Shmidt pointed out that the entire collegium of the Narkomtrud should consist, as far as possible, of VTsSPS members and he pledged to never interfere with the rights of trade unions.[106] In fact, the VTsSPS had essentially appointed Shmidt as the new Narkomtrud Commissar. On the commissariat's own collegium, when Shmidt and Tomsky disagreed, Tomsky's views usually carried the day.[107] As Shmidt himself stated, the role of Narkomtrud

> must be to give obligatory effect to the recommendations and plans worked out by the trade unions. Moreover, not only must the Commissariat of Labour not interfere with the rights of the unions, but even the organs of the Commissariat ... should as far as possible be formed by the unions themselves.[108]

The historian E.H. Carr noted there was still ambiguity as to whether the unions would be absorbed by the state or the state by the trade unions.[109] In any case, through their domination of Narkomtrud, Tomsky and the VTsSPS exerted considerable weight in the formulation of governmental labour policy.

The right to strike once again came up for debate at the Second Trade-Union Congress. Tomsky, over the objections of Menshevik delegates, held firm in his

---

103   Quoted in International Labour Office 1927, p. 32.
104   VTsSPS 1919, p. 69.
105   Shlyapnikov, who had appointed relatives to the Narkomtrud board, was accused of engaging in nepotism and removed: Allen 2015, pp. 119–20.
106   VTsSPS 1919, p. 98. Tomsky remained on the board, as did other prominent VTsSPS members such as Melnichansky: Gimpel'son 1998, p. 86. Shlyapnikov had filled significant positions in Narkomtrud with trade unionists: Allen 2015, p. 109.
107   This was also true when Shlyapnikov had been the labour commissar. For example, in the fiery debate in June 1918 over how much leave workers would be entitled to receive: Cook 2013, p. 11. Tomsky was one of the 12 members of the commissariat's collegium. The trade unions also had 35 representatives on VTsIK: Sorenson 1969, p. 79.
108   Quoted in Sorenson 1969, p. 79.
109   Carr 1952, p. 201.

belief that strikes should be banned. He argued that this was especially true following the nationalisation of all major industry, with the state now virtually the sole employer.[110] Despite whatever misgivings Tomsky might have felt, he emphatically argued that 'at a time when the trade unions regulate wages and working conditions, when the appointment of the commissar for labour also depends on our congress, no strikes can take place in Soviet Russia. Let us put the dot on this i'. He concluded this statement with this: when 'seven-eighths of the workers are fighting for socialism, it is intolerable that one-eighth should go against them' by striking.[111]

The debate over the state functions of the trade unions reached what appeared to be its climax in March 1919 at the Eighth Party Congress. Facing a surge of discontent with all the centralising trends, the delegates, in replacing the old Social-Democratic programme of 1903, passed a resolution – Point Five of the 'economic section' of the party platform – whose framework centred on workers' control.[112] Even though other clauses of the platform seemed to cancel it out, Point Five explicitly stated that trade unions, not the government, should run industry. Since its thrust would be the source of so much heated controversy over the next two years, it is worth quoting at some length. After a short preamble criticising 'craft unions', the resolution declared:

> Trade unions, which are already according to the laws of the Soviet republic and established practice participants in all local and central organs for the administration of industry, must proceed to the actual concentration in their hands of the management of the whole economy as a single economic unit. The trade unions, thus securing an unbreakable union between the central state administration, the economy, and the broad masses of workers, must persuade the latter to participate immediately in the direct management of the economy. The participation of trade unions in the management of the economy, and the attraction by them of the broad masses into this work, are moreover the principal method in the

---

110 VTsSPS 1919, p. 96. With the first clashes with the White Armies and the beginning of foreign intervention, the government accelerated the nationalisation of industries because they feared private enterprises would not fulfil the Red Army's needs: Deutscher 1950, p. 25.

111 VTsSPS 1919, p. 96. Tomsky at the same time tried to limit the repercussions for workers who went on strike. When the Orgburo on 6 April 1919 considered a proposal of repressive measures for striking workers, Tomsky argued that the party should instead respond in 'a spirit of reconciliation' with 'some concessions'. But his position did not receive support: Borisova 2006, p. 114.

112 Brinton 1970, p. 53.

FIGURE 3 Tomsky, behind Stalin and Lenin, with Delegates of the Eighth Party Congress
WIKIMEDIA COMMONS

struggle against the bureaucratisation of the economic apparatus of the Soviet government and provide the opportunity to establish truly popular control over production.[113]

The Workers' Opposition as well as other Bolshevik groups would later base their case on this Point Five. Although Lenin and the Bolshevik leadership were not prone to slipping up because of feelings of gratitude, the historian Isaac Deutscher stated that, 'in all probability, Point Five was a syndicalist slip committed by the Bolshevik leadership in a mood of genuine gratitude to the trade unions for the work performed by them in the Civil War'.[114] Another historian, Manya Gordon, suggests Lenin had not 'taken the trouble to visu-

---

113 Egorov and Bogoliubov (eds) 1983–84, vol. 2, pp. 84–5.
114 Deutscher 1950, p. 29. As noted in a footnote in Chapter 1, syndicalism is a radical philosophy that advocates for workers' control of the economy and the destruction of the centralised state.

alise what the management of industry by inexperienced toiling masses really implied'.[115]

Tomsky clearly enjoyed broad support in party circles. At the end of the Eighth Party Congress, the delegates elected him to the now 19-member Central Committee. Tomsky received the eighth largest number of votes, which put him ahead of Trotsky, among others.[116] At Central Committee sessions Tomsky regularly presented reports on domestic and international trade-union issues. Earlier in 1918 he was also elected to be a member of VTsIK. From 1920 he was a member of its Presidium.[117] During these years he was also appointed to other positions and given a seat on various commissions. But his primary focus remained the trade unions.

It was Trotsky, the intellectually flamboyant and spellbinding public speaker, who with Lenin's backing put the extraordinarily divisive, so-called trade-union debate in motion.[118] Given the truly horrendous economic conditions facing the country – so severe that less than half the populations of Petrograd and Moscow remained – with the impending demobilisation of the Red Army, Trotsky, as commissar of war, submitted on 16 December 1919 a set of 24 theses (propositions) to the Central Committee on the economic transition from war to peace. Using the same kind of authoritarian methods he had employed in the Red Army, Trotsky called for the militarisation of the labour force to restore economic production. While demobilised skilled workers were to be relocated to factory work, he called for unskilled soldiers, no longer needed for military purposes, to be sent to work in various forms of manual labour.[119] Since the government, given the collapse of the economy, could not provide sufficient incentives to these workers by providing adequate real wages, or goods to buy with those wages, Trotsky bluntly stated that all able-bodied people should be subject to working under harsh military discipline in 'labour armies', which were to be modelled on military units and 'run in a military fashion'. Trotsky argued, 'labour conscription must be supported by measures of a compulsory character ... by the armed force of the proletarian state'.[120] The commissariats of

---

115   Gordon 1941, p. 79.
116   Lenin received 262 votes, Stalin 258, Bukharin 258, Zinoviev, 255, Kamenev, 252, Dzerzhinsky 241, Krestinsky 235, and Tomsky 226: RKP(b) 1933b, p. 361. Tomsky would remain a member of the Central Committee until 1934.
117   Eighteen trade unionists were on the VTsIK, while Tomsky was one of five trade unionists on its presidium: Tomskii 1928a, p. 100.
118   The historian Alexander Rabinowitch characterised Trotsky as 'one of the greatest orators of modern times': Rabinowitch 1978, p. xx.
119   Kaplan 1968, pp. 354–5.
120   Quoted in Day 1973, p. 23.

FIGURE 4 Alexander Shlyapnikov
WIKIMEDIA COMMONS

war and internal affairs, along with the Cheka, would implement these policies, with the trade unions essentially ignored.[121] In some factories, workers were to be tied to their workplaces like tsarist industrial serfs.[122] Those who 'deserted' these labour armies, which meant being absent for more than three days, could

---

121 Leggett 1981, p. 242.
122 Stites 1989, p. 51.

be sent to concentration camps.[123] Trotsky even went so far as to suggest replacing the commissariat of labour with the commissariat of war.[124] Trotsky's draconian proposals for labour armies seemingly enjoyed Lenin's wholehearted support.[125] Since his theses would have, for all practical purposes, eviscerated the trade unions, their publication in *Pravda* sparked an outpouring of indignation from Tomsky and other union members.[126] They argued that instead of expanding and intensifying such harsh measures, more efforts should be devoted to providing higher rations, which they argued would be far more effective than compulsion for keeping workers on the job. Tomsky had shared his deep concerns in a report to the Politburo on 27 December 1919.[127]

Matters came to a head when Lenin and Trotsky jointly took the trade-union leadership head-on when they appeared before the VTsSPS to advocate for their policies on 12 January 1920. Although Tomsky shared their assessment of the dire state of the economy and the need to raise labour productivity, he stood up to them and the other party leaders who accompanied them.[128] Tomsky led the successful opposition to Trotsky's call for an increase in 'labour armies', which had already undertaken such tasks as peat mining, timber cutting, and railroad repair.[129] At this congress, Lenin and Trotsky suffered an almost unanimous defeat. Fifty-eight of the 60 Bolshevik trade-union leaders followed Tomsky's lead in rejecting Trotsky's proposal. In the words of Isaac Deutscher, 'never before had Trotsky or Lenin met with so striking a rebuff'.[130]

Tomsky also opposed Lenin's call to replace the collegial system of enterprise administration with one-man management [*edinonachalie*].[131] In the collegial

---

123 Likewise, workers expelled from a trade union could be assigned to a 'labour army': Kaplan 1968, p. 355; Day 1973, pp. 23–4.
124 Deutscher 1954, p. 492.
125 Bunyan 1967, p. 92.
126 They were perhaps published inadvertently. Trotsky submitted his theses to the Central Committee apparently with the sole purpose of provoking discussion within it: Deutscher 1954, p. 487. The theses were published in the party newspaper, which Bukharin edited: *Pravda*, 17 December 1919.
127 Khordina (ed.) 2000, p. 49.
128 Two of these party leaders, Rykov and Yury Larin, did take Tomsky's side: Borisova 2006, p. 69. A similar confrontation took place during January at the Sovnarkhoz congress. Tomsky along with Bukharin and Alexei Kiselev had worked together to prepare a report for that congress: Khordina (ed.) 2000, p. 51.
129 Various trade unionists joined the attack on Trotsky's plans for the militarisation of labour, including Shlyapnikov: Allen 2015, p. 140.
130 Deutscher 1954, p. 493.
131 William Chase provocatively suggests that for Lenin one-man management and collegial administration were not contradictory, but complimentary since workers would still be able to oversee and advise management: Chase 1987, pp. 39–40.

system that had emerged by this time, trade-union representatives served on managerial boards alongside officials from VSNKh. In fact, 50 percent of the members of these boards at all levels of management were trade-union representatives.[132] Tomsky enjoyed the strong support of his fellow trade-union leaders on this issue, although apparently no vote was taken on one-man management at the January meeting.[133] Rykov, the head of VSNKh, also spoke in defence of collegial management.[134] Some of the various individual trade-union central committees passed resolutions of support, stating that one-man management was not a communist form of management.[135]

Trade unionists recognised that one-man management meant hiring people according to their qualifications and experience, which in practice would mean hiring the so-called bourgeois specialists and perhaps even the old owners. Tomsky accepted that significant measures needed to be taken to raise labour productivity given the state of the Soviet economy, and the disintegration of the working class as a result of unskilled workers leaving industry in droves to return to the villages in search of food, while more skilled workers began to staff the state, party, and trade-union bureaucracies. But he nevertheless opposed the removal of trade unionists from factory management.[136] Tomsky felt they needed to be there in order to supervise the work of those colloquially and derogatorily referred to as *spetsy* [an abbreviation of the Russian plural *spetsialisty*]. But Lenin at the communist caucus of the VTsSPS meeting remained staunchly in favour of one-man management. He poked fun at Tomsky and other defenders of collegial management 'as chatterboxes who loved to sit around and waste time at meetings'.[137] Tomsky, not surprisingly, took offence at such jabs by Lenin.[138]

Tomsky, while taking what he thought was a more realistic approach than such militants as Shlyapnikov, who called for placing management entirely

---

132 Nosach 2005, p. 114.
133 One-man management did not come up for a vote perhaps because Lenin did not want a repeat of the embarrassing defeat he had suffered on the issue at the Third VSNKh Congress in January 1920, which voted against his call for one-man management and in favour of collegiality. Both Tomsky and Trotsky participated in the debate about labour conscription at the VSNKh congress: Dewar 1979, p. 54.
134 RKP(b) 1934a, p. 558. Sapronov, Ossinsky, and Maksimovsky were prominent members of the so-called Democratic Centralists.
135 Such as the Central Committee of Textile Workers' Union in December 1919: Husband 1990, p. 138.
136 Allen 2015, p. 142; Tsuji 1989, pp. 37, 57, 60. By mid-1920 industrial production was one-seventh of what it had been in 1914: Rosenberg 1989, p. 357.
137 Tomskii 1928a, pp. 501–2n83.
138 Tomskii 1928a, p. 100.

in the hands of workers, tried to preserve for the trade unions some presence in management as well as some autonomy from the party and government in order to defend the economic interests of workers.[139] Trotsky mocked Tomsky's desire for some trade-union autonomy and opposition to one-man management. He characterised it as that of an outmoded, old-fashioned type of trade unionist, which from pre-revolutionary practice encouraged workers' 'consumptionist' viewpoint and showed no understanding of the 'productionist viewpoint of the socialist state'.[140] Trotsky, who in debates had a seemingly uncontrollable impulse to try to humiliate his political opponents, even went so far as to disparage Tomsky as the 'Gompers' of the Russian trade-union movement.[141] Samuel Gompers, the president of the American Federation of Labor (AFL), was the quintessential 'bread and butter' trade unionist, who steadfastly opposed any thought of revolution while continuously attacking Bolshevism.[142] This was the beginning of the deep antipathy Tomsky developed toward Trotsky.

Tomsky, to counter Trotsky's propositions, published on 10 March 1920 his own 25-point theses, entitled 'On the Tasks of the Trade Unions', in the newspaper of VSNKh *Ekonomicheskaia zhizn'* (Economic Life). Tomsky based his argument on practical issues, rather than principle, by claiming that collective management was the only way 'to guarantee the participation of the broad, non-party mass of workers' and revive the economy.[143] He argued that 'the trade unions are the most competent and interested organisation in the matter of restoring the country's production'.[144] Tomsky insisted that except for in very limited cases, and in those cases only as a result of a mutual agreement between VSNKh and VTsSPS, collegiality should be applied from the top to the bottom of the economy, 'from the Presidium of VSNKh down to the management of factories'.[145] Make no mistake for those historians who consider Tomsky to be

---

139 Tomsky thought Shlyapnikov was 'naïve': Allen 2015, p. 142.
140 Deutscher 1959, p. 82.
141 Trotsky 1921, p. 250; Swain 2006, p. 12.
142 Gompers was the son of a Dutch-Jewish family that immigrated to the United States from England when he was 13. He was trained by his father as a cigar maker and became president of the Cigar Makers' Union in 1875. Gompers helped found the AFL in 1886. According to his biographer, Gompers condemned 'even the mildest liberals as socialists, pacifists, and revolutionaries': Mandel 1963, p. 437.
143 RKP(b) 1934a, p. 534. Reprinted from *Ekonomicheskaia zhizn'*, 10 March 1920. This was Tomsky's Fifth Point.
144 Quoted in Daniels 1960, p. 124.
145 RKP(b) 1934a, p. 535. This was the Seventh Point. Those limited cases of one-man management, the Democratic Centralist Sapronov proposed, should be confined to small factories: Rousset 1982, p. 63.

Lenin's lackey, by forcefully reiterating his strong support for collective management over one-man management, Tomsky was criticising Lenin's as well as Trotsky's views. Tomsky also continued to insist on the need for workers to oversee the 'bourgeois specialists' and on the right of trade unions to address fundamental questions of economic policy together with VSNKh.[146] While emphasising they were inextricably linked, Tomsky argued in some of his other points that trade unions needed to focus on improving both the economic situation of workers and worker productivity.[147] Tomsky, who made no reference to the use of compulsion, implicitly emphasised that his differences with Lenin and Trotsky were not about goals but about how to best to achieve them.

The VTsSPS's party caucus met on 15 March to discuss Tomsky's theses. In the intervening few days between their publication and the meeting of the caucus, Tomsky's theses had been discussed in a commission created by the caucus, which expressed its support for all of Tomsky's principal positions.[148] Lenin attended and a number of times voiced his strong objections to Tomsky's positions. So did Bukharin, who enthusiastically supported Trotsky, including his policy of the militarisation of labour, and whom the Central Committee had appointed to the VTsSPS Presidium along with Karl Radek, over Tomsky's objections.[149] Lenin argued that he was not opposed in principle to placing workers in managerial positions, but given the lack of experienced, competent workers, 'collegial management is inadmissible'.[150] Lenin believed the trade unionists' preference for collective management reflected their inadequate understanding of how desperate conditions had become. 'The country is so ruined, poverty has reached such an enormous scale with famine, cold, and general want, that we cannot continue to live like this any longer ... the very existence of Soviet Russia is at stake'.[151] He denounced workers who failed to appreciate that restoring production depended on turning management over to economic specialists, just like military leadership had been turned over to military specialists during the Civil War.[152] But the trade unionists were of course fully cognisant of how bad conditions were economically.

---

146 RKP(b) 1934a, p. 535. This was the Eighth Point.
147 RKP(b) 1934a, p. 536. These were the Fourteenth and Fifteenth Points.
148 Lenin 1958–65, vol. 40, p. 395–6n91.
149 GARF, f. 5451, op. 2, d. 3, ll. 163–4. Bukharin presented the theses in support of one-man management: RKP(b) 1934b, pp. 5, 71. Lenin also stated his objections that same day to the Third Congress of Transport Workers: Lenin 1958–65, vol. 40, pp. 213–24.
150 Lenin 1958–65, vol. 40, p. 222. There is little question that workers with the competency to run a factory were in short supply.
151 Lenin 1958–65, vol. 40, p. 216.
152 The expedient use of tsarist officers had also provoked strong, prolonged opposition within party ranks: Daniels 1960, p. 105.

Lenin once again was rebuffed and went down to defeat, if only temporarily.[153] The delegates not only rejected Lenin's arguments; they emphatically defended collegial management by adopting Tomsky's theses by a substantial majority. As these votes and actions demonstrated, Tomsky and his fellow union leaders were not afraid to stand up to Lenin, and at least on their own turf were able to successfully reject his proposals. But Lenin did not accept this defeat lying down. He immediately wrote a decree, which the Politburo adopted two days later on 17 March that attacked the VTsSPS caucus, singling out by name Tomsky and Yury Lutovinov for violating party discipline. In response, the members of the VTsSPS's caucus's bureau, at a hastily called secret meeting, drafted a declaration that emphatically protested that Lenin's call for party discipline was being used as a way to try his impose his resolution on the VTsSPS caucus. The bureau appealed to the Central Committee for permission to present the resolutions of the VTsSPS caucus. But the Central Committee's Politburo stood behind Lenin.[154]

Tomsky's position, it should be reiterated, was relatively moderate in comparison with those put forward by Shlyapnikov, whose own theses, entitled 'On the Question of Relations between the Communist Party, Soviets, and Production Unions', presented the position of the embryonic Workers' Opposition. Shlyapnikov envisioned a three-way 'separation of power and functions', with the party maintaining control over political matters, the soviets controlling the state apparatus, while the trade unions were to manage the economy.[155] The Workers' Opposition's position was that not a single person should be appointed to an administrative economic post without the agreement of the trade unions.[156] But one of the most prominent Workers' Oppositionists, Lutovinov, with the goal of having the trade unions present a united front at the congress, had moved away from Shlyapnikov and fallen in line behind Tomsky and other VTsSPS leaders' position on collective management. Lutovinov praised Tomsky's position, in the words of Shlyapnikov's biographer Barbara Allen, 'as one around which most trade unionists could rally'.[157] Tomsky went to great lengths to ensure everyone understood that he did not support Shlyapnikov's position

---

153   Lenin 1958–65, vol. 40, p. 404n112.
154   Lenin 1958–65, vol. 40, pp. 395–6n94.
155   Aves 1966, p. 27.
156   Deutscher 1950, p. 47. Osinsky, on behalf of the Democratic Centralists, supported Shlyapnikov's theses: Daniels 1960, p. 125. The Democratic Centralists, in contrast to the Workers' Opposition, primarily consisted of Bolshevik intellectuals. Their primary demand was a restoration of soviet and party democracy as well as greater political freedom within the party.
157   Allen 2015, pp. 145–6.

FIGURE 5 Tomsky, on the far right, with Trotsky
ALAMY

at a joint meeting of the communist caucuses of the VTsSPS and the Moscow trade-union council, held right before the convening of the Ninth Party Congress in March 1920. Tomsky told the caucus that if it supported Shlyapnikov, it would cause party leaders to suspect that trade unionists want to create a party within the party. Tomsky's position completely carried the day. All but one delegate favoured his positions over those of Shlyapnikov.[158] The fact that neither Shlyapnikov nor any of the other Workers' Oppositionists were on the Central Committee, even as a non-voting candidate member, no doubt helped to undercut their political clout.[159]

---

158   Allen 2015, p. 146. Similarly, at the Third Congress of the Water Transport Workers' Union on 15 March, even though Lenin again argued that 'very existence of Soviet Russia is at stake', the delegates refused to support his call for the introduction of military discipline at the workplace: Rousset 1982, p. 61. Lenin and Bukharin would be somewhat more successful the following day, 16 March, when Moscow's party organisation refused to choose between Bukharin's theses and Tomsky's: RKP(b) 1934b, p. 571.
159   Shlyapnikov had been a candidate member of the Central Committee previously in 1918–19 and would become a full member in 1921–22. It also obviously did not help that

Tomsky during the long and heated debates at the Ninth Party Congress would fare far worse than he had at the trade-union meetings, although not without a fight. Tomsky, alongside Bukharin, Radek, Lutovinov, and Stalin, was on a Central Committee commission that prior to the congress worked on the resolution on trade unions.[160] At the congress itself, the issue of whether factories should be collectively managed or managed by a single boss predictably provoked the stormiest debates. Trotsky made the case for one-man management vehemently and vociferously.[161] Tomsky, who had also tried to make the VTsSPS's case at the Politburo meeting the previous week, put forth the trade unions' support for maintaining the existing principle of collegiate management. He argued it was necessary so that trade unionists could continue to supervise the work of the technical specialists.[162] Tomsky also argued that collegial management should be maintained in principle while conceding that one-man management could be adopted on a case-by-case basis.[163] In addition, he argued that one-man management was not some sort of sure-fire panacea. He claimed it had been introduced in various places with minimal impact, if any, on increasing production.[164] To bolster his case that many managers were not necessarily experienced experts, he brought up an example of a coalmining manager who was in fact a former St. Petersburg lawyer.[165] There was indeed a widespread problem of 'false specialists' who embellished or fabricated their credentials so they could receive the specialists' high salaries.

Tomsky quickly realised that attacks on the specialists seemed to strike a more responsive chord at the party congress than attacks on one-man management.[166] While Lenin and other party leaders were doing everything possible to lure specialists back to work, including offering them extremely high salaries, special rations, and augmented control of factory affairs, Tomsky argued that specialists should be appointed to managerial positions cautiously and

---

Shlyapnikov was not at the congress but on a party mission to Western Europe. Even though Lutovinov had defected away from Shlyapnikov to join with Tomsky, it was he, in Shlyapnikov's absence, who presented the Workers' Opposition's proposals to the hostile congress: Allen 2015, pp. 143, 146.

160 RKP(b) 1934a, p. 276. Stalin, incidentally, did not say a word at the congress.
161 Trotsky, in addition, argued that the trade unions should themselves carry out the militarisation of labour: Swain 2006, p. 126.
162 GARF, f. 5451, op. 42, d. 11, l. 3, and d. 6, l. 28; RKP(b) 1934a, pp. 513, 535, 537–9; Khordina (ed.) 2000, p. 59.
163 RKP(b) 1934a, pp. 174–5.
164 RKP(b) 1934a, p. 159.
165 RKP(b) 1934a, p. 171.
166 Azrael 1966, p. 44.

FIGURE 6   The Presidium of the Ninth Party Congress. Sitting from left: Yenukidze, Kalinin, Bukharin, Tomsky, Lashevich, Kamenev, Preobrazhensky, Serebryakov, Lenin, and Rykov.
WIKIMEDIA COMMONS

only with the approval of the trade unions.[167] Tomsky added, 'We consider it necessary for specialists to become accustomed to working with workers in a collegium in a comradely atmosphere. We consider it imperative that between them and workers there is a living bond, which will be attained when the specialists and the collegium treat each other as equals'.[168] Tomsky's suspicion and distrust of the specialists reflected the hostility most workers felt toward them.

As he had at the VTsSPS caucus, Lenin came out firing in his speech against Tomsky's 25-point theses. Lenin declared that the time for theoretical discussions and big ideas was over. He insisted that the shattered economy made it urgently necessary to focus on practical solutions instead. Lenin noted that, after spending 15 years before the revolution discussing such theoretical points,

---

167   Industry suffered from a shortage of 'specialists', especially engineers, since a large number of them had emigrated following the Bolshevik seizure of power: Husband 1985, p. 36.
168   RKP(b) 1934a, p. 173.

now that they were in power they needed to embrace practical, business-like approaches.[169] Lenin argued that whether there was one-man management instead of collegial management was essentially irrelevant since 'the victorious proletariat has abolished property'.[170] For Lenin the bottom line was that 'iron discipline while at work, unquestioning subordination to a single will' were what was needed to bolster productivity. He denounced Tomsky's theses as 'terribly confused' and belittled them as 'sheer nonsense'.[171] He said there was 'not one iota of practicality, nothing businesslike' in Tomsky's 'fundamentally wrong' theses, which he said had created 'a very malodorous' scandal.[172] Zeroing in on Tomsky's defence of collegial management, Lenin declared, 'such thinking cannot be tolerated. Such thinking drags us back theoretically'.[173] Trotsky chimed in, mocking Tomsky's understanding of basic issues.[174]

Fellow members of the Central Committee joined Lenin in criticising Tomsky. The attacks they hurled at him shocked Tomsky. Nikolai Krestinsky went so far as to accuse Tomsky and Lutovinov of having counter-revolutionary tendencies, a sentiment Lev Kamenev echoed.[175] Trotsky joined the chorus of criticism, stating, 'I regretfully have to say that Comrade Tomsky has been weaker on these issues than anyone else' at the congress.[176] He demanded that the trade unions implement the militarisation of labour, stating it was necessary to establish a system in which every worker feels himself 'a soldier of labour'. Trotsky reiterated, with theatrical *élan* and a complete lack of discretion, that the trade unions should punish workers who failed to carry out orders like deserters in the Red Army and throw them into concentration camps or penal labour battalions.[177] With the majority of party delegates supporting Lenin's rejection of Tomsky's proposals, Tomsky tactfully, if reluctantly, refrained from forcefully defending his theses beyond laying out the reasoning behind them. He did lash back at some of the Central Committee members, including Rykov, the head of VSNKh, who had earlier supported collegial management. Rykov now spoke out strongly against workers' role in management and generally took a hard line

---

169   Lenin 1958–65, vol. 40, p. 258.
170   Farber 1990, p. 74.
171   Lenin 1958–65, vol. 40, pp. 260, 270, 272.
172   Lenin 1958–65, vol. 40, p. 265.
173   Lenin 1958–65, vol. 40, pp. 259–61.
174   Service 1995, p. 114. In the words of Jay Sorenson, 'Trotsky play the role of the *enfant terrible* at this congress and he did it with zeal': Sorenson 1969, p. 102.
175   Daniels 1960, p. 127.
176   RKP(b) 1934a, p. 207.
177   RKP(b) 1934a, p. 101.

on the role of the trade unions. Rykov's proposals, Tomsky said, would 'squeeze the guts' out of the trade unions.[178]

Trying to salvage some important role for the unions in management, Tomsky introduced an amendment that stated that factories could be administered, depending on 'the interests of each particular enterprise', either through management by a single individual or collegially. The majority of the delegates rejected this initial amendment.[179] But later in the congress, the delegates accepted another amendment by Tomsky, which was a watered-down version of the original resolution. The final resolution, as a result, did not call for an across-the-board introduction of one-man management but the formation of factory administrations, in agreements with the VSNKh and VTsSPS, which would be a combination of specialist directors with worker assistants or vice versus, worker directors with specialist assistants.[180] The adopted resolution also stated that those trade unionists who participated in management should be selected in consultation with the trade unions, on the basis of the candidates' 'practical experience, technical competence, firmness, organisational capacity, and business sense'.[181] In contrast to the steadfast views of the Workers' Oppositionists and Democratic Centralists, who single-mindedly defended collegial management and insisted that workers could assume managerial functions, Tomsky reluctantly conceded that even most skilled workers were ignorant of the challenging complexities of factory management, lacked any experience in executing managerial functions, and were so utterly exhausted that they would not be able to handle 'the extraordinary nervous strain' that holding such positions would entail as production continued to decline.[182] But in one of his parting shots, Tomsky declared that when the party stops treating trade unionists as second-class members of the party, and instead treated them 'seriously and thoughtfully', then the disagreements between the

---

178 Rykov, according to Tomsky, now opposed giving trade unions the right to appoint factory management, although just a few months earlier, in January 1920, he had orchestrated VSNKh's endorsement of collegiality over one-man management: RKP(b) 1934a, p. 174. Rykov before long would give even more full-throated support of the specialists: Oppenheim 1972, p. 250.
179 RKP(b) 1934a, pp. 205, 217.
180 Aves 1996, p. 17.
181 RKP(b) 1953, p. 492.
182 Quoted in Allen 2015, p. 142. The Ninth Party Congress did encourage the VTsSPS Presidium to work with VSNKh to identify workers who could be trained in managerial responsibilities and then promoted to become, initially, the managers of small enterprises: Malle 1985, p. 135.

party and trade unions would vanish. This was met with applause by the delegates.[183]

In recognition of his ability to work out an apparent compromise with Lenin and other members of the party leadership, delegates to the party congress re-elected Tomsky to the Central Committee. They also appointed him a candidate member of the Organisational Bureau (Orgburo) shortly after the congress.[184] The Orgburo, like the Political Bureau (Politburo), was formally a subcommittee of Central Committee.[185] Both were gradually taking over some of the powers of the Central Committee, although the lines between these three bodies remained blurry for some time.[186] But it is striking how quickly Tomsky was back in the good graces of the party leadership.

Tomsky's willingness to work out a compromise did not sit well, however, with many trade-union leaders, especially after one-man management began to be introduced on a wide scale.[187] Under pressure to raise output, managers not only shut trade unions out of managerial decisions, but they increasingly engaged in various illicit or illegal actions, which infuriated Tomsky as well as his fellow trade unionists. As the historian Jay Sorenson summarised: managers' conduct 'violated or ignored trade-union instructions and labour laws ... skimped on funds allocated for labour and safety devices; did not pay overtime; shifted manpower within the plan at will; hired outside the established procedures; and of all things, resorted to blacklists'.[188]

Tomsky, as a result, quickly regretted his decision to compromise with Lenin and decided to once again fight back. A week after the Ninth Party Congress, at the Third Trade-Union Congress in early April 1920, Tomsky in his speech

---

183 RKP(b) 1934a, p. 263. But the congress also rejected a draft resolution by Tomsky that stipulated that all trade-union party caucuses should be subordinate to the VTsSPS. The resolution the congress adopted made the subordination of the trade unions to the party explicit, stating that the VTsSPS's communist caucus was subordinate to the Central Committee, while the caucuses of each trade union should be subordinated to the local party committee: Egorov and Bogoliubov (eds) 1983–84, vol. 2, pp. 255–6.
184 Kupcha and Popov (eds) 1991, p. 116. Rudzutak and Andreev, two other VTsSPS Presidium members, were also elected to the 19-member Central Committee.
185 Party congresses officially were the sovereign body in the party, but increasingly real power was located in the party's executive organs.
186 Rigby 1979, p. 55. The Orgburo administered party affairs and checked on the execution of party directives. In Lenin's words, in principle, 'the Orgburo allocates forces, while the Politburo decides policy': quoted in Schapiro 1960, p. 240.
187 In 1918 only 3.4 percent of firms were under individual management, and in 1919 only 10.9 percent, but in 1920 the percentage shot up to 71.2 percent and in 1921 to 90.7 percent: Sirianni 1982, pp. 211–12.
188 Sorenson 1969, p. 77.

insisted on the right of trade unionists, not just to be consulted, but to actually appoint managers in conjunction with the local body of VSNKh (Sovnarkhoz).[189] But even more than the specific issue of one-man management, what particularly troubled Tomsky was Trotsky's seemingly gratuitous, wholesale attacks on the trade unions. In a speech at the trade-union congress that had been approved beforehand by the Politburo, Trotsky called for a 'shake-up' of the unions. Trotsky demanded the dismissal of all trade-union leaders and their replacement by nominees who would put the need to revive the shattered economy above the interests of individual workers.[190]

Shortly before this trade-union congress, the Central Committee had appointed Trotsky, on his own suggestion, as head of the Commissariat for Transport (Narkomput). Tomsky was the only member of the Central Committee to object.[191] This position made Trotsky responsible for fixing a railroad system that was so badly ruined during the Civil War that it was grinding to a complete stop. Only about a quarter of the total miles of railroad lines and about half of the locomotives were operational and almost no fuel or raw materials were reaching Moscow and other cities.[192] Trotsky blamed the leadership of the railway union for the problems with the railroads. Over Tomsky's objections, he replaced the Railroad Workers' Union on 3 September with a new Joint Central Transport Committee and made himself head of it.[193] This new union, which was known by its acronym, Tsektran, merged the Railroad Workers' and Transport Workers' Unions under conditions of rigid military discipline. Tomsky correctly feared that Trotsky intended to move on from there to thoroughly 'reorganise' the trade unions in all industries, using the same sort of tough methods in the trade unions he had used in reorganising the Red Army.[194]

Trotsky, who had been advocating for compulsory labour for some time, at the Third Trade-Union Congress in April 1920 foolishly presented a whole theory of forced labour, rather than justifying the militarisation of labour as just a temporary, expedient response to desperate circumstances. As the historian Isaac Deutscher put it, Trotsky made an ideological virtue out of a bitter necessity.[195] 'Because man is by nature a rather lazy animal', Trotsky argued,

---

189   Aves 1996, p. 29; Tomskii 1928a, p. 119. The Central Committee had insisted that the trade-union congress be postponed until after the party congress concluded, so they would be faced with a fait accompli on the issue of one-man management: Allen 2015, p. 142.
190   Volkogonov 1996, p. 216.
191   Daniels 1960, p. 130.
192   Hobson and Tabor 1988, p. 116; Chase 1987, pp. 18–19.
193   GARF, f. 5451, op. 42, d. 12, l. 15. Everyone on the Central Committee, except Tomsky, supported the proposal to create Tsektran: Daniels 1960, p. 130.
194   Broué 1988, p. 281; Swain 2014, p. 84.
195   Deutscher 1950, p. 38.

compulsory labour is absolutely necessary. Trotsky went even further, arguing that 'the transition to socialism is unthinkable without compulsory labour' and it was 'the right of the state, the workers' state, to punish the working men or women who refuse to carry out the orders of the state, who do not subordinate their will to the will of the working class and to its economic tasks'. Trotsky went so far as to argue that the trade unionists' belief that compulsory labour is unproductive 'is the most wretched and miserable liberal prejudice: chattel slavery, too, was productive ... Compulsory serf labour did not grow out of the feudal lords' ill will. It was [in its time] a progressive phenomenon'.[196] While Tomsky and the other leading Bolshevik trade unionists vociferously objected, it was one of the Mensheviks in attendance whose outraged question best captured the mood of many at the congress, including Tomsky. Rafail Abramovich stated, 'If socialism requires the militarisation of labour, how does it differ from the Egyptian slavery' used to build the pyramids?[197] Trotsky, undaunted, insisted the trade unions needed to abandon any fight for better conditions for workers to instead focus exclusively on the fight to raise labour productivity. He argued for classifying as desertion workers' failure to follow orders, which should be treated just like it was in the Red Army.[198] This was not idle talk on Trotsky's part. Revolutionary tribunals during the first half of 1920 convicted and sentenced over 1,000 railroad workers for violating labour discipline, with some even executed.[199] By the end of 1920, Trotsky and his supporters had managed to militarise some three thousand enterprises, primarily in munitions and coal mining.[200] The historian Robert Daniels, who characterised Trotsky as the first Stalinist in his economic thinking, argued that Trotsky's call for trade unions to assume responsibility for labour discipline and productivity was 'a foretaste of Stalin's *Gleichschaltung* of the unions after 1929'.[201]

Trade-union discontent, particularly Tomsky's, with Trotsky's programme of militarisation burst into a full-scale party crisis at the Fifth Trade-Union Conference, which convened on 2 November 1920.[202] Tomsky, in his opening speech as

---

196 VTsSPS 1920, pp. 87–97; Trotsky 1961, pp. 110–11, 142–50. Bukharin, Rykov, and Radek, among others, echoed Trotsky's support for compulsory labour: Carr 1952, pp. 213–16.
197 Quoted in Volkogonov 1996, pp. 215–16.
198 Swain 2014, pp. 81–2, 141.
199 Between February and July 1920, 3,666 railroad workers and white-collar employees were convicted for various workplace crimes, including absenteeism, with 82 executed: *Pravda*, 22 July 1920, cited in Aves 1996, p. 33.
200 Figes 1996, p. 724.
201 Daniels 1960, p. 122.
202 A preview of the 'trade-union debate' erupted at the Ninth Party Conference, held in

chair of the VTsSPS, argued that since the Civil War had now ended, such emergency methods as the militarisation of labour should be stopped and the trade unions should return to the tactics and positions they held prior to militarisation.[203] Tomsky also stated there was no longer any excuse for using coercive methods, including requiring workers to become members in trade unions, or for there to be undemocratic elections.[204] Tomsky was making a nod to the Workers' Opposition, which had been stridently advocating for the democratisation of the trade unions.[205] In the fierce back and forth between Tomsky and Trotsky on the floor of the conference, in which Tomsky became heated, Trotsky refused to budge. He bluntly made it clear that he would not back down on his call for a wholesale reorganisation of the trade unions in order to improve production, no matter what the delegates of the trade-union conference thought. Trotsky's recommendations would entail the forced merger of the trade unions with the state apparatus, wide-scale labour conscription, and the appointment rather than the election of all union leaders, as was the case in Tsektran. If Tomsky continued to balk at this, Trotsky again argued that the trade unions should be 'shaken up from top to bottom'. Trotsky, with his usual tactless bluntness, also called for 'tightening the screws' of War Communism and the immediate statification of the trade unions through their absorption into the party-state.[206] Trotsky, who thoroughly enjoyed provoking Tomsky and his fellow trade-union leaders, also called for extending the Tsektran system to the entire economy, with the conversion of all trade [*professional'nye*] unions into production [*proizvodstvennye*] unions. After a barrage of criticism of Trotsky's programme within the closed communist caucus, on the floor of the congress the overwhelming majority of trade unionists supported Tomsky against Trotsky. In addition, Tomsky enjoyed the support of the VTsSPS when he pointed out that Trotsky and his supporters had violated party rules by bringing the divisive debate before non-party delegates on the floor of the conference.[207]

September 1920. This is where the Workers' Opposition made its first public appearance: Allen 2015, p. 162; Tsuji 1989, p. 36.

203   Tsuji 1989, pp. 45–6.
204   Kulikova and Khazanov 1988, p. 72.
205   Tsuji 1989, p. 46.
206   Lenin 1960–70, vol. 31, p. 573; Lenin 1941–50, vol. 32, p. 24; Zhuravleva (ed.) 1995, p. 101; Tsuji 1989, p. 37. Economic policies during the Civil War were only subsequently dubbed War Communism.
207   Tomsky called for the Central Committee to prosecute in a 'party court' Trotsky and his supporters for their violation of party discipline: Allen 2015, p. 167. Shlyapnikov joined with Tomsky in the appeal to the Central Committee.

The trade unionists' opposition to Trotsky became the focus of a Central Committee Plenum (plenary meeting) as well as a Politburo meeting, which were held while the Fifth Trade-Union Conference was still in session. Knowing many fellow Central Committee members had by this time joined Tomsky in criticising Trotsky's labour programmes, an infuriated Tomsky, with the support of the VTsSPS Presidium, denounced Trotsky and Tsektran at the November Central Committee Plenum.[208] In addition to repeating the trade unionists' various reasons for opposing Tsektran, Tomsky criticised Trotsky's behaviour at the trade-union conference.[209] An 'unprecedentedly excited' Tomsky, along with Yan Rudzutak, then rushed off to the Politburo, where they directly pleaded their case to Lenin, who as noted above had earlier wholeheartedly favoured Trotsky's calls for creating labour armies.[210] But Lenin, who had become extremely irritated with how Trotsky had brought the trade-union debate out into the open and had denigrated Tomsky, made a quick, unexpected about-face and switched his support from Trotsky to Tomsky.[211]

Lenin's decision to side with Tomsky is not as surprising as it might seem. Although Lenin had supported Trotsky's call to create labour armies, he continued to hold Tomsky in high regard. Lenin praised Tomsky's leadership of the trade unions while criticising Trotsky for mistakenly implying that 'in a workers' state it is not the business of the trade unions to stand up for the material and spiritual interests of the working class'.[212] Conceding that the Soviet Union was not yet a workers' state, Lenin argued that defending workers' interests against the government was very much the role of the trade unions, which were a vital link between the party and the mass of workers.[213] It may be that Lenin also recognised that labour armies, as the historian Richard Sakwa noted, could achieve little other than alienating workers since most of them could join other workers seeking refuge with their relatives in the countryside, where there was more food than in the cities despite grain requisitioning.[214]

---

208   Sorenson 1969, p. 107; Garvy 1958, p. 92. According to Pierre Broué, a large minority of the VTsSPS had supported the creation of Tsektran: Broué 1988, p. 279.
209   Daniels 1960, p. 130; Tsuji 1989, p. 36.
210   Lenin 1960–70, vol. 32, p. 75; Aves 1996, p. 81. At this time the Central Committee was the true governing body, not the Politburo. That was reversed in 1922, when the Central Committee began to meet far less frequently. The five full members of the Politburo at this time were Lenin, Kamenev, Stalin, Trotsky, and Krestinsky.
211   Trotsky's attacks on Tomsky also outraged most members of the Central Committee: Tsuji 1989, p. 40.
212   Lenin 1941–50, vol. 32, p. 6.
213   Lenin 1941–50, vol. 32, p. 2.
214   Sakwa 1988, p. 92.

But Trotsky was not about to back down from his argument that the interests of workers and their state were identical, which further outraged Lenin. As a result, in a passionate speech, Lenin accused Trotsky of needlessly, and dangerously, alienating the trade unionists. 'If the party quarrels with the trade unions', an agitated Lenin exclaimed, 'then it is the party's fault, and this is certainly the end of Soviet power'.[215] Lenin presented the Central Committee with a new draft resolution, 'The Tasks of the Trade Unions and the Methods of Their Implementation', which called for strengthening trade unions and condemned any 'petty tyranny' over the trade unions by the party.[216] The Central Committee's response on 8 November to the rival theses of Lenin and Trotsky was almost evenly divided. Eight voted for Lenin's theses with six against, while seven voted for Trotsky's theses and eight voted against. Afterwards, Lenin wrote to Tomsky, along with Rykov and Rudzutak, stating 'If you are dissatisfied with [my] theses on the trade-union movement, please prepare a revision or a new set of theses immediately'.[217]

Ten Central Committee members, who wanted to alleviate the increasingly bitter tension between Trotsky and Lenin, the next day created a so-called buffer group apparently at the behest of Bukharin. Tomsky was also a member of it, along with Zinoviev, Rykov, Radek, Krestinsky, Kamenev, Dzerzhinsky, Leonid Serebriakov and Fedor Sergeev. Its chimerical aim was to eliminate the differences of opinion within the Central Committee over the role of trade unions.[218] As a result, it came up with proposals that tried to please both Trotsky and Tomsky: for Trotsky there was some vague promise of production unions while for Tomsky a promise of more trade-union participation in management.[219] The Central Committee Plenum adopted these proposals by a vote margin of only eight to six.[220]

The Central Committee, in a further attempt to resolve the apparently irreconcilable views and reach a consensus, created yet another Trade-Union Commission. The task of this subcommittee was to determine how best to increase democracy in the unions and their participation in management. It was also asked to review the employment of specialists. The Central Committee appointed Tomsky, along with Zinoviev, Rudzutak, and Rykov, to the commission. Lenin suggested that Trotsky should be left off the subcommittee, but Serebria-

---

215 Lenin 1941–50, vol. 32, p. 37.
216 Lenin 1941–50, vol. 32, pp. 24–5.
217 Tsuji 1989, pp. 40.
218 Tsuji 1989, p. 41.
219 Sorenson 1969, p. 111.
220 Tsuji 1989, p. 42.

kov, a member of the 'buffer group', insisted that he be added. Although Zinoviev was appointed chair, Tomsky played perhaps the key role in getting Trotsky to angrily walk out. Trotsky refused to participate because he felt the composition of the commission made it impossible for his views to prevail, for which Lenin severely criticised him.[221] Four members of the VTsSPS were immediately added to the commission – Shlyapnikov, Lutovinov, Andreev, and Alexander Lozovsky – which gave the VTsSPS a majority on the commission.[222] The VTsSPS proposal, written by Rudzutak, while not contesting the Central Committee's right to appoint economic managers, called on the Central Committee to do so in consultation with trade-union leaders.[223] Before long, Shlyapnikov also resigned when his recommendations were not integrated into the subcommittee's draft proposals.[224]

The trade-union commission's report would serve as the basis for an alternate set of theses, passed by a ten to four vote with one abstention. As a result, the winning faction became known as the 'Ten' and when their programme was later adopted in a modified form in January 1921, it was known as the 'Platform of the Ten'.[225] To the members of the commission, the fact that Tomsky, the head of the trade unions, supported it and voted for it was critical.[226] The 'Ten' rejected the 'statification' of the trade unions, arguing it would cut the union leadership off from the masses. They also refused to demand that unions drop their defence of workers' interests to focus only on increasing production, although it did state that should be their principal task. The 'Ten' bluntly called for the elimination of Tsektran and labour militarisation.[227] Tomsky, in addition, insisted that if trade unions were to protect workers' interests, they must retain certain rights, such as the right to negotiate collective agreements and to appeal violations of those agreements. The 'Ten' also agreed to stress the role of the trade unions as 'transmission belts' between the party and the masses and as 'schools of communism' in providing training to potential party members.

---

221   Carr 1952, p. 222n1. Zinoviev, in the words of one historian, was hardly the best choice for a peacemaker: Sakwa 1988, p. 248.
222   Tsuji 1989, p. 42. There were of course significant differences of opinion among these leading trade unionists.
223   Allen 2002, p. 74.
224   Barbara Allen also suggests Shlyapnikov resigned because of his distrust of Tomsky: Allen 2015, p. 167.
225   The ten who voted for it were Lenin, Zinoviev, Tomsky, Stalin, Rudzutak, Kalinin, Kamenev, Artem, Lozosky, and Grigory Petrovsky. Andreev, Krestinsky, and Rykov joined Trotsky in voting against it, while Preobrazhensky abstained.
226   Koenker 2005, p. 74.
227   Daniels 1960, p. 131.

While the 'Ten' stated that the trade unions were under the directing control of the Central Committee, they nonetheless called for giving the trade unions autonomy in order to defend the sectional interests of workers. They called upon the party to take into account the opinion of the trade-union leaders and emphasised that 'normal proletarian democracy should be strengthened and developed in the trade unions'.[228] Although Tomsky had to make concessions on various points, he appeared to have won a victory in maintaining the trade unions' separate identity. Trotsky, in contrast, had suffered a seemingly categorical defeat.

Although the vote won by the 'Ten' was supposed to end the debate about the role of trade unions before the upcoming Tenth Party Congress, it did not. The debate now burst into full public view despite Lenin's concerted attempt to confine it to the upper echelons of the party. The 'trade-union debate' filled the party press and became a source of widespread public interest from December 1920 to the beginning of the delayed Tenth Party Congress, which would finally open in March 1921. All 600,000 party members seemingly joined in the debate.[229] The various protagonists bitterly debated each other at rallies, meetings, and conferences. They did so on a couple of occasions before crowds numbering in the thousands.[230] Trotsky reviled Tomsky for ignoring the producers' concerns. He repeatedly denounced the 'backward', *'tred-iunionist* conservatism' of the VTsSPS and condemned Tomsky's approach to the trade unions as so old and outdated they were 'covered with mould'. In response Tomsky, along with other leading trade unionists and prominent members of the Central Committee, warned, 'if the working class is stripped of trade unions in their present form, they will have to create underground trade unions', probably organised by Mensheviks and Socialist Revolutionaries.[231] Tomsky also vehemently argued in opposition to Tsektran that trade unions 'must be strengthened not by creating a parallel organ outside it, but by pouring party folk into it'.[232] Tomsky's main points were the need for democracy not militarisation; the repudiation of Tsektran; and the lack of any need for trade-union reorganisation since no crisis specific to the trade unions existed. He insisted the party and soviets suffered from similar problems.[233] Lenin went even fur-

---

228   Tsuji 1989, p. 46.
229   Tsuji 1989, p. 43.
230   Kossior, Ryazanov, Lozovsky, Lutovinov, and Boguslavsky also spoke: Tsuji 1989, pp. 57, 59, 60, 75.
231   Tsuji 1989, pp. 60–1, 75; Thatcher 2003, pp. 109–10.
232   Tsuji 1989, p. 57.
233   Tsuji 1989, p. 81.

ther, arguing 'it is not a crisis of the trade unions but of the party'.[234] Tomsky added that 'we must draw the masses into production by way of the trade unions and make every worker at the bench feel himself the boss [*khoziain*], running production'. Tomsky concluded his 24 December speech in Moscow's Bolshoi Theatre by stating that 'Trotsky's fallacy is that he regards as ideal what an emergency has obliged us to do'.[235] It should also be noted that various major groupings, primarily the Workers' Opposition, also put forth their platforms on the trade unions in *Pravda* and at the various meetings. The Workers' Opposition, as we have seen, advocated for putting the trade unions in total charge of the economy. During the debate the Workers' Opposition enjoyed some success as they attempted to mobilise rank-and-file trade unionists' support.[236]

At the Eighth Congress of Soviets, which met jointly with the party caucus of the VTsSPS in the Bolshoi Theatre, Lenin on 30 December gave a speech entitled 'On the Trade Unions, the Present Moment, and the Mistakes of Comrade Trotsky', in which he ripped into Trotsky. Lenin denounced Trotsky's programme as full of 'theoretical mistakes and glaring blunders'.[237] He also suggested that Trotsky's criticisms of Tomsky raised the danger of creating a split in the party.[238] But while complimenting Tomsky for 'working very smoothly with the trade-union movement', he also poked fun at him for what he considered his 'many partial theoretical mistakes', stating 'I never heard that Tomsky was an eminent theoretician or claimed to be one' and wondered why Trotsky would get into a 'battle of principles' with him.[239] Tomsky's lack of distinction as a theorist would occasionally be thrown in his face in the years to come. Tomsky's common response was that reality itself, not theory, should determine their actions. He stated, for example, as early the First Trade-Union Congress, that resolutions and theory cannot force reality into their mould.[240]

There is no need to go into further detail about the fierce, but redundant, polemics between Trotsky and Tomsky other than to note that Lenin, in the two months that followed, repeatedly came to Tomsky's defence. He reproached

---

234 Quoted in Tsuji 1989, p. 76.
235 Quoted in Tsuji 1989, pp. 60–1.
236 Allen 2015, pp. 159, 169. The so-called Democratic Centralists were the other major grouping.
237 Lenin 1941–50, vol. 32, p. 1.
238 Tsuji 1989, p. 75. Lenin was becoming increasingly obsessed with a fear that the party might split, stating in late January, 'Any disagreement, even the most petty, can become politically dangerous if there is the chance of it developing into a split, and I mean the kind of split that could shake and destroy the whole political edifice': Lenin 1960–70, vol. 32, p. 57.
239 Lenin 1958–65, vol. 42, p. 209.
240 Kaplan 1968, p. 183.

Trotsky for antagonising Tomsky, who Lenin argued faithfully 'reflected the feelings and thoughts of the mass of workers'.[241] He also complemented Tomsky for his relative restraint in the face of Trotsky's attacks.[242] Under duress, Trotsky as a result retracted his harsh criticism of Tomsky. 'In the sharpest polemic with Comrade Tomsky I have always said – even when the polemic against Tomsky was at its bitterest – that it is absolutely clear to me that only men with his experience and authority are able to be our trade-union leaders'.[243] Trotsky added that Tomsky was frequently correct that the Central Committee intruded too much into the trade unions' internal affairs and the composition of the various trade-union bodies.[244]

Tomsky succeeded, despite serious opposition, in getting the VTsSPS to go along with the concessions he made in the 'Platform of the Ten', after it was rewritten by Zinoviev and formally adopted by the Central Committee's trade-union commission on 14 January 1921. A few weeks later a majority of the 117 delegates to a VTsSPS party caucus, who represented the 21 unions, voted for it. But this was after a heated debate between Tomsky and Andrei Andreev, the presidium member who presented Trotsky's theses to the caucus. Lutovinov presented the views of the Workers' Opposition because Shlyapnikov mysteriously did not show up.[245] In the vote at the caucus, the 'Platform of the Ten' received 70 votes, Trotsky's platform 23, and the Workers' Opposition platform 21.[246] But many of the 70 trade unionists who voted for Tomsky's theses did so with serious reservations. They wanted the unions to have a greater role in economic management than under Lenin's plan.[247] Likewise, the vote was split in the caucus's bureau, where five voted for the 'Platform of the Ten', three voted for Trotsky's platform, and one voted for the Workers' Opposition's platform.[248]

During these debates within the party and trade-union leadership in early 1921, the country descended into a full-blown domestic crisis. Now that the Civil War was over, at least for the most part, waves of peasant and worker

---

241 Quoted in Sorenson 1969, p. 97. The public fight between Lenin and Trotsky over the role of the trade unions shocked most party members, who had little inkling there was any serious divergence of views between them: Service 1995, p. 172.
242 Lenin 1960–70, vol. 32, p. 73.
243 Lenin 1960–70, vol. 32, pp. 105–6; Eastman 1925, p. 137.
244 Chechevishnikov 1990, p. 176.
245 Allen 2015, p. 178.
246 Six voters abstained.
247 Gorelov 2000, pp. 84–5.
248 Tomsky, Rudzutak, Lozovsky, Shmidt, and Grigory Tsyperovich voted for the 'Platform of the Ten', while Adam Goltsman, Andrei Andreev, and Stanislav Kosior voted for Trotsky's platform and Lutovinov for the Workers' Opposition's platform: Gorelov 1989, p. 41.

unrest swept across Russia. Strikes and demonstrations erupted in most of the industrial centres, including in Moscow and Petrograd. Workers suffering from hunger and cold protested the still woefully insufficient food rations and their appalling living conditions, among other serious grievances. This was primarily a spontaneous upsurge in worker dissatisfaction, but Mensheviks and other political elements were active in fomenting the discontent.[249] Outraged at the rigging of elections in the soviets and trade unions, workers increasingly booed party agitators.[250] This worker unrest contributed to Tomsky's belief that the sort of increased pressure on workers that Trotsky had been advocating could fatally undermine the Soviet state.[251] The unrest culminated in March when the sailors at the Kronstadt naval base, 'the pride and glory of the revolution' in 1917 according to Trotsky, revolted against what they saw as the Bolshevik elite's betrayal of the revolution. The mutineers, for example, adopted a resolution demanding the re-election of soviets by secret ballot.[252] But their fury focused principally on Trotsky for his policies of militarisation and regimentation.[253] The party leadership, rather than trying to appease the mutineers with some timely reforms, ordered the Red Army to launch its first assault against Kronstadt on the very day the Tenth Party Congress opened on 8 March.[254] One hundred and forty delegates, over a quarter of the attendees of the congress, left to join the fight against the rebels.[255] That included members of the Workers' Opposition and Democratic Centralists, who were determined to demonstrate their loyalty, but they must have also shared the exaggerated, yet widespread belief within the party that the uprising was a threat to the regime's survival.[256]

It is not clear if the crushing of the revolt two weeks later troubled Tomsky, but he was fully informed as it unfolded and was one of the handful of party leaders who were privy to the investigations of it afterwards. As one of the now 26 Central Committee members, Tomsky heard a report on 16 March about the Kronstadt revolt, but the protocols reveal nothing about the discussion, so it

---

249 Aves 1996, pp. 111–57.
250 Serge 1963, p. 123.
251 Service 1995, p. 153.
252 Discontent with the replacement of elections to the soviets with 'appointism' [*naznachesnstvo*] was widespread.
253 Avrich 1970, p. 178.
254 Trotsky orchestrated the attack.
255 RKP(b) 1933a, p. 339.
256 Avrich 1970, pp. 194–5, 211. Fifteen of them were killed in the fighting. In addition, many of Petrograd's leading trade unionists, including N.M. Antselovich, Ivan Lepse, Iu. Mileikovsky, and I.F. Zholnerovich, participated in the crushing of the uprising as commissars of regiments, divisions, and military groups: Nosach 2001, p. 291.

is impossible to know how he responded. Likewise, he was one of 25 Orgburo members who heard reports on 21 and 24 March about how to reward congress delegates who participated in the suppression of the revolt.[257] He also attended an Orgburo meeting on 25 March and a Central Committee Plenum on 16 May that were devoted to studying the causes of the Kronstadt Revolt.[258] But what is clear is that Tomsky did not join Lenin, Trotsky, Bukharin, Radek, Lev Sosnovsky, Emelyan Yaroslavsky, Yury Steklov, and other party leaders in their utterly false public statements about the rebels' leaders and motives, which they denounced as a 'White Guardist plot'.[259] He recognised in front of trade unionists, if only in passing, that the revolt resulted from mass discontent with party policy.[260]

At the Tenth Party Congress itself, the platform Tomsky supported easily prevailed. The resolution on the trade unions, which Tomsky along with Rykov and Zinoviev drafted as a yet again revised version of the 'Platform of the Ten', stated that 'the rapid statisation' of the trade unions would be 'a serious mistake'.[261] Yoshimasa Tsuji, a historian of the 'trade-union debate', argues the final version of the 'Platform of the Ten', which as a result of Lenin's influence 'stood halfway between Trotsky and Tomsky', was a 'theoretical mess'.[262] Regardless, since it enjoyed the support of a huge majority of the delegates, only a perfunctory debate occurred at the Tenth Party Congress. It was limited to a single three-hour session, with each of the seven speakers allotted only 10 minutes.[263] Tomsky, in his speech, occupied the moderate position between the two extreme blocs. He criticised Shlyapnikov and the Workers' Opposition for not taking into sufficient account the devastated condition of the country and argued they were speaking only for skilled workers.[264] But Tomsky also said trade unionists would fight any future 'pernicious attempts' by Trotsky to introduce 'strict military discipline'.[265] Shlyapnikov criticised Tomsky for abandoning his earlier support for the 'active participation' of the trade unions in the management of

---

257   Khordina (ed.) 1999a, pp. 468, 578, 609, 640.
258   Khordina (ed.) 1999b, pp. 6, 142–3. The Orgburo meeting might have discussed Trotsky's plan for a 'Political [Show] Trial of Kronstadters', which the Politburo had seriously discussed the day before, 25 March. The political trial ended up never being staged: Getzler 2002, p. 39.
259   Getzler 1983, p. 256.
260   Tomskii 1927b, pp. 26–7.
261   Carr 1952, p. 226.
262   Tsuji 1989, pp. 86, 88, 92.
263   RKP(b) 1933a, pp. 339, 378.
264   RKP(b) 1933a, pp. 370–2.
265   RKP(b) 1933a, pp. 372–3.

the entire economy, while Trotsky criticised Tomsky for 'baiting' him.[266] Following the debate, the congress overwhelmingly passed the resolution based on the 'Platform of the Ten'. It received 336 votes while Trotsky's draft calling for the annexation of the trade unions to the state received just 50, and Shlyapnikov's Workers' Opposition theses calling for their independence received only 18 votes.[267] Although subordination of the unions to the party was reaffirmed, the autonomy of the unions from the government was also confirmed.[268] The labour armies were disbanded.[269] Barbara Allen, Shlyapnikov's biographer, justifiably argued that because the Tenth Party Congress's vote was taken in the context of the Kronstadt revolt, worker unrest, and peasant uprisings, it undercut the power of the Workers' Opposition's criticisms, which were viewed in this context as a threat to the Soviet government's very survival.[270] The extent of their support among workers was undoubtedly much more than the vote indicated given the virulence with which Lenin attacked the Workers' Opposition afterwards.

The party leadership then added two resolutions, hastily drafted by Lenin, which were introduced on the very last day of the congress. The first resolution 'On Party Unity', which would henceforth ban any faction within the party and thus became the true turning point in the party's organisational history, took place after only a brief discussion.[271] The ban, which was said to be temporary, would become the basis in the years and decades to come for crushing any dissent against decisions by the Central Committee, although neither Lenin, Tomsky, nor other party leaders appear to have fully appreciated its far-reaching consequences at the time.[272] All but 30 delegates voted for the resolution, although some did confess their uneasiness in doing so. Karl Radek, for example, told the congress that 'I have a feeling that there was perhaps being established here a rule which can be turned against anyone as yet unknown ... We still do not know how this will be carried out.... The best Central Committee may make a mistake, but this is less dangerous than the wavering that is now observable'.[273] Even fewer delegates voted against a second resolution, 'On the Syndicalist and Anarchist Deviation in Our Party', which

---

266 RKP(b) 1933a, p. 358; Shliapnikov 1921, p. 292.
267 RKP(b) 1933a, p. 402.
268 Egorov and Bogoliubov (eds) 1983–84, vol. 2, p. 347.
269 Avrich 1970, pp. 9, 233.
270 Allen 2002, p. 75.
271 Daniels 1960, p. 148.
272 Allen 2015, p. 186; Figes 1996, p. 765.
273 RKP(b) 1933a, p. 540; Daniels 1960, p. 148.

specifically condemned membership in the Workers' Opposition as incompatible with membership in the party.[274] Tomsky, who undoubtedly voted for both these momentous resolutions, would not have to wait long before they would be used against himself.

Tomsky enjoyed widespread popularity in party circles for brokering the compromise resolution. In fact, in the voting for the next Central Committee at the end of the Tenth Party Congress, Tomsky came in third, behind only Lenin and Radek.[275] Trotsky, with whom Lenin was still furious, came in a humiliating tenth.[276] This undercuts Sorenson's argument that if Trotsky, a 'first-rate political leader', had led the trade unions, they would have fared much better than they did under Tomsky.[277] Be that as it may, Tomsky seemed to be fully ensconced as one of the handful of top party leaders. But that quickly proved illusory.

The Fourth Trade-Union Congress, which opened a couple months later on 17 May 1921, was the first opportunity for most trade unionists to discuss the role of unions following the decisions of the Tenth Party Congress. The Central Committee, which feared the Workers' Opposition might attempt to seize control of the trade unions at this congress, rumours to that effect had been circulating, entrusted Tomsky, as chair of the VTsSPS, with heading a subcommittee to prepare for the congress. Stalin, Molotov, Zinoviev, and Vasily Mikhailov were also members of this Politburo commission. They were given the responsibility of preparing draft resolutions on all the major issues to be discussed at the congress.[278] One resolution reaffirmed the Central Committee's views of the role of trade unions as subservient to the party, though independent from the state. Tomsky was also given the responsibility of ensuring the acceptance of the Central Committee's subcommittee's positions by the congress's party caucus. Then, at the commission's last meeting before the congress, Zinoviev handed Tomsky a handwritten note that stipulated that David Ryazanov was not to be nominated to the VTsSPS Presidium. Ryazanov was a long-time trade unionist

---

274 Gregor (ed.) 1974, p. 116. The resolution stated that it was 'fundamentally incorrect' for the Workers' Opposition and their supporters 'to defend their mistaken views' by citing the Point Five adopted at the Eighth Party Congress, which as we have seen called on the trade unions to concentrate in their hands the administration of the entire economy: Egorov and Bogoliubov (eds) 1983–84, vol. 2, p. 338.
275 Radek (born Sobelsohn), a Polish Jew from Austrian Galicia, was an influential figure in the Comintern, where his cleverness as a polemicist became legendary.
276 RKP(b) 1933a, p. 405.
277 But Sorenson seemingly contradicted himself when he wrote a few pages later that Trotsky hurt rather than helped Lenin's cause: Sorenson 1969, pp. 97, 103.
278 Chechevishnikov 1990, p. 172; Nosach 2015, p. 116.

and respected Marxist theoretician, who had long criticised the party leadership for interfering in trade-union affairs. Tomsky later said he considered Zinoviev's note only a draft and thus subject to revision.[279]

This put Tomsky in a difficult spot. When the more than 3,000 delegates arrived at the congress, most of them were still passionately debating what their role as trade unionists should be under the new and still incomplete New Economic Policy (NEP) and many were itching for a fight.[280] Many were also upset at the suppression of the Kronstadt revolt.[281] As the delegates assembled, Tomsky felt threatened from all sides.[282] In addition to the party leadership's pressure from above, he recalled that 'on my left were the Workers' Oppositionists led by Shlyapnikov. From below were dissatisfied provincial trade unionists'.[283] It was apparent that Tomsky's support within the trade-union bureaucracy had been called into question as never before by his political deals during the 'trade-union debate', with most of the delegates still wanting the unions to be granted 'maximum organisational autonomy' from the party at the central, provincial, and individual trade-union level. The Metalworkers' Union's Central Committee, in particular, came to the congress determined to oust Tomsky.[284] Shlyapnikov, its leader, blasted Tomsky for having helped to remove Workers' Oppositionists from their positions in various trade unions.[285] He characterised Tomsky as 'spineless' in how he negotiated with his fellow members of the party Central Committee, which no doubt infuriated Tomsky.[286] But Tomsky managed to calmly respond to the accusation by insisting the situation had required diplomacy. The Central Committee, he suggested, would break the back of the VTsSPS Presidium if it tried to buck it.[287] As we will see, that is exactly what happened to Tomsky when he did not follow a Central Committee 'directive'.

---

279   Allen 2002, p. 81; Nosach 2005, p. 117.
280   Of the over 3,000 delegates, 555 were non-Bolsheviks.
281   Nosach 2005, pp. 47–8, 116.
282   Even so, Tomsky curiously resisted the effort by various party leaders, as well as by Shlyapnikov, to remove Trotsky's supporters from the VTsSPS leadership: Allen 2015, p. 198.
283   TsA FSB, R33718, d. 499061, vol. 41, l. 195. I am grateful to Barbara Allen for generously sharing the notes she took in the Federal Security Service (FSB) archives of the report of the special commission set up by the Central Committee to investigate Tomsky's actions at the trade-union congress.
284   While the Workers' Opposition enjoyed little support within the party, it retained considerable trade-union support.
285   TsA FSB, R33718, d. 499061, vol. 41, ll. 200–1; Allen 2015, p. 198.
286   TsA FSB, R33718, d. 499061, vol. 41. ll. 195, 199. Shlyapnikov had previously said Tomsky was 'spineless' at the Tenth Party Congress: RKP(b) 1933a, p. 390.
287   Allen 2002, p. 85.

The first flare-up occurred on 16 May at the pre-congress communist caucus. More than 80 percent of the delegates to the congress were party members and thus attendees at the party caucus.[288] The eruption concerned the nomination to the VTsSPS Presidium, by shouts from the floor, of Ryazanov. Tomsky did not voice any objection to Ryazanov's nomination even though the Central Committee had told him before the congress they did not want Ryazanov to be on the presidium. It outraged party leaders that Tomsky failed to inform anyone at the congress of their objection to Ryazanov's nomination. The best that Tomsky could say in his own defence later was that he thought that the Central Committee's list for membership on the presidium was 'not a directive' and that he felt he had to remove any suspicion among the trade unionists that the Central Committee wants 'to interfere [with the unions' decisions]'.[289] The trade-union leadership did indeed feel threatened by the prospect of more vigorous oversight by the Central Committee, especially since, as noted above, Bukharin and Radek had recently been appointed over Tomsky's objections to the VTsSPS Presidium to represent the party leadership. Tomsky understandably felt they had been sent to serve as 'political commissars' since neither had any experience in the trade-union movement. Lenin disingenuously claimed they had been appointed simply because they were 'people who have an excellent theoretical knowledge of the trade-union movement'.[290]

The members of the Politburo and the Central Committee in attendance were further infuriated by Tomsky's and Ryazanov's speeches to the caucus. In his 45-minute 'political report' Tomsky diplomatically criticised the Central Committee for its interference in trade-union affairs while also arguing that the VTsSPS had 'to indisputably obey' the party leadership. But it was Ryazanov's speech at the podium following Tomsky's that particularly infuriated the party leaders in attendance.[291] In Valerian Kuibyshev's opinion, Tomsky laid the groundwork for Ryazanov's speech by implicitly blaming all the VTsSPS's failings on 'petty interference' by the Central Committee.[292] The eccentric Ryazanov, who had a well-deserved reputation for bluntly criticising party policies, fearlessly lit into Tomsky as well as into the Central Committee, to considerable

---

288 Chechevishnikov 1990, p. 173. Unlike in other Soviet institutions, non-party members, including Mensheviks and SRs, continued to be represented and have voting rights at trade-union congresses.
289 TsA FSB, R33718, d. 499061, vol. 41, ll. 196–7, 199.
290 Lenin 1941–50, vol. 30, p. 438.
291 TsA FSB, R33718, d. 499061, vol. 41, l. 211; Allen 2015, p. 20. Ryazanov was known for his willingness to say what everyone else was afraid to say: Ulam 1965, p. 544.
292 TsA FSB, R33718, d. 499061, vol. 41, ll. 199, 204.

FIGURE 7 David Ryazanov
WIKIMEDIA COMMONS

applause from the floor.[293] He was eager to challenge the party's undemocratic measures and penchant for exerting pressure on the VTsSPS. Ryazanov criticised the congress's proposed resolution, namely its omission of the phrase 'normal methods of proletarian democracy', which had been included in the

---

293 Ryazanov had also earned a reputation as an eccentric crank with an 'ironic, stormy temperament': Serge 1963, p. 250; Beecher and Fomichev 2006, p. 125.

resolution adopted at the Tenth Party Congress just two months earlier.[294] Upon concluding his speech, Ryazanov sat down and hastily scribbled an amendment reinstating the missing phrase as well as inserting such statements as 'one of the reasons for the VTsSPS's inability to work is the abnormal relationship between central party institutions and the VTsSPS's caucus'. He argued the deficiencies of the trade unions were for the most part the party's fault. Ryazanov then read his amendment to the caucus 'with machine-gun speed', according to one of those in attendance.[295] While granting the party the right to a general supervision of the trade unions, the amended resolution demanded that most of the power in union affairs be left in the hands of the trade-union leadership and that union members should be allowed to democratically choose their own leaders, who should be responsive to their memberships' hopes and desires. The delegates voted overwhelmingly in favour of Ryazanov's amendment, with 1,500 voting in favour and only 30 opposed.[296]

Tomsky, who would claim he had been surprised by Ryazanov's amendment, did not object to it, presumably since it used language almost identical with the Tenth Party Congress's resolution on trade-union democracy, which he had helped to write. Tomsky also probably sympathised with it. In any case, he did not speak out against it. In his concluding comments to the caucus meeting, Tomsky ignored Ryazanov's amendment and instead focused on criticising Shlyapnikov who, as everyone expected, had attacked the VTsSPS and Tomsky's leadership in his speech to the caucus.[297]

After the divisive debates of the previous year, the Soviet leadership was determined to put the trade-union debate to rest once and for all and to crack down on all violations of party discipline. The passing of Ryazanov's amendment and his nomination to the VTsSPS Presidium particularly outraged Lenin. Ryazanov, who was thrilled at his apparent triumph, was startled that night to receive a phone call in his apartment from Lenin.[298] Sophia Brichkina, Lenin's secretary, had never seen Lenin so angry. She remembers Lenin's face was 'as dark as a storm cloud, with his eyes literarily like lightning bolts'.[299] Members of the party leadership, including Lenin on behalf of the Central Committee, called for the caucus to remove the offending language and adopt the original

---

294 RKP(b) 1953, p. 540. The theses were the product of a Central Committee commission of which Tomsky, Stalin, Zinoviev, Vyacheslav Molotov, and Vasily Mikhailov were members.
295 TsA FSB, R33718, d. 499061, vol. 41, ll. 201, 204, 209, 214; RKP(b) 1961, p. 262.
296 RKP(b) 1961, pp. 262–3.
297 TsA FSB, R33718, d. 499061, vol. 41, ll. 204, 209, 211.
298 Balabanoff 1964, p. 99.
299 Golikov (ed.) 1969, p. 407.

party resolution.³⁰⁰ Stalin crudely attacked Tomsky, Ryazanov, and others in the caucus, which provoked protests in the hall. When Ryazanov vociferously objected, a furious Stalin boorishly told him 'to shut up, you buffoon'.³⁰¹ When an equally furious Lenin took the floor to address the caucus on behalf of the Central Committee and to impose party discipline, some defiant delegates shouted, 'You promised to abolish the statification of the unions. You deceived us'.³⁰² To the shocked delegates, Lenin denounced Ryazanov's resolution as 'anti-party' and questioned whether Tomsky 'made a mistake or committed a crime'.

The Central Committee immediately set up a special commission to investigate Tomsky's management of the congress, in particular his failure to implement party directives, and yanked him from the congress. Following Tomsky's speech to the delegates officially opening the congress on the morning of 17 May, Shmidt took his place and Tomsky never reappeared at the congress, which shocked the delegates.³⁰³ The following day Tomsky was summoned to appear behind closed doors before the commission.³⁰⁴ The members of this commission – Stalin, Dzerzhinsky, Alexei Kiselev, and Mikhail Frunze, the commission's chair – grilled Tomsky on 19 May.³⁰⁵ The commission also questioned seven other members of the trade-union party caucus: Shlyapnikov, Ryazanov, Artem, Andreev, Shmidt, Kuibyshev, and Abram Ginzburg. Shlyapnikov severely criticised Tomsky's leadership of the VTsSPS, but it is doubtful that carried much weight given how the party leaders viewed the Workers' Opposition and Shlyapnikov's refusal to criticise Ryazanov's amendment.³⁰⁶ In any case, neither Shlyapnikov nor any of the others called in to testify thought that Tomsky had conspired against the party leadership.³⁰⁷ When given the chance to

---

300 Nosach 2005, p. 212. There is no record of Lenin's speech in the central party archives: Lenin 1960–70, vol. 42, p. 563n343.
301 Nosach 2005, pp. 118, 213; Rokitianskii 2009, p. 293. Stalin's treatment of delegates to the congress earned him the biting nickname of the 'trade union hussar' [*profgusar*].
302 *Sotsialisticheskii vestnik*, 19 June 1921, p. 12.
303 Nosach 2005, pp. 49–50, 118.
304 RGASPI, f. 46, op. 1, d. 3, ll. 8–9.
305 Frunze, although he lacked any military training, was a brilliant Red Army commander who along with Stalin supported Lenin on trade-union issues, while Dzerzhinsky, the head of the Cheka, had supported Trotsky's position. Kizelev was an especially curious choice for the Central Committee to place on the commission since this former worker had previously chaired the Miners' Union and had been a member of the Workers' Opposition: Allen 2015, p. 201.
306 TsA FSB, R33718, d. 499061, vol. 41, l. 201. Allen speculates that Shlyapnikov's criticism 'possibly played a role' in the commission's recommendation regarding Tomsky: Allen 2002, p. 89.
307 Allen 2015, p. 201.

talk, Tomsky defended himself and tried to get the commission to appreciate the extent of the opposition he faced within the congress's party caucus. He also tried to argue that he had been given no directive from the Central Committee since it was just a handwritten note from Zinoviev. Frunze fired back, 'But you had the definite opinion of the Central Committee. And in my opinion, it's the same as in the military, opinion is equal to directive. Ryazanov's candidacy was unacceptable and you informed no one of this'.[308]

The commission found Tomsky guilty of 'a blatant violation of party discipline and criminal negligence toward party interests, which requires the most severe party punishment', even though one of the four commission members, Dzerzhinsky, refused to sign the reprimand.[309] Tomsky, although he had not supported Ryazanov's resolution, by allowing the party caucus to express its independent views was held responsible for letting the caucus become 'disoriented'. The Central Committee, after a speech by Lenin, in which he angrily denounced Tomsky's 'anti-party conduct', ousted Tomsky from his position as head of the trade unions, demoted him to candidate membership in the VTsSPS Presidium, and prohibited him from any further participation in the trade-union congress.[310] The trade-union caucus was bound by party statutes to ratify the Central Committee's dismissal of Tomsky, although many delegates expressed their dismay at the news he had been removed and protested against it.[311] One of them declared, 'We think the Central Committee very well knows how dear comrade Tomsky is to us and how deeply we respect him'.[312] The caucus added to Tomsky's disgrace by publishing the commission's reprimand. Rudzutak, the general secretary of the VTsSPS was made to share some of the responsibility for Tomsky's mistake, but unlike Tomsky he was re-elected at the end of the congress as a full-member of the VTsSPS Presidium.[313] Ryazanov, for his part, was barred from ever engaging in trade-union work again, also over the objections of caucus members. The caucus actually voted to reinstate Ryazanov, by a vote of 945–500, but the Central Committee overrode that vote.[314] But rather than being sent off into exile in disgrace, which as we will see was Tomsky's fate, he remained in Moscow to become the first director of the

---

308   TsA FSB, R33718, d. 499061, vol. 41, l. 199.
309   TsA FSB, R33718, d. 499061, vol. 41, l. 216.
310   RGASPI, f. 593. op. 1, d. 2, l. 24; Nosach 2005, p. 119.
311   Deutscher 1950, p. 57.
312   Quoted in Chechevishnikov 1990, pp. 174–4.
313   VTsSPS 1921, pp. 18, 185.
314   Ryazanov would, however, continue to address trade-union issues at various party congresses and conferences during the 1920s.

Marx-Engels Institute.³¹⁵ Afterwards Ryazanov and Tomsky maintained their personal relationship, which proved to be a temporary lifesaver for Ryazanov later, as we will see.³¹⁶ Other trade-union leaders were also reprimanded and transferred to various posts.³¹⁷

When the trade-union congress finally began its regular deliberations two days later, no further mention was made of what had happened to Tomsky. Barbara Allen suggests Shlyapnikov was happy that Tomsky had been removed as chair of the VTsSPS, but perhaps also concerned that he had alienated delegates who believed that he had 'intrigued' against Tomsky.³¹⁸ The thesis 'On the Role and Tasks of the Trade Unions' was restored back to its original form and the intimidated caucus voted nearly unanimously to pass this resolution and repeal its own.³¹⁹ Andreev surprisingly succeeded Tomsky as chair of the VTsSPS after the congress. This was surprising because Andreev had supported Trotsky's platform at the Tenth Party Congress and as a result had not been re-elected to the Central Committee.

At the Tenth Party Conference, which opened on 26 May in the Sverdlov Hall in the Kremlin, just a day after the conclusion of the Fourth Trade-Union Congress, delegates demanded that a report on the trade-union congress be put on the agenda. Following a summary report by Molotov, a still furious Lenin demanded the right to speak. He went beyond just denouncing Tomsky for betraying the trust the party had placed in him. He again questioned whether this was 'a mistake or a crime'.³²⁰ Lenin, who was suffering from extreme fatigue and seemed to be a nervous wreck, apparently concluded it was a crime. He shocked the conference's delegates by demanding that Tomsky be expelled not just from the Central Committee, but from the party itself.³²¹ This was the first time the Tenth Party Congress's ban on factions had been invoked. But Lenin was defeated because 'only an insignificant majority' of the Central Commit-

---

315 Ryazanov was widely recognised as the party's foremost Marxist scholar. Six months after Ryazanov's appointment as director, the institute was placed under the jurisdiction of the Executive Committee of the All-Russian Congress of Soviets. This put Ryazanov outside the party's direct control and allowed him to hire non-Bolshevik Party translators and scholars: Beecher and Fomichev 2006, p. 127.
316 Beecher and Fomichev 2006, pp. 140–1; Daniels 1960, p. 379.
317 The Central Committee plenum also censured Artyom, Shlyapnikov, and Ivan Kutuzov for not criticising Ryazanov's resolution: Nosach 2005, p. 120.
318 Allen 2015, p. 203.
319 VTsSPS 1921, pp. 66–8, 70.
320 RGASPI, f. 46, op. 1, d. 2, l. 2.
321 RGASPI, f. 46, op.1, d. 3, l. 18. All the leading members of the Central Committee suffered from one serious ailment or another: Service 1995, p. 210.

tee supported treating Tomsky so harshly.[322] According to a secret part of the resolution 'On Party Unity', a member could be expelled from the Central Committee only if two-thirds of the Central Committee supported it.[323] For days afterward, Lenin remained in a rage about his failure to push through Tomsky's removal.[324]

The Politburo informed Tomsky he was to be removed from the VTsSPS and sent on a party mission to Central Asia. Although he remained a member of the Central Committee, one can only imagine what a shock this must have been to Tomsky when he received the news. Tomsky, who had played such a pivotal role since the Bolshevik seizure of power, particularly in trade-union affairs, and who had risen into the top circle of the party, found himself disgraced, with his political career seemingly permanently crippled. His failure to maintain the delicate, perhaps impossible, balancing act between fulfilling his role both as a top party leader and as head of the trade unions proved to be his undoing, if as it turned out, only temporarily.

In sum, as we have seen, the role of the trade unions in the new Soviet state preoccupied Bolshevik leaders during 1920 and into 1921. Tomsky sought to protect, within limits and with caution, workers' demands and wage claims. The unions under Tomsky were a powerful interest group in early Soviet Russia. In the words of Jay Sorenson, the trade unions 'were able to prevent the introduction of many measures they opposed and to force the adoption of those they considered important'.[325] But Tomsky's proclivity to compromise did not sit well with many Bolshevik leaders and trade unionists. He faced fierce criticism from both extremes of the Bolshevik political spectrum. On one side sat the hard line of Trotsky's push for 'shaking up' the trade unions in order to impose one-man management and create labour armies. On the other extreme sat Shlyapnikov, with his steadfast demand for complete worker control of the

---

322 Service 1995, pp. 206, 211.
323 The previously secret provision of this resolution (Point Seven) became public only with Stalin's report at the Thirteenth Party Conference in 1924: RKP(b) 1953, pp. 529–30. A couple months later, in August 1921, Shlyapnikov was brought before a party court for violating the ban on factions, but the Central Committee and the Central Control Commission here too voted to allow him to remain in the Central Committee: Allen 2015, pp. 216–18.
324 Service 1995, p. 211. Years later, in November 1928, Tomsky surprisingly said that Lenin had removed him from the trade-union leadership because he suspected Tomsky wanted to form a bloc with the Trotskyists Andreev, Goltsman, and Kosior. Tomsky said he simply wanted the best associates for the trade-union leadership able to combat the Workers' Opposition and that Andreev had recovered from his previous support of Trotsky: Chechevishnikov 1990, p. 175.
325 Sorenson 1969, p. 78.

economy. Tomsky occasionally succeeded at working out compromises with Lenin during the trade-union debate, including getting Lenin to switch sides to support his position against Trotsky's. But that too failed when Lenin and some Central Committee members turned on him with a vengeance in May 1921. Tomsky as a result was in political disgrace and was about to face completely different challenges in Central Asia.

As a final note for this chapter, you might be wondering what happened to Kanatchikov following the Bolshevik seizure of power. He worked in relative obscurity during the Civil War, including in various governmental and party posts in Siberia. But in 1919 he returned to Moscow for a few months. Posted to the 'cultural front', Kanatchikov helped to found Sverdlov Communist University in Moscow, one of the most prominent centres for the political education and training of party agitators. Required to give a series of lectures on the history of the Bolshevik Party, Kanatchikov struggled to get over his phobia about public speaking. In 1921 he assumed a prestigious position as rector of the Zinoviev Communist University in Petrograd, despite having only four years of elementary-school education. During the three years Kanatchikov held this position, he finished his autobiography.[326]

---

326   Zelnik 1995, pp. 6–7, 28; Kanatchikov 1986, p. 389; Slezkine 2017, p. 184; David-Fox 1997, pp. 1, 11. The lecture hall for the Communist University was located in the Merchants Club on the Boulevard Ring, which had been the main social and entertainment centre for prosperous Moscow merchants. It was named after Yakov Sverdlov, its initiator, who had died a premature death in March 1919. The university was housed in what became the Higher Party School just off Tvserskaya Ulitsia. Kanatchikov also played a key role in the nationalisation of private theatres: Fitzpatrick 1970, p. 143.

CHAPTER 3

Detour East: From Disgraced Exile in Tashkent to Redemption inside the Kremlin

> Rudzutak, Tomsky's friend, told me yesterday that if I am three-quarters colonialist, Tomsky is five-fourths.
> LENIN

∴

> Tomsky sometimes makes mistakes, but that is nothing; we all make mistakes.
> LENIN

∴

Tomsky's political disgrace in the spring of 1921 landed him in Central Asia. The Politburo, following the Fourth Trade-Union Congress in May, informed Tomsky that he was ordered to go to Central Asia on what the party leadership, and Lenin in particular, considered a critical mission of trying to stabilise Bolshevik power in the region while at the same time engendering support from the Indigenous population, or at least not alienating them.[1] It proved to be an extremely challenging assignment. As a moderate Bolshevik, he quickly found himself trying to rein in someone he considered to be one the party's most extreme and violent fanatics, Georgy Safarov, against the wishes of many in Moscow, including Lenin. Tomsky's handling of the situation in Turkestan, primarily his opposition to the forcible expulsion of peasant settlers from the region, would

---

1 Khordina (ed.) 2000, vol. 1, p. 104. Tomsky's assignment was perhaps on the recommendation of Mikhail Frunze, who as the commander of the Turkestani Red Army had spent much of 1920 battling the Basmachi movement, and had served on the Turkestan Commission that will be discussed below. That Tomsky's mission in exile was considered critical highlights both the regime's shortage of experienced, capable administrators and the difference with how the party leadership treated oppositionists later during the 1920s, when they were exiled to minor posts in even more remote locales.

ultimately be vindicated over Lenin's objections. Surprisingly, Tomsky's sudden, shocking fall from political grace would be matched by his equally sudden and even more shocking redemption. Seemingly against all odds, Tomsky was recalled to Moscow, and less than a year after his ouster as head of the unions, was far more powerful than ever before. In addition to resuming his position as head of the trade-unions, the Central Committee appointed Tomsky to the most powerful positions in the party: a full, voting member in both the Politburo and the Orgburo. As a result, Tomsky and his family entered the world of material privilege that top party officials increasingly enjoyed. Tomsky's time in Central Asia, though, remains largely a black hole in the literature. Typically, in Tomsky's authorised biographical entry in the *Granat Encyclopedia*, Peter Kashin skipped over this period in his life except for a single sentence, stating his assignment in Turkestan meant 'he temporarily left trade union work'.[2] But it was far more significant than that. His short time in Central Asia helped shape many of the moderate positions Tomsky adopted later during the 1920s.

While his time in Tashkent certainly was a form of banishment, Tomsky had been appointed to an important position: the new chair of the Turkestan Commission (*Turkkomissia*), which the Soviet regime created in October 1919 as the top governmental body in the region.[3] He worked alongside his good friend and fellow moderate trade unionist during the 'trade-union debate', Yan Rudzutak, who had served under Tomsky on the Presidium of the VTsSPS. Rudzutak had been named a few months earlier, in March 1921, to head the Turkestan Bureau (*Turkburo*), which was the top party body in the region.[4] The Latvian Rudzutak, like Tomsky, was a former worker from an impoverished background with little formal education but a passion for self-improvement.[5] Bukharin's wife, Anna Larina, described Rudzutak as having 'a kind, generous face, with his tired

---

[2] Tomsky's biographical entry was published in 1924 or 1925 and reprinted in 1989: Gambarov et al. (eds) 1989, part 3, p. 150.

[3] Its full title: *Kommissia VTsIK i SNK RSDRP po delam Turkestana*. The Turkestan Commission could not be established until then because contact between Moscow and Tashkent had been blocked by the Whites' control of the rail link between the two cities. It was directly accountable to the Sovnarkom (Council of People's Commissars) in Moscow. Tomsky replaced an ailing Grigory Sokolnikov: Gorelov 2000, p. 91.

[4] Rudzutak received the sixth highest number of votes to the Central Committee at the Tenth Party Congress: RKP(b) 1933a, p. 221. Rudzutak, the son of farm labourers, became a factory worker in Riga and a Bolshevik during the 1905 Revolution.

[5] Rudzutak taught himself French in prison: Fitzpatrick 2015, p. 97. He would have friends in artistic circles (what Molotov would describe as 'a Philistine crowd'), develop strong cultural interests, and become an enthusiastic nature photographer: Montefiore 2004, p. 223.

FIGURE 8 Yan Rudzutak
WIKIMEDIA COMMONS

expressive eyes peering through glasses'.[6] Both Tomsky and Rudzutak had reputations as hardworking, modest, and honest. Lenin thought the two were 'the most even-tempered of men'.[7]

Since Tomsky obviously knew little if anything about the Turko-Islamic world in Central Asia, he might seem a curious choice for this assignment. But he was typical of the type of politically experienced, but ignorant Soviet administrators Moscow often assigned during the first years of the Soviet regime to

6 Larina 1993, p. 173.
7 Lenin 1960–70, vol. 32, p. 75.

advance the centre's various positions in what it considered the Asian 'periphery'.[8] Tomsky initially leaned on Rudzutak, seven years his junior, in his effort to understand how to implement the centre's nationality policies, since Rudzutak was more knowledgeable and experienced on various regional issues, having previously served on the Turkestan Commission when it was created in 1919.[9] But neither of them could speak the Turkic dialects needed to communicate with Turkestanis, which is how Russian colonisers referred to the Indigenous peoples.[10] This might have made them feel somewhat helpless given the challenges Moscow assigned to them, even if the Indigenous population viewed them as colonial masters.

Why Lenin, given his hopes to win the hearts and minds of the Indigenous Muslim population for the Soviet regime, would send officials ignorant of Central Asian culture and customs but also, as in the case of Tomsky as we will see, apparently with little respect for them, might seem mysterious. But it can be explained by the fact that the party leadership during these early years failed to recruit many Indigenous officials whom they considered to be politically dependable, that is, did not take the Bolshevik promises of national self-determination overly seriously, to take the place of the waves of party functionaries Moscow would send to Turkestan, only to remove them before long for their 'chauvinistic' attitudes, as in the case of Tomsky. When Tomsky weighed in on the debates over the 'national question' at the Eighth Party Congress in March 1919, he reluctantly and cautiously defended the right of national self-determination, including separation from Soviet Russia, but only as a necessary evil.[11] Tomsky stated, 'I don't think there is a man in this room who would say that the self-determination of nations, or even a national movement, is something normal or desirable. We regard such things as an unavoidable evil'.[12] While Stalin and Bukharin agreed with Tomsky, Lenin sharply objected, arguing that all nations have the right to self-determination.[13] But as Erik van Ree has argued, while Lenin gave lip service to national self-determination, he

---

8 Massell 1974, pp. 43–4, 55; Kotkin 2014, pp. 375–6. Curiously, many of the tsarist government's governors, or the staff members of its ministries in Central Asia, had initially been exiled there before the revolution: Kivelson and Suny 2017, p. 167.
9 Kulikova and Khazanov 1988, p. 73.
10 Virtually none of the Russians could speak the various Turkic languages and, with few exceptions, the Turkestanis could not speak Russian: Kaganovich 1996, p. 237. Those few Muslims fluent in Russian were rarely pro-Soviet: Blank 1987, p. 61.
11 One of the Soviet regime's first decrees in November 1917 guaranteed national groups not only autonomy but also the right to secede.
12 RKP(b) 1933b, p. 82.
13 Kivelson and Suny 2017, p. 283.

actually favoured recreating the boundaries of the Russian Empire under centralised authority in Moscow.[14] Other historians, such as S.A. Smith, take Lenin's support for national self-determination more seriously, although even Smith concedes that it 'took second place to the practical exigencies of suppressing anti-Bolshevik movements'.[15]

Tomsky, who had risen from his hardscrabble roots in working-class St. Petersburg to the apex of the Soviet regime in Moscow, was understandably upset at his demotion and this assignment thousands of miles away and in a cultural world so different from the metropole. He fell into a funk but agreed, as a disciplined Bolshevik, to accept the assignment and travel to Tashkent. But since the distraught Tomsky was reported to be a 'physically worn-out person', the Politburo decided to delay his departure until it received his doctor's assurance that he would be able to make the trip.[16] When Tomsky finally left Moscow he had only a vague sense of his mission. Tomsky left without bothering to ask Lenin to specify exactly what he wanted him to do in Tashkent.[17] This may have been due to Lenin's unavailability. In June 1921 the Politburo, alarmed by Lenin's deteriorating health, particularly his debilitating headaches and insomnia, caused at least in part by the bullet lodged in the back of his neck from the shot fired at him in 1918, required Lenin to take a month vacation.[18] If Tomsky's journey there was like others at the time, what should have been a five-day train trip took more than three weeks.[19] In addition to the problems resulting from the White army's determination to destroy rail lines as they retreated, the fuel shortage could be so severe that sometimes locomotives had to stop so passengers could pull down fences and scavenge for other wood to feed the firebox![20] After the long and trying trip, Tomsky finally arrived on 7 July at the Turkestan Commission's headquarters, a small, nondescript house with a simple signboard over the door.[21] When Alexander Barmine, a Soviet diplomat met him at the headquarters a little later, he immediately recognised Tomsky

---

14   van Ree 2002, pp. 77, 82.
15   Smith 2017, pp. 195–6.
16   RGASPI, f. 593, op. 1, d. 2, l. 25; Lenin 1960–70, vol. 45, p. 161; Sahadeo 2007, p. 28.
17   RGASPI, f. 5, op., d. 1403, reprinted in Amanzholova and Gorelov (eds) 2000, p. 10.
18   Clark 1988, p. 463; Watson 2005, p. 47. Robert Service calls into serious question that Fanya Kaplan was the attempted assassin: Service 1995, pp. 31–3.
19   Lazar Kaganovich's long and arduous trip took 23 days while Alexander Barmine's took 24: Rees 2012, p. 33; Barmine 1945, p. 98.
20   Riddell (ed.) 1993, p. 20.
21   Barmine 1945, p. 99. Tashkent was a city where the local Bolshevik organisation had intensely participated in the debate over the role of trade unions. Although the Leninist Platform carried the day in Tashkent, many of the Russian railroad workers there had strongly supported the Workers' Opposition: Khazanov 1969, pp. 40–4; Kaganovich 1996,

from all his portraits in the press: the short man with a 'cropped head and a large nose, his upper lip marked with a faint mustache'.[22]

Tashkent was the economic, cultural, military, and political epicentre of Central Asia. It was described by Barmine as a city 'with broad, quiet streets, lined with gardens and made pleasant by the sound of irrigation streams and singing birds'.[23] The symmetrically arrayed boulevards had been beautifully lined with acacias, poplars, mulberries, and other trees, but they had all been cut down for fuel by the time Tomsky arrived.[24] Barmine, it should be said, was referring to the separate, Russian quarter of Tashkent. Like the French had done in North Africa, tsarist Russia had built this 'New City', known as the European quarter or the Russian section, as a European colonial outpost, which the governor-general thought should 'radiate European civilisation and Russian power'.[25] It was at the eastern edge of the pre-existing Muslim city, which to many Russians seemed so alien and foreign that 'it could have been Istanbul or Baghdad'.[26] The Slavs and Indigenous populations generally lived in completely different worlds. Typically, Tashkent's privileged minority of Russians had limited contact with the Muslim population outside the bazaars or shops, although for some members of the intelligentsia, the city's exotic, 'Eastern' character was enthralling, and they loved to explore the maze of steep and winding, narrow alleys of the 'Old City', known as Asian Tashkent. But they would not get much of a glimpse of the Indigenous population's world as the individual, one-story mud-brick homes, and the courtyards around them, were walled off from passers-by.[27] Tomsky apparently did not engage in such romanticisation of Tashkent. His arrival there did not improve his mood. Having had

---

pp. 244–8; Rees 2012, p. 36. When Tomsky went to work there, he wisely steered clear of again jumping into that debate.

22 Barmine, who had arrived early in the morning to avoid the heat of the day, had simply walked in past the drowsy porter. He surprised the half-dressed Tomsky and Rudzutak who had been asleep on mattresses and cushions on the floor in an otherwise bare room: Barmine 1945, p. 99.

23 Barmine 1945, p. 99; Amanzholova and Gorelov (eds) 2000, p. 3. Barmine prefaced that quote with the Orientalist statement that Tashkent combined 'occidental modernity with oriental languor'.

24 Bailey 1946, pp. 32–3.

25 Sahadeo 2007, p. 33; Stronski 2010, p. 19.

26 Comment by the writer Anna Akhmatova, who had been evacuated to Tashkent during World War II: Manley 2009, p. 149. The two cities were equal in area in 1910, but while 47,00 lived in the Russian enclave 188,500 lived crowded together in Asian Tashkent: Fraser 1987, p. 2.

27 Sahadeo 2007, p. 16; Manley 2009, pp. 161–4; Stronski 2010, p. 27. Much of that old city was destroyed in the 1966 earthquake, with the one-story houses replaced by Soviet-style apartment blocks on tree-lined, wide boulevards.

to leave his wife and sons behind in Moscow, and hating the extreme heat of Central Asia and fearing its tropical diseases, he found conditions in Tashkent to be generally 'vile' [*gnusnye*].[28]

It is beyond the scope of this chapter to examine all the dizzying and constantly changing assortment of institutions created by the Bolsheviks as well as by Muslims during the first years after the Bolshevik seizure of power, but background on some of the developments in early Soviet Turkestan is necessary before turning to Tomsky's role there. During the early years of the Soviet regime the Bolsheviks referred to all of Central Asia as Turkestan, like the tsarist authorities before them. Turkestan, from the Persian for the 'land of the Turks', occupied an area even larger than Texas, with a variety of cultures and languages.[29] It proved to be a trouble spot for the tsarist state, the Provisional Government, and Soviet authorities as they all tried to manage it from afar without much knowledge of conditions there. During World War I tsarist troops and local settlers had brutally crushed the mass unrest and violent revolt of 1916, which had been triggered by the autocracy's ill-conceived call to conscript from Turkestan, for the first time, hundreds of thousand Muslim men to serve in the manpower-strapped Imperial Army.[30] Violence continued under the Provisional Government in 1917, and as we will see, greatly escalated under the Soviets during the Civil War.[31]

The Tashkent Soviet of Workers' and Soldiers' Deputies, which consisted of mostly Russian Socialist Revolutionary railroad workers, garrison troops, and intellectuals, seized power after a few days of bloody fighting on 23 October 1917, without any involvement on either side of the political struggle by the Indigenous population.[32] The members of the Soviet, in which intellectuals

---

28   RGASPI, f. 5, op. 1, d. 1403, reprinted in Amanzholova and Gorelov (eds) 2000, p. 9. The temperatures during virtually Tomsky's entire time in Tashkent hovered around 46 degrees Celsius.

29   Turkestan was the name the tsarist government gave to the region in Central Asia it conquered from 1865–76. Today the vast region is divided into Kirghizstan, Uzbekistan, Kazakhstan, Tajikistan, and Turkmenistan.

30   Buttino 1993, p. 266. While some 10,000 Russians died, the number of Turkestanis killed in this racial war numbered in the hundreds of thousands: Sunderland 2014, p. 138. The Muslim conscripts were probably unaware that they would serve only in non-combatant positions. What heightened their outrage at being conscripted is that it came at the time when the cotton crop needed to be harvested: Fraser 1987, pp. 4, 13.

31   Brower 2003, pp. 1–2, 153, 157–62.

32   Park 1957, p. 12; Chokayev 1931, p. 406. Adeeb Khalid argues that while the fall of the tsarist regime was widely celebrated by the local Muslim population, its intellectual elite were far more interested in cultural rather than political change. The Indigenous intellectuals, the Jadids, sought to lift Central Asian society from what it perceived as its cultural isola-

outnumbered workers, soon proclaimed themselves to be Bolsheviks, although they lacked any links with the party in European Russia.[33] Like the Turkestan Committee created by the Provisional Government before it, the Tashkent Soviet excluded the leaders of the predominately Muslim population of the city, despite Lenin's promotion of non-Russian equality.[34] The Soviet passed a resolution that explicitly barred all native Turkestanis from serving in it or in other governmental posts, even though they constituted some 80 percent of Tashkent's population.[35] The members of the Soviet ostensibly adopted this racist resolution because they considered the Indigenous population insufficiently proletarian.[36] The Bolshevik Safarov thought it was inevitable that the Russian revolution in Turkistan should initially have a typically colonial character because the Turkestani working class was numerically small and did not have 'its own class programme or revolutionary tradition'.[37] Although some of the Indigenous population worked as unskilled labourers in the cotton processing plants or other enterprises, and at the railroad yard, employers in tsarist Russia closed skilled occupations to Central Asians.[38] But the critical issues in Turkestan, in any case, were about nationality, not class. In the words of Michael Rywkin, 'the espousal of "dictatorship of the proletariat" in a region

---

tion, which they believed led to the stultification and ignorance of their fellow Muslims: Khalid 1996, p. 276; Sahadeo 2007, p. 142.

[33] There had been neither a Bolshevik nor a Menshevik Party organisation in Turkestan prior to the February Revolution: Pianciola and Gaignebet 2008, p. 104; Park 1957, p. 124.

[34] Olcott 1997, p. 685.

[35] Safarov 1985, p. 109. Of Tashkent's total population of 234,000, Russians accounted for 47,500: Pierce 1960, p. 103. Turkestan as a whole had a population of approximately 12 million. The adopted resolution read: 'At the present moment one cannot allow the inclusion of Muslims into the organs of the higher regional revolutionary power, both because the attitude of the local population toward the Soviet of Soldiers', Workers', and Peasant Deputies is quite uncertain and because the native inhabitants are lacking any proletarian organisations that the [Bolshevik] faction could welcome into the organ of the higher regional government'. The Third Congress of Turkestan Soviets in November 1917, by a vote of 97 to 17, similarly decided to exclude Muslims from governmental positions because they lacked both a proletariat and 'political maturity': Safarov 1985, pp. 109–10; Blank 1987, p. 49; Park 1957, pp. 12–13.

[36] Safarov 1985, p. 109.

[37] Safarov 1985, p. 110.

[38] Park 1957, p. 9; Sahadeo 2007, pp. 188–9, 199. These railway skilled workers, many of whom were exiled to Turkestan for their participation in the oppositional underground, or chose to move there after being blacklisted in Russia, saw themselves as the leaders of their fellow Russians who were unskilled and 'uncultured', just like in Russia. They looked down upon them almost to the same extent as they looked down upon unskilled Indigenous workers: Sahadeo 2007, pp. 109, 123–4, 135.

where the proletariat was for all intents and purposes non-native became a justification' for Russian domination.³⁹ Russian skilled workers and soldiers would have lost their many privileges if the Tashkent Soviet allowed for majority rule.⁴⁰ Another reason for excluding the Indigenous population may have been the language barrier. In any case, clearly little effort had been made to propagandise the overwhelmingly illiterate Indigenous population, who indeed had little understanding of the Soviet agenda.⁴¹ The Tashkent Soviet, given the above, not surprisingly rejected calls by the Muslim population for national autonomy and the right of self-governance.⁴² Much of the Indigenous population saw the Bolshevik seizure of power, in the words of one historian, 'not so much as a revolution but as a restoration of the old colonial system'.⁴³

Soviet power in Tashkent, according to the Bolshevik Safarov, was mostly in the hands of 'adventurers, careerists, and plain criminal elements'.⁴⁴ The Soviet itself, even the Red Army Marshal Mikhail Frunze conceded, seemingly did 'everything possible to alienate the local population'.⁴⁵ The Soviet introduced anti-religious legislation, such as outlawing Koran schools and preventing Sharia (Islamic religious law) courts from making any decisions that conflicted with Soviet law.⁴⁶ One of the first acts of the Tashkent Soviet occurred on 13 December 1917 when troops were ordered to fire on crowds in Tashkent commemorating Mawlid (the celebration of Muhammad's birth) because the Soviet interpreted it as an anti-Soviet protest.⁴⁷ Violent house-to-house raids 'nationalising' urban residents' possessions became commonplace. The authorities also closed bazaars in favour of the quickly discredited state provision organs.⁴⁸ And if any Muslims dared to challenge the authority of the

---

39   Rywkin 1994, p. 89.
40   Steinberg 2017, p. 241; Sahadeo 2007, pp. 187–90.
41   In Syr-Darya in 1912, 95 percent of the Russian children received a primary education in Russian schools, while only two percent of Indigenous children did: Fraser 1987, p. 3. Most children of the Indigenous population, who received a primary education, received it in Muslim schools.
42   Lenin and Stalin, in contrast, assured the Turkestanis on 22 April 1918 that they supported autonomy. But they did so with the major caveat that only if it was on 'Soviet lines', that is, Moscow's line: Blank 1897, p. 54.
43   Buttino 1993, p. 257.
44   Safarov 1985, p. 110.
45   Quoted in Chamberlin 1935, p. 420.
46   In tsarist Russia the Muslim population in Turkestan had been able to use Islamic courts for personal law and for commercial disputes that didn't involve non-Muslims: Khalid 2015, p. 8.
47   Olcott 1997, p. 685.
48   Argenbright 2011, p. 443; Pianciola and Gaignebet 2008, p. 107; Sahadeo 2007, p. 224.

Tashkent Soviet, brutal repression followed. When some Muslim intellectuals petitioned the Tashkent Soviet to grant the mud-walled ancient Islamic city of Kokand its autonomy, the Tashkent Soviet, with Stalin's approval as head of the Commissariat for Nationality Affairs (Narkomnats), instead mobilised local garrison troops, armed Slavic railroad workers, and attacked the city in February 1918. They indiscriminately massacred more than 14,000 of the city's Muslim residents, looted all the stores, and seized the large grain stocks in the region.[49] The shelling of Kokand helped provoke armed Muslim resistance throughout the region.[50] The Tashkent Soviet, even if it wanted to do so, generally lacked the power to implement policies that might have won over at least some of the local population, such as Lenin's 8 November 1917 land decree calling for the nationalisation of all lands not directly worked by their owners and their redistribution to the poor.[51] As the leader of the Kazakh national party, Ahmed Baytursunoglu, put it, the Indigenous population knew nothing about the Soviet regime other than that it was 'accompanied by violence, pillage, the abuse of power, and a new dictatorship'.[52]

Most horrifically, somewhere between one-fifth to as much as one-third of the population died from either starvation or the accompanying epidemics of typhus, typhoid, and cholera during the 1917–20 famine in Turkestan.[53] In addition, 90 percent of the region's livestock perished.[54] The famine resulted primarily from the drought, the turmoil of the fighting during the 1916 revolt, which cut grain harvests in half, and from the Civil War, which prevented grain from arriving from European Russia.[55] The anti-Bolshevik Ottoman Cossacks under Ataman Alexander Dutov, had severed all rail links to Turkestan, which

---

49   Kotkin 2014, pp. 253–5; Park 1957, pp. 20–1; Omerkhan 1960, p. 10; Sahadeo 2007, pp. 202–3, 210. Some historians put the number massacred as high as 50,000: Broxup 1983, p. 59. The chair of the Tashkent Soviet, F. Kolesov, personally led the attack: Blank 1987, p. 50. Stalin was Commissar of Nationalities from 1918 until the position was dissolved in 1923 following the formation of the USSR.
50   Safarov 1985, p. 125; Keller 1992, p. 30.
51   Pianciola and Sartori 2007, p. 480. But even these land redistributions of rented land usually only benefitted the Russians: Buttino 1993, p. 269. It is also not clear that the Indigenous population would have supported this policy of the Tashkent Soviet even it could have been implemented. Colonisers notoriously saw grazing land, which the Indigenous population was much more likely to value, as not directly worked.
52   Quoted in Buttino 1993, p. 259n4.
53   Marshall, 2003, p. 7; Olcott 1981, p. 352; Khalid 2015, p. 109; Bennigsen and Lemercier-Quelquejay 1967, p. 146: Buttino 1990, p. 62.
54   Buttino 1993, p. 276.
55   Cameron 2018, p. 42.

isolated the region from European Russia until late in 1919.[56] Imported grain had long been vital to Turkestan since much of the cultivated land was increasingly devoted to cotton.[57] But the famine also resulted from the ceaseless grain requisitioning by armed detachments of the local revolutionary authorities and from simple plundering by rampaging Russian 'revolutionary soldiers', coupled with the local peasants' decision in response to the 'requisitioning' to curtail the amount of land they cultivated. In addition, the Tashkent government thought it was a much higher priority to divert any available resources to supporting the Red Army at the front rather than to expend them on mitigating the famine.[58] Members of the Indigenous population accounted for almost all of those who died.[59] Given all this, it is no surprise that the Turkestanis hated the Soviet regime. Soviet control of Turkestan did not extend beyond the city of Tashkent, and there only to the European part of the city.[60] Soviet authorities in the centre were limited to trying to apply pressure on the Tashkent Soviet, often to little effect. In the words of one historian, Marie Broxup, the Tashkent Soviet often 'sneered at directives from Moscow or Petrograd'.[61]

Lenin viewed the tensions between the nationalist aspirations of the Turkestanis and the arrogance of the Russian Bolsheviks in Tashkent with increasing concern.[62] The Basmachi, some twenty thousand well-equipped, anti-Soviet Muslim guerrillas, who were able to hide out throughout the region and draw supplies from Afghanistan, Persia, and India, controlled much of Turkestan at the end of 1919.[63] Lenin worried that the Tashkent Bolsheviks were

---

[56]   The Samara-Orenburg-Tashkent railroad line had been a primary focal point of fighting from the very beginning of the Civil War: Safarov 1985, p. 122. Dutov was a native Turkestani.

[57]   By then, one-fifth of Turkestan's arable land was devoted to cotton plants, robbing the region of its former agricultural self-sufficiency: Brower 2003, pp. 77–8. The tsarist government's price-fixing during the war contributed to destroying the viability of many small cotton farms.

[58]   Park 1957, p. 39.

[59]   Buttino 2014, p. 114.

[60]   Safarov 1985, p. 124.

[61]   Broxup 1992, p. 41. From the Czechoslovak offensive in the spring of 1918, until Admiral Alexander Kolchak's defeat in early 1920, except for one short break in the winter of 1918–19, the Soviet regime in Turkestan operated free of any oversight from Moscow.

[62]   Sahadeo 2007, p. 209.

[63]   Smele 2015, pp. 233–5; Sahadeo 2007, p. 214. It was the Soviets who dubbed them Basmachi ('Raiders'). They called themselves the Beklar Hareketi (Freeman's Movement): Rees 2012, p. 33. The Basmachi would fight at dawn or at night, but become invisible during the day as they melted away, easily blending in with the local residents: Broxup 1983, p. 63.

undermining Moscow's hopes for an Asian revolution.[64] Lenin anxiously wrote to the Turkestan Commission, 'It is no exaggeration to say that the establishment of proper relations with the peoples of Turkestan is now of immense, world-historical importance for the Soviet regime'.[65]

The body that Tomsky was to head, the Turkestan Commission, was directed to work to abolish discrimination against the Indigenous population, overcome their mistrust, and recruit them into governmental work.[66] But, not unlike the Tashkent Soviet in 1917, the Central Committee in Moscow seemingly disregarded completely any pleas by Lenin and Stalin to include Muslims on the Turkestan Commission, with the exception of Frunze, the only commission member originally from Turkestan and able to speak Kazakh.[67] In addition to Frunze, other initial members of the Turkestan Commission were Shalva Eliava, its chair, Valerian Kuibyshev, who along with Frunze was mostly concerned with military affairs, Rudzutak, who focused on economic matters, Filipp Goloshchekin, who focused on party affairs, and Gleb Boky, a Chekist who worked for Narkomnats.[68] They were all prominent Bolsheviks. The Georgian Boky was truly notorious for how, as the Cheka's plenipotentiary representative to Turkestan from September 1919 (when Frunze broke Dutov's blockade) to August 1920, he terrorised Tashkent and thoroughly outraged local sensibilities. Before long Safarov, Lazar Kaganovich, and Yakov Peters, another Chekist who had helped brutally suppress the Basmachi, were added to the Turkestan Commission while Frunze, Kuibyshev, and Boky were withdrawn.[69] Although the members of the commission all lacked any prior experience in Central Asia, they were supplemented with a staff of activists and propagandists with literature in the local languages.

Instead of including Muslims on the Turkestan Commission, in June 1920 the Chekist Peters oversaw the purging of some members of the party's 'Muslim National Section' on charges of conspiring to seize power and to replace com-

---

64   Zenkovsky 1960, p. 241.
65   Lenin 1941–50, vol. 30, p. 117.
66   Pipes 1974, p. 181; Carr 1950, pp. 339–40. Once the Turkestan Commission was created it superseded the Tashkent Soviet as well as Narkomnats in Turkestan: Park 1957, pp. 114–15, 120: Sahadeo 2007, p. 216.
67   Marshall 2003, p. 9. Frunze, the son of a Russified Rumano-Moldavian father and a Russian mother, was born in the Central Asian city of Pishpek (later renamed Frunze) in Semirech'e, where he went to the town school. Frunze then attended the gymnasium in Verny (now Almaty), where he entered a radical circle before entering the Polytechnical Institute in St. Petersburg.
68   Rywkin 1990, p. 27.
69   Leggett 1981, p. 225; Plekhanov and Plekhanov 2011, p. 56; Agabekov 1931, p. 264.

munism with pan-Islamism.⁷⁰ As a result of all these actions, the Turkestan Commission did little to improve relations with the Indigenous population. According to Eliava, a Georgian whom Lenin appointed the first head of the commission despite his lack of any previous familiarity with Central Asia, and the fact that he was only a recent convert from Menshevism to Bolshevism, the Soviet government was 'seen as worse than the former Nicholas's government by the Muslim masses'.⁷¹ Frunze remarked that in 1920 the local Russian party members still held blatantly colonial attitudes.⁷²

When Tomsky arrived several Turkestanis had finally been added to the Turkestan Commission. Turar Ryskulov, Iu. Ibragimov, Nazir Turakulov, Abdul Rahkimbaev, S. Khojanov, and Kaigisiz Atabaev joined the Turkestan Commission in early 1920.⁷³ Frunze was impressed by the 'intelligence and enormous energy' of the Kazakh Ryskulov, who was sent in August 1920 to Moscow to work for Narkomnats, where he became its Deputy Commissar.⁷⁴ But generally, the character and reputations of the Muslims the Turkestan Commission succeeded in recruiting into the party were such that they had little sway over the Indigenous population. Those with sway were often not recruited because it was suspected they held pan-Turkic views.

At the same time, accusations of 'great Russian chauvinism' led to the dismissal of soviet and party officials in the borderlands.⁷⁵ It is a charge Lenin liked to hurl about. In his words, 'Come across any Communist and you'll discover a Great Russian chauvinist'!⁷⁶ The historian Botakoz Kassymbekova provocatively suggests the Bolsheviks used the term chauvinism as opposed to colonialism to convey that 'it was an attitude, not a system'. In other words, they claimed that since chauvinism was an anti-Soviet deviation by individuals that could

---

70 Sahadeo 2007, pp. 217–18. Frunze sent multiple warnings to Lenin expressing his fear that the Muslims sought full independence from Moscow: d'Ecausse 2009, pp. 162–3. Stalin labelled pan-Islamism a deviation from communism towards 'bourgeois-democratic nationalism': Stalin 1935, p. 978.
71 Khalid 2015, p. 113.
72 Eudin and North 1957a, p. 49.
73 Keller 2003, p. 283.
74 Pianciola and Gaignebet 2008, pp. 108, 112; Smele 2015, p. 353n42. Ryskulov, the descendant of a Kazakh aristocratic family was appointed to Narkomnats even though he supported a pan-Turkic resolution of the national question. That was in opposition to those who favoured dividing Turkestan into ethnically based territorial states, which was the policy the Soviet government ultimately adopted in 1924: Smith 2017, pp. 194–5.
75 Park 1957, pp. 163–4.
76 Quoted in Service 1995, p. 78. Lenin would accuse Stalin, the Commissar of Nationalities, of 'great Russian chauvinism' for his treatment of Georgia in 1921: Warth 1977, p. 124.

be eliminated, it was not the same as ingrained, systemic colonialism.[77] Before Tomsky's arrival, the Turkestan Commission had purged nearly two thousand Russian members of the Communist Party in Turkestan.[78] Jeff Sahadeo notes, however, that many may have been guilty of abusing power or corruption rather than Russian chauvinism.[79]

The Tashkent government changed its attitudes with Tomsky's arrival, to some extent at least. Tomsky, who had been among the first to call for ending War Communism, with Lenin's encouragement called for the implementation of the recently announced policies of the New Economic Policy (NEP), namely replacing grain and cotton requisitioning with the fixed tax in kind and lifting all restrictions against small-scale private businesses and trading, which allowed the bazaars to reopen and businesses of various types and small industry to quickly flourish.[80] By August 1921, the Turkestan Commission had succeeded in ending all requisitioning in Turkestan.[81] But Tomsky argued that although these economic policies enjoyed some success in reviving the economy, they did not address other important discontents of the Turkestanis, who viewed the Soviet regime as a direct threat to Islam and their way of life, which of course it was.[82] Tomsky, again with Lenin's encouragement, insisted that the temporary concessions to religious freedom toward Muslims that had been adopted in January 1920 needed to be fully implemented.[83] Adat (customary) and Shari'ah (religious) law needed to be restored if the Muslim population was to be truly placated.[84] The Soviet government allowed mosques and

---

77   Kassymbekova 2016, p. 127.
78   Khalid 2015, pp. 115–16.
79   Sahedo, 2007, p. 216.
80   Park 1957, p. 167; Sorenson 1969, p. 97; Lorenz 1994, p. 297. Peasants were taxed based on the amount of land and livestock they had. The tax was progressive. It required the wealthier peasants to pay at a higher rate. It became a monetary tax with the stabilisation of the ruble in 1924.
81   Gorelov 2000, p. 13.
82   Olcott 1981, p. 357.
83   Lenin called for treating the Muslim's religious beliefs with sensitivity at the Eighth Party Congress in March 1919: Lenin 1941–50, vol. 29, pp. 150–1. While Turkestanis were ethnically and linguistically diverse, they were all Muslims.
84   The full power of the Shari'ah courts was indeed restored on 6 October 1921. This was near the end of Tomsky's tenure in Tashkent. Some initial concessions allowing Muslim judges to decide cases according to Islamic law occurred in December 1919, prior to Tomsky arrival: Sartori 2010, pp. 408, 415. This relatively tolerant attitude toward Islam stands in stark contrast to the merciless manner in which the Soviet regime treated the Orthodox Church at this time. From the beginning, party leaders in Moscow considered Islam of relatively minor concern compared to the Russian Orthodox Church, which had been a major pillar of the tsarist regime: Braker 1994, pp. 163–4; Crews 2006, p. 366. The regime

Muslim schools to reopen, which were taken out of Soviet control, and returned any previously confiscated waqf lands.[85] These measures were of course welcomed and had their desired result of weakening temporarily the appeal of the Basmachi network of anti-Communist guerrillas.[86] Some mullahs, the so-called red mullahs, even publicly supported or cooperated with the Soviet regime.[87]

However enlightened Tomsky may appear to be on the need to show some respect, if only for pragmatic reasons, to aspects of the Islamic way of life, it should be stressed that he shared the unquestioned, patronising views of virtually all Bolsheviks on the perceived ignorance and 'cultural backwardness' [*kul'turno-otstalost'*] of the Muslim masses and the Bolsheviks' 'civilising mission' there.[88] This was particularly true regarding gender roles and family relations. Tomsky was appalled that even the tiny minority of Muslims who had joined the Communist Party in Tashkent still had multiple wives and were not, in his words, 'brave enough to have them unveiled'.[89] For Bolsheviks the veils symbolised everything that was awful about Muslim women's lives.[90] Tomsky does not seem to have appreciated the dangers faced by women who unveiled. In addition to verbal attacks, they were commonly insulted and denounced as prostitutes. Some were raped, assaulted, and murdered.[91] Yet some strides toward altering the position of women in Central Asian society, at least on the books, had been made by Soviet authorities. In addition to the new

---

would back away from persecuting Christians during the 1920s. As Tomsky stated in 1928, 'If we dismissed all believers from our ranks, who would be left in the unions? The core of our unions would not be much larger than that of the party': quoted in Siegelbaum 1992, p. 163.

85   Olcott 1981, p. 357; Pipes 1974, p. 183. There were about 400 mosques in Tashkent: Crews 2006, p. 252. Waqfs were Islamic charitable endowments.
86   d'Ecausse 2009, p. 180; Lorenz 1994, p. 297.
87   Park 1957, pp. 214–15; Keller 1992, p. 43. For the Soviet leadership's ambiguous feelings about such 'red mullahs': Massell 1974, pp. 69–70.
88   Stalin, despite his position as the head of Narkomnats, like Tomsky viewed Central Asian Muslims as a 'culturally backward people' needing to be emancipated by the Soviet regime: Khalid 2001, p. 153. Party officials commonly referred to Central Asian societies as feudal-patriarchal, stagnant, primitive, semi-barbarous, or half-savage. Most Bolsheviks also commonly viewed the Slavic peasantry in similar ways. Muslims, like peasants, could successfully use their supposed 'backwardness' as a tactic to evade responsibility for implementing the Soviet project: Kassymbekova 2016, p. 2.
89   RGASPI, f. 122, op. 1, d. 264, l. 57, reprinted in Amanzholova and Gorelov (eds) 2000, p. 9.
90   Keller 2001, pp. 64–5. In Turkestan, the veil was a black robe (*paranji*) that covered a woman's body from head to toe, accompanied by a smaller face veil made of horsehair called a *chachvon*.
91   Northrop 2004, pp. 134, 235–6, 261; Kamp 2006, p. 144.

FIGURE 9   Negotiations with Basmachi
            WIKIMEDIA COMMONS

family laws adopted in Moscow by VTsIK (Central Executive Committee of the Soviet) in October 1918, such as making women the legal equal of men and recognising divorce at the request of either spouse. In June 1921, just before Tomsky's arrival, the Turkestan Executive Committee outlawed bride purchase [*kalym*] and raised the minimum age of marriage for females to 16 from the nine years of age nominally allowed by the Islamic religious code.[92] But Tomsky discouraged Lenin from entertaining any illusions that Alexandra Kollontai and her Slavic cohorts in Zhenotdel (Women's Department of the party) would succeed in liberating Eastern women, whose 'black veil cut them off from the rest of the world'.[93] And he no doubt recognised that the attack on

---

92   Massell 1974, p. 112; Goldman 1993, pp. 48–57. Girls had generally married between the ages of 12 and 16: Edgar 2004, p. 247.
93   RGASPI, f. 122, op. 1, d. 264, l. 57, reprinted in Amanzholova and Gorelov (eds) 2000, p. 9. One of the initial decisions of the Turkestan Commission had been to create a branch of Zhenotdel, which viewed Central Asian women as the worst victims of patriarchal oppression. Kollontai, the head of Zhenotdel, had brought some Turkestani women to Moscow for congresses, where to applause they would theatrically throw off their veils. But in their

traditional marriage customs angered Indigenous men, including their 'class allies', the poor rural dwellers whom the Soviets were trying to rally to their side.[94]

Tomsky shared other ethnic stereotypes and Russian racist prejudices against the native population. Most notably, he believed they all lacked a strong work ethic. This blatant example of bigotry can be found in a letter to Lenin, in which Tomsky wrote, 'Don't forget to replenish the Turkestan Commission, only not with Muslims. They are not hard working [*nerabotosposobny*]'.[95] Such attitudes remained common among Soviet bureaucrats in the decades to come. But Tomsky's reluctance to hire Muslims, in addition to his cultural prejudices, arguably owed more to their lack of education than their work ethic.[96] Some 80 percent of the Indigenous party members were still illiterate.[97]

Tomsky as head of the Turkestan Commission attended to a variety of other issues, such as helping members of the local intelligentsia. The renowned author Maksim Gorky, who often wrote to top party leaders to fight for members of the old intelligentsia during the Civil War, including those persecuted by the Cheka, sent a letter to Tomsky pleading with his old comrade to help a number of world-renowned scientists and scholars in Tashkent.[98] Gorky described their situation as utterly desperate. Devastated by severe food shortages, many of these starving scientists, Gorky argued, were on the verge of death.[99] Tomsky responded by ensuring that their rations would be raised. The weakening of Basmachi fighting near Tashkent, and the ending of grain requisitioning, had begun to improve food supplies in the city.[100]

---

early years, Zhenotdel reached only a small number of Muslim women, who were mostly troubled women, either because they had been disowned by their husbands, were suffering in abusive marriages, or were simply horribly poor: Khalid 2015, pp. 161–2, 204–5; Stites 1978, p. 333. Many of the women who cast off their veils in Moscow resumed wearing them when they returned to Central Asia: Kamp 2006, p. 141. However, a 'divorce wave' would occur in some Central Asian districts by mid-1926: Shelley 1982, p. 282.

94 Edgar 2004, pp. 11, 222.
95 RGASPI, f. 5, op. 1, d. 1403, l. 4, reprinted in Amanzholova and Gorelov (eds) 2000, p. 14.
96 Edgar 2004, pp. 78–9.
97 Keller 1992, p. 37. Central Asians, for their part, shared a stereotype of the poor Russians as lazy and drunken: Sahadeo 2007, pp. 73, 78.
98 These intellectuals presumably had been active in Tashkent's branches of the Imperial Russian Geographic Society and the Imperial Society of Lovers of Natural Sciences, Anthropology, and Ethnography: Sahadeo 2007, pp. 63, 67; Fitzpatrick 2015, p. 107. During these years pleas for help besieged Gorky, who it was commonly believed had a unique ability to provide assistance. His international stature stopped the regime from taking action against him.
99 The world-famous ornithologist Nikolai Zarudny had died in March 1919: Bailey 1946, p. 62.
100 Sahadeo 2007, p. 224.

Tomsky, in his capacity as head of the Turkestan Commission, also became directly involved in military affairs in the region. On 4 July he was appointed to the Turkfront Revolutionary Military Council and, in this capacity, devoted a good part of his daily work to it and frequently visited the Red Army's headquarters.[101] He once narrowly escaped with his life when a dagger-wielding Basmachi surprised a dozing Tomsky and attacked his carriage.[102] Although Tomsky had no military experience, he had to sign off on all the Red Army commander Vladimir Lazarevich's major operations against the Basmachi.[103] Tomsky also worked to meet Lazarevich's requests to provide the army with food provisions and fuel. On an almost weekly basis, from August through the middle of September, he sent resources to various forces in the region, some of whom were malnourished and suffered from other illnesses.[104] The Soviets, despite committing 120,000–160,000 forces to the effort and the Basmachi's lack of coordination and inability to muster more than 20,000 forces, fiercely struggled with these guerrilla forces until the end of the summer of 1922, before the fighting slowly subsided.[105] The political liberalism of the Turkestan Commission when Tomsky headed it was matched by absolute ruthlessness in military affairs.[106]

Lenin, faced with millions of people afflicted by mass starvation in European Russia, quickly undercut Tomsky's focus on implementing NEP by ordering him, just weeks after his arrival, to find ways to procure food from Turkestan to

---

101 Gorelov 2000, p. 93. Gorelov's book, from pages 90 to 96, consists of an interview with the military historian Andrei Bondarenko.
102 Tomsky's sheepdog saved him by going for the neck of the attacker: Gorelov 2000, p. 280. The Basmachi gained new momentum in November 1921 under the leadership of the colourful, but unsavoury Turk Enver Pasha, who Lenin had sent to help make peace with the Basmachi, but who instead double-crossed Lenin and defected to the other side.
103 This was probably pretty pro forma since the Soviet government had little reason to question Lazarevich's loyalty. He had voluntarily joined the Red Army in 1918 and had already commanded several military units during the Civil War before becoming the commander of the Turkestan Front in February 1921. During the Great Purges, Lazarevich was arrested and executed in 1938.
104 According to a report of the Fergana commander, vegetables were non-existent and meat only rarely available. Clothing was no better. The troops lacked greatcoats or winter uniforms and only 25 percent of them had tolerable boots. They also went unpaid: Fraser 1987, p. 40. On 24 September Tomsky rewarded the Thirty-Second Turkestan Rife Regiment with leave and 1,500 silver rubles for their success taking out a major Basmachi leader: Gorelov 2000, pp. 93–5.
105 Pipes 1974, pp. 256–60; Park 1957, pp. 51–4. The defeat of the White Army under General Dutov in early 1920 released a large part of the Red Army for service in Turkestan. The Basmachi resistance flared up again in the early 1930s in opposition to collectivisation.
106 Broxup 1983, p. 65.

send to the emerging famine in the Volga region, southern Ukraine, the Crimea, and the north Caucasus.[107] Lenin instructed Tomsky to obtain 250,000 puds of grain and to purchase mutton from sheep breeders.[108] Tomsky responded in a letter to Lenin dated 23 July that he would quickly carry out this mission after receiving sufficient funds from the Commissariat of Finance (Narkomfin). After Tomsky travelled to Bukhara, he wrote 'I think it is possible that another 500 wagonloads of grain can be squeezed out of Bukhara, even if I have to pay it another visit … If they give me half a million puds of grain for each visit, I'll make a habit of going there even if the Bukharan banquets destroy my stomach'.[109] Beginning on 29 July wagonloads of grain were being shipped out of Turkestan to the famine-afflicted areas.[110] Impressed by Tomsky's achievement and his assessment that he could possibly obtain four million sheep from Afghanistan and five million from China, Lenin wrote on 7 August that Moscow 'must have those nine million sheep. They must be obtained at all costs'![111] To achieve these goals, Tomsky developed diplomatic contacts with the governments in Afghanistan and China.[112]

---

107 Russia's total agricultural output had declined to 43 percent of the pre-war level: Nove 1992, p. 81. Lenin felt compelled to address the catastrophic situation by purchasing food from abroad in May and June 1921: Pipes 1994, p. 415. Ultimately some five million people lost their lives in the 1921–22 famine. Millions more would have lost their lives if Lenin had not relented and allowed American relief workers to provide aid on a massive scale: Patenaude 2002.

108 Amanzholova and Gorelov (eds) 2000, pp. 3–4. One pud equals about 36 pounds.

109 RGASPI, f. 5, op. 1, d. 1403, reprinted in Amanzholova and Gorelov (eds) 2000, p. 8. Uzbek dishes are not particularly spicy, but at dinner parties the copious and rich food combined with alcohol caused many guests to develop stomach problems. Tomsky's nine years in prison and Siberian exile had caused him to suffer from serious stomach ailments.

110 By September 600,000 puds of grain had been shipped: Khazanov 1969, p. 76. These forays to acquire grain did not endear Tomsky to local Bukhara party officials. In another letter to Lenin in mid-September, Tomsky complained, 'As before, [Bukhara leaders] continue to sabotage us over grain and to beg for money and so forth. The more one finds out about the political lines of the various "communist" groups here, the worse it gets. They try to outdo each other in their Russophobia. They make very good use of their own position and godlessly swindle us both politically and economically': RGASPI, f. 5, op. 1, d. 1403, l. 4, reprinted in Amanzholova and Gorelov (eds) 2000, p. 11.

111 RGASPI, f. 5, op. 1, d. 1403, reprinted in Amanzholova and Gorelov (eds) 2000, p. 9; Lenin 1958–65, vol. 53, p. 104. Taking advantage of the resources of areas such as Turkestan was very much on the minds of Soviet leaders besides Lenin. Frunze, as his troops overcame White resistance, triumphantly announced that the road to the cotton of Turkestan was now open: Park 1957, p. 261. Turkestan had previously accounted for 80 percent of the cotton raised in the Russian Empire.

112 Gorelov 2000, p. 94. Yakov Surits, the Commissar of Foreign Affairs for Turkestan and Cent-

Tomsky also focused on improving cotton production, 90 percent of which was carried out by small Indigenous farm plots of five to eleven acres.[113] He considered increasing the number of cotton farmer cooperatives as key to improving production. Tomsky's efforts to increase the number of cooperatives bore fruit. By the end of 1921, there were 60 cotton cooperatives with 105,000 Tajik peasant members.[114] The Soviet government also provided subsidies to cotton growers through the cooperatives.[115] The Turkestan Commission in addition provided poor, Indigenous cotton growers with easier access to credit from government sources. As one historian noted, 'because of the long period between one year's harvest and the following year's planting, the small cotton grower, operating on the narrowest of margins, could hardly survive without access to credit. Even the prosperous farmers required it'.[116] The Turkestan Commission also lowered taxes on these poor peasants. Tomsky in addition allocated large sums to restore the destroyed and damaged irrigation works. During 1921 five billion rubles of state funds were spent on the revival of ancient canal networks. In arid Turkestan, given the lack of rainfall and high rates of evaporation, land is unsuitable for cultivation without irrigation channels.[117] The Turkestan Commission required the Turkestani population to help in reconstructing the irrigation channels by providing building materials and labour so water could arrive in ditches from where it could flow or be physically carried to nearby fields.[118] Together with the Turkestan Commissar of Agriculture, Sanjar Asfendyarov, and the Head of the Turkestan Water Department, Erasmus Kadomtsev, Tomsky travelled around the region to oversee land and water reform in Semirech'e, Syr-Darya, and Fergana, and to organise local water management committees. As a result, the agricultural area able to be irrigated increased by nearly 300,000 acres in 1921.[119] Although this represented only about half of

ral Asia, was a member of the Turkestan Commission and helped Tomsky in these efforts. Shortly before Tomsky's arrival, Surits had signed a Soviet-Afghan 'treaty of friendship', which was a non-aggression pact. The Soviet Union was the first country to recognise Afghanistan's independence following the Third Anglo-Afghan War in 1919.

113 Peterson 2019, p. 139. Russian peasant settlers shunned cotton growing to focus on growing wheat instead: Park 1957, pp. 290–2.
114 Gorelov 2000, p. 92.
115 Park 1957, p. 314.
116 Park 1957, p. 313.
117 Peterson 2019, p. 8.
118 Peterson 2019, p. 233; Teichman 2018, p. 101. Later Soviet efforts to modernise what became the region's increasingly cotton monoculture led to ecological disaster, which is best captured by the shrinking of the Aral Sea.
119 Gorelov 2000, p. 92. Severe floods in the spring of 1921 had increased the challenges by washing out the control mechanisms on a number of restored irrigation systems: Peterson 2018, p. 226.

the previously irrigated land, Tomsky's efforts helped to reverse the downward course of cotton production in Turkestan and created favourable conditions for its revival.

But most consequentially for his time in Turkestan, Tomsky began to clash with Safarov almost immediately after his arrival. This extremely energetic, half Armenian-half Polish Old Bolshevik had served for several months as the political commissar of the *Krasnyi Vostok* (Red East) agitational train, which is how he arrived in Turkestan in November 1919.[120] Dismayed by the Europeans' domination over the Indigenous population, and with a charge from Lenin 'to establish comradely relations with the peoples of Turkestan' and 'to eradicate all traces of Great Russian imperialism', Safarov quickly became the primary Soviet advocate for the Muslim population in Tashkent.[121] But with Tomsky's arrival, he now had to serve under him on the Turkestan Commission.[122]

It was tricky for Tomsky to enter into conflict with Safarov since he was such a long-time friend and close collaborator with Lenin, who clearly held him in high esteem. While both Safarov and Tomsky had worked with Lenin before the revolution, Safarov had a much closer personal relationship. Safarov and his wife Valentina had socialised with Lenin and his wife Nadezhda Krupskaya at various times in Western Europe while Tomsky was stuck in Siberian exile.[123] At the recent Tenth Party Congress Lenin had entrusted Safarov with presenting a co-report to Stalin's on the nationality question, in which he condemned the continuance of colonial relations between Russians and the Indigenous population in Turkestan. After Stalin argued that under the Soviet regime 'there are no longer either oppressed or dominant nationalities, national oppression has been liquidated', Safarov successfully recommended that the resolution, over Stalin's objection, be augmented with a clause supporting national cultural self-determination for the peoples of the Soviet East. Safarov proposed that

---

120 The brightly decorated Red agitational train carried activists who distributed leaflets and pamphlets in the local languages, showed short films, and staged plays to propagandise the Muslim population. The train included a printing car, making possible the issuance of daily bulletins. Few native Turkestanis participated in the expedition: Argenbright 2011, pp. 437–54; Balabanoff 1964, p. 75.
121 Quoted in Carr 1950, p. 340.
122 Safarov was also a member of the Turkestan Bureau: Genis 1998, p. 49. Safarov, the son of an internationally recognised architect, had joined the Bolshevik Party in 1908. Although he had no previous experience in Central Asia and could not speak any Central Asian languages, Safarov was quickly seen by Moscow as the Bolsheviks' top local authority.
123 Krupskaya 1959, pp. 235, 241, 284, 303, 341, 344. In addition, Safarov, who travelled with his wife and children, was among the 20 Bolsheviks with Lenin and Krupskaya on the famous 'sealed train' from Zurich to Petrograd in April 1917: Merridale 2017, p. 149.

FIGURE 10
Grigory Safarov
WIKIMEDIA COMMONS

Turkestan be treated as a laboratory for Soviet views on the 'nationality question'. Safarov also called for the eviction of all 'kulak settlers' from Turkestan.[124]

Tomsky was not alone in finding working with Safarov extremely difficult. Safarov was known to sometimes fly into a rage against other members of the Turkestan Commission, and at times, he seemed to be suffering from some sort of psychosis.[125] A number of the members of the Turkestan Commission had for some time been calling for Lenin to remove him. The majority of the Bolsheviks in the Turkestan Bureau opposed Safarov's positions, with both Rudzutak and Peters deploring what they called the 'Safarovshchina'.[126] It is noteworthy that even Peters, who as Deputy Chair of the Cheka had never shied away from mercilessly applying mass terror, was appalled by Safarov's methods.

---

124 RKP(b) 1933a, pp. 102, 104, 108, 114. Kulak, a term for a 'rich' peasant, literally meant 'tight fist' and suggested a peasant who was miserly, greedy, and acquisitive.
125 Genis 1998, p. 49.
126 Chechevishnikov 1990, p. 176.

Once Tomsky arrived, Peters travelled to Moscow to try to get Safarov removed from the Turkestan Commission.[127] The Central Committee had in fact rebuked Safarov earlier for his 'extremism', but the Politburo refused to remove him from the Turkestan Commission.[128] An upset Tomsky told Lenin that if he was to succeed in Tashkent, in addition to the full support of the Central Committee, he needed Safarov to be withdrawn and for the Turkestan Commission to be staffed with disciplined, capable functionaries. 'Don't forget', he boldly told Lenin, 'I am here as the plenipotentiary of the Council of People's Commissars' (Sovnarkom).[129] Tomsky was determined to let Lenin know that he was not going to be unquestioningly subservient to him while serving as head of the Turkestan Commission.

As much as their personalities might have clashed, differences concerning the large number of Slavic settlers in Turkestan were at the heart of the conflict between Tomsky and Safarov. Russian peasant migration to Turkestan, which began with a trickle in the 1860s, had soared after 1907. The Stolypin agrarian reforms encouraged poor peasants in search of a better life to move out of provinces in European Russia to settle in Turkestan as well as in Siberia.[130] This encouragement of mass migration from European Russia included Ukrainians, Germans, Cossacks, and others, but the sources usually refer to these pioneers as simply Russians, which the vast majority were.[131] Facilitated by the completion of the Orenburg-Tashkent railroad line in 1906, the state-sponsored resettlement programme induced almost two million impoverished peasants to migrate to Turkestan, where they ploughed up the grazing land the tsarist government expropriated from the pastoral nomadic tribes. The tsarist government promoted peasant settlement both to reduce social and economic unrest in the land-hungry regions of European Russia and to strengthen its colonial hold over its Asian borderlands.[132] In the words of one historian, 'in a historic shift, this territory, a place long synonymous with pastoralism, a prac-

---

127   Genis 1998, p. 52; Leggett 1981, p. 267.
128   Smith 1999, p. 99; Park 1957, p. 170.
129   RGASPI, f. 5, op. 1, d. 1403, reprinted in Amanzholova and Gorelov (eds) 2000, pp. 9–10.
130   Of the roughly 400,000 immigrants who annually moved east, some two-fifths headed for Turkestan rather than Siberia: Katsunori 2000, p. 76. Most came from the Middle Volga and Ukraine: Cameron 2018, p. 35.
131   Parenthetically, the Cossacks had the best relations with the Indigenous population: Caroe 1967, p. 152.
132   Sahadeo, in contrast, states that 'Tsarist officials and intellectuals viewed poor migrant settlers not as a counterweight to the Central Asian majority or as a sign of successful economic development, but as a danger to the image of Russians as bearers of European culture and civilization': Sahadeo 2007, p. 135.

tice defined by the herding and management of animals, was now a mixed economic region, populated by large numbers of settled, agrarian peoples in addition to pastoralists'.[133] In the foothills and mountainous valleys of Semirech'e alone, where settlers primarily moved because of the relatively abundant land and fertile soils, they had received by 1914 over two million acres that a tsarist commission deemed were too valuable to be wasted on herding.[134] Some utterly destitute settlers also rented land from clan leaders, who pocketed the profits. This all came at the expense of impoverished nomads. As the number of colonists grew and upset the equilibrium between the human population, the size of herds, and pastureland, it led to a partial abandonment of the nomadic way of life, which had existed in Turkestan for at least 4,000 years. The Indigenous nomadic population often had little choice but to become day labourers on the farms of fellow Muslims or Russians.[135]

With similarities to what might be labelled the United States model, many of the settlers came to Turkestan well-armed while also receiving thousands of rifles from the government for the predictable ethnic conflicts. They joined the government troops in brutally repressing revolts by the Indigenous population. In the words of the historian Daniel Brower, 'their disdain for the nomads made use of these arms an easy matter'.[136] During the 1916 rebellion and following the Bolshevik seizure of power, some Russian farmers in Semirech'e took the opportunity to forcibly take additional land, property, and livestock from settled and nomadic Central Asians and to slaughter them when they resisted.[137] The local Soviet authorities initially supported the settlers, at least in part, in the hope of getting their grain during the 1917–18 famine.[138]

To work toward reversing the effects of the colonisation of the steppe, Safarov advocated initiating land reforms in Turkestan in June 1920 (which in some ways foreshadowed Stalin's vicious policy of dekulakisation in the first half of 1930).[139] The Turkestan Commission had resolved in November 1919 that it was necessary to expel from Turkestan a large number of Russian

---

133   Cameron 2018, p. 19.
134   Buttino 2014, p. 113; Pianciola and Gaignebet 2008, p. 103n3, Demko 1969, pp. 154, 200, 203; Pipes 1990, p. 171; Vaidyanath 1967, pp. 39–41, 63, 79; Rywkin 1990, pp. 15–16. At the same time an increasing number of Indigenous people began to request land from the tsarist government to become settled farmers, although many used it for livestock grazing.
135   Brower 2003, p. 136, Buttino 1993, p. 254. Some wealthy Muslim cotton growers had large land holdings: Engelstein 2018, p. 346.
136   Brower 2003, pp. 126, 130, 146–8.
137   Park 1957, p. 323; Pianciola and Gaignebet 2008, p. 110, 117; Pianciola 2001, p. 266.
138   Buttino 1993, p. 259.
139   Genis 1998, p. 45.

settlers, in addition to the tsarist police and governmental officials and owners of large enterprises who had already been sent to concentration camps.[140] But the expulsions were not implemented until Safarov began ruthlessly carrying out his land reform policies in January 1921. He was hardly a lone wolf in this. A directive from Moscow had authorised a programme of land reorganisation [*zemleustroistvo*] in order to address the 'unequal relationship' between Russian settlers and the Indigenous population.[141] The goal was to rid Turkestan of 'kulaks' and to inspire the Indigenous population to ditch nomadism for a more settled way of life.[142] In the words of one historian, 'the Bolsheviks perceived a settled lifestyle to be more progressive than a nomadic one and the agricultural economy more useful for the Soviet project'.[143] Soviet authorities thought the confiscations of the settlers' land would also help to undermine the influence of the wealthy clan leaders.[144]

The land reform programme thus sought to seize from 'predatory Great Russian kulaks' their 'excess' land with the goal of redistributing it to the Indigenous population, who on average owned a miniscule percentage of the land. Whereas the Central Asians owned 0.21 desiatinas of arable land per inhabitant, the settlers owned 3.17 (one desiatina equals 2.7 acres).[145] Although many of the poor migrants failed in Turkestan and returned to European Russia or Ukraine, the Slavic settlers in Semirech'e who most prospered were said to employ dozens of hired laborers and own hundreds of heads of cattle.[146] More commonly, village settlers were far from wealthy, but did own on average three horses and three cows before World War 1.[147]

Safarov quickly moved to disarm and then forcibly deport the Slavic 'kulak element' and redistribute their property, livestock, and inventory.[148] Safarov, who had a very broad definition of who was a kulak, often relying on the denunciations of local unsavoury characters in his efforts to identify them, argued there were hundreds of thousands of kulaks in Turkestan.[149] Safarov's efforts

---

140 Khalid 2005, p. 218; Genis 1998, p. 44.
141 The Politburo had adopted this policy on 29 June 1920: Genis 1998, p. 44; Khordina (ed.) 2000, p. 71.
142 Cameron 2018, pp. 49–50; Katsunori 2000, p. 83.
143 Kassymbekova 2016, p. 58.
144 Cameron 2018, p. 49.
145 Blank 1994, p. 195.
146 Carr 1950, p. 338.
147 Pahlen 1964, p. 4.
148 Holquist 2001, p. 130. For a provocative discussion of the Soviet use of the term 'element': Holquist 1997, p. 131.
149 RKP(b) 1933a, p. 95; Genis 1998, p. 47. Though the term kulak was pejoratively associated with exploitation and greed, by Western standards a kulak would be considered just a mildly successful small-scale farmer.

FIGURE 11   Settlers' homestead in Turkestan
            WIKIMEDIA COMMONS

were modelled on what the Bolsheviks considered a 'successful' 1920 operation on the prairies of the North Caucasus, where poor Chechens had received land expropriated from Cossack 'kulaks'.[150] The initial expulsion plans in Turkestan called for the displacement of 6,000 families, some 35,000 people, and a ban on any further Slavic settlement in Turkestan.[151] In the spring of 1921 poor Muslims began to be allotted land, including some pastureland, livestock, and farm tools

---

150   Service 1995, p. 96. Lenin, from the beginning of the Civil War until the introduction of NEP, had been inclined to blame food shortages on kulak hoarders and sabotage rather than disastrous government policies. Leone Musgrave shared with me that her research on the North Caucasus suggests the 'success' of this transfer of land did not last long.
151   Cameron 2018, p. 49.

seized from the 'colonising kulaks' in Semirech'e and Syr-Darya.¹⁵² Faced with this threatening prospect, a large number of settlers returned to European Russia on their own accord.¹⁵³

Tomsky and Safarov represented polar opposites in the Bolshevik Party. While Tomsky was arguably too solicitous of the settlers when they came under attack, Safarov was a true fanatic and, by this time, a hardened political operative. As we have seen, the Slavic settlers had taken the Turkestanis' land and often treated them atrociously, sometimes violently so, as Tomsky must have quickly come to appreciate. But however important it was to carry out some land reform to undo the decades of tsarist Russian settler colonialism, especially given Lenin's dreams of winning Muslim support, Safarov often acted like an emotionally unbalanced brute. This deeply offended Tomsky's moderate sensibilities. During the operations that Safarov personally directed, in which he liked to switch between wearing a British-style pith helmet and a worker's cap, he was fond of dressing down Slavic peasants and local Soviet officials who did not support him. Before gatherings of local Kirgiz, where he would show up with an army escort, he called them such names as bastards, shitheads, crooks, and swindlers.¹⁵⁴ Safarov subjected the most influential Slavic farmers to violent interrogations. He also encouraged natives to beat up colonisers in the dead of night. In his fanatical zeal, Safarov personally carried out a series of mass arrests along with fellow plenipotentiaries as they went from village to village. He even personally executed some 'colonisers' in Semirech'e.¹⁵⁵ This terror against Russian peasants apparently succeeded in winning him some popularity with the 'native party-intelligenty' and the Indigenous poor.¹⁵⁶

Rudzutak, as head of the Turkestan Bureau and simultaneously one of the members of the Turkestan Commission, denounced Safarov in his reports to

---

152 Akademiia nauk Kazakhskoi SSR 1959, p. 162; Pianciola and Gaignebet 2008, p. 123.
153 This was particularly true of Ukrainians: Buttino 2007, p. 357.
154 Complicating matters, Kazakhs were commonly referred to as Kirgiz. On his headgear: Kotkin 2014, p. 387. On the escort: Kassymbekova 2016, p. 46.
155 Genis 1998, p. 50; Pianciola and Gaignebet 2008, pp. 126–7.
156 Genis 1998, p. 49. Parenthetically, it was Safarov, as further evidence of his brutal zealotry, who was responsible for planning the execution of the royal family in July 1918 together with Filipp Goloshchekin: Steinberg and Khrustalev (eds) 1995, p. 390; Service 1995, p. 38. The 1930–33 famine in Kazakhstan, incidentally, is known as the Goloshchenkin genocide, because this Jewish 'Old Bolshevik', who ruthlessly enforced Stalin's policies, was the top official there until he was removed at the height of the famine in early 1933. Goloshchenkin was made the scapegoat for the food shortages even though he had petitioned Moscow in 1932 to soften its policies: Cameron 2018, pp. 9, 145, 160–1.

Moscow.¹⁵⁷ Shortly after Tomsky's arrival, presumably with Tomsky's support, Rudzutak on 16 July indignantly informed the Politburo that Safarov, with 'his characteristic fever', was carrying out land reform as a crusade against the Russian settlers and called for his removal.¹⁵⁸ Rudzutak reported that under Safarov, terrified Russian settlers, some of whom had lived in Semirech'e for decades, were being evicted without any sort of genuine plans regarding their future resettlement, not to mention any possibility of appealing the decision. The majority of these peasant households were given 48 hours to gather together their movable belongings in preparation for who knew what, often being sent on foot or in oxen-pulled wagons 60 or 70 miles to the nearest railroad station, where hundreds of terrified families were forced to live in open-air camps until rail transportation could be arranged.¹⁵⁹ Rudzutak reported, for example, that in the village of Vysokoe, where settlers had lived since 1888, policemen appeared on 16 April 1921 and with the help of Red Army troops, loaded 20 families on to trucks and transported them to the station of Abail on the Semirech'e railway, where they sat without shelter for three full days in a pouring rain. Most of the deportees were old men, women, and children, including even some infants, because men of working age commonly had either been arrested or put into the Red Army.¹⁶⁰ The victims of one of these operations forcefully protested, arguing that, 'when 25 million people are starving in Russia one should ensure that everyone sows as much grain as possible, but we are being deprived of a harvest which we have already sowed, which only increases the number of people starving ... Our 24 families are doomed to die of starvation ... And for

---

157   It should be noted that Rudzutak, who initially pressured the Tashkent Soviet to stop food requisitions from Central Asian villagers, earlier played a key role in creating provision brigades [*prodotriady*] composed of Russian workers to obtain food from the countryside through bartering goods or simple confiscations in early 1920 after starvation returned to the region: Sahadeo 2007, pp. 219–22. Rudzutak would become a member of the Politburo in 1926, serving alongside Tomsky who had been a member since 1922. Tomsky and Rudzutak remained friends during the 1920s: Fitzpatrick 2015, p. 66. Rudzutak later took Stalin's side against Tomsky in 1928, though not without some wavering and attempts to reconcile the two. In January 1932, he did timidly urge Stalin to moderate his policies on forced collectivisation: Khlevniuk 2009, p. 62; Volkogonov 1991, pp. 172, 180. In May 1937, the NKVD arrested Rudzutak at his home while entertaining friends. Rudzutak, who was accused of being a German spy and a member of the 'anti-Soviet Right-Trotskyist bloc', was interrogated and tortured for over a year before his execution on 28 July 1938: Nosach 2005, pp. 190, 219.
158   Genis 1998, pp. 46, 52.
159   Genis 1998, p. 46.
160   Ibid.

what? What have we simple, eternally hardworking peasants done'?[161] Similarly heartless and destructive operations against the families of Russian peasants branded as kulaks occurred elsewhere in Turkestan, such as in the Fergana valley.[162] All in all, the Soviet regime seized from European colonists a total of some 687,841 acres of land, which they turned over to clan leaders to be redistributed to Indigenous households.[163] Some 12,826 families also received confiscated cattle and agricultural tools in addition to the land.[164] Rudzutak also deplored how, 'in order to ensure the support of the native population, such demagogic-nationalist propaganda has been conducted that it repeatedly results in threats from the Kirgiz to slaughter the Russian population'.[165]

Tomsky was determined to work with Rudzutak, whom Lenin highly respected and considered a personal friend, to ensure that Safarov's coercive land reform policies were stopped.[166] Tomsky, as we have seen, had introduced in Turkestan the recently adopted NEP, with its fixed tax in kind replacing grain and cotton requisitioning. Ending requisitioning removed a principal source of rural dissatisfaction and unrest and eventually led to the revival of agriculture in Central Asia as elsewhere. In addition to Rudzutak's telegram to the Central Committee calling for Safarov's removal from the Turkestan Commission, Tomsky sent a telegram soon after his arrival calling on the Politburo to postpone Rudzutak's planned departure from Turkestan.[167] Both telegrams were discussed at the Politburo's 16 July 1921 meeting.[168] Rudzutak temporarily remained in Tashkent, but only because he was too ill to make the trip back to Moscow.[169] In addition, at the same time and in sharp contrast to what Safarov was doing, Tomsky headed an effort to temporarily settle in Turkestan over 300,000 workers and peasants from the famine-affected areas of the Volga region.[170]

---

161 Genis 1998, p. 47.
162 Ibid.
163 Park 1957, pp. 302, 323–5.
164 Pianciola and Gaignebet 2008, p. 139.
165 Genis 1998, p. 48.
166 Genis 1998, p. 53; Sorenson 1969, p. 99.
167 The Central Committee Plenum on 18 May 1921, following its expulsion of Tomsky from the VTsSPS Plenum, appointed Rudzutak its general secretary: Nosach 2005, pp. 213–14.
168 Khordina (ed.) 2000, p. 111.
169 Nosach 2005, p. 214. Rudzutak, who like Tomsky spent many years in prison and Siberian exile, suffered from migraine headaches: Trukan 1963, p. 53. Various illnesses, most seriously malaria and tuberculosis, eventually affected nearly all the Russian state officials sent to Central Asia. Tomsky fortunately avoided adding those illnesses to his long list of ailments.
170 Gorelov 2000, p. 93.

Safarov vehemently fought back. He argued that NEP did not fit Turkestan and an exception should be made for it. Safarov believed it was impossible to develop a free market and collect NEP's taxes in kind in Turkestan until 'class differentiation' had been completed.[171] Instead of advocating for a relaxation of class tensions along the lines of the policies of NEP, he wanted to intensify them.[172] He directed the *Koshchi*, a union of poor and landless peasants, to collect data for expropriation campaigns against the Russian settlers and to organise the rural proletarian and semi-proletarian masses for this purpose.[173] The *Koshchi* was a mass association that had sprung up in a disorganised way during the Civil War.[174] Safarov, who with reason accused Tomsky of being the spokesman for settlers, viewed NEP, which he correctly thought would mostly benefit Slavic merchants and settlers, as sure to antagonise Muslims.[175] Safarov was also surely correct that the settlers would also be the ones who could take advantage of NEP's legalisation of the leasing of land and the hiring of labour.

Tomsky, who insisted it was impossible to combine NEP with support for the *Koshchi* and their sharing out of the property and cattle of the so-called kulaks to poor or landless Central Asian peasants, led the resistance against Safarov's operations. Immediately after Tomsky's arrival, he and Rudzutak not only disrupted the forced expulsion of peasants from Semirech'e during the summer of 1921, but with the support of the Cheka plenipotentiary Peters, they reversed it.[176] Rudzutak wrote, 'a significant percentage of the expelled peasants (who

---

171   Smith 1999, p. 99.
172   Blank 1994, p. 67.
173   Pianciola and Gaignebet 2008, p. 126. The Muslim section of the Communist Party strongly opposed the *Koshchi* policy of promoting class conflict in Indigenous villages: Park 1957, p. 169.
174   The historian Alexander Park described the *Koshchi* as 'a mixture of rural trade union and cooperative with a predominantly political character, which included landless and small-scale peasants, agricultural workers, tenant farmers, share croppers, and village kustars'. Safarov also created a 'stratification commission' to pursue the goal of weakening village unity by driving a wedge between the tribal leaders and the mass of peasants: Park 1957, pp. 146, 149; Smith 1999, p. 99. Tomsky referred to the *Koshchi* as the local version of the Poor Peasant Committees [*Kombedy*], which had been established in European Russia following the seizure of power to carry out class warfare against suspected kulaks and aid the armed requisitioning brigades in grain seizures. The resentment and hostility created by the *Kombedy* turned the rest of the village against the poor peasants and resulted in the murdering of thousands of requisition brigade members: Hudson 2012, p. 21. Officially, the Soviet regime abolished the *Kombedy* in January 1919.
175   Fischer 1964, pp. 542–3; Pianciola and Gaignebet 2008, p. 130.
176   Pianciola and Gaignebet 2008, pp. 130, 143.

were by no means kulaks) were able to return. This has brought some calm to the tense atmosphere in Semirech'e'.[177]

As head of the Turkestan Commission, Tomsky wanted Lenin's support in his fight with Safarov and his numerous followers, which prompted him to write to Lenin on 23 July, a couple weeks after his arrival. Laying out his differences with Safarov, Tomsky wrote Lenin, 'I do not see how it is possible to combine the policy of the tax in kind with the ongoing redistributions from the well-to-do Russian peasants to the Indigenous poor. *Koshchi* can't operate in conjunction with "the freedom to sell surpluses"'.[178]

An indecisive Lenin, in separate letters to both Tomsky and Safarov on 7 August, wanted to split the difference between the two of them.[179] Although Lenin had allocated some of his responsibilities to others because of his deteriorating health, resolving the tensions in Turkestan remained one of Lenin's primary concerns.[180] After emphasising that the first priority was acquiring grain and meat, and the need for 'a number of concessions and bonuses to merchants' in order to achieve that, Lenin wrote Tomsky, 'I believe the two tendencies *can* and *must* be combined ... No question about the New Economic Policy [but] Muslim poor peasants' committees [are] indispensable ... the Muslim poor should be treated with care and prudence, with a number of concessions'.[181] Thus, while Lenin supported Tomsky on the need to implement NEP, he also undercut him by supporting Safarov on the *Koshchi's* desire to expropriate the settlers' land. The Politburo followed Lenin's lead and called for the collection of the tax in kind while also supporting the Muslims' *Koshchi*.[182] Lenin's mixed message and, at best, half-hearted support, understandably angered Tomsky, who was becoming increasingly frustrated during his tenure in Tashkent. As Lenin continued to waffle on whether to remove Safarov, Tomsky asked to be relieved of his post in Tashkent once he had completed a half-year of service.[183]

---

177   Genis 1998, p. 48.
178   Ibid.
179   Lenin 1958–65, vol. 53, pp. 105–6.
180   Lenin wrote Gorky in August 1921, 'I'm so tired I am incapable of the slightest work': Gorky 1932, p. 52.
181   Lenin 1958–65, vol. 53, p. 105.
182   Lenin 1958–65, vol. 53, p. 398n118; Smith 1999, pp. 99–100; d'Encausse 1967, pp. 234–6.
183   Lenin told Tomsky that the Central Committee would probably agree to his request to be relieved of this post after a half year, but he would first talk to Rudzutak about it: Lenin 1958–65, vol. 53, p. 105. As we will see, Tomsky's tenure in Turkestan, in the end, lasted less than four months.

Because of Lenin's desire to reverse tsarist imperialism, his inclination was to side with Safarov over Tomsky, especially after Safarov wrote to him on 21 August. Safarov euphemistically told Lenin that although some 'glass had been broken' in implementing his nationalist policies; work had to be conducted like a 'fireman' given the roadblocks Tomsky and others put in his way. Safarov assured Lenin that such instances were isolated and confined to Semirech'e. He accompanied the letter with a brochure he had published in 1921 entitled 'Current Questions of the Nationalities Policy' that Lenin found compelling.[184] Lenin told the Sovnarkom that Safarov's harsh treatment of kulaks in the name of land reform was 'completely correct'. It was Stalin, as Commissar of Nationalities, who objected. On 5 September Stalin expressed his concerns with what he characterised as two years of Safarov's 'unsystematic, imprudent, unreasonable policies'.[185]

Lenin in response decided he needed more information to better understand the conflict between Tomsky and Safarov.[186] He prompted the Politburo to send Adolf Joffe to investigate the tensions between them. Joffe, the Jewish son of a wealthy Crimean merchant, was a trusted and erudite aide of Lenin, to whom he often turned to when he needed a troubleshooter.[187] Joffe arrived in Tashkent with a brief that expressed the Politburo's determination to end the exclusion of Muslims from political power but without alienating the Russian population: 'We need to strike a balance, fighting against colonialism but not destroying our buttress in the republic, namely, the Russian labouring population, from whom the core of Turkestan's Red Army forces are taken'.[188] Joffe, as he began to investigate, while he appreciated how Safarov's reforms had created unprecedented support among the poor in the Indigenous population,

---

184 Lenin 1958–65, vol. 53, p. 399n120.
185 Genis 1998, p. 53.
186 Getting accurate information about conditions far from the centre would remain a perennial problem for officials in Moscow.
187 Joffe, for example, had headed the Soviet delegation to the Brest-Litovsk peace negotiations and, before accepting his assignment in Turkestan, negotiated the peace terms with Poland in the Treaty of Riga in March 1921. He was a long-time friend and collaborator of Trotsky, who characterised Joffe as 'a man of great intellectual ardor, very genial in all personal relations, and unswervingly loyal to the cause': Trotsky 1970, p. 220. An American foreign correspondent who became friends with Joffe and his family described him as 'short, thick set, bearded, with keen brown eyes and a rather prepossessing manner': Harrison 1921, p. 188.
188 Smith 1999, p. 100. The sickly, highly-strung Joffe suffered from tuberculosis, myocarditis, stomach ulcers, and polyneuritis: Service 2009, p. 111. The increasingly ill Joffe committed suicide in 1927 as an act of political protest, somewhat like a distraught Tomsky would do in 1936.

was utterly appalled at the extraordinarily low moral level of the Soviet regime's agents in Turkestan. He quickly realised that land reform had indeed been conducted with utter lawlessness, with 'methods of wild terror, including brutal beatings of Russians in the presence of Kirgiz, and orders for the Kirgiz to beat the Russians'.[189]

Joffe sent a telegram to the Politburo on 9 September describing his interactions with Tomsky and Safarov and his assessment of the source of the conflict.[190] In his report, Joffe stated that Safarov was often unable to control himself and was prone to hysterics in how he treated his colleagues, as had been reported to Lenin earlier by members of the Turkestan Commission.[191] Safarov's justification of his seemingly indiscriminate use of force, according to Joffe, was that 'it didn't matter if the less guilty ones suffer first, since all are guilty, and secondly, only in this way was it possible to show the Kirghiz poor that power was in their hands'.[192] Joffe reported that Safarov was continuing to pursue policies reminiscent of the 'most cruel forms' of the now discarded policy of War Communism, confiscating 'surplus' property and livestock from so-called kulaks and distributing it among the poor peasants, though he agreed to stop using 'draconian methods', including any further forcible evictions or arrests.[193] Joffe followed that up with a telegram on 14 October that stated the disagreements over policies between Tomsky and Safarov were 'enflaming the hostility between the Russian and native populations and between various nationalities'.[194]

Joffe also reported to the Politburo that Safarov's policies were having a devastating impact on agricultural production as one peasant hut after another was forcibly emptied. He reported seeing 'abandoned Russian huts and abandoned vegetable gardens, while alongside them Kirgiz artels lived in their yurts and neglected [all that had been confiscated] because they did not know to use a Russian stove or cultivate a Russian garden'.[195] Indeed, as a result of Safarov's land reform policies, in 1921 the Russian population of Turkestan fell by half a million people, from 2.7 to 2.2 million, and Russian arable landholdings fell

---

189 Genis 1998, p. 48.
190 Lenin 1960–70, vol. 45, p. 672n328.
191 This experienced diplomat succeeded in meeting with Tomsky and Safarov together, but that failed to ease tensions, with both of them insisting they could not work with one another: Genis 1998, pp. 52–3.
192 Quoted in Genis 1998, p. 48.
193 Genis 1998, pp. 48, 52.
194 Lenin 1958–65, vol. 53, p. 415n220; Fischer 1964, p. 543.
195 Genis 1998, p. 57.

by nearly half, from 3.3 million to 1.6 million desiatinas.[196] Joffe concluded that 'reckless' land reform had caused mass devastation and destruction.[197] He ended his telegram by stating that leaving Safarov in Turkestan was 'unacceptable' and would lead to endless squabbling.[198] But whether or not the Politburo agreed to remove Safarov, Joffe insisted the Politburo had to choose whether to support Safarov or Tomsky; it could not continue to support them both.[199] Tomsky wrote Lenin that he completely agreed with Joffe that it was impossible for Lenin to continue to advocate a 'middle position'.[200] The Politburo, on Stalin's suggestion, decided to put Safarov on medical leave.[201]

One might think that Lenin, after receiving these reports of Safarov's ruthless land reform policies, would have quickly come out in support of Tomsky and removed Safarov. But, of course, Lenin had himself never been shy about advocating brutally violent methods if he thought they were necessary. He protected the Cheka from condemnation and reform despite the approximately one hundred thousand 'enemies' it repressed and murdered, and under his leadership the Red Terror became an integral part of the Soviet system during the Civil War.[202] Most similarly to the terrible events in Turkestan, Lenin authorised mass terror against the Don Cossacks in 1919, as was noted above.[203] Before Safarov began carrying out his land reform operations in Turkestan, Lenin mused about what to do with the 'kulak settlers' there, wondering whether the local Bolsheviks should 'destroy them'.[204] On another occasion he suggested that one in ten of these kulaks should be sent to concentration camps.[205] Christopher Read argues that Lenin was not a violent person, but for him 'whatever

---

196 Hosking 2006, p. 57.
197 Genis 1998, pp. 57–8. Despite the famine in Turkestan, hundreds of thousands of refugees from the famine-stricken Volga region and from Turkestan itself flooded into Tashkent because of its reputation as 'The City of Bread'. Camps of desperate, starving people appeared all over the city, which led before long to outbreaks of such diseases as typhus and cholera: Cameron 2018, p. 42; Sahedo 2007, pp. 224–5. A large percentage of the refugees from the Volga region were Muslim Tatars and Bashkirs. Safarov tried to prevent the refugees from going to Semirech'e and Fergana because of the famine conditions there, but Moscow overruled him: Pianciola and Gaignebet 2008, pp. 115, 117.
198 Genis 1998, p. 53.
199 Fischer 1964, p. 543.
200 RGASPI, f. 5, op. 1, d. 1403, reprinted in Amanzholova and Gorelov (eds) 2000, p. 11.
201 Genis 1998, p. 53; Smith 1999, p. 100.
202 Figes 1996, p. 649. Lenin, to give just one example, had ordered the commander in Penza to 'carry out relentless terror against the kulaks, the priests, and White Guards': quoted in Volkogonov 1994, p. 201.
203 Holquist 1997, pp. 127–62; Genis 1994, pp. 42–55.
204 d'Encausse 1992, p. 202.
205 Lenin 1958–65, vol. 41, p. 433.

served the revolution was right' and that justified in Lenin's mind even the most horrifically violent means.²⁰⁶

Lenin, in his 13 September response to Joffe's report, admitted that there was some difference of opinion within the Central Committee on the conflict between Tomsky and Safarov. But Lenin nonetheless decided to take a hard line against Tomsky. Instead of supporting him, he began to question whether Tomsky was the right man for the assignment in Turkestan. Lenin wrote to Joffe that he wondered whether 'the natives (*tuzemtsy*) will be able to stand up for themselves against such a subtle and firm and stubborn man as Tomsky'. After posing such questions as whether or not it was true that Safarov was ruining cotton production, Lenin wrote 'I personally very much suspect Tomsky of engaging in Great-Russian chauvinism, or to put it more correctly, of deviating in that direction'.²⁰⁷ Lenin, who was becoming increasingly worried that a failure to win over Muslims in Central Asia would undermine the Soviets' hopes of revolution in 'the East', continued, 'it is terribly important to win the confidence of the natives; to win it again and again; to prove that we are not imperialists, that we shall not tolerate any deviation in that direction ... It will have an effect on India and the East; it is no joke, it calls for exceptional caution'.²⁰⁸ As the prospects of the communist movement in Europe looked increasingly bleak, Lenin and other members of the party leadership viewed Turkestan as the gateway to British India and beyond.²⁰⁹ But Lenin remained very confused, suggesting in the same letter that rather than Tomsky, 'perhaps it would be more correct to say Peters's line? Or Pravdin's line? etc. [were guilty] of engaging in great Russian chauvinism'.²¹⁰ In any case, Lenin cared far less about the brutal treatment the settlers received than he cared about the possibility that Safarov's policies

---

206 Read adds that 'to understand Lenin's position is not to condone it': Read 2005, pp. 246–52.
207 Lenin 1958–65, vol. 53, pp. 189–190.
208 Lenin 1958–65, vol. 53, p. 189.
209 Lenin had the Comintern trumpet the goal of 'setting the East ablaze', with India the initial target: Hopkirk 1984, p. 102. Lenin and Trotsky even dreamed of training an army of Central Asians to march into India through Afghanistan to aid the Indian revolutionary movement: Agabekov 1996, p. 56; Meijer 1964, p. 627; Eudin and North 1957a, pp. 76–7, 117–18. Stalin also believed that the consolidation of Soviet power in Turkestan 'could have great revolutionary impact on the entire East': Stalin 1946–51, vol. 4, p. 230.
210 Lenin 1958–65, vol. 53, pp. 189–90. As noted above, the Chekist Peters was a member of the Turkestan Commission from 1920 to 1922: Leggett 1981, p. 267. Alexander Pravdin, an Old Bolshevik who joined the party in 1899, led the Workers' Opposition during the intense debate in Tashkent: Rees 2012, p. 36; Allen 2015, pp. 255, 352. Later, in his 1933 purge testimony, Tomsky conceded he had come into conflict with the local party functionaries but did not state why: TsGAODM, f. 2870, op. 1, d. 296, reprinted in Karpachev and Minaeva (eds) 1992b, p. 103.

might serve as a means for persuading the Muslim elites of the seriousness of the Bolsheviks' anti-colonial project, which he hoped would ignite revolutions in Europe's colonies.

Tomsky was so exasperated with the decisions of the Central Committee and the Central Control Commission, that on the same day Lenin wrote back to Joffe, 13 August, Tomsky delivered a defence of the need to stand up for what one believed was best for the revolution, even if it came at great personal cost. At the Sixth Turkestan Party Congress, held in Tashkent on 11 and 12 August, at which he initiated various measures that significantly shaped party and governmental policies in the region, Tomsky urged delegates to follow his example and boldly expose the party's current shortcomings. 'I'm not afraid to criticise the Central Committee. I'm not afraid of being exiled. I recommend you do the same. Anyone who is afraid to do so is a bad communist. Anyone who is afraid to disrespectfully treat his superiors, who is afraid that if he does so he will be subject to exile and arrest, he is not a communist'.[211]

Tomsky, in the midst of all this controversy, nonetheless went about his business. He wrote to Lenin about economic conditions in Turkestan, especially the challenges he faced implementing NEP and purchasing sheep. Tomsky informed him that grain collections in Turkestan remained an enormous problem. 'I have tried to implement tough policies' to ensure local officials collect the tax in kind from peasants since they have been able to collect only 60 percent of what they had promised.[212] He resorted on 2 August to using some Red Army troops to help collect the tax in kind.[213] But he also emphasised that the lack of financial resources 'hampers everything'.[214] Tomsky repeatedly asked Moscow for additional funds if he was to fulfil the requests for more mutton without further antagonising the breeders. On 15 September, Lenin rejected Tomsky's request for an advance of another 100,000 rubles, adding two days later that, given the inflated prices the breeders were demanding, all further livestock purchases in Turkestan needed to stop.[215] After Tomsky objected to this decision, Lenin decided he needed to be brought back to Moscow to sort this and other issues out. Although Tomsky had been requesting that he be relieved of his position in Tashkent, for some reason it took another telegram

---

211 Quoted in Chechevishnikov 1990, p. 175. Tomsky also attended many plenary meetings of the Turkestan Communist Party's Central Committee and its Executive Bureau during his time in Tashkent.
212 RGASPI, f. 5, op. 1, d. 1403, l. 4, reprinted in Amanzholova and Gorelov (eds) 2000, p. 11.
213 Gorelov 2000, p. 94.
214 RGASPI, f. 5, op. 1, d. 1403, l. 4, reprinted in Amanzholova and Gorelov (eds) 2000, p. 11.
215 Lenin 1958–65, vol. 53, p. 399n119; Amanzholova and Gorelov (eds) 2000, p. 5.

FIGURE 12 Tomsky wearing Turkish sheepskin hat
ELEKTRONNAIA BIBLIOTEKA GPIB

before Tomsky agreed to come to Moscow. Perhaps he feared what Safarov might do in his absence. If so, Tomsky's fears were unwarranted, because on the day after Tomsky's departure, Safarov took the next train to Moscow out of Tashkent so he would be able to simultaneously make his case to Lenin. Tomsky arrived on 30 September and met with Lenin on 5 October.[216]

---

216 Amanzholova and Gorelov (eds) 2000, p. 6. Even without Safarov's presence, the Tenth Congress of the Turkestan Soviets passed a resolution voicing its strong support for the *Koshchi* while Tomsky was in Moscow: Park 1957, pp. 146–7. There is evidence to suggest that Tomsky arrived in Moscow shortly before that, in time to attend the Central Committee Plenum: RGASPI, f. 122, op. 1, d. 35, l. 27.

The Politburo, with Lenin in attendance, met on 14 October to hear a report from Tomsky on 'the Turkestan question'.²¹⁷ Following the meeting, the Politburo, for unspecified reasons, decided to remove Tomsky and appoint new members to the Turkestan Commission and Turkestan Bureau, with instructions on the need for circumspection in implementing NEP.²¹⁸ Lenin had apparently agreed with Safarov that how Tomsky implemented NEP antagonised many Muslims. Or perhaps it was a conversation Lenin had with Rudzutak that convinced Lenin that Tomsky should no longer head the Turkestan Commission. According to Lenin's message to the Politburo, 'Rudzutak, Tomsky's friend, told me yesterday [that] if I am three-quarters colonialist, Tomsky is five-fourths'. Rudzutak, who perhaps was also on the hot seat, told Lenin in addition that he marvelled at how quickly Tomsky had 'mastered an imperious tone' while in Turkestan.²¹⁹

Grigory Sokolnikov was appointed to replace Tomsky on 14 October as head of the Turkestan Commission and the Politburo set up another commission on 22 December to examine the question of Turkestan affairs.²²⁰ The brilliant, highly educated Sokolnikov had headed the Turkestan Commission in 1920 and served as a Red Army commander on the Turkestan front.²²¹ He was also a strong defender of NEP.²²² But he very much did not want to be dragged into the 'Safarov affair' as, in his words, the 'super-arbiter'. His request that someone

---

217 Khordina (ed.) 2000, p. 123.
218 The members of the newly constituted Turkestan Commission, besides Sokolnikov, were Victor Nogin, Ia. Z. Surits, Nazir Tiuriakulov, Abdula Pakhimbaev, Kaigisiz Atabaev, and briefly Peters: Genis 1998, p. 54.
219 Lenin 1958–65, vol. 53, p. 259.
220 Lenin 1967–81, vol. 54, pp. 86, 585n156.
221 One of the reasons the Central Committee had sent Tomsky to Turkestan was as a replacement for Sokolnikov, who was convalescing from an illness: RGASPI, f. 122, op. 1, d. 264, l. 57. Sokolnikov had commanded the Red Army's Turk Front beginning in August 1920. He took over for Frunze as the commander of the Fourth Army, which consisted of 21,650 infantry and 203 machine guns. Some 40 percent of those troops were Muslim soldiers and officers: Broxup 1983, p. 68.
222 Kotkin 2014, p. 451. The 'Old Bolshevik' Sokolnikov was a Jewish intellectual who had earned an economics degree from the Sorbonne while in exile and returned to Russia with Lenin in the sealed train in April 1917. He became Vice-Commissar for Finance before becoming Commissar for Finance in 1922. Sokolnikov introduced monetary reforms that are credited with successfully stabilising the currency. After his arrest in July 1936, Sokolnikov became one of the lead defendants in the second Moscow show trial in January 1937. At the trial Sokolnikov stated he had spoken with Tomsky about their shared opposition to collectivisation in 1935: Stalin 1937, p. 71. Unlike 13 of the 17 defendants, the court did not sentence Sokolnikov to be shot. But his cellmates murdered him in 1939, on Stalin's orders according to one historian: Slezkine 2017, p. 864.

else be appointed who had been 'less involved in the Semirech'e reforms than I have been, and consequentially less in danger of falling into despair from all the squabbling', was rejected.[223]

After arriving in Turkestan, Sokolnikov on 24 December sent a telegram to Lenin stating his assessment of the conflict between Tomsky and Safarov.[224] Implicitly corroborating Tomsky's assessment of Safarov, Sokolnikov was scathing in his criticism of Safarov's 'unconstitutional and immoral' policies. He confirmed that Safarov and his subordinates verbally abused and sometimes assaulted 'colonisers'. Sokolnikov wrote that the Russian population was intensely angry and aggrieved at how they had been 'terrorised'. Although Sokolnikov did note that the Kirgiz poor felt that Safarov had 'liberated' them, in a statement sure to get the party leadership's attention, he wrote that if they continued to support Safarov's campaign 'they will be responsible for the political murder of the Communist Party in Turkestan'.[225]

Lenin, who thought the attacks on Safarov were exaggerated, still proved reluctant to turn against him. He hastened to reassure Safarov while at the same time scolding him. 'Comrade Safarov, don't lose your nerve, it's intolerable and shameful. You're not a 14-year-old girl ... Continue your work, and don't give up any of your duties. You must learn to calmly collect the facts against those who have started this absurd case' against you.[226] The Central Control Commission on 3 January 1922 supported Lenin by ruling that the charges against Safarov, 'in the form in which they have put forward', were unfounded, although the commission went on to state that the way in which Safarov carried out his policies toward the 'colonisers' did not always maintain the 'proper restraint' and constituted an abuse of power. One of the members of the Central Control Commission, M.I. Chernyshev, objected to even this mild rebuke and instead suggested that everyone else was somehow 'responsible for creating the [Safarov] affair', stating by name Rudzutak, Tomsky, Joffe, Peters, and Pravdin.[227] Although Lenin's intervention had led the Central Control Commission to drop any charges against Safarov, Lenin finally went ahead and removed him from the Turkestan Commission the following day, on 4 January 1922.[228] But rather than demoting him, Lenin promoted Safarov to a post on the Comintern as head of its Middle East and Far East section and also gave

---

223 Quoted in Genis 1998, p. 56.
224 Lenin 1958–65, vol. 54, p. 585n157.
225 Genis 1998, pp. 55–6.
226 Lenin 1958–65, vol. 54, pp. 91–2, 585n155, 585n156.
227 RGASPI, f. 613, op. 1, d. 4, ll. 1, 3, quoted in Genis 1998, p. 56.
228 Khalid 2005, p. 219.

him a two-month leave to write a book on the first years of the Soviet regime in Turkestan.[229] Safarov would use the time to write what remains the most cited source for early Soviet Turkestan, *Kolonial'naia revoliutsiia* (Colonial Revolution). After the departure of Safarov many of his Muslim protégés were also removed.[230]

To the extent that Tomsky was guilty of 'Great Russian chauvinism', he was hardly alone. In the months after Tomsky had returned to Moscow the Central Committee was still urging the Turkestan communists to get rid of their 'colonialist deviation'.[231] Accusations of 'Great Russian chauvinism' continued to lead to the removal of thousands of party and soviet officials in the Central Asian borderlands in 1922–23.[232] Stalin, at the Twelfth Party Congress in April 1923, said 'Great Russian chauvinism' was not shrinking, but increasing.[233]

Tomsky's views on the implementation of NEP in Turkestan and the ending of attacks on the Russian settlers ultimately prevailed in Moscow. With Lenin increasingly side-lined by illness, and Tomsky now a member of the Politburo, in August 1922 the VTsIK commission headed by Mikhail Kalinin condemned the way land reform in Semirech'e had been implemented at the expense of Russian peasants. The use of land reform to achieve decolonisation was denounced as a 'nationalistic deviation' and brought to a close.[234] In late 1922 the OGPU organised the mass return of formerly expelled settlers and restitution for their confiscated agricultural tools.[235] In 1926 the party leadership explicitly forbade any future land reform that dispossessed Slavic farmers.[236]

---

229 Far from falling into disgrace, Safarov, in addition temporarily served as the Russian Secretary of the Comintern. He and Zinoviev gave the major speeches at the Moscow and Petrograd Congresses of the Revolutionary Peoples and Organisation of the Far East in January and February 1922. In November 1922, Safarov was officially selected a member of the Executive Committee of the Comintern. Safarov never changed his tune, proclaiming in December 1925 at the Leningrad provincial party conference that 'the kulak is a kulak, and as Lenin taught us, he is a verminous pig [*vrednaia skotina*] of the worst sort': quoted in Lenoe 2010, p. 65. He would be expelled from the Comintern because of his support for the Zinovievite Opposition in 1925 and then expelled from the party in 1927. He was executed in 1942: Genis 1998, p. 54; Lazitch with Drachkovitch 1986, pp. 411–12.
230 Pianciola and Gaignebet 2008, p. 131.
231 Carr 1950, p. 342.
232 Park 1957, pp. 129–30, 163–4.
233 Park 1957, p. 163.
234 Khazanov 1969, p. 131; Katsunori 2000, p. 83. Kalinin also thought nationality issues should take a back seat to economic ones: Blank 1994, p. 84. For a discussion of the Kalinin Commission, see Hirsch 2005, pp. 79–82.
235 Pianciola and Gaignebet 1998, p. 129.
236 Massell 1974, p. 71. Of course that would be reversed with Stalinist de-kulakisation, with

Following Tomsky's removal as head of the Turkestan Commission in October 1921, Lenin and the Politburo initially were not sure what to do with him. They initially proposed that Tomsky be appointed head of the Urals Industrial Bureau (*Prombiuro*), before Lenin wrote to Molotov opposing the idea. Lenin thought that Tomsky would not want to work under Grigory Lomov, who would be his VSNKh supervisor, and that the two would not mesh well together. It is hard to say why Lenin though this, since Lomov, too, had been a pre-revolutionary Bolshevik trade unionist and he and Tomsky had worked together in Moscow in 1917.[237] The Secretariat instead assigned Tomsky to temporarily work at the office of Gokhran, the State Depository of Precious Metals and Precious Stones, at its building in central Moscow, where valuables, such as the jewellery confiscated from the Romanovs and the Orthodox Church, were secretly transferred and assessed. Lenin had been concerned for months about reports of thefts by employees since the gold and precious stones were one of the few Soviet sources of hard currency.[238] Tomsky was sent to investigate a pardon for the former appraiser, Yakov Shelekhes.[239] The case against Shelekhes arose after the discovery that a large amount of diamonds was missing, and he was accused of the theft. Lenin obviously thought Tomsky was the sort of honest, capable person able to evaluate the level of corruption at Gokhran as well as the case against Shelekhes. Shortly after Tomsky looked into the case, he determined that Shelekhes was indeed guilty of the charge. As a result, Shelekhes was executed.[240]

---

tragic consequences for the 'kulak' households in the region, who were sent to remote regions of Kazakhstan, where they joined 'special settlers' from European Russia. In addition, 1.5 million Kazakhs nomads died as a result of collectivisation and forced sedentarisation: Cameron 2018, pp. 102, 118–19.

237 Kulikova and Khazanov 1988, pp. 73–4; Zalesskii 2000, pp. 282–3. Lomov, who had been the Commissar of Justice in Lenin's government of 1917, served in various capacities during the 1920s, including as the director of the Donbass Coal Trust (*Donugol*) during the 1928 Shakhty Affair.

238 Lenin complained that stealing was resulting in 'vast losses' the government could ill afford since the valuables produced hard currency needed for foreign grain purchases to alleviate the famine: Lenin 1960–70, vol. 45, pp. 159–60, 189–90. Gokhran sold precious stones to firms in Western Europe: Reswick 1952, p. 122. It was a subcommittee of the People's Commissariat of Finance (Narkomfin).

239 Amanzholova and Gorelov (eds) 2000, p. 7.

240 On 4 June 1921 the Politburo had decided to 'speedily mobilise' about 2,000 'honest' communists to work in shifts at Gokhran. Lenin was outraged when the Chekist Boky suggested the case against Shelekhes was 'highly exaggerated', and that in any case, while the Cheka was working to bring the stealing at Gokhran down to a minimum, 'it is impossible to stop it altogether': Lenin 1960–70, vol. 45, pp. 640n155, 651n205. Corruption in Gokhran would indeed persist in the years to come: Reswick 1952, pp. 122–3.

Tomsky's disgrace following the Fourth Trade-Union Congress proved to be short-lived. Party leaders continued to hold him in high esteem, although for his part, Tomsky initially had trouble letting go of the resentment he felt over how he had been treated, especially by the Central Control Commission.[241] The Politburo decided, on Lenin's recommendation, to return Tomsky to the VTsSPS Presidium over the objections of Andrei Andreev, who had taken Tomsky's place as chair. Andreev even threatened to quit the VTsSPS if the decision was not reversed.[242] But Andreev and other opponents on the VTsSPS quickly dropped their objections and on 9 January 1922, Tomsky was appointed to the number two position in the trade unions before regaining his former status as chair of the VTsSPS Presidium nine months later, in time to lead the Fifth Trade-Union Congress.[243] It was clear many of the Presidium members had greatly missed his leadership. They had stayed in touch with Tomsky while he was in Turkestan, sending him the protocols of meetings as well as other informational materials. He received a letter on 18 August 1921, for example, that stated that the VTsSPS Presidium meetings lacked any clear focus without him. The letter writers presumptuously concluded their message with 'We await your return'.[244]

The Central Committee also appointed Tomsky on 2 February to be one of the seven voting members of the Orgburo (Organisational Bureau).[245] The Orgburo, which developed an extensive collection of files on party members, was authorised to appoint and remove officials from party jobs, which were to be implemented by the Secretariat. Originally a sub-committee of the Politburo that supervised local party committees, the Orgburo in 1920 became independent in organisational and personnel questions up to the oblast level.[246] But the

---

241 This is according to a letter Rudzutak wrote to Lenin on 10 January 1922. Rudzutak added that he thought Tomsky would quickly regain his full equilibrium after he threw himself into his work on the VTsSPS: Kvashonkin et al. (eds) 1966, p. 235.

242 Alexander Dogadov and N.K. Antipov joined with Andreev in hotly expressing their opposition to Tomsky's return to the VTsSPS, with 'dragon speeches' according to Rudzutak: Kvashonkin et al. (eds) 1996, p. 234; GARF, f. 5451, op. 42, d. 46, l. 22.

243 The Fifth Trade-Union Congress was held 17–22 September 1922. Tomsky and Rudzutak received the most votes of those elected to the VTsSPS by the congress: VTsSPS 1922, pp. 511–12.

244 Chechevishnikov 1990, p. 176.

245 Addibekov (ed.) 2000, p. 151. Tomsky had earlier served intermittently on the Orgburo, including between the Ninth and Tenth Party Congresses. The other members of the Orgburo in 1922 were Stalin, Molotov, Rudzutak, Kuibyshev, Andreev, Dzerzhinsky, and Rykov.

246 By 1923, the party Secretariat, in the persons of Stalin and Molotov, succeeded in gaining complete control over the Orgburo.

overworked members of the Orgburo, at least in the early 1920s, usually did not initiate personnel appointments. They were done by the staff, who were more concerned with finding able administrators than with political considerations.[247]

The Eleventh Party Congress in April 1922 cemented Tomsky's return to political prominence. Tomsky, who delivered one of the major reports at the congress, had drafted with the increasingly ill Lenin the resolution 'On the Role and Tasks of the Trade Unions under the Conditions of NEP', which the congress adopted.[248] When the elections were held for the Central Committee, Tomsky received the sixth highest number of favourable votes of the 27 members elected, ahead of such party luminaries as Stalin, Kamenev, Zinoviev, and Rykov.[249]

Most shockingly, given the recent censoring of his leadership, Tomsky was selected on the heels of the congress to be one of the seven voting members of the Politburo (Political Bureau of the Party Central Committee), which was increasingly eclipsing the decision-making power of the Central Committee. Tomsky would be the only one of them who had been a worker and did not have any higher education. Beyond the fact that the elections to the Central Committee demonstrated that party leaders continued to respect Tomsky despite his recent fall from grace, it is not clear why they put him on the Politburo. Adam Ulam understandably speculated that Tomsky came back from Tashkent 'chastened and ready to support Lenin'.[250] But Tomsky's actions in Turkestan suggest otherwise. He stuck to his guns in calling on Lenin to abandon Safarov's brutal actions. In any case, Lenin was ill and no longer in control after suffering a major stroke on 25 May 1922, from which the only 52 years old Lenin never fully recovered. If Molotov's memoirs are to be believed, Frunze had suggested Tomsky's appointment to the Politburo. Although, as we have seen, it was Frunze who led the commission that recommended Tomsky's removal from the VTsSPS in 1921, he had also interacted with Tomsky in Tashkent and presumably came to respect his leadership of the Turkestan Commission.[251] According to

---

247   The staff were members of the Organisation and Instruction Department (*Orgotdel*) and Records and Assignment Department (*Uchraspred*): Gill 1990a, pp. 69–70, 73, 105. The Central Committee merged these departments into the Department for Assignments (*Orgraspred*) in 1926.
248   Egorov and Bogoliubova (eds) 1983–84, vol. 2, pp. 483–92.
249   Tomsky tied for sixth place with Karl Radek. Lenin and Trotsky tied for the top number of votes, with Bukharin, Kalinin, and Dzerzhinsky behind them: RGASPI, f. 48, op. 1, d. 19, l. 2, cited in Sakharov 2003, p. 172.
250   Ulam 1973, p. 201. Daniels similarly suggests Tomsky's exile to Turkestan had turned him into 'a pliant agent of the leadership': Daniels 1960, p. 158.
251   Gorelov and Shapovalova (eds) 2001, p. 154.

Tomsky's son Yury, Tomsky and Frunze became close friends in Turkestan.[252] Perhaps more to the point, Frunze shared Tomsky's animosity toward Trotsky and probably suggested placing Tomsky on the Politburo to provide another counterweight to him.[253] At the Eleventh Party Congress, Tomsky and Trotsky had resumed their bitter debates of 1920–21 over the role of trade unions, particularly their participation in the management of factories.[254] The debilitated Lenin, who had been attending Politburo meetings only sporadically since late 1921 and left the congress before Tomsky's appointment, expressed displeasure with the Central Committee's appointment of Tomsky but felt he had to agree and did not strongly object.[255] He seems to have been more opposed to the suggested appointment of Felix Dzerzhinsky.[256]

Whatever the case, it is clear that ultimately Lenin was willing to pardon Tomsky because he valued him so highly as an effective administrator. Lenin told his close, long-time friend and executive party secretary, Vladimir Bonch-Burevich, that 'we need dozens and hundreds of labour leaders like Tomsky'. Lenin summarised his feeling about Tomsky by stating that he 'sometimes makes mistakes but that is nothing; we all make mistakes'.[257] Lenin may have even considered naming Tomsky General Secretary of the party instead of Stalin. According to one account, Tomsky was Lenin's first choice for the post, but he refused because he preferred to focus on the trade unions.[258] Whether that offer actually occurred or not, Tomsky was certainly offered a position as

---

252   Gorelov 1988, p. 454.
253   The Old Bolshevik Frunze was an incessant critic of Trotsky on military issues. He would replace him as Commissar of War in January 1925.
254   RKP(b) 1961, p. 276.
255   Molotov 1993, pp. 142–3. The Central Committee also appointed Rykov to the Politburo at the same time. Frunze, the conqueror of the White Armies of Kolchak and Wrangel, enjoyed great sway in the party as well as in the army at that time: Medvedev 1989, p. 156.
256   Lenin, according to Molotov, had lost confidence in Dzerzhinsky. He could not forgive him for his lack of support during the Brest-Litovsk peace talks and during the 'trade-union debate': Molotov 1993, p. 107.
257   Bonch-Bruevich 1931, pp. 374–5. Bonch-Bruevich, the chief-of-staff for the Sovnarkom after the Bolshevik seizure of power, was from the nobility and his family's rural dacha in Finland is where Lenin hid in July 1917.
258   Kozlov 1991, p. 75. Kozlov's account is based on Tomsky family lore. According to Tomsky's son, Yury, Lenin twice met with Tomsky to convince him to take the position of general secretary: Shelestov 1988, p. 26. Kotkin argues that Lenin created the new position in March 1922 'expressly for Stalin', but he appears to be wrong about that: Kotkin 2014, p. 411. It seems clear that Lenin chose Stalin for the post at the suggestion of Kamenev, who suggested creating the position: Service 2009, p. 292; Volkogonov 1991, pp. 69–70; Mikoian 1999, p. 372. According to Trotsky, Zinoviev proposed Stalin's appointment over Lenin's objections: Warth 1977, p. 144; Trotsky 1980, p. 441.

one of the deputy chairs of the Sovnarkom in April 1922, which he turned down for the same reason.[259]

Thus, after being thrown into exile in May 1921, less than a year later, Tomsky was one of the party's top leaders. He was a member of the Politburo, the Orgburo, and head of the trade-union presidium. He, along with Stalin and Rykov, were the only party officials to be members of both the Politburo and Orgburo. The Politburo met on Thursday mornings at 11:00 and adjourned by 2 p.m., but often ended up meeting more than once a week if it could not finish the agenda, either on Friday or Monday.[260] The Orgburo was also a demanding post, which met once or twice a week in 1922. Its regular Monday meetings went well into the evening, from 7:00 to 11:00 p.m., if not later.[261] In addition, the Orgburo occasionally had meetings that lasted for days. All this was in addition to his day job as head of the trade unions. It would be the norm for officials such as Tomsky, who were suffering the lingering ill effects of years in prison and exile, to work 12–14-hour days.[262] All these responsibilities would obviously prove very taxing, especially when he also began regularly travelling to London and other sites in Europe on official business, as will be discussed in the next chapter. It also obviously meant he had little time to spend with his wife and children.

Tomsky as a result of his elevation to these posts was ensconced within the very top echelon of the Soviet political system, where he would remain until 1929. And despite all the party's propagandising about egalitarianism and the creation of a classless society, Tomsky and his family soon began to have access to a variety of material comforts. The Tomsky family moved into living quarters within the walls and towers of the Kremlin, the 64-acre fortress at the centre of Moscow, which in addition to serving as the seat of power, also housed a large apartment complex.[263] Tomsky and the other top party leaders who lived there were popularly known as 'Soviet aristocrats'.[264] The historian Sheila Fitzpatrick questionably asserts that, 'although they lived in the Kremlin like the tsars, they did not see themselves as heirs to the tsars, and had trouble even seeing themselves as rulers'.[265] Adam Ulam thinks 'only a misanthrope would

259 McNeal 1988, p. 76.
260 Getty 2013, p. 101.
261 Bazhanov 1980, pp. 50, 153. According to the archival source that J. Arch Getty cited, the Orgburo was supposed to meet on Mondays and Thursdays at 9 p.m.: Getty 2013, p. 102.
262 Gimpel'son 1998, p. 201.
263 The government moved from Petrograd to Moscow in March 1918.
264 Kuusinen 1974, p. 26.
265 Fitzpatrick 2015, p. 64.

begrudge the government figures who had spent their youth and early manhood in prison and exile some comforts inaccessible to the ordinary citizen'.²⁶⁶ One can only wonder whether Tomsky felt at least occasional pangs of guilt that his living conditions and life style differed so drastically from those of his trade-union constituents. Plus, the material privileges he and his family increasingly enjoyed were such an obvious violation of the revolution's egalitarian, socialist principles and ideals, they tried to keep them hidden behind a veil of secrecy.²⁶⁷ These privileges would multiple over time, though there were occasional efforts to scale them back.²⁶⁸

The Tomskys, like many other families in the Kremlin, now resided in the converted Cavalry Guards Barracks, an over 200-year-old, four-story structure located near the massive Trinity Gates, where generals and senior officials resided during the Old Regime.²⁶⁹ Constantly damp and hardly luxurious, unless in comparison to the grim, abysmal conditions in which almost all urban residents then lived, their modestly furnished, grey-walled apartment was cramped, with just a few small bedrooms.²⁷⁰ The Tomskys had three children after adopting an infant boy they named Yury in 1921.²⁷¹ Their older sons Victor and Mikhail were 13 and 18 in 1922 when the Tomskys moved into their

---

266   Ulam 1973, p. 211.
267   But the party elite's privileges became known and occasionally sparked unrest, even within the party. The Ninth Party Conference in September 1920 felt compelled to set up a commission to investigate Kremlin living conditions. The commission's report to the Tenth Party Congress, which was shown to only a few Central Committee members and otherwise buried, in the words of one historian, 'named and shamed senior Bolsheviks' for their privileged lifestyle: Pirani 2008, p. 58. Tomsky was obviously not one of those who were named and shamed since he did not yet live in the Kremlin.
268   Gimpel'son 1998, p. 200.
269   The Tomskys lived on the third floor: Gorelov 2000, p. 272. All the royal statues and icons in the Kremlin had been removed on Lenin's orders: Slezkine 2017, p. 186. The new regime also altered the bells of the Spassky Tower to play the tune of the Internationale instead of 'God Save the Tsar'. But the double-headed Romanov eagles remained on the Kremlin towers until 1935: Mawdsley 1991, p. 83; Figes 1996, p. 551.
270   The size of apartments depended on your place in the Kremlin's housing hierarchy. Lenin and Nadezhda Krupskaya had four rooms as did Trotsky's family: Colton 1995, p. 162; Service 2009, p. 341. Over time the Tomskys, like other Kremlin families, might have managed to get their apartment renovated or exchanged for a better one: Kun 2003, p. 256.
271   Many of the 'Old Bolsheviks' adopted children of deceased comrades as well as ordinary orphans: Fitzpatrick 2015, p. 70; Montefiore 2004, p. 12. The Tomskys made that decision almost immediately after Tomsky returned from Tashkent. The Tomskys had suffered earlier familial heartbreaks when a daughter died from diphtheria and another son broke a leg and died from blood poisoning: Gorelov 2000, p. 270.

FIGURE 13 Tomsky in the Kremlin
WIKIMEDIA COMMONS

high-ceilinged Kremlin apartment.²⁷² In addition, they had to share the same bathroom and dining room with another family. In these overcrowded quarters they freely socialised with their neighbours, especially Stalin, Kirov, Rudzutak, Bukharin, Kalinin, Voroshilov, and their families. Tomsky's wife, Maria Tomskaya (Efremova), was especially hospitable, but other families also kept an

---

272 Mikhail may have already left home. Yury talks about sharing time with his older brother Victor, but rarely mentions Mikhail.

open house, with neighbours casually dropping by and children from other families frequently coming and going.²⁷³ The children had free reign since the Kremlin was closed to the general public. Yury, when he got older, joined the thirty or so other Kremlin children racing around its courtyards and gardens or cross-country skiing among the palaces and cathedrals. They attended each other's birthday parties, in which they put on plays to which their parents and fellow children 'screamed with delight', before the whole gathering retired to the dining room for tea and cake and candies.²⁷⁴ The adults also held their own parties on birthdays and holidays.²⁷⁵ Yury, in addition, fondly remembered strolling around the Kremlin grounds with his father, who enjoyed describing the historical and cultural significance of the various palaces and fifteenth- and sixteenth-century cathedrals and churches.²⁷⁶ One historian described the Kremlin at this time as a 'village of unparalleled intimacy'.²⁷⁷ But residents paid for this with a lack of privacy. At least one party official turned down the opportunity to live there. He found the prospect of living in this closed community thoroughly unappealing and oppressive. 'Your every step was watched and one couldn't sneeze' without the GPU learning about it.²⁷⁸

Although Tomsky, like all the other top officials earned a modest salary, he had access to a vast array of free or heavily subsidised benefits, what has been characterised as the party elite's 'invisible earnings'.²⁷⁹ Their Kremlin apartment, including their heat and electricity, for example, was always cost-free.²⁸⁰ Maria Tomskaya, like the wives of most of the top leaders, had a job. Tomskaya

---

273   Service 2009, p. 341; Fitzpatrick 2015, p. 55.
274   Sullivan 2015, p. 26. Not all the children had fond memories. The Molotovs' daughter, Svetlana, remembered hating how she was continually told by her parents to be quiet in the Kremlin courtyard: Montefiore 2004, p. 40. Likewise, Andreev's daughter Natasha remembered 'we didn't want to live in the Kremlin. We were constantly told by our parents not to be noisy. You're not in the street now, they'd say. You're in the Kremlin. It was like a jail and we had to show passes and get passes for our friends to visit us': Brooke 2006, p. 227. One historian referred to the children as the 'Kremlin brats': Fitzpatrick 2015, p. 8.
275   Alliluyeva 1967, p. 31.
276   Gorelov 2000, p. 272.
277   Montefiore also described relations among the 'Old Bolsheviks' as similar to that of 'an incestuous family, a web of long friendships and enduring hatreds [and] shared love affairs': Montefiore 2004, pp. 14, 38.
278   Bazhanov 1990, p. 38.
279   Voslensky 1984, p. 185.
280   Shatunovskaia 1982, p. 42; Furhmann 1989, p. 386. There was, however, no central heating: Colton 1995, p. 162. It should be noted that until the stabilisation of the currency, much of the Soviet economy, including housing, was free, or virtually free, for everyone.

went to work in the Worker-Peasant Theatre Administration.[281] Although it originally exerted influence over urban and rural amateur groups' staging of plays, by the time Tomskaya went to work there its primary function was as an information-gathering body, amassing statistics about the social composition and repertoire of these amateur theatrical groups.[282] Like Tomsky, she earned 'the party maximum', initially set at 225 rubles.[283] She did not need to concern herself with housework. The Executive Committee's special Housekeeping Department provided free maids and cooks, some of whom were holdovers from the previous tsarist occupants.[284] The Tomskys also had access to an excellent restaurant in their own building, with cooks trained in France, which was colloquially known as the Kremlin Cafeteria.[285] It was ridiculously underpriced and limited to Kremlin residents and their friends and relatives.[286] They could shop at a grocery store next door to their apartment building for excellent quality foods and delicacies, unavailable outside such special stores, and payment was seemingly optional.[287] They also received regular deliveries of free food (the so-called *kremlevsky payok*) that were large enough to feed the whole family.[288] When it opened in 1926, the nearby Kremlin hospital, as it was known because it was built expressly for the Soviet elite, provided much better medical care than normal hospitals, stocked foreign medicine, and made house calls

---

281 Gorelov 2000, p. 272. The Worker-Peasant Theatre was a division of the Commissariat of Enlightenment (known by its acronym, Narkompros). The wives of many of the party's leaders also worked for Narkompros, including the wives of Kamenev and Kalinin, Olga Kameneva and Ekaterina Kalinina. In addition, Trotsky's wife Natalia Sedova had been appointed director of Narkompros's museums and ancient monuments department, while Lenin's wife Nadezhda Krupskaya directed primary education in Russia: Trotsky 1970, p. 356; Harrison 1921, p. 82; Bryant 1923, p. 79.
282 Mally 2000, pp. 22–3.
283 According to the party maximum, party officials, even those who held the highest offices, could not earn more than a skilled factory worker. It was repealed in 1934. Workers understood that Tomsky and other members of the party elite lived in relative prosperity, but might have wrongly thought it came from their high salaries. In September 1926 Tomsky faced many hostile questions during factory meetings, including one that asked, 'Comrade Tomsky, please tell us how much you earn in a year: 12,000 rubles, or a little more or a little less': quoted in Murphy 2005, p. 171.
284 Fuhrmann 1989, p. 386.
285 Ultimately there would be five restaurants in the Kremlin: Stites 1989, p. 142.
286 Shatunovskaia 1982, pp. 40–1; Kun 2003, p. 262; Fuhrmann 1989, p. 386; Figes 1996, p. 683; Colton 1995, p. 119. News of it would have caused outrage. When Kronstadt sailors learned during the Civil War that the party headquarters in Petrograd had three restaurants, they forcibly closed them: Stites 1989, p. 142.
287 Shatunovskaia 1982, p. 41. Shatunovskaia had lived in the Kremlin during the 1920s.
288 Kun 2003, p. 265.

to Kremlin residents, such as to the often-ailing Tomsky.[289] There was also a sauna and hairdresser in the Kremlin. The Tomskys' youngest son went along with other children in the Kremlin to a top day-care centre, school, and summer camp. Yury and Stalin's daughter Svetlana became friends there.[290] They could also reserve comfortable boxes at Moscow theatres or seats at the circus and the top movie house.[291] On at least one occasion Maria Tomskaya invited Lenin to accompany her to a performance of the Bolshoi Ballet at the House of Unions, in which the prima ballerina Yekaterina Geltser danced.[292] Tomsky, who received a chauffeured car for work, also received special travel passes that allowed him and his family to travel free on all the railways and waterways of the Soviet Union.[293] The family, however, did have to pay for its own clothes. According to one historian, 'Politburo wives could barely afford to dress their children'.[294] In almost all the photos of Tomsky at work he appears to be wearing the same brown suit.[295] But he was also fond of wearing on special occasions an embroidered, colourful shirt, devoid of a collar, with a red sash, and elegant high boots.[296]

Top officials such as Tomsky, who socialized almost entirely with one another, also had access to exclusive health spas, sanatoria, and resorts ('rest homes') in the North Caucasus around Kislovodsk and around Sochi on the Crimean Riviera, as well as elsewhere, which had previously been pre-revolutionary gentry and merchant estates.[297] With billiards the most popular

---

289 Shatunovskaia 1982, p. 43; Slezkine 2017, p. 190. But according to an American member of the Comintern, who visited the Kremlin hospital in 1928, it would be considered 'a very poor and dilapidated hospital in the United States': Gitlow 1940, p. 467.
290 Runin 1995, p. 187. Kremlin children went to an elite school, where they studied and socialised alongside the children of intelligentsia celebrities and foreign communists: Fitzpatrick 2015, p. 71.
291 Slezkine 2017, p. 190.
292 Gorelov 2000, p. 273.
293 Slezkine 2017, p. 190. Cars, such as the one provided to Tomsky, had been expropriated following the seizure of power: Kun 2003, p. 269. Kamenev made a point of securing for himself a Rolls Royce: Bazhanov 1980, p. 153.
294 Montefiore 2004, p. 42.
295 Tomsky did have a white summer suit as well. The tuxedo he wore on trips abroad may have been provided to him for such occasions: Gorelov 2000, p. 274. One resident, Sergei Dmitrievsky, doubted there were more than three dinner jackets among all the Kremlin residents during the 1920s: Merridale, 2013, p. 318. Robert Service disagrees, stating that top politicians dressed well; most notably Trotsky: Service 2009, p. 341.
296 Lee 1928, p. 128; Avtorkhanov 1959, p. 97.
297 Although sanatoria were often regarded as just another type of vacation home [*doma otdykha*], they provided a health regimen of exercise, diet, and rest under medical supervision for the sort of chronic ailments that plagued Tomsky and other top party officials: Fitzpatrick 1999, p. 246.

amusement at the resorts, Tomsky often had an opportunity to display his prowess.[298] But for Tomsky, the main attraction was hunting. When Tomsky stayed at one of the rest homes in the North Caucasus, he and his buddies from the party elite found it relaxing to go out hunting.[299] During one Politburo meeting, Voroshilov passed a slip of paper to Tomsky, asking where he wanted to go hunting. 'Are you just hunting bears, or are there some wolves around there, too? I find it really hard to shoot bears'. Tomsky replied on the back of the note, 'There are bears there, but there are lynx too'.[300] One of this avid hunter's cherished possessions was his gun collection, which consisted of gifts to Tomsky from Rudzutak, Frunze, Stalin, Dzerzhinsky, Georgy Ordzhonikidze, Vasily Bliukher, and the Tula arms factory.[301]

Tomsky's most prized privilege was the summer country house (dacha) allotted to him and his family. All the top party leaders received dachas, which formerly belonged to Moscow's pre-revolutionary elite. Although they did not own them, they enjoyed de facto ownership.[302] The Tomskys' bucolic dacha was in Bolshevo, a suburban village about 20 miles northeast of Moscow, away from where most of the party elite had dachas.[303] Unpretentious, yet impressive in a rustic sort of way, it was an elongated, one-story log house with no nearby neighbours. At the centre of the house was a huge fireplace, with bearskins on the floor in front of it (probably from one of Tomsky's hunting trips). All of the rooms had parquet floors and electric lighting. The family enjoyed dining in one of the two glassed-in verandas on each end of the house, where there was a long wooden table that sat 10. Other than flower beds in front of the verandas, there was no landscaping. The house sat in the middle of an untouched pine forest, which the Tomskys had left uncleared, although there was a high green fence enclosing their spacious plot. The family enjoyed strolling through the tall pine trees. But at the same time the dacha lacked basic modern comforts.

---

298   Slezkine 2017, p. 536.
299   Service 2009, p. 341. Seemingly, all the top party officials, including Lenin, Trotsky, and Stalin, hunted.
300   Kun 2003, p. 284.
301   Gorelov 2000, p. 279.
302   The one requisitioned for Lenin southwest of Moscow had been the property of a tsarist general, while the one for Trotsky, which had previously belonged to the Yusupovs, had been one of the most lavish landed estates in tsarist Russia: Pipes 1994, p. 442. The largest concentration of dachas for top officials was in Serebrianyi Bor, in an unspoiled pine forest west of the city, along the Moscow River: Lovell 2003, pp. 131–2. The Main Guard Directorate was responsible for supplying these dachas with food, consumer goods, and servants as well as providing protection: Khlevniuk 2015, pp. 34–5.
303   Teshkin (ed.) 1992, p. 24; Razumovsky 1994, p. 279.

Running water had to be fetched from a well. There was an unheated primitive shower outside and since the house lacked a sewage system, the toilet was also outside. It obviously was not very usable during the winter even if the family could make it through the snowdrifts to get to the house from the not distant railroad station.[304] Tomsky, who loved to play billiards, enjoyed using the dacha's exquisite billiards table.[305] He often played games with Nikolai Bukharin and other visitors. And since hunting in the North Caucasus was Tomsky's favourite form of relaxation, he had a shooting range built on the dacha property to improve his shot.[306] Like a member of the pre-revolutionary aristocracy in his country home, Tomsky also had a large library of books. He did not pay a kopek for them because publishers would send him and other top officials all newly published political and literary works.[307] An ardent reader, the favourite authors of this autodidact included Mikhail Saltykov-Shchedrin, the nineteenth-century satirist, and Sergei Esenin, the twentieth-century lyrical poet.[308] In the words of Molotov, 'all of us had our weaknesses and had acquired some ways of the gentry. We were seduced into that life-style, there is no denying that. Everything was provided for us, all our wishes were attended to'.[309] Their privileged life was, of course, hidden from visiting foreign delegations as well as ordinary citizens.[310] But Tomsky knew that many lower party officials were fully aware of the Kremlin elite's special privileges, which they understandably resented. They angrily complained that the elite's enjoyment of material privileges undercut the party's moral authority.[311] Rank-and-file party

---

304   This description of the dacha is primarily from Teshkin (ed.) 1992, pp. 252–66; Kudrova 2004, pp. 21–2, 29; Schweitzer 1992, pp. 348–9. After Tomsky's suicide, his family was evicted from the dacha. The poet Marina Tsvetaeva and members of her family lived in half of the house for five months in 1939, after it had been converted to a safe house for the NKVD.

305   Perhaps it was left over from the wealthy owner, who had abandoned the house after the revolution, as was the case with the player piano Stalin obtained along with his dacha: Kotkin 2014, p. 467. If so, perhaps that is why this particular dacha especially appealed to Tomsky. Stalin had a detached billiards hall at his Sochi dacha: Kotkin 2017, p. 311. It is worth noting that, for the population at large, Soviet officials condemned billiards as an 'uncultured and decadent' way to spend your leisure time and launched campaigns against it: Hoffmann 2003, p. 32.

306   Gorelov 2000, p. 280.

307   Voslensky 1984, pp. 234–5, 238.

308   Gorelov 2000, p. 274. Saltykov-Shchedrin was also a lifelong favourite of Kanatchikov's since his days first reading him in prison: Kanatchikov 1986, pp. 125–6.

309   Molotov 1993, p. 225.

310   British Labour Delegation 1920, p. 6.

311   For example, an angry Moscow Party Committee stated exactly that in November 1921: Pirani 2008, p. 125.

members particularly liked to target the wives of party leaders for flaunting their privileges. They, for example, denounced the evil of party members wives wearing of jewellery or travelling to their dachas 'sporting huge hats with bird-of-paradise feathers'.[312] Wearing the sapphire-and-pearl necklace Maria Tomskaya was to receive from British trade unionists in 1925 would certainly have opened her up to being the target of such attacks.

While Tomsky and other top officials seemingly had access to almost anything they desired, all these privileges obviously could be abruptly revoked if the recipient fell out of political favour. But it is worth noting that Tomsky in fact did not lose many of his key privileges when he fell out of favour in 1929. He and his family kept their Kremlin apartment until April 1935, after which they were moved to another exclusive residence, the House of Soviets just a couple blocks away from the Kremlin. The Tomsky family kept their dacha until Tomsky committed suicide there in August 1936.

In conclusion, Tomsky went from extreme disgrace to total redemption during the year spanning the spring of 1921 to the spring of 1922. But even in disgrace, during his less than five months in Tashkent, Tomsky was grappling with two of the major issues that confronted the Soviet regime at its inception. On the 'nationality question', Tomsky like other party leaders gave lip service to 'national self-determination', but more honestly than others he characterised it as an 'unavoidable evil'. Tomsky clearly shared the prejudices and stereotypes of fellow Russians, Bolshevik or not, that the Indigenous population was lazy, as revealed in his statement telling Lenin to refrain from putting any more Muslims on the Turkestan Commission because they are not hardworking. But he was hardly alone as the policy under the Provisional Government, and the Soviet government initially, had been to exclude Muslim from participation on such governmental bodies. Tomsky obviously identified far more with the 'Russian settlers' in the region as he came to their defence against their mistreatment by Safarov and fellow Bolshevik zealots. This brought Tomsky face-to-face with another major issue confronting the early Soviet regime, how to respond to the prospect of growing inequality in the countryside during the 1920s under the policy of NEP; in particular, how to treat the so-called kulaks. Tomsky's denunciation of their brutal mistreatment in Turkestan would be vindicated in the early 1920s. And as we will see, Tomsky continued to favour following a moderate course toward the kulaks during the rest of the 1920s before vehemently opposing Stalin's ultimate, vicious resolution of the issue with the introduction

---

312 Pirani 2008, pp. 121. Pirani noted that 'the sexist manner of these complaints ... does not mean they were never valid'.

at the end of the 1920s of forced collectivisation, including an enormous, far worse replica of Safarov's policy of de-kulakisation. Despite Lenin's immediate anger at Tomsky's handling of the Fourth Trade-Union Congress and his accusations of Russian chauvinism against him, it is clear that Tomsky was viewed as one of the most capable Bolshevik leaders and one with a real connection with the mass of Soviet workers. Tomsky's shocking appointment to the Politburo and return to his post heading the VTsSPS underscored that. Tomsky's mishaps at the Fourth Trade-Union Congress and problems in Turkestan, in the end was a detour in his career, rather than the fatal derailment it appeared to be at the time, although Stalinists would use Lenin's displeasure with Tomsky in 1921 against him later.

CHAPTER 4

Getting Together Then Falling Apart: Tomsky and British Trade Unionists

> I cannot see why your Western European workers should be communists. I do not see any possibility of revolution in the West.
> TOMSKY to a German member of the Comintern

∴

Mikhail Tomsky, the chair of the USSR's huge trade-union bureaucracy and a member of the Politburo during the 1920s, played a leading role in early Soviet foreign policy as well.[1] Tomsky orchestrated one of the Soviet Union's few foreign policy achievements of the period, the creation of the Anglo-Russian Committee, linking British and Soviet trade unions together.[2] He also made some headway toward unifying the wider European trade-union movement despite fierce resistance by non-communist socialists. Tomsky achieved these successes by charming British trade unionists while holding his hard-line critics in Moscow at bay.[3] Tomsky's prominent role in Soviet foreign policy has been obscured by historians' focus on the intra-party combat between supporters and opponents of Leon Trotsky's policy of 'Permanent Revolution' and Stalin's alternative theory of 'Socialism in One Country'.[4] But early foreign policy positions within the party leadership were far more diverse than that.[5] Tomsky's more pragmatic and less ideological position explains his success in England,

---

1 Part of Chapter 4 has been previously published in 'Getting Together and then Falling Apart: Tomsky and British Trade Unionism during NEP', *Russian Review*, 73, 4: 571–95.
2 European countries' recognition of the Soviet regime as the legitimate government of Russia, and the Soviet Union's virtual alliance with Germany in the 1922 Treaty of Rapallo, constitute the other main foreign policy achievements of the 1920s.
3 Tomsky's colleagues in the Soviet leadership, in recognition of these achievements, authorised the British to translate and publish a number of Tomsky's speeches on international trade-union affairs: Tomskii 1926a. In addition, the sixth volume of his collected writings and speeches is devoted to the international trade-union movement: Tomskii 1928d.
4 See, for notable exceptions to that, Calhoun 1976 and Gorodetsky 1977.
5 See, for an example, the discussion in Jacobson 1994.

where compromises and alliances rather than revolutionary agitation or strategic rigidity produced results. This chapter will account for Tomsky's accomplishments in the international arena as well as his ultimate failure following the collapse of the British general strike in 1926.

Tomsky, as we have seen, was a self-confident, pragmatic leader. He proved to be among the most moderate Bolsheviks in international as well as domestic affairs. Tomsky broke with Trotsky and other Soviet leaders who believed a European revolution was just around the corner. In 1923, on his own initiative, he began promoting closer ties with the British Trades Union Congress (TUC) and with the International Federation of Trade Unions (IFTU), which became known as the Amsterdam International because of the location of its headquarters.[6] Tomsky's moderate proclivities, at least in comparison with other members of the Soviet leadership, were reinforced by his growing exposure to life in Europe. Tomsky, who had travelled to Western Europe before the Bolshevik seizure of power to attend various Bolshevik conferences, during the early 1920s gained a greater appreciation of the comparatively high standard of living of workers in Britain and other European countries. Unlike Trotsky, who continued to think Europe was ripe for communist revolutions, Tomsky came to doubt the possibility of a European revolution anytime soon. Tomsky in 1925 told a German member of the Communist International (Comintern), 'I cannot see why your Western European workers should be communists. I do not see any possibility of revolution in the West'.[7]

Tomsky worked on international trade-union issues almost from the moment the Bolsheviks seized power. He initially hoped that Soviet trade unionists might be able to recreate the international trade-union movement that had fallen apart because of European trade unions' support for their respective countries' military efforts during World War I.[8] Following the Soviet's First Trade-Union Congress in January 1918, Tomsky tried to establish connections with Western European trade unions, whether they were 'reformist' or 'revolutionary'. He wrote, 'We believe that despite our differences of opinion with the reformists, as fellow trade unionists we still share something in common that would allow us to unite on some sort of platform'.[9] The European Social Democrats not only ignored Tomsky's appeals, but in the summer of 1919 succeeded in re-establishing the International Federation of Trade Unions without includ-

---

6 The IFTU's communist rivals originally gave it this nickname: Van Goethem 2006, p. 11n3.
7 Quoted in Deutscher 1967, p. 402n2. Deutscher was told this by a former German vice-president of the Comintern.
8 European Social Democrats launched the IFTU in 1901.
9 Tomskii 1928d, pp. 39–40.

ing the Soviet trade unions.[10] Tomsky, angered by the snub, lashed out at what he characterised as the Amsterdam 'farce' and portrayed the European trade unionists as 'bourgeois lackeys'.[11]

Tomsky, in response to the IFTU's rejection, intensified his efforts to create a Soviet-led international trade-union organisation to counter the Amsterdam International and hopefully lure some foreign unions away from it. Prior to Tomsky's appointment to the Communist International's (Comintern's) Executive Committee in August 1920, in July 1920 he became the general secretary of a provisional body called the International Trade-Union Council (ITUC), the forerunner of the Red International of Labor Unions (commonly known as the Profintern).[12] Tomsky was chosen to head this body over fellow trade unionist Alexander Lozovsky, even though Lozovsky spoke three foreign languages – German, French, and English – and had considerable international experience.[13] Tomsky and Lozovsky would be at loggerheads during the 1920s, which will be a focus later in this chapter, so some background on their relationship is important. The Soviet leadership preferred to put Tomsky in the top leadership position, at least partly because Lozovsky had been a Menshevik.[14] But it was also already apparent that foreign representatives much preferred Tomsky. The Spaniard Angel Pestaña, for example, remarked that, 'from the very first moment, Tomsky turned out to be much easier to get on with than Lozovsky'.[15] The British communist, John Murphy, also quickly picked up on the rivalry that existed between Tomsky and Lozovsky. According to Murphy, 'Tomsky regarded Lozovsky as a new-comer who was trying to appear more Bolshevik than the Bolsheviks in order to supersede Tomsky in the leadership of the Russian trade unions'.[16] Even so, after the ITUC elected its Bureau on 11 August, which consisted of Tomsky, as its general secretary, the Frenchman Alfred Rosmer, and a representative of the Comintern to be appointed later, Tomsky proposed to a Central Committee Plenum that Lozovsky be assigned

---

10 Representatives of trade-union confederations from 14 countries attended this first IFTU congress. All but two of those federations, the British and Dutch, forbid communist organisations from becoming members of their national federations: Van Goethem 2006, p. 92.
11 Tomskii 1928d, pp. 14–18.
12 The other Soviets appointed to the Comintern Executive Committee, in addition to Tomsky, were Zinoviev, Bukharin, and Radek: Adibekov (ed.) 2004, p. 56.
13 Calhoun 1976, pp. 12–13. Other sources state Lozovsky started to learn English only in 1939: Rubinstein and Naumov (eds) 2005, p. 179. E.H. Carr described Lozovsky as 'an able and ambitious intellectual': Carr 1952, p. 62.
14 Lozovsky, who left the Bolshevik Party in 1912, rejoined it in 1917.
15 Quoted in Tosstorff 2018, p. 178.
16 Murphy 1941, p. 161.

to collaborate with him, in order to lighten his work load somewhat, given his other competing responsibilities, primarily his position as chair of the VTsSPS. The Central Committee, which clearly did not want to appoint Lozovsky to even this subordinate position, refused to accept Tomsky's proposal.[17] In the words of the historian of the Profintern, Reiner Tosstorff, 'all Lozovsky's international experience could not alter the fact that Tomsky was a man of much great political stature'.[18] But not of physical stature: while Tomsky was short, Lozovsky was tall and far more physically imposing.

Tomsky's exile to Turkestan not only temporarily deprived him of his position as head of the VTsSPS, but also as head of the ITUC. Even before the ITUC was renamed the Profintern at its founding congress in July 1921, Lozovsky managed to move into Tomsky's place.[19] Although Tomsky did not resume his former position as head of the Soviet's international trade-union organisation, after the Politburo returned Tomsky to the VTsSPS in January 1922, and then to its chair in September, Tomsky did assume a leading position in the Profintern. In early 1922, before his appointment to the Politburo, it was Tomsky, sometimes along with Rudzutak and Melnichansky, who discussed Profintern issues with the Politburo.[20] By the time of the Profintern's Second Congress in November 1922, Tomsky was one of the 12 members of the Profintern's Executive Committee and one of the three members of its Secretariat, along with Lozovsky and the Spaniard Andrés Nin.[21]

Tomsky, despite his efforts toward promoting the Profintern, behind the scenes wanted to carve out a significant role for the VTsSPS in foreign affairs by independently improving relations with the Amsterdam International and the British Trades Union Congress. Tomsky at this point already had begun working to overcome opposition within the Profintern to establishing these closer international ties.[22] But his influence within the Profintern took a hit when Lenin in December 1922 decided he needed to lessen Tomsky's workload. Always solicitous of his comrades' health, Lenin wrote to Stalin that he did not want Tomsky

---

17 Tosstorff 2018, pp. 179, 305.
18 Tosstorff 2018, p. 306. In contrast, the historian of the IFTU wrongly argued that the Soviet party leadership had more confidence in Lozovsky: Van Goethem 2006, p. 79.
19 Lozovsky became head of the Profintern in May 1921, just before its founding congress in July 1921. In exile before the revolution, he became the head of the primarily Jewish Hatters' Union of the *Confederation Generale du Travail*, the most influential syndicalist union in Europe, which had joined the IFTU, though they denounced it as reformist: Tosstorff 2003, pp. 84, 96n20.
20 See the Politburo protocols for 9 and 23 February 1922: Khordina (ed.) 2000, pp. 152, 159.
21 Tomsky had previously attended the second enlarged Comintern Plenum in June 1922.
22 Langsam 1973, p. 235.

FIGURE 14   Alexander Lozovsky
            WIKIMEDIA COMMONS

to spend more than an hour a day with Profintern responsibilities because he was overloaded with work in the VTsSPS.[23]

The utter failure of the uprising in Germany in October 1923 confirmed Tomsky's pessimistic views about the prospects for a successful communist revolu-

---

23   Lenin's message on cutting back time in the Profintern also applied to Rudzutak. Lenin said they should have the assistance of 'two or more secretaries who know foreign languages and who are capable of keeping Tomsky and Ruzutak informed in every detail': Lenin 1960–70, vol. 45, p. 599; RGASPI f. 17, op. 3, d. 327, l. 2.

tion in Europe anytime soon. This defeat also crushed the high hopes of Trotsky and other party leaders who believed Europe, particularly Germany, was on the verge of a communist revolution.[24] In response to this and earlier fiascos, the Soviet party line was that conditions in Europe had temporarily stabilised and communists should adopt the tactic of pursuing 'united fronts' with non-communist workers' organisations.[25] Tomsky whole-heartedly embraced the new policy he had a hand in crafting. He called for Soviet trade unionists to 'join hands' with socialists and other non-communists in Europe.[26]

To make this happen, Tomsky reached out to the British General Council of the Trades Union Congress. The General Council consisted of the leaders of the main British trade unions, including the small group Tomsky considered 'wobblers', leaders with left-wing leanings.[27] Although the British were the most conservative affiliate in the IFTU next to the Americans, they were Amsterdam's most numerous and influential members and were the only affiliate to demonstrate any willingness to consider bringing the Soviet trade unions into the IFTU.[28] In this outreach, Tomsky may have been able to carry out simple conversations without his interpreter. He had begun to learn English after a visit of British labour leaders to Soviet Russia in 1920.[29] As a result of that visit many of the British trade-union leaders had a chance to get to know Tomsky and observe his public speaking prowess. They were in attendance when Tomsky opened the proceedings on 18 May 1920 of a special session of the Moscow Soviet and they also attended a VTsSPS plenum meeting on 24 May. The Labour delegation, upon their return to London, blamed the deplorable economic conditions in the Soviet Union primarily on the foreign intervention and blockade rather than Bolshevik policies.[30]

---

24   Bayerlein 1999, pp. 252–4, 257–8. Uprisings also failed at that time in Bulgaria and Estonia.
25   The Comintern had formally adopted the united front strategy earlier, on 18 December 1921. The Comintern called for 'the greatest possible unity' of all workers' organisations, including negotiating with 'the treacherous social-democratic and Amsterdam leaders': Degras 1956, p. 424. The united front policy was reaffirmed at the Fourth Comintern Congress in November 1922: Carr 1964, p. 534.
26   Tomskii 1926b, p. 61.
27   Langsam 1973, p. 190.
28   The TUC also provided much of the IFTU's funding, which curtailed the IFTU's leadership's prerogatives, as this statement conveys: 'Unfortunately, we are at present financially dependent on the English and therefore have to accept many things that would otherwise be dismissed': quoted in Van Goethem 2006, p. 37.
29   Kun 1992, p. 273.
30   White 1994, pp. 630–4, 638. The Labour delegation attended another VTsSPS session on 10 June.

The formation of the first-ever Labour Government in Great Britain, on 22 January 1924, provided Tomsky with the opportunity to court the General Council. Prime Minister Ramsay MacDonald's minority government extended de jure diplomatic recognition to the Soviet Union just over a week after gaining office on 1 February 1924 and invited the Soviet government to send representatives to draw up a treaty to resolve all remaining issues between the two countries.[31] Tomsky was the second-ranking member of the 11-member Soviet delegation, which arrived in April.[32] Though formally a diplomat, with the Politburo's approval, Tomsky quickly made contact with the TUC leadership after arriving in London.[33] The British trade unionists welcomed him with open arms. Fifteen of the General Council's 32 members held a dinner on 14 May 1924 for Tomsky and the three other trade unionists in the Soviet delegation: Ivan Kutuzov (Textile Workers' Union), Nikolai Shvernik (Metal Workers' Union), and Zhitkov (Railway Workers' Union).[34] The TUC leaders had earlier indicated at their congress in September 1923 that, while representatives from the Profintern were unwelcome at their congresses, they were willing to meet with Soviet trade-union representatives.[35]

Tomsky seized the opportunity to turn the reception at a London restaurant into a mini conference. Following an extremely warm welcoming address by Alf Purcell, the president of the TUC, Tomsky, through his translator, delivered a tactically skilful speech in which he happily flattered his hosts. He lauded the members of the General Council for providing a model that Russian trade unionists had tried to emulate in their infancy, decades earlier. Tomsky, a member of the Politburo, also made a backhanded slap at Soviet and British political

---

31 France and then all other the major powers except the United States followed the British lead and recognised the Soviet Union. The British hoped the bilateral Trade Agreement would limit Soviet support for foreign revolutionary groups, particularly in India: Hughes 1997, pp. 185–6.

32 The Romanian Christian Rakovsky, who was from an aristocratic background, headed the Soviet delegation and was the chief Soviet negotiator. This was a fast-developing situation since Tomsky had been entrusted by the Politburo on 20 March to attend the German Communist Party's Congress that opened on 7 April 1924, along with Bukharin, Sokolnikov, and Lozovsky. Tomsky now obviously had to decline attending that congress: Adibekov (ed.) 2004, p. 251.

33 Zinoviev presented a report to the Politburo on the VTsSPS delegation to England on 13 March 1924: Khordina (ed.) 2000, p. 280.

34 One of the diplomatic attachés and a translator also attended the dinner: Tomskii 1926a, pp. 14–15; 'Report of Reception with Russian Delegates at Gatti's Restaurant, London, May 1924', TUC Archive, MSS. 292/947/1/36. All the references to the TUC Archive are from the Modern Records Centre at the University of Warwick.

35 Carr 1964, p. 130.

leaders when he remarked that 'trade unionists are the most practical and sensible people in the world'. He acknowledged that 'transient political differences' will continue to separate British and Russian trade unionists, but he dismissively characterised these differences as superficial. He then informed his audience point-by-point about the diplomatic negotiations with the Labour Government and, in particular, the reasons why he thought a 'mutual canceling of debts' was just.[36]

Tomsky completely won over his audience. The leaders of the TUC responded enthusiastically to his speech. 'We shall be ready', Purcell promised, 'to use all our influence to do everything we possibly can to ensure that an understanding shall be reached'. He hoped that this meeting would mark the beginning of a link between the British and Soviet trade union movements. Ben Tillett ecstatically declared that 'Comrade Tomsky has outlined the picture with a master hand ... In this invigorating atmosphere, I feel young once more, rejuvenated'.[37] While these trade unions leaders had antagonistic relations with members of the Communist Party inside Britain itself, they quickly came to see Tomsky as a fellow trade unionist with whom they could talk and work. Tomsky was clearly touched by the unexpectedly enthusiastic response to his speech.[38]

Following his charm offensive in London, Tomsky reached out to the IFTU leadership in Amsterdam. Tomsky apparently believed he could win over the IFTU's leaders with left-wing leanings just as he had won over leaders of the TUC.[39] His hopes seemed justified when the British General Council, which clearly believed that international unity could be achieved, agreed to serve

---

36 Tomskii 1926a, pp. 27, 33; Great Britain Foreign Office 1984, p. 366. Tomsky had played a central role in formulating how to approach the negotiations with England along with Rakovsky, Georgy Chicherin, and Maksim Litvinov. They gave multiple reports to the Politburo on 20 March and 27 March 1924: Khordina (ed.) 2000, pp. 282, 284. The Soviet government ultimately agreed, in principle, to pay British citizens for the tsarist debts and reimburse English bondholders and proprietors for property that the Soviet government had nationalised: Jacobson 1994, p. 136.

37 Tomskii 1926a, pp. 34, 39; 'Report of Reception', TUC Archive, MSS. 292/947/1/36.

38 About the dinner, the historian Daniel Calhoun wittily remarked, 'The enthusiastic response of his hosts testifies to the quality either of Tomsky's rhetoric or of the restaurant's wine list. One assumes it was a little of each': Calhoun 1976, p. 54. An article in the British press delighted in writing that Tomsky requested beer instead of wine at the conference, which Tomsky felt necessary to refute when back in Moscow: GARF, f. 5451, op. 42, d. 20, l. 66.

39 Tomskii 1926, p. 58; Langsam 1973, pp. 188–90. It is worth noting that the Social-Democratic leadership of the IFTU was initially almost as hostile to Samuel Gompers, as well to other leaders of the American Federation of Labor, as they were to Tomsky and the VTsSPS: Van Goethem 2006, p. 27.

as an intermediary between the Soviet Union's VTsSPS and the IFTU. Fred Bramley, the TUC's general secretary, who characterised himself as a member of the extreme Right of the British trade-union movement, forcefully argued the Soviet case at the IFTU's annual Congress in Vienna in June 1924 and at the Amsterdam Congress in February 1925.[40] In his February speech he said that excluding Russia is a disastrous policy that stems from 'the almost savage ferocity that you get into when you are discussing Russian affairs … Get rid of the panicky fear that seems to invade and dominate your minds in dealing with Russia'.[41] Tomsky and his colleagues are not, Bramley insisted, 'the wild-eyed, red-tied, long-haired, irresponsible revolutionaries' that you seem to imagine.[42]

The British advocacy for unity succeeded against all odds. The majority of the IFTU's Executive Committee, primarily French and German Social Democrats, had come to their Vienna congress in June 1924 determined to put an end to any future overtures towards the Soviet trade unions. They objected to communist tactics in their countries, including 'unwarranted attacks upon the character and honesty of trade-union officials'.[43] Part of the British trade-union leaders' initial success was simply fortuitous. During the congress, Purcell, the most pro-Soviet member of the General Council, was elected president of the IFTU because Jimmy Thomas, among the most anti-Soviet members of the General Council, resigned the IFTU presidency to join MacDonald's Labour Government.[44] Purcell forcefully argued that Soviet trade unions needed to be

---

40   Calhoun 1976, p. 54; Bramley 1925, p. 2.
41   Bramley 1925, pp. 8, 17.
42   Bramley 1925, p. 18. Unlike the Western European Social-Democratic leaders of the IFTU, the British trade unionists seemed happy to ignore aspects of the Bolshevik Party that should have troubled them and the fact that Tomsky was not just the chair of the VTsSPS but also a leading member of the Soviet government.
43   *Russia and International Unity: Report to Affiliated Societies Trades Union Congress*, TUC Archive, MSS. 36/R30/55.
44   The strongly anti-Communist Secretary of the British Miners' Union, Frank Hodges, resigned as well to become a minister in the government. The General Council of the TUC required the resignation of any of its members who accepted a position in the government, while the unwritten rules of the IFTU reserved the presidency to the national federation that gave the largest financial contribution, although in this case the IFTU leaders did so only very reluctantly and were determined to undercut Purcell at every opportunity: Van Goethem 2006, p. 91. It was also chance that allowed Purcell to become president of the TUC. He stepped into the presidency after Margaret Bondfield became parliamentary secretary of the Ministry of Labour. Purcell previously had a chance to get to know Tomsky from his visit to Moscow as part of the British Labour delegation in May-June 1920, when he played a role along with Tomsky in the creation of the Profintern: Morgan 2013, p. 68; Tomskii 1928a, pp. 196, 513.

admitted if the IFTU hoped to become an actual international organisation.⁴⁵ The discussions off stage entailed lots of back-and-forth arguments and, in the end, were very encouraging. The General Council's efforts succeeded in obtaining an invitation for the Soviet trade unions to join the IFTU.⁴⁶

But Tomsky would never have a chance to charm the IFTU leadership like he had charmed the General Council. The IFTU delegates had only agreed to invite the Soviet Union grudgingly, and they stipulated that the VTsSPS would have to agree to accept all pre-existing IFTU statutes, including the statute forbidding trade-union organisations in the IFTU from being affiliated simultaneously with the Profintern.⁴⁷ Because Tomsky knew the IFTU's demand to disassociate Soviet trade unions from the Profintern would be unacceptable back in Moscow, he characterised the terms as 'preposterous'. But he was clearly intrigued by the unexpected invitation.⁴⁸

Tomsky's involvement in foreign affairs brought him into conflict not only with many of the leaders of the Amsterdam International, but with Lozovsky, the general secretary of Profintern, as well.⁴⁹ This was quickly apparent at the Fifth Congress of the Comintern, 24 June–8 July 1924, and the Third Congress of the Profintern, which opened immediately afterwards.⁵⁰ At both these congresses, as well as at the Politburo meeting on 11 July, the most contentious issue concerned whether to seek unity with the Amsterdam International.⁵¹ The previously uncompromising Lozovsky had been put on the defensive by the IFTU's offer.⁵² He was sensitive to charges of 'splitting' the international trade-union

---

45 Tosstorff 2016, p. 685.
46 From the Comintern's multilingual newspaper (it was published in English, German, Spanish, and French), the English version of which was the *International Press Correspondence (Inprecorr)* 19 June 1924, p. 352; 7 August 1924, p. 596; 12 August 1924, p. 600.
47 'Special Supplement to the Monthly Circular of the Labour Research Department, 1925', TUC Archive, MSS. 292/778.1/4/35; International Labour Office 1927, p. 230.
48 Tomskii 1926a, p. 70.
49 Born Solomon Abramovich in 1878. The son of a Hebrew schoolteacher in a Ukrainian *shtetl* Lozovsky always spoke with a heavy Yiddish accent. As a secondary-school graduate, Lozovsky had far more formal education than Tomsky. Lozovsky, joined with Zinoviev, Aleksander Dogadov, and Andrei Andreev, to make a presentation to the Politburo on 27 June on Tomsky's relations with the Amsterdam International: Khordina (ed.) 2000, p. 305.
50 The other Soviet leaders to attend the Fifth Comintern Congress were Zinoviev, Bukharin, Stalin, Kamenev, Rykov, Trotsky, and Lozovsky. The Politburo commission included besides Tomsky, Lozovsky, Rudzutak, Andreev, Melnichansky, Dogadov, Ivan Lepse, and Nikolai Antipov: Adibekov (ed.) 2004, pp. 257, 260.
51 Tomsky, Zinoviev, Lozovsky, Dogadov, Andreev, and Iosif Pyatnitsky all addressed the Politburo at this July meeting: Adibekov (ed.) 2004, p. 259.
52 In the colourful description of one Comintern member, when Lozovsky was attacked 'his

movement (though that is precisely what he wanted to do), so at both congresses Lozovsky gave lip service to the goal of uniting the two internationals and praised by name Purcell, Bramley, and A.J. Cook (the militant leader of the British Miners' Union) as 'honest revolutionary proletarians'.[53] But he made it clear that he remained reluctant to deal with the IFTU on any terms other than its full capitulation to the Profintern.

Tomsky was undeterred by Lozovsky's criticisms. At the Profintern Congress, he vigorously defended the policy of interacting with the Western European 'reformists', stating that to let the chance of negotiations with Amsterdam and the British left wing slip away would be 'a grave error, a short-sighted policy'.[54] Tomsky went on to argue that Lozovsky needed to face the fact that millions of workers in Europe were led by 'reformists', and that the idea of one trade-union international, which included Soviet trade unions, was steadily gaining popularity.[55] Tomsky succeeded in getting Lozovsky and the 70 Profintern delegates to soften their opposition to negotiations with the IFTU while also convincing the British delegates in attendance of his sincerity in reaching out to them and the IFTU.[56] He also won the support of key Soviet leaders, including Grigory Zinoviev, the widely disliked, demagogic president of the Comintern.[57] Zinoviev, who also served alongside Tomsky on the Politburo, wholeheartedly supported him by optimistically, if hyperbolically, proclaiming, 'The chief task of the Communist International is now transferred to England in all fields'.[58] Bukharin, in a formal speech of welcome from the Comintern, argued that the emergence of a left wing in the IFTU was 'one of the most important facts in our present political life'.[59] The Profintern Congress, despite strong opposition from some non-Soviet 'ultra-leftist' delegates, authorised Tomsky to negotiate with the IFTU. He was to do so either directly with the IFTU or through the TUC's General Council, with the goal of achieving international trade-union unity

---

        eyes, narrow and squinting, lit up like those of a fanatical dervish doing a holy dance': Gitlow 1940, p. 458.
53   *Inprecorr*, 19 August 1924, pp. 665–7; Tosstorff 2018, p. 687.
54   Tomskii 1926a, pp. 52, 60.
55   Tomskii 1926a, p. 54.
56   GARF, f, 5451, op. 42, d. 92, l. 17.
57   *Inprecorr*, 19 August 1924, p. 626. Many of Zinoviev's associates thought he was personally repulsive. Most harshly, Angelica Balabanoff, who served as secretary of the Comintern at its inception, said that 'after Mussolini ... I consider Zinoviev the most despicable individual I have ever met': Balabanoff 1973, p. 220. Another member of the Comintern, Aino Kuusinen, recalled that Zinoviev 'was heartily disliked by all who knew him well': Kuusinen 1974, p. 78.
58   Quoted in Tosstorff 2018, p. 690.
59   Quoted in Carr 1964, p. 560.

while also maintaining a role for the Profintern. The resolution, which the Politburo approved, called for the convocation of an international unity congress in which all the trade unions adhering to either the Amsterdam International or to the Profintern would take part 'on the basis of proportional representation'.[60] Although Tomsky and his fellow Soviet trade union leaders had been instructed not to take any major steps without the sanction of the Profintern, they were also contradictorily encouraged to take the initiative and not ignore any opportunity to negotiate with the IFTU. According to the preeminent historian of the Profintern, 'It was an open secret at the congress that the Russian trade unions aimed to secure entry into the IFTU ... and that this would automatically bring with it the liquidation of the RILU [Profintern]'.[61] Lozovsky clearly was the loser and Tomsky the victor in the debates at the Comintern and Profintern congresses.[62] Tomsky had left the Profintern without any clear role, and as a result it went into 'cold storage', in the words of one historian.[63] Its Central Council did not even meet again until March 1928. Not surprisingly, from here on out, the tug-of-war between Tomsky and Lozovsky, and between the VTsSPS and Profintern, intensified. Tomsky and Lozovsky increasingly disliked one another. It grated on Tomsky that Lozovsky, who unlike Tomsky had never been a worker, was so adamantly militant in his hostility toward the European Social Democrats. Tomsky also resented Lozovsky's claim that the Profintern should set policy for the Soviet trade-union council. Lozovsky, for his part, resented Tomsky's unilateral negotiations abroad.[64] As their personal animosity grew, Lozovsky, an adroit speaker and writer, worked hard to undermine Tomsky's efforts. So for Tomsky, an added benefit of any successes in the West was that it came at the expense of Lozovsky, while also increasing the prestige of the VTsSPS at the expense of Profintern.[65]

Tomsky was not alone in taking a dislike to Lozovsky. Most harshly, an American member of the Comintern described Lozovsky as 'an inveterate intriguer ... a dirty, unscrupulous fighter, with the cunning of a cat and the treachery of a rat'.[66] Victor Serge, another member of the Comintern, argued more positively that Lozovsky was 'open-minded, lively, and easy-going.' But even he

---

60   Degras 1956, p. 132; *Inprecorr*, 29 August 1924, pp. 665–6. The Politburo resolution called for six representatives each from the VTsSPS and the IFTU: Adibekov (ed.) 2004, p. 296.
61   Tosstorff 2018, pp. 699–701.
62   Calhoun 1991, p. 254.
63   Swain 1987, p. 72.
64   Cohen 1973, p. 231.
65   Carr 1964, p. 550n1.
66   Gitlow 1948, p. 177.

FIGURE 15   Tomsky at British Trades Union Congress in Hull
WIKIMEDIA COMMONS

conceded that Lozovsky had 'the air of a slightly fastidious schoolmaster amidst his world-wide assortment of trade-union militants'.[67] Lozovsky 'relished his pose as cosmopolitan sophisticate in marked contrast to the native, blunt, sometimes raw openness of Tomsky', according to the historian Daniel Calhoun, who concluded that 'everybody who knew them both preferred dealing with Tomsky'.[68] Certainly the British trade-union and Communist party leaders did. They took an immediate aversion to Lozovsky.[69] Tomsky played this up during his trips to England. One British observer compared him to a dove flitting around London 'cooing I'm not Lozovsky, I'm Tomsky'!"[70]

67   Serge 1963, p. 146.
68   Calhoun 1976, p. 13. Also see Murphy 1941, p. 161.
69   Morgan 2013, p. 123.
70   Quoted in Morgan 2013, p. 128.

Tomsky returned to Britain a couple months after the Profintern Congress to attend the annual TUC Congress in Hull in September 1924.[71] This was the first time a Russian trade-union leader had been invited to the congress as a fraternal delegate. The official purpose of this trip was to ratify the Anglo-Soviet trade treaties signed a month earlier, but Tomsky's true goal was to urge the TUC to facilitate talks without any preconditions between the VTsSPS and the IFTU, and to lay the groundwork for creating an Anglo-Russian Committee for trade-union unity. The Politburo had earlier given Tomsky the authority to work toward bringing the Russian and English trade unions together in such a committee.[72] When they arrived at the congress hall, Tomsky and his three fellow Soviet trade-union leaders were so enthusiastically welcomed by the 1,040 delegates that one delegate, Charlie Cramp, the strongly anti-communist leader of the Railroad Workers' Union, felt compelled to tell the congress that although the Soviet trade unionists were not 'angels', he found them to be 'sincere and straightforward men'.[73] In the words of the official report, Tomsky, who spoke immediately after the head of the IFTU, Jan Oudegeest, received 'a very hearty reception', whereas Oudegeest had been only 'cordially received'.[74] Walter Citrine, the assistant general secretary of the TUC remembered all the delegates were 'on the tiptoe of expectation', as a smiling Tomsky mounted the podium. Citrine characterised him as 'a little man with small twinkling eyes, large protruding ears, and a rather sallow complexion. His voice was harsh and metallic, with excellent carrying power'.[75] In response to Cramp's comment, Tomsky conceded the Soviets were 'very far from angels ... angels did not make revolutions (hear, hear) [but] just plain working people like yourselves'.[76]

In this 45-minute speech, Tomsky confronted the issue of the Profintern delicately and ambiguously, in a way that suggested his lack of dedication to it. He certainly did not defend it, saying the Profintern 'may be a good thing, or it may be a bad one' and 'a great many people may not like it', but the TUC needed to

---

71 Tomsky had arrived in England more than a month earlier to be with one of the five Soviet signees of the Anglo-Soviet General Treaty on 10 August: Fischer 1930, p. 490.

72 RGASPI, f. 17, op. 3, d. 433, ll. 5, 13, 14, 22, reprinted in Adibekov (ed.) 2004, p. 257.

73 Bramley (ed.) 1924, p. 317. At the 1922 British Labour Party Conference, Cramp introduced a resolution, which carried, denouncing the trial of SRs in Moscow: *Inprecorr*, 17 July 1922, p. 420. The other members of the delegation were Lepse, A.M. Amosov, and A.M. Gorbachev: Pankratov 1972, p. 195.

74 Bramley (ed.) 1924, pp. 393–5.

75 Citrine 1964, p. 89.

76 Tomskii 1926a, p. 88. The stenographic report counted six cheers, seven 'hear hears', and four outbursts of laughter during Tomsky's speech: Morgan 2013, p. 129.

accept the fact that 'it exists'.⁷⁷ Tomsky concluded his speech with a passionate appeal for international working-class unity and called on the TUC to make it happen. Tomsky, as he had less than five months before, won over his British listeners.⁷⁸ The standing ovation at the end of his speech lasted for such a long time that one observer described it as 'the greatest éclat ever known in a Labour conference'.⁷⁹ The Congress unanimously resolved to push the Amsterdam International to offer more concrete steps toward unifying the workers' movement into one international. Some of the press reports were almost as enthusiastic as those by the delegates. The liberal *Daily News* praised Tomsky's smooth, diplomatic touch, pleasant voice, and skilful use of humour.⁸⁰

Tomsky returned to Moscow in a triumphant, if physically exhausted state.⁸¹ After a couple of weeks in a hospitable bed, he reported on 24 October 1924 to the Moscow province's Metalworkers' Union's Congress that, as a move toward achieving a single, new world organisation, 'we have offered to liquidate Profintern if Amsterdam would be liquidated as well'.⁸² This announcement utterly infuriated Lozovsky.

After the Hull congress, British trade-union leaders accepted Tomsky's invitation for a reciprocal visit to Moscow to attend the Soviet's Sixth Trade-Union Congress.⁸³ At this November 1924 congress in the trade unions' Hall of Columns, when Tomsky welcomed the seven British delegates in his opening address, they were greeted with enormous applause. Zinoviev opened the congress by grandiosely proclaiming that 'the international unity of the trade-union movement is as necessary to us as air is to man'.⁸⁴ Tomsky in his speech shared the fruitless nature of the correspondence he had been conducting over the last couple months with the IFTU. To Amsterdam's questions about whether the Soviets wanted a marriage based on love or simply one of convenience, he had told them, in his typically humorous way, that since he had a genial disposition, he wanted to enter into a marriage of love, though the

---

77 Tomskii 1926a, pp. 89–90.
78 Bramley (ed.) 1924, p. 400.
79 Quoted in Morgan 2013, p. 129.
80 Shapovalova 1989, p. 92.
81 GARF, f, 5451, op. 42, d. 89a, l. 1.
82 Tomskii 1928d, p. 193.
83 The large and top-level delegation received lavish attention during its 36 days in the Soviet Union. Tomsky even postponed the opening of the congress just so the British delegates could attend it. Upon their return to London they would write a strongly pro-Soviet report: TUC General Council 1925; Great Britain Foreign Office 1984, p. 452; International Labour Office 1927, p. 234.
84 Quoted by Carr 1964, p. 570.

exchange of letters with the IFTU felt like a romance in which 'both sides love one another and at the same time abuse each other'. But after years of 'firing at one another with small arms and with heavy artillery', this exchange of letters, Tomsky argued, was a big move forward.[85] Tomsky was clearly making some headway. On 6 November Oudegeest wrote in a confidential letter to Leon Jouhaux, an IFTU vice-president and the most prominent spokesperson of the IFTU's right wing, that he thought Tomsky's messages showed 'a sincere desire on the part of the Russians to co-operate with us'.[86]

The British delegates found the trade-union congress's atmosphere 'charged with a revolutionary fervor' that they found impossible to resist.[87] Purcell lauded Russian workers' 'magnificent achievements'. Bramley declared British trade unionists were also striving for 'control over the means of production', while Tillett paid homage to Lenin, 'the great fighter and leader of the working class'.[88] The impetuous Purcell, recently elected president of the IFTU, pledged in his fiery speech to the Sixth Trade-Union Congress that the General Council would bring about unity with the Russians if Amsterdam failed to do so.[89] The congress passed a resolution, drafted by Tomsky, which gave the VTsSPS full authority to form an Anglo-Russian Committee in order 'to coordinate the activities of the trade-union movements of both countries in their struggle for international trade-union unity', which was followed by loud, prolonged cheering.[90] The resolution also asserted that such a committee would be 'a sure guarantee against the continuing threat of a new world war and a bulwark in the struggle against fascist reaction and the offensive of capital'.[91] At an impromptu

---

85   Tomskii 1926a, pp. 50, 66, 71; VTsSPS 1925, pp. 178–80.
86   But Oudegeest, the Dutch trade-union leader and social-democratic politician, added that this meant it was time to attack Tomsky. The exact wording was: 'I send you herewith copy in French of the letter we have received from Tomsky. It was in very bad English. It appears to me to show a sincere desire on the part of the Russians to cooperate with us, and, therefore, it seems to me it is time we passed to the attack': quoted in Dunn, 1928, p. 226. It caused an uproar in 1927 when a British IFTU official made the contents of this message public: Tosstorff 2018, p. 703.
87   Bramley 1925, p. 10.
88   *Inprecorr*, 20 November 1924, p. 906. The other members of the delegation were John Bromley, Alan Findlay, Herbert Smith, and John Turner.
89   TUC Archive, MSS. 292/947/59/74–75. Purcell, to prolonged applause, ended his speech with 'Hurrah for the international unity of the world's working class and down with capitalism'! Bramley and Tillet also presented speeches that were translated into Russian, with Tillet, in his tribute to the memory of Lenin, proclaiming that 'I believe this Lenin's name will still be honoured after the memory of the Caesars has long since been forgotten': *Inprecorr*, 16 December 1924, p. 978.
90   *Inprecorr*, 16 December 1924, p. 995; Morgan 2013, p. 130.
91   Quoted by Carr 1964, p. 571.

meeting behind the scenes, the British delegates voiced their strong support for creating such a committee. At the close of the congress, amid a booming rendition of 'The Internationale', and enthusiastic applause from every part of the vast Hall of Columns, delegates rushed the stage and threw both Tomsky and Purcell, who was hardly sylph-like, up into the air.[92]

Tomsky enjoyed the adulation of both the Soviet and British delegates to the congress. The VTsSPS paid a special tribute to all the work he done to build up the Soviet trade unions. One VTsSPS Presidium member, after recounting Tomsky's years of imprisonment before the revolution, announced to the congress the impending multi-volume publication of Tomsky's articles and speeches to commemorate the twentieth anniversary of Tomsky's membership in the Bolshevik Party. The affectionate report in the *Workers' Weekly* conveys well how the British representatives viewed Tomsky. 'As this quiet, modest looking man stepped forward it seemed impossible to believe he was the leader of six million trade unionists. But in his short, sharp phrases, every sentence conveyed a direct thought. In his keen eyes, his love of a joke, one saw at once he was a leader of men, and one that not only thinks of today, but looks far ahead'.[93] Even Lozovsky, despite continuing reservations, felt compelled to give a full-throated endorsement for the establishment of an Anglo-Russian Committee. It would be, Lozovsky stated, of 'tremendous significance, both from the point of view of principle and practice. It shows where there is a will for unity, where there is a desire to join the various detachments of the working class, it can be achieved'. Lozovsky also voiced his reservations, stating that in creating the committee we should 'never for a moment close our eyes to the differences between us'.[94]

Zinoviev, who at least temporarily shared Tomsky's doubts about the prospects of revolution in Europe, stated that the Anglo-Russian Committee was 'the greatest hope of the international proletariat', and that revolution in Bri-

---

92   Calhoun 1976, p. 98; *Inprecorr*, 16 December 1924, p. 995; Morgan 2013, p. 135. The British press responded to the British delegation's positive report with a barrage of criticism: Klugmann 1969, p. 15. The newspapers of the German, French, Dutch, and Hungarian social-democratic newspapers also unleashed attacks on the British delegation. The German newspaper, *Vorwärts* (Forward) suggested that the published report of Purcell's speech was a forgery, which Purcell denied. The Belgian newspaper, *Le Peuple*, with some justification, accused the British delegation of seeing 'what they hoped and wished to see' during their visit to the Soviet Union: 'Special Supplement to the Monthly Circular of the Labour Research Department, 1925': 'Special Supplement to the Monthly Circular of the Labour Research Department, 1925', TUC Archive, MSS. 292/778.1/4/35, pp. ii–x.
93   'The Minority Movement, Special Supplement', TUC Archive, MSS. 229/947/59/1.
94   'The Minority Movement, Special Supplement', TUC Archive, MSS. 229/947/59/1.

tain was as likely to come 'through the door of the unions as through the door of the Communist Party'.[95] There was no getting around the fact that the British Communist Party remained extremely weak and insignificant. It never had more than four thousand members from the end of 1921 to 1924, and half of those members failed to pay their dues.[96] Tomsky told Purcell that the British communists were just 'babes'.[97] The British Communist Party did establish the National Minority Movement (NMM) in August 1924, which affiliated with the Profintern and enjoyed some success in building up factions in various unions, most impressively in the miners' union, which elected Cook, the Minority Movement candidate, as their general secretary.[98] Tomsky, though, wisely kept the NMM at arm's length because of his desire to not offend the General Council. The General Council asked him not to attend or even send VTsSPS delegates to the January 1925 conference of the NMM, which Tomsky respected.[99]

Tomsky's brainchild, the Anglo-Russian Joint Advisory Council, was ratified in early April 1925. Tomsky led a delegation of five top members of the VTsSPS to London to formally sign the agreement.[100] For Tomsky and his fellow trade unionists, according to Citrine, the Anglo-Russian Committee was 'the greatest victory yet achieved for working-class solidarity and unity'.[101] At the three-day meeting, the British delegation of 14 leading British trade unionists agreed to convene a conference between the VTsSPS and the IFTU 'without

---

95 Summary of Zinoviev's report to the plenary meeting of the Executive of the Communist International on 25 March 1925: quoted in Borkenau 1938, p. 279. Upon his return to Moscow, Tomsky had to fend off criticism for trying to join the IFTU at the Central Committee Plenum and even from some members of the VTsSPS itself: RGASPI, f. 17, op. 2, d. 179, ll. 38–40.
96 Thorpe 2000, p. 45. In contrast, the strong French Communist Party had 131,000 members in 1921: Drachkovitch and Lazitch 1966, p. 186.
97 Quoted in Morgan 2013, p. 71.
98 The miners held the election because their previous leader, the strongly anti-communist Hodges, had resigned to become first lord of the Admiralty in MacDonald's government. Purcell, who refused to join the British Communist Party, was known to sympathise with the Minority Movement.
99 MacFarlane 1966, pp. 115, 151–2; Bramley 1925, pp. 14–15.
100 The Soviet delegation consisted of Tomsky, Melnichansky, Lepse, Olga Chernysheva, Vasily Mikhailov: Tomskii 1928d, p. 682n234. According to the British report, a sixth delegate, Nikolai Glebov-Avilov, was also part of the Soviet delegation: *Russia and International Unity: Report to Affiliated Societies Trades Union Congress*, TUC Archive, MSS. 36/R30/55. They set off without visas in hand because the Tory government delayed granting them for nearly two weeks before the Home Office caved in to TUC pressure.
101 Van Goethem 2006, p. 94.

prior conditions' and to act as a mediator between the Soviet trade unionists and Amsterdam.[102] In response, Tomsky assured the British delegates that the Soviet attacks on the Amsterdam International were over.[103] He also told the assembled representatives that each of the 23 affiliates of the VTsSPS had removed wording in their statutes about membership in Profintern and had applied for membership in the IFTU.[104]

Tomsky's breakthrough with the British trade unionists enjoyed the support of the majority of Soviet leaders, particularly Stalin and Bukharin.[105] Even Trotsky gave it his qualified support.[106] As a result, the Fourteenth Party Conference at the end of April 1925 ratified the creation of the Anglo-Russian Committee.[107] And though Lozovsky was upset with Tomsky's overtures to the IFTU, the Profintern's Executive Committee adopted a resolution that also attached 'the greatest importance to the coming together and co-operation of the English and Soviet trade unions'.[108] The VTsSPS appointed Dogadov, Melnichansky, Andreev, and Lepse to serve under Tomsky on the joint advisory council.[109]

Tomsky and the British trade-union leaders continued to speak fondly of each other at the next British Trades Union Congress, held in Scarborough in September 1925. The TUC's general secretary, Bramley, characterised Tomsky and the Soviet trade unionists who accompanied him 'as steady, as constructive, as logical, as clear, as well informed as any trade-union leaders that you will find in any part of the world'.[110] The effusive hospitality went beyond words when Purcell put the TUC's gift of a sapphire-and-pearl pendant around the neck of Tomsky's wife. An appreciative Maria Tomskaya said she had never worn anything like it.[111] Tomskaya might have insisted on coming on this trip,

---

102 *Russia and International Unity: Report to Affiliated Societies Trades Union Congress*, TUC Archive, MSS. 36/R30/53.
103 Dewar 1976, p. 58.
104 Calhoun 1976, p. 206.
105 See, for example, Stalin's 22 March 1925 article in *Pravda*: Stalin 1952–67, vol. 7, p. 56.
106 See the Introduction by George Novack in Trotsky 1973a, p. 12. The April 1924 Central Committee plenum approved Tomsky's moves toward trying to create a single trade-union international: RGASPI, f. 17, op. 2, d. 166, ll. 3, 38.
107 There was some limited criticism voiced when a VTsSPS Plenum met to ratify the formation of the Anglo-Russian Committee: Tosstorff 2018, p. 713.
108 *Inprecorr*, 29 April 1925, p. 529.
109 Carr 1964, p. 578.
110 Bramley 1925, p. 18. Scott Nearing, an American socialist, characterised Tomsky in a less flattering manner as an 'under-sized, stooping product of European proletarian life': quoted in Morgan 2013, p. 223.
111 Citrine (ed.) 1925, p. 482.

FIGURE 16 Tomsky with Alf Purcell
TUC LIBRARY COLLECTIONS

or Tomsky might have felt he owed it to her, because Tomsky on an earlier trip abroad had fathered an illegitimate child.[112]

Tomsky began his speech by emphasising the progress made since the previous annual congress in Hull, in particular the visits by the British trade-union leaders and other foreign delegations to Moscow. He warmed up the audience by humorously characterising those who dismissed their positive reports on conditions in the Soviet Union with a Russian saying: 'if you go to the zoo and you see a peacock in a cage, but the label of the cage says "a camel" don't believe your eyes; it is not a peacock but a camel'.[113] Tomsky thanked the British trade

---

[112] Tomsky had confessed to Tomskaya that he had an affair with his VTsSPS stenographer when he had brought the child, Mikhail Ambrazhevich, home one day. Tomsky apparently talked through what had happened with Tomskaya. The child temporarily lived with Tomsky's family because things were not going well for his mother: Gorelov 2000, p. 282.

[113] Citrine (ed.) 1925, p. 475. The British press, including *The Times*, had harshly criticised various statements by the TUC delegation while in the Soviet Union, in particular those by

unionists for their courage and friendship and once again made a powerful argument for unconditional talks with the IFTU. Tomsky gave no inkling of the opposition he faced back in Moscow from Lozovsky. The General Council passed by a large majority a resolution approving Tomsky's proposal that if the IFTU continued to oppose an 'unconditional conference', the TUC should itself convene a conference in which it would serve as an intermediary between the VTsSPS and the Executive Committee of the IFTU.[114] The Anglo-Russian Committee issued a declaration that argued the growing threat of war made establishing a 'World Trade-Union International' especially urgent.[115]

Tomsky was on a roll. Immediately afterward, Citrine and George Hicks accompanied Tomsky and the rest of the Russian delegation back to Moscow.[116] Tomsky wined and dined them, including an invitation to his dacha, where he grilled shish kabobs for them.[117] Tomsky, who had an opportunity to speak at length with many of them, clearly turned their heads.[118] The usually rather cautious and conservative Citrine, at a session of the Moscow trade-union organisation, very uncharacteristically stated 'our task is to exhaust all means at our disposal to create such an International of Trade Unions which will embrace the trade unions of the entire world and which will provide the proper means for the abolition of Capitalism; such an International would be capable of building on the foundations laid down by your October revolution'.[119] A number of other foreign delegations soon followed in coming to the Soviet Union and making proclamations such as denouncing 'the great crime' of opposing international trade-union unity.[120]

But Tomsky soon after lost all this momentum. The Scarborough Congress, the first meeting of the Anglo-Russian Committee, and the visit of Citrine and Hicks to the Soviet Union, would prove to be the pinnacle in Anglo-Soviet

---

Purcell: 'Interim Report of Trades Union Congress Delegation to Russ (Press Cuttings)', TUC Archive, MSS. 292/947/59/23–25.

114   TUC Archive, MSS. 292/947/25/2.
115   Quoted in Carr 1964, p. 579.
116   By this time the VTsSPS, which had a standing committee for foreign relations, had considerable experience hosting foreign delegations. They had hosted more than one hundred official and unofficial delegations from a wide variety of nations: Dunn 1928, pp. 222–3.
117   Kozelev 1996, p. 159.
118   Riddell 2000, p. 291.
119   *Trud*, 16 October 1925. This statement stands in stark contrast to the sceptical, critical conversations Citrine had with Tomsky and other Soviet officials during his visit to the Soviet Union, at least according to his memoir: Citrine 1964, pp. 95–122. Tomsky duly reported to the Central Committee during its plenum on 9 October 1925 what happened at the Anglo-Russian Committees first meeting: RGASPI, f. 17, op. 2, d. 192, l. 1.
120   Carr 1964, pp. 579–80. That statement was by the French and Belgian delegations.

FIGURE 17　Walter Citrine
　　　　　　TUC LIBRARY COLLECTIONS

trade-union cooperation. This was largely due to changes in the British government and changes in the composition of the General Council. In the British general elections on 29 October 1924, the strongly anti-Soviet Conservative Party, led by Stanley Baldwin, won a sweeping victory over the Labour Party, which had been in power for just nine months.[121] This was the result, in some part, of the sensational publication four days before the election of the

---

121　The Liberals had withdrawn their support from the minority Labour Government largely because of its negotiations with the Soviet Union.

famous, almost certainly forged, 'Zinoviev Letter'. This letter, allegedly sent by the Comintern to British communists, called on them to mobilise 'sympathetic forces' in the Labour Party to support the ratification of the Anglo-Soviet treaty and instructed them on how to promote revolution among the country's factory workers and armed forces.[122] The Soviet government immediately denounced the letter as a forgery, but the damage was done.[123]

Even more foreboding for the future of Anglo-Soviet trade-union relations, conservative and moderate leaders dealt leftists a crushing defeat in the elections to the General Council.[124] Figures on the right wing of the Labour Party, who had stepped down from their positions on the General Council to serve in the MacDonald Government, were re-elected, including Arthur Pugh, Ernest Bevin, and Jimmy Thomas. The Soviets particularly disliked and distrusted Thomas. In addition, Citrine became the TUC's new general secretary after Bramley suddenly died, to Tomsky's dismay, on 10 October 1925.[125] Bramley had been the chief proponent of an alliance with Russia, while Citrine had sobered up after his uncharacteristic remarks in Moscow.[126] *The Times* reported that within the General Council the 'passion for unity with the Russians at all costs' had considerably abated.[127]

---

122 Gorodetsky 1977, pp. 35–52.
123 *Pravda* and *Izvestiia* published articles on 28 October that presented evidence supporting the government's contention it was a forgery: Adibekov (ed.) 2004, p. 281. Historians today have little doubt that it was a forgery.
124 Gorodetsky 1977, p. 119.
125 Tomsky had become alarmed as Bramley's health, which had been poor for some time, deteriorated. He wrote a heartfelt letter to Bramley on 19 September 1925: 'We are so few in number and the Cause we defend is so enormous that our common task is to keep healthy … The continuance of your illness and even the temporary abstinence from work may bring about great difficulties'. Tomsky, who evidently offered some medical advice, asked Bramley 'to forgive our somewhat rough and impertinent interference with you in the form of a cure for your health … let me express to you all the respect I am feeling for you and the hope that you will soon recover': 'Letter to Fred Bramley from Mikhail Tomsky, 9 September 1925', TUC Archive, MSS. 292/21.12/1/43.
126 Citrine was only 'acting' general secretary until he was confirmed at the September 1926 Trades-Union Congress, which might have encouraged him to tread warily regarding the Anglo-Russian Committee. He would become general secretary of the IFTU in 1928. Although an autodidact who left school at age 12, like Tomsky, Citrine would become such a part of the British establishment that he was knighted in 1935 and became Lord Citrine in 1947.
127 *The Times*, 30 November 1925. Citrine, in the words of the historian of the IFTU, normally was 'not a man of emotion and action, but of consultation and negotiation': Van Goethem 2006, p. 44.

The situation regarding the IFTU was no better. To Tomsky's great disappointment, but not surprise, the creation of the Anglo-Russian Committee seemed to have had little impact on the IFTU's leadership.[128] The IFTU's Executive Committee, which was still dominated by German and French Social Democrats, at its February 1925 meeting voted 14–6, and at its December meeting 14–7, to reaffirm its previous preconditions for any meeting with Tomsky, despite the best efforts of such British trade unionists as Hicks.[129] They were partly motivated by their anger toward Purcell, the IFTU president, for statements he made in the Soviet Union, which they characterised as 'singing the praises of the saints of Moscow'.[130]

A few days after the December IFTU meeting, when the Anglo-Russian Committee met for the second time in Berlin, an impatient Tomsky was itching to revert to open attacks against the IFTU.[131] Returning to the marriage metaphor, Tomsky joked, 'our romance could not end with a marriage, as no Amsterdam bride consented to meet the Moscow bridegroom'.[132] He said he did not understand why the IFTU's leaders would not meet with leaders of the Soviet trade unions. 'Are Oudegeest and Sassenbach afraid ... we shall corrupt them if they sit at the same table with us'?[133] The British contingent persuaded him to wait a little longer by forcefully denouncing Amsterdam's 'unprovoked attacks' on Tomsky's proposal for a unity conference.[134]

In the months that followed, Tomsky appears to have moved toward following the General Council's advice to soften his criticism of the Amsterdam International and to try to join the IFTU 'unconditionally'.[135] Trotsky thought Tomsky and his colleagues in the VTsSPS were not at all bothered that follow-

---

128 RGASPI, f. 593, op. 1, d. 4, l. 44.
129 Tomskii 1928d, p. 682n231; 'Special Supplement to the Monthly Circular of the Labour Research Department, 1925': 'Special Supplement to the Monthly Circular of the Labour Research Department, 1925', TUC Archive, MSS. 292/778.1/4/35, pp. x–xi.
130 Morgan 2013, p. 135. Purcell had also been a part in 1920 of the British Labour delegation to Soviet Russia where he shared that he hoped that Britain too would have a socialist revolution: White 1994, p. 629. The leaders of the IFTU had for some time disliked Purcell. Sassenbach considered him 'a man without culture, knowledge, or experience': quoted in Van Goethem 2006, p. 91.
131 Joining Tomsky as delegates at the meeting were seven leading officials of the VTsSPS: 'Minutes of the Second Meeting of the Anglo-Russian Joint Advisory Council, Berlin, 8–9 December 1925', TUC Archive, MSS. 292/947/25/2.
132 *Inprecorr*, 28 May 1925, p. 594. Tomsky was clearly fond of this metaphor. He had used it before at the April 1925 Anglo-Russian Committee meeting: Tomskii 1926a, p. 109.
133 *Inprecorr*, 28 May 1925, p. 595.
134 *Inprecorr*, 17 December 1925, p. 1319.
135 Tomskii 1928d, p. 298; Carr 1964, p. 585.

ing such a course would mean closing down Profintern. Tomsky no doubt was thinking along those lines. As noted above, liquidating the Profintern would have undercut Tomsky's persistent antagonist Lozovsky, who was continuing to do his best to sabotage the Anglo-Russian Committee. More broadly, liquidating the Profintern would also have freed the VTsSPS from its officially subordinate position internationally under the Profintern.

Tomsky did his best to reassure the Bolshevik leadership. At the Central Committee plenum on 10 October 1925, he claimed he was still enjoying success cultivating the left wing of the TUC, pronouncing that Purcell and Hicks were 'almost communists, though not Bolsheviks'.[136] At the Fourteenth Party Congress, which opened in Moscow on 18 December 1925, the primary focus was the attack on Zinoviev and Kamenev and the so-called Leningrad or Zinovievite Opposition. This is not the place to discuss in any detail Tomsky's part in the unfolding power struggle, other than noting that he played a major role in the attack against the oppositionists at this congress. The debate on trade-union policy was put off until the last days of the congress.

When Tomsky rose to open the debate on the Anglo-Russian Committee at the congress, he was vigorously applauded. Tomsky emphasised that he had done nothing without clearing it first with the Central Committee, the Profintern, and the Comintern. At the same time, he lightly touched on the most controversial part of his speech, which was to suggest that although he hoped unity could be achieved 'over the head of Amsterdam', serious consideration should be given to the possibility of the Soviet trade unions joining the IFTU on its terms. He noted how the British trade unionists had been working as 'super arbiters' to bring this about.[137] This predictably outraged Lozovsky, who emphatically demanded that the Soviet unions be forbidden from joining Amsterdam. Lozovsky argued that such a 'capitulation', would splinter the Profintern and weaken the Communist Parties in several countries.[138] Tomsky, who excelled in these sorts of spontaneous exchanges, argued that Lozovsky was 'of course' just doing his job by defending the interests of the Profintern, and suggested that the TUC would eventually call a world unity conference with or without the IFTU.[139] Rather than following Lozovsky's 'empty rhetoric', or his propensity for continually saying 'under no conditions whatever [will we] affiliate with the Amsterdam International', Tomsky argued that Soviet leaders

---

136   Tomsky argued they were not Bolsheviks because of their different tactics and traditions: RGASPI, f. 17, op. 2, d. 196, p. 10.
137   RKP(b) 1926, p. 746.
138   RKP(b) 1926, p. 776.
139   RKP(b) 1926, p. 802.

should, if necessary, be prepared to go even 'to hell or to the Pope', to further the cause of trade-union unity. To do otherwise, Tomsky argued, would be 'un-Bolshevik'. Tomsky also defended the Anglo-Russian Committee from charges that it was too moderate to denounce the leaders of the Amsterdam International as traitors and reformists, arguing it would be counter-productive to abuse those with whom you wanted to negotiate.[140] Tomsky also laid out the three purposes of the Anglo-Russian Committee as leading the fight against war, against the 'economic offensive of capital', and for the unity of the international workers' movement.[141] Other trade-union leaders spoke in support of Tomsky's position. The Fourteenth Party Congress's adopted resolution praised the VTsSPS's work toward achieving international trade-union unity.[142] Tomsky repeated at the twelfth session of the Enlarged Executive of the Comintern on 2 March 1926 his argument that extreme slogans should not be used when attempting to win support from non-communist workers in Europe.[143]

The various rebuffs from both foreign reformists and domestic hardliners, after all his strenuous work and travels, took their toll on Tomsky. As he had during other politically tense moments in the past (and as he would in the future), Tomsky fell ill.[144] He left Moscow in February 1926 for the spa and sanatorium in Kislovodsk. But he recovered quickly enough to speak at the Comintern meeting in March, where he gave a lengthy speech reporting that negotiations with the IFTU were completely deadlocked. He however urged the delegates to be patient, while a British delegate urged Tomsky to stay strong.[145]

The 1926 general strike in Great Britain would bring to the breaking point, not only the possibility of achieving international trade-union unity, but the continuation of the Anglo-Russian Committee as well. The general strike began following a royal commission recommendation that the wages of workers in Britain's inefficient and decreasingly profitable coal industry, which had already been savagely cut by an average of 50 percent since 1921, be cut by a further 13.5 percent and that shifts be increased from seven to eight hours. After Cook, the leader of the British miners, answered on 1 May with the fiery slogan 'Not a penny off the pay, not a minute on the day'! nearly one million miners

---

140   Carr 1964, p. 586.
141   Carr 1964, pp. 586–7.
142   RKP(b) 1926, p. 803; *Inprecorr*, 26 January 1926, p. 14.
143   *Inprecorr*, 25 March 1926, p. 351.
144   RGASPI, f. 593, op. 1, d. 4, l. 4.
145   Tomskii 1928d, pp. 298, 318; *Inprecorr*, 25 March 1926. At the Central Committee plenum in April Tomsky gave a speech in which he discussed in some detail why the Soviet Union had not been able to achieve the same sort of success in France as had been achieved in Britain: RGASPI, f. 17, op. 2, d. 218, ll. 176–82.

found themselves locked out of the country's roughly three thousand pits. The miners appealed to the TUC for help. To Tomsky's surprise, when no face-saving compromise developed at the eleventh hour in the negotiations with the government, on 4 May the General Council felt compelled, albeit reluctantly, to declare a general strike in 'defence of miners' wages and hours'. Tomsky thought that 'none of them believed the strike could succeed, did not want it, and strongly feared it'.[146] Tomsky was not the only one who was shocked that the General Council went ahead anyway. The Politburo, the Profintern, the Comintern, and the British Communist Party were all also taken by surprise.

The General Council, which had done little to prepare for a conflict they had so wanted to avoid, were stunned by the British workers' response to the strike, which surpassed all their expectations. In a massive display of working-class solidarity, millions of workers went on strike to support the miners. Because the General Council never thought the dispute with the miners would lead to a general strike, it failed to plan for such basic issues as how to provide food for the strikers or how to publicise their side of the dispute.[147] In contrast, the Conservative Government, which overtly took the coal owners' side, had prepared for the conflict for months. It quickly began winning the battle for public opinion. Though the general strike, of course, greatly inconvenienced the public, the government's supply and transport organisation, with a network of middle-class volunteers, gave the appearance of neutralising the general strike. More importantly, the government succeeded in defining what was at stake. While the General Council vigorously insisted it was engaged in only an industrial dispute, without political objectives, the Conservative Government rallied support by characterising the general strike as a political offensive against parliamentary democracy and played up the supposed communist threat.

The General Council felt the Soviets were doing their best to make the government's case that the trade-union leaders were essentially dupes of the Soviet Union. Lozovsky, for example, declared that 'the victory of the miners is our victory and their defeat is our defeat'.[148] Some Soviet leaders reacted as if the revolutionary moment in Europe had come at last when the general strike broke out.[149] 'However events may develop', Zinoviev declared, 'one thing is certain: what has already happened in Great Britain has opened a new era in the

---

146   GARF, f. 5451, op. 42, d. 129, l. 46.
147   Laybourn 1992, pp. 36, 53–4, 119.
148   *Pravda*, 10 May 1926.
149   Degras 1960, p. 299. Perhaps influencing their wildly optimistic evaluations of the British strike were memories of how in 1905 the October general strike compelled the tsarist government to make concessions, including a national legislature.

British and international labour movement. No power in the world can now arrest the rapid Bolshevisation of the vanguard of the British proletariat, and the strengthening of communist ideas among the British proletariat'.[150]

Tomsky quickly sprang into action. He convened a special session of the VTsSPS on 5 May and declared his determination to promptly organise a campaign in support of the British workers. That same day, on Tomsky's recommendation, the Politburo created commissions in Moscow and Paris to respond to developments in the general strike.[151] Tomsky left for Paris on 6 May to head the international commission there, which included a number of French, German, and Czechoslovakian Communist Party leaders. Its first order of business was to offer a substantial sum of money to the General Council to help finance the strike since strike pay was quickly haemorrhaging the TUC's funds. At the Politburo's direction, the VTsSPS instructed Soviet trade-union members to donate a quarter of one day's pay for a relief fund to support the miners and the VTsSPS immediately sent the General Council a cheque for £26,247.[152]

The General Council, which had accepted donations from the trade-union organisations in other countries, to Tomsky's surprise, rejected the unsolicited offer. Adding insult to injury, it was George Hicks, one of the left-wingers on the General Council whom Tomsky had told the Central Committee eight months earlier was 'almost a communist', who introduced the motion to reject the Soviet money.[153] On 8 May, the General Council, which shared Hicks' opinion that the aid would be 'wilfully misinterpreted and misunderstood', issued a terse statement in the TUC's newspaper, the *British Worker*, that 'the Council has courteously informed the Russian Trade Unions that they are unable to accept the offer and the check has been returned'.[154] Citrine later recalled that 'the General Council, already faced with the baseless charge of instituting a strike

---

150 *Inprecorr*, 13 May 1926, p. 657.
151 RGASPI, f. 17, op. 162, d. 3, ll. 62–3. The members of the Moscow commission were Lozovsky, Dogadov, Stalin, Zinoviev, Chicherin, and Molotov. Rykov would be added to the commission on 10 May. The commission would meet daily: Vatlin 2009, p. 166.
152 RGASPI, f. 17, op. 162, d, 3, ll. 57–9. Soviet workers, the British Foreign Office accurately reported, commonly resented 'being forced to contribute to the support of those who were better off than they': Bourne and Watt (eds) 1986, vol. 25, pp. 312, 321. One historian disagrees, stating that the workers' lack of resistance suggests their contributions were voluntary. He also takes at face value an OGPU report that workers wanted to contribute more than what the VTsSPS was asking for. He does concede that at mass meetings, while some workers expressed their exasperation with British trade-union leaders, others challenged Tomsky's concern for British workers since they earned more than Soviet workers: Murphy 2005, pp. 84–5.
153 Borkenau 1938, p. 281; Tomskii 1928d, p. 334; RGASPI f. 17, op. 2, d. 196, p. 10.
154 Klugmann 1969, p. 319.

to overthrow the constitution, felt that however well-intentioned the Russian offer was, its acceptance would be misrepresented'.[155] The General Council certainly had good reason to believe that the Conservative Government would use the aid to portray the General Council as a tool of the Bolsheviks. And indeed, when the government got wind of the offer, the House of Commons denounced the proffered donation as 'Red Gold'.[156] An angry Tomsky offered substantially more money, £383,895, directly to the Miners' Federation, which readily accepted it.[157]

The General Council was already looking to end the general strike by 10 May. Some of its most influential members, particularly Thomas, who was the General Council's chief negotiator and someone whom the miners as well as the Soviets had long distrusted, claimed that many workers were drifting back to work and the general strike was on the verge of collapse.[158] This was not the case. Historians generally agree that the general strike remained remarkably solid until the very end, with some even arguing that support for the strike was still growing when the General Council called it off.[159] More likely causes for the General Council's decision were their frustration with the miners' refusal to accept any wage cuts and their fear that the longer the strike lasted the more radical it would become as control of the strike was clearly shifting to the rank and file.[160] In any case, on 11 May, without consulting the miners, the General Council decided to call the strike off on the following day. They knew their abject surrender would be greeted with rank-and-file outrage. 'We will get it in the neck for sure', said Tillett.[161] Shocked workers, who at first were led to believe a great victory had been won, angrily denounced the General Council's betrayal

---

155   Citrine 1964, p. 91.
156   Kocho-Williams 2008, p. 3. The Soviet government dishonestly responded that it had played no role in sending the funds and could not legally prohibit the VTsSPS from sending money to the Trades-Unions Congress: Eudin and Fisher 1957b, pp. 341–2.
157   Warth 1958, p. 118; International Labour Office 1927, p. 235.
158   Thomas publicly declared on 9 May that he had never supported the principle of a general strike: Farman 1972, p. 220.
159   Laybourn 1992, pp. 74, 120; Morris 1976, pp. 94, 97; McDonald 1975, pp. 82–3; Callaghan 1990, p. 108.
160   Lee 1996, p. 92. Thomas told the House of Commons on 13 May: 'What I dreaded about this Strike more than anything else was this. If by any chance it should have got out of the hands of those who would be able to exercise some control, every sane man knows what would have happened ... That danger, that fear, was always in our minds': Farman 1972, p. 152. But this was delusional, especially since roughly half of the Communist Party's members were arrested during the strike: Eaden and Renton 2002, p. 54. Other simply feared a breakdown in law and order: Riddell 2000, p. 292.
161   Quoted in Callaghan 1990, p. 120.

of the Miners' Union, whose embittered members remained locked out, while conservatives exulted.[162] The sudden, ignominious termination of the general strike after just nine days would prove to be a disaster for the General Council. The TUC would lose more than a half a million members and see its funds depleted by the drain of the strike pay.[163] In addition, that it was not Thomas, but the left-wing Purcell, who as head of the strike committee, announced the termination of the strike undercut their standing with rank-and-file workers. The failure of the more leftist members of the General Council to oppose the ending of the strike was a boon for the British Communist Party. It enjoyed a large influx of new members.[164]

When Tomsky received news in the Soviet embassy in Paris of the end of the general strike, he apparently took at face value the General Council's initial representation of it. The TUC's newspaper, the *British Worker*, ran three editions that day, each implying victory, with the last edition including a bogus manifesto by the General Council stating they had terminated the general strike because they had received 'assurances' that negotiations would be 'resumed to secure a settlement in the coal-mining industry, free and unfettered from either strike or lock-out'.[165] Or it may be because Tomsky, who had trouble maintaining lines of communication with London on 12 May, was misled by a report that morning from the French Communist Party's daily newspaper *L'Humanité* that the British strike was liquidated on the basis of a compromise that was a victory for the workers.[166] Whatever the basis for his initial evaluation of the strike's outcome as a success, the telegram Tomsky sent to the Politburo that day would be the source of much criticism in the days and weeks to come. He wrote that he had recommended that the British Communist Party proclaim that the aborted strike constituted 'the partial moral victory of the proletariat', and that they optimistically proclaim that it will contribute 'toward the ultimate suc-

---

162   Callaghan 1990, p. 90; Mowatt 1955, p. 327. Each of the three 13 May editions of *British Worker* sounded triumphant: Farman 1972, pp. 235–6.
163   Van Goethem 2006, p. 37; McDonald 1975, p. 84.
164   Purcell's biographer insists that he did not view the outcome of the strike as a 'victory', in opposition to assertions to the contrary. British communists derided Purcell for lapsing after the announcement into 'cowardly silence': Morgan 2013, pp. 261, 263. Membership in the British Communist Party grew from 4,900 in January to 11,127 in December 1926, primarily as a result of recruited miners: Worley 2002, pp. 56, 61; Pelling 1987, 188. The six months after the strike were among the best in the history of the British Communist Party: Thorpe 2000, p. 94.
165   Quoted in Farman 1972, p. 236.
166   RGASPI, f. 17, op. 2, d. 225, l. 529. The British Communist Party was unable to communicate with Moscow as well as Paris: Thorpe 2000, p. 93.

cess of the proletarian struggle' in conditions 'more favourable than the current ones'.[167] When it became apparent the next morning that the General Council had completely capitulated by terminating the strike without any concrete gains, Tomsky's commission sent the British Communist Party another directive.[168] The British Communist Party now denounced the ending of the strike, calling it 'the greatest crime that has ever been permitted, not only against the miners, but against the working class of Great Britain and the whole world'.[169]

Tomsky's failure to question the General Council's initial justifications for terminating the general strike may have reflected his overriding goal of preserving the Anglo-Russian Committee, as some have suggested.[170] Regardless, the now Oppositionist Zinoviev and Kamenev enthusiastically seized the opportunity to attack Tomsky, and indirectly Stalin. Zinoviev sent an angry letter to the Politburo denouncing Tomsky's evaluation of the outcome of the strike. Although the Politburo rejected Zinoviev's letter at its meeting on 14 May, it did resolve to ruthlessly criticise the General Council. Stalin sent a telegram to Tomsky in Paris, in which he stated that the Politburo believed 'what happened was not a compromise but capitulation and treason'. Although Tomsky had already done so, Stalin ordered the commission to replace its initial directive 'in the spirit of our telegram' and, after that, to dissolve the commission immediately.[171] At the same time he sent Tomsky a cryptogram alerting him that Zinoviev 'is raising hell against your commission and you personally'.[172]

Tomsky's support for the TUC and the failure of the general strike now became embroiled in the emerging new phase of the post-Lenin power struggle. Zinoviev on 26 May demanded a Politburo meeting be convened to discuss 'the lessons of the British strike'.[173] The heated Politburo sessions that followed proved to be a catalyst for the formation of what came to be known as the United Opposition, with Trotsky, Zinoviev, and Kamenev joining together to denounce the General Council's 'cowardice' and 'fainted-heartedness'.[174] On 3 June, the Politburo spent six hours debating Zinoviev's resolution, which

---

167 RGASPI, f. 558, op. 11, d. 723, l. 84, reproduced in Adibekov et al. (eds) 2001, p. 368. The text of the entire telegram has not been found.
168 GARF, f. 5451, op. 42, d. 129, l. 56.
169 Quoted in Laybourn 1992, p. 100.
170 Souvarine 1939, p. 428; Fischer 1948, p. 561.
171 RGASPI, f. 17, op. 162, d. g, 3, l. 65, 67–70, reproduced in Adibekov et al. (eds) 2001, pp. 123–4.
172 RGASPI, f. 558, op. 11, d. 34, l. 75, reproduced in Adibekov (ed.) 2004, p. 369.
173 RGASPI, f. 17, op. 162, d. 3, ll. 65, 67–70, reproduced in Adibekov et al. (eds) 2001, pp. 121–3; Vatlin 2008, p. 68.
174 For a discussion of how the debate within the Politburo over the British general strike was a catalyst for the formation of the 'United Opposition': Vatlin 2008, pp. 57–77.

denounced the Anglo-Russian Committee as a bloc with bankrupt, reformist traitors, and called for its dissolution.[175] During this meeting Zinoviev blasted Tomsky's initial response to the ending of the general strike as 'a dangerous political mistake'. When Tomsky defended the 12 May telegram as based on 'incorrect information' from London, Zinoviev proclaimed, 'you don't need to be a rocket scientist' to have appreciated the 'scandalous' outcome of the strike.[176] Zinoviev also proclaimed that Tomsky was 'dancing with the dead' by dealing with the reactionary British trade unions and accused him of deliberately ignoring communist mass movements.[177] Trotsky chimed in that he had warned of the pitfalls in relying on non-Communist allies. Tomsky said both sides 'threw away all restraints' during the bitter back and forth, which made him feel like he was on trial, a 'defendant' for supporting what were denounced as 'opportunistic' policies.[178]

Tomsky nevertheless stuck to his guns as a moderate, pragmatic Bolshevik. He forcefully defended the policy of a united front with the British trade-union movement and argued that he had built the Anglo-Russian Committee with Zinoviev's complete approval, stating he had kept Zinoviev fully informed each step of the way.[179] And indeed, as we have seen, Zinoviev had profusely praised the creation of the committee and celebrated the outbreak of the general strike. Tomsky also argued that Trotsky's and Zinoviev's criticism of his policy was based on 'unrealistic expectations of a revolution in Britain'.[180] Trotsky shot back, 'And yours depends upon the assumption that it will never take place'. Tomsky, who was of course correct that Britain was not in a revolutionary situation, insisted that British communists needed to continue working in the trade unions, not leave them. He argued that if Zinoviev's resolution was adopted it would lead to the Soviets losing any influence in the British trade unions and forfeiting everything the Soviets had gained during the last couple years, which needless to say, meant everything he had gained. John Murphy, the British Communist Party leader and a prominent member of the Profintern as well as the Comintern, wrote to the Politburo on behalf of the British Communist Party Central Committee on 15 July agreeing with Tomsky's assessment. 'There is a danger', Murphy argued, 'of overestimating the strength of the

---

175   I.P. Tovstukha sent Stalin a telegram summarising the meeting: Stalin 1995, p. 112. To label opponents in the international arena as 'traitors' was nothing new for the Bolshevik leadership.
176   RGASPI, f. 17, op. 163, d. 686, reproduced in Vatlin (ed.) 2007, p. 747.
177   RGASPI, f. 17, op. 163, d. 686, reproduced in Vatlin (ed.) 2007, p. 751.
178   RGASPI, f. 17, op. 163, d. 686, reproduced in Vatlin (ed.) 2007, pp. 820–1.
179   RGASPI, f. 17, op. 163, d. 686, reproduced in Vatlin (ed.) 2007, p. 755.
180   Vatlin 2008, p. 70.

revolutionary forces in Britain and underestimating the power of the labour aristocracy or bureaucracy'.[181] In the end, the Politburo adopted the counter-theses by Bukharin, Tomsky, and Molotov, with encouragement from afar by Stalin, who had returned to Sochi. The Politburo took the position, which would prove untenable, of both criticising the 'traitors' of the Anglo-Russian Committee while arguing that the preservation of the Anglo-Russian Committee remained 'a necessity'.[182]

The members of the Politburo devoted other sessions in the coming weeks and months to rehashing the British general strike and Tomsky's 'notorious' telegram. During these sessions of party infighting, Bukharin, Rykov, and Stalin would continually come to Tomsky's defence.[183] In the session on 15 July, Rykov emphasised how 'much capital' the exceptionally popular Tomsky had built up with workers.[184] Stalin argued that while Tomsky had demonstrated 'some carelessness, some gullibility' in how he had let the reports in *L'Humanité* mislead him, 'we must still recognise that his mistake was minimal, insignificant'.[185] While Tomsky appreciated this support, he recognised the blow his political standing suffered from Zinoviev's and Trotsky's hard-hitting attacks.[186]

That Tomsky had lost some political clout, not just in the Politburo but in the VTsSPS as well, became all too clear at the VTsSPS plenary session on 7 June. Tomsky tried to convince his trade-union colleagues that the general strike would strengthen, not weaken the Anglo-Russian alliance.[187] He ended his speech by arguing that the Anglo-Russian Committee 'should not interrupt its work for one minute' and the VTsSPS should 'put all its strength behind preserving' it.[188] He also tried to placate his opponents by criticising the General Council, including its left wing, for 'dragging their feet' during the general strike. But that was not enough to satisfy those who wanted to attack the General Council more harshly. Tomsky had temporarily lost control of the VTsSPS.

---

181 Murphy argued for maintaining the Anglo-Russian Committee while trying 'to strengthen and develop its revolutionary work while working for a change in the representatives of the English working class', which he conceded was a 'very remote' possibility: RGASPI, f. 17, op. 2, d. 225, ll. 658–61.
182 RGASPI, f. 17, op. 163, d. 686, reproduced in Vatlin (ed.) 2007, pp. 830–44. See the 3 June telegram from Stalin to Molotov: Stalin 1995, pp. 108–10. Trotsky voted in favour of Zinoviev's defeated theses.
183 RGASPI, f. 17, op. 2, d. 224, l. 129.
184 RGASPI, f. 17, op. 2, d. 225, ll. 442–4.
185 RGASPI, f. 17, op. 2, d. 225, l. 529.
186 Rykov tried to minimise that, stating Tomsky's 'capital had decreased only slightly' as a result of the general strike debacle: RGASPI, f. 17, op. 2, d. 196, l. 443.
187 *Inprecorr*, 17 June 1926, p. 772.
188 Tomskii 1928d, p. 345.

The plenum, over Tomsky's vigorous opposition, adopted a resolution blaming the failure of the general strike on the 'capitulation' of Purcell and other leftist leaders in the TUC.[189] The plenum, more harmfully, compelled Tomsky to issue a manifesto 'To the International Proletariat' denouncing the General Council.[190] But the plenum also agreed to entrust the VTsSPS with doing everything possible to preserve and strengthen the Anglo-Russian Committee.[191]

The manifesto predictably outraged the General Council. Citrine protested Tomsky's 'misleading and inaccurate' representation of the strike.[192] The General Council seemingly had no sense of the internal fight within the Soviet political leadership and Tomsky's need to appease his critics, although a decade later Citrine did wonder if Tomsky, whom he continued to hold in high esteem, had 'really believed the nasty things he said about us'.[193]

The British Communist Party was so dismayed by the sharp tone of the manifesto issued under Tomsky's name that it suppressed publishing its translation for six full weeks.[194] Like Tomsky, its leaders feared that such an attack overestimated the left wing's influence on the General Council and, more importantly, was likely 'to hamper' the preservation of the Anglo-Russian Committee.[195] The British Communists' Central Committee, in the letter it sent to Moscow on 15 July, argued that it was difficult to change the trade-union leadership in England and, in any case, to expect some new revolutionary leadership in the General Council would be 'exceedingly utopian'. Breaking with the Anglo-Russian Committee, they concluded, would only strengthen the hand of British right-wing trade-union leaders.[196] In fact that is exactly what happened. Citrine

---

189   *Inprecorr*, 17 June 1926, p. 772; 'Reports of the Third and Fourth Meetings of the Anglo-Russian Joint Advisory Council', TUC Archive MSS. 292/947/26/3, p. 8.
190   *Pravda*, 8 June 1926; *Inprecorr*, 17 June 1926, p. 772. The resolution also attacked the 'treacherous tactics' of Thomas, MacDonald, and the other Labour Party leaders, who 'infamously allowed themselves to be a tail wagged by the lackeys of capital'.
191   'Reports of the Third and Fourth Meetings of the Anglo-Russian Joint Advisory Council', TUC Archive, MSS. 292/947/26/3, p. 50.
192   Gorodetsky 1977, p. 190. Purcell was no more willing to accept the legitimacy of the manifesto's criticisms: Morgan 2013, p. 265.
193   Citrine 1964, p. 9. When the Soviet authorities, after considerable resistance, allowed Citrine to meet with Tomsky in Moscow in 1935, he told him 'all your trade union friends in England wished me to give you their good wishes': Citrine 1936, pp. 81–2, 132.
194   When they finally capitulated, it was not prominently featured in the 9 July 1926, issue of the *Workers' Weekly*: Thorpe 2000, p. 98.
195   Thorpe 2000, p. 97. The leaders of the British Communist Party were also upset that the VTsSPS issued the manifesto without consulting them: Degras 1960, p. 301.
196   RGASPI, f. 17, op. 2, d. 225. l. 660.

and Bevin had already begun to consolidate their dominance of the General Council. Arguing that the defeat of the general strike showed the limitations of 'direct action', they began to move the TUC away from class conflict toward pragmatic cooperation between unions and employers.[197]

The British communists, before long, would do exactly what they had argued against, by adopting a staunchly anti-TUC stance. It predictably backfired. After their brief upsurge of support following the collapse of the general strike, they sank back into political insignificance as the membership rolls of the CPGB precipitously decreased from 10,800 at the end of 1926 to only 2,555 in November 1930.[198]

The prospects for the first meeting of the Anglo-Russian Committee since the end of the general strike were obviously bleak. Tomsky failed to join the Soviet delegation for the 30 July meeting in Paris. Upset by the hardening Soviet line against the Anglo-Russian Committee, he instead sent a letter explaining that, 'to his regret', his doctor had ordered a two-month convalescence due to 'excessive overwork'. The stresses of the last year had undoubtedly aggravated the physical ills that plagued him.[199] In his letter, Tomsky did seek to repair the damage caused by the harsh statements of the VTsSPS manifesto of 7 June. He expressed his hope that the Anglo-Russian Committee, 'which has always been dear to me', would not let our differences of opinion 'disturb our co-operative work'.[200] The British delegation sent 'a letter of sympathy' to Tomsky expressing their hope that he would quickly recover.[201]

Tomsky's hope that the Anglo-Russian Committee would be able to continue its fraternal work was not to be. Andrei Andreev, a tough hardliner as it would become all too clear in the years to come, took Tomsky's place as head of the Soviet delegation.[202] This felt like sweet revenge for Andreev. Back in 1921, Andreev had briefly taken Tomsky's place as head of the VTsSPS when Tomsky had been sent packing to Tashkent for 'violating party discipline' at the

---

197 Callaghan 1990, p. 117; Riddell 2000, pp. 286, 293.
198 McDermott and Agnew 1996, p. 106.
199 Although E.H. Carr wrongly concluded that Tomsky's illness was 'certainly diplomatic', he was probably correct to suggest that for Tomsky to meet in Paris with the British members of the Anglo-Russian Committee, individuals with whom he had close personal ties, would have been extremely embarrassing: Carr 1976, pp. 329–30.
200 *Inprecorr*, 26 August 1926, p. 989; *Sotsialisticheskii vestnik*, 25 August 1926, p. 8.
201 'Reports of the Third and Fourth Meetings of the Anglo-Russian Joint Advisory Council', TUC Archive, MSS. 292/947/26/3.
202 Though he backed Trotsky's faction during the 1920s, Andreev would become, along with Molotov, Kaganovich, Mikoyan, and Voroshilov, part of the core group around Stalin during the 1930s. In fact, he would remain so until 1952: Fitzpatrick 2015, pp. 3, 28.

Fourth Trade-Union Congress. But, as we have seen, Tomsky's exile and demotion lasted just four months. The Politburo brought Tomsky back to Moscow, and over Andreev's strong objections, gave him the number two position in the VTsSPS.[203] Not long after that, Tomsky replaced Andreev as head of the trade unions. Now, in 1926, Andreev seemingly was only too happy to do what he could to undercut Tomsky.[204]

After Andreev read Tomsky's conciliatory letter to the British members of the Anglo-Russian Committee, the meeting quickly gave way to bitter recriminations. The British delegation began the session with Citrine calling for the VTsSPS to 'unreservedly repudiate and publicly withdraw' its 'insulting' and 'abusive' 7 June manifesto. Andreev refused. The British, for their part, refused to apologise for rejecting the VTsSPS offer of aid during the general strike. They also refused to discuss possible financial support for the still ongoing miners' strike on the grounds that it was a domestic, British matter.[205] These criticisms and counter-criticisms continued over the course of two days before the disastrous meeting was indefinitely adjourned.

In the months that followed, the alliance Tomsky had worked so hard to build up over the previous two years came crashing down. When the Anglo-Russian Committee met next, in Berlin on 23–25 August, Tomsky again failed to appear.[206] As before, no headway was made on improving relations, as the Soviet delegation continued to press that aid to the miners be the first order of business. They proposed vigorously supporting the British miners by heeding the British Communist Party's call for an embargo on coal imports to Great Britain.[207] The British trade-union leaders continued to refuse to even discuss the miners' strike.[208] For two days they went round and round on this proced-

---

203   GARF, f. 5451, op. 42, d. 46, l. 22.
204   Boris Kozelev, a leading trade unionist as head of the Metalworkers' Union until 1930, as well as a friend and hagiographic biographer of Tomsky, wrote in his diary that Dogadov had a very different perspective. Dogadov believed that the Politburo was using Andreev, over his objections, against Tomsky: Kozelev 1996, p. 154.
205   *Inprecorr*, 26 August 1926, p. 1026; *Inprecorr*, 30 September 1926, p. 1091.
206   This time he certainly was not seriously ill since he gave a speech to the VTsSPS on 25 August: Tomskii 1928d, p. 368. Another Soviet member of the Anglo-Soviet Committee, Dogadov, the VTsSPS Secretary, also failed to attend because he was indeed ill: *Inprecorr*, 16 September 1926, p. 1057. Dogadov had been the member of the VTsSPS delegation at the Paris meeting who most tried to salvage it: 'Reports of the Third and Fourth Meetings of the Anglo-Russian Joint Advisory Council', TUC Archive, MSS. 292/947/26/3.
207   Stalin 1995, pp. 29, 126.
208   In defiance of the General Council, the Soviets invited a delegation of British coal miners to travel to Moscow. They arrived at the end of August. During their visit Tomsky pledged his continued support for the miners' four-month strike and offered substantial financial

ural issue.[209] The British delegation, which thought Andreev was working to rupture the Anglo-Russian Committee, again protested 'the most unjustifiable and bitter attacks' on the General Council as 'an unwarranted interference in the internal affairs of the British trade-union movement'.[210] The meeting did, however, pass a resolution that the General Council would fulfil its promise to call again for a preliminary conference between the IFTU and the VTsSPS, without any restrictive conditions.[211] Not surprisingly, little was to come of that.

The British delegation suggested that the meeting might have been more fruitful if the Soviet delegation had been headed by Tomsky instead of Andreev.[212] At the VTsSPS Presidium immediately convened after the Berlin meeting, Tomsky felt compelled to state that it was an 'illusion' of the General Council to think there was any dissent within the Soviet trade-union leadership over the Anglo-Russian Committee.[213] But on 8 September, Tomsky conceded in a speech in Moscow that the Soviets had been perhaps too 'coarse' and 'uncultured' in their dealings with the General Council, and said he reiterated his opposition to those who wanted to dissolve the Anglo-Russian Committee.[214]

Despite all the abuse that Tomsky and the Soviet leadership had flung at the General Council, he was appointed a fraternal delegate to the 1926 TUC Congress in Bournemouth.[215] But in September 1926 the British government rejected Tomsky's request for a visa.[216] Tomsky blamed the General Council, and

---

support. The Politburo on 4 September, in a voice vote, accepted Tomsky's statement from the VTsSPS to the British Federation of Miners: Lih et al. (eds) 1995, p. 120.

209 'Reports of the Third and Fourth Meetings of the Anglo-Russian Joint Advisory Council': TUC Archive, MSS. 292/947/26/3.
210 *Inprecorr*, 15 September 1927, p. 1183.
211 *Inprecorr*, 23 September 1926, p. 1075. The British members of the Anglo-Russian Committee argued that the reason the committee existed was to work toward international trade-union unity, and as a result that needed to be the first piece of business: 'Reports of the Third and Fourth Meetings', TUC Archive, MSS. 292/947/26/3, p. 26.
212 The British noted during the meeting that Schwarz and Ugarov were more 'conciliatory' than the 'frank, verging on rude' Andreev: 'Reports of the Third and Fourth Meetings of the Anglo-Russian Joint Advisory Council', TUC Archive, MSS. 292/947/26/3, p. 34.
213 Tomskii 1928d, p. 372.
214 Tomskii 1928d, pp. 410, 412.
215 Tomsky had been invited, along with Melnichansky and their interpreter Yarotsky, at the end of the Anglo-Russian Committee meeting in Berlin, even though Tomsky had failed to attend that meeting: 'Reports of the Third and Fourth Meetings', TUC Archive, MSS. 292/947/26/3, p. 48.
216 The government, in contrast, granted visas to representatives of the IFTU and the American AFL: 'Published Correspondence between the All-Russian Central Council of Trade Unions and the TUC, September 1926', TUC Archive, MSS. 292/947/6/38.

indeed, *The Times* reported that the General Council was probably glad the government refused Tomsky a visa: 'The action of the Home Office will relieve the General Council from a rather embarrassing position ... there will be a secret satisfaction that Tomsky will not be able to deliver the peculiar kind of fraternal speech which it is believed he had in contemplation for the occasion'.[217] The blistering three-page telegram Tomsky sent to the congress certainly confirmed the General Council's suspicions. Tomsky accused the General Council of going 'over to the enemy' with its 'bend-the-knee attitude toward the government'. If the General Council had not betrayed the general strike and sabotaged the miners' strike, Tomsky asserted, 'it would have led to a glorious victory and you would already have long been free of your government of aristocrats and mine owners'. He also insisted on the Soviets' right to voice such harsh criticisms. 'We may be accused of being too sharp', Tomsky wrote, 'but when it comes to choosing between empty compliments ... to the leaders, and to serving the working masses, we will always choose the latter course'.[218] The *New York Times* reported the 'bomb-like blast' of the 'fiery' Tomsky 'scorched' the General Council 'to the very marrow', sending 'them into a frenzy of anger'. The General Council, which resented the tone as well as the substance of the telegram, struck back at Tomsky, denouncing his 'most regrettable abuse of the ordinary courtesies expected of fraternal delegates'.[219] According to a communist observer, the delegates responded to the General Council's rebuttal with such a roar of approval it was 'enough to frighten anyone'!'[220] Any remaining feelings of camaraderie in the General Council toward Tomsky were rapidly evaporating.

Tomsky would still try to preserve the Anglo-Russian Committee despite these acrimonious exchanges. He told the General Council that he was fighting against 'individual comrades' in the Soviet Union who wanted to dissolve the Anglo-Russian Committee.[221] And indeed, he had to defend the policies he had long pursued towards the Anglo-Russian Committee at the VTsSPS meeting on 19 September.[222] Then, at the Fifteenth Party Conference, 26 October–3 November 1926, in the few minutes Tomsky devoted to the Anglo-Russia Committee at the end of his lengthy speech on trade-union affairs, he criticised the United Oppositionists of Trotsky, Zinoviev, and Kamenev for wanting to make

---

217 *The Times*, 3 September 1926.
218 The telegram sent by Tomsky and VTsSPS Secretary, Dogadov, and the response by the General Council, appeared in the *Manchester Guardian*, 10 September 1926 and was reprinted in Lozovsky 1926, pp. 44–6.
219 *New York Times*, 10 September 1926, p. 6.
220 Quoted in Morgan 2013, p. 266.
221 *Inprecorr*, 7 October 1926, p. 1106.
222 GARF, f. 5451, op. 42, d. 129, ll. 108–10.

a 'revolutionary gesture' by calling for the dissolution of the Anglo-Russian Committee. Tomsky again argued that doing so would lead British communists to leave the trade unions in droves and lose what influence they had with workers.[223] Tomsky appeared to have regained some support.[224] Bukharin, who replaced Zinoviev as president of the Comintern, also spoke out against the Opposition's proposal to disband the Anglo-Russian Committee.[225] The conference ratified the theses by Tomsky and Bukharin, which insisted the Anglo-Russia Committee must be maintained at 'any cost' even though it meant sitting with 'traitors'.[226] Hand-in-glove with Stalin, Tomsky began to redefine the primary purpose of the Anglo-Russian Committee as working to help defend 'socialism in one country' by deterring the anti-Soviet offensive of the British conservative government had launched, which had led to a 'war scare' in the Soviet Union.[227]

Although the General Council continued to lack any appreciation of the pressures Tomsky faced in Moscow and the sincerity of his efforts to salvage the Anglo-Russian Committee, it agreed to his insistent demand for another meeting.[228] In what turned out to be its last formal meeting, held 29 March–1 April 1927 in Berlin, Tomsky once again led the Soviet delegation. He recognised that the General Council was itching for an excuse to dissolve the connection with Soviet trade unions.[229] Hoping to preserve the Anglo-Russian Committee, he evidently decided to accept everything the British wanted, including an addition to its by-laws requiring both sides to refrain from interfering in each other's internal affairs.[230] Tomsky said the British told him during the course of the meeting, 'you must moderate your abuse a little. It makes a very bad impression on public opinion in Great Britain when you abuse us and mention names'. When Citrine brought up some particularly offensive language in Lozovsky's pamphlet entitled *British and Russian Workers*, Tomsky responded

---

[223] RKP(b) 1927c, p. 294.
[224] Gorodetsky 1976, pp. 304–5.
[225] Degras 1960, p. 314.
[226] RKP(b) 1927c, p. 294; Great Britain Foreign Office 1984, p. 386; *Inprecorr*, 11 November 1926, p. 1271.
[227] Tosstorff 2018, p. 718.
[228] The General Council, it should be noted, was also subjected to outside criticism as various newspapers mocked its willingness to 'meekly' tolerate all the insults from the VTsSPS: *The Times*, 28 June 1927.
[229] Andreev, Lepse, Melnichansky, Dogadov, along with the translators Yarotsky and Rothstein, accompanied Tomsky: 'Minutes of the Fifth Meeting of the Anglo-Russian Joint Advisory Council', TUC Archive, MSS. 292/947/25/5.
[230] The members of the TUC insisted they too wanted to preserve the Anglo-Russian Committee: Citrine 1964, p. 92.

'Oh, that's just Lozovsky. Well what can you expect from Lozovsky'![231] Tomsky agreed to stop repeating, in the press or elsewhere, his criticisms of the General Council's decisions during the general strike and the miners' strike (the ending of the miners' strike after a few more months of post general-strike resistance had reduced that source of friction). The British delegates, who felt that Tomsky and his fellow Soviet representatives on the Committee were sincere in wanting to avoid any further conflicts and misunderstandings, promised to push again for a conference without pre-conditions with the Amsterdam International.[232] The British did initiate an informal meeting between Jouhaux, Oudegeest, and Soviet trade-union representatives, which took place in Geneva a month later.[233] The TUC also agreed to hold the next meeting of the Anglo-Russian Committee, either immediately before or after the IFTU's Congress in Paris.[234] Tomsky later reported the sessions had been 'cordial', the decisions 'unanimous', and that 'the hopes of the enemies of the working class that the Committee would be dissolved have been completely shattered'.[235] But, in what could have only embarrassed Tomsky, and added to the uneasiness of his remaining allies back in Moscow, the headline of *The Times* article on the meeting was 'Russian Unions Surrender'.[236]

Opponents of Tomsky's attempts to maintain the Anglo-Russian Committee again seized the opportunity to criticise him. Denouncing the 'Berlin capitulation', Trotsky wrote it was wrong for Tomsky to talk of 'unanimity' and 'cordial relations' with those who had betrayed, and would again betray, the working class.[237] In Berlin, at the meeting of the Comintern Presidium on 11 May, Tomsky was harshly criticised by Voja Vujovich, the Yugoslav representative to the Comintern, who was close to Zinoviev.[238] Here and elsewhere Tomsky argued that the Soviet delegation had not suffered a defeat. It had just made the sort of compromises that were inevitable if the Soviet Union hoped to maintain or develop alliances with non-communist trade unionists.[239] But the criticism stung.

---

231   *Inprecorr*, 7 July 1927, p. 867.
232   *Inprecorr*, 15 September 1927, p. 1183; Van Goethem 2006, p. 95.
233   Lepse apparently led the Soviet trade-union delegation: Tosstorff 2018, pp. 719–20.
234   'Minutes of the Fifth Meeting of the Anglo-Russian Joint Advisory Council', TUC Archive, MSS. 292/947/25/5.
235   *Inprecorr*, 7 April 1927, p. 481; Tomskii 1928d, p. 450.
236   Calhoun 1976, p. 341.
237   Fel'shtinskii (ed.) 1988b, pp. 52, 56, 62; Degras 1960, p. 370.
238   Vatlin 2009, p. 183.
239   Tomskii 1928d, pp. 448–9. Bukharin did come to Tomsky's defence: *Manchester Guardian*, 1 July 1927.

Under this pressure, on 13 May 1927, in an interview with a correspondent from the British communist newspaper, *Workers' Life*, Tomsky blatantly violated the just recently signed Berlin agreement not to interfere in British domestic affairs.[240] Tomsky criticised individual members by name and lambasted the General Council as a whole for its failure to rally the British working class against the increasingly bellicose attitude of the British Government toward the Soviet Union and against the 'fascist' anti-trade-union bill in Parliament.[241] Tomsky was obviously trying to fend off the attacks from Trotsky and others that he had capitulated to the British on the Anglo-Russian Committee, but his statements predictably outraged the General Council. Citrine fired off a letter expressing the Council's disbelief that 'you, as the responsible leader of the Russian trade-union movement, have made such declarations'. Citrine generously offered Tomsky an out by asking if the translation of his comments was 'a travesty of what you actually said'.[242] Tomsky did not take up the offer. He bluntly wrote three weeks later, on 6 June, that he was surprised the General Council considered it worth its time to ask such a question, and insisted that yes, the translation was substantially accurate. Tomsky added that he resented the idea of anyone trying to restrict his freedom of speech. 'In my personal utterances, I do not feel myself bound by any resolutions of the Anglo-Russian Committee'.[243] The General Council was understandably outraged at what they thought was his flippant response considering their recent agreement. No longer willing to put with the endless stream of abuse, all the Soviet criticisms of them as traitors and capitalist lackeys, the General Council voted on 22 June to suspend relations with Tomsky and the VTsSPS.[244]

Despite all this bad blood, Purcell declared in his presidential address at the IFTU's Congress in Paris in early August 1927 that 'international trade-union

---

240 Citrine (ed.) 1927, p. 206.
241 Citrine (ed.) 1927, pp. 207–9; *Inprecorr*, 12 May 1927, pp. 587–8; *Inprecorr*, 15 September 1927, p. 1184. The key provisions of the recently passed Trades Disputes Act outlawed sympathy strikes and any strike that sought to 'coerce the government'. There was no prosecution of the Act up to its repeal by the Labour government in 1946: Laybourn 1992, p. 140.
242 Citrine (ed.) 1927, p. 209.
243 Citrine (ed.) 1927, pp. 209–10; *Inprecorr*, 7 July 1927, p. 868.
244 *Inprecorr*, 15 September 1927, p. 1184; Citrine (ed.) 1927, p. 207. Just prior to the General Council vote, there was a meeting in Berlin on 18–19 June of a truncated Anglo-Russian Committee, consisting of just Tomsky, Melnichansky, Hicks, and Citrine, to discuss the possibility of calling a meeting of the committee to oppose the threat of a British war against the Soviet Union: 'Report of Meeting between Representatives of the General Council of the Trades Union Congress and the All-Russian Council of Trade Unions, 18–19 June 1927', TUC Archive, MSS. 292/947/25/6.

unity must take precedence over everything ... How miserable are the follies that have kept ourselves and the Russian workers apart. We need the young and powerful Russian Trade-Union Movement in our International'.[245] But that speech was merely the last hurrah for Purcell and the Anglo-Russian Committee. The IFTU Executive Committee rebuked Purcell for his accommodating attitude toward the Soviet trade unions and removed him from his position as IFTU president.[246] Oudegeest even went so far during a heated exchange as to call Purcell a 'Russian agent'.[247] The ineffective British delegation felt it had no choice but to walk out of the conference. Purcell's failure to overcome opposition within the IFTU meant the Anglo-Russian Committee had lost whatever remained of its original raison d'être. With any remaining hope of international trade-union unity gone, the VTsSPS held nothing back in its vilification of the IFTU leaders, calling them 'a clique of venal careerists and lackeys of capitalism and imperialism who place their own interests before the interests of the proletariat'. They needed to be replaced by 'fresh, bold, honest working-class leaders'.[248]

The British General Council unanimously recommended bringing the Anglo-Russian Committee to a formal end at the Trades Union Congress in Edinburgh on 17 September 1927. Its report stated that 'no useful purpose will be served by continuing negotiations' with the VTsSPS 'so long as their attitude and policy are maintained'.[249] After a lengthy debate, during which some speeches caused considerable commotion on the floor of the congress, the resolution carried. When the congress's decision to dissolve the Anglo-Russian Committee was put to a vote by all the members of the TUC, it passed overwhelmingly. Only 620,000 of the 3,171,000 voters opposed dissolving the Anglo-Russian Committee.[250] Relations had become so bad that the TUC would

---

245 Citrine (ed.) 1927, p. 374.
246 Martin 1969, pp. 84–5; *Inprecorr*, 11 August 1927, p. 1026. The IFTU initially offered the position to Hicks, but he refused to accept it. In 1928 the TUC general secretary Citrine replaced Purcell as IFTU president. Equally unsuccessfully, at the IFTU General Council meeting, Hicks again called for the convening of a conference 'without preliminary conditions' between representatives of the IFTU and the VTsSPS: Citrine (ed.) 1927, p. 216.
247 Tosstorff 2018, p. 720.
248 *Inprecorr*, 8 September 1927, p. 1172; *Inprecorr*, 15 September 1927, p. 1187.
249 Officially, the TUC suspended relations 'until Moscow changed its conduct ... We have not bolted or barred the door'. In reality the General Council appeared to completely lose interest in relations with the Soviet Union after the collapse of the Anglo-Russian Committee: Citrine (ed.), pp. 359–60. See also Williams 1989, pp. 29, 37, 44.
250 Citrine (ed.), pp. 358–70.

not have agreed to attend the Bolsheviks' tenth anniversary celebrations in Moscow, if invited.[251]

In the aftermath of the collapse of the Anglo-Russian Committee and the last hopes of achieving international trade-union unity, some members of the General Council and the IFTU leadership speculated about Tomsky's motives in negotiating so enthusiastically with them earlier.[252] The evidence indicates that Tomsky acted in good faith. He genuinely sought a working alliance with the Western non-communist Left. His instrumental role in the creation of the Anglo-Russian Committee, through which the Soviets were able to forge close ties with a major element of the international labour movement, was a notable achievement, of which he was justifiably proud. But, as we have seen, Tomsky's success at building a collaborative relationship with the British trade unions proved ephemeral. The shakeup in the composition of the General Council in November 1925 brought to the fore trade-union leaders with relatively little interest in working with Tomsky to establish an international trade-union organisation that included the Soviet trade unions. And Tomsky's hopes of bringing Soviet trade unions into the Amsterdam International ran up against the IFTU's steadfast refusal to meet with him because of the Politburo's unwillingness, after briefly flirting with the idea, to close down the Profintern, which meant Tomsky never had a chance to work his charms on the leaders of the IFTU. Following the failed general strike, Tomsky's balancing act between the General Council and the Profintern proved untenable because he needed to adopt a radical posture in response to all the criticisms from Zinoviev and Trotsky for his initial response to the ending of the general strike. The Soviet leadership's subsequent barrage of attacks on the British trade-union leaders, in which Tomsky reluctantly participated, doomed his attempt to preserve the Anglo-Russian Committee and the policy of the 'united front'. The British trade-union leaders' feelings of friendship and camaraderie with Tomsky gave way to feelings of acrimony and anger.

The dissolution of the Anglo-Russian Committee, coupled with the British government's decision to sever diplomatic relations, and the disaster in China that resulted from the Soviet policy of forcing Chinese communists to submit to the nationalists (Kuomintang), led the Comintern in 1927 to drop the 'united front' policy in favour of 'a turn to the left'.[253] The attempt to form competing communist unions, with the Profintern denouncing leftists such as Cook as 'social fascists', would prove to be a total flop, just as Tomsky had long argued

---

251   Morgan 2013, p. 296. A large British delegation did attend the anniversary.
252   Calhoun 1976, p. 23.
253   McDermott and Agnew 1996, pp. 68–70.

it would be. The dissolution of the Anglo-Russian Committee also undercut Tomsky's political clout in Moscow. The sort of moderate foreign policies Tomsky personified lost their foothold in the Soviet leadership. As we will see, once Stalin vanquished Zinoviev and Trotsky, Tomsky became one of the next victims in the leadership struggle. In the aftermath of his foray into foreign policy, he would lose what proved to be a fatal challenge to his leadership of the trade unions at the end of 1928, while Lozovsky, now a Stalinist, remained general secretary of the Profintern until its dissolution in 1937.[254]

[254] Lozovsky piled on in the attacks on Tomsky in 1930: Tosstorff 2018, p. 770.

CHAPTER 5

Tomsky during NEP: Trade Unions and the Intra-Party Struggle

> When our workers' government does all that is possible to meet our needs, we do not think of it as the enemy because it cannot do more.
> MIKHAIL TOMSKY

∴

> All the leaders of the Bolshevik Party, even those whose reputation as Moderates has been firmly established, indulge freely in the habit of using spicy revolutionary rhetoric.
> MICHAEL FARBMAN

∴

Tomsky played contradictory roles during NEP. As head of the trade unions he was the quintessentially moderate Bolshevik. His instincts for realism, pragmatism, and evolutionary policies were on full display in the VTsSPS Presidium and in his interactions with other trade-union and party officials as he tried to advance workers' short-term interests while also supporting the Soviet government's more long-term goals of reviving the economy and building an industrialised, socialist society. Trade unionists and workers seemed to recognise Tomsky had their best interests at heart and as a result he enjoyed, at least among many of them, enormous personal popularity. At the same time, Tomsky was in the thick of all the party disputes and policy decisions of the 1920s. That included being in the centre of the behind-the-scenes power struggle. His role in this party infighting essentially revolved around his conflict with Trotsky, his determination to defend the moderate policy of NEP, and his distrust of 'bourgeois specialists'. Tomsky, in this party infighting, was hardly a voice for Bolshevik pluralism and tolerance. Examining these contrasting aspects of Tomsky's domestic record during NEP, before the showdown at the Eighth Trade-Union Congress in 1928, is the subject of this chapter.

Tomsky had always appeared to enjoy partisan wrangling, going back to how he had first made a name for himself at the Fifth Party Congress in 1907. A consistent opponent of the 'leftists' in the party, Tomsky supported Iosif Stalin, Grigory Zinoviev, Lev Kamenev, and Alexei Rykov against Leon Trotsky first, and then, along with Nikolai Bukharin, Stalin, and Rykov against the 'Leningrad Opposition' of Zinoviev and Kamenev, and finally against the self-proclaimed United Opposition of Trotsky, Zinoviev, and Kamenev. Tomsky's commitment to maintaining the moderate policies of NEP, with its conciliatory policies towards the peasantry and the promise of gradually improving wages for workers, was certainly a key factor behind his woefully mistaken decision to align himself with Stalin. But Tomsky's personal aversion to the leadership's prima donnas, in particular Trotsky and Zinoviev, also helps explain his positions during the power struggle. In the words of Adam Ulam, 'the ruling group's cohesion was forged as much by hatred of Trotsky and Zinoviev as it was by loyalty to Stalin'.[1] Tomsky never forgot or forgave Trotsky for his attacks during the 1920–21 'trade-union debate'. As fatally wrongheaded as it was in hindsight, Tomsky considered Stalin a political ally as well as a personal friend, who shared his moderate approach to economic policy and his antagonism to Trotsky.

Tomsky, as we will see, unwittingly adopted positions that would ultimately destroy his own political fortunes. When in power, he proved to be a harsh opponent of those he perceived to be serious threats to NEP, party unity, or workers' interests. In doing so, Tomsky inadvertently gave Stalin and his cohorts weapons to use against him and his allies after the crushing of the United Opposition in 1927. The ways in which Tomsky had excoriated Trotsky, Zinoviev, and Kamenev would undercut his efforts to mount an effective counter-attack when the Stalinists turned their fire against him. In addition, Tomsky shamefully exerted enormous influence in the attacks against the so-called bourgeois specialists during the Shakhty Affair in early 1928. Stalin, a skilful and tactical politician, although devoid of personal magnetism, would cleverly use those attacks to help undermine Tomsky's leadership of the trade unions. Tomsky, like his cohorts Bukharin and Rykov, failed to appreciate the threat Stalin posed to their policies of economic moderation until it was too late. It was only when Stalin coercively began to implement the so-called extraordinary measures against the peasantry in early 1928 that the blinders finally came off and convinced Tomsky that Stalin posed an existential threat to the pragmatic, moderate economic policies of NEP as well as to his standing within the party leadership.

---

1 Ulam 1973, p. 274.

Before turning to Tomsky's role in the unfolding power struggle, it is important to underscore that he had many official responsibilities during the 1920s. Tomsky had to juggle the time and focus he devoted to his various official capacities, never able to focus on one to the exclusion of the others.[2] As head of the VTsSPS Presidium, Tomsky continued to devote much of his energy primarily to the trade unions during NEP, including the trade-union movement's foreign policy, as was examined in chapter four. But at the same time he served as one of the seven members of the Politburo, the highest policymaking body in the country, where Tomsky participated in the heated debates over various issues.[3] Tomsky's particular role on the Politburo was to focus on various trade-union and other worker-related issues, including presenting regular reports on labour issues.[4] For Tomsky, this meant he once again faced many of the same dilemmas he had confronted during the Civil War. Tomsky's dual roles as both a member of the Politburo and head of the trade unions would continually leave him torn between his support of party and government policies to revive the economy, which he helped formulate, and fulfilling the trade unions' more traditional function of representing and protecting workers' interests. Tomsky's other main responsibilities were as a member of the Orgburo, from April 1922 until January 1926.[5] Tomsky's heavy workload also included serving on the Executive Committees of the Comintern and on the Presidium of the Central Executive Committee of the Soviets (VTsIK).

The trade unions were a major pillar of the Soviet regime during NEP as the one mass organisation that connected the party with workers, in whose name the revolution had been carried out. In his leadership of the trade unions, Tomsky accepted, over the objections of some trade unionists, the party's ultimate oversight of the trade unions.[6] But Tomsky tried to ensure that non-union party officials would not interfere in the trade unions' day-to-day affairs, pointing out that party members from working-class backgrounds increasingly occupied all

---

2 That was not unusual. All the members of the Politburo had other full-time positions, from which they derived additional power and influence, at both the central and regional level.
3 Khordina (ed.) 2000, pp. 170–300; Vilkova 2004, p. 145. The Politburo meetings were not dry and sedate debates: Gill 2018, p. 80.
4 The other members of the Politburo were Lenin, Trotsky, Stalin, Zinoviev, Kamenev, and Rykov. Bukharin, Molotov, and Kalinin were candidate (non-voting) members of the Politburo then.
5 Tomsky was not the only member serving on both the Politburo and Orgburo. With 50 percent of Politburo members also on the Orgburo in 1922, there was a considerable overlap between the members of the two bodies. Gill 1990a, pp. 65–6, 67, 81. During his last two years on the Orgburo Tomsky was only a candidate member.
6 RKP(b) 1961, pp. 248–51; Tomskii 1927b, p. 312.

FIGURE 18 Composite Poster of Soviet Officials in 1924: top row Bukharin, Zinoviev, Lenin, Trotsky, Tomsky; second row Rakovsky, Chicherin, Rykov, Stalin, Dzerzhinsky; third row Yenukidze, Kamenev, Kalinin, Lunacharsky, Frunze; front row Budenny, Semasko.
WIKIMEDIA COMMONS

the full-time positions in the unions. It is also important to note that industrial managers were also subject to party oversight. Both the trade unions and managers competed for the party's favour. Tomsky also did his best to exert his political influence on behalf of the trade unions. It was Tomsky's firm belief that the trade-union leaders could successfully defend workers' interests through their dealings with the other leaders of the party as well as the heads of the various economic bodies. He thought that, in addition to his positions on the Politburo and Orgburo, the large number of fellow trade unionists in key institutions, including the Central Executive Committee of the Soviets as well as the Central Committee of the Bolshevik Party, meant that the state and the party were subject to the influence of the trade unions.[7] With considerable justification, Tomsky repeatedly stated that not a single law, circular, or order affecting workers or working conditions could be passed without the sanction of the VTsSPS.[8] Tomsky also boasted in late 1926 that the 'the unions have the right to call on any people's commissar to appear before them to make a report, and not one of them has the right to refuse on the grounds than he is not formally responsible to the unions'.[9] While Tomsky may have overstated the trade unionists' influence, the trade unions did enjoy considerable autonomy and power during the 1920s, contrary to the portrayal of them in much of the historiography on NEP.

While Tomsky's leadership of the trade unions during NEP will be examined in considerable detail, it does not warrant a separate chapter from the simultaneous intra-party struggle. Most of Tomsky's positions on trade-union policy during this period were similar to what they had been during the Civil War, which were examined in Chapter 2. Tomsky was essentially on the same page as other top party leaders when it came to the role of trade unions during NEP. There was no repeat of anything resembling the intra-party conflict over labour policy during War Communism that erupted in the 'trade-union debate'. It would also be redundant to provide a comprehensive examination of NEP

---

7 Tomsky 1927a, p. 18; Tomskii 1928b, pp. 19, 39. In this report to the Profintern in 1923, Tomsky stated that five of the 13 members of the Presidium on the Central Executive Committee of the Soviets were trade unionists: Tomsky 1923, p. 15. Three of the 25 members of the Central Committee in 1921 were also trade unionists. In addition to Tomsky, the secretary of the VTsSPS, Rudzutak, and the head of the Miners' Union Fedor Artem, were elected to the Central Committee. Tomsky's aide Alexander Dogadov and the Miners' Union head Isaak Shvarts were added in 1924, with Shvarts taking the place of Artem, who died in 1921.
8 Tomsky 1923, p. 16.
9 Quoted in Kuromiya 1988, p. 40.

trade-union policy since so much of that history has been addressed in the secondary literature on trade unions and workers during the 1920s.[10]

While reviving agriculture by ending grain requisitioning was the main impetus behind the party's introduction of NEP, reviving the industrial economy was also a top priority. After the catastrophic damage done by seven years of war, revolution, and civil war, as well as by the policies of War Communism, overall production at the beginning of 1921 was approximately one-seventh of pre-war levels. NEP, in addition to privatising all enterprises employing less than 40 persons, required large-scale, nationalised industrial enterprises, the most damaged sector of the economy, to operate according to cost-accounting procedures [*khozraschet*], which meant they had to compete on a commercial basis with private enterprises and other nationalised enterprises.[11] NEP largely eliminated the state subsidies many industrial enterprises had received during War Communism regardless of their efficiency or profitability.[12] In even those large-scale industrial enterprises that continued to receive some state funding during NEP, sales were increasingly required to provide the means to purchase materials and to pay workers. Tomsky strongly supported this change in policy, arguing that given the desperate need to revive the economy 'we don't have the luxury of allowing even a single enterprise to operate at a loss'.[13]

Although trade unions, together with economic bodies, discussed all candidates nominated for administrative positions in enterprises, during NEP the Soviet government required trade unions to relinquish any role in enterprise management beyond negotiating the terms of collective agreements and ensuring their implementation.[14] Influenced perhaps by his earlier failure to maintain the trade unions in managerial roles during War Communism, Tomsky believed that it would be impossible for trade unions, at the same time, to manage a factory on the basis of cost accounting and to defend the economic

---

10   NEP labour policy has been covered extensively in the secondary literature. For some examples beginning with the very exhaustive work by E.H. Carr: Carr 1952; Carr 1953; Carr 1958; Carr and Davies 1969b; Dunn 1928; Zagorsky 1930; Gordon 1941; Bergson 1944; Deutscher 1950; Schwarz 1951; Morrell 1965; Sorenson 1969; Langsam 1973; Dewar 1979; Sirianni 1982; Hatch 1985; Chase 1987; Kuromiya 1988; Nosach 2001; Koenker 2005; Murphy 2005; Borisova 2006; Lobok 2006; Jo 2007.
11   It was not until February 1922 that the principle of *khozrachet* was firmly established.
12   The trade unions also lost their subsidies.
13   Tomskii 1927b, p. 29.
14   Tomskii 1927b, p. 10; RKP(b) 1961, p. 235. While Tomsky believed that managers generally lived up to the terms of the collective agreements, that was challenged at the party caucus of the Fifth Trade-Union Congress, where delegates argued that it was not the case out in the provinces: GARF, f. 5451, op. 42, d. 39, ll. 56–7.

interests of workers.[15] Embracing this role as the defender of workers' interests, Tomsky urged trade unionists at the February 1922 plenum of the VTsSPS, and in a widely cited article at the time, to defend workers economic interests by bargaining hard for higher wages in nationalised as well as private enterprises.[16] Additionally, the VTsSPS would set a minimum wage below which 'wages in Soviet Russia must not fall'.[17]

Tomsky and other trade-union leaders abandoned completely the goal of collective management, not just because they thought it was impossible to simultaneously serve in managerial positions and defend workers' interests. Tomsky also argued, as he had before, that 'we are too poor and the general economic conditions are too unfavourable' to place workers in management now.[18] He added that it was important, however, to educate workers on economic issues 'in the spirit of management' and to prepare the most talented among them to eventually become managers themselves.[19] Tomsky's unwillingness to fight for any formal trade-union role in management angered some fellow trade unionists, namely the leaders and supporters of the Workers' Opposition. Because of such criticism, and no doubt still bristling from Shlyapnikov's role in his banishment to Turkestan, at a closed session of the Eleventh Party Congress in March 1922, Tomsky proposed an amendment that called on the Central Committee to purge from the party the top three Workers' Oppositionists – Alexander Shlyapnikov, Alexandra Kollontai, and Sergei Medvedev – if they engaged in any future violations of party discipline.[20] It passed overwhelmingly.

The trade unions in NEP were supposed to perform a function that in some respects was analogous to the role trade unions played in the capitalist West.[21]

---

15 Tomskii 1927b, p. 10; Nosach 2005, p. 123.
16 Tomskii 1927b, p. 9.
17 Aves 1996, p. 170. Sometime that simply meant making sure the Labour Code was enforced.
18 Tomskii 1927b, p. 85. Many individual trade unionists had in fact become industrial managers: Deutscher 1950, p. 63. It is not at clear why Deutscher incorrectly states on this same page that Tomsky was temporarily removed from the VTsSPS Presidium at the Fifth Trade-Union Congress.
19 RKP(b) 1961, p. 235. Tomsky conceded later in the year that most workers' 'brains were too exhausted' to take advantage of such opportunities: VTsSPS 1922, p. 129.
20 The Workers' Oppositionists were under fire for their protests, including an appeal to the Comintern, against the introduction of NEP. At the same time, Tomsky as part of an Orgburo commission, along with Andrei Andreev and Sergei Syrtsov, worked to undermine Shlyapnikov's base in the metalworkers' union's central committee: Allen 2015, pp. 234–5, 251.
21 One historian compared them to the American Federation of Labour in their focus on 'bread and butter' issues: Straus 1990, p. 555. As we saw earlier, when Trotsky during the

As had already been the case during War Communism, especially following the Ninth Party Congress, when the party had abandoned its original goal of workers' control in the face of economic collapse, trade unions during NEP were to work to defend the interests of workers while not interfering in the running of industries. But in reality, the Central Committee repeatedly criticised the trade unions for their interference in management. The tension between VSNKh and the VTsSPS became one of the central features of NEP. Tomsky tried to work with his friend Valerian Kuibyshev, a leading figure in VSNKh, to smooth over these tensions, while pursuing the trade unions' traditional economic goals to benefit their worker constituents.[22] But relations between managers and the trade unions often remained adversarial. Tomsky recognised their different roles in the economy made some conflict unavoidable. Just as managers strove to cut costs and show a profit, the trade unions' mission was to defend the material interests of their members. Tomsky particularly resented how managers often blamed workers for their own mismanagement.

While defending the policies of NEP, Tomsky felt it was important for the trade unions to articulate workers' grievances and work to alleviate them. This was particularly true when it came to the enterprises' non-party managers and technical specialists, attacks on whom would play a major role in the power struggle. While Bolshevik intellectuals generally thought it was possible, if warily, to work with the specialists, Tomsky argued workers, even those who were party members, remained deeply suspicious and distrustful of them. As we saw in Chapter 2, one of the reasons Tomsky had opposed one-man management and supported collegial management was the perceived need to supervise those derisively referred to as 'bourgeois specialists' (*spetsy*).[23] Workers on the factory floor continued to greatly resent the remuneration the *spetsy* received and viewed with scepticism, to say the least, the party leadership's claim that their high salaries served the workers' own long-term interests. But at the Eleventh Party Congress Tomsky and his cohorts in the trade-union leadership were instructed not only to acquiesce to the monetary incentives, but to explain the *spetsy*'s economic value to their members. Such instructions had little if any impact. According to Tomsky, trade unionists had a hard time defending

---

Civil Ware compared Tomsky to Samuel Gompers, the head of the AFL, he greatly resented it.

22 GARF, f. 5451, op. 2, d. 42, l. 4. Kuibyshev would become head of VSNKh following the death of Felix Dzerzhinsky from a heart attack in July 1926.

23 Sixty-five percent of managers in 1922 were officially classified as workers, but already by 1923 only 36 percent of them were so classified: Carr 1954, p. 40.

party policy on the specialists at factory meetings.[24] That was at least partly because their hearts were not really in it; no doubt because they too resented the high salaries specialists received. So although the trade-union leadership felt compelled to continue to accept, at least in principle, the rationale that it was necessary for industrial development to provide managers and technical specialists with substantial monetary incentives, in practice they often balked because they recognised that the privileged position of the *spetsy* created widespread resentment and envy among their rank-and-file union members. The mood of the mass of workers as a result of their poverty and desire to achieve equality, Tomsky argued, is of course against the specialists because 'the specialist lives better and is paid better. The specialist gives orders and makes demands. He is an alien entity who did not make the October Revolution. That is how people evaluate the specialists'.[25] Tomsky worked with Stalin to respond to trade-union and worker discontent with the *spetsy*. They presented to the Orgburo on 13 March 1922 a proposal to establish parameters for the maximum pay for specialists, which was adopted.[26] The salaries of engineers and technical personnel were reduced between 10 and 20 percent. But unionists remained so angry about the specialists' salaries that Narkomtrud forced further concessions from specialists in late 1923.[27]

In addition to workers' resentment of the specialists' salaries, they also resented the role of the *spetsy* in pushing workers to increase their productivity.[28] Some miners in the Donbass and the Urals so hated the engineer specialists in their mines they had gone so far as to murder them.[29] Throughout NEP, criticism of the 'bourgeois specialists' was repeatedly aired at party and trade-union congresses, before it fully erupted during the 'Shakhty Affair' in 1928.

Tomsky did, however, use the same sort of logic, which justified the higher wages 'bourgeois specialists' received, to justify paying skilled workers much higher wages than unskilled workers. Under War Communism all workers were paid basically the same. But industry suffered from a serious shortage of skilled workers because so many had been promoted into positions of authority in the trade unions or other bureaucracies during the Civil War, or after they were demobilised if they survived the fighting. In addition to pursuing the goal of

---

24 RKP(b) 1961, p. 279.
25 RKP(b) 1961, p. 279. 'Specialist-baiting' (*spetseedstvo*) predictably was most pronounced in industries with depressed wage levels: Hatch 1985, p. 58. Sometimes specialists were driven to the point of suicide by the harassment they endured: Stites 1989, p. 75.
26 GARF, f. 5451, op. 4, d. 46, l. 4.
27 Pirani 2008, p. 189.
28 Dewar 1979, p. 125.
29 Lenin 1960–70, vol. 42, p. 383.

retaining skilled workers in industry, Tomsky also advocated using material benefits and monetary incentives to encourage workers to raise their skill level. The wage differential between skilled and unskilled workers as a result skyrocketed from 4 percent in 1920 to 65 percent in 1922.[30]

This disparity in wages resulted from the complex and detailed collective agreements the trade unions continued to negotiate with economic administrators following the introduction of NEP, in both the public and private sector.[31] The signing of the collective agreements were supposed to be preceded by meetings in which workers would be given a chance to discuss the various clauses, including wages and the output norms.[32] But Tomsky conceded in 1922 that all too often workers were not consulted and the negotiations over the collective agreements merely meant 'a talk between the trade-union representative and the representative of the administration, who in the silence of an office signed an agreement about which the workers knew nothing'.[33] And inflation, especially during early NEP, would often undermine wage increases and lead workers to demand that the collective agreements be re-negotiated.[34]

Even so, conditions for rank-and-file workers did begin to improve. With Tomsky's support, Narkomtrud introduced a new Labour Code in 1922, which replaced the 1918 code.[35] It established guarantees for all workers, including a minimum wage, an eight-hour day, and paid vacations. And despite Tom-

---

30   Bettelheim 1978, p. 249. Tomsky had worked on a Politburo sub-committee in February 1922, before he became one of its seven members, to establish a general framework for wage levels. Sokolnikov, Rudzutak, and Melnichansky also served on the sub-committee: Khordina (ed.) 2000, p. 152.

31   These negotiations took place on two levels. Central trade-union authorities negotiated general industry-wide agreements with the relevant economic organisation. At the local level, the district trade-union committee became involved in order to work out with management how to implement the collective agreements at the enterprise level, including setting wage-rates for each grade of workers and the output quotas and piece-rates.

32   Tomskii 1927b, p. 12. The collective agreements were fairly standardised in their general form but varied considerably in their details. They could have nearly 200 clauses.

33   Tomskii 1927b, p. 12. Despite Tomsky's demands that this practice be decisively abandoned, it apparently did not improve over time. In 1926 Tomsky likewise conceded that unfortunately in the majority of cases workers for whom the collective agreement is signed do not know what is being signed on their behalf: RKP(b) 1926, p. 731.

34   GARF, f. 5451, op. 42, d. 137, l. 139; *Sotsialisticheskii vestnik*, 21 July 1928, p. 14.

35   The VTsSPS, however, had been bypassed when the Commissariat of Labour made the final revisions of the code, although the Commissar of Labour Vasily Shmidt insisted it had been a joint effort of Narkomtrud and the VTsSPS until then: Allen 2015, pp. 237–8; Sorenson 1969, p. 175. In any case, as a member of the Narkomtrud Presidium, Tomsky presumably had input in those final revisions. In many instances Narkomtrud remained subservient to VTsSPS.

sky's endlessly repeated statements about how wage increases must be tied to increases in productivity, and about how the interests of today must be subordinated to the general class interests of tomorrow, during early NEP the bargaining of the trade unions in the negotiations over the collective agreements generally enabled workers' wages to rise much faster than output.[36] In 1921, before the introduction of NEP, wages were probably only a third of what they had been in 1913 in real terms.[37] By spring 1923 wages might have risen to over 50 percent of their pre-war level.[38] By this time the unions had also begun to succeed in reducing the scandalous disparity between the wages of workers in heavy and light industry, which corresponded to the disparity between the wages in the slowly recovering state enterprises and the flourishing private enterprises.[39] In addition, the rapid revival of agriculture after the horrific 1921–22 famine made food easily available in urban markets. In addition, there was on top of the wage differentials based on skill, large differences in wages between different branches of the economy. For example, workers in printing earned 50 percent more than workers in mining.[40] Workers, especially metalworkers and miners, made it known that they did not buy Tomsky's pleas for them to be patient until further increases in production would allow for more substantial improvements in their conditions.[41]

Tomsky and his fellow trade unionists struggled to deal with a dramatic increase in unemployment, which was the most injurious by-product of the introduction of NEP. Many enterprises, which were compelled to cut costs, laid off substantial portions of their workforces. The complete closure of some unprofitable enterprises led to further workforce reductions. Tomsky and others in the party leadership recognised they were treading an uncomfortably fine line, for although closures were necessary to lower costs, a full unleashing of market forces would have resulted in even more massive layoffs. As a

---

36 Sometimes it would take many months of bargaining by the trade unions to hammer out the collective agreements: VTsSPS 1927, pp. 89–90.
37 Zaleski 1971, p. 390.
38 Carr 1954, pp. 72–4. Labour productivity might have already risen from 30 percent of the pre-war level in 1920/21 to 50 percent a year later: Lobok 2006, p. 156.
39 Carr 1954, p. 75. The collective agreements with private enterprises in 1922 called for wages much higher (often double) than what was agreed to in the negotiations with state firms, which led to many private enterprises refusing to sign collective agreements: GARF, f. 5451, op. 6, d. 4, ll. 11–12; GARF, f. 5451, op. 42, d. 137, l. 140. These private enterprises, which usually were very small, generally engaged in consumer industries, unlike the state industries, which engaged in heavy industry and took longer to recover following the introduction of NEP.
40 Langsam 1973, p. 125.
41 VTsSPS 1922, p. 130.

result, the party leadership, despite the policy of *khozraschet*, in the end refrained from closing many large, unprofitable enterprises. Even so, Tomsky estimated that hundreds of thousands of workers were laid off as a result of the introduction of NEP.[42] Most of those thrown out of work were unskilled women, 'yesterday's peasants', or juveniles.[43] Few skilled or experienced male workers, the trade unions' core constituency, and the workers with whom Tomsky most identified, had to worry about unemployment.[44]

Tomsky and the trade unions had reason to assert that the unemployment picture was not as bleak as it seemed. The main driver of unemployment, once NEP successfully began to revive the Soviet economy, was not layoffs. Since NEP succeeded in producing dramatic, continual increases in the number of employed workers, high unemployment was primarily the result of the massive influx of peasant migrants into industrial areas. As paradoxical as it seems, high unemployment would continue at the same time as the number of employed workers steadily rose because economic hardships drove rural residents to migrate in such enormous numbers that it continually drove up the number of unemployed.[45] High unemployment rates would subject Tomsky, the VTsSPS, and the Politburo to harsh attacks from oppositionists during the 1920s.

Tomsky reaffirmed his earlier opposition to strikes with the introduction of NEP, although not initially. At the VTsSPS Plenum in February 1922, Tomsky argued that if unions opposed strikes, the most powerful weapon in the unions' arsenal, they would lose their influence with the mass of workers.[46] 'In instances of the exploitation of women or the insulting treatment of workers', Tomsky argued, 'the trade unions should have short, organised strikes to get the attention of administrators'.[47] But just a month later, at the Eleventh Party Congress in March 1922, which explicitly did not ban strikes, Tomsky argued, as he had during War Communism, that strikes were an unsuitable way to

---

42 Tomsky 1923, p. 9. A Soviet scholar, O.I. Shkaratan, estimated that more than 260,000 workers, a quarter of the industrial workforce, lost their jobs: Goldman 2002, p. 11.
43 Chase 1987, p. 103.
44 Carr 1954, p. 49. The shortage of skilled workers continually limited increases in labour productivity: GARF, f. 5451, op. 42, d. 136, l. 105. Even though unemployed workers, unlike under the autocracy, did receive some unemployment support, losing a job brought serious privation since that support was so minimal during early NEP.
45 GARF, f. 5451, op. 42, d. 137, l. 52; Chase 1987, pp. 86, 96. In addition, the revival of the industrial economy served as a pull factor.
46 Tomsky's opposition to strikes was less adamant than what was expressed by such other leading trade unionists as Alexander Dogadov and Andrei Andreev: Lubok 2006, p. 157.
47 Chechevishnikov 1990, pp. 176–7.

settle workers' grievances since they hurt the efforts to rebuild the shattered economy.[48] Tomsky thought they could be used against the private enterprises legalised by NEP, but they should not be carried out against state enterprises, or if so, only as a last resort.[49] In almost all cases, Tomsky argued, the mediation or arbitration procedures established between representatives of the concerned trade unions and economic administrations should be adequate to bring about a peaceful resolution of labour disputes, assuming, as he did, that the trade unions, management, and the courts would all act in good faith.[50] And indeed, according to a report at the Fifth Trade-Union Congress in September 1922, nearly 80 percent of the disputes in state enterprises were resolved in favour of the workers; in most cases completely so.[51] But because most employed workers remained impoverished, if no longer utterly destitute, wildcat strikes broke out in 1922 and 1923.[52]

Tomsky was attending the usually twice-weekly, three-hour Politburo meetings as well as the long Orgburo meetings, while dealing with trade-union issues.[53] In the Politburo, as noted above, Tomsky weighed in on the various worker and trade-union issues as well as the wide variety of other issues being discussed. Right from the get-go, he often staked out more moderate positions than other Politburo members. In May 1922, during his first days and weeks on the Politburo, over the objections of the majority, Tomsky advocated a more lenient approach to arrested Socialist Revolutionaries and physicians who had come under suspicion. Tomsky had defended a group of the accused Socialist Revolutionaries and asked for mercy, understanding, and 'moral rehabilitation', unlike Trotsky, who became the spokesperson for those advocating a

---

48   RKP(b) 1961, pp. 237–8. Tomsky, for example, said that a strike of railway workers, even though there were among the most poorly paid workers, would be intolerable 'from the point of view of the general tasks of the working class' because the railroads were so critical to 'the construction of socialism': VTsSPS 1922, pp. 51, 109, 529–30; Tomskii 1928c, p. 8.
49   RKP(b) 1961, p. 238.
50   Tomskii 1927b, pp. 21–3. Shlyapnikov agreed with Tomsky on the need to rely on arbitration rather than strikes to get management to enforce the collective agreements: Allen 2015, p. 236.
51   VTsSPS 1922, p. 51.
52   GARF, f. 5451, op. 6, d. 3. Failure by management to fulfil the terms of the collective agreements, in particular the late payment of wages to workers living hand-to-mouth, was the cause of most of the strikes: Hatch 1985, pp. 193–4; Pospielovsky 1997, p. 13; Kuromiya 1998, pp. 128–9. Since many enterprises were operating at a loss and were having trouble meeting their payment obligations, these late payments were not necessarily due to managerial indifference to workers' plight: Brovkin 1998, p. 174.
53   Tomsky's level of participation in the labour-intensive Orgburo is unclear given all the other demands on his time.

FIGURE 19 Leon Trotsky in 1925
WIKIMEDIA COMMONS

hard line.[54] Only Tomsky, in regard to the physicians, abstained from voting for repressive measures, stating, 'we need a different approach'.[55] As for Lenin's September call for the Politburo to elevate Trotsky to be his deputy chair on the Sovnarkom, with special responsibility for the VSNKh, although no one opposed it, Tomsky and Kamenev abstained in the vote, before Trotsky 'categorically refused' the appointment, as he had before.[56] Trotsky's admirers see this one of Trotsky's biggest mistakes because they claim it would have made him Lenin's heir.

Tomsky was quickly drawn into the emerging power struggle and its various factional intrigues. He quickly became aware of the growing tension between

---

54 Jansen 1992, pp. 45, 60, 123, 134, 137; Finkel 2007, pp. 157–63, 168; Khaustov, Naumov, and Plotnikova (eds) 2003, p. 31; Pipes 1994, p. 406.
55 Quoted in Volkogonov 1994, p. 367.
56 Service 2009, p. 300; Deutscher 1959, p. 66; Pipes 1994, pp. 466–7. Figes thinks Trotsky refused because he thought the position of deputy chair was beneath him: Figes 1996, p. 796. Tomsky and Trotsky, in addition to all their previous clashes over the role of trade unions, had another bitter fight at the Eleventh Party Congress: Service 1995, p. 253.

Trotsky and the troika of Stalin, Zinoviev, and Kamenev.[57] This troika, beginning in the summer of 1923, if not even earlier, met together on the eve of Politburo meetings to set the agenda and discuss and decide issues before the actual meetings.[58] Historians have endlessly debated whether serious policy disagreements, personal ambitions, political rivalries, or past resentments were paramount in driving the discord within the Politburo. In the case of the moderate Tomsky, he had good reason to oppose Trotsky on all these counts. If Tomsky, still angry over Trotsky's earlier attempts to undermine the role of the trade unions, had any thoughts of softening his attitude toward Trotsky, the authoritarian rhetoric Trotsky directed at workers at the Twelfth Party Congress in 1923 squashed them. Trotsky, espousing his theory of 'primitive socialist accumulation', argued that the capital for industrial reconstruction would have to come from workers.[59] He frankly told workers, 'There may be moments when the government pays you no wages, or when it pays you only half your wages and when you, the worker, have to lend [the other half] to the state'.[60] In contrast to the positions of the calculating Stalin, Trotsky's advocacy for such harsh policies obviously showed little concern for the everyday needs of workers. Fearing the coercion Trotsky's harsh policies would necessarily entail, Tomsky in the Politburo, along with the fellow moderate Rykov, joined these secret sessions designed to thwart Trotsky.[61] Rykov had been appointed to the Politburo by the Central Committee along with Tomsky in 1922.[62] As a result, as early as

---

57 E.H. Carr suggests Stalin was the weakest of the three and still highly vulnerable because of Lenin's 'Testament': Carr 1954, p. 284.
58 The goal of this shadow Politburo was to undercut Trotsky, who they thought would be Lenin's likely successor, although it is not certain he wanted to be: Service 2009, p. 303. Trotsky had earlier stated that 'we should not give our enemies the opportunity to say that our country was being ruled by a Jew': quoted in Kotkin 2014, p. 523. Melnichansky, a Jewish trade unionist, shared Trotsky's opinion that the leader of the party should not be Jewish because of the widespread anti-Semitism. But he also opposed Trotsky because of his treatment of the trade unions: Citrine 1964, p. 101.
59 Carr 1954, p. 24.
60 Quoted in Deutscher 1959, p. 102. Later in the 1920s Trotsky followed the lead of Evgeny Preobrazhensky, a theorist of the left, who argued the capital had to be primarily 'pumped' (*perekachal*) out of the peasantry instead of workers. Preobrazhensky, a critic of NEP since its inception, impoliticly argued that the workers' state needed to 'exploit' the peasantry, when all he meant was that the terms of trade needed to be turned against the peasantry: Millar 1990, p. 68. He certainly had nothing in mind like the forced collectivisation of agriculture Stalin adopted in 1929.
61 Trotsky argued that 'the state could take "half their wages" only by force; and to do this it had to deprive them of every means of protest and to destroy the last vestiges of a workers' democracy': Deutscher 1959, p. 131.
62 Rykov, like Tomsky, had often been the target of Trotsky's broadsides: Day 1973, p. 33.

29 March 1923, with Lenin seriously incapacitated, Tomsky joined with fellow Politburo members Zinoviev, Stalin, Kamenev, and Rykov to write a letter to the Central Committee condemning Trotsky's continual, 'indiscriminate criticism' of the Politburo's work.[63] In addition to such policy differences, Trotsky's arrogant, aloof personality, and condescending manner, intensified how much both Tomsky and other leaders from working-class backgrounds disliked him.[64] Kanatchikov, who had painstakingly overcome his inhibitions about public speaking, is said to have 'viciously' attacked Trotsky at the peak of the party leadership's campaign against Trotsky. In 1924 he also wrote two extremely polemical anti-Trotsky brochures.[65] Trotsky also won no friends or support by frequently degrading the other members of the Politburo as 'ignoramuses' and 'technical incompetents'.[66] Even such an admirer of Trotsky as his biographer, Isaac Deutscher, recognised that Trotsky 'not only did not suffer fools gladly – he always made them feel that they were fools'.[67]

Trotsky, although increasingly isolated within the Politburo, initially held back from directly responding because he was hoping for Lenin's recovery after his first stroke in May 1922.[68] As late as the spring of 1923, he continued to fully share the orthodox Bolshevik emphasis on the need for party unity and discipline.[69] But by the fall of 1923, when Lenin's recovery seemed decidedly unlikely, Trotsky decided to hit back against the ruling coalition.[70] He was aware by then that the rest of the Politburo was conspiring against him.[71] Apparently that was

---

63 Startsev 1989, pp. 33–4.
64 Rudzutak and Shlyapnikov, for example, shared Tomsky's intense dislike of Trotsky: Fitzpatrick 2015, p. 37; Service 1995, p. 174. Rudzutak once said to his face, 'Comrade Trotsky, I know you have a clever head; what a pity it belongs to a scoundrel': Service 2009, p. 337.
65 Zelnik 1995, pp. 7–8; Kanatchikov 1986, p. 389.
66 Swain 2006, p. 162. Alienating potential friends and allies seemed to be Trotsky forte.
67 Deutscher 1959, p. 34.
68 The stroke paralysed Lenin's right side and he suffered a temporary loss of speech.
69 Daniels 1960, p. 194.
70 Lenin suffered a second stroke on 23 December 1922 that left him paralyzed and often speechless.
71 Trotsky 1937, p. 126. A memo from Zinoviev to Stalin, Kamenev, Rykov, and Tomsky at the Politburo meeting on 8 December 1923 formalised the formation of the seven Politburo members aligned against Trotsky, the so-called *semyorka*: Vilkova 1996, pp. 220–1. By August 1924, the Politburo candidate members Dzerzhinsky, Kalinin, Molotov, Uglanov and Frunze also joined the pre-Politburo meetings: Rees 2012, p. 49. Valerian Kuibyshev, as the head of the Central Control Commission, was also included in the Politburo meetings and joined the *semyorka*. The Central Control Commission's nine-member presidium had the right to attend Politburo meetings. The Central Control Commission, which had been created in September 1920, had dramatically expanded from five members to 50 following the Twelfth Party Congress in April 1923. It was the party's disciplinary body. As one

FIGURE 20 Stalin, Rykov, Zinoviev, and Bukharin relaxing together in 1924
WIKIMEDIA COMMONS

made explicit during a fight at one of the Politburo meetings, when Zinoviev shouted at Trotsky, 'Can't you see you're in a "ring"? Your tricks don't work anymore, you're in the minority, a minority of one'.[72] Tomsky, for his part, did his best to help prevent Trotsky from effectively fighting back. It was Tomsky who reported to the Politburo on 23 September 1923, along with the political police head Felix Dzerzhinsky, that all party members were obliged to immediately notify the Central Committee and the GPU if they became aware of 'any groupings in the party'.[73] That such directives could in the future be used against him-

---

of its members, S.I. Gusev, put it, 'the Central Committee establishes the party line, while the Central Control Commission sees that no one deviates from it': quoted in Daniels 1960, p. 167.

72 Quoted in Volkogonov 1996, p. 241. As this conspiracy increasingly dominated Politburo interactions, Tomsky joined the others in all sorts of petty digs at Trotsky: Trotsky 1970, p. 504. Trotsky responded by contemptuously reading French novels during Politburo and Central Committee meetings as well as the April 1923 sessions of the Twelfth Party Congress: Warth 1977, p. 129; Service 1995, p. 173.

73 This was the report of the so-called Dzerzhinsky commission, established by the Central Committee Plenum. It also reported on economic conditions and the spring 1923 strike wave: Khordina (ed.) 2000, p. 242; Hincks 1992, p. 138. Incredibly, Trotsky welcomed the directive, although he thought party members should report only to the Central Committee, not to the political police. Trotsky believed it was directed solely against various

self apparently did not concern Tomsky, perhaps because he had just received 99 percent of the possible votes at the Twelfth Party Congress in April 1923 and now seemed so firmly ensconced in power.[74] Tomsky, at the same time, did have some misgivings about such use of the political police to enforce such directives. As recently as the 29 June 1922 Politburo meeting, Tomsky had expressed his concerns about the excessive empowerment of the OGPU and criticised its lack of competence.[75]

Trotsky's main way to retaliate was to appeal directly to the broader party leadership, which had no inkling of the infighting within the Politburo. But if Trotsky thought his counterattack of vehement letters of protest would be effective, he severely underestimated what he was up against.[76] Trotsky began these oppositional letters on 8 October 1923 with a 15-page, 18-point letter, which he submitted to the Central Committee and the Central Control Commission. It was an all-out indictment of the Politburo's political and economic policies. Portraying himself as the champion of internal party democracy, Trotsky criticised the 'absolutely abnormal and unhealthy intra-party regime' in which the Orgburo (of which Tomsky was one of its nine full members) increasingly appointed party members to important posts rather than allowing them to be elected.[77] And indeed, between April 1922 and March 1923, the Orgburo ratified the appointment of at least 1,000 party members to various jobs, including at least 42 provincial party bosses.[78] How many of these appointments were made to create so-called clients is open to question though.[79] But, in any case,

---

workers' oppositional groups rather than also against himself: Pirani 2008, p. 215; Vilkova 1996, pp. 46, 58–9.

[74] Bukharin, Dzerzhinsky, Kalinin, Rykov, and Stalin had also received 99 percent of the possible votes, with Lenin alone receiving 100 percent. Zinoviev received 93 percent of the votes cast, while Trotsky received 87 percent: Mawdsley and White 2000, p. 38.

[75] Plekhanov 2006, pp. 292–3.

[76] Trotsky did defeat an attempt in September to curb his power over the Red Army, but only by threatening to resign in protest from all the posts he held, including the Politburo and Central Committee: Deutscher 1959, p. 111. If Trotsky had decided to enter into a full-scale challenge to the party leadership earlier, he might have enjoyed more success.

[77] The Orgburo was authorised to appoint and remove officials from party posts. Trotsky argued that not even during the most difficult period of the Civil War was the scale of appointments one-tenth of what it was in 1923: RGASPI, f. 17, op. 2, d. 685, reprinted and translated in Vilkova 1996, p. 51.

[78] Kotkin 2014, p. 432.

[79] While party and state organisations promoted from within, the Organization and Instruction Department (*Orgotdel*) and the Department for Records and Assignment (*Uchraspred*), which the Central Committee merged into the Department for Assignment (*Orgraspred*) in 1926, did so independently of much oversight from the party leadership: Harris

it seemed hypocritical to Tomsky and other party leaders for Trotsky to now become the champion of democracy since he had so strongly defended the practice of 'nominating from above' when he was running Tsektran and attacking Tomsky in 1920 during the 'trade-union debate'.[80] Trotsky also blamed the Politburo's economic policies, which resulted in what he labeled the 'scissors crisis', for widespread worker and peasant discontent.[81] The Politburo, at its 11 October 1923 meeting, rather than addressing the letter's substance, instead subjected Trotsky to harsh criticism for violating party discipline. A couple days later, the Politburo adopted a resolution, which Tomsky wrote along with Vyacheslav Molotov, which denounced as 'disloyal' the broad circulation in 'party circles' of Trotsky's letter.[82]

Undeterred, Trotsky's closest political associates began circulating their 'Declaration of the 46' that same day.[83] Although Trotsky did not sign it, presumably because he still did not want to come out quite so openly against the Politburo, this platform echoed his criticisms of the party leadership's economic policies and lack of internal party democracy.[84] The Politburo members' point-by-point rebuttal, to which Tomsky was a signee, accused Trotsky and his associates of the 'monstrous mistake' of attacking the Central Committee in an 'undisguised attempt at creating factionalism'.[85] Others in the trade-union leadership shared Tomsky's opposition to the Trotskyist platform.[86] Like Tom-

---

2005, p. 79. But regional leaders could stack national congresses and conferences with their supporters: Gill 1990a, p. 143.

80   Carr 1954, p. 296n1. Party leaders more broadly thought Trotsky's use of 'party democracy' was insincere, a phony issue, given his advocacy for authoritarian methods and iron discipline throughout the Civil War: Getty and Naumov 2008, p. 70.

81   Trotsky used the nickname of the 'scissors crisis' to describe the economic fact that the blades of industrial and agricultural prices were rapidly widening, with the prices of the relatively scarce manufactured goods rising substantially while agricultural prices fell because of the good harvest of 1922. What made this a 'crisis' was the danger that peasants would respond by increasingly withholding their grain from the market.

82   Trotsky argued that the letter had been circulated without his knowledge, claiming he wanted his letter to be discussed only by the Politburo: RGASPI, f. 17, op. 2, d. 685, reprinted and translated in Vilkova 1996, pp. 74–5.

83   Volkogonov 1991, p. 86.

84   The Central Committee blocked their efforts to read the Platform at lower-level party meetings: Hincks 1992, p. 139.

85   The rebuttal was sent to all Central Committee and Central Control Commission members on 19 October. The signees included all the Politburo members except of course Trotsky. Trotsky wrote an even longer rebuttal on 23 October. Both are reprinted and translated in Vilkova 1996, pp. 105–26, 139–64.

86   Only one of the signees of the 'Declaration of the 46' occupied an important post in the trade unions and only two others had any background in the unions: Pirani 2008, p. 217.

sky, they remembered Trotsky's call for the militarisation of labour and the creation of labour armies during the Civil War, which most of the signees of the 'Trotskyist Manifesto' had also supported.[87] At the October 1923 Central Committee and Central Control Commission Plenum Trotsky put forth a powerful defence.[88] But the plenum was unmoved and condemned Trotsky's letter and the 'Declaration of the 46' by the nearly unanimous vote of 102–2.[89] Zinoviev and Kamenev demanded that Trotsky be expelled from the Politburo, but they were overruled.[90]

Just as political tensions within the leadership ratcheted up, Lenin died from a massive stroke on 21 January 1924. Lenin's funeral was significant for the power struggle partly because of who was, or was not, visible during these critical days when so many party members felt deeply anxious about the Soviet Union's future. Tomsky was one of a handful of party leaders who played an extremely prominent role. Along with Zinoviev, Bukharin, Kalinin, Stalin, and Kamenev, he drove out to Lenin's mansion in Gorki on a motorised sled the day after Lenin passed away, with Tomsky captured on film the following day helping to carry Lenin's coffin, covered with red cloth and flowers, after it was lowered from the train at the Paveletsky railroad station.[91] The thousands of Muscovites, who braved the extremely bitter cold to follow the funeral cortege along the five-mile route to the House of the Trade Unions, must have been surprised at Trotsky's absence.[92] Lenin was laid in state in the trade union's elegant

---

Likewise, though it is open to debate, it appears that relatively few workers supported the Trotskyist Opposition during its short life span. Priestland argues that support for the Trotskyist Opposition came from students, soldiers, and members of the Moscow party organisation rather than from workers: Priestland 2007, p. 160. Daniels agrees they failed to win worker support while Carr suggests they made little effort to do so: Daniels 1960, p. 228; Carr 1958, p. 423. Murphy and Thatcher, in contrast, suggest that the opposition enjoyed considerable worker support: Murphy 2001, pp. 332–4; Thatcher 2003, p. 127. Sakwa argues the oppositionists' emphasis on planning alienated workers who interpreted it as support for the specialists and increased productivity rather than improved conditions for workers: Sakwa 1995, pp. 60–1.

87 Chase 1987, p. 234; Deutscher 1959, p. 82.
88 Figes 1996, pp. 803–4. It was long thought that Trotsky was too sick to attend the October Plenum, but that was incorrect.
89 RGASPI, f. 51, op. 1, d. 21, reprinted and translated in Vilkova 1996, p. 316. There were 10 abstentions.
90 Rees 2012, p. 47.
91 Carr 1954, p. 345; Tumarkin 1983, p. 138. Rudzutak met them at the train station and helped to carry Lenin's coffin.
92 Anastas Mikoyan said he was astonished by Trotsky's absence: Gill 2018, p. 89n9. Trotsky was recuperating in the Caucasus. Rykov, who was in Moscow, was indeed too ill to appear at the funeral. Moscow, with temperatures at minus 49 Celsius, was in the midst of the

FIGURE 21 From left to right: Rudzutak, Krupskaya, Kalinin, and Tomsky at Lenin's funeral
WIKIMEDIA COMMONS

Hall of Columns, which was a favourite spot for major party events, including the traditional site for the public mourning of Soviet leaders. Tomsky was part of the rotating honour guard who flanked the open coffin as hundreds of thousands of grieving mourners filed past in respectful and sometimes tearful silence.[93] Four days later, Tomsky was also one of the eight honorary pallbearers who carried Lenin's casket, accompanied by bands playing martial music, less than a mile away to the hastily erected wooden, temporary mausoleum on Red Square, where they lowered the casket into the vault prepared below the Kremlin wall.[94] Tomsky gave a long speech at a meeting in the Bolshoi Theatre in which he eulogised Lenin for all he had done for workers and the trade unions.[95]

---

deepest freeze the city had experienced in years. The cortege stopped every half mile or so to change coffin bearers.

93 Kozlov 1991, p. 121. Orlando Figes puts the number of mourners waiting to pay their respects at half a million: Figes 1996, p. 805.

94 This moment was marked by the unleashing of a cacophony of every possible noisemaker, from factory sirens and locomotive whistles, salvos of cannons and rifles, foghorns, to the bells in the Kremlin towers: Service 1995, p. 320; Sebestyen 2017, pp. 500–2. The other honorary pallbearers were Kamenev, Zinoviev, Stalin, Bukharin, Rudzutak, Dzerzhinsky, and Molotov.

95 Tomsky 1928a, pp. 227–30. Many of the top party leaders also spoke. Zinoviev, always a

Tomsky's attempt to unify the European trade-union movement took much of his time and preoccupied his attention as the power struggle heated up following Lenin's death. As noted in Chapter 4, he travelled to London in April 1924 as the second-ranking member of the Soviet diplomatic delegation to discuss the terms of British recognition of the Soviet Union, where Tomsky took the opportunity to charm the leaders of the British trade-union movement at a restaurant gathering. Many of the Politburo meetings at this time focused on Soviet policy toward the British Trades Union Council and the Amsterdam International, with Tomsky as well as others presenting reports. Tomsky's trips abroad would require him to miss many Politburo meetings.[96]

Tomsky, to his discredit, helped squash the publication of Lenin's 'Testament' [*Zaveshchanie*].[97] Although its provenance has been questioned, the party leadership certainly viewed it as authentic.[98] Lenin in the 'Testament', in which he failed to name a successor, spoke most highly of Trotsky, calling him the ablest party leader, while its postscript called for Stalin's removal from his powerful position as general secretary on the grounds that he was too rude.[99] Trotsky called for the publication of the 'Testament'. At this moment, when Tomsky could have heeded Lenin's advice and helped undercut Stalin's power base, he played a pivotal role at a Politburo meeting and a Central Committee and Central Control Commission Plenum by refusing to do so. Driven by his opposition to Trotsky, and displaying an elitist, condescending view of the party's rank and file as well as ordinary Soviet citizens, Tomsky declared, 'I am in favor of Comrade Zinoviev's proposal that it should be shared only with members of the Central Committee. It should not be published, as the general public will understand nothing in it'.[100] Members of the Central Committee, who had not suspected a breach between Lenin and Stalin, were caught off guard by the revelation that Lenin wanted Stalin removed as general secretary

---

brilliant orator, gave a particularly powerful speech, while Stalin's speech, using litany-like exhortations, had a religious tone: Tumarkin 1983, pp. 152–7.

96 The 22 May, 12 June, 27 June, 11 July, and 24 July meetings: Khordina (ed.) 2000, pp. 296, 299–300, 305, 309, 313.

97 Lenin, although he had suffered two massive strokes earlier in 1922, apparently dictated the 'Testament' in a series of sessions on 23, 24, 26, and 29 December. Lenin lost the power of speech after suffering a third stroke on 9 March 1923.

98 Stephen Kotkin suggested that Lenin was too incapacitated to have dictated it and that Krupskaya or others in the household were its actual authors. He does concede, however, that it could be authentic, and regardless, in all probability, it reflected Lenin's views: Kotkin 2014, pp. 498–501. Kotkin's doubts stem from a book by V.A. Sakharov, who claimed the dictations were forgeries: Sakharov 2003.

99 Krupskaya later told Mikoyan that Lenin wanted to replace Stalin with Rudzutak as general secretary: Mikoian 1999, p. 365.

100 Quoted in Volkogonov 1996, p. 243.

(Lenin realised Stalin was quickly turning the post into the most powerful in the party).[101] Despite Krupskaya's opposition, they ultimately followed Zinoviev's lead, who stated 'the fears of Ilich have not been realised'. They voted 30–10 against reading the 'Testament' at the upcoming Thirteenth Party Congress as well as against its publication in *Pravda*. They did agree to provide provincial delegations with the gist of the 'Testament' at closed meetings.[102] It was in fact read to members of the Central Committee and heads of local party organisations a week before the congress in May 1924.[103] Although Stalin survived the bombshell, it continued to haunt him in the years that followed as reports of its contents continually resurfaced.[104] His knowledge that Old Bolsheviks were familiar with it was one of the reasons he later wanted to eliminate them in the Great Purges.

Trotsky recognised that the Politburo's decision to squash dissemination of the 'Testament' meant his political defeat. He appeared to completely capitulate at the Thirteenth Party Congress in May 1924, where he expressed the sort of blind loyalty to the Politburo's majority that was already expected of leaders who found themselves in the minority. 'Comrades, none of us wants to be or can be right against the party', Trotsky declared. 'In the last analysis, the party is always right'.[105] And he accepted, to applause, the right of the party to discipline him regardless of whether he was mistaken or not.[106] This set the template for the capitulation ritual that Tomsky and so many others would perform in the years to come.

Tomsky, in addition to his opposition to Trotsky's policies and personality, aligned with Stalin because he believed that Stalin, along with Bukharin

---

101 Party leaders were so surprised because Stalin was the only member of the Politburo who had never openly defied Lenin: Daniels 1960, p. 70.

102 Daniels 1960, p. 239; McNeal 1988, p. 110; RKP(b) 1963b, p. xxii. Provincial delegations were also provided a confidential, draft resolution that authorised Stalin's continued service as general secretary, with the understanding that he would address Lenin's criticisms of him: Gill 2018, p. 63.

103 Toker 2008, p. 136.

104 In a dramatic example, Max Eastman, an American journalist who had been Trotsky's longstanding supporter and friend, in the summer of 1925 published a slender book entitled *Since Lenin Died*, which at Trotsky's request accused the Politburo of deliberately suppressing Lenin's 'Testament'. A Central Committee commission, consisting of Stalin, Zinoviev, Kamenev, Bukharin, and Tomsky, compelled Trotsky to disavow Eastman's account as a fabrication and 'a slander on the Central Committee': Broué 1988, p. 470; Rubenstein 1988, p. 140; Warth 1977, p. 144.

105 RKP(b) 1963b, p. 158.

106 RKP(b) 1963b, p. 159. To at least one historian, not only was Trotsky not sincere, his confession was clearly intended to be sarcastic: Daniels 2007, p. 182.

and Rykov, would continue the moderate policies of NEP, including in foreign policy, and because he thought Stalin had limited political ambitions.[107] Tomsky would of course be proven spectacularly wrong on both counts. But Stalin, we should remember, succeeded in portraying himself to his fellow Politburo members in the 1920s as a measured and even-handed colleague.[108] James Harris questions whether Stalin's position as general secretary was as powerful as is conventionally thought, arguing instead that it was his skill at managing to be always in the majority within the Politburo that explains his ability to defeat the oppositionists.[109]

Tomsky seemingly had no inkling of the potential threat Stalin posed, or if he did have such concerns, Stalin effectively reassured him. For example, when Zinoviev and Kamenev demanded at the end of 1924 that the Central Committee immediately expel Trotsky from the party, Stalin presented himself as the voice of moderation and restraint.[110] He not only opposed treating Trotsky and his fellow 'Left Oppositionists' so harshly, Stalin said it was 'inconceivable' that Trotsky would not be a member of the party leadership.[111] In a perversely ironic, as well as prophetic, statement given the Great Purges he launched after he was able to fully consolidate his power, Stalin argued, 'We did not agree [to Trotsky's removal] because we know that the policy of chopping off heads is fraught with major dangers for the party ... this method of bloodletting – and they did demand blood – is dangerous and contagious. If today you cut off one, tomorrow it will be another, and the day after tomorrow a third'.[112] As one historian aptly noted, 'the tyrant lay dormant in the skillful politician'.[113]

One other factor explaining Tomsky's alignment with Stalin, although to what extent is unclear, was that Tomsky and his wife Maria Tomskaya were personal friends of Stalin and his wife Nadezhda Alliluyeva. According to Tomsky family lore, Maria often came to the aid of Stalin and Nadezhda. This happened, for example, when Stalin, feeling humiliated and victimised by Lenin's 'Testament', and in bad health, with his marriage going through one of its regular

---

107 Bukharin had been appointed a full voting member of the Politburo to take Lenin's place. Stalin's support for peaceful coexistence in foreign policy aligned with Tomsky's desire to unify the international trade-union movement, unlike Trotsky's policy of permanent revolution, which argued that it would be impossible to sustain the revolution without workers seizing power in the West.
108 Lars Lih's introduction in Lih et al. (eds) 1995, pp. 62–3.
109 Harris 2005, p. 79.
110 Daniels 1960, p. 254.
111 Deutscher 1967, p. 297.
112 RKP(b) 1926, p. 502.
113 Ulam 1973, p. 237.

rough patches, in August 1924 submitted to the Central Committee a letter of resignation from the Politburo, Orgburo, and Secretariat (one of the six times he threatened to resign during these years). Stalin requested a two-month medical leave followed by an assignment to a minor post in Siberia.[114] Stalin had left Moscow in the middle of a Central Committee plenum and locked himself up in a dacha, refusing to speak to anyone except Tomsky's wife. Tomskaya managed to calm Stalin down, after sitting with him for two full days and nights. She supposedly 'looked after him like a child' before she could persuade him to go back to Moscow. Upon his return to Moscow, where the Central Committee retained him as general secretary, Stalin was still brooding and stayed with the Tomsky family for a few nights.[115] Tomskaya and Alliluyeva were also good friends, perhaps especially because of Nadezhda's turbulent marriage with Stalin.[116] In 1926, fed up with Stalin's constant rudeness and foul-mouthed attacks, the sensitive and often depressed Alliluyeva decided to leave him, six months after their daughter Svetlana was born. Nadezhda took their daughter and son to her parent's home in Leningrad (as Petrograd was renamed after 1924) to start an independent life.[117] When Stalin's pleas for her to return fell on deaf ears, he turned to Tomskaya again. As she had done with Stalin, Tomskaya managed to persuade Alliluyeva to come back to Moscow, in this case with Stalin's promise that she could pursue a higher education and hire a governess.[118] At the same time, Stalin and Tomsky were good, collegial friends until the end of the 1920s. Neighbours in the Kremlin, Stalin frequently dropped by for a visit.[119] Tomsky's son Yury remembered that his parents usually called Stalin by his pre-revolutionary pseudonym, Koba, and that on their mantelpiece was a photograph of Stalin that he had affectionately signed in 1926 'to my good pal Mishka Tomsky'.[120] The Stalin and Tomsky families also got together

---

114 Khlevniuk 2015, pp. 79–80. Although usually vaunted for his extraordinary powers of self-control, Robert Service argues that the 'psychologically complex' Stalin was impulsive and 'when his pride was offended lost his composure': Service 2004, pp. 223–4.

115 Gorelov and Shapovalova (eds) 2001, p. 158. Tomsky enjoyed sharing stories about his life with his young, adopted son, Yury, such as on fishing trips to Karelia or simply going camping in the woods near their dacha: Gorelov 2000, pp. 267, 271.

116 Stalin could go for days without speaking to his wife or responding to her questions: Bazhanov 1990, pp. 110–11.

117 Alliluyeva hoped to find a job and 'build a life of her own' there: Alliluyeva 1967, p. 103.

118 Gorelov and Shapovalova (eds) 2001, p. 158; McNeal 1988, p. 47. Alliluyeva began to study chemistry at Moscow's Industrial Academy. There is reason to think she was already suffering from a serious mental illness: Montefiore 2004, p. 12.

119 Fitzpatrick 2015, p. 55.

120 Mishka is a very familiar diminutive form of Mikhail: Fitzpatrick 2015, p. 286n10. That is what Tomskaya called her husband: RGASPI, f. 17, op. 2, d. 579, l. 49.

on occasion to celebrate such holidays as birthdays and name days and sometimes vacationed together in Sochi on the Black Sea coast. Stalin and Tomsky in addition often relaxed together, along with others, on hunting trips, where they enjoyed Stalin's hospitality.[121] But it should also be noted that regardless of their friendship, for all the 'Old Bolsheviks', friendship was extremely conditional. None of them, including Tomsky, would ultimately put friendship ahead of politics. As the unsentimental Stalin stated in a speech after their falling out, 'Ours is not a family circle, not a coterie of personal friends, but a political party of the proletariat'.[122]

To reiterate, Tomsky, like other members of the party leadership, failed to appreciate, at least fully, Stalin's dark side. However vindictive and thin-skinned the party leaders all thought he could be, no one perceived Stalin as a potentially criminal tyrant.[123] As one historian put it, the Stalin of the 1920s largely succeeded in concealing the ruthless, unscrupulous Stalin of the 1930s.[124] Or as another historian stated, 'No contemporary ... saw in the Stalin of 1923 the menacing and towering figure he was to become'.[125]

In the mid-1920s, Tomsky continued to emphasise his serious commitment to improving conditions for trade-union members. At the Sixth Trade-Union congress in November 1924, Tomsky could point to areas of substantial progress over the past two years as the party and the trade unions' promise of improving living standards continued to be realised as wages, in a now stable currency, continued to grow.[126] But with industry still at only 46 percent of its pre-war level, the issue of how to raise labour productivity also continued to dominate much of Tomsky's attention.[127] The so-called rationalisation campaign that the party introduced in 1924, and its 1926 successor the 'regime of economy', tried to improve labour productivity by increasing output norms.[128] Increases in output norms, even when accompanied by a steady rise in nominal and real

---

121   Gorelov and Shapovalova (eds) 2001, p. 159; Alliluyeva 1967, p. 32.
122   Vatlin et al. (eds) 2000d, p. 452. These sorts of collegial friendships didn't survive Stalin's consolidation of his power, when mutual suspicions among members of his inner circle would be encouraged: Fitzpatrick 2015, p. 6. Later, during the Great Purges of 1936–38, Stalin would routinely order the killing of former friends and colleagues. And during the war, a similar harshness could extend even to members of his own family. In the words of his daughter, 'Years of friendship and fighting side by side in a common cause might as well never have been ... he could wipe it out in a stroke': Alliluyeva 1967, p. 86.
123   Kotkin 2014, p. 597.
124   Kuromiya 2005, p. 57.
125   Deutscher 1959, p. 93.
126   Pirani 2008, p. 235; *Inprecorr*, 16 December 1924, pp. 871, 980.
127   Tomskii 1924, pp. 30–5; Erlich 1960, p. xvi.
128   Chase 1987, pp. 142, 235–6, 239.

wages, angered workers and were one of the major causes of strikes from 1925 onwards.[129] But, even so, increases in wages continued to outpace increases in productivity.[130] Tomsky, although always torn on the issue, at the Seventh Trade-Union Congress in December 1926 called on the party to prioritize wages over productivity.

It was issues concerning the peasantry, not workers, that were the main concern of most party leaders during the mid-1920s. Tomsky joined with them to offer various concessions to the peasantry, who began to enjoy unprecedented freedom and relative prosperity during NEP. With Trotsky increasingly marginalised, the ruling coalition, in its campaign entitled 'turn the face of the party to the countryside', reduced peasant taxes and raised state procurement prices.[131] Tomsky whole-heartedly supported those policies. He pointedly argued that industrialisation should not be built at the expense of the peasantry. 'The villages and the peasantry are not the colony of the cities', he declared.[132] But it was the policy toward the small percentage of relatively well-off peasants, who were labelled kulaks, that would be the main issue of controversy during 1925, just as it had been for Tomsky in 1921 in Turkestan. Although the kulak officially remained a figure of opprobrium among party members for their presumed exploitation of fellow peasants, early in 1925 all the members of the Politburo except Trotsky favoured conciliatory policies toward them, which allowed kulaks to lease additional land and hire rural labour, on the grounds that this would benefit the overall economy. And indeed, grain harvests reached their pre-war level by 1926.

Tomsky in December 1925 played a major role at the extremely contentious Fourteenth Party Congress.[133] Although he gave a report at the congress on his progress with the British trade unionists toward getting the Soviet trade unions into the Amsterdam International, as well as a report on labour issues, it was his political attacks that attracted the most attention.[134] To understand his vitriolic role at this congress it is necessary to provide some background. In the run-up to the congress, Tomsky and Stalin, in contrast to Rykov and

---

129 Pospielovsky 1997, p. 16; GARF, f. 5451, op. 42, d. 137, l. 36.
130 Wages increased 12 percent in 1926–27, while productivity increased only nine percent: Carr and Davies 1969b, p. 493.
131 Hughes 1991, p. 57.
132 Tomskii 1928a, p. 328.
133 Tomsky had not given a speech at either the Twelfth Party Congress in April 1923 or the Thirteenth Party Congress in May 1924. He was in London during the Thirteenth Party Congress.
134 Two separate short books of his political speech at the congress were published: Tomsky 1925a; Tomsky 1926c.

FIGURE 22   Nikolai Bukharin
WIKIMEDIA COMMONS

Bukharin, were cautious in how they formulated their support for the leadership's agrarian policy. While Rykov enthusiastically advocated for the pro-kulak policy, it was Bukharin who would make the major political faux pas.[135] As he would later prove to be as the leader of the 'Right Opposition', Bukharin was far less politically astute than his coalition partners. Tone deaf, he foolishly made statements that could easily be used against him. In a speech addressing the regime's economic policies at a party meeting in the Bolshoi Theatre on 17 April 1925, Bukharin went so far as to encourage peasants to get rich. Rejecting calls

---

135   Rykov, the former head of VSNKh, who had been born in the countryside, had long been a defender of individual farming. When told that any peasant who owned two horses and two cows was a kulak, Rykov said in February that he hoped within two years every peasant would be a kulak: Carr 1958, p. 266; Oppenheim 1977, p. 423.

by Trotsky and his supporters to accumulate the funding for faster industrialisation by raising taxes on the kulaks, Bukharin instead urged the party to further incentivise peasants. 'To the peasants, to all the peasants, we must say: enrich yourselves, develop your farms, and do not fear that constraints will be put on you. However paradoxical it may appear, we must develop the well-to-do farm in order to help the poor peasant and the middle peasant'.[136] Bukharin quickly felt compelled to renounce the inflammatory phrase, 'enrich yourselves', under pressure from the Central Committee.[137] But the damage had been done. Bukharin would never live down his frank assessment. For six months various oppositionists made him the special target of abuse. This put Tomsky and other leaders in the awkward position of having to address, ad nauseam, Bukharin's use of the phrase.[138]

In this context, the previous anti-Trotsky coalition within the Politburo split apart. At the Fourteenth Party Congress in December 1925, with the party more divided than ever before, Zinoviev and Kamenev switched tack and joined with Grigory Sokolnikov and Nadezhda Krupskaya to form a new opposition. Now fearful of Stalin's growing power, and for the first time publicly voicing their opposition to the party's economic policies, especially toward the peasantry, they submitted to the Central Committee a document entitled the 'Platform of the Four'.[139] The platform attacked the role of kulaks in rural areas, who they claimed were holding the regime for ransom, called for increasing industrial workers' wages by 20 percent, and argued there needed to be less reliance on the market in favour of state planning. The document also stressed the importance of collective leadership.[140] Still incensed at Zinoviev's and Kamenev's sus-

---

136   Quoted in Carr 1958, p. 280. The kulaks were indeed responsible for much of Soviet agriculture's marketable surplus. It quickly became clear that making such a reasonable case, on such a fraught issue, in the midst of the intra-party factional conflict was virtually impossible, if not done with considerable tact.
137   Erlich 1960, p. 28. Stalin criticised Bukharin's slogan behind the scenes: Carr 1958, pp. 260, 284. While politics forced Bukharin to grudgingly retract the slogan, he continued to believe it was the correct policy: Cohen 1973, p. 177; Gluckstein 1994, p. 144.
138   Bukharin made a subsequent major indiscretion, when he pessimistically declared that to achieve socialism, 'we shall have to creep forward at a snail's pace': RKP(b) 1926, p. 135. This statement also became a favourite target for attacks from oppositionists.
139   Sokolnikov apparently joined the opposition only because of his antipathy toward Stalin. As commissar of finance he strongly supported the leadership's gradualist economic policies: Trotsky 1975, p. 395; Deutscher 1959, p. 247; Priestland 2007, p. 140. Khlevniuk condescendingly suggests Lenin's widow joined the opposition simply because of her long-standing friendship with Zinoviev and Kamenev: Khlevniuk 2015, p. 82.
140   Pogorelskin 2000, p. 393; Merridale 1990, p. 31.

tained earlier attacks on him, including their efforts to have him expelled from the party, Trotsky stood aside as this new split within the leadership emerged.

Tomsky was the most strident critic of Zinoviev, Kamenev, and their supporters at this congress, where they hoped to rally opposition against the ruling coalition. Zinoviev and Kamenev, in addition to criticising how the leadership had implemented NEP, publicly attacked Stalin, which they had never done before.[141] But the oppositionists were hopelessly outnumbered. They had hoped to have the support of the Moscow and Ukrainian delegations at the congress, but only Zinoviev's Leningrad delegation was willing to offer support.[142] When Tomsky reached the rostrum, the delegates greeted him with exuberant, prolonged applause. Tomsky portrayed Zinoviev's and Kamenev's criticism at the congress as disingenuous, as a case of political opportunism. Tomsky emphasised that earlier in the year they had not criticised the 'kulak concessions' or even offered any amendments to resolutions.[143]

Tomsky did his best to defend Bukharin while attacking Zinoviev as well as his supporters within the Leningrad Komsomol. 'You don't want the slogan "enrich yourselves" to be disavowed', Tomsky told the oppositionists, but instead simply want to discredit Bukharin. Tomsky pointed out that Bukharin himself had renounced the phrase any number of times. Tomsky also criticised how the 'Leningrad Oppositionists' had gradually escalated their attacks (these oppositionists were also referred to as the 'Zinovievites'). To applause, Tomsky stated, 'First you whisper doubts, then undermine confidence, then express outrage, before finally preparing a minority report'.[144] Tomsky, who was often at loggerheads with the Komsomol's leadership over the trade unions' policies toward young workers, also devoted a good part of his speech to criticising the Leningrad branch of the Komsomol.[145] Tomsky essentially dismissed their criti-

---

141   Stalin, who for the first time delivered the opening political report, cleverly did not bring up the conflict with the opposition, to make it look like the opposition had initiated it: Kotkin 2014, p. 580.
142   During the congress only 82 of the 803 delegates supported the oppositionists, with the vote on the Central Committee's report, 559 to 65: RKP(b) 1925, p. 524.
143   Tomsky argued that Zinoviev and Kamenev had sworn allegiance to the party line at the Fourteenth Party Conference held earlier that year in April, and noted that nothing of consequence had happened between then and the October plenum, when their criticism of the regime's economic policy first came out into the open: RKP(b) 1926, pp. 276–8; Pogorelskin 2000, p. 392. That is not altogether accurate. Kamenev and Zinoviev had given speeches attacking the kulak policy in the intervening months: Swain 2006, pp. 162–3. Conferences were smaller and less authoritative than congresses.
144   RKP(b) 1926, p. 277.
145   The Komsomol leadership had issued a collection of documents on the leadership's agricultural policies, annotated with critical comments: Daniels 1960, p. 260.

cisms as the products of youth and a lack of experience.[146] Tomsky complained, 'We are always busy with them, like with a child who has grabbed a knife'.[147] As we will see in the following chapter, Stalin would later skilfully exploit Tomsky's dismissive attitude toward Komsomol complaints.

Tomsky notably also attacked Nadezhda Krupskaya, Lenin's widow and a major party figure in her own right, even though they were good friends and he held her in high esteem.[148] In her speech to the Fourteenth Party Congress, in addition to criticising Bukharin's 'enrich yourselves' slogan, Krupskaya attacked the leadership for suppressing internal party democracy and packing the congress.[149] Tomsky in his response chose to focus on Krupskaya's questioning the nature of truth.[150] To her declaration that 'for us Marxists, truth is what corresponds to reality', Tomsky replied in words he would surely come to regret. 'Comrade Krupskaya said that the concept of what is true and untrue is a subjective concept. For the working class, led by its party, there can be only one measure of truth – the will of the majority of the Leninist party'.[151] This attitude would leave Tomsky largely defenceless when the Politburo majority turned against him.

Tomsky next focused his attack on Kamenev, which would be the high point, or perhaps more accurately, the low point of his speeches at the congress. Tomsky, who the party leadership had slotted to appear right after Kamenev's speech because of his combative skills, with zeal undertook the job of repudiating Kamenev's criticism of the amount of power Stalin had amassed, and how he had wielded it. Kamenev had created a commotion in the congress by concluding his long speech by stating:

> We object to the theory of creating a leader (*vozhd*) ... We object to the idea that the Secretariat, which combines both politics and organisation, should stand above the main political organ [the Politburo] ... We can-

---

146 RKP(b) 1926, p. 276.
147 RKP(b) 1926, p. 281.
148 According to Sheila Fitzpatrick, Tomsky and Krupskaya's friendship went back to the 1890s, when they had worked together in St. Petersburg: Fitzpatrick 2015, p. 54.
149 RKP(b) 1926, pp. 159–66.
150 Tomsky also criticised Krupskaya's statement that the party majority was not always right. Krupskaya was referring to the spring 1906 Party Congress in Stockholm. Tomsky justifiably argued it was a false analogy because the context was completely different since Mensheviks had dominated that congress. 'Then we were a two-faction Social Democratic Party; now we are a single, united Communist Party', he declared: Carr 1959, p. 150.
151 RKP(b) 1926, pp. 165, 288.

not regard it as normal, and we think it is harmful to the party, to prolong a situation in which the Secretariat combines politics and organisation, and in fact decides policy in advance ... Precisely because I have often said this to Comrade Stalin in person and precisely because I have frequently said this to a number of Leninist comrades, I repeat this at the congress: I have come to the conclusion that Stalin cannot fulfil the role of uniting the Bolshevik general staff.[152]

Despite the enormous uproar this statement provoked in the hall – including shouts of 'long live Stalin'! – an undaunted Kamenev ended by reiterating, 'We are against the doctrine of one-man rule, we are against the creation of a leader'.[153] Tomsky should have stopped to consider this warning about Stalin, but instead responded with: 'It is ridiculous to speak as if someone has concentrated power in his hands ... A system of individual leaders cannot exist, and will not, no, will not'.[154] Tomsky concluded his speech by telling Kamenev and Zinoviev to 'apply to yourselves the lesson you taught Comrade Trotsky ... to recognise your mistakes and bow your heads before the will of the party'. The delegates responded to Tomsky's speech with exuberant applause that turned into a standing ovation.[155]

Stalin, for his part, continued to skilfully reassure Tomsky and other party leaders while outmanoeuvring the oppositionists. Stalin in his speech to the congress forcefully defended collective leadership, which he claimed the 'Zinovievites' had been trying to undermine. How, he demanded, was the party to be led 'without Rykov, without Kalinin, without Tomsky, without Molotov, without Bukharin'?[156] 'It is impossible', he concluded, 'to lead the party other than collectively. Now that Lenin is no longer with us, it is stupid to think about such a thing, it is even stupid to talk about it'.[157] And in fact, the still cautious Stalin appeared to embrace the goal of collective leadership as he worked in close

---

152 RKP(b) 1926, p. 274.
153 RKP(b) 1926, pp. 274–5.
154 Rykov similarly stated, 'The party has never fallen on its knees, and never will fall on its knees before anyone, neither Stalin, Kamenev, nor anyone else': RKP(b) 1926, pp. 289, 418.
155 RKP(b) 1926, p. 292. Kamenev's speech was the only explicit reference at the congress to Stalin's growing consolidation of political power or the need to remove him as general secretary.
156 RKP(b) 1926, p. 506. Rykov's, Tomsky's, and Bukharin's names were removed from the sentence when Stalin's collective works were published first in 1947, and then in English translation in 1954: Stalin 1952–67, vol. 7, p. 398.
157 RKP(b) 1926, p. 508.

harmony with Bukharin, Rykov, and Tomsky. All decisions continued to be promulgated as the decisions of collective bodies rather than individual party members, with Stalin often taking a low profile.[158]

In the months that followed in early 1926, Stalin, Bukharin, Rykov, and Tomsky purged followers of Zinoviev and Kamenev. Although Tomsky opposed ousting Zinoviev and Kamenev from their party posts – he characterised them as still 'valuable, authoritative leaders' – the party leaders replaced the leadership of the district committees and the Komsomol in Leningrad and shook up the Central Committee.[159] Not unlike how Tomsky had been treated in 1921, the party leadership transferred many prominent 'Zinovievites' to Turkestan or other remote locations, although they were generally given far less important responsibilities.[160] Zinoviev remained on the Politburo for the time being, but Kamenev was demoted to a candidate member, while Sokolnikov, previously a candidate member, was totally dropped.

Kanatchikov, whose life we have been tracking alongside Tomsky's, chose to align himself with Zinoviev's 'Leningrad Opposition' in the fall of 1925. After the three years at the Communist University in Moscow, he had moved to Leningrad, where in 1924 he became head of the Central Committee's Press Department (*Otdel pechati*). In 1925–26, Kanatchikov became director of the Central Committee's Department of Historical Research (*Istpart*) and deputy chief of the Commissariat of Enlightenment's Chief Administration of Scientific Institutions (*Glavnauka*). During these years, in addition to attending party congresses and delivering public lectures, Kanatchikov wrote various articles and brochures. As a supporter of the 'Leningrad Opposition', in used his position as director of Istpart to criticise party historians whom he argued were guilty of underestimating Lenin's 1905 doubts about the peasantry. This sort of 'historical' criticism was correctly understood to be an attack on the party leadership's view of the peasantry. After Bukharin denounced Kanatchikov a few months later, he was removed from his position as Istpart director in July 1926. Kanatchikov's biographer, Reginald Zelnik, finds it mysterious that Kanatchikov supported the 'leftist' opposition since, like Tomsky, he had always been a party moderate previously. Zelnik suspects it had more to do with his long collaboration with Zinoviev than any attraction to 'leftist' positions. Following the defeat of the Leningrad Opposition, Kanatchikov enjoyed a far

---

158   Gill 1990a, pp. 191, 193.
159   Tomskii 1925a, p. 23. Tomsky helped carry that out in Leningrad immediately following the Fourteenth Party Congress.
160   Lenoe 2010, p. 73.

FIGURE 23 Stalin with Tomsky and Kalinin in 1926
WIKIMEDIA COMMONS

better posting in exile than others in the opposition. The Central Committee sent him in October 1926 to Prague as a TASS correspondent, where he remained for a year and a half.[161] Kanatchikov would be back in the regime's good graces after writing a letter to Stalin, his 'esteemed comrade', following the

---

161   Zelnik 1995, pp. 7–8, 30; Kanatchikov 1986, pp. 389–90.

Fifteenth Party Congress in December 1927. In the letter he apologised for his oppositional past and professed his loyalty to the party line.[162]

With the demotion of Kamenev and the promotion of Voroshilov, Molotov, and Kalinin to full members, the size of the Politburo fatefully increased from seven to nine on 1 January 1926.[163] Although these three are generally described as Stalin devotees, that was really only true of Molotov at this time.[164] Tomsky and Rykov, along with Bukharin, who had earlier been appointed to full membership in the Politburo following Lenin's death, thought they could count on Voroshilov and Kalinin to share their commitment toward maintaining the moderate policies of NEP. That was especially true of Kalinin since he had long favoured conciliatory policies, particularly toward the peasantry. Kalinin, who considered himself the peasants' defender, had long opposed the use of any force against them.[165] When Kalinin ultimately joined Stalin's team, he did so only with the greatest reluctance.[166]

Tomsky continued to grapple with various trade-union issues in the context of NEP's continued success at growing the economy. Although unemployment remained a serious problem, with over a million officially unemployed in 1926, economic output had returned to its pre-war level, with heavy industry finally outpacing light industry.[167] After Tomsky convinced his members of the Politburo to raise the wage pool of industrial workers in July 1926, wages had also almost reached the pre-war level.[168] One of Tomsky's top priorities at this time was to reduce the wage gap that had developed, with his previous support, between skilled and unskilled workers. In announcing a policy of wage levelling at the Seventh Trade-Union Congress in December 1926, Tomsky stated that in addition to being a matter of 'elementary class justice', it was a source of embarrassment when he hosted foreign delegations. 'When foreigners travel here they are surprised most of all by the difference between the pay of skilled and unskilled labour, which does not exist on such a colossal scale

---

162 Slezkine 2017, p. 306; Zelnik 1995, p. 9.
163 Trotsky remained a member of the Politburo.
164 Ulam, for example, described all three of them as already Stalin's lieutenants: Ulam 1973, p. 257.
165 Fitzpatrick 2015, p. 29.
166 Lewin 1968, p. 361.
167 Dewar 1979, pp. 115, 122. A million peasants moved to urban areas from 1923 to 1926: Carr and Davies 1969b, p. 454. Tomsky stated that the hundreds of thousands of peasants fleeing rural over-population inflated the unemployment numbers by moving to cities for the brief building construction season and then registering for unemployment benefits for the rest of the year: RKP(b) 1927c, p. 287.
168 This was according to a report by Kuibyshev, the head of VSNKh, to the Seventh Trade-Union Congress in December 1926: Dewar 1979, p. 122; Rees 2012, p. 56.

FIGURE 24   Tomsky with Rykov at Seventh Trade-Union Congress
WIKIMEDIA COMMONS

in Western Europe'.[169] After the congress the VTsSPS subtly, but deliberately, pushed wage policy towards egalitarianism rather than efficiency. Together with Narkomtrud, the VTsSPS conducted an extensive revision of the wage scales, which substantially narrowed the wage differential between skilled and unskilled workers.[170] For his success at raising the wages of the most poorly paid workers, Stalinists would accuse Tomsky of promoting 'petty bourgeois egalitarianism' at the Eighth Trade-Union Congress in December 1928.

Strikes, which were not banned by law, were occurring in increasing numbers, but they tended to be extremely short, with the vast majority lasting no more than a couple days and involving fewer than one hundred workers.[171] Only 3 percent of all workers participated in strikes in any particular year from

169   VTsSPS 1927, p. 51.
170   Bergson 1944, p. 187: Davies, Harrison, and Wheatcroft (eds) 1994, p. 94; Kuromiya 1988, p. 88. Wage egalitarianism enjoyed the support of the vast majority of workers: Straus 1990, pp. 545–5.
171   Pospielovsky 1997, p. 25.

1925 to 1928.[172] Large-scale work stoppages were largely avoided during NEP because of workers' willingness to turn to official channels to resolve labour disputes: the arbitration hearings of the Assessment and Conflict Commissions (RKKs). These commissions, which had an equal number of management and trade-union representatives, handled an astonishingly large number of cases. They dealt with a wide variety of worker grievances and factory issues, such as basic wage rates and the fixing of norms and piece-rates, compensation for dismissals or unused vacations, procedures for hiring and firing, and various alleged managerial violations of the collective agreements and the labour code.[173] Since workers could be fired only with the approval of the RKK, unions essentially enjoyed veto power over management's attempts to enforce its disciplinary regulations.[174] In slightly over 50 percent of the cases the RKK sided with the workers, with another 20 percent a compromise between the trade unions and management, all of which won the trade unions considerable goodwill from workers.[175] The author of a study of a Moscow metal factory, Kevin Murphy, concluded 'workers themselves viewed the trade unions as an effective source of power in pressing their grievances with management'.[176]

Unlike during War Communism, when membership was compulsory, membership in the trade unions was voluntary under NEP. After a dramatic decline in 1921–22, almost 90 percent of Soviet workers chose to join the unions and pay their dues, which were two percent of their earnings, because they also received in addition to access to jobs, priority in case of layoffs. Their dues also helped fund workers' clubs. Workers also enjoyed a long laundry list of various indirect wages, such as access to low-cost housing, sickness and disability benefits, paid vacations, free medical care, free or subsidised education, paid maternity leave, retirement pensions, and free summer camps for their children.[177] The various free or heavily subsidised social insurance benefits enjoyed

---

172   Pospielovsky 1997, p. 28.
173   For example, according to the 1922 Labour Code, the workday should not exceed eight hours (six hours for workers aged 16 to 18 and miners working underground), with each worker entitled to two days off a week. Women should receive eight weeks both before and after birth of paid maternity leave: Dewar 1979, pp. 231–2.
174   Filtzer 1986, p. 103.
175   Carr and Davies 1969b, pp. 563–4; Murphy 2005, p. 93; Langsam 1973, p. 154. Some RKK almost always sided with workers: Hatch 1985, p. 188.
176   Murphy 2005, p. 93.
177   Non-union workers lost out on many of these benefits. They, for example, received only 50 percent of the sickness benefits paid to union members: Deutscher 1950, p. 123. By 1928, with 11 million trade union members, their rolls exceeded the 8.4 compulsory members in 1921: Smith 2017, p. 276.

by Soviet workers were unmatched anywhere in the world.[178] For all the problems still besetting workers, and for all of the trade unions' shortcomings during the 1920s, 'the individual worker enjoyed far greater rights and liberties than her or his capitalist counterpart', as the leading labour historian Donald Filtzer concluded.[179] According to another labour historian, Manya Gordon, the period from 1923 to 1927 was 'the most gratifying, active, and useful period' in the history of Soviet trade unions.[180] By the tax year of 1927–28, the pre-war wage levels had been substantially exceeded.[181] During the latter half of the 1920s Tomsky and his fellow trade-union leaders' success in defending workers' economic interests, albeit within the limits dictated by the party, made it in the words of Blair Ruble a kind of 'golden age' for the trade unions.[182] Moshe Lewin likewise concluded that trade unions had become 'quite attuned to the interests of workers'.[183]

In the midst of NEP's successful revival of the economy, with workers' and peasants' standard of living slowly but surely improving, the Politburo members were startled in the early spring of 1926 by the emergence of a new, seemingly unlikely oppositionist alliance, and one that was initially directed specifically at Tomsky. Zinoviev and Kamenev, despite their vociferous denunciations of Trotsky in 1923–24, and he of them, joined together with Trotsky to form what they called the United Opposition.[184] As we saw in Chapter 4, the immediate catalyst for the formation of the United Opposition was the collapse of the general strike in England in May 1926. The bitter attacks on Tomsky over this issue in June, which were repeated in numerous follow-up meetings

---

178 Siegelbaum 1992, p. 204.
179 Filtzer 1986, p. 21. Perhaps at the top of these shortcoming was the bureaucratisation of the trade-union apparatus. A more specific problem was workers' widespread embezzling of trade-union funds: Dewar 1979, p. 148. At one of the trade-union meetings, where he discussed the difficulty of preventing their bureaucratic ranks from swelling, Tomsky said it reminded him of the brave knight who cuts off the head of a dragon but instead of one head the dragon grows two. 'So it is with us: we reduce the staff to 200, and see in four months that it has increased to 500': Tomskii 1928a, p. 322.
180 Gordon 1941, p. 91.
181 Pre-war real wages had been exceeded by somewhere between 11 and 24 percent by 1927. This was made possible by an upward surge in labour productivity, even though the average workday had been decreased from 10 hours in 1913 to seven and a half hours. Labour productivity, between just 1926 and 1928, rose by 28 percent: Kuromiya 1988, pp. 80–1; Service 1999, p. 74. But it should be noted, labour productivity remained extremely low if compared to Western Europe or the United States.
182 Ruble 1981, p. 12.
183 Lewin 1985, p. 25.
184 Many of the party's most talented and prestigious Old Bolsheviks supported the United Opposition: Deutscher 1959, 265.

in the weeks and months to come, was the very first appearance of the United Opposition.[185] Zinoviev and Trotsky harshly attacked Tomsky for his support of the Anglo-Russian Committee and his initial acceptance of the Trades Union Congress's justification for ending the general strike. How sincere those criticisms were is open to question. A recent biographer of Trotsky, Geoffrey Swain suggests his foreign-policy critiques were rhetorical, just 'camouflage', for his attacks on Tomsky and other members of the party leadership.[186] Another recent biographer of Trotsky, Robert Service, argues that if the United Opposition had come together earlier, 'Stalin would have been helpless against it. Trotsky, Kamenev, and Zinoviev would have dominated the Politburo, the Central Committee and the Comintern, and Sovnarkom would have been theirs for the taking'.[187] It is not clear why Service thinks this, since the three of them still would have lacked the majority of votes on the Politburo. Likewise, the oppositionists' marriage of convenience did not enjoy mass support within the party, where no more than 8,000 of its 750,000 members rallied to its cause.[188] In any case, all three were expelled from the Politburo in October 1926.[189] A month later, Tomsky agreed to join with Stalin, Molotov, and Bukharin to also remove Zinoviev as the leader of the Comintern.[190] Bukharin replaced Zinoviev as head of the Comintern.

In this context, a 'war scare' took centre stage in 1927. Although it has sparked considerable debate, historians have generally treated it as a sham.[191] Stalin is commonly accused of manufacturing it as part of his drive against the United Opposition, but it was Bukharin, as the new head of the Comintern, who in January gave the speech that first sounded the alarm, by warning of a British-led campaign against the Soviet Union.[192] Stalin initially tried to calm the popula-

---

185 Vatlin 2008, p. 57.
186 Swain 2006, pp. 3–4.
187 Service 2009, p. 328.
188 Le Blanc 2015, p. 52.
189 Kamenev, as we have seen, had been demoted to a candidate (non-voting) member earlier. At this time, just before he was expelled from its membership, Trotsky angrily denounced Stalin at a Politburo meeting as the 'grave-digger of the revolution': Carr and Davies 1971, p. 17; Deutscher 1959, p. 296.
190 Adibekov (ed.) 2004, p. 11.
191 Alfred Meyer called the war scare 'essentially a phony issue, manipulated by politicians': Meyer 1978, p. 2. But some historians argue the fear was authentic: Sontag 1975, p. 71; Uldricks 1979, pp. 55–83.
192 Meyer 1978, pp. 2–6; *Inprecorr*, January 1927, pp. 189–94. In addition to its anger over Soviet support for the general strike, Britain's Conservative government was also anxious about losing control of India and its hegemony over Afghanistan to the Soviets: Hudson 2012, p. 146.

tion by downplaying the danger, as did Rykov and other members of the leadership.[193] Tomsky, for his part, remained focused on trying to maintain the Anglo-Russian Committee, one of whose explicit purposes was to prevent any possible new war. It was partly on these grounds that Stalin continued, even after the general strike debacle, to offer his support for the Anglo-Russian Committee.[194] Then most dramatically, in May, the British Conservative government, which accused the Soviets of interfering in British domestic affairs, broke off diplomatic relations with the Soviet Union and cancelled their trade agreement.[195] A month later, a young Russian émigré assassinated the Soviet ambassador in Poland. For Stalin this appeared to be the final straw. He argued this assassination was not merely the action of an individual fanatic, but was intended to play a role similar to that of the Sarajevo assassination in 1914 by drawing the Soviet Union into a war with Poland. He called for a get-tough policy against the Soviet Union's perceived enemies both at home and abroad.[196] The United Oppositionists, while they pounced on the ruling coalition's string of foreign policy failures, also succumbed to the hysteria, with Zinoviev writing in July that 'a war with the imperialists is not only probable, it is inescapable'.[197]

Stalin adroitly used the 'war scare' against the United Oppositionists at the joint Politburo and Central Control Commission Plenums held in July and September 1927. He accused them of irresponsibly increasing intra-party disunity at a dangerous time. Stalin cynically, indeed ludicrously (although a foretaste of the sort of charges made during the Moscow show trials), warned that the Soviet government faced 'a united anti-Soviet front from Chamberlain to Trotsky'.[198] Tomsky expressed alarm at Stalin's hard line. While emphasising the

---

193 Meyer 1978, pp. 4–6.
194 Stalin 1952–67, vol. 8, p. 195.
195 Tomsky, along with Stalin, Bukharin, Rykov, and Molotov, was part of a commission the Politburo created to decide what measures should be taken in retaliation for the provocative British raid in London on Moscow's All-Russian Cooperative Society and the Soviet trade mission: RGASPI, f. 17, op. 162, d. 5, ll. 7–8, reproduced in Adibekov (ed.) 2001, p. 149. Tomsky sent a futile letter to the Trades Union Congress calling on it to protest against the raid: Khaustov, Naumov, and Plotnikova (eds) 2003, p. 131.
196 Warth 1958, pp. 136–7. The OGPU, the political police, responded by immediately rounding up and shooting 20 alleged enemy agents, which provoked widespread outrage in the West: Jacobson 1994, pp. 222–4.
197 Quoted in Sontag 1975, p. 71. Prominent among the other failures the United Oppositionists seized upon was Bukharin's and Stalin's disastrous policy toward China, where they had supported Generalissimo Chiang Kai-shek, the leader of the Chinese Nationalist Party, who in April ordered the wholesale slaughter of Chinese Communist Party members and their sympathisers.
198 Deutscher 1967, p. 310; Tucker 1977, p. 567. The reference is to the British foreign secretary

FIGURE 25   United Opposition leaders Trotsky, Kamenev, and Zinoviev
TATE IMAGES

risks of isolation in a hostile world and the value of a rapprochement with the West, Tomsky, along with Bukharin, Rykov, Kalinin, and Chicherin, got Stalin to back off from his harsh rhetoric.[199] Whether or not Stalin ever considered the threat to be genuine, the war scare created widespread panic within the country. To prepare for war shortages, workers made a run on food shops, while peasants began to hoard grain, flour, and various staples.

There is evidence that Tomsky and the other moderates were by this time becoming increasingly uneasy with Stalin's leadership and talked of replacing him with Tomsky as general secretary of the party. At the July 1927 Central Committee Plenum, according to the historian Michal Reiman, in addition to dealing with the United Opposition,

> plans apparently ripened within the moderate wing of the leadership to use the increasingly complicated internal party situation to make fundamental changes in top party posts. The details are hard to determine

 in the Conservative government, Austin Chamberlain, who actually favoured improved relations with the Soviet Union.
199   Jacobson 1994, p. 225; Reiman 1987, p. 15.

today. But it remains a fact that rumors were circulating – even reaching diplomatic channels – that in the interest of making peace within the party, Stalin should be replaced in his post by someone else.[200]

Reiman, who relied on documents in the German Foreign Ministry, states that Tomsky was mentioned as Stalin's possible replacement. He also argues that Stalin increasingly thought that the moderates would eventually turn against him.[201] Four months later, on 10 November the head of the political police, Vyacheslav Menzhinsky, sent two reports to Stalin that described secret plans in the offing to replace him with Tomsky.[202] Be that as it may, the moderates never made a move to replace Stalin with Tomsky or anyone else. Tomsky, for his part, continued to focus his public attacks on the United Opposition, who while not calling for the total abandonment of NEP, criticised the leadership's concessions to the peasantry while advocating more investment in heavy industry. Tomsky understandably continued to see Trotsky, Zinoviev, and Kamenev as a greater threat to the moderate policies he supported than Stalin.[203] Like virtually everyone else, he would underestimate or be fooled by Stalin until it was too late to stop him.[204]

As the United Opposition engaged in a wave of activity during 1927, Tomsky and the rest of the party leadership used two events to attack them and their supporters, including those within the VTsSPS.[205] The first was a partly spontaneous demonstration that took place on 9 June 1927 at the Yaroslavl railroad

---

200   Reiman 1987, p. 28.
201   Reiman 1987, pp. 18, 28. In response, Stalin in the fall of 1927 began thinking about how to remove Tomsky from his post as head of VTsSPS: Shmelev 1989, p. 58.
202   Broué 1988, p. 530. There had been similar, earlier rumours that Tomsky and the other moderate members of the Politburo wanted to oust Stalin and replace him with Dzerzhinsky: Cohen 1973, p. 141. Although notorious as head of the political police during the Civil War, Dzerzhinsky seems to have repented and become 'decidedly right wing'. He favoured moderate, gradualist economic policies as chair of VSNKh: Graziosi 1991, p. 548; Pirani 2008, p. 140. As head of the OGPU, Dzerzhinsky was well aware of the extent of peasant dissatisfaction and its economic roots: Hudson 2012, pp. 54–8. In any case, Dzerzhinsky unexpectedly died in July 1926.
203   Similarly, Rykov told the American journalist, William Reswick, that despite his recognition of Stalin as 'a growing menace', he feared far more what he saw as Trotsky's determination to make Russia a centre of world revolution, which he feared would result in war and the destruction of the Soviet Union: Reswick 1952, p. 120.
204   With the exception of Trotsky, all the Soviet party leaders during the 1920s, starting with Lenin, were blind to the danger Stalin posed until it was too late.
205   Trotsky, for example, claimed 20,000 supporters met in secret meetings in workers' apartments in Moscow and Leningrad: Trotsky 1970, p. 530.

station in Moscow. A crowd of as many as two thousand United Oppositionists and their friends had gathered at the station to say goodbye to one of its leaders, the respected and popular 'Old Bolshevik', Ivar Smilga, who the Central Committee was transferring to the Siberian city of Khabarovsk, where an insignificant administrative post awaited him.[206] Even though in their speeches Trotsky and Zinoviev focused primarily on foreign policy, without explicitly criticising the party leadership, Tomsky characterised the rally as 'anti-party' at a time when there was a direct danger of war.[207] That it was staged in a busy public place in central Moscow, within view and earshot of the throngs of non-party passers-by coming and going from the three railroad stations on Kalanchovskaya Square, meant it was virtually a counter-revolutionary demonstration in the eyes of Tomsky and the other members of the party leadership.[208] There had been a consensus among the party leaders ever since the 'trade-union debate' that oppositionists should never take their criticisms public.[209] The second event was a sting operation organised by Stalin. The operation revealed Stalin's increasing willingness to engage in devious intrigues as well as his increasing control of the political police. Stalin had learned that the United Opposition, in desperation, was trying to initiate an underground propaganda campaign. In September 1927, Stalin sent an undercover OGPU agent, who was a former officer in the White Army during the Civil War, to help the United Opposition establish a clandestine printing press, which the OGPU then immediately raided as an 'illegal printing shop'.[210] Stalin openly acknowledged that the United Oppositionists had been set up, but defended it as a way of discovering their plots.[211] Hundreds of United Oppositionists were expelled from the party as a result.[212]

---

206 Smilga, who helped organise the Bolshevik seizure of power as leader of the Baltic Fleet, became the political commissar overseeing Mikhail Tukhachevsky's army in the Civil War and a respected economist during NEP. The party leaders had been sending leading oppositionists to party posts in remote locations to get them out of Moscow and in reprisal for their oppositional actions. This, of course, was not unlike how Tomsky had been banished to Tashkent in 1921.
207 Deutscher 1969, p. 339.
208 Carr 1959, p. 27; Reiman 1987, p. 22. In early August the Central Committee and Central Control Commission Plenum devoted the session to attacking Trotsky's and Zinoviev's actions. Trotsky managed to speak for an hour and a half despite constant interruptions by Stalin and Grigory Ordzhonikidze, who chaired the session: Astakhovoi et al. (eds) 2007b, p. 626; Service 2009, p. 72.
209 Gill 2018, p. 41.
210 Reiman 1987, p. 31; Khlevniuk 2015, pp. 84–5.
211 Burtsev 1927, p. 267.
212 GARF, f. 5421, op. 42, d. 140, l. 27. The OGPU imprisoned one of the oppositionists, Sergei

The United Oppositionists tried to recruit support within individual trade-union branches, particularly in the Metalworkers' Union. Trotsky and Zinoviev, for example, on 29 June 1927 wrote a letter to the Metalworkers' Union's Central Committee in which they tried to get it to disavow a VTsSPS resolution, adopted a day earlier, condemning the 'splitting activity' of the opposition. Copies of this letter were sent to oppositionists in all the other major trade unions. It apparently was not endorsed by any of them.[213] In fact, in some unions, such as the Construction Workers' Union, it had the reverse effect as oppositionists found themselves removed from leading positions within the union.[214]

At the VTsSPS Plenum in October 1927 the United Oppositionists nonetheless brought the intra-party conflict into Tomsky's bastion, the central trade-union leadership. Whereas Bukharin's 'enrich yourselves' exhortation provided the primary target for the opposition's attacks in 1925, Tomsky's support for the Anglo-Russian Committee was the primary target in 1926–27, even though the committee was in its last throes. Although supporters of the United Opposition in the VTsSPS introduced a resolution that attacked the VTsSPS for insufficient wage increases, deplorable living conditions, and other problems, their most potent attack at both plenums appeared to be their criticism of the VTsSPS's foreign policy. Their proposed resolution stated that, 'despite timely warnings about the inevitable collapse of its policy', the VTsSPS remained in the Anglo-Russian Committee, thereby allowing 'those notorious enemies of the dictatorship of the proletariat, the English trade-union bureaucrats, to use the authority of the Russian socialist revolution in the interests and service of international capital'.[215] These oppositionists expressed outrage that that they had been accused of giving 'Menshevik speeches' at the VTsSPS plenum while such 'agents of imperialism' as Alf Purcell, George Hicks, and Ben Turner are referred to as comrades and friends.[216] Tomsky faced similar criticism at factory meetings.[217]

In his nearly hour-long speech, Tomsky chose not to defend his years of work on the Anglo-Russian Committee. He in fact did not even mention it. He instead hammered the supporters of the United Opposition on the various

---

Mrachkovsky. This was the first time a prominent member of the opposition was imprisoned: Deutscher 1967, p. 358.

213 Voskrenskii and Subbotin 1996, p. 115.
214 Voskrenskii and Subbotin 1996, p. 117.
215 GARF, f. 5421, op. 42, d. 140, l. 2. The oppositionists had launched similar criticisms at VTsSPS Plenums in June and September: Voskrenskii and Subbotin 1996, p. 114; Kozelev 1996, pp. 158–9.
216 GARF, f. 5421, op. 42, d. 140, l. 27.
217 Murphy 2005, pp. 84–5, 171.

points voiced by fellow members of the leadership in other settings. On the Smilga demonstration, he declared that, 'Trotsky and Zinoviev know that you can say things in the Hall of Columns here in the Trade Unions' headquarters that you can't say at the Yaroslavl railroad station'.[218] Tomsky also accused the oppositionists of committing 'a colossal crime' when they turned to a former White officer in order to set up a non-party printing operation.[219] When the oppositionists complained that this was a 'vile slander' because he was an OGPU agent, a communist, Tomsky adopted Stalin's defence and fired back that you did not know that at the time. Tomsky threatened the oppositionists: 'If you think the party will tolerate all this, you are mistaken; if you think that we have ceased to be Bolsheviks and have become vegetarians, you are mistaken; if you think we are Tolstoyans, you are mistaken; if you think our patience is inexhaustible, you are mistaken'. Tomsky then added, 'if you choose to fight, do not beg for mercy later', to which there was 'stormy applause'.[220] Tomsky not only argued that the oppositionists should be expelled from the party – 'you do not have the right to speak against the decisions of the party and remain in the party' – he argued they deserved to be arrested for such crimes as demoralising non-party workers or spreading ideas that encourage them to conspire against the party.[221] He also suggested it was criminal to mock the trade-union leadership.[222] Tomsky apparently failed to appreciate the potential danger to himself or others of criminalising oppositional sentiments. He would come to ruefully regret this and similar statements when he became a party outcast and fully ensnared in the web that he had played such a crucial role in helping to weave.

As party discourse continued to coarsen, at the Central Committee and Central Control Committee Plenum a couple weeks later in October 1927, the leaders of the United Opposition were subjected to an onslaught of insults from the opening bell. As Trotsky rose to the podium he was met with such a general uproar, with delegates banging their fists on tables and loud shouts to 'get down from the dais', that he could not be heard as he read his resolution.[223] Various delegates yelled such insults as 'Liar', 'Slanderer', 'No One Believes You', 'Scum', 'Traitor', while Kaganovich yelled out 'Menshevik, Counterrevolution-

---

218 GARF, f. 5421, op. 42, d. 140, ll. 145, 151. When the trade-union oppositionists tried to insist they were against splitting the Bolshevik Party, voices shouted out, 'What about the railroad station demonstration'?
219 GARF, f. 5421, op. 42, d. 140, ll. 155–7.
220 GARF, f. 5421, op. 42, d. 140, l. 159.
221 GARF, f. 5421, op. 42, d. 140, l. 149.
222 GARF, f. 5421, op. 42, d. 140, l. 154.
223 Kudriatsev (ed.) 2018, pp. 24–5. As a result, Trotsky's speech was not included in the stenographic report of the plenum.

ary'!²²⁴ Emelyan Yaroslavsky and Nikolai Shvernik went so far as to throw heavy books at Trotsky's head. Nikolai Kubyak threw a glass. Others threw inkwells. While no one threw anything at Zinoviev, his speech was also drowned out and he too left the rostrum amid a chorus of boos.²²⁵ Tomsky, appalled at the complete breakdown in decorum and stung by all the United Oppositionists' criticisms of the Anglo-Russian Committee, did not join the attacks, unlike Stalin, Bukharin, and Rykov. In fact, he did not say a word during the plenum, though he did vote for a number of resolutions against the United Opposition. The plenum in the end, by a vote of 201–11, expelled Trotsky and Zinoviev from the Central Committee.

Tomsky may also have been silent at the plenum because he was reeling from the startling 'surprise' by VTsIK, a week before the start of the plenum, that a seven-hour workday with no reduction in pay would be introduced to celebrate the tenth anniversary of the Bolshevik seizure of power. The manifesto was obviously a political gesture rather than a considered economic plan.²²⁶ It apparently was in response to the United Opposition's attempts to exploit workers' discontents, including complaints that they commonly continued to work beyond the statutory eight-hour workday.²²⁷ The announcement of the seven-hour day infuriated the oppositionists. Grigory Yevdokimov described it as 'a fairy tale for small children'.²²⁸ Tomsky likewise made known his displeasure with the stunt, which was obviously done without any serious consultation or planning.²²⁹ It would be three weeks after the original announcement before a commission was even formed to develop 'practical proposals' for the eventual introduction of the seven-hour working day. The commission consisted of the Labour Commissar, a representative from VTsSPS (presumably Tomsky), and a representative from VSNKh.²³⁰ In the meantime, Tomsky decided, despite his grave doubts, that he might as well go ahead and join other members of the Politburo majority in celebrating the promised 35-hour workweek. He proclaimed on 5 November 1927 that 'the wages of workers and the length of the

224 Kudriatsev (ed.) 2018, pp. 24–5, 296–7; Kotkin 2014, pp. 646–8.
225 Serge 1963, p. 225; Volkogonov 1996, pp. 295, 299.
226 Kudriatsev (ed.) 2018, pp. 319–20n20. It was addressed 'to the workers, peasants, and Red Army men of the USSR and to the proletariat and oppressed peoples of the world'.
227 The manifesto is translated and reprinted in Dewar 1979, p. 264.
228 Kudriatsev (ed.) 2018, p. 60.
229 Deutscher 1959, p. 364; Kudriatsev (ed.) 2018, pp. 47–51; Fel'shtinskii (ed.) 1988b, p. 222; Reiman 1987, p. 38.
230 The Sovnarkom decided on 17 January 1928 to give the commission until July 1928, eight months after the original announcement, to submit their practical proposals: Dewar 1979, p. 265.

FIGURE 26   Tomsky on the Lenin Mausoleum in November 1927
MARXISTS INTERNET ARCHIVE

work day are the chief indicators of the trade unions' achievements'.[231] But the first 'experimental trials' of the shorter workday in the textile mills were hardly promising.[232]

The United Oppositionists made one last desperate stand after the October 1927 Central Committee plenum. They attempted a dramatic act of resistance, by going into the streets during the parades in Moscow and Leningrad on 7 November to celebrate the tenth anniversary of the revolution. They carried their own banners with such slogans as 'Strike against the Kulak, the NEPmen, and the Bureaucrat'! 'Carry Out Lenin's Testament'! and 'Preserve Bolshevik Unity'! An occasional soldier would shout out 'Down with Stalin' as soldiers passed before Stalin, Tomsky, and the other party leaders atop the

---

231 Tomskii 1928a, p. 449 with Rykov, Bukharin, Kalinin, and Stalin in November 1927.
232 In these experiments, a three-shift workday was introduced in which textile workers were required to work on several machines at once. The haste in which it was introduced, coupled with the worn-out condition of much of the machinery and the increased intensity of work, led to many accidents: Reiman 1987, pp. 54–5. There appears to have been a deep generational split among workers over how they responded to the change. Archival evidence suggests young workers hoped the change would alleviate the high levels of unemployment and lead to higher pay, while older workers almost universally opposed the seven-hour day: Hagenloh 1994, p. 49.

Lenin Mausoleum.[233] The demonstrations were an utter failure. Squads of activists and police, presumably with Tomsky's approval, pounced on the oppositionists, tore their banners to shreds, and beat many of them with truncheons, while arresting others.[234] It was not only to no avail, this clear violation of party norms backfired. As recently as August, Tomsky had joined with Ordzhonikidze, Rykov, and Kalinin to oppose Stalin's, Molotov's, and Bukharin's desire to purge Trotsky and Zinoviev.[235] But at the Central Committee and Central Control Commission Plenum held a week after the demonstrations, Tomsky joined the nearly unanimous decision to expel Trotsky and Zinoviev from the party for inciting the 'counter-revolutionary demonstrations' and giving 'anti-party speeches'. It passed by a vote of 210–2.[236] But Tomsky and other members of the Politburo apparently blocked Stalin's desire to have Trotsky and Zinoviev arrested.[237] The plenum also expelled Kamenev and many others from the Central Committee, although they were not ousted from the party.[238]

The primary goal of the Fifteenth Party Congress, when it finally opened in December 1927, was for Tomsky and other members of the leadership to finish off the United Opposition once and for all.[239] Tomsky's speech denouncing the United Oppositionists enjoyed the support of virtually all of the delegates. Tomsky ridiculed its leaders' 'division of labour', declaring, 'When they need a man of war, a warhorse, they launch Trotsky … When they need peace, they launch Kamenev. When a tear has to be shed, they launch Zinoviev'.[240] Tomsky argued that the views of Trotsky and Zinoviev, which he labelled 'Trotskyism', were fundamentally incompatible with those of the party.[241] Since Trotsky and

---

233 Trotsky 1970, p. 534.
234 Deutscher 1967, pp. 372–9. In Leningrad, Zinoviev barely escaped a crowd intent on beating him up: Merridale 1990, p. 43.
235 Broué 1988, p. 520.
236 The Fifteenth Party Congress confirmed their expulsions. The Politburo concocted a resolution, which Tomsky signed, forcing Trotsky, Zinoviev, Kamenev and other leaders of the United Opposition to promise to end any oppositional activity and to denounce other non-United Opposition dissidents such as Shlyapnikov: Allen 2015, p. 274.
237 McNeal 1988, p. 106.
238 Gregor (ed.) 1974, p. 308; Daniels 1960, pp. 316–17. Those with apartments in the Kremlin were evicted since only members of the Central Committee were entitled to live in the Kremlin. Trotsky, who moved out before they could evict him found a small room at the Fifth House of the Soviets: Service 2009, pp. 364–5. This is where Tomsky and his family would move when they left the Kremlin in 1935.
239 The lapse of two years since the Fourteenth Party Congress was unprecedented. Party statutes called for congresses to meet annually.
240 RKP(b) 1928, p. 299.
241 Quoted in Kulikova and Khazanov 1988, p. 79.

Zinoviev, having been expelled from the party before the congress, were not in attendance, Tomsky, as he had at the Fourteenth Party Congress, trained his fire on Kamenev, who had tried in vain to defend the principle of opposition within the party. Kamenev's first sentence, stating that he came to the tribune with the goal of finding a way to reconcile the United Opposition with the party, was met with shouts of 'lies'.[242] To the charges accusing him of insincerity and evasive statements, Kamenev pleaded, 'Why don't you believe my honest words'?[243] Tomsky gave no countenance to Kamenev's long service in the party:

> If we put on one side of the scale your service for the party and the working class, and on the other side what you have done and made a mess of during these past two years, the second side of the scale will outbalance the first. In settling accounts with you, the services you have rendered to the working class have long been erased from the pages of history.[244]

Tomsky mocked Kamenev's requests for amnesty by bringing up all the times that the oppositionists had promised to dissolve their faction over the previous two years. He likened the United Opposition's tactics of playing for time to those of the Basmachi during the Civil War in Turkestan, when he had been exiled there:

> Throughout the summer we gave them a licking. When winter set in, the fields became bare and there was no grass, with their horsemen worn out, their horses starving, and with no cartridges to be had. They came to us and said, 'We are coming over to your side, we recognise the Soviet government, but we shall keep our weapons'. We told them they could join us and serve as our guards. After they spent the winter on our side and grew fat, in the spring, as soon as there was grass to be seen, they left and started fighting us all over again.

Tomsky, to laughter and applause, continued with the analogy:

> Comrade Kamenev, your horsemen are shattered both ideologically and morally. You have no bullets with which to carry on your factional battles. You have no grass fields, no suitable political field for your oppositional

---

242   RKP(b) 1928, p. 251.
243   RKP(b) 1928, p. 255.
244   RKP(b) 1928, p. 305.

cavalry. You want to feed on our bread until you can attack us again. This will not work. Not a bit of it.[245]

Tomsky even characterised Kamenev's role in the 7 November demonstrations as 'a criminal betrayal of the party'.[246] Tomsky, who had long shared the Bolsheviks' unwillingness to tolerate any dissent within their ranks, categorised the United Oppositionists as Mensheviks for whom there was no place within the Leninist Party.[247] To reiterate, Tomsky's lines of attack against the United Opposition would be strikingly similar to the ones the Stalinists would later use against Tomsky. In words that in particular must have haunted him later, he joked that 'under the dictatorship of the proletariat, two, three, or four parties may exist, but only on the single condition that one of them is in power and the others in prison. Anyone who doesn't understand this doesn't know a damn thing about the dictatorship of the proletariat, about the Bolshevik Party'.[248] But despite his attacks and accusations, Tomsky, along with Bukharin and Rykov, opposed the Politburo majority's decision to exile Trotsky to Alma-Ata in Central Asia following the congress.[249]

The Fifteenth Party Congress in December 1927 proved to be far more momentous than Tomsky and others appreciated at the time. The five-year plan, which the congress adopted, projected moderate rates of growth in line with the gradualist philosophy that still seemed to predominate within the party leadership. The leadership certainly did not speak as if economic policies were about to be radically reversed. While Stalin bemoaned agriculture's slow rate of growth and attributed it largely to the continued use of strip farming,

---

245   RKP(b) 1928, p. 300. This was indeed a tactic adopted by the Basmachi, who as a result were dubbed 'Winter Bolsheviks': Broxup 1983, p. 63; Olcott 1981, p. 363.
246   RKP(b) 1928, p. 303.
247   RKP(b) 1928, p. 302.
248   Tomsky said this at a Leningrad Oblast Party Conference: *Pravda*, 19 November 1927. As Victor Serge, who quoted this statement and a similar quip by Bukharin earlier in the year, stated, 'Tomsky, Bukharin, and their friends did not have long to wait before experiencing at their own expense the virtues of the prison-state': Serge 1937b, p. 92.
249   The Swiss communist who became a top official in the Comintern during the 1920s, Jules Humbert-Droz, heard that Tomsky as well as Bukharin and Rykov opposed Trotsky's banishment: Humbert-Droz 1971, p. 276. Trotsky heard the same thing: Deutscher 1959, p. 469. Fitzpatrick states that Kuibyshev also voted against the expulsion, but Bukharin in the end switched his vote to side with the majority of the Politburo: Fitzpatrick 2015, p. 42. Exiling other oppositionists to the far reaches of the Soviet Union soon followed. Later, Tomsky, along with Bukharin and Rykov, would strongly oppose the Politburo's decision in mid-January 1929 to kick Trotsky out of the Soviet Union, which was carried out the following month: Deutscher 1959, p. 469; Cohen 1973, p. 304; Service 2009, p. 373.

and argued that the only solution to that was collective farming, he stressed that increased collectivisation should not be implemented by exerting pressure on the peasantry. Stalin appeared to agree with Tomsky and other moderates, who were arguing that collectivisation should be conducted voluntarily and in a measured manner. Stalin explicitly stated that 'we need to collectivise gradually, by example and persuasion'.[250] Stalin also did not call for an attack on kulaks, arguing that 'comrades are wrong who think that it is possible and necessary to put an end to the kulaks through administrative measures, through the GPU'. The kulak, Stalin insisted, 'must be defeated through economic measures and on the basis of socialist legality'.[251] All in all, as Moshe Lewin concluded in his classic study of the decisions that led to collectivisation, the delegates of the Fifteenth Congress 'saw nothing unusual in the decisions [that were taken at the congress], and failed to attribute any real significance to them'.[252] The United Oppositionists thought that Bukharin, Rykov, and Tomsky had won a mandate at the congress for a gradualist approach to industrialisation and collectivisation.[253]

But even before the congress ended, contradicting his other statements, Stalin pushed for the adoption of 'extraordinary measures' to address the 'grain crisis'. The party only now announced that the 1927 marketing of grain had dropped to 80 percent of the grain procured in 1926. This was partly because of bad weather, but also because peasants began to 'hoard' in response to the war scare and in hopes of holding out until the state raised its grain procurement prices, which had been lowered in 1926–27.[254] The shortfall, which had taken the party leadership by surprise, not only undermined plans to increase grain exports in order to purchase machinery for the five-year plan, it even fell below what was adequate to feed urban areas and the Red Army.[255] Tomsky joined with his fellow moderates Bukharin and Rykov to correctly identify low government grain prices and the severe shortage and high price of manufactured goods, especially textiles, as the primary causes for the fall-off in the peasantry's willingness to sell grain to the state.[256] But the previously moder-

---

250 RKP(b) 1928, p. 56.
251 Stalin contradictorily added, however, that 'this does not exclude, of course, the possibility of administrative measures being used against kulaks. But the application of such measures must not take the place of economic measures': RKP(b) 1928, p. 60.
252 Lewin 1968, p. 206.
253 Deutscher 1966, p. 313.
254 Viola (ed.) 2005, p. 17; McNeal 1988, p. 116. Some peasants began to demand that they be paid in gold for their grain: Hudson 2012, p. 152.
255 Hughes 1991, p. 104.
256 Many workers shared this assessment of what was causing the shortages: GARF, f. 5451, op.

ate and pragmatic Stalin, now that the 'leftist' leaders had been vanquished, essentially adopted Trotsky's and Zinoviev's positions. Stalin, who had no economic expertise, suddenly began to view the grain shortfall in radical, strictly political terms. He argued that a 'grain strike' by greedy kulaks, coupled with the 'complacency and sluggishness' of local officials, was to blame and called for 'extraordinary measures' to forcibly requisition grain.[257]

Even though the coalition in the ruling leadership was suddenly coming apart, the Politburo nonetheless unanimously decided on a limited, emergency collection of grain on 5 January.[258] Although this was not his preferred course of action, Tomsky, after vacillating, voted for the 'emergency measures' as a regrettable, though 'absolutely necessary', temporary expedient to rectify the food shortages appearing in urban areas.[259] He and the other moderates, who had been taken aback at the extent of the shortfall, envisioned an orderly, short-term campaign against 'kulak speculators'.[260] But as reports came in, Tomsky, Bukharin, and Rykov quickly became alarmed at how the 'extraordinary measures' were being implemented and the mass discontent and resistance it provoked among the peasantry. They were stunned that Stalin, who had changed seemingly overnight from the embodiment of caution and moderation, had pushed far beyond the boundaries of what Tomsky and other members of the Politburo had authorised.[261] It was, in the words of one of Stalin's biographers, Alex De Jonge, 'the first time that Stalin took a major step on his own initiative'.[262] Until then, according to Graeme Gill, Stalin preferred 'to take a low profile in open leadership initiatives. He appeared to be the epitome of collective leadership'.[263] Oleg Khlevniuk concluded that Stalin chose this radical course with the goal of 'intentionally destroying the system of collective leadership'.[264]

While most of the Politburo remained in Moscow, and no mention of it was made in the press, Stalin rushed off to western Siberia, where the shortfall was

---

42, d. 159, l. 32. It was more profitable for peasants to focus on livestock, since the prices of meat and dairy products were determined by the market and thus outside government control: Davies 1980, p. 40.
257   Viola (ed.) 2005, pp. 18–19.
258   Khordina (ed.) 2000, pp. 581–4; Hughes 1991, p. 127.
259   Vatlin et al. (eds) 2000, pp. 422, 424.
260   Cohen 1973, p. 278.
261   Nove 1992, p. 152.
262   De Jonge 1986, p. 219.
263   Gill 1990, p. 193.
264   Khlevniuk 2015, p. 101.

particularly large, while Molotov headed to the Urals, Kaganovich to Ukraine, and Mikoyan to the North Caucasus.[265] During his more than two weeks in Siberia, from 18 January to 2 February, Stalin personally instructed large, roving contingents of urban party brigades and local officials to replicate the brutal and economically disastrous methods of War Communism, not unlike those implemented earlier by Safarov in Turkestan.[266] Stalin's posse, often brandishing guns, ordered Siberian peasant settlers to sell their grain and sanctioned the OGPU's arrest of any peasants who failed to do so, including the so-called middle peasants.[267] So much was requisitioned from some farms that they were completely ruined.[268] Stalin mocked and angrily disregarded the advice of local officials, who warned him that using the anti-speculation Article 107 of the Criminal Code against 'kulaks' would be counter-productive and worsen the situation in the countryside.[269]

When Stalin returned to Moscow with trains loaded with seized grain, an angry confrontation took place in the Politburo between Stalin and Bukharin, Rykov, and Tomsky. They deplored Stalin's use of violence. An outraged Rykov cursed Stalin, arguing that criminal charges should be filed against you for forcing local officials to employ illegal methods of coercion.[270] Tomsky later admitted that he deeply regretted his initial support for the emergency methods. He confessed that how they had been implemented had shaken him to his core.[271]

---

265 Other Stalin supporters, such as Andrei Zhdanov, Nikolai Shvernik, and Andrei Andreev, fanned out to other regions.
266 For the grain confiscations, Stalin and other senior party officials managed to have 30,000 urban party cadres at their disposal: Jacobson 1994, p. 257.
267 Molotov reportedly said, 'We must strike at the kulak in such a way that the middle peasant comes to heel': Carr and Davies 1969a, p. 55. The procurement prices were actually lowered rather than raised as the moderates wanted: Karcz 1967, p. 423. On the brandishing of guns: Manning 2001, p. 26.
268 Khlevniuk 2015, p. 103.
269 Stalin 1952–67, vol. 11, pp. 5–6. Although it had never been a crime to refuse to sell grain at state prices, the OGPU now equated peasant refusal to sell with illegal speculation by the so-called NEPmen, who were for the most part small-scale private entrepreneurs, tradespeople, or urban traders, rather than the speculators in scare commodities party propagandists portrayed them to be. Those charged under Article 107 could be sentenced to one year of imprisonment along with the confiscation of their property: Beerman 1967, p. 127. Enraged peasants responded with violent attacks on grain-requisitioning brigades: Viola 1987, p. 26.
270 *Sotsialisticheskii vestnik*, 23 July 1928, p. 15; Cohen 1973, pp. 178–9; Montefiore 2004, p. 36; Kotkin 2014, p. 686.
271 TsGAODM, f. 2870, op. 1, d. 296, reprinted in Karpachev and Minaeva (eds) 1992b, p. 104.

Rykov, Tomsky, and Bukharin, with Kalinin's and Voroshilov's support, succeeded in getting Stalin to back off somewhat from this 'reign of terror'.[272] There were also signs that other key Stalinists were also having serious second thoughts, including Rudzutak and Kuibyshev, who had just been elevated to the Politburo to replace Zinoviev and Kamenev. Only Molotov and Kaganovich offered their unqualified support for Stalin on the Politburo.[273] Thrown on the defensive, within a week of his return, Stalin issued a directive to all party organisations condemning the use of force as unauthorised 'excesses' [*peregiby*] (just as he would do two years later following the disastrous implementation of forced collectivisation). Although Stalin had denounced NEP to local party and government officials, he now soothingly insisted that NEP was the 'basis of our economic policy and will remain so for a long historical period'.[274] But the Stalinists' confiscations of 'surplus grain' had not only created a deep rift within the Politburo; it had dealt a serious, arguably fatal blow to NEP, by destroying the peasantry's confidence in the government. It was a truly pivotal event. Tomsky later attributed the origins of his, Bukharin's, and Rykov's so-called Right Deviation to how the Stalinists implemented the 'extraordinary measures'.[275] Although it should be said, as the historian Michael David-Fox correctly noted, they did not consider themselves rightists or deviationists.[276]

Tomsky and the conciliatory policies of NEP were thrown further on the defensive by what became known as the 'Shakhty Affair' [*Shakhtinskoe delo*], even though, as we will see, Tomsky played a central role in bringing it about.[277] It began in June 1927 when OGPU officials in the North Caucasus arrested engineers and technicians who had been trained before the revolution and were now serving in managerial positions in Donbass coal mines.[278] As we have seen, trade unionists and workers had long viewed 'bourgeois specialists' with dis-

---

272   Lewin 1968, pp. 229–30.
273   Volkogonov 1991, p. 180; Manning 2001, p. 1; McNeal 1975, pp. 95–6. Oleg Khlevniuk, in contrast, argues Stalin, 'with careful calculation', was provoking Bukharin, Rykov, and Tomsky. He adds that by projecting himself as an energetic, revolutionary leader he succeeded in casting 'moderation in an unflattering light and made radicalism look more effective': Khlevniuk 2015, p. 104.
274   Stalin 1952–67, vol. 11, pp. 18, 20–1; Hughes 1991, pp. 209–10.
275   RKP(b) 1934c, p. 249; TsGAODM, f. 2870, op. 1, d. 296, reprinted in Karpachev and Minaeva (eds) 1992b, p. 104.
276   David-Fox 1997, p. 182.
277   Before the revolution, the town of Shakhty, which means Mine Shafts, was Aleksandorvsk-Grushevsk.
278   Two more waves of arrests followed in the winter of 1927 and the spring of 1928: Krasil'nikov (ed.) 2011, pp. 22–3. This is one of two volumes that reprinted a large amount of the party, government, and OGPU documents pertaining to the Shakhty Affair.

trust and jealousy. Historians have commonly thought that Stalin concocted the case while Tomsky, along with Rykov and Bukharin, opposed the move against the 'bourgeois specialists'.[279] But whether out of naiveté, trust in the OGPU, or a longstanding suspicion of the *spetsy*, Tomsky would prove to be anything but moderate during the Shakhty Affair. In his defence, Tomsky, along with other party leaders, was presumably unaware of the coercive methods the OGPU had begun to use to extract confessions.[280] Regardless, Tomsky's adamant belief in the validity of the charges proved key in the Politburo's treatment of the Shakhty Affair. Tomsky's attacks on the 'bourgeois specialists' would play right into Stalin's and Molotov's hands.

Another key figure in the case is Yefim Yevdokimov, the OGPU boss of the huge Northern Caucasus district, who initiated the investigation.[281] Yevdokimov, 'a strange man with an immovable stony face', could rely on a nucleus of loyal subordinates to wring confessions out of the arrested managers and engineers.[282] Two of these OGPU officers, Nikolai Gavrishenko and Venedikt Belenko, led the intense interrogations of the arrested managers and engineers. Although they did not resort to physical violence, their methods included the 'conveyer belt' (constant interrogations without allowing the accused much opportunity to sleep).[283] The OGPU interrogated Abram Bashkin, an engineer, almost daily for three months, sometimes day and night. The accusations followed along three tracks: their sabotaging and wrecking of production, intolerable treatment of workers, and anti-revolutionary activities before the revolution and during the Civil War. Although they succeeded in extracting detailed confessions from many of the arrested engineers and managers, the interrogations sometimes proved as taxing to the interrogators as those they interrogated.[284]

---

279 See, for example, Stone 2000, p. 65.
280 The formulaic nature of the confessions, and that over 90 percent of the accused confessed, should have raised Tomsky's suspicions: Cassiday 2000, pp. 115, 130.
281 Despite an indeterminate past, Yevdokimov had risen fast within the ranks of the political police. Often characterised as a common criminal before the revolution, Yevdokimov according to Kotkin had been an anarchist syndicalist: Kotkin 2014, p. 688.
282 Conquest 1985, p. 25.
283 Two of the arrested specialists told the writer Varlam Shalamov this when they were in the gulag together: Medvedev 1989, p. 259.
284 Gavrishenko, who became increasingly unbalanced during the uninterrupted interrogations, on 30 January 1928 killed himself during one of the interrogations by jumping out of an OGPU building's fourth-story window! Bashkin suffered such severe emotional problems as a result of the interrogations, the OGPU sent him temporarily to a clinic: Krasil'nikov, Savin, Ushakova 2011, pp. 25–7.

When Stalin and Molotov presented the OGPU's report to the Politburo on 2 March, many party members expressed scepticism about the charges, especially Rykov, but not Tomsky.[285] Yet Stalin or Molotov, somehow, indeed almost unbelievably, successfully pressured Rykov into being the Politburo member who would inform the public for the first time about the Shakhty Affair. Rykov grudgingly agreed, presumably because he was in a poor position to question the authenticity of the case because of his background in industry and longstanding support of the 'specialists'.[286] In his widely reprinted speech on 'The Counter-Revolutionary Conspiracy in the Shakhty Area of the Donets Basin', while warning against unwarranted 'specialist baiting', Rykov stated that according to their confessions, conspiring engineers sought to overthrow the Soviet regime and restore capitalism by such underhanded means as wasting resources, extracting coal from non-lucrative shafts, and purchasing unnecessary equipment from abroad. Despite failing to provide any specific examples, Rykov declared, 'If I did not know that these facts have been established beyond all doubt by documentary evidence, I would say they were malicious inventions brought forward to the detriment of the Soviet Union. But they are facts'![287]

Rykov's speech set off a flurry of activity. *Pravda* published under a banner headline a four-page unsigned editorial denouncing the engineers. *Pravda* also reported that Tomsky had instructed the VTsSPS to create a commission to investigate the case and the trade unions' involvement in it.[288] That same day, 55 engineers and managers were indicted.[289] The bill of indictment placed as much emphasis on the ideology of the engineers and their supposed communication with the former owners as any alleged counter-revolutionary actions.[290]

Rykov quickly reversed course and called the case into question a couple days later, on 12 March. He informed the Politburo that he had just received reports from the prosecutor general, who considered the OGPU's case against

---

285 Krasil'nikov, Savin, Ushakova 2011, p. 46. Rykov, as chair of the Sovnarkon, in an attempt to reconcile the intelligentsia with the Soviet state, in December 1924 provided a charter of rights to 'the specialist, the engineer, the man of science and technology': Carr 1958, pp. 134–5. Both Kuibyshev and Ordzhonikidze, the present and future heads of VSNKh, shared Rykov's concerns about the damaging economic consequences of the 'Shakhty Affair': Fitzpatrick 1978, p. 13; Tucker 1990, p. 77.
286 Reiman 1987, p. 60; Fitzpatrick 1992, p. 119.
287 *Inprecorr*, 22 March 1928, p. 376.
288 Bailes 1978, p. 79.
289 *Pravda*, 10 March 1928. In contrast, the VSNKh's newspaper, *Torgovo-promyshlennaia gazeta*, put the announcement on page two: Bailes 1978, p. 79.
290 *Inprecorr*, 17 May 1928, pp. 509–10.

the engineers suspicious. The documents presented to the government by the Ukrainian OGPU, Rykov argued, 'did not correspond at all to reality'.[291] Rykov, with the support of Menzhinsky, the head of the OGPU, raised enough serious doubts that the Politburo, the following day, decided to postpone until 5 April the upcoming Central Committee Plenum and to send Tomsky, Molotov, and Yaroslavsky to Donbass coal mining towns to investigate the situation on the ground.[292] For 10 days they were 'to acquaint themselves with the local situation, evaluate the work of trade-union, party, economic, and other organisations and make recommendations for practical measures'.[293] Molotov went to Stalino, Yaroslavsky to Artemovsk, while Tomsky went to Shakhty, the primary focal point of the investigation.[294]

Tomsky appears to have conducted a serious investigation, even though he was clearly biased against the *spetsy* and presumed those arrested were indeed guilty. Before he left he had sent a circular to all trade unionists stating that the overwhelming majority of the old specialists were beyond reproach, but there was a group who were guilty of systematic sabotage at the behest of the former, pre-revolutionary owners.[295] Tomsky also reported that workers and trade unionists in the Donbass resented the 'bourgeois specialists' since the managers and engineers received wages many times higher than skilled workers and also enjoyed various privileges, especially in housing. This had long been Tomsky's own view of the specialists, as we saw above. While Tomsky conceded that the non-party managers were pressured from above to cut costs, and lacked the necessary funds to improve conditions, workers had reason to blame them for the hardships within enterprises. As did the local trade unionists, who the specialists often attacked for trying to protect workers from their attempts to improve labour productivity. Workers, in addition, resented the arrogance and rudeness of the technical elites, who commonly referred to them in the first person 'you' (*ty*), with its connotations of subordination, and failed to fully implement collective agreements.[296] Workers commonly charac-

---

291 Rykov's message to Vyacheslav Menzhinsky, head of the OGPU, on 12 March 1928: translated and reprinted in Reiman 1987, p. 146.
292 On 15 March, the Politburo had formed a top-level investigatory team including Politburo members Tomsky and Molotov and Central Control Commission chair Yaroslavsky.
293 RGASPI, f. 17, op. 3, d. 677, l. 3, reproduced in Krasil'nikov (ed.) 2011, p. 650.
294 Kislitsyn 1993, pp. 48–9. Stalino, which was Iuzovka before the revolution, had briefly been named Trotsk before Trotsky fell out of favour. It is now Donetsk.
295 Alexander Dogadov, the VTsSPS secretary, co-signed the VTsSPS Presidium circular: RGASPI, f. 17, op. 3, d. 677, ll. 7–9, reproduced in Krasil'nikov (ed.) 2011, pp. 652–6.
296 In Russian only close friends and children should be addressed in the informal first person.

terised the role of engineers in production as 'parasitic'.[297] Workers frequently brutally attacked the specialists, including sometimes trying to kill them.[298] It is safe to assume that the 'bourgeois specialists' were extremely unpopular, with most trade unionists and workers welcoming the OGPU's attack on their 'class enemies'.[299]

Tomsky, who travelled around the Donbass, went to two mines in Shakhty and also went to a mine and factory in nearby Lugansk. At the Shakhty mines he went underground to assess conditions for himself, which he claimed the *spetsy* rarely if ever did. Tomsky arranged to talk to engineers and managers, but he distrusted them and felt they were trying to deceive him. He also met with groups of workers and personally examined their living conditions.[300] The Shakhty miners themselves appear to have focused their comments to Tomsky on how the engineers abused and mistreated workers rather than suggesting any instances of actual industrial sabotage.[301] Tomsky also met with OGPU officials.[302] Tomsky in addition spoke with some regional party administrators. These activities all suggest Tomsky tried to conduct a fairly serious investigation.

Rykov, who knew Molotov and Yaroslavsky would side with Stalin, pinned his hopes on Tomsky. But his hope proved misplaced. Unlike the other members of those soon to be denigrated as 'Right Deviationists', Tomsky's lack of sympathy for the *spetsy* proved unshakeable.[303] He unequivocally believed the OGPU reports, accepted the confessions of the accused, and supported the new campaign. Tomsky wrote, 'I consider it unquestionable that the information previously given by the OGPU has been fully confirmed'.[304] Furthermore, he continued, 'it is indisputably proven that there are direct ties between the engineers of the Donets Coal trust (*Donugol*) with Polish diplomats and the old French owners'.[305] Tomsky, who was outraged at the reports he received

---

297 Lampert 1979, pp. 128–9.
298 Kuromiya 1998, p. 142.
299 The attack against the technical specialists enjoyed almost unanimous worker support: Lenoe 2004, pp. 94–7. But it should also be noted that OGPU, party, and trade-union officials had long stoked such feelings: Kislitsyn 1993, pp. 27–8.
300 Vatlin et al. (eds) 2000a, p. 30; RGASPI, f. 17, op. 3, d. 677, ll. 19–20, reproduced in Krasil'nikov (ed.) 2011, p. 662.
301 This was the focus in the letters that Shakhty miners wrote to the prosecutor: Kuromiya 1997, p. 50.
302 RGASPI, f. 17, op. 3, d. 677, l. 50, reproduced in Krasil'nikov (ed.) 2011, p. 691.
303 Priestland 2007, p. 238. Trade unionists, and workers more generally, were predisposed to make scapegoats of the technical specialists.
304 Tomsky underlined 'fully confirmed': Krasil'nikov, Savin, Ushakova 2011, p. 50.
305 RGASPI, f. 17, op. 3, d. 677, ll. 19–20, reproduced in Krasil'nikov (ed.) 2011, p. 662.

about managers' treatment of the miners and appalled at the working and living conditions he observed, devoted most of his report to how to improve conditions in the Donbass.[306] Tomsky seemed surprised to learn that the wages there still had not reached pre-war war levels.[307] The only mention of actual acts of possible sabotage were in his report to the VTsSPS Presidium, where he stated that the engineers often failed to repair underground ventilation systems.[308] Good ventilation is a deadly serious issue since it is essential to avoid coalmine explosions. But even there, he attributed the high rate of accidents in the Donbass mines more to the old and worn-out condition of the equipment, and to the inexperience of so many miners given the high labour turnover rate there, than to any acts of 'sabotage' or 'wrecking' by the mining administrators.[309] Likewise, it is worth emphasising that at the forthcoming trial, the engineers' confessions and statements of mistreatment by workers were the only evidence presented. The prosecution introduced not a single incriminating document, including not even one intercepted letter with damning information.[310]

Tomsky, despite this lack of specificity and the inflated nature of the charges, made his conclusions perfectly clear in an exchange with Voroshilov shortly after he returned. At the 29 March meeting of the Politburo, Voroshilov, who grew up in the Donbass, worked up the nerve to ask Tomsky whether any wrecking actually occurred and whether they should 'plunge into open court' given the suspicions about the local officials, particularly those in the OGPU. 'Won't we get into shit if we hold an open trial in the case of the mining engineers? Perhaps the local authorities have exaggerated the affair, in particular the men of the OGPU'? Tomsky rejected this out of hand. He responded that there was nothing to fear, 'the picture is clear'. As noted above, Tomsky apparently did not think it was conceivable that the OGPU had extracted confessions using harsh methods.[311] Tomsky displayed little concern for the fate of the accused 'bour-

---

306 RGASPI, f. 17, op. 3, d. 677, ll. 50–5, reproduced in Krasil'nikov (ed.) 2011, pp. 690–700.
307 GARF, f. 42, d. 152, l. 46. For pre-revolutionary wages in the Donbass see Wynn 1992, pp. 44–6.
308 GARF, f. 42, d. 155, l. 32; RGASPI, f. 17, op. 3, d. 677, ll. 7–9, reproduced in Krasil'nikov (ed.) 2011, p. 653. The VTsSPS Presidium had created a commission to look into the Shakhty Affair that included besides Tomsky, Dogadov, Ginzburg, and Shvarts, who was the head of the Miners' Union.
309 GARF, f. 42, d. 152, l. 43.
310 Bailes 1978, p. 91.
311 RGASPI, f. 74, op. 2, d. 45, ll. 4, 6, reproduced in Kvashonkin et al. (eds), p. 28; Vatlin et al. (eds) 2000a, p. 30; Kun 2003, p. 284. Tomsky went on to tell Voroshilov, 'In my opinion [besides the non-party engineers] it would be good to lock up a half-dozen communists

geois specialists' and stated that he welcomed the opportunities for workers' upward mobility their removal would entail.[312] Even Stalin thought Tomsky had 'over-criticised' the 'specialists'.[313]

Tomsky was thus only too willing to believe the reports that the *spetsy* were hostile to the Soviet state and engaged in sabotage and treason against it. Although most historians consider the charges fabricated, Tomsky was hardly alone in his beliefs. Even Trotsky, despite his years of mistreatment at the hands of the OGPU, accepted the validity of the confessions and charges against the 'wreckers' (*vrediteli*). He could not imagine at this time the OGPU engaging in a frame-up.[314] The historian Hiroaki Kuromiya, citing a OGPU report, argued that while the 'evidence for wrecking was not strong ... "the sabotage" (accidents, flooding, waste of foreign currency, etc.) cited at the trial as a crime did in fact take place. Many observers found it difficult to know whether such incidents were due to carelessness and negligence or to malice'.[315] While many Western reporters based in the Soviet Union accepted the validity of the confessions, with reservations, others ridiculed the case.[316] What seems clear is that what was interpreted as wrecking generally was simply the sorts of subterfuges or manoeuvres Soviet managers, engineers, and bureaucrats had to use if they were to meet their production targets, such as hoarding stocks of scarce spare parts.[317]

The Shakhty Affair was, along with the 'extraordinary measures', the focus of the April 1928 Central Committee plenum. Rykov, who prepared his report on the Shakhty Affair on the basis of materials provided by the OGPU and the commission consisting of Molotov, Tomsky, and Yaroslavsky, stated that 10

[in the region] as well'. In her most recent book, Sheila Fitzpatrick wrongly states that Tomsky was the only Politburo member to view the charges with scepticism: Fitzpatrick 2015, p. 50.

312   Fitzpatrick 1978, pp. 12–13. There would be massive upward social mobility during the First Five-Year Plan along with the dramatic drop in wages and conditions for workers on the factory floor.

313   Quoted in Priestland 2007, p. 238.

314   Trotsky continued to believe such confessions were valid until 1936: Trotsky 1981, p. 88; Trotsky 1973b, p. 219; Glotzer 1989, pp. 241–2.

315   Kuromiya 1997, pp. 44–5.

316   For examples, the *United Press* correspondent who attended the trial found the charges 'generally convincing': Lyons 1937, p. 118. But in contrast, the *Associated Press*'s William Reswick found the charges 'a mixture of nonsense and flagrant lies': Reswick 1952, p. 246. Others, such as the *New York Post*'s Louis Fisher, 'did not know how much to believe. I believed part. I wondered about the remainder': Crossman (ed.) 1949, p. 189.

317   Stone 2000, pp. 73–4.

percent of the *spetsy* were 'wreckers'.[318] Rykov, nevertheless, stated that many party members questioned whether the affair had been 'artificially inflated' into criminal charges and called for exercising extreme caution toward all those specialists who work well but fail to express support for Soviet power.[319] He reminded the delegates that Lenin thought they had no alternative but to work with the 'bourgeois experts' for the foreseeable future. It was 'communist conceit', he argued, to think otherwise.[320] But about a dozen top officials, including Tomsky, gave speeches at the plenum on the grave problems resulting from 'wrecking'. Tomsky provided an overview to the Central Committee of the Shakhty Affair in his speech. While not questioning the guilt of the arrested engineers and managers, he did inject some words of caution. Tomsky argued the primary danger would be to panic since the problems with the 'bourgeois specialists' were generally manageable, even if some of them acted like 'English kings'.[321]

When Stalin weighed in at the April plenum, these were his first comments on the Shakhty Affair outside the Politburo. Taking the guilt of the accused for granted, Stalin began his speech by focusing on the need for 'self-criticism' [*samokritika*]. He argued that with the opposition defeated at the Fifteenth Party Congress, there was a danger of the party 'resting on its laurels, beginning to take things easy, and closing its eyes to the shortcomings in our work'.[322] In encouraging 'ordinary' workers and peasants to criticise 'Old Bolsheviks', Stalin argued it was 'utopian' to expect their criticism to be 100 percent correct. 'If their criticism is only 5–10 percent true, it should be welcomed and listened to attentively'.[323] Stalin would use this campaign of self-criticism to great effect against Tomsky. He ended his speech by criticising party and governmental organisations generally, including Tomsky's bailiwick, the trade unions. Stalin argued that the trade unions, which were technically responsible for overseeing the non-Bolshevik specialists, had been lax in their supervision and had been silent about all their violations of labour laws. According to Stalin, the lack of vigilance of various organisations, including the trade unions, 'could not have been worse'.[324] This was the beginning of the offensive against Tomsky.

---

318   Kislitsyn 1993, p. 52; Priestland 2007, p. 213.
319   Senin 1993, p. 172; Kislitsyn 1993, p. 52.
320   Vatlin et al. (eds) 2000a, p. 164; Fitzpatrick 1992, p. 156.
321   Vatlin et al. (eds) 2000a, p. 254.
322   Vatlin et al. (eds) 2000a, p. 232.
323   Vatlin et al. (eds) 2000a, p. 233.
324   Vatlin et al. (eds) 2000a, pp. 239–40.

Tomsky seems to have been caught completely unawares by how Stalin and his cohorts would use the Shakhty Affair as a weapon against his leadership of the trade unions. Andreev, now a member of Stalin's entourage, quickly piled on and accused the trade unions of not being sufficiently vigilant and working poorly with the various planning departments.[325] Molotov said the trade unions and the party had 'insufficient influence' over the *spetsy*.[326] Tomsky objected, rejecting the notion that the trade unions were solely responsible for these and other problems in the Donbass. He insisted that party organisations shared responsibility.[327] He also pointed his finger at the Donbass Coal Trust for failing to improve equipment.[328] But Tomsky recognised that Stalinists could use the attacks against the trade unions to tap into workers' anger that more had not been done to improve Donbass working-class conditions. He also conceded the trade unions should have done more to embolden workers to speak out against the 'bourgeois specialists'.[329]

While the Politburo decided to go ahead and hold a major trial to punish 'the evil saboteurs and wreckers', the April Central Committee Plenum adopted a compromise resolution that Tomsky played a role in crafting, which stated that the wrecking activity had been possible only because the Red Directors lacked the expertise necessary to manage their enterprises.[330] The resolution also denounced specialist baiting, stating 'it is essential to improve the working conditions of the vast majority of honest and devoted specialists', while calling for the gradual replacement of the older specialists with graduates of higher technical institutions.[331] The resolution though was also implicitly critical of Tomsky. It deemed the performance of trade unions in checking the specialists 'completely inadequate'.[332]

---

325 Vatlin et al. (eds) 2000a, p. 256.
326 Vatlin et al. (eds) 2000a, p. 219.
327 Tomsky conceded that the trade unions were guilty of not pushing harder for the education of Red specialists. He called for creating a Soviet intelligentsia from the Komsomol while noting that such former workers as himself, Voroshilov, and Uglanov, would have benefitted from receiving a higher education. Vatlin et al. (eds) 2000a, pp. 260, 263. It obviously continued to deeply rankle Tomsky that he had been deprived of such opportunities.
328 Vatlin et al. (eds) 2000a, p. 257.
329 Vatlin et al. (eds) 2000a, p. 262.
330 Stalin argued the specialists were effectively in charge even when there was a Red Director: Fitzpatrick 1992, p. 153.
331 Krasil'nikov, Savin, Ushakova 2011, p. 58; Harris 1999, p. 89. The other members of the resolution commission for the plenum were Yaroslavsky, Molotov, Kuibyshev, and Stanislav Kosior.
332 Vatlin et al. (eds) 2000a, pp. 326–7.

FIGURE 27 Delivery of interrogation protocols, the only 'evidence' produced in court during the Shakhty Trial
WIKIMEDIA COMMONS

The Shakhty trial was the first Stalinist show trial.[333] The kangaroo court was pure melodrama, with Tomsky and the Politburo signing off on the verdicts well ahead of time. The six-week trial, which was at least partly intended to bolster working-class support for the regime, was indeed quite a spectacle.[334] It was held not in a courtroom, but in the large, marbled Hall of Columns of the House of Trade Unions from 18 May to 6 July, which was decorated in red bunting with incendiary inscriptions.[335] The orchestrators of the Shakhty trial, which was a dress rehearsal for the future show trials that would also be held in the trade unions' building, sought to achieve maximum publicity,

---

333 The first major show trial was the 1922 trial of 34 Socialist Revolutionaries. In that trial, Krylenko, then an official in the Commissariat of Justice, drafted the indictment. Richard Pipes quotes him as stating, 'We must execute not only the guilty. Execution of the innocent will impress the masses even more': Pipes 1995, p. 224. Like the Shakhty trial it was held in the House of the Trade Unions.

334 Priestland 2007, p. 202.

335 Hingley 1970, p. 150. Tomsky replaced Molotov as head of the Politburo Commission on the Shakhty Affair the day before the trial opened, so Molotov could go on vacation: Krasil'nikov (ed.) 2011, p. 150.

with movie cameras and more than one hundred journalists, foreign diplomats, and high officials in attendance.[336] One journalist felt the trial had a carnival atmosphere, while another described it as more riveting than any theatrical performance, 'a marvelous human drama where lives are at stake'.[337] Unlike at the later Moscow show trials, many of the defendants refuted the charges and maintained their innocence.[338] But like in the later trials, the prosecution presented very little evidence of any actual wrongdoing by the defendants.[339] Nonetheless, the craven judge, the notorious Andrei Vyshinsky, sentenced 11 of the managers and engineers to death.[340] Stalin, who sometimes still played the role of the restraining moderate, had proposed that the death penalty not be imposed. But apparently Tomsky as well as Bukharin and a seriously ill Rykov voted for it.[341] Five of the convicted were eventually executed on 9 July but the death sentences of the six other defendants were reduced to life imprisonment.[342] But while all the publicity devoted to the case, including a propaganda

---

336 Foreign as well as Soviet newspapers ran front-page articles on the Shakhty Affair and then on the trial itself. Four thousand one-day attendees, mainly groups of factory workers, peasants, and school children, were ushered in past OGPU soldiers standing in attention with their fixed bayonets. They served, in the words of one historian, as 'an accusing chorus, mocking the pitiful attempts of some of the prisoners to defend themselves': Cassiday 2000, p. 123.
337 Lyons 1937, p. 114; Wood 2005, p. 193.
338 Those pleading not guilty and acquitted included all three Germans. Two of them, Ernst Otto and Max Maier, vigorously defended themselves. The Soviets had earlier released two of the Germans after the initial announcement that five German engineers had been arrested. Germany nonetheless terminated talks to renew the 1925 commercial treaty. Members of the Politburo during the trial began to have second thoughts about putting the Germans on trial: Rosenbaum 1962, pp. 240, 251.
339 One of the reporters remembered: 'We waited in vain for a genuine piece of impersonal and unimpeachable testimony – an intercepted letter perhaps, a statement or document that did not carry the suspicion of OGPU extortion. The far-reaching "international intrigue" never did emerge': Lyons 1937, p. 118.
340 Roy Medvedev suggests Vyshinsky was chosen to make the trial appear objective since he was a former Menshevik lawyer and the Rector of Moscow State University from 1925–31: Medvedev 1989, p. 258. Vyshinsky became especially notorious after he switched roles from judge to become the prosecutor in the Moscow show trials during the Great Purges.
341 Bukharin told Kamenev this in their conversation on 11 July 1928: *Sotsialisticheskii vestnik*, 22 March 1929, pp. 10–11; Reiman 1987, p. 65.
342 Bailes 1978, p. 94. After the trial, from 1928–31, it is estimated that the OGPU arrested between 2,000 and 7,000 engineers, perhaps as much as 20 percent of that workforce: Beissinger 1988, p. 95. Yevdokimov was rewarded with his fourth 'Order of the Red Banner' for uncovering the Shakhty Affair: Avtorkhanov 1959, p. 30; Kotkin 2017, p. 23. He would become a victim of the Great Purges in 1940.

film afterwards, served Stalin's political goals, the arrests and show trial had a terrible impact on industry, particularly on labour discipline, by undermining the authority of managers.

In this acrimonious context, party meetings and plenums became increasingly contentious and uncivil. Molotov embraced his role as Stalin's lieutenant in the attacks on those soon to be pejoratively labelled Right Deviationists. He fashioned himself increasingly as the Stalinists' foremost 'theoretician'.[343] With Stalin continuing to keep a more low-key profile, Molotov sharply attacked Rykov and Tomsky in Politburo discussions of economic plans. But it was Bukharin, whom Molotov had long disliked, who particularly attracted his venom. Tomsky found Molotov's nasty tone of voice in these attacks utterly appalling.[344] An atmosphere of distrust increasingly permeated the various party meetings.

The July, as well as the April 1928, plenums of the Central Committee and Central Control Commission focused on the 'extraordinary measures' as well as the Shakhty case. Prior to the April plenum, under pressure from the moderates, the leadership strongly condemned 'excesses' and called for the end of any compulsory measures.[345] Tomsky peppered Mikoyan, who delivered the report on the 'extraordinary measures' at the April plenum, with critical comments, but Bukharin and Rykov, as well as Stalin, remained silent.[346] Tomsky, in the hallways away from the floor of the plenum, reiterated his previous advocacy for higher grain prices as well as the necessity of making concessions to the middle peasants.[347] The plenum endorsed the criticism of the 'excesses' of local grain-seizing authorities, which reflected the mood of many of the provincial delegates, but in late April Stalin sought to revive the 'extraordinary measures', apparently with even greater intensity and scope than earlier in the year.[348] Bukharin, Tomsky, and Rykov, with the support of Uglanov, a candidate member of the Politburo, managed to convince the Politburo to cancel Stalin's attempt to resuscitate the 'extraordinary measures' and to increase

---

343 Vatlin et al. (eds) 2000a, p. 32; Carr and Davies 1971, p. 71.
344 Watson 2005, p. 81.
345 Tomsky condemned Kaganovich at the plenum for reintroducing the 'extraordinary measures' in a 'badly prepared form': Taniuchi 1995, p. 86.
346 Vatlin et al. (eds) 2000a, p. 57.
347 TsGAODM, f. 2870, op. 1, d. 296, reprinted in Karpachev and Minaeva (eds) 1992b, pp. 104–5. Tomsky later remembered making a speech calling for these changes from the floor at the April plenum, but such a speech does not appear in the stenographic report: Vatlin et al. (eds) 2000a.
348 Cohen 1973, pp. 282–3.

grain prices.[349] In addition to Kalinin and Voroshilov, Andreev, Ordzhonikidze, and Yagoda might have sided with them against Stalin.[350] The Central Committee followed up at its July 1928 plenum by again passing a resolution prohibiting any continued use of the 'extraordinary measures'. The resolution bluntly stated that the application of the 'extraordinary measures' had evolved into a political crisis that threatened the alliance [*smychka*] between the state and peasants and would not substantially alleviate grain shortages. The resolution called for a return to the previous, market-based methods of grain collection.[351] But Stalin's agreement to do so was a mere manoeuvre.[352] He explicitly stated that the government might have to resort again to the 'extraordinary measures' if circumstances made it necessary to do so.[353]

In conclusion, Tomsky had overseen a gradual, if uneven, improvement in workers' standard of living, with trade unions free to articulate the needs of workers against those of the industrial managers, within the framework of NEP and support for the party's efforts to improve the industrial economy. But in contrast to his moderate views on economic policy, Tomsky had made many intemperate statements and, at least in hindsight, serious missteps in the struggle against oppositionists during the 1920s. Most notably, his antagonism toward Trotsky and his policy proposals, coupled with Stalin's apparent moderation, threw him into siding with Stalin during the first half of the 1920s. Later in the decade there were rumours that Tomsky, along with Bukharin and Rykov, wanted to remove Stalin. But overall, Tomsky failed to appreciate the threat Stalin posed both to himself and the moderate policies he favoured. Tomsky had vehemently attacked Kamenev when the latter tried to warn the party. The Shakhty trial, along with the renewal of forced grain procurements, signalled Stalin was moving toward abandoning the class-conciliatory New Economic Policy. When Stalin and his cohorts began to target Tomsky and to work toward pushing him out of his power base in the trade unions, the harsh attacks Tomsky had made against oppositionists, particularly those in which he had excoriated their tactics, would make it extremely difficult for him and his moderate associates to mount effective opposition, as we will see in the following chapter. In his attacks on the United Opposition, after all, Tomsky had argued that the party was infallible and any opposition to the decisions of the majority of the Politburo was grounds for expulsion from the party.

349 Karpachev and Minaeva (eds) 1992b, p. 118; TsGAODM, f. 2870, op. 1, d. 296, reprinted in Karpachev and Minaeva (eds) 1992b, p. 105.
350 Langsam 1973, p. 251.
351 Taniuchi 1995, p. 79; Egorov and Bogoliubov (eds) 1983–84, vol. 4, pp. 348–53.
352 Nove 1992, p. 152.
353 Vatlin et al. (eds) 2000a, p. 362.

CHAPTER 6

NEP's Last Stand: The Eighth Trade-Union Congress

> It would good if we could have NEP without Nepmen, without kulaks, and without making concessions to anyone. This would be a wonderful NEP ... But it would no longer be NEP.
> MIKHAIL TOMSKY

∴

> It could be said that [the Stalinists' takeover of the trade-union leadership] was a violation of proletarian democracy, but comrades it has long been known that for us Bolsheviks, democracy is no fetish.
> LAZAR KAGANOVICH

∴

Forced collectivisation and breakneck industrialisation, with all their attendant hardships and suffering, as well as the brutal terror that followed, could have been prevented if the defenders of NEP within the party leadership had been able to block Joseph Stalin and his supporters' drive to power.[1] While historians have argued, from various perspectives, that the Stalinist outcome was all but inevitable, Stalin's victory over the so-called Rightists was far more contingent than that.[2] It was hardly a foregone conclusion to contemporary participants and observers. Many expected the more moderate members of the Politburo to prevail.[3] Leon Trotsky, for one, predicted they would soon 'hunt

---

1 Part of Chapter 6 has been previously published in 'NEP's Last Stand: Mikhail Tomsky and the Eighth Trade Union Congress', *Canadian-American Slavic Studies*, 53, 1–2: 149–75.
2 Stephen F. Cohen's biography of Bukharin remains the most important challenge to the dominant historiography: Cohen 1973. Sheila Fitzpatrick notes that Tomsky and his fellow Politburo moderates enjoyed 'weight in the leadership and visibility in the country': Fitzpatrick 2015, p. 53.
3 Stalin's insistence in early 1928 that coercive economic policies toward the peasantry be more than a stop-gap measure seemed to have led Mikhail Kalinin and Kliment Voroshilov to join with Nikolai Bukharin, Alexei Rykov, and Mikhail Tomsky to form an anti-Stalinist 'group of five' within the nine-man Politburo: *Sotsialisticheskii vestnik*, 21 February 1928, p. 15.

down Stalin'.[4] It was even widely rumoured, as we saw in the previous chapter, that Mikhail Tomsky might replace Stalin as general secretary.[5] While Nikolai Bukharin primarily articulated the defence of NEP, Tomsky in his dual roles as a member of the Politburo and as head of the huge trade-union bureaucracy, played a central part in the attempt to preserve NEP and prevent the predictably catastrophic First Five-Year Plan.

The friction between the Tomsky-led trade unions and advocates of a dramatic increase in the pace of industrialisation was a central feature of NEP-era politics. It has even been said that the dominant feature of 1928 was the existence of a dual regime – a labour regime at the trade-union headquarters in Moscow's House of Labour, on the one hand, and a party regime in the Kremlin on the other.[6] While this is certainly an overstatement, trade unionists did enjoy considerable autonomy and power in the latter half of the 1920s, contrary to the assumption in most of the historiography of the period.[7] In addition, trade unionists were well represented on every important state and party committee during the 1920s. As a result, they not only executed state policies, trade unionists also helped to formulate them.

Catherine Merridale argued that it was only in Moscow that the 'Right Opposition' in 1928, through its control of the party there, had 'a real organisational base'.[8] But that is not the case. The trade unions' huge administrative machine gave the 'Right Opposition' another, and indeed far more substantial organisational base. Contemporaries commonly thought that through the VTsSPS, which consisted of representative of the 23 national unions, the 'Rightists' could mobilise the seemingly formidable political power of the nearly 100,000 trade-union administrators, strategically located in all industrial centres, to obstruct Stalin's abandonment of NEP. The trade unions were also an influential interest group since they possessed an impressive media network. It included a large number of daily, weekly, and monthly publications, with a combined circulation of two million, as well as a national radio service.

Tomsky, in addition, enjoyed enormous personal popularity, particularly among the upper echelon of the trade unions, a self-perceived 'party within the party' and the party's most homogeneous element.[9] These top trade unionists – Grigory Melnichansky, Alexander Dogadov, Yakov Yaglom, Vasily Mikhailov,

---

4 Quoted in Deutscher 1959, p. 428.
5 Reiman 1987, p. 28; RGASPI, f. 17, op. 2, d. 35, ll. 3–8.
6 Avtorkhanov 1959, p. 98.
7 A notable exception is Kuromiya 1988, p. 45.
8 Merridale 1990, p. 47.
9 Cohen 1973, p. 229.

Boris Kozelev, Fedor Ugarov, Ivan Lepse, and Vasily Shmidt, the Commissar of Labour – were 'comrades' who Tomsky justifiably noted 'had become accustomed in the course of years to see in me their leader'.[10] Nikolai Uglanov, the Moscow party boss and formerly a leading trade unionist, reportedly said Tomsky had earned the right to head the trade unions for as long as he lived.[11] The top trade unionists, who were thought to be '150 percent NEPists', counted on Tomsky using his position on the Politburo to fight for the trade unions' interests.[12] Other trade unionists besides Tomsky had political power, with eight trade unionists among the 71 members of the Central Committee elected at the Fifteenth Party Congress. The trade unionists saw themselves, according to the historian Stephen Cohen, as a 'party within the party'.[13] Reflecting the trade unions relative moderation, they continued to be a politically pluralistic institution. In April 1928, 27.8 percent of senior officials in the VTsSPS and 20.7 percent of the members of union central committees had been members of non-Bolshevik parties before 1917.[14]

In mid-1928, when Stalin was gaining the advantage over those soon to be labelled Right Deviationists, he considered the trade unions the major obstacle to his plans to abandon NEP and push forward with forced collectivisation and breakneck industrialisation.[15] The final showdown between the Stalinists and trade-union leadership occurred at the Eighth Trade-Union Congress, which met 10–24 December 1928. The broad outline of Tomsky's defeat at the congress and in the power struggle has long been known, but this episode remains largely unexplored. Examining how Stalin outmanoeuvred Tomsky during 1928, and whether the trade unionists went down without a fight at the congress, is the primary focus of this chapter.

One might question why Tomsky, a former worker and the leader of the trade unions, would oppose a programme calling for more rapid industrialisation since it would dramatically increase the size of the labour force and therefore increase trade-union membership. Tomsky was not an opponent of rapid industrialisation per se, especially if it would eliminate unemployment, but as a long-time advocate for moderate, pragmatic domestic policies, Tomsky accurately feared that calls for breakneck industrialisation would inevitably

---

10   Quoted in Cohen 1973, p. 229.
11   Gaisinskii 1932, p. 209.
12   Pyatakov, quoted in Langsam 1973, p. 248.
13   Cohen 1973, p. 229.
14   Jo 2007, pp. 94–5.
15   Stalin, with his superior political skills, successfully labelled Bukharin, Rykov, and Tomsky deviationists even though they were defending the party orthodoxy that NEP was to be implemented 'seriously and for a long time', in Lenin's words: Merridale 1990, pp. 48–9.

de-emphasise consumer goods production, while also entailing longer working hours, lower wages, and a greater reliance on coercion to improve labour discipline.[16] And in terms of institutional interests, he justifiably feared it would further increase the powers of the economic administrations over the trade unions.

The VTsSPS refused to sanction any further sacrifices from the trade union's eleven million members, such as making the collective agreements less advantageous, increasing the rights of management, or waging an administrative struggle for increased 'labour discipline'. It proudly noted that wages and working conditions had been slowly improving under NEP. Stalin, while holding his cards very close to his chest, seemed to agree. In April he stated, 'it would be foolish to speak of ... suppressing NEP, of a return to food requisitioning, etc. Only enemies of Soviet power could think of this'.[17] But, in fact, peasant withholding of grain in response to the war scare, and Stalin's implementation of 'extraordinary measures' to requisition it, had led to long lines for bread and shortages in other foodstuffs in Moscow and other major cities, which a concerned Tomsky noted led to increased absenteeism and workers either arriving late to work or leaving early.[18] It also led to a spike in food prices, especially by private traders, and as a result a slight decrease in the purchasing power of workers' wages.[19] This decline in workers' standard of living was not due to a decrease in wage growth. Wages continued to rise but as noted above, Tomsky's priority at the end of the 1920s was to narrow the gap between the wages of skilled and unskilled workers, which he achieved.

Stalin, who had been a personal friend of Tomsky and his whole family, very methodically began to lay the groundwork for the attack on Tomsky by exploiting the tensions between the Komsomol and VTsSPS. For years the leadership of the trade unions and the Komsomol had bitterly criticised each other over issues regarding juvenile labour.[20] Stalin unmistakably, if indirectly, encouraged the Komsomol leadership to start attacking Tomsky in his closing address at the Komsomol's Eighth Congress in May 1928. To laughter and applause, he

---

16   During the first three years of the First Five-Year Plan, the average real wages of Soviet workers would in fact decline about 40 percent in the total economy and 50 percent in industry: Schwarz 1951, p. 139; Filtzer 1986, p. 91.
17   Souvarine 1939, p. 480.
18   Siegelbaum 1992, p. 204; Carr and Davies 1969b, p. 701.
19   The real wages of Moscow workers, because of the rise in the price of agricultural goods, decreased by 1.3 percent from the first half of 1927/28 to the first half of 1928/29: Kuromiya 1988, p. 81. The private traders charged double or triple the prices of state stores. The government in response introduced rationing in early 1929: Chase 1987, p. 180.
20   Carr and Davies 1971, p. 552.

said 'We sometimes have to trample on the toes of some of our comrades who have past services to their credit, but who are now suffering from the disease of bureaucracy ... For their past services we should take off our hats to them, but for their present mistakes and bureaucracy it would be quite in order to give them a good drubbing'.[21] A week later, while stating that 'the strength of our revolution lies in the fact that there is no division between our old and new generations of revolutionaries', Stalin hailed *Komsomolskaia Pravda* as 'a warning bell' for its attacks on 'the bureaucratism of our institutions'.[22]

Stalin orchestrated the assault on the union leadership that began appearing in the Komsomol's newspaper, *Komsomolskaia Pravda*, which spearheaded the attacks on Tomsky. On the surface, the attacks appeared to be largely spontaneous, reflecting the discontents of the Komsomol's young rank-and-file workers. The demoralisation and pessimism common among young communists during the 1920s, coupled with the new emphasis on militancy in the Komsomol campaigns of 1928, certainly played a role. But Stalin just as certainly fanned the conflict between the Komsomol and the trade-union leadership.[23] He had his protégé, Georgy Malenkov, secretly provide the editors of *Komsomolskaia Pravda* with materials attacking Tomsky and other 'Rightists' in the VTsSPS.[24]

Stalin's 'surprise assault' initially caught Tomsky off guard. Tomsky's close assistant, Boris Kozelev, noted in his diary that they recognised Stalin was secretly egging on 'the boys' in the Komsomol to discredit Tomsky.[25] An outraged Tomsky telephoned Stanislav Kosior, the Polish-born former worker, who was the Ukrainian general secretary and presumably someone Tomsky thought had sway over the Komsomol leadership, to demand an explanation.[26] When none was given, and the attacks continued on the union's 'bureaucratism', insufficient 'self-criticism,' and inadequate attention to the needs of youth, Tomsky fought back.[27] The trade unions denounced the Komsomol's criticisms as

---

21 VLKSM 1928, p. 538.
22 *Komsolskaia Pravda*, 27 May 1928.
23 Sheila Fitzpatrick convincingly argues: 'Stalin, it is true encouraged the Komsomol attacks on bureaucracy in 1928, probably because the campaign against the "bureaucratic" trade-union leadership, in particular, was serving a useful purpose from his point of view. But it would be considerable oversimplification to see the Komsomol simply as a Stalinist tool in its cultural revolution campaign against the bureaucracy': Fitzpatrick 1978, p. 25.
24 Pavlov 2001, p. 99. I am grateful to Gleb Albert for directing me to this source.
25 Kozelev 1996, p. 62.
26 Vatlin et al. (eds), 2000d, pp. 55–6; Kozelev 1996, p. 164. Kosior's political rise derived from his close association with Stalin since 1919.
27 Tomsky's associate Kozelev thought the self-criticism campaign served Stalin like Jewish

'scandalous rubbish' and criticised other members of the party leadership for their failure to intervene in this 'fratricidal war in the press'.[28] On 10 June, at the graduation ceremony at the trade-union college named after him, Tomsky proudly highlighted the trade unions' achievements while perfunctorily acknowledging trade-union 'deficiencies'. He stated, 'the task of the period of self-criticism lay in honestly revealing and bringing all our deficiencies to the attention of the proletarian public, but I suppose, not only deficiencies. To fall silent about our achievements would be the greatest and deepest mistake'.[29]

Tomsky's pushback succeeded. The Politburo and Sovnarkom came down on the side of the trade unions against the Komsomol, throwing Stalin on the defensive.[30] He quickly retreated and reversed course. On 26 June, Stalin accused *Komsomolskaia Pravda* of criticising '*for criticism's sake*', turning criticism into a '*sport*', into '*sensation mongering*'. Stalin characterised as 'impermissible caricatures' *Komsomolskaia Pravda*'s attacks on Tomsky and his lieutenants Alexander Dogadov and Grigory Melnichansky.[31] But such statements were completely disingenuous. At roughly the same time, Stalin invited *Komsomolskaya Pravda*'s editorial board to the Kremlin, where he told them over cups of tea to disregard the reprimand. 'It was a mere formality', he told them.[32]

Tomsky also came into serious conflict with Valerian Kuibyshev, the Stalinist head of VSNKh, during the second half of 1928 as the already tense relations between the industrial managers and the trade unionists escalated further.[33] The educated Kuibyshev, whose father like Lenin's had earned noble status, played a prominent role drafting the First Five-Year Plan and increasingly served as a zealous spokesman for the very high growth rates the Stalinists

---

pogroms did for the tsarist system: Kozelev 1996, p. 162. The Central Committee, in an attempt to manipulate worker grievances, launched the self-criticism campaign in June 1928 with an attack on the Smolensk party leadership, which was accused of being infested with 'corruption, drunkenness, and sexual degeneration': Graziosi 2000, p. 185; Murphy 2005, p. 90. The campaign was abandoned in the winter of 1929–30 following the defeat of the 'Right Opposition': Lenoe 2004, p. 211.

28 NIPTS, f. 2, op. 1, d. 76, l. 11.
29 *Trud*, 26 June 1928.
30 Vatlin et al. (eds), 2000d, p. 56.
31 Stalin 1952–67, vol. 11, p. 142 (italics in the original).
32 Pavlov 2001, pp. 99–100.
33 Kuibyshev became head of VSNKh following the February 1926 death of Felix Dzerzhinsky, who had headed VSNKh since February 1924. Perhaps surprisingly, Dzerzhinsky, the ruthless head of the Cheka, as head of VSNKh was a strong supporter of NEP, in particular he called for seriously maintaining the *smychka*, and according to Stephen Cohen became the 'angriest and most effective voice in the debates with industrialisers of the Left': Cohen, 1973, p. 233; Davies 1960, pp. 381–8.

began advocating.³⁴ In fact, there is reason to believe that it was Kuibyshev who convinced Stalin to push for a faster tempo of industrialisation than he had previously considered.³⁵ In the proposed plan Kuibyshev reduced the role of trade unions over the objections of Tomsky, who insisted that the unions should continue to be the champions of workers' interests in their dealings with economic administrators and industrial managers. In addition, the union leadership condemned VSNKh for envisioning for 1928/29 a 19.2 percent growth in industrial output, while envisioning only a 4.7 percent increase in the number of workers.³⁶ When it became clear the Stalinists had no intention of compromising, the union leadership, in the words of Hiroaki Kuromiya, 'entered into a state of war' with VSNKh.³⁷

While still trying to maintain a façade of unity, the debate became cantankerous and relationships within the party leadership turned increasingly bitter, with many members no longer on speaking terms.³⁸ At the 4–12 July 1928 Central Committee Plenum, as well as at the Politburo meeting that preceded it, Bukharin, Rykov, and Tomsky repeatedly clashed with Stalin and Molotov. Tomsky in his long speech strongly objected to Stalin's notion that industrialisation would be based on a 'tribute' [*dan'*] from the peasantry and workers.³⁹ He argued that preserving the *smychka* [alliance] between workers and middle and poor peasants was the major historical task confronting the party, which could be achieved by raising some prices and lowering others as the party had done in the 'scissors crisis' in 1923.⁴⁰ Making an analogy with the situation in 1921, Tomsky insisted the party leadership needed not to panic, but to remain true to NEP, to 'the Leninist formula', and disavow the forced grain requisitions of the 'extraordinary measures', which were rupturing relations with middle peasants. With the Stalinists publicly claiming they were sticking to NEP, Tomsky's biting attack on Molotov near the end of his speech would become widely

---

34 Daniels 1960, p. 338.
35 Azrael 1966, p. 89.
36 Jo 2007, p. 38.
37 Kuromiya 1988, p. 43.
38 Tomsky shared with his top lieutenants how bad relations had become in the Politburo: NIPTS, f. 2, op. 1, d. 76, l. 12.
39 Stalin argued at the plenum that a tribute or a super tax was necessary, if only temporarily, to continue industrial development and criticised Tomsky's failure to appreciate that: Vatlin et al. (eds) 2000b, pp. 354, 513.
40 According to Roy Medvedev, grain prices in 1927 were so low that they were lower than the cost of production: Medvedev 1989, p. 203. Appeasing the peasantry, in addition to raising grain prices, primarily entailed lowering the price on textiles, which were the main peasant consumer good. Stalin, in the plenum, asked Tomsky where he thought the money would come from to raise grain prices: Vatlin et al. (eds) 2000b, pp. 419–22, 519.

known: 'It would good if we could have NEP without Nepmen, without kulaks, and without making concessions to anyone. This would be a wonderful NEP'. After the laughter subsided, he added that this however 'would no longer be NEP'.[41]

Tomsky and his fellow moderates once again appeared to carry the day. The July Central Committee Plenum's resolution on agricultural policy acknowledged the discontent within the peasantry created by the Stalinists' coercive 1927–28 'extraordinary measures' to increase grain procurements. The plenum voted unanimously to repeal the 'extraordinary measures'.[42] The resolution called for an increase in wholesale grain prices and the 'immediate elimination' of illegal searches for grain. The plenum also repudiated any notion of repealing NEP.[43] Outside observers, such as the British foreign ministry, concluded that the Soviet leadership had repudiated the left and was returning to 'normal conditions'.[44]

But the moderates knew their apparent victory was illusory. Even while the July plenum was still going on, an emotionally distraught Bukharin was so alarmed he decided, with Tomsky's approval, to see if it might be possible to find allies among the 'Left Oppositionists' by secretly meeting with the recently expelled Lev Kamenev in Kamenev's apartment.[45] He told Kamenev that Tomsky and Rykov agreed it would be much better if you and Zinoviev were in the Politburo instead of Stalin, who they hoped to oust as general secretary. 'The differences between us and Stalin are many times more serious than all our former differences with you'. Bukharin shared his fear that Stalin, the 'unprincipled intriguer has made concessions now, so that [later] he can cut our throats … Stalin knows only one method … to plant a knife in your back'. Comparing Stalin to Genghis Khan, Bukharin said his policies would lead to civil war, to terror and bloodshed. But Kamenev rejected Bukharin's appeal and nothing came of the meeting.[46]

---

41 Vatlin et al. (eds) 2000b, p. 426.
42 Stalin in his speech at the plenum did call for doing away completely with the 'extraordinary measures' but he again suggested if conditions changed, they might be necessary again. He primarily argued that the way forward was through collective farming: Vatlin et al. (eds) 2000b, pp. 362, 365.
43 Egorov and Bogoliubova (eds) 1983–84, vol. 4, pp. 348–55. Donny Gluckstein states that Bukharin had either personally drafted the resolutions or they were based on his memoranda: Gluckstein 1994, p. 236.
44 British Foreign Office 1928, vol. 13,311, p. 13.
45 Grigorii Sokolnikov, who in 1926 was removed from the Politburo and demoted from Finance Commissar to deputy chair of Gosplan, also attended this meeting with Kamenev. Stalin had permitted Kamenev and Zinoviev to return from Siberian exile in June 1928.
46 Trotsky 1981, pp. 83, 379; Fel'shtinskii 1993, pp. 30–7. Bukharin met with Kamenev on a

Tomsky's fears were reinforced the day the plenum closed. In what struck some observers as a crude attack, Stalin especially criticised Tomsky for thinking we have no policy options but to make concessions to the peasantry. Stalin stated all Tomsky had to offer was 'concessions today, concessions tomorrow, and concessions the day after tomorrow. This is a defeatist attitude'.[47] Stalin commonly referred to Tomsky's views as 'the theory of permanent concessions' or 'the theory of continuous concessions' in meetings afterwards.[48] He labelled Tomsky a defeatist, whose attitude 'would not strengthen Soviet power'.[49] One of the delegates described Stalin during this attack on Tomsky as 'swarthy, sour, vindictive, wrathful. A forbidding sight ... The rudeness of it was astonishing'.[50] In addition, two of the nine members of the Politburo on whom Bukharin, Rykov, and Tomsky thought they could count – Voroshilov and Kalinin – at the last minute reversed themselves and unexpectedly lined up on Stalin's side.[51] Kalinin's reasons in particular struck observers as completely lacking in conviction.[52] Bukharin sadly deduced that 'Stalin had some special hold on them'.[53] Rudzutak also ended up siding with Stalin perhaps for the same reason.[54] If they had stuck with Bukharin, Rykov, and Tomsky, Stalin would have been in the minority and they could have moved toward removing him as general secretary and perhaps replacing him with Tomsky.[55] They could have definitely blocked forced collectivisation.

---

   number of further occasions, as did Tomsky: RGASPI, f. 17, op. 2, d. 575, reprinted and translated in Getty and Naumov 1999, p. 319; Cohen 1973, pp. 290–1; Khlevniuk 2015, p. 107.
47   Vatlin et al. (eds) 2000b, p. 516.
48   Vatlin et al. (eds), 2000d, p. 57.
49   Vatlin et al. (eds) 2000b, p. 647.
50   Fel'shtinskii 1993, pp. 36–7; Trotsky 1981, p. 385; Lewin 1968, p. 306. The delegate was Sokolnikov.
51   Tucker 1973, p. 417; Souvarine 1939, p. 480. Trotsky quotes Kalinin as earlier expressing serious doubts about Stalin's leadership, 'That horse will some day drag our wagon into a ditch'.
52   Lewin 1968, p. 361.
53   Cohen 1973, p. 289.
54   Like Bukharin, Trotsky concluded that 'Stalin managed to keep Kalinin and Voroshilov loyal to himself only by the threat of exposing them': Trotsky 1941, p. 388. Recent archival revelations confirm the Stalinists had access to pre-revolutionary police records that could have been used to blackmail Politburo members in 1928. According to the records, both Kalinin and Rudzutak had provided the tsarist police with detailed information about members of their underground organisations: Khlevniuk 2009, p. 7. It has also been suggested that Stalin used Kalinin's fondness for ballerinas to blackmail him: Service 2004, p. 260.
55   Cohen 1973, p. 287. *Sotsialisticheskii vestnik* reported that it had learned from a member of the Bolshevik 'old guard' that a coup against Stalin was in the offing: 23 July 1928, p. 15.

With their failure to elicit Kamenev's support, Tomsky desperately sought to find other allies. He met, for example, with Grigory Pyatakov, an eminent Trotskyist who had very recently 'capitulated'.[56] Stalin became seriously concerned that Tomsky might be able to win to the moderates' side one or more of his supporters and protégés. In August Stalin wrote to Molotov that 'apparently Tomsky tried to "corrupt" [Andreev] ... but he wasn't able to "lure Andreev". And under no circumstances should Tomsky (or anyone else) be allowed to "turn" Kuibyshev or Mikoyan'.[57]

The political and personal animosity between Tomsky and Stalin grew increasingly bitter. During the fight over whether to abandon NEP, Stalin came to loathe Tomsky more than the other so-called Right Deviationists.[58] He denounced Tomsky, projecting his own character onto his opponent, as 'a malicious fellow not always clean in his methods'.[59] Tomsky angrily protested that a radical departure from NEP would exploit workers and peasants and warned Stalin they would resist the inevitable deterioration in their standard of living.[60] Though he was normally rather calm, when heated Tomsky was prone to 'hysterics', his face becoming 'full of fire'.[61] And when drunken, he lacked tact, to say the least. At a family barbecue in Sochi in 1928, while Stalin was grilling *shashlik*, a very drunk Tomsky shockingly whispered into Stalin's ear, 'soon our workers will start shooting at you, they will'.[62] Tomsky may have made a similar threat in 1929.[63]

---

56   Lewin 1968, p. 298.
57   RGASPI, f. 82, op. 2, d. 1420, ll. 200, 220.
58   Ulam 1973, p. 416.
59   Stalin 1952–67, vol. 11, p. 229.
60   *Sotsialisticheskii vestnik*, 28 October 1928, p. 12; 25 February 1929, p. 12.
61   Kitaeff 1954, p. 12; Lee 1928, p. 128.
62   Related by Bukharin to Kamenev during their clandestine meeting on 11 July 1928: Fel'shtinskii 1993, p. 36; Trotsky 1981, p. 385. Bukharin told a somewhat similar account of the incident at the 7 December 1936 Central Committee plenum, when he said 'an absolutely insane' Tomsky threatened Stalin. Bukharin stated that he believed Stalin at the time thought it was nothing more than 'a drunken prank': Gorelov and Shapovalova (eds) 2001, p. 173. Kaganovich also brought it up at this plenum: RGASPI, f. 17, op. 2, d. 574, l. 98. Similarly, according to Leonid Naumov, a drunken Tomsky 'farsightedly' promised to shoot Stalin in 1928: Naumov 2010, p. 38. Tomsky's son remembered a more convivial gathering that summer, where after Stalin grilled with Tomsky's wife Maria at Rykov's place in Sochi, everyone sang revolutionary songs and went for a walk along the sea: Gorelov and Shapovalova (eds) 2001, p. 173. It was common for top party officials to socialise and drink vodka together.
63   There is at least one account in which Tomsky threatened to shoot Stalin himself. Pavel Sapozhnikov, in a 1 October 1936 note, stated that the 'peaceful' Tomsky threatened Stalin with bullets in 1929: APRF, f. 3, op. 24, d. 245, l. 158, cited in 'Fragmenty' 1995, p. 22n13.

Tomsky's dacha in Bolshevo, some twenty miles northeast of Moscow, served as a favourite meeting place for the 'Right Oppositionists' to get together to discuss the various tactical issues they were considering and vent about the 'slanderous inventions' that Stalin and his supporters within the Central Committee were hurling at them. Usually these gatherings took place on Sundays. Rykov, Bukharin, Uglanov, Vasily Shmidt, Aleksandr Smirnov (Foma), V.I. Polonsky, Konstantin Ukhanov, Fedor Ugarov, Nikolai Antipov, and Vasily Kotov were regular attendees during 1928.[64] Rykov was prone to talk about the necessity of removing Stalin from his post as general secretary while Tomsky shared with them his suspicion that the Stalinists wanted to undercut him by placing a 'commissar from the Politburo' on the VTsSPS.[65] Tomsky also visited with Yagoda, the head of the OGPU, who at the time had 'rightist' sympathies, as well as with the writer Maksim Gorky.[66]

This was all clearly taking a physical toll on Tomsky, although he could rouse himself to emphatically make a point. At the end of June, Tomsky spent two weeks abroad seeking medical treatment.[67] Ann McCormick, a roving correspondent for the *New York Times*, interviewed Tomsky in his office around this time. She remarked that he 'was so tired that his face was as pasty and gray as the faded tunic he wore'. She also noted that, 'Tomsky looked years older than his forty-seven years'. She thought Tomsky looked like 'a weary old woman'. But as the interview proceeded, she noted his 'tired blue eyes kindled. Once, when he jumped to emphasise and argument, he was suddenly transformed into the fiery agitator'. She thought 'Everything in Tomsky was exhausted, save his ardor for the cause'.[68]

In one of the few instances in which the 'Right' went public with their views, Bukharin caused a sensation when he published in *Pravda* on 30 September, without the approval of the Central Committee, a long article entitled 'Notes of an Economist'.[69] Under the guise of an attack on Trotsky, Bukharin criticised Stalin and Kuibyshev for their 'adventurism' in calling for what he labelled an unrealistically rapid, hyper-centralised industrialisation.[70] What was needed

---

       Bukharin, however, stated to the December 1936 Central Committee Plenum, that he never heard Tomsky threaten Stalin again: Gorelov and Shapovalova (eds) 2001, p. 173.
64   Khaustov and Samuel'son 2010, p. 368.
65   TsA FSB, R27744, d. 3257, tom 1, l. 81.
66   Bykovtseva and Iokar (eds) 1996, pp. 216, 224–5.
67   RGASPI, f. 593, op. 1, d. 6, l. 148.
68   McCormick 1929, pp. 106–7.
69   Carr and Davies labelled it the Right's manifesto: Carr and Davies 1971, p. 75.
70   Wolfe 1957, pp. 295–315; Carr and Davies 1969a, p. 318. Kuibyshev, with Stalin's encourage-

FIGURE 28   Tomsky and Tomskaya socialising with Gorky and Yagoda in May 1928. From left to right in front row: Koltsov, Yagoda, Ugarov, Gorky, Tomsky, and Tomskaya
WIKIMEDIA COMMONS

was both the correct balance between agriculture and industry: 'our industrialisation must not impoverish the village' and we need to have a realistic budget. We cannot build factories today out of 'future bricks'.[71] It was a desperate effort to take the fight outside the confines of the party apparatus, in the words of one of Tomsky's closest associates.[72] Tomsky thought Bukharin should have written what the Stalinists characterised as the 'Platform of the Right Deviationists' in a more popular, less esoteric style.[73] In any case, within the week, the Politburo meeting erupted into acrimonious exchanges. An emotional Bukharin denounced Stalin as 'a petty Oriental despot'.[74] But the Politburo majority, over Bukharin's, Rykov's, and Tomsky's objections, supported Stalin in condemning

ment, had called for a radical acceleration of investment in heavy industry a couple weeks earlier: Cohen 1973, p. 295.
71   Wolfe 1957, pp. 307, 309–11.
72   Kozelev 1996, p. 166.
73   Vatlin et al. (eds) 2000d, pp. 58–9.
74   Volkogonov 1991, p. 181.

the 'unauthorised' publication of the 'Notes'.[75] And around the same time, the Stalinist press began to attack Tomsky and the trade-union leadership for obstructing industrial productivity.

Tomsky and those in the party leadership who shared his views, to their great disadvantage, essentially confined their opposition to the Stalinists to within the party elite. Tomsky later stated they consciously refused to take their disagreements over Stalinist policies 'out into the streets'.[76] Fearing this might lead to splitting the party or worse, they never seriously considered appealing to the non-party masses. Rykov confided to an American journalist, 'we could have forced a showdown and won. But there was always the haunting fear of an intra-party fight turning into a civil war'.[77] The crushing defeat of the United Opposition's demonstrations in November 1927, and their own roles in denouncing those demonstrations, also no doubt forestalled any consideration of open opposition to try to rally party members to their side. Afraid of being accused of undermining party unity, those soon to be labelled 'Rightists' limited the expression of their profound concerns, in Tomsky's words, to 'within the walls of the Central Committee', rather than taking them to the party at large.[78] Tomsky was a moderate Bolshevik, who opposed Stalin's increasingly radical proclivities, but he was also a loyal Bolshevik who believed in party discipline. He never for a second imagined advocating for some sort of multi-party democracy.

By October the Stalin group clearly had the upper hand. Stalin, without uttering their names, delivered a long speech on 19 October to the plenum of the Moscow Party Committee and Moscow Control Commission on the 'Right Danger' in the party, arguing that it favoured policies that would lead to the 'restoration of capitalism'.[79] The Stalinists proceeded at this meeting to successfully undermine Moscow's first party secretary, and Tomsky's close friend, Uglanov, who had come out strongly against the Stalinists' peasant policy and against Kuibyshev's plans to rapidly increase the tempo of industrialisation.[80]

---

75   Cohen 1973, p. 296.
76   Vatlin et al. (eds) 2000d, p. 84.
77   Reswick 1952, p. 254. Similarly, see *Sotsialisticheskii Vestnik*, 25 February 1930, p. 12.
78   Vatlin et al. (eds) 2000d, p. 84.
79   Stalin did make a thinly veiled reference to Tomsky when he mentioned how Lenin had sent a Central Committee member to Turkestan: Stalin 1952–67, vol. 11, p. 247.
80   Uglanov, who came from a poor peasant background and like Tomsky began working in St. Petersburg at the tender age of 12, denounced the 'extraordinary measures' at the July 1928 Central Committee plenum: Merridale 1988, pp. 29, 72–3. Uglanov's views on industrialisation were diametrically opposite those of Kuibyshev: Shimotomai 1983, p. 19. Stalin considered Uglanov to be 'to the right of Bukharin': Colton 1995, p. 205.

He was deposed and replaced by Molotov.[81] Since Uglanov was a tough and determined adversary, as well as a candidate member of the Politburo and a full member of the Orgburo and Secretariat, the Stalinists' easy defeat of the Moscow party organisation devastated Tomsky.[82] At the same time, the Stalinists deposed Shmidt, who had occupied the post of People's Commissar of Labour for 10 years and was also a long-time Tomsky supporter.[83] By the late fall, Tomsky had to wonder if the moderates had any chance of holding on to their last significant bastion, the trade-union bureaucracy, which was regarded by the Stalinists as the 'fortress of the Right'.[84] *Sotsialisticheskii vestnik* reported that Stalin and his henchmen were scheming in every possible way against Tomsky.[85] Without naming Tomsky, Bukharin, or Rykov, virtually every one of Stalin's major speeches at the time spoke about the 'Right Danger' or 'Right Deviation' in the party or foreign communist parties.[86] Even so, Tomsky's support remained strong among the various union leaders in Moscow and in the provinces. Although all of Stalin's innuendos associating him with the anonymous 'Right deviation' had begun to rack the lower echelons of the trade unions, at the VTsSPS's regular plenary session, held on 25–29 October, the union leaders did their best to disregard all the Stalinist criticisms swirling around Tomsky.[87] The plenum chose instead to adopt a resolution to honour Tomsky for his 10 years of service as VTsSPS chair.[88]

With the Stalinist noose tightening, and their options narrowing, Bukharin, Rykov, and Tomsky debated among themselves how best to respond. Just days before the mid-November opening of the Central Committee Plenum, all three of them, on Tomsky's recommendation, took the extreme step of jointly writing a declaration that requested that they be relieved of their positions of responsibility: Tomsky from the trade unions, Rykov from Sovnarkom, and Bukharin from the Comintern. Tomsky, who thought Stalin would not accept their resig-

---

81   Merridale 1990, p. 59; Nosach and Zvereva 2007, p. 35; Carr and Davies 1969, p. 81. Uglanov was not formally removed until 27 November: Cohen 1973, p. 296. Karl Bauman served as Uglanov's replacement as Moscow party boss until Kaganovich assumed that post in 1930.
82   Cohen 1973, pp. 296–8; Shimotomai 1983, p. 17.
83   Uglanov briefly replaced Shmidt as head of Narkomtrud before he too was deposed.
84   Jo 2007, p. 365.
85   *Sotsialisticheskii Vestnik*, 28 October 1928, p. 12. It has been suggested that Tomsky and Rykov might have kept some Menshevik contacts open and served as the source of the paper's information about high Soviet politics: Liebich 1997, p. 141.
86   Most notably on 19 October, 19 November, and 19 December 1928: Stalin 1952–67, vol. 11, pp. 231–48, 255–302, 307–24.
87   The members of the 'Right Deviation' continued to go publicly unnamed until April 1929.
88   VTsSPS 1929a, p. 53.

nations, argued that this would be the best way to demonstrate to their colleagues the seriousness of their condemnation of Stalin's policies. It did cause considerable consternation. Ordzhonikidze wrote to Rykov, 'It is ridiculous, of course, to talk about "replacing" you, or Bukharin or Tomsky. That would be insane'.[89] The joint resignation reportedly so shook up Stalin his hands were said to have trembled, with his face turning pale as he read the letter of resignation.[90] Stalin felt compelled to backtrack and state 'it is time to get rid of the gossip' that there is a Right Deviation in the Politburo.[91] The Politburo refused to accept the resignations of Bukharin, Rykov, and Tomsky, while Stalin tried to placate them with various concessions.[92] Unlike the arrogant Trotsky, Bukharin, Rykov, and Tomsky were well liked by their Politburo colleagues.[93]

But as soon as Bukharin, Rykov, and Tomsky withdrew their resignations, Stalin again adroitly reversed course and devoted his speech at the November Central Committee Plenum to attacking the so-called Right deviation as 'the chief danger in our party'. Stalin stated this danger was 'growing and gaining strength' in the trade-union bureaucracy among other places.[94] The trade unions were criticised for failing to mobilise for the tasks of 'socialist construction'. *Pravda* joined the attack against Tomsky and his fellow leading trade unionists, even though Bukharin was still officially its editor, with articles calling for strengthening party leadership over the trade unions, and accusing the unions of 'a conspiracy of silence' about the important issues confronting the country.[95] While many in the Central Committee supported the 'Rightists', including among others Shmidt, Uglanov, Sokolnikov, E. Kulikov, D. Rozit, Fedor Ugarov, and N. Osinsky, it was clear the majority of the Central Committee supported the course Stalin was advocating.[96] Tomsky and Bukharin chose not to say a word at the November plenum.[97]

---

89 RGASPI, f. 669, op. 1, d. 30, ll. 133–142, reprinted in Kvashonkin et al. (eds) 1999, p. 58.
90 *Bulleten' Oppozitsii*, November 1929, p. 16.
91 Daniels 1960, p. 342.
92 Stalin, for example, agreed to remove three Stalinists from some key positions.
93 Mikoyan remembers that when Stalin told him, Ordzhonikidze, and Kirov that he wanted to elevate them by elbowing aside Tomsky, Rykov, and Bukharin, they were shocked and wondered how that could be since those three were so much more experienced and work so much better than the three of us: Mikoian 1999, p. 289.
94 Stalin 1952–67, vol. 11, pp. 280, 298, 301.
95 *Pravda*, 24 November, and 30 November 1928. Over Bukharin's objections, Emelyan Yaroslavsky and G.I. Krumin, among others, were added to *Pravda*'s editorial board. Tomsky mocked the stated justification of their appointments that it was necessary to bring in some young blood: Vatlin et al. (eds) 2000d, pp. 60, 64.
96 Shapovalova 1989, p. 93.
97 Rykov delivered a major address at the plenum.

Everyone who was aware of the split within the Politburo – and rumours of the 'heated disputes' by then had spread to the lowest levels of officialdom[98] – realised that the Eighth Trade-Union Congress slated to open on 10 December would offer the Stalinists their best opportunity to undermine Tomsky's sway over the trade unions. But the Stalin group faced a problem. The delegates to the congress had been selected months earlier, before the public unfurling of the Stalinist campaign against the 'Right deviation', and the VTsSPS insisted on upholding the method of delegate selection.[99] On this and other issues, the VTsSPS, over the objections of Alexander Lozovsky and the few other Stalinists on its Presidium, refused to buckle.[100] Seeing Tomsky come under attack by Stalin must have been satisfying to Lozovsky, after the conflicts between the trade unions and Profintern earlier, which encouraged him to hitch his political fortunes to Stalin.[101]

The Politburo majority, in response, decided (over Tomsky's strong objections) to create a commission regarding the Eighth Trade-Union Congress. They placed a number of leading Stalinists on the commission, including Molotov and Kaganovich.[102] Although the Politburo appointed Tomsky the chair of the body, he refused at first to agree to participate in its meetings, which he predicted would take place in 'an atmosphere of distrust'.[103] When the commission met, Kaganovich did not even pretend to take the meetings seriously. Rather than reading the report Tomsky had prepared for the congress, Kaganovich just doodled in the margins.[104] Tomsky knew the commission had a simple charge: to add delegates to the congress to dilute Tomsky's support. And indeed, it did

---

98   Daniels 1960, p. 328; Vatlin et al. (eds) 2000d, p. 60.
99   Carr and Davies 1969b, pp. 553–554; *Trud*, 13 November 1928, p. 1.
100 GARF, d. 5451, op. 42, d. 152, l. 232.
101 Although Lozovsky was never part of Stalin's inner circle, he would later become one of Molotov's three deputies in the foreign commissariat. Lozovsky survived the purges before coming under attack after the war as the former head of the Jewish Anti-Fascist Committee. He then starred in the 'trial of Jewish poets' in May 1951 during which he refused to plead guilty and cooperate despite having been brutally beaten. He was executed in August 1952: Montefiore 2004, pp. 306, 545–6, 587–8, 620; Rubinstein and Naumov 2005, p. 58.
102 Others on the commission were Kuibyshev, Bukharin, Dogadov, Melnichansky, Shmidt, Rudzutak, Ordzhonikidze, Lozovsky, Ivan Akulov, Vasily Mikhailov, I.I. Shvarts, Ivan Lepse, Fedor Ugarov, Aleksandra Artiukhina, Aleksander Milchakov, and Ivan Moskvin: Vatlin et al. (eds) 2000d, pp. 33, 701n31; RGASPI, f. 17, op. 3, d. 712, l. 4; GARF f, 5451, op. 42, d. 152, l. 200.
103 Nosach and Zvereva 2007, p. 24; Vatlin et al. (eds) 2000d, p. 61.
104 RGASPI, f. 81, op. 3, d. 35, l. 4.

exactly that. Most of these added delegates were not trade-union members of any standing but could be counted on to support the Stalin group.[105]

Simultaneously, attacks in the press on the trade-union leadership intensified. *Komsomolskaia Pravda* featured a series of articles that criticised the trade unions in particular for not 'drawing the masses' into the pre-congress discussions.[106] *Trud* [Labour], the trade unions' national newspaper, edited by Tomsky's close associate Yakov Yaglom, did its best to vigorously defend the trade unions. It ran a series of articles criticising *Komsomolskaia Pravda*.[107] But the trade unions then suffered a media attack on a second front during November when the industrialists' newspaper, *Torgovo-promyshlennaya gazeta* [Commercial-Industrial Newspaper], began to run a series of articles criticising trade unionists for what it saw as their lack of cooperation in the planning for the launching of breakneck industrialisation.[108] *Pravda* chimed in with similar criticisms.[109] One of Tomsky's supporters, a leader of the Metalworkers' Union, criticised these articles for their 'attitude of disdain' toward workers' interests and its revival of the 'Trotskyism' of War Communism.[110]

Molotov told the trade unionists they were overreacting to what was often a 'misunderstanding', although he insisted the Komsomol's critiques of the trade unions were as often correct as incorrect.[111] Tomsky again successfully pushed the Politburo to adopt a motion criticising *Komsomolskaia Pravda*. The Politburo also agreed to remove its editor, Taras Kostrov, over the strong objections of the Komsomol Central Committee and *Komsomolskaia Pravda*'s editorial board.[112] But Tomsky was far from mollified. He threated to boycott the trade-union congress. To convince him to take part, the Politburo gave him a week off from his other responsibilities and a guarantee that he would be able to formulate the list of candidates for the new VTsSPS Presidium.[113] The Politburo also agreed to the VTsSPS's draft of the report and the resolutions to be presented

---

105 Nosach and Zvereva 2007, p. 24, 25; GARF, f. 5451, op. 42, d. 150, l. 15.
106 See *Komsomolskaya Pravda* on 6, 11, 14, 29 November 1928.
107 See *Trud*, 10, 13, 21, 30 November 1928; GARF, f. 5451, op. 42, d. 152, ll. 196–248; Murphy 2005, p. 178.
108 *Torgovo-promyshlennaya gazeta*, 11, 17, 18, 29, 30 November 1928.
109 *Pravda*, 12 December 1928.
110 Bettleheim 1978, p. 454.
111 GARF, f. 5451, op. 42, d. 150, l. 48.
112 RGASPI, f. 17, op. 3, d. 714, ll. 5, 7; Lenoe 2004, pp. 191–2. Kostrov had been the editor since August 1925. The Politburo also criticised the editor of *Ekonomicheskaya zhizn'* for its 'incorrect criticisms' of the VTsSPS.
113 RGASPI, f. 17, op. 3, d. 713, l. 9. Shortly afterwards, it also gave Kuibyshev a week off to prepare for the congress: RGASPI, f. 17, op. 3, d. 715, l. 8.

at the congress. With these promises, Tomsky chose to chair the congress, but he did not underestimate Stalin's craftiness and the sneakiness of his cohorts. He suspected they were preparing a series of additional 'surprises' and during the congress frequently met in his Kremlin apartment with other leading trade unionists as well as Bukharin and Rykov to plan his response.[114] A few months later he recounted, did you think that 'us old Bolsheviks didn't understand the old methods of struggle? "Discredit, surround with your people ... and then crush"'.[115]

Tomsky enjoyed the delegates' enthusiastic support. When the formal sessions of the congress opened inside the vast, beautiful Hall of Columns in the trade union's building in central Moscow, the delegates responded to his appearance at the rostrum with a standing ovation.[116] During his four-hour opening address, which was broadcast live on the radio, Tomsky systematically rebutted all the attacks against the trade unions, one by one. Tomsky downplayed Stalin's role in the leadership and avoided addressing the 'Right danger' or paying much attention to the economic programme ratified at the recent November Central Committee plenum.[117] But he did say he feared that the Five-Year Plan's drive for heavy industry would wear workers out and underscored the importance of the unions fighting to defend workers' economic interests. Insisting that the trade unions 'exist to serve the worker masses', he said it would be wrong to use trade unions only to raise worker productivity and improve labour discipline as the Stalinists were calling for.[118] That would reduce the trade unions, he argued, to little more than 'propaganda services' and transform them into 'houses of detention'.[119]

During the trade-union congress, an impassioned Kuibyshev revealed for the first time the revised Five-Year Plan. It called for industrial production to increase by a ridiculously ambitious 250 percent. Stating that the Rightists favoured industrialisation at 'a snail's pace', he criticised Tomsky and the union leadership for supporting 'a purely workers' point of view' at the expense of rapid industrialisation. Tomsky vigorously fought back. He argued industrialisation needed to take 'civilised forms'; by which he meant it needed to be

---

114 Nosach and Zvereva 2007, pp. 25–6; RGASPI, f. 17, op. 2, d. 578, l. 12.
115 Vatlin et al. (eds) 2000d, p. 60.
116 VTsSPS 1929b, p. 24. Lenin's widow, Nadezhda Krupskaya, was the only other speaker to receive a standing ovation during the congress.
117 Tomsky later said he did not think it necessary to address the internal party squabbles at a trade-union congress: Vatlin et al. (eds) 2000d, pp. 33, 63, 116; Vaganov 1970, p. 192.
118 The Stalinists had introduced a new slogan: 'Trade Unions – Face toward Production'!
119 VTsSPS 1929b, pp. 6, 38, 44; Sorenson 1969, p. 239; Murphy 2005, p. 178.

balanced, gradual growth. He also argued such a high tempo of industrialisation could only be achieved by improving workers' living conditions and raising wages by 50 percent. He characterised Kuibyshev and his fellow planners as blinded by everything but their own numbers. 'Very often pathetic things are concealed behind planning', he argued.[120]

But the main source of tension occurred when the ugly feud between the Komsomol and Tomsky erupted on the floor of the congress.[121] The Komsomol's earlier biting attacks against Tomsky had clearly stung and, although it could have been seen as merely a distraction from the far more serious conflicts with the Stalinist leadership, Tomsky came ready to fight. He said he had previously refrained from responding to all the falsehoods published in *Komsomolskaia Pravda* in the hope that this would all blow over. Tomsky, who from a young age had to fend for himself on the working-class streets of St. Petersburg stated, 'We did not speak out because we know that when a fight takes place, it is impossible to be courteous; a fight is a fight, shirts are torn to shreds and hair is ripped out'.[122] Tomsky angrily made it clear he viewed Komsomol members as ungrateful, undignified whiners. 'Adult workers carried out the revolution, knowing that they would not live to see developed communism ... We fought for the young, but now we are accused of not paying attention to the needs of youth'.[123] The problem, in Tomsky's view, was that the Komsomol saw only the present conditions; they failed to appreciate what had been achieved because they did not know first-hand what it had been like back in tsarist Russia. 'As a result they raise demands that are impossible for us to satisfy at the present time, demands that will be quite legitimate in five years'.[124] Telling them to wait patiently for five years was arguably not the most strategic way to respond.

Central to the Komsomol leadership's discontent was the large number of youths unable to find jobs. Nearly half of the country's juveniles were said to be unemployed during the 1920s.[125] The trade unions had reason to assert that the employment picture was not as bleak as the Komsomol argued. As noted above, NEP had succeeded in producing dramatic, continual increases in the number of employed workers.[126] In the view of the trade unionists the prob-

---

120 VTsSPS 1929b, pp. 42–4; Lobok 2007, p. 167.
121 Forty-five of the 1,500 delegates at the congress were members of the Komsomol.
122 VTsSPS 1929b, p. 189.
123 VTsSPS 1929b, p. 48.
124 VTsSPS 1929b, p. 29.
125 Nearly 43 percent of workers between the ages of 18 and 24 were unemployed in 1928: Carr and Davies 1969b, pp. 457–8.
126 The number of industrial workers increased by 23 percent from 1926 to 1929, while construction workers more than doubled: Carr and Davies 1969b, p. 453.

lem was not that young people were not finding jobs, but rather the continual influx of young, unskilled and inexperienced peasant jobseekers into urban areas, which made a high rate of youth unemployment unavoidable.[127] Even so, there was a sense, even among trade unionists, that Tomsky and the top leadership had failed to devote sufficient attention to the unemployment crisis facing young workers. In his reports to party and trade-union congresses, Tomsky had usually referred only cursorily to juvenile unemployment and at the congress he sarcastically stated, 'We are a class organisation ... If we put serving the young in first place, and in second place serving women, who will defend male adult workers, the poor old devils'.[128] After the laughter subsided, Tomsky further belittled the Komsomol complaints by stating that as an organisation of the whole working class the unions represented all workers regardless of their age, gender, 'or even the colour of their hair'.[129]

There clearly was merit to the Komsomol's complaint that Tomsky made the interests of skilled adult workers his primary concern. Tomsky's formative experiences before the revolution, like those of most of his fellow members on the VTsSPS Presidium, was as a skilled worker, and he shared his fellow trade-union functionaries' disdain for the mass of young, unskilled workers, especially those illiterates fresh from the countryside.[130] Many rank-and-file workers shared such attitudes. Younger workers disruptive, hooliganistic behaviour at worker clubs, and their absenteeism and general lack of discipline on the factory floor, also often angered older workers.[131]

Whatever the merits of Tomsky's perspective, the Komsomol was understandably outraged at his condescending dismissal of their complaints. On financial matters Tomsky portrayed the Komsomoltsy as ungrateful profligates incapable of properly handling their funds. He explicitly characterised their relations with the trade unions as that of a child to his father. 'You complain when we criticise you for wasting workers' hard-earned money and you say

---

[127] GARF, f. 5451, op. 42, d. 136, l. 105.
[128] VTsSPS 1929b, p. 49.
[129] VTsSPS 1929b, p. 48.
[130] VTsSPS 1929b, p. 32. In addition to generational tensions, skilled workers felt condescension toward their fellow workers fresh from the countryside, who they saw as 'country bumpkins': Siegelbaum 1992, p. 207.
[131] See GARF, f. 5451, op. 42, d. 137, ll. 77, 179; Hatch 1994, pp. 97–117. Anxiety about youths' lack of discipline was a major preoccupation also of party and Komsomol leaders during the 1920s: Gorsuch 2000, pp. 4, 53, 64–6, 71, 92–3, 183; Gooderham 1982, p. 511. It should be noted, working-class rank-and-file youths generally seemed at least as disenchanted and disengaged with the Komsomol leadership as with the trade-union leadership: Guillory 2009, pp. 192–210, 354.

we are tightfisted ... But if you want to receive money from your papa's purse then you need to be careful with that money and you need to pay heed to your father's advice'.[132] To the demand that youths be provided with holidays at sanatoria, rest homes, and summer dachas, and hot breakfasts and lunches in school, Tomsky stated that if someone makes such demands without indicating how they are to be paid for, they are nothing but 'chatterboxes'.[133] And even if it were feasible, 'adult men and women would justifiably protest against the creation of a privileged stratum within the working class'.[134] Tomsky characterised the Komsomol demands as mindless; their slogans 'beautiful, but empty'.[135] These and other condescending gibes at the Komsomol met with the approval of the delegates who repeatedly interrupted Tomsky with laughter and applause.

Tomsky also refused to give any credence to the Komsomol complaints about the lack of opportunity for Komsomol members to assume important positions within the trade-union bureaucracy. After claiming that it hurt him to have to criticise the young, Tomsky justified not providing more responsible administrative positions to members of the Komsomol by castigating the performance of the representatives the Komsomol had sent in the past to work as functionaries within trade-union organisations. He stated that they did not even pretend to apply themselves. According to Tomsky, after self-importantly appearing for work, with their briefcases in hand, they quickly vanished, commonly failing to attend important meetings. And after stating that criticism is a good thing, that it would be stupid to assert that the trade unions worked mistake free, he declared to laughter from the delegates, that 'one response to Komsomol criticism might be that the only ones who do not make mistakes are those who do not work ... or [who are] newspaper columnists'.[136] Tomsky and the trade-union delegates obviously refused to take the Komsomol seriously despite Stalin's support for its complaints. Or perhaps he took them deadly seriously and was using humour and pandering to the friendly crowd to go on the offensive.

But if Tomsky thought his haughty, dismissive attitude toward the Komsomol would put them in their place, he was badly mistaken. The Komsomol representatives expressed outrage at the patronising manner in which Tomsky dismissed their grievances. Alexander Milchakov, who represented Ukraine

---

132   VTsSPS 1929b, pp. 49–50.
133   VTsSPS 1929b, p. 50.
134   VTsSPS 1929b, p. 51. Tomsky of course occupied just that sort of privileged stratum.
135   VTsSPS 1929b, p. 191.
136   VTsSPS 1929b, p. 52.

on the Komsomol Presidium, bristled, 'It is wrong to make fun of the Komsomol ... We are not chatterboxes ... We are not little children'.[137] The Komsomol Stalinist I.P. Zhdanov stated that rather than being mocked, the two million members of the Komsomol had a right to expect a serious response to the issues they raised.[138] Zhdanov proceeded, in a slightly veiled, but carefully prepared statement, to call for Tomsky's removal from the trade-union leadership. He proposed that we don't need as the leader of the trade unions a person 'who cannot recognise the full depth of our principled arguments with the trade unions on labour issues and cannot understand the principles on which our joint work is based'.[139] This was the first time anyone had publicly called for Tomsky's removal. It angered the trade unionists. One delegate interrupted Zhdanov's speech, shouting, 'Who gave you the right to cast absolutely unjustified aspersions on the trade-union movement'?[140]

These Komsomol attacks on the leadership of the trade unions, as well as those of the preceding months, helped to lay the foundation for the intervention from the Stalinists that now took place. For as dramatic as the tense exchanges had been on the floor of the congress between Tomsky and Kuibyshev, and particularly between Tomsky and his Komsomol critics, the final showdown occurred behind closed doors: first within the Politburo's trade-union commission, then within the Politburo itself, followed by within the bureau of the trade-union party caucus, and finally within the caucus itself.[141] These meetings were scheduled at virtually the last minute. Stalin decided to strike before he would allow the delegates to the Eighth Trade-Union Congress to leave Moscow.

The bitter feuding on the floor of the congress erupted into a full-fledged political war at a quickly called meeting of the Politburo's trade-union commission on 22 December. The 19 members of this commission, which included Bukharin and Tomsky as well as Kaganovich and Molotov, split closely between supporters of Tomsky and supporters of Stalin.[142] In addition to attacks on Tomsky for his treatment of the Komsomol, the Stalinists were particularly outraged

---

137 VTsSPS 1929b, pp. 164–7.
138 I.P. Zhdanov, head of the Komsomol Central Committee's labour and education department, should not be confused with Andrei Zhdanov, who soon became part of Stalin's inner circle: Fitzpatrick 1979, p. 289n99.
139 VTsSPS 1929b, pp. 110–1.
140 VTsSPS 1929b, p. 116, quoted in Fitzpatrick 1979, p. 131.
141 The proceedings of the congress's party caucus meetings, unlike those of the congress itself, were not published. Only the 72.5 percent of the congress's delegates who were party members could attend the meetings of the party caucus: GARF, f. 5451, op. 42, d. 150, l. 105.
142 RGASPI, f. 17, op. 3, d. 706, l. 7.

by accusations by Tomsky's close associate, Kozelev, that *Pravda* had published 'libelous' [*klevetnikcheskii*] attacks on the trade unions during the congress.[143] Kozelev also characterised *Komsomolskaia Pravda* as a Menshevik newspaper.[144] The meeting concluded deep into the night with a vote on a resolution formulated by Molotov. The final vote on this resolution, which affirmed party leadership over the trade unions and the need for a determined struggle against the 'Right Deviation' was carried by only a single vote: 10–9. The Stalinists clearly had only a razor-thin majority, even on the commission whose composition the Politburo had chosen.[145]

The Stalinists then revealed their next, most shocking surprise. After the vote, at 4:00 in the morning, Molotov suddenly handed Tomsky a note that asked, 'What do you think about putting Kaganovich on the VTsSPS Presidium'? Tomsky told Molotov he was absolutely opposed to it.[146] While there was nothing against the rules in Molotov's proposal, Tomsky expressed his outrage at this surreptitious move and the Stalinists' betrayal of their recent promise not to add anyone to the presidium. The following day, at a specially called meeting of the Politburo, Stalin further ambushed Tomsky by proposing that besides Kaganovich four more Stalinists be appointed to the VTsSPS Presidium (bringing the total Presidium membership to 21).[147] These appointees were all from Stalin's immediate entourage. Although the justification for adding members to the VTsSPS leadership was supposed to seem innocuous enough – simply to strengthen ties between the Central Committee and the VTsSPS – Tomsky accurately interpreted the proposed appointees as a vote of no confidence in his leadership and the opening shot in the Stalinists' attempt to gain control of the unions.[148]

The elevation of Kaganovich, who had not participated in the open sessions of the congress, particularly drew Tomsky's wrath and, in his words, provoked

---

143 VTsSPS 1929b, pp. 95, 178. Kozelev was a delegate from Moscow's Hammer and Sickle metal factory: Murphy 2005, p. 178.
144 Vatlin et al. (eds) 2000d, p. 33.
145 Vatlin et al. (eds) 2000d, p. 63.
146 Vatlin et al. (eds) 2000d, p. 63.
147 RGASPI, f. 17, op. 3, d. 721, ll. 6–7; Khordina (ed.) 2000, p. 658. The other four were Kuibyshev, Ordzhonikidze, Rudzutak, and Andrei Zhdanov: Broué 1963, p. 291. Rudzutak by this time sided with Stalin against his old friend Tomsky, although how firmly is open to question.
148 Tomsky pointed to the fact that eight of the current members of the VTsSPS Presidium were Central Committee members, with an additional two who were candidate members, and that two other Presidium members served on the Central Control Commission.

FIGURE 29
Stalin with Kaganovich
WIKIMEDIA COMMONS

'furious resistance' from his like-minded supporters in the VTsSPS.[149] Tomsky saw it as an attempt to neutralise his influence by introducing a 'political commissar' to oversee the unions.[150] Kaganovich had a history as a trade unionist, but he was a strong, articulate advocate for Stalin's plans for rapid industrialisation, which Tomsky and other VTsSPS leaders had so clearly and persistently opposed. Kaganovich shared Kuibyshev's criticism of Tomsky's belief that

---

149 TsGAODM, f. 2870, op. 1, d. 296, reprinted in Karpachev and Minaeva (eds) 1992b, p. 110.
150 Vatlin et al. (eds) 2000d, p. 64; RGASPI, f. 17, op. 3, d. 718, l. 4. Tomsky had similarly complained when the Central Committee appointed Bukharin and Radek to the VTsSPS over his objections in 1919.

the main purpose of the trade unions was to defend workers' interests.[151] He instead supported tightening up labour discipline and generally was Stalin's most unquestioning and most fanatical supporter. Molotov considered Kaganovich a '200 percent Stalinist. He felt I didn't praise Stalin well enough'.[152] Tomsky said he knew Stalin's intent with the appointment of his loyal henchman was to create a 'dual centre' in the trade-union leadership, which would, he argued, 'weaken and create divisions in the trade-union movement'.[153] Tomsky told Emelyan Yaroslavsky that he and his fellow Stalinists should not imagine the union leaders were 'naïve children'.[154]

The ensuing, heated Politburo meeting lasted four hours. Reflecting Stalin's still tenuous control of the Politburo, Voroshilov and Kalinin again wavered. But in the end, over the vehement objections of Tomsky, as well as those of Rykov and Bukharin, the Politburo adopted the resolution adding the Stalinists to the VTsSPS leadership. It passed by a vote of 5–3, with one member abstaining.[155] Tomsky stated that, given this vote of no confidence in his leadership, he could no longer participate in the trade-union congress.[156] But the Politburo, which considered that to be an act of 'insubordination', rejected Tomsky's request to step down from the VTsSPS chair and adopted another resolution requiring him to continue to serve as chair of the congress.[157] At the same time, as a loyal member of the party, Tomsky was not going to publicly expose the intra-party disputes.

Tomsky, who had been so combative on the floor of the congress, knew his position had been fundamentally undermined by these votes behind closed doors. When he failed to appear in the morning at the party caucus meeting, he told a representative of the Politburo commission who called on him, that he had fallen ill. Tomsky's claim that he was sick may have well been true. But

---

151 Later, at the Sixteenth Party Congress in 1930, Kaganovich said all one had to do was read Tomsky's 1922 article, entitled 'Trade Unions on New Paths', in order to see his 'opportunistic ideology' that it was necessary for the trade unions 'to concentrate all their attention on defending the economic interests of workers': RKP(b) 1931, p. 63. VTsSPS reissued the article in 1923, and it was reprinted in Tomsky's collected works: Tomskii 1928a, p. 150.

152 Molotov 1993, p. 229. Kagnovich had spent the previous three years as the Ukrainian Party boss, where his heavy-handed methods ultimately alienated other members of the Ukrainian leadership.

153 Quoted in Nosach 2005, p. 126.

154 Vatlin et al. (eds) 2000d, p. 116.

155 GARF, f. 5452, op. 42, d. 150, l. 30. Rudzutak was presumably the abstaining member.

156 Vatlin et al. (eds) 2000d, p. 568.

157 Vatlin et al. (eds) 2000d, p. 91. The Politburo did grant Tomsky a holiday leave following the conclusion of the congress: RGASPI, f. 17, op. 3, d. 718, l. 4; GARF, f. 5451, op. 42, d. 150, ll. 45–6, 51, 55; Reiman 1987, p. 98.

Tomsky's failure to appear no doubt also reflected his displeasure with the Politburo's decision. Kirov later said Tomsky did not appear because he knew he 'lacked the gunpowder' to reverse the Politburo's decision and did not want 'to go down the path that Kamenev and Zinoviev had gone down toward an open struggle against the party'.[158] But Tomsky probably also wanted to send an unspoken signal of his displeasure with the Stalinists to the VTsSPS.

In any case, his doctor certified that Tomsky was suffering from the flu and severe fatigue and needed to remain in bed for the next few days and then be sent out of Moscow for one to two weeks in order to regain his strength.[159] Indeed, as the power struggle had heated up over the last few months, Tomsky often appeared to be thoroughly exhausted. 'An over-taxed man to whom rest seemed the prime reward', in the words of one observer.[160] If so, this would not be the first time, nor the last, that intense political infighting debilitated this otherwise strong-willed man.

Whether Tomsky refused to continue fighting because he was truly too sick to do so, or because of a perhaps misguided sense of Bolshevik discipline, he was hardly alone in his vehement opposition to the Politburo's decision.[161] When the bureau of the trade-union party caucus met early the next day, many infuriated members expressed their outrage at the Politburo's decision to place Kaganovich on the VTsSPS Presidium. They decided to put forward a proposal calling on the Politburo to reconsider its decision. It lost by just four votes, 28–24.[162] The Stalin group had again prevailed, but again by only a very narrow margin, and only by packing the caucus before the congress began.

Despite this setback, vehement opposition to the Politburo's decision to appoint five Stalinists to the VTsSPS Presidium once again erupted when the forum shifted to the whole party caucus. Tomsky's support within the caucus remained strong even with his failure to attend the meeting, perhaps partly because he might have met secretly with some of them prior to the caucus meeting to plot strategy.[163] This was evident when the caucus meeting opened with the routine sanctioning of the leadership. The mere announcement of

---

158   RKP(b) 1931, p. 158.
159   The Politburo would agree to Tomsky's request and the doctor's prescription for a two-week vacation: RGASPI, f. 593, op. 1, d. 2, ll. 193–203.
160   McCormick 1929, p. 108.
161   Tomsky, when interrogated later by the 1933 purge commission, stated he had indeed refused to continue working in the trade unions. He made no mention of being too sick to work: TsGAODM, f. 2870, op. 1, d. 296, reprinted in Karpachev and Minaeva (eds) 1992b, p. 110.
162   GARF, f. 5451, op. 2, d. 150, l. 30.
163   TsA FSB, R27744, d. 3257, tom 1, l. 82.

Tomsky's name received a loud, standing ovation. In contrast, everyone else enjoyed less applause. Then, when Kaganovich's name was announced, the delegates generally refused to applaud. In the virtual silence someone even dared to shout sarcastically, 'Who'?[164] Many members of the trade-union leadership were determined to resist the Politburo's decision, despite the Stalin group's determination and Tomsky's absence.[165] They realised what was at stake.

Rather than openly opposing all five of the Stalinist appointees, Tomsky's supporters concentrated their fire on the unpopular, but powerful Kaganovich, who, like Tomsky, they saw as the primary threat. Their tactic, like that at the caucus bureau meeting earlier that day, was to formally request that the Politburo reconsider its decision to place Kaganovich on the VTsSPS Presidium. Tomsky's supporters evidently thought the Politburo might well rescind its earlier decision if faced with sufficient VTsSPS opposition.

The Stalin group's initial response was to downplay the significance of Kaganovich's appointment. Molotov insisted that Tomsky and all the other members of the VTsSPS Presidium continued to enjoy the Politburo's full support, although a few minor 'mistakes' and 'misunderstandings' had occurred.[166] Delegates refused to let such innuendoes pass unchallenged. Interrupting Molotov's speech, delegates demanded he identify those mistakes and misunderstandings. Molotov, using the attacks on Tomsky that had occurred on the congress's floor, responded that the trade unionists needed to recognise that the Komsomol's criticisms were often correct.[167]

Members of the trade-union leadership willing to come to the rostrum to challenge Molotov also rejected the Politburo's justification for imposing Kaganovich on the VTsSPS Presidium. Among the first to come forward to contest Molotov's speech was Ugarov, the chair of the Leningrad council. He refused to accept the official line that Kaganovich's assignment was just a routine attempt to minimise mistakes rather than a move against Tomsky's leadership. Ugarov declared that Kaganovich was assigned not to improve ties between the Politburo and the VTsSPS Presidium but to provide new leadership. Ugarov also bluntly stated that 'the inaccurate attacks on the VTsSPS by the Komsomol and press were the problem, not weak ties between the VTsSPS and the Politburo'. He also bristled at the Stalinists' charge that questioning Kaganovich's appointment was a violation of party discipline: 'The Central

---

164   GARF, f. 5451, op. 42, d. 150, l. 45.
165   TsGAODM, f. 2870, op. 1, d. 296, reprinted in Karpachev and Minaeva (eds) 1992b, p. 110; *Sotsialisticheskii vestnik*, 12 April 1929.
166   GARF, f. 5451, op. 42, d. 150, ll. 45, 48.
167   GARF, f. 5451, op. 42, d. 150, ll. 45–7.

Committee shouldn't question whether we are violating discipline, rather it should consult with the congress's party caucus on the important question of the composition of the VTsSPS. It should honour the opinion of the caucus'.[168] Glukhovtsev in particular stuck out his neck by criticising the Politburo directly, arguing that since 'lively ties' already exist, with so many VTsSPS members occupying top party positions, no one should take Molotov's argument seriously.[169] 'It seems to me it is necessary to look much deeper ... and question whether the proposal to place Kaganovich on the trade-union presidium indicates uneasiness with the trade-union leadership'. Glukhovtsev ended by declaring that any such concern was 'completely unfounded'.[170] M.G. Nefedov emphasised that the caucus should understand that the majority of the trade-union leadership opposed the Politburo's decision.[171] Yaglom, the editor of *Trud*, directly rejected the charge made elsewhere that Tomsky had turned the trade unions into his personal domain, into 'a feudal principality'.[172] He emphasised that the dismissal of Tomsky was connected with political disagreements. The congress delegates responded with applause to Yaglom's rousing endorsement of Tomsky, whom he characterised as a superior trade unionist, a superior member of the party.[173]

The few Stalinists in the trade-union leadership fought back alongside Molotov. They jumped on Tomsky's failure to come to the caucus meeting, denouncing it as an outrageous act of insubordination, a clear violation of the Politburo's order that he remain in his post. After stating that he was in no position to ascertain Tomsky's physical wellbeing, Molotov insinuated that Tomsky was guilty of violating party discipline, and that if members of the caucus followed his example it could lead to 'deep political splits in the ranks of our party'.[174] Yaroslavsky chimed in, 'We need to fully and unconditionally support ... the entire party line'.[175] Yaroslavsky condemned Tomsky for making what he viewed as an ultimatum to the party, warning the caucus that if it supported him it too would be guilty of threatening the party with 'an ultimatum'.[176] Lozovsky, who had long bitterly fought with Tomsky, challenged the logic of those opposed to

---

168 GARF, f. 5451, op. 42, d. 150, l. 61.
169 Members of the VTsSPS occupied 10 positions in the Party's Central Committee, three in the Orgburo, and one in the Politburo.
170 GARF, f. 5451, op. 42, d. 150, ll. 74–5.
171 GARF, f. 5451, op. 42, d. 150, ll. 65–6.
172 Stalin himself had made that charge earlier.
173 GARF, f. 5451, op. 42, d. 150, l. 71.
174 GARF, f. 5451, op. 42, d. 150, ll. 37, 51–2.
175 GARF, f. 5451, op. 42, d. 150, l. 163.
176 GARF, f. 5451, op. 42, d. 150, ll. 55–8.

Kaganovich, stating that the Central Committee had previously placed other members on the VTsSPS without objection.[177] The debate further sharpened when A.M. Amosov put Kaganovich's opponents' backs against the wall by demanding they recognise the party's predominant role. 'Comrade Tomsky leads the trade-union movement under the guidance of our Bolshevik party and the Party Central Committee. It is only through joining together his personal qualities and the wisdom of the party leadership that we have a powerful trade-union movement, such as the world has never seen before'.[178]

Opponents of Kaganovich's appointment nonetheless were able to muster enough votes to defeat an attempt by the Stalinists to end the debate, which had already lasted for hours. The Stalinists responded to this defeat by raising the stakes higher. They began to label the opposition to Kaganovich's appointment an act of anti-party political resistance, no longer downplaying or denying the appointment's political motivation. Molotov directly threatened the delegates. He stated, 'It is forbidden for any of you to ignore or oppose a decision of the Central Committee'.[179] Milchakov, one of the Komsomol leaders who had led the attack on the floor of the congress, confirmed the VTsSPS's fear that Kaganovich's appointment was 'a political move'. He stated that the resistance being expressed at the caucus clarified why just such a check on the trade-union leadership by the party was not only necessary, but urgent. Milchakov concluded by stating that the trade unionists resisting this appointment were engaging in 'a political demonstration against the Central Committee'.[180]

The trade unionists' will to resist began to crumble. In this secret arena, as in the more public one we are familiar with, the Stalinists were able to exploit the ingrained Bolshevik culture of party discipline. It was impossible for most of the members of the trade-union party caucus to flatly reject a direct Politburo resolution. But according to a report in *Sotsialisticheskii vestnik*, breaking the trade unionists' surprisingly stubborn resistance occurred only after Yaroslavsky threatened that measures would be taken against those who resisted, not only by the party, but by the GPU as well![181] In the end, by a vote of

---

177 GARF, f. 5451, op. 42, d. 150, ll. 67–8. As we saw in chapter four, the conflict between Tomsky and Lozovsky went back to Lozovsky's opposition to Tomsky's efforts to reach out to Western European Labourite and Social-Democratic trade unionists in the mid-1920s.
178 GARF, f. 5451, op. 42, d. 150, ll. 76–7.
179 GARF, f. 5451, op. 42, d. 150, l. 51.
180 GARF, f. 5451, op. 42, d. 150, ll. 82–3. Milchakov was the General Secretary of the Komsomol Central Committee at the time.
181 *Sotsialisticheskii Vestnik*, 1 July 1929, p. 14. Yaroslavsky, as Secretary of the Party Collegium of the CCC, would oversee the preparations and implementation of the May 1929 to May 1930 purge, which expelled 170,000 Party members: Rigby 1968, pp. 178–9.

474 to 92, the caucus accepted the appointment of Kaganovich and the four other Stalinists into the trade-union leadership. But the final vote was not as lopsided as it appeared to be. Almost half of those eligible to vote in the party caucus – 568 delegates – did not vote.[182] It is impossible to be certain whether they did so because they were afraid to vote for fear of Stalinist retribution, but that is the most plausible explanation.

In their final bit of business, the caucus 'unanimously' adopted the Stalinist resolution, that as the historian Robert Daniels noted, had 'a tone distinctly different from the regular congress proceedings: it was the new harsh voice of Stalinism'.[183] The call for an increased industrial tempo was endorsed, while 'groundless, panicky assertions' about collectivising agriculture and strengthening the offensive against kulaks were denounced. Most pointedly, the resolution repudiated 'a purely workers' view of the trade-union movement's role while endorsing an 'intensified struggle against the Right Danger and any compromise with it'.[184] *Pravda*'s predictably false summation of the congress stated the congress had expressed its 'full solidarity with all the decisions of the party in its unyielding struggle with all deviators from the correct Leninist line'.[185] As for the 92 dissenting voters, they would all be quickly removed from their posts or forced to repent.[186]

If all the Komsomol attacks before and during the congress were, at least in part, an attempt to bait Tomsky, it worked. While his condescending attitude toward the Komsomol appealed to the congress's delegates, it outraged the Komsomol and provided Stalin with a rationale for the appointment of Kaganovich and others from his group to the VTsSPS Presidium. Following Tomsky's defeat, issues concerning juvenile workers, having served their purpose as the driving force in the attack on Tomsky's authority in the trade unions, fell off the radar as a pressing concern.[187]

Tomsky, Bukharin, and Rykov defiantly tried to keep fighting the Stalinist takeover of the party leadership during the first four months following the Eighth Trade-Union Congress at a party conference, and at joint plenums of the Central Committee and Central Control Commission. At the 9 February

---

182   Nosach and Zvereva 2007, p. 38.
183   Daniels 1960, p. 347.
184   VTsSPS 1929b, pp. 504–5.
185   *Pravda*, 29 December 1928, p. 1. *Trud* published Tomsky's report to the congress and his replies during the debates as if nothing untoward had occurred: Carr and Davies 1969b, p. 559.
186   Tomsky later argued that party rules allowed delegates to vote as they wanted: Vatlin et al. (eds) 2000d, p. 65. All 92 would later be swept up in the Great Purges: Nosach 2007, p. 81.
187   Carr and Davies 1969b, p. 481.

1929 plenum, Tomsky, Bukharin, and Rykov made their last effort to win the party leadership over to their side with an alternative plan, which they considered still viable.[188] The meeting was marked by substantial animosity and rancour during and after Rykov presented their 30-page platform, which reiterated in detail their criticism of Stalin's polices. They proposed a lower tempo for industrialisation and criticised Stalin's demand for a peasant 'tribute'.[189] The platform characterised the Stalinists' attitude toward the peasantry as one of 'exploitation', of treating the peasantry as if they were a 'colony' of the party.[190] Tomsky bluntly declared, 'What is this new form of *smychka*? ... There is nothing new here; it is the extraordinary measures and the ration book'.[191] These harsh criticisms predictably outraged the Politburo majority. The platform also made reference to Lenin's 'Testament', which had called for Stalin's removal as general secretary, while also deploring the destruction of the collective leadership in the party and the 'bureaucratisation of the inner party', much as the successive Left Oppositions had done before them.[192] Tomsky also complained about the complete collapse of any sort of comradely tolerance for different viewpoints within the Politburo since Stalin gained control of it.[193]

Stalin and members of his team began a merciless campaign of vilifying Bukharin, Rykov, and Tomsky, for the first time by name, as 'pro-kulak Right Deviationists'.[194] A resolution of the February plenum repeated the accusation that Tomsky had established in the trade unions 'a feudal principality'. The revelation only now that Bukharin had secretly met with Kamenev in July 1928 brought a chorus of criticism. But Tomsky and his cohorts refused to admit

---

188 Alex Nove thinks that Bukharin's programme was viable economically, but questions how viable it was politically: Millar 1990, p. 85. Kotkin, in contrast, argues that 'the rightists possessed an alternative programme that – whether of or not it could possibly work to achieve socialism – commanded support. Indeed, it is striking how much potential power that the right wing of the party had possessed *within the politburo* and how Stalin crushed them anyway': Kotkin 2017, p. 68.
189 The word *dan'* connoted the tribute Russian princes were required to extract from their subjects during the Mongol yoke to pay the Tatar khans: Tucker 1990, p. 84.
190 Vatlin et al. (eds) 2000d, p. 607.
191 Quoted in Cohen 1973, p. 311.
192 For their entire platform: Vatlin et al. (eds) 2000d, pp. 604–19.
193 Kumanev and Kulikova 1994, p. 148.
194 It was originally labelled the 'Right Deviation', because unlike the oppositions of Trotsky, Zinoviev, and Kamenev earlier, Bukharin, Rykov, and Tomsky did not take their opposition outside the confines of the party elite. But the party leadership soon began to use the labels 'Right Deviation' and 'Right Opposition' interchangeably. Robert Daniels observes, 'the history of the Right Opposition offers the singular spectacle of a political group defeated first and attacked afterwards': Daniels 1960, p. 362.

their views were wrong. They again tried to explain their positions at the April 1929 Central Committee and Central Control Commission plenum. Here too they were denounced and continually interrupted, although some courageous delegates voiced their disapproval of how they were being treated, including Lenin's sister Maria Ulyanova.[195] Stalin, in a seven-hour speech, one of his longest ever, engaged in a point-by-point attack on the 'Rightists'. He called Tomsky a petty political intriguer who refuses to recognise the need for a radical change in the methods of the trade unions, adding that 'Tomsky answers us that all this is nonsense, that no such new tasks confront us'.[196] The plenum's resolution declared:

> On the trade-union question, comrades Bukharin, Rykov, and Tomsky have taken the highly dangerous course of setting the unions against the party. In fact, they are doing this by pursuing a policy of weakening the party leadership of the trade-union movement, by obscuring the deficiencies in trade-union work, covering up trade-unionist tendencies and instances of bureaucratic ossification in parts of the union apparatus, and wrongly portraying the party's struggle against these deficiencies as a Trotskyist 'shake-up' of the trade unions.[197]

Kalinin, at the Sixteenth Party Conference, which followed the plenum, argued the 'Rightists' were especially dangerous because 'their inner purity, idealism, personal qualities, and individual traits' made them attractive to rank-and-file members of the party.[198] But the April Central Committee Plenum and Sixteenth Party Conference made it clear to anyone who still doubted it that the Stalinists had prevailed in the power struggle against the 'Right' and were going full speed ahead with the maximum variant of the First Five-Year Plan.

Tomsky, who during the first months of 1929 had remained the VTsSPS's nominal chair, refused to resume his position or responsibilities. Tomsky not only declined to carry out his duties as VTsSPS chair, he stopped attending its meetings.[199] The party leadership finally allowed Tomsky to resign from his pos-

---

195 Khlevniuk 1996, p. 21.
196 Stalin 1952–67, vol. 12, pp. 2, 20.
197 Egorov and Bogoliubov (eds) 1983–84, vol. 4, p. 434.
198 Quoted in Oppenheim 1972, p. 431. Kalinin's backhanded tribute to the 'Rightists' clearly indicates that he still had mixed feelings about signing on with the Stalinists. Many of the 'Stalinist' members of the Politburo continued to be on good personal terms with the 'Rightists': Lih et al. (eds) 1995, p. 148. Tomsky and Kalinin had been friends since 1907.
199 GARF, f. 5451, op. 42, d. 162; RGASPI, f. 593, op. 1, d. 2, l. 198. Some other trade unionists, in contrast, continued to fight. For example, Ugarov on 3 January 1929, denounced the Polit-

ition as head of the trade unions in May 1929. Tomsky had asked the Politburo earlier, on 10 January 1929, but it was rejected despite Tomsky's lengthy explanation for why he could no longer lead the trade unions and should be reassigned to some other work.

To 'refresh' the trade unions, Kaganovich oversaw a massive purge of the leadership of the trade unions, from the bottom to the top over the course of 1929 and early 1930.[200] By 1 April 1930, the purge removed 59.5 percent of the VTsSPS, 51.7 percent of the VTsSPS Presidium members, and 67.5 percent of the trade union's central committee members.[201] Almost every member of the VTsSPS representing Moscow and Leningrad was removed. The 'refreshing' of trade-union officials was as great or greater at lower levels, such as in the Urals and Ukraine, where six out of seven officials were removed.[202] In addition, the Stalinists dramatically cut the power, prestige, and budgets of the trade unions.[203] Tomsky's associate Boris Kozelev, writing in the journal *Metallist*, nevertheless bravely criticised Stalin's treatment of the trade unions as a revival of Trotsky's treatment of trade unions.[204]

In conclusion, the Eighth Trade-Union Congress proved to be NEP's last stand. As we have seen, the union leadership resisted the Stalinist takeover of the trade unions even after Tomsky collapsed in a fit of fatigue and outrage. The imposition of Kaganovich on the VTsSPS carried by only the thinnest of margins within the bureau of the party caucus, and in the caucus itself only because various threats, including ultimately the threat of arrest, intimidated 568 of the delegates into not voting. As Kaganovich himself put it, 'It could be said this was a violation of proletarian democracy, but comrades it has long been known that for us Bolsheviks, democracy is no fetish'.[205] With the takeover of the unions, the Stalinists' victory was complete. The hope of maintaining the moderate

---

buro's decision to 'shake-up' the trade unions by adding Kaganovich and the others to the VTsSPS Presidium: RGASPI, f. 17, op. 21, d. 2643, l. 2.

200 Khordina (ed.) 2000, p. 661; RGASPI, f. 593, op. 1, d. 2, ll. 195, 261–5; Vatlin et al. (eds) 2000d, pp. 568–71.
201 Kuromiya 1988, p. 46.
202 Morrell 1965, p. 60; Rigby 1968, pp. 182–3. An even larger number of Stalinist trade unionists were swept up in Great Purges in 1937: Jo 2006, pp. 68–115.
203 No trade-union Congresses occurred between 1932 and 1949 and during this period the unions had almost no representatives on the Central Committee: Mawdsley and Smith 2000, p. 50.
204 Lobok 2007, p. 169. Kozelev was expelled from the party shortly afterwards when a colleague discovered his diary and turned it over to the political police. He was arrested in 1936 and shot in 1937: Hellbeck 2006, p. 49.
205 RKP(b) 1931, p. 63. Stalin had previously said the Bolsheviks did not 'fetishise the question of democracy' at the Thirteenth Party Congress: Rees 2012, p. 50.

policies of NEP, including the trade union's ability to push for higher wages and defend workers against abuses by management, was dead. There was no stopping the Stalinist Revolution, which was about to throw the Soviet people into the hardships and famine of the First Five-Year Plan.

CHAPTER 7

Tomsky Outcast: Tormenting a 'Right Deviationist'

I am not able to live when I am put on a par with fascists.
MIKHAIL TOMSKY

∴

The ultimate fate suffered by the leaders of the Left Oppositions and the so-called Right Deviation in the Great Purges is well known.[1,2] But relatively little attention has been devoted to the years between their ousters from power and their deaths.[3] This is especially true in the case of Mikhail Tomsky, since unlike most of the others he did not undergo a show trial. This chapter, which examines the last seven years of his life, questions the characterisation of Tomsky as 'a lost and beaten man' who 'had no present and no future. All he could do was stand by and suffer in silence as Stalin ran roughshod over the nation, the unions, and the party'.[4] While that is basically accurate, Tomsky's final years were more mixed than that. Tomsky did indeed suffer bouts of psychological and physical collapse, but he performed ably in the important administrative position the Stalinist leadership entrusted him with, and he continued to meet privately with other former leading oppositionists to share their discontents with Stalin and Stalinist policies. The party leadership was unsure how strongly to attack this respected 'Old Bolshevik' before the crises of 1932–33 increased

---

1 Part of Chapter 7 has been previously published in 'The "Right Opposition" and the "Smirnov-Eismont-Tolmachev Affair"' in *The 'Lost' Politburo Stenograms: From Collective Rule to Stalin's Dictatorship*, edited by Paul Gregory and Norman Naimark, New Haven: Yale University Press, pp. 97–117.
2 The term Great Purges is used here instead of the more commonly used Great Terror because the focus is on the elite purges. Great Terror seems a more apt term for the wave of arrests and executions in the NKVD's 'mass operations' and 'nationalities operations', which primarily targeted ordinary people.
3 The major exceptions are Nicholas Bukharin and Leon Trotsky. Regarding Bukharin, see Cohen 1973; Gregory 2010; Medvedev 1980; Kun 1992. Innumerable books have covered Trotsky's life following his ouster from power.
4 Sorenson 1969, p. 243.

their sense of political vulnerability and the attacks on Tomsky intensified. Initially Tomsky demonstrated considerable fortitude in the face of these attacks until he totally capitulated in 1934 and, in response to the first Moscow show trial, decided to take his own life in 1936. Many in the West, saddened by his death, viewed him as a 'tragic hero'.

Tomsky, following the Eighth Trade-Union Congress, incongruously remained a member of the Politburo whose formal weekly meetings Rykov continued to chair, even as Stalin launched his disastrous programme of forced collectivisation, coercive grain requisition, and dekulakisation during the winter of 1929–30.[5] Stalin claimed he had held back other members of the leadership who wanted to remove Tomsky and Bukharin at the April 1929 Central Committee Plenum. Continuing to pose as a conciliator, Stalin stated, 'In my opinion, for the time being, we don't need to resort to such an extreme measure'.[6] At the plenum in November 1929, while Bukharin, Rykov, and Tomsky did recant their opposition to collectivisation, if half-heartedly, they nonetheless boldly asserted in a 12-point declaration that the alternative approach they had proposed at the April plenum could have attained the desired results in 'a less painful way'.[7] Although Tomsky was accused of holding 'Menshevik views', he not only still remained on the Politburo, he regularly presented reports to it, until Stalin finally ousted him in August 1930.[8] Stalin may have lacked the votes within the Politburo to oust Tomsky before then.[9] The November plenum obediently affirmed the campaign for wholesale collectivisation, with plenum members suppressing whatever doubts they had.

The first opportunity to publicly humiliate Tomsky came at the Sixteenth Party Congress, held in June-July 1930, while the turmoil of draconian industrialisation and forcible collectivisation was unfolding.[10] In a long speech in

---

5   Stalin before long put an end to this 'comedy': Kotkin 2017, p. 26.
6   Stalin 1946–51, vol. 12, p. 107.
7   Khlevniuk et al. (eds) 2000, pp. 158–65.
8   Khlevniuk et al. (eds) 2000, pp. 133–4, 183–6. Bukharin had been removed from the Politburo in November 1929, while Tomsky and Rykov were severely 'warned' against continuing to fight against the party line, even in the slightest way: Egorov and Bogoliubov (eds) 1983–84, vol. 5, p. 49.
9   Kotkin 2017, p. 15.
10 In the runup to the congress, the Central Committee sent Tomsky to the Transcaucasian conference held in Tbilisi to give its official report. Tomsky in his speech gave only lip service to Stalin's push for collective farms and refused to say a single word about his 'opportunistic work' in the VTsSPS, despite being under considerable pressure to do so. Tomsky was repeatedly censored for that at the Sixteenth Party congress. Rykov, who had been sent to a party gathering in the Urals, where he was said to have been even more

which Tomsky utilised his characteristically wry wit to elicit laughter from the audience nearly three dozen times, he recognised he had made various 'mistakes', such as advocating concessions to the peasantry at the July 1928 Central Committee plenum and displaying 'trade-unionist tendencies'.[11] But he insisted he had not engaged in the sort of factional behaviour banned at the Tenth Party Congress or conducted open opposition like Trotsky and Zinoviev. In contrast, he accurately argued, he had confined his opposition to inside the Politburo and the Central Committee.[12] Perhaps with an eye on the newer delegates to the party congress, he subtly reminded them of the large role he had played in the party since its inception.

Speaker after speaker, over the course of many hours, harshly criticised what they perceived as Tomsky's lack of sincerity and the inadequacy of his 'admission of errors'. The delegates, who also attacked Rykov, denounced the 'Rightists' for their 'kulak programme' and demanded they acknowledge the correctness and great achievements of the party's policies (even though forced collectivisation had been so catastrophic that Stalin just a few months before felt compelled to retreat and hypocritically condemn local activists for their 'dizziness with success').[13] Tomsky's close personal friend Sergei Kirov demagogically argued that the policies of the 'Right Deviationists' would deliberately lead to the restoration of capitalism in the Soviet Union.[14] Stalin ridiculed the 'Right-

---

defiant, suffered similar treatment at the congress: RKP(b) 1931, pp. 109, 118, 125, 161; Gaisinskii 1932, pp. 250–1. Bukharin escaped the ordeal of being sent to a regional conference because he had come down with pneumonia.

[11] The resolutions adopted at the end of the congress did not focus on the opposition of the 'Rightists' to Stalinist agricultural policies. They focused instead on the trade unions, in particular 'the opportunistic leading group on the old staff of the VTsSPS', for its 'anti-Leninist, right-deviationist position on all the fundamental questions facing the trade-union movement during this new stage'. The congress formally approved the purging of its ranks: Egorov and Bogoliubova (eds) 1983–84, vol. 5, pp. 173–4. Stalin continued for months, in his correspondence with Molotov, to harp on the need to break with Tomsky's 'petit bourgeois traditions', including, for example, the relatively lenient treatment of workers guilty of absenteeism: Lih et al. (eds) 1995, p. 220.

[12] RKP(b) 1931, pp. 142–8.

[13] Bukharin, who did not attend the Congress, was criticised to a lesser extent. Bukharin was still too sick to attend. Only Nadezhda Krupskaya, Lenin's widow, had the nerve to refuse to criticise the 'Right Deviationists' or to insufficiently praise Stalin, but after a considerable amount of heckling she backed down and mildly criticised the speeches of Tomsky and Rykov while emphasising their contributions to the party and their admittance of mistakes: RKP(b) 1931, pp. 210–4; McNeal 1972, p. 281. Krupskaya had similarly protested against their treatment at the earlier April Plenum: Kumanev and Kulikova 1994, pp. 148–50.

[14] RKP(b) 1931, p. 157. They were of course defending Lenin's policy of NEP, not advocating

ists', stating that as soon as any 'difficulties arise, when the tiniest cloud appears on the horizon', the Right Deviationist leaders get frightened. Stalin tried to match wits with Tomsky despite the disastrous conditions and mass unrest in the countryside.[15] To loud laughter Stalin put forth an analogy belittling their concerns about the consequences of collectivisation and dekulakisation: 'Should a cockroach make a rustling sound somewhere, they fall back terror-stricken even before it has had time to crawl out of its hole, and they begin to howl about a catastrophe, about the downfall of the Soviet regime'.[16] At the same time, Stalin rejected the charge by the 'Rightists' that he had abolished NEP.[17]

While admitting his 'errors', Tomsky tried to fight back, which did not go over well. It only further incriminated him in the minds of the Stalinists. Mendel Khataevich, who himself would be executed later during the Great Purges, denounced Tomsky for his lack of sincerity, stating 'Comrade Tomsky gave a very clever speech, which could be called a model of the diplomatic art, but the sincerity in this speech was insufficient ... the speeches of Comrades Uglanov and Rykov were more sincere'.[18] Alexei Badaev brought up Lenin's exile of Tomsky to Turkestan in 1921.[19] Tomsky denied he had ever conspired to set up his own faction within the party, which he argued he always thought was wrong since any long-term opposition against the party line and its leadership would inevitably lead to a struggle against the party by its enemies.[20] But Tomsky

---

for the restoration of capitalism. According to Tomsky's youngest son, Tomsky and Kirov remained friends even after Kirov sharply attacked him. Tomsky visited Kirov at his home in Leningrad when he went there on business, and sometimes they went hunting together as they had in earlier years. In the fall of 1934, again according to Tomsky's son, Kirov visited Tomsky in Moscow, which seems highly doubtful: Gorelov and Shapovalova (eds) 2001, pp. 155–6.

15   There were many thousands of instances of mass, anti-government unrest, in which approximately 3.4 million peasants took part during the course of 1930: Khlevniuk 2015, p. 114.
16   RKP(b) 1931, pp. 289, 293. Stalin also mockingly dismissed various notes handed up to the congress presidium by delegates, including those expressing concerns about collectivisation's impact on livestock. *Razbazarivanie*, the peasantry's wholesale slaughtering of their livestock, was a nearly fatal blow to the new collective farm system: Viola 1996, p. 70.
17   Stalin held onto the ludicrous position that he had not abandoned NEP until 1937: Rees 2012, p. 106.
18   RKP(b) 1931, p. 163. Only six of the 24 delegates who vociferously condemned the 'Right Opposition' during the congress survived the purges of the 1930s: Oppenheim 1979, p. 447.
19   RKP(b) 1931, p. 237.
20   RKP(b) 1931, p. 145. Although it seems far-fetched, Graeme Gill suggests it was Tomsky's renunciation of oppositional activity that may explain the re-election of Tomsky, Bukharin, and Rykov as full members to the Central Committee, Rykov's re-election to the

forcefully resented the endless calls for him to repent. He sarcastically asked if the delegates wanted him 'to put on a hair shirt and go seek penance in the Gobi Desert, living on wild honey and locusts'. To Stalin's complaint that Tomsky had not 'expiated his sins', Tomsky demanded, 'permit us to work and not merely to repent', adding that 'repentance was a religious, not a Bolshevik term'.[21] Most defiantly, when the delegates demanded that Tomsky give a second speech to further debase himself, he refused.[22] Though most commentators noted how demoralised all those under attack at the Sixteenth Party Congress appeared to be, the Yugoslav delegate Ante Ciliga was among those who thought that 'of all the speeches only that of Tomsky contained a note of human dignity'.[23] Alexander Barmine who like Ciliga was in attendance, wrote 'Tomsky tried to strike a note of dignity, when announcing his surrender by refusing to insist on his mistakes and on those of his friends'.[24] In addition to sharing these views, Trotsky also thought that 'the ruling clique was not mistaken when in the notes of Tomsky's repentance it heard a discreet amount of hatred'.[25]

Tomsky's former colleagues at the VTsSPS took heat at the party congress for supporting Tomsky during the Eighth Trade-Union Congress. The most tumultuous interactions during the entire Sixteenth Party Congress came when Tomsky's long-time assistant at the VTsSPS, Alexander Dogadov, took the podium. Delegates hounded this Central Committee member for his opposition to introducing Kaganovich onto the VTsSPS at the congress. Dogadov, who had been a Bolshevik since 1905, clumsily tried to defend himself by stating that he did not understand the political significance of trying to deny Kaganovich a

---

Politburo, and why Zinoviev and Kamenev were allowed to re-enter the party: Gill 1990, p. 406n147.

21 RKP(b) 1931, pp. 142, 146–7, 157, 160.
22 TsGAODM, f. 2870, op. 1, d. 296, reprinted in Karpachev and Minaeva (eds) 1992b, p. 111.
23 Ciliga 1979, p. 185.
24 Barmine 1945, p. 199. Tomsky generally 'grovelled less' than his fellow oppositionists according to L. Toropetskii (alias), writing in Pavel Miliukov's émigré publication in Paris, *Poslednie novosti* (*The Latest News*), reprinted in Gorelov and Shapovalova (eds) 2001, p. 213. The historian George Katkov wrote that Rykov's statement was less defiant and subtle than Tomsky's: Katkov 1969, p. 72. Kirov and other speakers particularly disliked the cheerful tone in which Tomsky delivered his speech: RKP(b) 1931, pp. 155, 159, 169.
25 Trotskii 1988, p. 229. Trotsky was of course writing from afar and thus presumably relying on informers. He also wrote that Tomsky carried out the humiliating ritual of humbly repenting 'with more dignity than the others'. Rykov, to his credit, refused to renounce Bukharin. 'I am responsible for what I have done, for the mistakes I have made, and I am not going to use Bukharin as a scapegoat. You cannot demand that from me. For the mistakes I've made, I should be punished, not Bukharin'. But he did implicitly criticise Tomsky for his leadership of the trade unions: RKP(b) 1931, pp. 148–54.

seat on the VTsSPS. Raucous shouting erupted every time Dogadov opened his mouth to the point where Kalinin, who was moderating, at one point could not make himself heard when he tried to restore some order. Dogadov nonetheless remained calm and dignified. While ultimately admitting his mistake regarding Kaganovich, he refused to criticise Tomsky beyond stating that his speech at the trade-union congress was 'completely unsatisfactory'.[26] The party congress passed a resolution denouncing the 'opportunistic' old leadership of the VTsSPS for its 'bourgeois trade-unionist tendencies', especially its failure to understand its role in this new reconstruction period.[27] The envisioned new role for the trade unions was to be almost entirely disciplinary in nature.

The Soviet leadership proceeded to purge tens of thousands of 'Rightists' from its rolls, but they moved slowly against Tomsky.[28] Even though he had been dubbed an 'accomplice of the kulaks', Tomsky was not expelled from the party leadership following the Sixteenth Party Congress.[29] Although dropped from the Politburo, Tomsky was 're-elected' onto the Central Committee.[30] 'He measured things out in doses' is how Bukharin characterised Stalin's piecemeal treatment of oppositionists.[31] Tomsky emphatically agreed, noting 'they were gradually refashioning us by means of a special system – every day a little brushstroke – here a dab, there a dab' ... as a result of this clever bit of work they have turned us into "right-wingers"'.[32] The American former Stalinist, Louis Fischer, noted that 'Stalin can wait. He possesses consummate patience. It is one of his crowning virtues ... He tears down his enemies and rivals in installments'.[33] It is unclear whether the incremental step-by-step approach, when it came to removing the alleged 'Rightists', might have been a result of Stalin's caution or lack of firm control over the Politburo. Many members of the Politburo, who did not yet have reason to fear Stalin, had enjoyed good personal relationships with

---

26   RKP(b) 1931, pp. 276–7; Nosach and Zvereva 2007, pp. 398–9.
27   Egorov and Bogoliubov (eds) 1983–84, vol. 5, pp. 173–4. Dogadov, for the time being, incongruously remained on the VTsSPS and was appointed its head of administrative and managerial functions: GARF, f. 5451, op. 13, d. 9, l. 218.
28   The party purged 250,000 members between 1929 and 1931, a significant percentage of whom because they shared the views of the 'Right Deviationists': Khlevniuk 1996, p. 21.
29   Khlevniuk 1996, p. 22.
30   Stalin had removed Bukharin from the Politburo in November 1929 while allowing him to remain a member of the Central Committee and appointing him director of *Izvestiia*. Rykov, on the other hand, remained not only a member of the Politburo, but the chair of the Sovnarkom until the end of 1930. He was later appointed commissar of the Postal and Telegraph Administration.
31   Quoted in Rogovin 1998, p. xv.
32   Quoted in Agnew and McDermott 1996, p. 76.
33   Fischer 1941, p. 230.

Tomsky and still respected him and did not want him removed from the Central Committee.[34] Ordzhonikidze stated, for example, 'We did everything possible to keep comrades Rykov, Bukharin, Tomsky, and Uglanov in leading posts within the party'.[35] Stalin was determined not to increase sympathy for them among Politburo members by moving against them too quickly or harshly.

Stalin's incremental approach to the former oppositionists, however, may have been the result of neither his caution nor his lack of political control, but rather because he remained unsure of how he wanted to treat them. Peter Whitewood, in his study of Stalin's purge of the Red Army, demonstrates that it was not a matter of Stalin simply waiting until he consolidated his personal power before rooting out possible sources of opposition. An indecisive Stalin was convinced to massacre former oppositionists in the military only after years of suspicions, hesitations, and attacks. In Whitehead's view, the purge of the military leadership was neither long planned nor carefully premeditated.[36] This line of argument dovetails with J. Arch Getty's portrayal of Stalin as an erratic leader who was 'not a master planner ... he stumbled into everything'.[37]

In any case, the Stalinist leadership, given the shortage of experienced administrators, continued to entrust Tomsky with significant non-political power after the Sixteenth Party Congress. The Politburo initially proposed sending Tomsky, in the summer of 1929, to do diplomatic work in Great Britain, but the suggestion was withdrawn after the British Labour Party leader Ramsay MacDonald objected. This became something of a joke inside the Politburo, where Bukharin proposed appointing Tomsky prime minister in London and MacDonald party secretary in Kyshtym.[38] The Politburo appointed Tomsky instead to be the head of a number of commissions in various industries, including most importantly a commission that focused on relations between *Yugostal'* (the Ukrainian iron and steel trust) and military industries.[39] Tomsky's leadership earned the respect of the other 10 members of that commis-

---

34   Fitzpatrick 2015, pp. 35–6. 58–9, 66; Khlevniuk 2009, pp. 6, 10; Rees 2004, pp. 46–7.
35   Quoted in Cohen 1973, p. 452.
36   Whitewood 2015, pp. 276–81.
37   Getty 1993, p. 62.
38   RGASPI, f. 17, op. 3, d. 754, l. 4; Bazhanov 1990, p. 198; Kvashonkin et al. (eds) 1999, pp. 85–6. Kyshtym was a provincial town on the eastern slope of the Ural Mountains.
39   Tomsky was appointed head of the *Yugostal* commission on 6 June 1929: Kvashonkin et al. (eds) 1999, pp. 90–1; Khordina (ed.) 2000, p. 700. *Yugostal* is an acronym of the State Southern Metallurgical Trust. Regional trusts combined large industrial enterprises producing similar products.

sion.⁴⁰ In addition to an appointment as deputy chair of VSNKh, which was especially surprising given his opposition to forced collectivisation and breakneck industrialisation, the Politburo made him head of the Committee on Chemical Production (*Vsekhimprom*) on 19 August 1929.⁴¹ In the 11 months he held that position Tomsky assumed responsibility for a number of projects, including putting a giant chemical plant (one of the Soviet Union's largest) into operation. To the later charges that he had done nothing for the five-year plan, Tomsky pointed with pride to completing this 'difficult assignment'.⁴²

Tomsky, however, had trouble holding up under the prolonged stress from the political attacks, both physically and mentally. One sexist observer described Tomsky in 1930 as having 'nerves like an old *baba*'.⁴³ And indeed, two weeks after the Sixteenth Party Congress and the accompanying vilification of him in the press, Tomsky suffered a serious seizure and complete psychological collapse.⁴⁴ Rykov wrote to Kuibyshev that Tomsky was in such a state that he did not even recognise me.⁴⁵ The doctor, who diagnosed it as a nervous breakdown, also noted that Tomsky suffered from emphysema and an enlargement of his heart.⁴⁶ Overwhelmed and depressed, he became completely unable to carry out his managerial functions. On 16 September 1930, the Politburo granted Tomsky's request, which was encouraged by his Kremlin doctor, to resign as head of the chemical industry.⁴⁷ In agreeing to Tomsky's resignation, Stalin

---

40   Kvashonkin et al. (eds) 1999, p. 89; Khordina (ed.) 2000, p. 713. Perhaps partly on the Tomsky commission's recommendation, *Yugostal'* was abolished in 1930 and its metallurgical factories were incorporated into *Stal'* as part of a major reorganisation of the administration of industries by VSNKh's leaders: Shearer 1996, p. 170. *Stal'* is the abbreviation of the All-Union Association of the Iron and Steel, Iron Ore, and Manganese Industry.
41   Khordina (ed.) 2000, p. 742. This position made Tomsky responsible for the control of the chemical industry at the republican and local level as well as for its direct management at the national level: Carr and Davies 1969a, p. 355.
42   TsGAODM, f. 2870, op. 1, d. 296, reprinted in Karpachev and Minaeva (eds) 1992b, pp. 104, 117.
43   Kitaeff 1954, p. 121. Tomsky was far from alone in suffering from what were diagnosed as nervous disorders. That was the cause of virtually half of all visits to medical clinics by members of the political elite: Kotkin 2014, p. 576. The Commissar of Health, Nikolai Semashko, conceded that 'exceptional nervous strain' was a common feature of Soviet life: quoted in Pinnow 2010, pp. 218–19. Tomsky had earlier agreed, stating 'the atmosphere in which we work today is indeed nervous, unhealthy ... The cream of our human material has exhausted itself': quoted in Halfin 2003, p. 102.
44   TsGAODM, f. 2870, op. 1, d. 296, reprinted in Karpachev and Minaeva (eds) 1992b, p. 104.
45   Nosach and Zvereva 2007, p. 57.
46   RGASPI, f. 593, op. 1, d. 2, 63, l. 71.
47   RGASPI, f. 593, op. 1, d. 2, ll. 62, 69. Tomsky's 30 August 1930 letter to the Politburo is reprinted in: Kvashonkin et al. (eds) 1999, pp. 133–4.

noted that by this time 'he is doing nothing for us in the chemical industry'.[48] Although they continued to have their Kremlin apartment, Tomsky and the family increasingly retired to his dacha when the weather permitted. But his chronic depression and anxiety, along with his increasingly serious heart problems, were so severe the party sent him to Italy and then Germany for treatment, where he slowly recovered, although the doctors there were not the psychiatrists Tomsky probably also needed.[49] Tomsky returned to Germany for medical care in January 1931, following what the doctors again diagnosed as a nervous breakdown.[50] On doctor's orders Tomsky began to follow a simple diet and swore off alcohol, although he clearly often fell off the wagon.[51] Despite his new status as an outcast, there is no evidence Tomsky considered not returning to the Soviet Union during these trips abroad, even though Tomsky's family was able to accompany him to Berlin in 1931.[52] Tomsky, in addition to his hobby of drawing, loved to read, and with all this down time Tomsky, ever the autodidact, read numerous classics as well as various works of contemporary literature.[53]

After nearly two years of leave, Tomsky in April 1932 went to work as the chair of the Association of State Publishing Houses (OGIZ), the government's massive publishing conglomerate created as part of the Stalinist centralisation of the economy.[54] The 30 individual, specialised publishing houses, which collectively published 90 percent of all the books and journals in the RSFSR, were made subordinate to Tomsky and OGIZ's central administration.[55] The interna-

---

48   Lih et al. (eds.) 1995, pp. 210–1. It was Rykov who provided the Politburo with updates on his condition: Khordina (ed.) 2001, pp. 79, 82.
49   Tomsky arrived in Genoa on the ship 'Mikhail Tomsky' for treatment before going to a top specialist in Breslau, where he spent months convalescing: RGASPI, f. 593, op. 1, d. 6, l. 2; Gorelov 2000, p. 278.
50   RGASPI, f. 593, op. 1, d. 6, l. 148.
51   Citrine 1936, p. 132.
52   Gorelev 2000, p. 25. Trotsky travelled with his wife Natalya to a medical clinic in Berlin in 1926. Likewise, Bukharin, when the treatment of the 'oppositionists' became increasingly brutal, in early 1936 travelled to Paris in an unsuccessful attempt to acquire the archives of the German Social-Democratic Party. He was able to travel with his pregnant wife, which may have been an implicit invitation to emigrate: Fitzpatrick 2015, p. 123. Apparently, Bukharin never considered emigrating.
53   Tomsky's knowledge of English literature impressed the British trade unionist Walter Citrine: Citrine 1964, p. 89.
54   TsGAODM, f. 2870, op. 1, d. 296, reprinted in Karpachev and Minaeva (eds) 1992c, p. 107. Tomsky had been appointed in August 1931, but because of his poor health was not able to begin work until April 1932. OGIZ, the *Ob'edinenie gosudarstvennykh knizhno-zhurnal'nykh izdatel'stv*, had been established shortly before, in July 1930. It superseded Gosizdat.
55   Tomskii 1934, p. 6; Kassof 2015, p. 91. OGIZ was also supplied with its own book distribu-

tionally acclaimed writer, and his old friend, Maksim Gorky had recommended Tomsky for the position, even though Tomsky had only three years of formal education.[56] Despite his long history as the head of the trade unions and his recent experience as head of the chemical industry, one might think he would not be able to handle the job of directing the largest publishing enterprise in the world, which was facing enormous problems as a result of the introduction of the First Five-Year Plan, either because of his still poor health, or because he lacked any expertise in publishing.[57] For a simple editor in one of the subordinate publishing houses, the party ideally sought experienced and 'politically aware' Bolsheviks who had more than a minimal education as well as some background in journalism or academia.[58] But it is not as if Tomsky had never weighed in on cultural policies. He had been, for example, a member of a 1925 Politburo commission that had written the party's first policy statement on literary and artistic policies.[59] From another perspective, Tomsky arguably was the perfect candidate for the job not only because of his experience directing a large organisation, but because he was so politically vulnerable.[60]

Tomsky may have very much wanted to again assume such a position of responsibility, to be, so to speak, back in the ring again, but he himself knew he was not qualified for this assignment. Given his serious doubts about his ability to perform well in this new capacity, Tomsky must have wondered why Gorky had recommended him for the post.[61] During his first days on the job, Tomsky wrote to Gorky, with whom he had been corresponding for a quarter of a century, stating in a panic, 'until now I have only been a reader'. He asked Gorky, 'the great proletarian writer' who was still living outside the Soviet Union in

---

tion network, *Knigotsentr* (Book Centre), and direct ties with the Soviet Union's 16 largest printing plants. Ministerially, OGIZ was subordinate to Narkompros, the acronym for the Commissariat of Enlightenment.

[56]   Spiridonova 2013, p. 220. Nadezhda Krupskaya also supported Tomsky's appointment: Shapovalova 1989, p. 95. Ironically, Artashes Khalatov, who had been ousted to make room for Tomsky, had led the effort to try to convince Gorky to return to the Soviet Union: Slezkine 2017, p. 458.

[57]   Tomsky had been a printer by trade in his younger years and had been editor or served on the editorial board of numerous Bolshevik publications, beginning in 1906, as noted in chapter one. Gorky, incidentally, also lacked much formal education.

[58]   Because editorial work was not well paid and did not carry much status within the party, the publishing houses had trouble finding editors who met these criteria. Many in fact were former Mensheviks: Kassof 2000, pp. 341, 564.

[59]   Kemp-Welch 1991, p. 32.

[60]   Kassof 2000, p. 341.

[61]   Gorelov 2000, p. 220.

Sorrento, the seaside resort in fascist Italy, to provide whatever support and advice he could from his years of experience in the publishing world.[62] 'The party has entrusted me with a difficult assignment about which I know so little and you know so much. Don't refuse to provide comradely help'.[63] And in fact Gorky, who proved to be a loyal friend, remained in constant contact despite the increasingly dark clouds hanging over Tomsky's head.[64] Both Tomsky and Gorky increasingly battled depression and anguished over the course the revolution had taken under Stalin's leadership as well as their various compromises, or worse in Gorky's case, they would make to try to remain in the Stalinist regime's good graces.[65] Gorky wrote in one of his notebooks after he returned to the Soviet Union, '[I'm] like a dog: I understand everything, yet I am silent'.[66]

Tomsky's health proved to be perhaps a much bigger obstacle than his lack of any experience in publishing. His doctor would regularly request that he be granted a week or two of time off, or be allowed to conduct business from home, because of debilitating spells of 'general malaise, severe headaches, or a depressed mood'.[67] It is unclear what sort of treatment Tomsky received for his periodic bouts of incapacitating mental strain and melancholia, which would

---

62 Gorky, who had left the Soviet Union in September 1921, after often spending the warmer months in Moscow beginning in 1928, returned permanently in May 1932, after years of Stalin encouraging him to do so.

63 Quoted in Ivanova 1989, p. 6. Ivanova based this article on the unpublished correspondence between Tomsky and Gorky she found in the Gorky and OGIZ archives. Unfortunately, she does not provide any archival citations.

64 They regularly discussed various issues. For example, with Gorky's encouragement and through his contacts in England and Germany, Tomsky in January 1933 pursued the possibility of foreign editions of Soviet works: Spiridonova 2013, pp. 220–1.

65 Gorky in August 1933 pulled together a group of 37 prominent Soviet writers for a notorious book about the building of the 141 miles of the White Sea-Baltic Canal, or Belomor for short, which was constructed by gulag labour using only wooden spades, handsaws, and pickaxes, and cost the lives of at least 12,000 prisoners; perhaps many thousands more. It was of minimal value because it was too shallow for oceangoing ships. OGIZ, under the collective editorship of Gorky, Leopold Averbakh (a literary figure whom Gorky considered his protégé), and Semyon Firin (head of the Belomor prison camp), in January 1934 published a beautiful volume with the book's 'uplifting stories' celebrating re-education through work that was immediately translated into English: Levin 1965, pp. 291–3, 295–8. It has aptly been compared to writing a Nazi travelogue about Auschwitz: von Geldern and Stites (eds) 1995, p. 190.

66 Quoted in Ruder 1998, p. 39.

67 RGASPI, f. 593, op. 1, d. 2, ll. 3, 5, 48, 53, 55, 145. These requests for time at home or leave would be repeatedly discussed by the Politburo: Khordina (ed.) 2001, pp. 350, 454, 495, 557, 616, 678, 726, 760, 793.

continue to plague him for what remained of his life, beyond some time away from his office to rest.⁶⁸

Worn out as he was, Tomsky nonetheless proved able to throw himself into his work as director of OGIZ. He led an organisation of 36,000 employees, which was responsible for the planning, financing, and equipping, as well as for the marketing and distribution of all Soviet books and journals.⁶⁹ Although one of OGIZ's primary responsibilities was to develop plans for the individual publishing houses, Tomsky's predecessor, Artashes Khalatov, had failed to do so. Tomsky had the plan reworked five times before he was satisfied.⁷⁰ Tomsky also hired experienced assistances with whom he developed a plan on how to supervise OGIZ's large publishing houses, which published 49,990 titles in 1932, increasing to 53,800 titles in 1933.⁷¹ He quickly realised the nature of the enormous problems he faced, namely the poor quality and insufficient amount of paper, woefully outdated printing presses, and an acute shortage of editors.⁷² The last problem was worsened by the recent dismissal of many experienced editors and employees because of their political 'unreliability'.⁷³

One editor who was not dismissed was Semen Kanatchikov, whose life we have been tracking in parallel with Tomsky's. Despite his association with Zinoviev's 'Leningrad Opposition' during the intra-party struggle and his own lack of education, Kanatchikov became a top editor and literary administrator in sensitive literary-journalistic posts following the Stalinists' consolidation of power.⁷⁴ From 1929 to 1935, Kanatchikov edited the newly founded *Litera-*

---

68 It was thought that an extended period of rest could restore one's equilibrium, so it was often prescribed: Pinnow 2010, p. 219.
69 RGASPI, f. 81, op. 3. d. 179, ll. 27–8, 70; RGASPI, f. 593, op. 1, d. 2, ll. 14–25.
70 RGASPI, f. 81, op. 3, d. 179, l. 22; Walker 1991, p. 68.
71 A slight majority of those titles were pamphlets (4–32 pages) as opposed to books (more than 32 pages): Jaryc 1935, pp. 19–20.
72 The publishing industry had only gradually recovered from the serious damage it had suffered during War Communism, including the deterioration of printing presses and the disruption of the distribution network: Kenez 1985, pp. 44–5, 239, 243. But during the second half of 1932 the amount of paper unexpectedly plummeted due primarily to a lack of chemicals.
73 Ivanova 1989, p. 6. For example, Anatoly Vinogradov, the director of the Lenin Library from 1921 to 1925, who at OGIZ worked with Gorky on the publication of foreign literary classics and had edited and written numerous books during the 1930s, was fired for his 'ideological vacillations'. But in addition, many had been dismissed for such non-political reasons as embezzlement: Gorelov 2000, pp. 221–2. Like at OGIZ, most of the employees of the Marx-Engels Institute, the translators, librarians, archivists as well as scholars, were not party members, including former Mensheviks, SRs, and even Kadets. They were all fired after Ryazanov's arrest and ouster as director in 1931: Beecher and Fomichev 2006, pp. 127, 141.
74 The Central Committee assigned Kanatchikov, beginning in 1928, to the editorial board

turnaia gazeta (The Literary Newspaper), which under his watch became in 1934 the organ of the Soviet Writers' Union.[75] Tomsky probably had a hand in the publication of the second volume of Kanatchikov's acclaimed autobiography, which OGIZ reissued in 1934.[76]

Tomsky assumed his position as head of OGIZ at the exact time that the Central Committee decided to abolish the Russian Association of Proletarian Writers (RAPP), which had militantly and rigidly advocated for avant-garde experimentation. The Stalinists instead proclaimed a new method for literature, Socialist Realism, that would be 'accessible to the masses' with positive plots that contributed to the general mobilisation for industrialisation by focusing on the 'heroism of socialist construction'.[77] Between 1932 and 1934, as the party leadership largely succeeded in making publishing houses and fictional writers wholly subservient to the ideological demands of the party leadership, OGIZ's revamped editorial boards worked to ensure that all accepted works conformed to Socialist Realism.[78] Although these OGIZ editors had only a vague sense of what the new aesthetic actually entailed, published works quickly became formulaic, mostly of the so-called production novel variety. In the words of the literary scholar Katrina Clark, 'If a writer wanted his novel to be published, he had to use the proper language (epithets, catch phrases, stock images, etc.) and syntax (conventional ordering of events in accordance with the master plot)'.[79]

OGIZ also felt pressure to replace experienced writers with young writers from among the *udarniki* (shock-brigade workers) and collective farmworkers who displayed some literary talent.[80] When Tomsky began work at OGIZ, the Central Committee was celebrating the new writers and artists who have

---

member of the 'thick' journal *Krasnaia Nov'* (Red Virgin Soil) and named him secretary of the Soviet Writers' Federation: Zelnik 1995, p. 9.

75   Zelnik 1995, pp. 9–10. Kanatchikov wrote a number of propagandistic pamphlets during these years, including a semi-fictional glorification of collectivization: Kanatchikov 1986, pp. 390–1.

76   Kanatchikov's autobiography was first published in 1924. The first volume was reissued in 1929: Zelnik 1976a, p. 294n2.

77   Fitzpatrick 1978, p. 28; Clark 1978, p. 194; Brown 1982, p. 168. Stalin also called on writers to cheer on the five-year plans by becoming 'engineers of the human soul': Hellbeck 2006, p. 291.

78   Yedlin 1999, p. 198; Robin 1992, p. 43. Stalin attended a gathering of writers in October 1932 at Gorky's mansion, where he interjected that 'If the artist is going to depict our life correctly, he cannot fail to observe and point out what is leading it towards socialism. So this will be socialist art. It will be socialist realism': James 1973, p. 86.

79   Clark 1985, p. 13.

80   Clark 1978, p. 197; Slonim 1977, p. 161.

come forward from the plants, factories, and collective farms to replace 'alien elements'.[81] Although Tomsky was in no position to challenge the new policy, he publicly argued that there was still a need for the 'old intelligentsia' and privately complained that Socialist Realism left him with authors without much ability or professionalism and he deplored the dull character of much of what OGIZ published.[82] He even called it 'trash' in one of his messages to Gorky.[83] Even though Gorky is viewed as the primary originator of Socialist Realism, he also wanted Soviet literature to uphold certain standards, writing to Tomsky in March 1933, 'What sort of rubbish is being published'![84] 'The work of hacks, and the indulgent attitude towards it, constituted the greatest evil on the cultural front', Tomsky wrote to Gorky in another letter.[85] Tomsky lamented how contemporary authors, as censorship tightened, only seemed concerned with showing their 'ideological fidelity' by implementing any shifts in the general line, rather than, in Tomsky's quaint words, bothering to address 'the meaning of life'.[86] Tomsky concluded, shortly after he assumed the helm, that OGIZ was in a very sorry state of affairs.

It might seem hard to explain why the party leadership would appoint Tomsky to the politically sensitive position of head of OGIZ. Surveillance over publishing was obviously thought to be of critical importance to the Stalinist leadership. Stalin may have assumed, as suggested above, that Tomsky in this post would try to prove his loyalty by slavishly following party dictates. And indeed, despite his personal views, Tomsky in an OGIZ publication in 1934, explicitly referring to Stalin's infamous letter to the editors of *Proletarskaia revoliutsiia* (Proletarian Revolution), stated that in the struggle for ideological purity 'any

---

81   At the meeting of the First Congress of the Writers' Union in 1934, held in the columned hall of the House of the Trade Unions, nearly three-quarters of the delegates were of worker or peasant origin while less than 20 percent were from the 'working intelligentsia': Garrard 1990, pp. 29, 32.

82   Gorelov 2000, p. 222; Tomskii 1934, p. 7; Harris 2017, pp. 215–16. This was not a new view on Tomsky's part. At the Seventh Trade-Union Congress in 1926, Tomsky argued that the literature workers created was generally of poor quality – vulgar and ungrammatical – and called for greater cooperation between amateurs and professionals: Mally 2000, p. 101.

83   Ivanova 1989, p. 6; Spiridonova 2013, p. 10.

84   Quoted in Yedlin 1999, p. 202.

85   Ivanova 1989, p. 6. Gorky became utterly appalled at the state of Soviet letters and feared it would only get worse given the party hacks who quickly came to control the Writers' Union, some of whom he characterised as 'ignoramuses' and men of 'decrepit intellect' in a letter to Stalin in August 1934: Gorky 1997, pp. 306–7, 351–3.

86   Gorelov 2000, p. 220. This section of Gorelov's book, pages 219–27, consists of an interview with the historian Galina Ivanova.

form of conciliation or tolerance toward opportunism was inadmissible'.[87] In addition, a good part of the explanation for Tomsky's appointment is that the Central Committee intended for Tomsky to focus on economic-administrative issues. One of his deputies, the scholar Ivan Luppol, 16 years Tomsky's junior, was to focus on ideological issues.[88] Yet even though it was Luppol who was supposed to be primarily responsible for ensuring that the books OGIZ published were in line with the pronouncements of Stalin and the Central Committee, Tomsky had to continually deal with the concerns of staff members who were directly responsible to the Central Committee.[89] To address that, the Tomsky-led board of OGIZ established in the summer of 1932 an editorial council to oversee the publishing houses, with the stated purpose of providing ideological leadership'.[90]

As the director of OGIZ, Tomsky did occasionally engage in profiles in courage. For example, despite the risks involved, he provided his old friend and combatant, David Ryazanov, with over two years of work as a translator. Ryazanov was in extremely difficult straits. After his ouster from the trade unions along with Tomsky during the Fourth Trade-Union Congress in 1921, he became the first director of the Marx-Engels Institute until he was dismissed and expelled from the party in 1931 for allegedly participating in a plot to overthrow the regime with a group of Mensheviks. He had been, for all practical purposes, barred from working.[91] Despite the extremely dark political clouds hovering

---

[87] Tomskii 1934, p. 5. Stalin initiated the purge of publications in October 1931 with his article-length letter attacking the editors of *Proletarskaia revoliutsiia* for their 'rotten liberalism'. He condemned party historians as 'archive rats' and called for revamping party textbooks to emphasise accessibility as well as political education. Although party intellectuals mocked it, Stalin's letter proved to be a key turning point in the relations between the regime and the intelligentsia because editors and publishers understood it as an order for conformity to the party line not just in history, but in all cultural and theoretical fields: Brandenberger and Zelenov (eds) 2019, p. 2; Priestland 2007, p. 268; Barber 1976, pp. 25, 32; Fitzpatrick 2015, p. 107.

[88] Luppoll was assigned to OGIZ a month after Tomsky assumed the directorship. Luppol was a philosopher and historian who had been a party member since 1920: Kassof 2000, p. 549.

[89] Since the powers of Glavlit (the Main Directorate of Literature and Publishing Houses), which had been responsible for censorship during the 1920s, had been sharply curtailed, ideological responsibility fell on the shoulders of Luppol and the directors and 'political editors' under Tomsky at each of the publishing houses. Many directors of publishing houses and their 'political editors' quit when censorship responsibilities were placed on their shoulders. When they were compelled to return to their posts, they did so reluctantly: Kassof 2015, pp. 92–3. Luppol managed to avoid arrest until 1941. He would die in the gulag in 1943.

[90] Kassof 2000, pp. 547–8.

[91] Rokitianskii and Muller 1996, p. 123.

over Ryazanov, Tomsky courageously published in 1935, in two volumes, Ryazanov's translation of the speeches and letters, with commentary, of the influential British economist David Ricardo, an important precursor of Marx. Tomsky had OGIZ publish them in editions of 20,000 copies, although wisely not under Ryazanov's name. Tomsky also arranged for him to be paid 11,000 rubles for his work.[92] Tomsky surely was aware that Ryazanov, as the director of the Marx-Engels Institute earlier, helped leading Bolshevik oppositionists by discreetly providing them with various paid assignments, including giving Trotsky translation work when he was in Central Asian exile.[93] Ryazanov had also bravely spoken out against the hounding of Tomsky at the Sixteenth Party Congress, which undoubtedly earned Tomsky's gratitude.[94]

Given Stalin's determination to subject publishing to party control, almost as remarkable as Tomsky's appointment to head OGIZ was the appointment of the disgraced Lev Kamenev as director of the prestigious, internationally renowned Academia (*Akademiia*) publishing house.[95] Kamenev, who Tomsky had mercilessly attacked during the power struggle, as we have seen, assumed this post within OGIZ immediately upon his return from exile in December 1933, when he was also readmitted into the party. Like Tomsky's appointment, Kamenev's appointment was also at the behest of Gorky, although Tomsky had to presumably sign off on it.[96] In this position Kamenev, again with Gorky's

---

[92] Rokitianskii 2009, p. 482. As director of the Marx-Engels Institute, Ryazanov had published, in addition to works by Marx and Engels and various other Marxists such as Plekhanov, Russian editions of a wide variety of classical thinkers besides Ricardo, including G.W.F. Hegel, Ludwig Feuerbach, Thomas Hobbes, Adam Smith, Denis Diderot, and Baron d'Holbach: Beecher and Fomichev 2006, pp. 130, 143. Ryazanov was arrested on 22 July 1937 and executed on 21 January 1938: Tomsky's son Yury would visit the apartment of Ryazanov's widow Anna Lvovna after they were both allowed to move back to Moscow following their years in the gulag. He may have crossed paths there with Rykov's daughter Natalia Rykova and Bukharin's wife Anna Larina among other victims of Stalinist repression who frequently visited the apartment.

[93] Beecher and Fomichev 2006, pp. 140, 143. Ryazanov also helped Mensheviks and SRs: Nosach 2005, p. 53.

[94] Rokitiansii and Muller 1996, p. 57.

[95] The Academia Publishing House, despite its name, was not the official publisher for the Academy of Sciences, which had its own publishing house. The Academy of Science was one of the few institutions from tsarist Russia to survive.

[96] Spiridonova 2013, pp. 220–1; Krilov and Kichatova 2004, pp. 63–4. Gorky used his 'friendly terms' with the OGPU head Yagoda to successfully intervene to assist various oppositionists: Yedlin 1999, p. 180; Krilov and Kichatova 2004, p. 74. But Gorky and Tomsky could not protect everyone. The former Trotskyists Ivar Smilga and Aleksandr Voronsky, who also worked under Tomsky at OGIZ, were arrested in early 1935: Slezkine 2017, pp. 773–84.

backing, organised and directed the Institute of Literature in 1934.[97] A scholarly man who spoke many languages, Kamenev edited the works of the great nineteenth-century Russian radical Alexander Herzen and published 'memoirs and world classics of a quality and with an objectivity not seen in the Soviet Union before or since', in the words of one literary scholar.[98] Academia also published Russian fiction from the twelfth century to the beginning of the twentieth century.[99] Kamenev joined with Tomsky to courageously help Ryazanov, by publishing under the Academia imprint, his translations of Etienne Cabet's utopian French novel *Travel and Adventures of Lord William Carisdall in Icaria*. Here too Ryazanov's name did not appear on the title page.[100]

The Stalinists had thus brought together at OGIZ the former 'Rightist' Tomsky and the former 'Leftist' Kamenev, whom they already suspected of colluding with one another against the Stalinist leadership.[101] And they apparently did. They met at least a couple of times in Tomsky's office in OGIZ, where they talked 'about everything and anything'.[102] In effect, if not intent, Kamenev's appointment under Tomsky amounted to entrapment, which would be used against both of them later.[103] Kamenev was arrested on 16 December 1934 for his supposed role in Kirov's assassination.

Tomsky could not protect Kanatchikov, even if he tried. Kanatchikov was ousted as editor on 4 December 1935. His successor, Lev Subotsky, a 35-year-old

---

97   Krylov and Kichatova 2004, p. 85. The Institute of Literature was retitled the Gorky Institute of World Literature during Kamenev's tenure as director in 1934. Luppol became Kamenev's successor as director.
98   Rayfield 2004, p. 221. Kamenev, the son of an engineer who had gone to law school, came from a much more privileged background than Tomsky. A 'return to the classics' was part of the new cultural conservatism under Stalin: Hellbeck 2006, p. 230. Kamenev was also put in charge of organising the Pushkin jubilee. In addition to 13.4 million copies of Pushkin's complete works, OGIZ published in the millions the complete works of Turgenev, Chekhov, and Tolstoy.
99   Krylov and Kichatova 2004, p. 65.
100   Beecher and Fomichev 2006, pp. 143–4. Anatoly Lunacharsky also did what he could to help Ryazanov: Rokitianskii 2009, p. 483.
101   Kun 1992, p. 359.
102   *Pravda*, 22 August 1936. They had undoubtedly discussed, for example, what Ryazanov had told them about how Stalin had fabricated charges against him through one of his underlings: Rokitianskii 2009, p. 492.
103   Similarly, Rykov met with Kamenev in 1929, which Kaganovich later suggested had some sinister purpose. Rykov, as head of the Sovnarkom, met with Kamenev since he was then head of the Soviet government authority in charge of foreign concessions (Glavkontsesskom), which answered to the Sovnarkom: RGASPI, f. 17, op. 2, d. 584, l. 180.

military prosecutor and sometime literary critic, turned *Literaturnaya gazeta* into the spearhead of a campaign denouncing 'enemies of the people' in the literary world.[104] Kanatchikov, as a result, was unsurprisingly arrested in 1936. In desperation, he wrote a letter from prison to his 'deeply esteemed' leader, in which he asserted that Stalin knew him 'better than anyone else' and therefore could not conceivably imagine that he was a traitor. Kanatchikov tried to impress upon Stalin that he had 'struggled in the area of literature against every kind of deviation'.[105] Like similar letters of capitulation to Stalin during the Great Purges, including by Bukharin, it was to no avail. Kanatchikov was sentenced to eight years of hard labour. He would die in the gulag on 19 October 1940 at age 61.

One of Tomsky's primary responsibilities at OGIZ was to oversee the publication of school textbooks and to ensure that they presented the 'correct general line' when accusations of 'wrecking' were swirling around all state institutions.[106] The party had begun sending inspectors to the various publishing houses on the lookout for any lack of vigilance in blocking 'the perspective of the class enemy'.[107] With publishing under this sort of extraordinary scrutiny, OGIZ refused to release 88 books in 1933 that were ready for distribution and removed many textbooks from circulation or had them radically rewritten.[108] Tomsky would later be accused of wasting one million rubles on 'ideologically flawed' manuscripts.[109] In addition, around this time troikas, drawn from the political police, censors, and propagandists, removed around 50 percent of the books in every field of knowledge from libraries across the country.[110] The confiscated writings included those by Tomsky himself.[111] The Central Committee in this context adopted on 12 February 1933 a resolution that called for an all-out effort to publish ideologically acceptable elementary and middle school

---

104 Zelnik 1995, pp. 10–11, 37. Subotsky survived the Great Purges and the entire Stalin era, although as a Jewish critic, he became a target of Stalin's vicious post-war 'anti-cosmopolitanism' campaign.
105 Quoted in Zelnik 1995, p. 11.
106 Citrine was appalled at how propagandistic these textbooks were in their negative portrayal of British life: Citrine 1936, pp. 305–6.
107 Gorelov 2000, p. 221.
108 Brandenberger 2011, p. 34; Gorelov 2000, p. 224. Party leaders received secret lists of all the authors and texts pulled from circulation: Kassof 2015, p. 92; Plamper 2001, p. 531.
109 TsGAODM, f. 2870, op. 1, d. 296, reprinted in Karpachev and Minaeva (eds) 1992a, p. 111.
110 Rayfield 2004, p. 234. Libraries and archives created 'special sections' to store these 'dangerous' books: Boberowski 2016, p. 114. That meant it was only in private libraries such as Tomsky's where many earlier Soviet publications could be found: Polonsky 2010, pp. 72–3.
111 Ermolaev 1997, p. 56.

textbooks in all the basic subjects.[112] The Central Committee instructed the tough, no-nonsense Stalinist Andrei Bubnov as Commissar of Enlightenment, and Tomsky as head of OGIZ, to work together with a number of scholars to publish 77 textbooks with a print run of more than 45 million copies by 15 July 1933, just six months later.[113] It called for an all-out push, with presses working three to four shifts a day, and it consumed most of OGIZ's paper reserves, hurting other planned publications.[114] Remarkably, the schools received the textbooks on time, although the quality of the paper was extremely poor.[115] A Stalinist-era history of Soviet publishing, without of course mentioning Tomsky's name, described this as 'a great achievement of Soviet socialist culture'.[116] The secretary of the OGIZ party cell, A.I. Udalov, attributed this success almost exclusively to Tomsky.[117] But since Tomsky and others were 'working day and night', they predictably made some careless mistakes, for example, on the map in one of the textbooks. Tomsky would have to answer for that later. In the midst of this massive effort, when OGIZ had already published 30 of the 45 million copies, Tomsky was hauled before a purge commission, as will be discussed below.[118]

---

112 Fitzpatrick 1979, p. 225. Textbooks would constitute a significant portion of what OGIZ published. The demand for traditional textbooks increased after the Soviet regime introduced universal primary education in 1930 and the Central Committee subsequently repudiated further experimenting in progressive education. Likewise, the number of students in higher education and technical training institutes dramatically increased during the 1930s.
113 Karpachev and Minaeva (eds) 1992a, p. 114; Fitzpatrick, 1979, p. 136; McNeal 1972, p. 276. Bubnov, a former Trotskyist, had little administrative experience in the field of education before he replaced Lunacharsky as Commissar of Enlightenment on 12 September 1929. Tomsky had known him since at least 1922, when he had nominated Bubnov to be one of three members of an editorial commission at the Eleventh Party Congress: RKP(b) 1961, p. 5. They were neighbours in the Kremlin: Gorelov 2000, p. 272. Bubnov, who had joined the attacks against Tomsky at the Sixteenth Party Congress, albeit in a cursory manner, would be arrested on 17 October 1937 and executed on 1 August 1938: RKP(b) 1931, p. 181.
114 Gorelov 2000, p. 224.
115 Tomsky wrote to Gorky at the beginning of March 1933 that the quality of the paper was 'unspeakably bad': Ivanova 1989, p. 7.
116 Nazarov 1952, pp. 173–4. Textbooks continued to be a primary focus of OGIZ in the following years, with editions of hundreds of million copies, including in many of the languages of the Soviet Union. There would be a similar Central Committee resolution on textbook publications in May 1934: Schlogel 2012, p. 158; Fitzpatrick 1976, p. 216n10. Tomsky along with his associates presented a report about textbook publications to the Politburo on 2 July 1935: Khordina (ed.) 2001, p. 667.
117 TsGAODM, f. 2870, op. 1, d. 296, reprinted in Karpachev and Minaeva (eds) 1992a, p. 108.
118 TsGAODM, f. 2870, op. 1, d. 296, reprinted in Karpachev and Minaeva (eds) 1992a, p. 108.

The long working days coupled with the stress that he might fail to meet the publication deadline for this enormous number of textbooks, along with the increasingly harsh political attacks, all predictably took a toll on Tomsky's emotional and physical wellbeing. In 1933 Tomsky suffered from influenza and a variety of other ailments. When he failed to improve after 10 days of rest, the Kremlin doctor Vyshnepolsky recommended at least two more weeks of rest, during which he was instructed to ignore all his responsibilities at OGIZ.[119] In his correspondence with Gorky at this time, a note of despair began to permeate his messages.[120]

Clearly accustomed to the lifestyle of the party elite, Tomsky also felt stressed over his family's finances. Although the publishing industry was relatively poorly paid, it is not clear why he felt financially strapped since he still received the use of his apartment in the Kremlin (with all the privileges that came with that) as well as his dacha in Bolshevo and a chauffeur-driven car. He would write to Abel Yenukidze a couple times a year asking for additional financial support.[121] He also complained to his old colleague and friend Kalinin that he had 'no way of earning extra money from literary activity or other work' and asked for financial support from the Kremlin's special, secret fund.[122]

Tomsky displayed impressive resilience despite all the stresses. Tomsky quickly returned to work, where despite various obstacles he became increasingly pleased with what he was able to achieve at OGIZ. This was partly due to his success at getting the party leadership to provide greater resources to OGIZ, including additional paper and the importation of foreign printing presses.[123] In his campaign for more funding, Tomsky even arranged a have a short personal meeting with Stalin, who agreed to Tomsky's request for an additional 4.5 million rubles of funding.[124] OGIZ managed to publish books by popular,

---

119   RGASPI, f. 593, op. 1, d. 6, ll. 53, 145.
120   Gorelov 2000, p. 224.
121   'Uncle Abe', the popular secretary of Central Committee from 1922 to 1935, was known as 'a soft touch' who had trouble saying no: Fitzpatrick 2015, p. 116; Merridale 2013, p. 323; Dmitrievskii 1932, p. 32.
122   Kvashonkin et al. (eds) 1999, p. 306. This was a little later, in 1935. Kalinin did not reply to Tomsky's plea. Stalin abolished in 1932 the decree prohibiting party officials from earning more than the 'party maximum' of 500 rubles, except from writing or teaching: Matthews 1978, p. 68; Tucker 1990, pp. 111–12.
123   RGASPI, f. 593, op. 1, d. 2, ll. 20–7; RGASPI, f. 593, op. 1, d. 6, ll. 20, 25, 27, 31. When he wrote to Stalin, he addressed him as 'Dear Koba': RGASPI, f. 593, op. 1, d. 6, l. 20. Whereas European printing presses were replaced every 10 years or so, many of the Soviet presses were 35 years old.
124   RGASPI, f. 593, op. 1, d. 6, l. 14.

pre-revolutionary authors, especially by Pushkin, in editions so large that it makes 'a foreign publisher gasp', in the words of one German visitor to the Soviet Union.[125] Tomsky proudly told a British visitor in September 1935 that OGIZ would publish over a 100 million books that year, including books in English, such as Dickens' *Pickwick Papers* and Thackeray's *Vanity Fair*, and showed him, in the visitor's words, 'many fine specimens of good printing on quite excellent paper'.[126] As Molotov put it, in a backhanded slap, Tomsky had grown into 'a real bureaucrat'.[127]

One of OGIZ's most impressive publications fell victim to the Great Purges. Tomsky in 1933 commissioned the celebrated avant-garde artists and couple, Alexander Rodchenko and Varvara Stepanova, to produce a lavish album to celebrate the tenth anniversary of the Uzbek Soviet Socialist Republic. *Ten Years of Uzbekistan* was a remarkable achievement in graphic design. They used such techniques as gatefolds acetates and embossing, with bold, large-scale photo collages and full-colour and duotone printing. Besides the reproductions of painting and drawings by Uzbek artists, it included photographs of members of the political elite, including at least two who had worked there alongside Tomsky in 1921: Yan Rudzutak and Yakov Peters. The Russian edition appeared in 1934, and the Uzbek edition in 1935. Following Tomsky's suicide in 1936, many of the party bosses photographed in *Ten Years in Uzbekistan* were purged and executed and possession of the book became a crime. Rodchenko and Stepanova chose to deface their personal copy of their own book by covering the photos of the 'enemies of people' with thick black India ink. This blackening or cutting out the faces of photographs was, in the words of Yuri Slezkine, one of the ways people 'cleansed' their life 'of all connections to the excommunic-

---

125 Feuchtwanger 1937, p. 46. OGIZ published a total of 19 million copies of Pushkin's works: Hoffmann 2018, p. 86.
126 Tomsky conceded to the visitor, the British labour leader Citrine, that OGIZ 'could not possibly satisfy the demand for books. The Russia people were devouring everything they could lay their hands on'. What particularly impressed Citrine was 'a finely illustrated book', an edition of the epic poem 'Slovo o polku Igoreve', which Citrine translated as the *Saga of the Legion of Igor*: Citrine 1936, p. 132. Tomsky had good reason to be particularly proud of this book. For the illustrations, Tomsky, on Gorky's recommendation, recruited the famous founder of the Palekh school of lacquer art, Ivan Golikov, who with Tomsky's encouragement worked on the project at one of OGIZ's buildings in Peredelkino, the writers' colony outside Moscow. Tomsky returned the favour by providing valuable help to Gorky, who was overseeing an ambitious project to publish an inexpensive, popular history of the Civil War: Ivanova 1989, p. 7; Vedlin 1999, pp. 193–4, 201, 213; Spiridonova 2013, p. 294; Krilov and Kichatova 2004, pp. 89–90.
127 Molotov 1993, p. 283.

FIGURE 30   Tomsky and Kalinin with party functionaries
TATE IMAGES

ated'.[128] The couple, partly as a result, survived the Great Purges. Party members with photos of Tomsky in them would similarly blacken his face.

Despite his achievements at OGIZ, Tomsky continued to be subjected to political attacks. This was at least partly because the party leadership correctly suspected he was having 'anti-party conversations' with other ousted Old Bolsheviks who shared his outrage over Stalin's policies.[129] In 1932 the old split between the 'right' and 'left' oppositional wings of the party had given

---

128   Slezkine 2017, p. 818; King 1997, pp. 126–33. Rodchenko lived until 1956 and Stepanova until 1958. Terrified party members associated with someone arrested also burned books and letters, cut faces out of photographs, gave their children a new last name, and avoided any contact with their neighbours and relatives.

129   According to Trotsky, the letters he received during the fall of 1932 reported that the most popular saying in party circles, especially in Moscow, was 'Down with Stalin'. Trotsky thought all the discontented people in and out of the party 'must be gravitating to the Right': Trotsky 1979, pp. 168, 174.

FIGURE 31   Same photo with Tomsky's and K. Lebedev's faces blacked out
TATE IMAGES

way to a shared desire to remove Stalin and change the party line.[130] Tomsky met with prominent former oppositionists including Zinoviev as well as Kamenev, Bukharin, and Rykov. Tomsky was particularly close to Rykov, whom Tomsky often invited to the drinking parties he held at his dacha.[131] Tomsky also met with former colleagues who had been purged from the union leadership for supporting him during the showdown with the Stalinists at the Eighth Trade-Union Congress in December 1928.[132] As we saw in the previous chapter, Tomsky's dacha in Bolshevo served as a favourite meeting place for weekend

---

[130]   Deutscher 1967, p. 333. Davies argues that shared hostility to Stalin's policies emerged among members of the 'left' and 'right' in 1930, although they did not yet associate with one another: Davies 1981, pp. 37, 45. By 1932, party criticism of Stalin was at a high point among Old Bolsheviks of all political stripes, unifying all the oppositionists, as the OGPU recognised: Starkov 1992, p. 73; Service 2004, p. 286; Broué 1990, p. 104; RGASPI, f. 17, op. 2, d. 579, l. 51.

[131]   RGASPI, f. 17, op. 2, d. 582, ll. 16, 59.

[132]   RGASPI, f. 17, op. 2, d. 582, l. 11; RGASPI, f. 17, op. 2, d. 511, l. 3.

gatherings.¹³³ Plus, for any especially private conversations, free from being overheard, there were the surrounding woods for walks among the pine trees. During the upcoming Moscow show trials, the prosecution declared that it was in private conversations at dachas that the 'counter-revolutionaries' hatched their conspiratorial plots. The German historian Karl Schlogelm concurs. He writes, 'the dacha was where intimate conversations and consultations took place, texts and letters were exchanged, and plots were hatched'.¹³⁴ Tomsky, it should be noted, agreed. He stated in his speech at the Sixteenth Party Congress, when he was under intense political pressure, that there was no such thing as private conversations among Soviet leaders since they inevitably all became political.¹³⁵ 'If two people, one of whom is a member of the top leadership and the other one is too, get together and talk about political matters, even in the course of a private conversation, then those are no longer private conversations'.¹³⁶ Sometimes these conversations also took place during strolls around the Kremlin grounds or in one another's offices.¹³⁷ It was said that Tomsky, 'with open arms', met in 1932 with Zinoviev in his Narkompros office.¹³⁸

Given the catastrophic results of Stalin's policy of forced collectivisation and dekulakisation, if there ever was a propitious moment to remove Stalin, this was it. The criminally high procurement norms imposed on the recently formed collective farms were bringing death in their wake on a vast scale, with millions succumbing to starvation and disease. The masses of hungry, desperate peasants fleeing to industrial centres brought typhus and other diseases

---

133 Koshelevoi et al. (eds) 1992, pp. 6–7, 28; RGASPI, f. 17, op. 2, d. 580, 39–41; APRF, f. 3, op. 24, d. 319, reprinted in Khaustov and Samuel'son 2010, pp. 368, 373.
134 Schlogel 2012, p. 330. Yagoda testified in the 1938 Moscow show trial that he went to Tomsky's dacha in 1931: Tucker and Cohen (eds) 1965, p. 490.
135 This was in the context of being questioned, under pressure, about his previous conversations with Bukharin and Kamenev: RKP(b) 1931, p. 147.
136 Quoted in Slezkine 2017, p. 304.
137 RGASPI, f. 17, op. 2, d. 584, l. 123.
138 RGASPI, f. 17, op. 2, d. 581, l. 265. Tomsky later testified to that during a 1932 meeting of Narkompros, Zinoviev invited Tomsky to come chat with him in his office, where Zinoviev complained about both his personal difficulties and the conditions in the country: RGASPI, f. 17, op 2, d. 574, l. 85. Zinoviev had been appointed a member of Narkompros's board in 1931. Zinoviev worked there for only a short time as the editor of *Bolshevik* before his was again expelled from the party in October 1932 and sent into exile: Zalesskii 2000, p. 185. According to Kaganovich, at another meeting of Tomsky with Zinoviev in his Narkompros office, Nadezhda Krupskaya participated: RGASPI, f. 17, op. 2, d. 574, l. 85.

with them.[139] As a result of Stalin's disastrous economic policy, the Soviet economy was, in the words of the economic historian Alec Nove, in the midst of one of 'the most precipitous peacetime declines in living standards in recorded history'.[140] The dramatic drop in wages and the severe shortages of food, including even in privileged Moscow and Leningrad, sparked mass discontent. An OGPU official reported that people in food lines talked about how much better conditions were under Bukharin, Rykov, and Tomsky.[141] A worker at one factory stated that after the party banished Tomsky, 'there's nobody to defend us'.[142] Peasants and workers engaged in various forms of mass unrest, including a wave of riots and strikes.[143] The crisis also created mass discontent and turmoil in the ranks of the Red Army's peasant soldiers.[144] This inevitably increased the popularity of the former oppositionists, especially the 'Right Deviationists'.[145] In various places in the country, the political police apprehended dissident party members who, to give one example, declared that 'the mass of workers and peasants were not on the side of the Central Committee and Stalin but on the side of Bukharin, Tomsky, Rykov, Zinoviev, Uglanov, and Kamenev'.[146] The party leadership felt no better about newer recruits to the party.[147] Since their warnings had proven to be accurate, the 'Rightists' certainly had reason to believe their stature among party members, including those who had earlier supported Stalin, had grown significantly.[148] Many contemporaries likened the situation in 1932 to the conditions at the time of the Kronstadt revolt in 1921, which led to a dramatic change in state policies and the introduction of NEP.[149] And indeed the Politburo in May belatedly decided to dramatically decrease the grain procurement plans for the 1932 harvest and allow peasants to sell their surpluses at market rates in what was unofficially labelled a policy of

---

139 In 1932–33 there were over 1.1 million registered cases of typhus and more than half a million cases of typhoid fever: Khlevniuk 1996, p. 60; Fitzpatrick 1993, pp. 28–33.
140 Nove 1992, p. 210.
141 Khlevniuk 1996, p. 20.
142 Quoted in Rossman 2005, p. 142.
143 Filtzer 1986, pp. 83–4; Khlevniuk, 1992, pp. 10–11; Rossman 2002, pp. 44–5.
144 Whitewood 2015, pp. 125–7.
145 Khlevniuk 2009, p. 9.
146 Quoted in Kuromiya 1998, p. 177. For similar examples, from letters to *Pravda*, see Starkov 1992, p. 77.
147 Resistance to Stalin's policies was widespread among lower-level oppositionists: Getty and Naumov 1999, p. 52; Merridale 1990, p. 82.
148 Katkov 1969, p. 79; Kuromiya 1998, pp. 177–80; Taubman 2003, p. 73.
149 See, for example, Nicolaevsky 1965, p. 28.

'neo-Nep'.[150] According to Katherine Merridale, 'a severe political crisis, if not the regime's collapse', was widely predicted in 1932.[151]

Leading 'Rightists' may well have been discussing the possibility of 'a palace coup', in which Tomsky would be appointed general secretary. Bukharin asserted during the 1938 Moscow show trial that the plan was for Tomsky to replace Stalin as general secretary.[152] Yagoda, the head of the OGPU, who had shared the 'Rightists' fears about Stalin, during the summer of 1931 accepted an invitation to Tomsky's dacha to speak with him, Rykov, and Alexander (Foma) Smirnov.[153] During his interrogation in April 1937 Yagoda confessed that Tomsky had said that given the situation in the country, 'we Rightists don't have the right to remain simple observers, the moment requires action'.[154] They specifically talked about the possibility of arresting all the members of the Politburo in the Kremlin, if one of Yagoda's biographers is to be believed.[155] On a number of occasions in the spring, summer, and fall of 1932, Tomsky got together at his dacha to discuss the 'Ryutin Platform' with Rykov, Uglanov, Shmidt, and a number of his friends who formerly served on the VTsSPS Presidium.[156] But Tomsky

---

150 Rees 2012, pp. 133–4; Deutscher 1966, p. 334. 'Neo-Nep' was arguably motivated more by concern with worker protests and demonstrations than with peasant unrest or the mass famine: Davies, Ilic, and Khlevnyuk 2004, pp. 111–12.
151 Merridale 1990, p. 89.
152 People's Commissariat of Justice of the USSR 1938, pp. 394–6. Bukharin spoke of the idea of a 'palace coup' during his first confession on 2 June 1937, well before the lengthy bouts of interrogations leading up his show trial in March 1938: Furr and Bobrov 2007, p. 50. Earlier, Bukharin testified that Tomsky was being prepared to replace Stalin as general secretary at the July 1928 Central Committee Plenum. When grilled about it, Bukharin said there was 'nothing funny' about the proposal: RGASPI, f. 17, op. 2, d. 582, l. 144.
153 Khaustov, Naumov, and Plotnikova (eds) 2004, p. 140. Yagoda was one of Rykov's friends: Slezkine 2017, p. 745. Bukharin had told Kamenev when they met in July 1928 that 'Yagoda and Trilisser are ours': Trotsky 1981, p. 381. Meer Trilisser, who served as Second Deputy of the OGPU in 1928, like Yagoda was an 'Old Bolshevik'. Victor Serge, writing in 1937, stated Yagoda sympathised with the 'Rightists', but 'not for long': Serge 1937a, p. 129.
154 Khaustov, Naumov, and Plotnikova (eds) 2004, p. 141. Tomsky and Uglanov, the former Commissar of Labour and Moscow party boss, met to discuss how best to fight back against the Central Committee: Teptsov 1992, vol. 1, p. 63; RGASPI, f. 16, op. 163, d, 1009, reprinted in Koshelevoi 2007c, pp. 569–70.
155 Il'inskii 2002, pp. 129, 170–1, 226–31, 236–7. Yezhov stated at the Central Committee Plenum in February 1937 that various forms of a palace coup were widely discussed in Rightist circles: RGASPI, f. 17, op. 2, d. 579, l. 46.
156 RGASPI, f. 17, op. 2, d. 578, ll. 22–4, 80; RGASPI, f. 17, op. 2, d. 583, l. 17. Bukharin was not there because he was away on holiday. A worker apparently came to Tomsky's dacha with a printed document from the Ryutin group: Koshelevoi et al. (eds) 1992, p. 14; RGASPI, f. 17, op. 2, d. 583, l. 124. Rykov, when grilled about it at the February 1937 Central Committee

and his cohorts in the end shied away from directly challenging Stalin's pre-eminence despite Stalin's apparent drop in popularity.[157] Talk of a palace coup, if it actually occurred, was exactly that, just talk. As much as Tomsky might have fantasised about removing Stalin, he continued to subscribe to the Bolshevik view that any opposition ran the risk of splitting the party and perhaps even unleashing another civil war, a prospect he could not abide. At the same time, the Stalinists had no compunctions about ousting from the party anyone who publicly voiced their discontent.

Discovery of the 'Ryutin Platform' in 1932 allowed the Stalinist leadership to zero in on the former oppositionists. Copies of the seven-page, compressed version of the Old Bolshevik Martemian Ryutin's 194-page anti-Stalinist treatise, 'Stalin and the Crisis of the Proletarian Dictatorship', had been clandestinely circulating within Moscow and other party circles since March 1932.[158] He was a peasant-born, former Central Committee member and well-known party secretary of the Krasnaya Presnya district in Moscow, who had been expelled from the party in October 1930 for his 'rightist' views.[159] Ryutin characterised conditions within the country as 'catastrophic' and demanded the party reverse course by liquidating collective farms and removing the party leadership.[160] Though he censured the leaders of the 'Rightist Opposition' for their capitulation at the Sixteenth Party Congress in 1930, Ryutin argued 'the right

---

Plenum, stated he learned only later that the document was the Ryutin platform: RGASPI, f. 17, op. 2, d. 582, l. 61. Kaganovich asserted that Rykov had not only read the platform, he had edited it: RGASPI, f. 17, op. 2, d. 583, l. 269. Shmidt, like Tomsky, was a former worker. As an early member of the VTsSPS and then the Commissar of Labour from 1923 until the end of 1928, Shmidt and Tomsky had long worked together on trade-union issues and were close friends. In 1930 Shmidt was the Deputy Commissar of Agriculture, then in 1931 the Deputy Chair of Sovnarkom.

157 A correspondent in Trotsky's émigré newspaper, *Bulleten' oppozitsii* (Bulletin of the Opposition), reported that on 23 February 1932 Stalin's appearance at a party meeting in the Bolshoi Theatre was greeted with an 'icy silence' instead of the usual applause: quoted in Merridale 1990, p. 86.

158 Reprinted in Iakovlev (ed.) 1991, pp. 334–443. Ryutin had supported the central party leadership of Stalin, Bukharin, Rykov, and Tomsky during the 1920s. He became such a fierce opponent of the United Opposition, including preventing them from speaking publicly and breaking up private meetings of their sympathisers, that he became known as the leader of 'Uglanov's hooligans': Clark 2015, pp. 385–7; Daniels 1960, pp. 303–2.

159 He had earlier been purged from his positions as a candidate member of the Central Committee and a member of the VSNKh Presidium.

160 Fifteen Moscow party officials in August 1932 heard a report by Ryutin on the platform at a meeting in a village 40 miles outside Moscow, where they took the name of the 'Union of Marxist-Leninists': Clark 2015, pp. 395–6.

wing has proved correct in the economic field'.[161] He also condemned how the post-Tomsky trade unions had gone from defending workers' interests to being Stalin's 'obedient tool' as real wages were lowered and workers' overall standard of living declined drastically.[162] Denouncing Stalin and his clique for their 'crimes' and characterising Stalin as 'the evil genius of the Russian revolution', the Ryutin Platform called on 'new forces' within the party and the working class 'to destroy Stalin's dictatorship'. The Ryutin Platform explicitly stated that, since Stalin and his clique would not give up their positions voluntarily, they needed to be removed by 'force' and 'as soon as possible'. Failure to act would result in 'the collapse of the proletarian dictatorship'.[163] Stalin and his cohort, when they got wind of the Ryutin Platform from an informer, were both rattled and utterly outraged.[164]

Since forced collectivisation and breakneck industrialisation had led to precisely the economic and political problems that Bukharin, Rykov, Tomsky, and other moderate Bolsheviks had predicted, Stalin and the party leadership feared the widespread emergence of Ryutin-like groups within the party.[165] How many could have had an opportunity to read the actual Ryutin Platform before the political police swooped down and arrested Ryutin and over 20 of his collaborators in September 1932 was unclear to Stalin and other members of the party leadership, but OGPU investigators argued it had passed 'from comrade to comrade, group to group, city to city', and it had even reached government and diplomatic circles abroad.[166] Then, on 8 November 1932, the day after the

---

161 Quoted in Conquest 1990, p. 24. Some historians suggest Stalin used Ryutin to entrap the 'Right Opposition': Clark 2015, pp. 393–4.
162 Ryutin 1992, p. 234. On the drop in real wages and workers' standard of living: Filtzer 1986, pp. 208–9.
163 Kurilov et al. (eds) 1990, p. 12. In his February 1933 confession, the young Bukharinist Alexander Slepkov stated that he and his fellow oppositionists envisioned replacing the Stalinist leadership with a 'collective leadership', in which Bukharin, Rykov, Tomsky, Kamenev, and Zinoviev would all play leading roles: reprinted in Artizov et al. (ed.) 2004, vol. 3, pp. 287–8.
164 Montefiore 2004, p. 91. The Ryutin Platform may have come as no surprise to Stalin since Ryutin had been arrested in November 1930 for 'counter-revolutionary agitation and propaganda' and somewhat inexplicably released from prison a couple months later. Years later the Ryutin Platform's withering indictment of Stalin and his policies obviously continued to rankle. Andrei Vyshinsky used the Ryutin Platform extensively in his prosecution of Bukharin, Rykov, and others at their show trial in March 1938.
165 The political police had been discovering Ryutin-like groups in various industrial cities: Kuromiya 1998, p. 177. Leonard Schapiro concluded it was 'probable that a number of minor groups of this nature existed': Schapiro 1960, p. 391.
166 Rogovin 1993, pp. 289–90; Harris 2017, p. 111. A group of middle-ranking officials in Moscow had discussed and edited Ryutin's 'platform': Merridale 1990, p. 85. According to Shlyap-

country celebrated the fifteenth anniversary of the Bolshevik seizure of power, Stalin's wife, Nadezhda Alliluyeva, shot herself in the heart with her small pistol.[167] Much about her death, including what provoked her to take her life, is shrouded in mystery and gave rise all sorts of rumours.[168] Although hardly beyond doubt, there is reason believe there was a suicide note full of political as well as personal accusations against Stalin. In addition, if Stalin's chief personal bodyguard General Nikolai Vlasik is to be believed, a copy of the Ryutin Platform was found in her bedroom. 'She left me like an enemy' Stalin is said to have bitterly concluded.[169] In the words of the historian Robert Daniels, this period was 'one of the most desperate of [Stalin's] career'.[170] Although usually impressively calm during times of crisis, Stalin was devastated and close to losing his nerve.[171] He even suggested in perhaps a fit of pique that he might resign from the Politburo and he threatened to kill himself.[172] Some historians go so far as to argue the system's very survival was in danger.[173]

In this context of economic crisis and widespread discontent inside the party, Stalin quickly regained his nerve and forcefully cracked down on former oppositionists. As noted above, a large number of party members who had opposed the collectivisation campaigns were expelled during 1932.[174] Because the Stalin group could not tolerate prominent party members criticising government policies and Stalin's leadership, even in small-group discussions, when conversations criticising Stalin's polices by the 'Rightists' Nikolai Eismont, Vladimir Tolmachev, and Smirnov were brought to their attention, they

---

nikov, on vacation in Kislovodsk, rumours about the Ryutin Platform created a sensation there: Allen 2015, p. 313.

167   Kun 2003, p. 209.

168   But it should be kept in mind that Alliluyeva was mentally unstable. Montefiore suggests she suffered from a bipolar disorder: Montefiore 2007, p. 329.

169   Montefiore 2004, pp. 20, 108. According to their daughter Svetlana, who heard it second hand and isn't always a reliable source, only a few people had a chance to read the damning personal and political letter, 'full of reproaches and accusations', which Nadezhda Alliluyeva wrote Stalin before it was destroyed: Alliluyeva 1967, pp. 112–13; Service 2004, p. 293. Although there is no hard evidence that Nadezhda opposed collectivisation, she may well have: Larina 1993, pp. 141, 291; Khlevniuk 2015, p. 255; Kuromiya 2005, p. 108. The Industrial Academy she attended had been a bastion of the 'Right' during the power struggle and she may have encountered opposition to collectivisation there.

170   Daniels 1960, p. 380.

171   Rieber 2001, p. 1663.

172   Deutscher 1966, p. 334. Daniels argued Stalin threatened to resign in order to get a vote of confidence from the Politburo: Daniels 1960, p. 380.

173   Rees 1988, p. 50.

174   For example, nearly half of the Kuban party membership were purged: Harris 1999, p. 139.

summoned Tomsky along with others before a special joint session of the Politburo and the Central Control Commission (CCC) on 27 November 1932.[175] Stalin wrote to Voroshilov that he thought this case of opposition was analogous to the 'Ryutin Affair', albeit 'less well defined and thoroughly saturated with alcohol'.[176]

This Politburo session, held just three weeks after the death of Stalin's wife Nadezhda, convened as it always did in the beautiful Imperial Senate building inside the Kremlin. Chaired by Molotov, the tough, quintessential Stalinist, the nine members of the Politburo were joined by 21 members of the Presidium of the CCC and seven invited Central Committee members.[177] The entire CCC Presidium was brought into Politburo meetings, as well as Central Committee plenums, when the leadership planned a full-scale attack on oppositionists.[178] According to party rules, failure to answer control commission questions truthfully was grounds for immediate expulsion from the party.[179]

Tomsky, Rykov, Smirnov, and Shmidt were caught by surprise by the serious nature of the accusations when they arrived at the Politburo and CCC Presidium session. These men, all of whom had seen their health seriously deteriorate over the last couple years under the onslaught of Stalinist attacks, were confronted with Eismont's and Tolmachev's signed depositions and told the meeting had been convened to evaluate them. A stunned Tomsky incredulously asked 'Today'? Once he regained his wits, Tomsky persuaded the Politburo to give them a full hour to read the 'materials'.[180] When the session began,

---

175   As J. Arch Getty has argued, 'This government and its leaders were afraid of their own shadow and of anything that might challenge their political monopoly and privilege': Getty 1998, p. 189. Eismont was Commissar for Supply of the RSFSR. Smirnov had been Commissar of Agriculture of the RSFSR and was currently a member of VSNKh's Presidium. In early 1929, Smirnov met with Bukharin, Rykov, and Tomsky, but refused to sign their platform: Heinzen 2004, p. 215. Tolmachev had been RSFSR Commissar for Internal Affairs from 1928–30 and was currently head of the road transportation administration of the RSFSR.
176   Kvashonkin et al. (eds) 1999, p. 196; van Ree 2002, p. 119.
177   The party congresses elected members of the CCC, which was created in 1920 as an independent party body.
178   Service 2004, p. 279.
179   The official functions of the CCC were mainly to maintain party discipline ('ensuring in all respects the party line'), to investigate and punish 'incorrect behaviour' among Communists, and to supervise the Politburo by sending three CCC presidium members and three deputies to all Politburo meetings: Gill 1988, pp. 141–2, 148n5; Kharkhordin 1999, p. 37. In 1934, in response to a proposal by Kaganovich, the Seventeenth Party Congress disbanded the CCC.
180   Koshelevoi et al. (eds) 2007c, p. 551.

members proceeded to denounce and question Tomsky, Rykov, and Smirnov, who gave lengthy speeches in response to this questioning. Their attempts to defend themselves were continually interrupted. It might seem puzzling that Bukharin, the leading figure of the 1928–29 'Right Opposition', was not also compelled to appear and be questioned in connection with this 'affair'.[181] The most plausible reason is not only that Bukharin did not attend the dacha get together, but that the leadership recognised that Bukharin was in fact no longer engaging in any oppositional activity.[182]

For most of this session, despite the mass famine stalking the countryside, or perhaps because of the need to find scapegoats for it, members of the Politburo and CCC Presidium acted as if they had nothing more pressing to do than interrogate these 'Old Bolsheviks'.[183] But though Stain dismissed party reports of the famine as fairy tales, and the Soviet media adamantly denied a famine was occurring – to even mention it made one liable to being labelled a Right Deviationist or even a counterrevolutionary – certain members of the party leadership, Stalin in particular, did feel the need to devote part of this Politburo session to addressing the rural crisis.[184] In his lengthy speech Stalin defended

---

181 According to a number of sources, Bukharin had remained friends with Stalin's wife Nadezhda after he stopped meeting with Stalin. Bukharin and Alliluyeva reputedly discussed their shared opposition to Stalin's disastrous agricultural policies: Larina 1993, p. 141; Medvedev 1980, p. 9; Shishkin 1989, pp. 51–2; Montefiore 2004, 14. The NKVD defector Alexander Orlov, who may have been in a position to learn this, believed Nadezhda heard about the horrors of the collectivisation campaign from her classmates at the Industrial Academy: Orlov 1953, p. 317.

182 Documentary evidence and the memory of his wife, Anna Larina, suggest Bukharin did not engage in oppositional activity since the beginning of 1930: Rogovin 1998, p. 233; Larina 1993, 262. According to Valentin Astrov, Bukharin told him during 1932 that given what had happened in the country and the party over the last few years, it was no longer possible to implement the 'old Rightist platform': Artizov et al. (eds) 2004, p. 29. That of course was not the Stalinist view at later plenums, particularly the February 1937 Central Committee Plenum, when Molotov and Kaganovich, among others, accused Bukharin of getting together with Tomsky and Rykov to discuss the Ryutin Platform: RGASPI, f. 17, op. 2, d. 583, ll. 92, 257.

183 It is thought that somewhere between five and eight million men, women, and children lost their lives in the 1932–33 famine.

184 Stalin responded to a brave plea for aid from a party official in Ukraine by telling him, 'It seems you are a good story-teller. You've concocted a story about famine, thinking to frighten us. But it won't work. Wouldn't it be better for you to leave your party post and the Ukrainian Central Committee and join the Writers' Union? Then you can write your fables and fools will read them': Kemp-Welch 1991, p. 138. To speak of famine even in starving villages, according to Robert Conquest, became 'an offense bringing 10-year sentences, or sometimes death': Conquest 1991, p. 165; Kuromiya 1998, p. 169. In later years delegates freely admitted at Central Committee plenums that 1930, 1931, and 1932 were 'very tough

collectivisation while finding scapegoats for its problems.[185] The party's 'small difficulties' in the collectivisation campaign, was how one member characterised what had become by then a horrendous human tragedy.[186] Ordzhonikidze stated that 'we don't hide' the fact that the party has had difficulties in implementing collectivisation while arguing that anyone who thought the party would not is not 'a politician but a naïve child'.[187] Tomsky and Rykov were told they should recognise that any problems in collectivisation and industrialisation were 'unavoidable', not evidence of an incorrect party policy.[188]

The primary focus of the 27 November session was 'unmasking' the 'Right Oppositionists'. The party leaders, Stalin especially, were tormented by the notion that behind the façade of party unity and uncritical support of the leadership, many party members secretly opposed the leadership and were trying to sabotage its work. In the villages, Stalin stated, 'they don't come out openly against the collective farms. They express their "solidarity" with the kolkhozes just like our Right Deviationists express their "solidarity" with the party's general line'.[189] The 'Rightists', Stalinists believed, were simply waiting for a more favourable moment to push for a change in party policy. There was indeed some talk of this, as noted above. Whether Stalin was being paranoid, as he is commonly portrayed, it is not unreasonable to think he 'genuinely feared a genuine conspiracy'.[190]

What especially agitated Stalin and the party leadership, and provoked their determined effort to blame Tomsky for the 'Smirnov-Eismont-Tolmachev group', was Tomsky's and Smirnov's failure to attend the joint Central Committee and CCC plenum devoted to the Ryutin Group, held less than two months earlier, from 28 September to 2 October 1932.[191] The plenum had expelled

---

years'. See, for example, Voroshilov at the February 1937 plenum: RGASPI, f. 17, op. 2, d. 580, l. 125.
185   Koshelevoi et al. (eds) 2007c, pp. 581–91.
186   Koshelevoi et al. (eds) 2007c, p. 609.
187   Koshelevoi et al. (eds) 2007c, p. 576.
188   Koshelevoi et al. (eds) 2007c, p. 592.
189   Koshelevoi et al. (eds) 2007c, p. 588.
190   Mawdsley and White 2000, p. 106n106. Rees argues that Stalin was 'a high-functioning psychopath' who was able to control his 'paranoid delusions': Rees 2012, p. 220. Other historians have come to similar conclusions.
191   Stalin personally wrote the resolution 'On the Counter-Revolutionary Group of Ryutin and Slepkov', which called for the immediate expulsion from the party of anyone who read, or even knew about, the Ryutin Platform and failed to report it to the party leadership: Starkov 1992, p. 75. Historians have long argued that at a Politburo meeting around this time Stalin demanded that Ryutin be shot because his platform could inspire acts of terrorism, but this desire to institute the death penalty for oppositional activity was blocked

Ryutin's 'White-Guardist counter-revolutionary group' from the party, denouncing them as 'enemies of the party and the working class'.[192] A number of high-profile former oppositionists, who had read the Ryutin Platform and kept quiet about it, such as Zinoviev, Kamenev, and Uglanov, were interrogated by CCC members at that plenum and called upon to recant.[193] Uglanov, whom Yaroslavsky labelled the guiltiest of the three, broke down and cried after trying to trying to justify himself.[194] The resolution the plenum adopted called for the immediate expulsion from the party of anyone who had read these 'counterrevolutionary documents' and failed to inform the Central Committee and CCC. As 'concealers of enemies of the party and the working class', Zinoviev, Kamenev, and Uglanov were expelled from the party and sent into Siberian exile.[195]

At the November plenum, speaker after speaker fervently attacked Tomsky, who proved particularly unwilling to kowtow to the Politburo and play his part in the party's self-criticism ritual. Kirov crudely demanded that Tomsky not only 'smash the mug' of any oppositionist, but do so twice as hard as other party members to demonstrate 'you've actually broken with your past'.[196] Tomsky tried to maintain some dignity while admitting his 'mistakes'. But it was difficult. Although the OGPU lacked evidence that Tomsky had read the Ryutin Platform, the leadership had good reason to question Tomsky's sincerity and he had no way to effectively deflect the repeated charge that he was

---

by a moderate bloc of Politburo members led by Kirov. J. Arch Getty has called into question the sources used for this account, which he labelled a 'unsubstantiated rumour': Getty and Naumov 1999, p. 54. E.A. Rees agrees with Getty and questions 'whether politically Stalin could at that time have presented such a demand to his colleagues': Rees 2004, p. 45. Ryutin, in any case, was instead sentenced to 10 years in prison.

192 Donkov et al. (eds) 1989, p. 107.
193 The primary focus of the OGPU and CCC functionaries immediately following the arrests of Ryutin's 'group' was to investigate the possible involvement of leading 'Rightists' in formulating the Union of Marxist-Leninists' arguments: Anfer'tev (ed.) 2003, p. 66.
194 Anfer'tev (ed.) 2006, pp. 73, 80. In his February 1933 confession, Uglanov characterised his discussions with other oppositionists during the second half of 1932 as 'Rightist conferences': Artizov 2004, p. 290. Later, at the December 1936 Central Committee plenum, Bukharin was accused of meeting at Tomsky's apartment to discuss the Ryutin platform with him and other Rightists. While Bukharin denied such a meeting took place at the plenum, in his final letter to Stalin in December 1937, he stated that he had concealed that 'the gang had met, and a report was read': Getty and Naumov 1999, pp. 317, 557.
195 Iakovlev (ed.) 1991, pp. 95–6, 151. Zinoviev and Kamenev, unlike Uglanov, were readmitted to the party in 1933 in time to praise Stalin and admit their sins at the Seventeenth Party Congress in January 1934. Also, unlike Zinoviev and Kamenev, Uglanov was not a defendant in a show trial before his 1937 execution.
196 RGASPI, f. 17, op. 163, d. 1010, l. 281. In Kirov's stenographic 'edit' [*pravka*] he changed the phrase from 'smash the mug' to 'politically beat': Khevniuk 2010, p. 166.

masking his true thoughts.[197] Tomsky became angry at being accused of party disloyalty; that his former fellow members of the Politburo would attack so harshly someone who, as Tomsky described himself, had devoted his life to the party for nearly 30 years.[198] He exclaimed that there was no defence against the charge that 'you don't say what you think, you don't vote like you think'.[199] Why are my statements 'never enough', an exasperated Tomsky asked time and again. 'If I say 10–15 words ... I'm asked why did you not say 20'.[200] Tomsky may have sadly remembered, as he made this defence, how he and other delegates made light of Kamenev's similar pleas at the Fourteenth Party Congress. Kaganovich, who questioned whether he had truly 'disarmed', told Tomsky that he had evaded the central issues and that he had not talked sufficiently about his mistakes.[201] Kuibyshev stated that Tomsky 'needs to understand our psychology, our demands'.[202] Far from being placated by his responses, the plenum raised the possibility of arresting Tomsky and handing him over to the OGPU.[203]

For Tomsky, still a Central Committee member, albeit a lame duck in political disgrace, to miss the plenum session devoted to Ryutin was considered by Politburo and CCC Presidium members to be 'an act of political protest'.[204] They accused Tomsky of 'boycotting' the session by going wild boar hunting with Smirnov and Shmidt. Tomsky insisted it was completely 'innocent', nothing more than a needed vacation, and 'I love to hunt while I'm on leave'.[205] He argued that his doctor had prescribed that he rest three times a year.[206] But many questioned how Tomsky could plead he was ill and yet had still gone hunting. Molotov mocked his excuse, with Ordzhonikdze adding that Lenin loved to hunt, 'but he did not do so during plenum meetings'.[207] The Politburo

---

197 Koshelevoi et al. (eds) 2007c, pp. 622–4.
198 Koshelevoi et al. (eds) 2007c, p. 623.
199 Koshelevoi et al. (eds) 2007c, p. 622.
200 Koshelevoi et al. (eds) 2007c, p. 624.
201 Koshelevoi et al. (eds) 2007c, p. 613.
202 Koshelevoi et al. (eds) 2007c, p. 633. Tomsky was not conforming to the rules of what J. Arch Getty calls the Stalinists' 'apology ritual': Getty 1999, pp. 49–70.
203 Koshelevoi et al. (eds) 2007c, p. 565.
204 Koshelevoi et al. (eds) 2007c, pp. 590, 634.
205 According to his youngest son, Tomsky always preferred to spend his holidays hunting: Gorelov and Shapovalova (eds) 2001, p. 150. Hunting had long been a favourite activity for most of the Bolshevik leaders, including Stalin: Medvedev and Medvedev 2004, p. 287. Tomsky, like Stalin, probably fell in love with hunting when he was in Siberian exile: Svanidze 1953, p. 206.
206 Koshelevoi et al. (eds) 2007c, p. 558.
207 Koshelevoi et al. (eds) 2007c, p. 663. Ordzhonikidze, Kirov, and Kuibyshev, unlike Molotov

and CCC Presidium members demanded to know what Tomsky discussed with Smirnov and Shmidt while they were away. That they shared the same railroad car, lived together, and 'drank from the same samovar' during their two-week vacation was viewed with great distrust. Molotov argued they must have talked about more than 'the quality of the wine and the charms of nature; they must have discussed political issues'.[208]

Tomsky did not help his case by holding firm to his position that he never talked politics when hunting. As he joked when questioned by party interrogators on another occasion about this hunting trip, 'If I had been talking about politics, I would have returned empty-handed'.[209] But Rykov inadvertently undercut Tomsky's defence by acknowledging during his questioning that he of course discussed politics with Tomsky and other political leaders when they got together.[210] Tomsky conceded they had indeed talked about their 'extremely difficult position in the party'.[211] Tomsky in the end stated, 'I now see my trip was a big political mistake', but he continued to insist he had not discussed the agricultural crisis or politics while on the hunting trip.[212] Tomsky pointedly asked the Politburo and CCC Presidium why they thought he would need to go on such a long trip to engage in political discussions.[213] Recognising he often talked in a way that 'could be easily distorted', Tomsky insisted it was 'laughable' to say Smirnov had proposed replacing Stalin with Voroshilov.[214] But in fact, as we have seen, Tomsky met with Smirnov and Rykov to discuss the Ryutin Platform before he decided to skip out on the Central Committee plenum devoted to the Ryutin Affair.

Tomsky tried to use his still nimble sense of humour during the questioning to defuse the attacks. Tomsky joked that since he was deaf in one ear, coming to the Ryutin meeting would have been completely useless unless he was given a front row seat.[215] Tomsky's attempt to fend off attacks with jokes elicited laughter. Some of the Stalinists – Ordzhonikidze, Kuibyshev, and Kirov –

---

and Kagonovich, still used the familiar 'you' (*ty*) when addressing Tomsky at the plenum: Fitzpatrick 2015, p. 87.

208   Koshelevoi et al. (eds) 2007c, p. 605.
209   TsGAODM, f. 2870, op. 1, d. 296, reprinted in Karpachev and Minaeva (eds) 1992b, l. 112. Even though Tomsky said this during his 1933 purge interrogation, his response elicited laughter and applause from those in attendance.
210   Koshelevoi et al. (eds) 2007c, p. 578.
211   Koshelevoi et al. (eds) 2007c, p. 624.
212   Koshelevoi et al. (eds) 2007c, p. 621.
213   Koshelevoi et al. (eds) 2007c, p. 621.
214   Koshelevoi et al. (eds) 2007c, p. 559.
215   Koshelevoi et al. (eds) 2007c, p. 561.

continued to be on familiar (*ty*) terms with him and responded in a similarly humorous manner. They seemed to be conflicted on how harshly to treat Tomsky.[216] But others, while conceding that Tomsky was 'a very witty person as everyone knows', criticised him for looking for laughs when he responded to serious political issues'.[217] Molotov denounced his 'rotten jokes'.[218]

Tomsky also outraged party leaders when he attempted to minimise the significance of the Eismont gathering by characterising it as simply 'drunks talking about drunken things'. Tomsky characterised Eismont as someone 'who chatters irresponsibly when drunk, saying whatever comes into his head'.[219] CCC Presidium members refused to accept this excuse. Andreev argued it was 'ridiculous' for Tomsky and Rykov to portray the 'Eismont-Smirnov group as simply a drunken affair'.[220] Tomsky felt compelled to add that, as much as he would like to drink given how the party was treating him, for health reasons he had not had a drink in years.[221] Any acceptance of the alcohol defence might have offered hope for Rykov, who had long been renowned throughout the party for his love of vodka.[222] But Stalin and other party leaders had no sympathy for the drunkenness excuse.[223]

Various Politburo and CCC Presidium members argued that Tomsky, and Rykov to a lesser extent, shouldered the 'primary responsibility' for the Rightist oppositional activity of the early 1930s – 'they arm the party's enemies, inspiring all those elements within the party who are vacillating or directly disagree with party policy'.[224] That Tomsky and Rykov had not attended the social gatherings in question was apparently irrelevant. More important in the minds of the Politburo and CCC Presidium members was that Smirnov's conversation with Eismont and Tolmachev took place shortly after he returned from his vacation with Tomsky.[225] This was sufficient evidence for Stalin and other members of the leadership who were determined to draw a direct connection between

---

216 Fitzpatrick 2015, p. 87.
217 Koshelevoi et al. (eds) 2007c, p. 566.
218 Koshelevoi et al. (eds) 2007c, p. 594.
219 Koshelevoi et al. (eds) 2007c, p. 560.
220 Koshelevoi et al. (eds) 2007c, p. 590.
221 Koshelevoi et al. (eds) 2007c, pp. 559, 625. As noted above, Tomsky only intermittently followed his doctor's orders to stop drinking alcohol: Citrine 1936, p. 132.
222 Many party members called vodka *rykovka*. A well-connected foreign correspondent described Rykov as 'one of those amazing Russians who can drink vodka as if it were water ... without any visible effect on the lucidity of his mind or the evenness of his speech': Reswick 1952, p. 88.
223 Kuromiya 2008, p. 47.
224 Koshelevoi et al. (eds) 2007c, pp. 592, 616.
225 Koshelevoi et al. (eds) 2007, p. 611.

the Ryutin Platform, the 'Smirnov-Eismont-Tolmachev group', and the leaders of the earlier 'Rightist Opposition'. In Mikoyan's words, 'Tomsky was primarily responsible for the Smirnov affair'.[226] Stalin suggested that Tomsky's and Rykov's belief that the collectivisation and the industrialisation campaigns had failed inspired Smirnov, Eismont, and Tolmachev.[227]

It was not enough that Tomsky had stopped any open oppositional activity. He was taken to task for his public silence over the past two years.[228] Politburo and CCC Presidium members questioned his failure to speak up in defence of Stalinist policies. Tomsky, for example, was asked why he did not write an article in the press criticising the 'Ryutin Platform'.[229] Andreev suggested Tomsky was lying low until he believed the party would be forced to reverse course, while Kirov accused him of bragging of his, as well as Rykov's and Bukharin's, 'secret reserve' of oppositionists.[230] Tomsky fired back, asking why, if the party considered him 'an insufficiently trustworthy person', it kept him as head of OGIZ. Tomsky's various objections were dismissed as 'whining'.[231]

The attacks at the November 1932 Politburo and CCC session were preparations for the somewhat more public performance that would come shortly afterwards at the Central Committee plenum, which convened on 7 January 1933. The Stalinist leadership demanded that the 'Rightists' capitulate unconditionally in this larger forum. Bukharin, who had abandoned any oppositional conversations, obligingly lambasted Tomsky and Rykov at the plenum for their 'extremely serious and grave political errors'. Bukharin, who his biographer Stephen Cohen lionised as the leader of the Right Opposition, demanded 'the utmost ruthlessness' against his former cohorts.[232] Bukharin hysterically declared that 'such factions must be hacked off without the slightest mercy, without [our] being in the slightest troubled by any sentimental considerations concerning the past, personal friendships, relationships, respect for a person, and so forth. These are all totally abstract formulations, which cannot serve the interests of an army that is storming the fortress of the enemy'.[233] Why Bukharin thought that incriminating Tomsky and Rykov would be an effective way to allay Stalin's suspicions is unclear.

---

226   Koshelevoi et al. (eds) 2007c, pp. 616, 618.
227   Koshelevoi et al. (eds) 2007c, pp. 581–2.
228   Koshelevoi et al. (eds) 2007c, p. 553.
229   Koshelevoi et al. (eds) 2007c, p. 573.
230   Koshelevoi et al. (eds) 2007c, p. 638.
231   Koshelevoi et al. (eds) 2007c, pp. 560, 637.
232   Cohen 1973.
233   RGASPI, f. 17, op. 2, d. 575, translated and reprinted in Getty and Naumov 1999, p. 96.

Tomsky, while abjectly admitting his own 'grave mistakes' against the party and praising the supposed successes of the First Five-Year Plan, proved to be less repentant and more stubborn and loyal to his friends and fellow oppositionists than Bukharin and pretty much everyone else.[234] Tomsky outraged delegates by having the gumption to state during his 45-minute speech that his oppositional views stemmed from Lenin's emphasis on the importance of the *smychka* (alliance) between the working class and peasantry.[235] Gorky thought Tomsky's 'repentance speech' was 'courageous and full of self-respect', but the following day speaker after speaker attacked him, often as much for what he did not say as for what he said.[236] Tomsky was accused of never recognising Stalin as the leader of the party. Indeed he had not uttered his name during his speech. He was mocked for thinking of himself as still a party leader.[237] Voroshilov, who identified himself as still his friend, told Tomsky that he had 'slept through the past four years [and] you poured out such rubbish here that I am simply ashamed for your sake'.[238] Nikolai Shvernik, who beginning in March 1930 occupied Tomsky's former post as chair of the VTsSPS, accused him and his fellow 'trade-union Right Opportunists' of trying to undermine the First Five-Year Plan by continuing to advocate for 'trade-unionist policies' rather than 'mobilising the masses'.[239] Tomsky's defence of Smirnov, his close friend since 1906, and the Russian Republic's Commissar of Agriculture during NEP, particularly provoked outrage throughout the hall.[240] The deputy chair of the OGPU, Ivan Akulov, stated, 'the kind of negative opinion, as expressed by Comrade Rykov toward the faction headed by Smirnov, is lacking in the case of Tomsky'. Despite knowing the outrage that he would provoke, Tomsky while under questioning initially made light of the charges. Akulov expressed disgust that 'Even today, at this critical juncture ... Comrade Tomsky is making jokes'.[241] Voroshilov proclaimed 'I believe Bukharin a hundred times more than Rykov

---

234 RGASPI, f. 17, op. 2, d. 504, ll. 87–128. Typescript with Tomsky's corrections.
235 RGASPI, f. 17, op. 2, d. 504, ll. 93, 103, 169–170. Cohen characterised the *smychka* as a euphemism for the party's conciliatory policies toward the peasantry: Cohen 1973, pp. 145–6.
236 Spiridonova 2013, p. 276.
237 RGASPI, f. 17, op. 2, d. 575, translated and reprinted in Getty and Naumov 1999, pp. 86, 99.
238 RGASPI, f. 17, op. 2, d. 511, translated and reprinted in Getty and Naumov 1999, p. 100.
239 RGASPI, f. 17, op. 2, d. 508, l. 139. Shvernik, who would become only a candidate member of the Politburo in 1939, never became part of Stalin's inner circle: Fitzpatrick 2015, p. 177.
240 TsGAODM, f. 2870, op. 1, d. 296, reprinted in Karpachev and Minaeva (eds) 1992b, p. 113. Tomsky and Smirnov had known each other for 37 years, since meeting as fellow workers in St. Petersburg in 1896. Ten years later they worked together in the Bolsheviks' party organisation in St. Petersburg.
241 RGASPI, f. 17, op. 2, d. 575, translated and reprinted in Getty and Naumov 1999, p. 81.

and a thousand times more than Tomsky. Tomsky is being sly ... We expected a different kind of speech from you'.²⁴² Outraged at the demand that he humiliate himself before the Politburo, Tomsky lost his temper, exclaiming 'Why are your lashing out at me, what use is it to you? Is it enough that the people have already spoken out against me'.²⁴³ Summarising the Politburo's and the Presidium of the CCC's contention that Tomsky's self-criticism was totally insincere, Matvei Shkiriatov declared, 'There is not a single Bolshevik word in what Tomsky says when he speaks from this podium'.²⁴⁴ Convinced that Tomsky had not genuinely abandoned his opposition to Stalin's policies, the party leadership denounced his 'double dealing' [*dvurushnichestvo*], a derogatory term that meant one continued to oppose the party line inwardly while insincerely supporting it in public. The Central Committee's resolution at the end of the plenum, prepared by Stalin and Rudzutak, reprimanded Tomsky, Rykov, and Shmidt for giving 'anti-party elements grounds for counting on the support of the former leaders of the Right Opposition' and threatened them with 'severe measures' if they continued to do so.²⁴⁵ The repercussions of this resolution spread widely, as Khlevniuk and Naumov have noted: 'These dramatic events in Moscow sent smaller shock waves throughout the country. Provincial GPU officers who received the relevant decrees on these cases concocted their own local "counterrevolutionary groups"'.²⁴⁶

These attacks were followed six months later, in July 1933, by Tomsky's appearance before the purge commission of the OGIZ party cell. During the January plenum, which had disparaged even his achievements at OGIZ, Joseph Vareikis suggested that Tomsky was in his element with all the 'aliens' and Mensheviks who filled OGIZ's bureaucracy.²⁴⁷ Tomsky's summons was part of a nationwide purge [*chistka*].²⁴⁸ The hundreds of thousands of workers and

---

242 Voroshilov stated during his attack that he and Tomsky were once close friends: RGASPI, f. 17, op. 2, d. 575, translated and reprinted in Getty and Naumov 199, p. 100.
243 Quoted in Boberowski 2016, p. 190.
244 RGASPI, f. 17, op. 2, d. 575, translated and reprinted in Getty and Naumov 199, p. 86. The speeches of Tomsky, as well as of Bukharin and Rykov, were subsequently published in full in *Pravda*.
245 Rykov and Shmidt received the same reprimand: Egorov and Bogoliubova (eds) 1983–84, vol. 6, p. 33. Rudzutak somewhat mysteriously fell out of favour with Stalin and was arrested in 1937. He refused to confess, despite being cruelly tortured, before his execution in 1938: Baberowski 2016, p. 240.
246 Lih et al. (eds) 1995, p. 226.
247 RGASPI, f. 17, op. 2, d. 504, l. 114.
248 The January 1933 joint Central Committee and CCC session approved the Politburo's decision to carry out a purge, which had been adopted on 10 December 1932 because 'an enemy with a party card in his pocket is more dangerous than the open counter-

peasants who had joined the party during the mass recruitment drive during collectivisation and the beginning of the First Five-Year Plan, rather than Old Bolsheviks, were the primary targets of the purge.[249] But the unspoken backdrop to this purge was the Stalinist leadership's sense of insecurity given the widespread misgivings within the party over collectivisation and the resulting famine. As Getty argues, 'Although they publicly celebrated the victory of their new policies, in their inner councils the Stalinist leaders felt more anxiety than confidence, and they perceived that their position was more fragile than secure'.[250] This purge, nonetheless, was part of the party's regular 'cleansing' of its ranks. The consequence for those found guilty was expulsion from the party, not the arrest and execution or shipment off to the gulag of the Great Purges of a few years later.

Tomsky's appearance in the nationwide purge campaign came before the OGIZ party cell because, as elsewhere, the Central Purge Commission dictated that the applicable local control commission conduct the purge sessions.[251] According to the resolution adopted at the January Central Committee and CCC Plenum, the purges were to be conducted at open party cell meetings, which non-party fellow employees and workmates were encouraged to attend.[252] They were intended to be public spectacles with a didactic message. Kaganovich, the official chair of the central Purge Commission, had seized control of the campaign, bypassing the CCC, to ensure that only hard-line Stalinists conducted the purges.[253] The local purge commissions reported straight to him.

Tomsky's OGIZ purge commission session began with an obligatory account of his life and career in the party. Tomsky was held to account for his various 'political mistakes', principally what was called 'his theory of constant concessions to the peasantry' and his defence of workers' economic interests over efforts to increase their productivity. Over the course of three days, members

---

revolutionary and must be punished with every severity of revolutionary law': quoted in Haslam 1986, p. 401. According to the instructions issued in April 1933, the purge was to target 'double-dealers', 'violators of discipline', and 'degenerates': Getty 1985, pp. 48–57. The 1933 purge ultimately removed 182,500 party members from its ranks, including many 'Old Bolsheviks', such as Shlyapnikov, for double-dealing, although most were purged simply for being 'inactive members': Allen, 2015, pp. 320, 323, 328; Rees 2012, p. 130.

249   Rigby 1968, p. 203; Getty 1985, pp. 53–4.
250   Getty and Naumov 1999, p. 15.
251   Getty 1985, p. 43. For a vivid portrayal of one of the local 1933 purge sessions: Kravchenko 1946, pp. 132–47.
252   Getty 1985, p. 51; Rigby 1968, p. 202.
253   Kaganovich thus bypassed Rudzutak, Tomsky's old friend and comrade in Turkestan and on the VTsSPS, who then headed the CCC. The CCC had conducted all the previous purges, except in 1919: Getty 1985, p. 42.

of the purge commission also attacked Tomsky for the 'ideological defects' in some of the textbooks that OGIZ was in the midst of publishing for primary and middle schools, as noted above.[254] In his long, many hours opening speech and in hours of cross-examination the following day, Tomsky spoke in great detail about his life-long service to the party, nine years in tsarist prisons and exile, the reasons he had opposed the 'extraordinary measures', and why he objected to Kaganovich's appointment to the VTsSPS Presidium at the Eighth Trade-Union Congress in 1928.[255] He conceded that since his ouster from the leadership, he had been guilty of failing to speak out against 'anti-party elements'.[256] But he failed to appease those intent on attacking him, especially since he refused to say why he had remained silent about 'Rightists' since the Sixteenth Party Congress.[257] Tomsky's jokes making light of the criticisms nonetheless did elicit laughter from those in the audience nearly a dozen times, beginning from almost his first words to the commission, when he joked that for 'a man to have lived for almost 54 years without making mistakes means he hasn't done anything'.[258]

It became obvious at his purge session how popular and respected Tomsky had already become among his colleagues at OGIZ during his short tenure there. Trotsky wrongly argued from abroad that at OGIZ, 'Tomsky was surrounded on all sides by carefully chosen enemies. Not only his assistants, but even his personal secretaries were undoubtedly agents of the GPU'.[259] Trotsky's speculation, though understandable, appears to be completely off base. The report sent to Stalin and Kaganovich deplored how members of the party cell 'had fallen under [Tomsky's] influence and related to him completely uncritically', even after they had been informed of the resolution denouncing him at the January Central Committee meeting. The report noted the 'intemperate praise' Tomsky received from his top aides, including by Udalov, the party secretary

---

254   RGASPI, f. 593, op. 1, d. 6, 1; TsGAODM, f. 2870, op. 1, d. 296, reprinted in Karpachev and Minaeva (eds) 1992a, pp. 108–15; 1992c, pp. 106–7. Luppol was also held to account for these 'defects' immediately after the purge commission was finished with Tomsky, during which he praised Tomsky's leadership of OGIZ while criticising Tomsky's failure to speak out against the 'Right Deviation': RGASPI, f. 81, op. 3, d. 179, pp. 60–2.
255   TsGAODM, f. 2870, op. 1, d. 296, reprinted in Karpachev and Minaeva (eds) 1992b, pp. 106–10.
256   RGASPI, f. 81, op. 3, d. 179, l. 57.
257   Tomsky did not speak at the Central Committee Plenums in 1931 and 1932: Koshelevoi et al. (eds) 2007c.
258   TsGAODM, f. 2870, op. 1, d. 296, reprinted in Karpachev and Minaeva (eds) 1992b, p. 100.
259   Trotsky was in Norway when he wrote his portrait of Tomsky during the fall of 1936: Trotsky 1988, pp. 228–31. As will be discussed, over one hundred of Tomsky's former staff members at OGIZ were arrested during the Great Purges.

of the OGIZ party cell. According to the report, Udalov had 'a wholly positive view' of Tomsky. Shockingly, despite the pressure the party cell was under to disavow him, Udalov is quoted as solemnly stating, 'we surrounded Mikhail Pavlovich with love'.[260] Several speakers testified that Tomsky's leadership was far superior to that of his predecessor, the inept bohemian Artashes Khalatov, the first chair of OGIZ.[261] One of them, M.P. Kuznetsov, declared that Tomsky's first report after he arrived 'intoxicated us'.[262] Tomsky clearly had lost none of his charisma and ability to charm, or his administrative skills. Members of the purge commission were not pleased, to say the least. Members of the OGIZ party cell were reprimanded by the purge commission for their failure to criticise Tomsky's political mistakes.[263] But when the purge commission's insults of Tomsky were especially venomous, the unbowed audience reacted with outbursts of disapproval.[264]

Failing to find sufficient support for attacking Tomsky among the ten members of the OGIZ party cell, outsiders from local districts were brought in. These 17 speakers taunted Tomsky for his 'failure to speak in detail of his mistakes', particularly his involvement with the 'counter-revolutionary group of Eismont-Tolmachev-Smirnov'.[265] Tomsky, to his credit, continued to try to

---

260 RGASPI, f. 81, op. 3, d. 179, l. 56; TsGAODM, f. 2870, op. 1, d. 296, l. 21, reprinted in Karpachev and Minaeva (eds) 1992a, p. 108. This outpouring of support may not have been as unusual as it sounds. At Shlyapnikov's purge, some party members similarly refused to denounce him: Allen 2015, p. 318.

261 RGASPI, f. 81, op. 3, d. 179, 59; TsGAODM, f. 2870, op. 1, d. 296, reprinted in Karpachev and Minaeva (eds) 1992c, p. 116. The Armenian Khalatov, who came from a middle-class upbringing in Baku, was renowned for his long curly hair, full beard, and trademark Astrakhan hat, which he rarely removed: Slezkine 2017, pp. 277, 382. The Politburo had dismissed Khalatov with little warning on 4 April 1932, evidently primarily because of his poor relationship with many OGIZ staff members and production problems in 1931, as well as his general incompetence during some five years of complete control over Gosizdat and then OGIZ. Sheila Fitzpatrick has a much more favourable assessment of Khalatov, at least earlier in his career, characterising him as 'an unusually capable organizer, popular in the party and (as head of Sovnarkom's All-Russian Commission for the Improvement of the Life of Scholars in the early 1920s) with non-party intelligentsia': Fitzpatrick 1970, p. 305.

262 TsGAODM, f. 2870, op. 1, d. 296, reprinted in Karpachev and Minaeva (eds) 1992a, p. 108.

263 TsGAODM, f. 2870, op. 1, d. 296, l. 23, reprinted in Karpachev and Minaeva (eds) 1992a, p. 109.

264 It was recorded in the stenographic report as 'noise in the hall': TsGAODM, f. 2870, op. 1, d. 296, reprinted in Karpachev and Minaeva (eds) 1992c, pp. 108–10.

265 RGASPI, f. 81, op. 3, d. 179, l. 121; TsGAODM, f. 2870, op. 1, d. 296, reprinted in Karpachev and Minaeva (eds) 1992a, pp. 105–6, 110. Tomsky continued to defend his opposition to the 'extraordinary measures' in 1928, stating that attacks on the kulaks hurt middle peasants, adding that history had proven him correct in that. Tomsky stated that his mistake was in thinking that NEP needed to be 'some pristine thing' while also going on to add

defend Smirnov, which stands in stark contrast with Bukharin's failure to defend his young adherents, members of the so-called Bukharin school, when they came under attack.[266] But Tomsky's attackers did succeed in getting him to state that the treatment the so-called Right Opposition received from the Central Committee was 'entirely correct'.[267] Tomsky also emphasised that unlike the 'leftists', he never took his opposition 'outside the gates of the party'.[268] He also thought he should get some credit for rebuffing offers from the 'bourgeois press' to provide information about the desperate conditions in the countryside.[269] But it was all to no avail since the purge commission viewed all of Tomsky's attempts at self-defence as just further evidence of his guilt.[270] They had no interest in forgiving Tomsky for his oppositionist past, much less granting him the sort of redemption he received after returning from his banishment to Turkestan in 1921.

The OGIZ purge commission, which called for the removal of 84 of the 572 members of OGIZ's senior management and editorial staffs as 'socially alien elements', in its concluding resolution also called for purging Tomsky from the party.[271] But the Central Purge Commission not only refused to implement this recommendation, it kept Tomsky in his position as head of OGIZ.[272] And interestingly, after Kaganovich received the OGIZ Purge Commission's report on

---

that he recognised 'it was impossible to create a powerful industry on the basis of a small, backward technical base'. A former St. Petersburg worker, who had grown up in its factories, it was ridiculous to think he opposed industrialisation. This was hardly the sort of full-fledged admission of guilt the purge commission was demanding.

266 Karpachev and Minaeva (eds) 1992a, pp. 107–8. Tomsky even offered that Smirnov often now said that when he was in charge of the Commissariat of Agriculture 'everything was good, but now everything is bad'. He was referring in particular to horse breeding, but the implication was far broader: TsGAODM, f. 2870, op. 1, d. 296, reprinted in Karpachev and Minaeva (eds) 1992b, p. 113.

267 TsGAODM, f. 2870, op. 1, d. 296, reprinted in Karpachev and Minaeva (eds) 1992b, p. 114; 1992c, p. 101. Smirnov would be purged from the party in 1934.

268 TsGAODM, f. 2870, op. 1, d. 296, reprinted in Karpachev and Minaeva (eds) 1992b, pp. 114–15. The refusal by the 'Right Oppositionists' to take their views outside the confines of the Politburo and Central Committee into an open confrontation in public was, as we have seen, a key factor in their defeat.

269 TsGAODM, f. 2870, op. 1, d. 296, reprinted in Karpachev and Minaeva (eds) 1992c, p. 108.

270 See, for example, the response to Shlyapnikov's attempts at self-defence: Allen 2015, p. 311.

271 TsGAODM, f. 2870, op. 1, d. 296, reprinted in Karpachev and Minaeva (eds) 1992a, p. 113. The quality of the staffs at OGIZ predictably deteriorated even lower following the purging of 'ideological vacillators' as little educated incompetents often took their places: Gorelov 2000, p. 222.

272 TsGAODM, f. 2870, op. 1, d. 296, reprinted in Karpachev and Minaeva (eds) 1992a, pp. 109, 115.

Tomsky, he cut whole portions that went into detail about Tomsky's opposition to forced collectivisation and dekulakisation. He obviously thought it best to leave that unmentioned given the horrific famine continuing to extend through a large part of the country.[273]

Tomsky could not sustain his resistance to the continual onslaught of political attacks and endless demands that he engage in degrading repudiations of his past views. Although he had a history of holding onto his principles, he abandoned his attempts to alternate between supplication and self-defence. During the following year, Tomsky capitulated completely at the Seventeenth Party Congress in February 1934, which billed itself as the 'Congress of Victors', where all the leading former oppositionists felt compelled to make public declarations of self-criticism. A weary and dispirited Tomsky delivered a short speech from the rostrum, without any attempts to elicit laughter, and with only a few of the usual derisive interruptions from the delegates.[274] Tomsky, who was demoted from full member to the rank of candidate member of the Central Committee, did maintain some of the dignity that had characterised his speeches at earlier meetings.[275] While renouncing the 'Rightist platform', including both its defence of NEP and its refusal to recognise 'the necessity of forced dekulakisation', he did explain the reasons he had continued to support the moderate policies of NEP after the party line changed, including the need to provide 'concessions' to kulaks as well as offering peasants higher grain prices. Tomsky also once again renounced his 'mistake' of attempting to preserve the NEP-era trade-union movement.[276] He may have felt some sense of vindication when he apologised for the fact that his policy views had found resonance both inside and outside the party.[277] But after watching the failure of party members still in good standing to mount any concerted opposition to Stalin during the disastrous 1932–33 famine, coupled with the upswing in the economy, Tomsky had obviously concluded that any further resistance on his part, however min-

---

273   RGASPI, f. 81, op. 3, d. 179, l. 123.
274   Rykov and Bukharin, especially Bukharin, spoke at greater length.
275   The congress also demoted Bukharin and Rykov to candidate members. In the published ranking of the 68 candidate members, Bukharin had dropped to 59, Rykov to 65, and Tomsky to 67. Even so, Tomsky received 801 of the possible 1,059 votes cast: Wheatcroft 2004, p. 81; Mawdsley and White 2000, p. 40.
276   RKP(b) 1934c, pp. 249–51. Kaganovich and Shvernik accused Tomsky of pitting the trade unions against the party in 1928–29: Rees 2012, p. 118. All the former oppositionist leaders – Bukharin and Rykov, as well as Zinoviev, Kamenev, Radek, and others – capitulated at the Seventeenth Party Congress.
277   RKP(b) 1934c, pp. 250–1.

imal, was utterly hopeless and only self-defeating, at least for the time being.²⁷⁸ As a result, Tomsky lavishly praised Stalin as 'the most consistent, the brightest of Lenin's pupils ... [who] was leading the party along the correct Leninist path'.²⁷⁹ While Kirov expressed some sympathy, and even understanding of the former oppositionists, a triumphant Stalin dismissed them as 'utterly demoralised and smashed'.²⁸⁰ The humiliated Tomsky certainly acted dejected and defeated.

Tomsky tried to put on a good face despite his political disgrace and poor mental health. Walter Citrine, the top British trade unionist, remarked after visiting with him in his OGIZ office in September 1935, 'I looked at Tomsky very carefully ... He seemed just the same as when I saw him eight years ago. His hair was somewhat greyer, but he had all his old vigour and his little slanting eyes glittered just as merrily as ever'.²⁸¹ But Tomsky, in fact, was suffering from a deep depression that no one could alleviate. According to Rykov, who occasionally continued to meet with him, Tomsky often thought about committing suicide.²⁸² In desperation, the head of the OGIZ Secretariat, N.I. Voinov, went to

---

278   Rykov implausibly testified at his show trial in 1938 that Tomsky favoured carrying out a coup at the Seventeenth Party Congress but it was rejected because no one else supported it: Tucker and Cohen (eds) 1965, p. 178. The congress has been dubbed the Congress of Victims, instead of its official name as the Congress of Victors, because within a few years over half of those in attendance had been shot or sent to the gulags, according to Khrushchev's 1956 de-Stalinisation 'secret speech': Khrushchev 1970, pp. 572–3.
279   RKP(b) 1934c, p. 250. The repentant tone and extravagant praise of Stalin by the 'Right Deviationists' might have been the quid pro quo for not being removed from the Central Committee entirely: Clement 1987, p. 186.
280   RKP(b) 1934c, pp. 28, 253.
281   Numerous British trade-union leaders had been unsuccessful in their attempts to contact Tomsky when they visited the Soviet Union during the 1930s. Both Citrine and another British labour leader, George Hicks, had been trying to 'renew their friendship' with Tomsky for over a year before a determined Citrine finally succeeded. He stated that he had mentally resolved to interview him or to be kicked out in the attempt'. He told Tomsky that 'all your trade-union friends in England asked me to give you their good wishes'. To Citrine's surprise he thought that Tomsky remained an enthusiastic defender of the Soviet system despite his own bitter experiences, although he recognised that their translator was probably an NKVD agent so he could not be sure: Citrine 1936, pp. 4, 81, 132–5. Sidney and Beatrice Webb, who had also hoped to visit Tomsky in Moscow, sent their best wishes to Tomsky's wife and children in a letter that was intercepted by the NKVD: RGASPI, f. 593, op. 1, d. 7, ll. 6–7, 10–11.
282   According to Rykov, Tomsky had also thought about suicide earlier during bouts battling depression and various physical ailments: RGASPI, f. 17, op. 2, d. 574, l. 35. In his testimonies at the December 1936 and February 1937 Central Committee Plenums, Rykov testified that he had met with Tomsky a number of times between 1934 and 1936. One of them was a large gathering that included many actors and actresses: RGASPI, f. 17, op. 2, d. 574,

Bukharin at *Izvestiia* to ask him to go see Tomsky and try to cheer him up. But Bukharin, who had been steering clear of Tomsky, later admitted he was afraid to do so.[283] Socially and politically ostracised, Tomsky would occasionally visit with some top officials outside OGIZ including former oppositionists, such as Zinoviev during 1934, but such outings became increasingly rare, not just for him but for all the former oppositionists.[284]

Tomsky did his best to immerse himself in his work at OGIZ and live life as normally as possible, including with his family and those friends still willing to socialise with him, even as the barrage of political attacks continued to intensify.[285] Despite the despair eating away at his soul, he appears to have remained deeply engaged in his responsibilities as head of OGIZ, judging by the directives he issued on a daily basis and his occasional messages to the Politburo explaining the need for additional funds for OGIZ.[286] He continued to attend Central Committee Plenums, such as in June 1936. A workaholic, when his health permitted, he commonly worked from six in the morning until 11 or 12 at night.[287] Occasionally he was able to spend time relaxing on hunting trips with colleagues or simply spending time with his family. That summer, Tom-

---

l. 32. Other occasions involved both Tomsky and Rykov's families at their respective dachas and apartments: RGASPI, f. 17, op. 2, d. 580, ll. 39–42. For his part, the normally cheerful, sociable, and witty Rykov was also increasingly irritable and rarely socialised: Senin 1993, pp. 214–15.

283 Bukharin 1993, p. 2; RGASPI, f. 593, op. 1, d. 2, l. 25. Voinov, who had followed Tomsky from VTsSPS to OGIZ, had been Tomsky's secretary since 1927. Their families were close: TsGAODM, f. 2870, op. 1, d. 296, reprinted in Karpachev and Minaeva (eds) 1992b, p. 112. Bukharin, under questioning at the February 1937 Central Committee Plenum, stated he had not seen Tomsky, Rykov, Uglanov, or Shmidt in either 1935 or 1936: RGASPI, f. 17, op. 2, d. 584, ll. 103, 124.

284 Khaustov and Samuel'son 2010, p. 373. Tomsky visited Zinoviev at his dacha in 1934 because Zinoviev had complained to him about 'his isolation, his lack of friends': Rogovin 1998, p. 104.

285 For example, *Pravda*, 13 March 1936, published an article by Central Committee member Peter Pospelov, who accused Tomsky as well as Bukharin and Rykov of 'foul anti-party activity' and criminal links with the Trotskyites: Conquest 1990, p. 273. This is the same Pospelov who headed the commission that laid the basis for Khrushchev's de-Stalinisation speech at the Twentieth Party Congress. The denunciations intensified behind the scene as spring turned into summer, according to the questionable source Abdurakham Avtorkhanov, writing under the pseudonym Alexander Uralov, who wrote that Stalin convened an Extraordinary Meeting of the Central Committee and the Control Commission in the summer of 1936 to focus on the 'Bukharin Affair', and that the NKVD kept Tomsky as well as Bukharin and Rykov informed about the depositions Yezhov extracted from Zinoviev and Kamenev: Uralov 1953, pp. 34–5.

286 GARF, f. 533, op. 1, d. 10, l. 13; RGASPI, f. 593, op. 1, d. 2, l. 4; Rogovin 1998, p. 80.

287 Gorelov 2000, p. 226.

FIGURE 32 Tomsky in 1936
WIKIMEDIA COMMONS

sky took his 15-year-old son Yury on a weeklong fishing trip in Karelia.[288] He also occasionally continued to meet with former oppositionists. Tomsky's and Rykov's families had socialised together in 1934, during which Rykov insisted that he and Tomsky were not apart from their families for 'a single minute',

---

288 Gorelov 2000, p. 267. During the years Tomsky worked at OGIZ, he requested extra vacation time from the Politburo on numerous occasions, including during the week before his suicide: RGASPI, f. 17, op. 3, d. 898, 929, 937, 948, 956, 967, 980.

and in any case, no longer talked about politics when they got together.[289] That same year, against Rykov's advice, Tomsky accepted an invitation from Zinoviev to come to his dacha to drink tea, after which they drove in Tomsky's car to pick out a dog for Zinoviev. This seemingly innocuous visit would be the focus of political attacks later.[290] Tomsky also got together in 1935 with the prominent former Left Oppositionist Gregory Pyatakov. According to the show-trial testimony of Sokolnikov, he did so in the capacity of the Rightists' representative to the 'Trotskyist centre'.[291]

The all-union discussion of the drafts of the new Soviet Constitution in the summer of 1936 was attracting much of the nation's attention before the first of the infamous, major Moscow show trials opened on 19 August 1936, in the stately House of Unions. The trial took place in the relatively small, upstairs October Hall, which had space for just about 350 spectators, most of whom presumably were NKVD agents. But there were also foreign diplomats and correspondents in attendance. To great fanfare, 16 former oppositionists stood in the dock, including most prominently Zinoviev and Kamenev, both of whom were ill, deeply depressed, and psychologically broken after years of political attacks, imprisonment, exile, and finally months of interrogations.[292] In this first trial of formers members of the Bolshevik leadership, Zinoviev and Kamenev pleaded guilty to organising 'a terrorist centre' on behalf of Trotsky and the Gestapo and to having assassinated Kirov and making plans to assassinate Stalin, Voroshilov, and other members of the Politburo. On 20 August, as the chief prosecutor Vyshinsky led them through their testimony, Zinoviev and Kamenev unexpectedly implicated Tomsky as well as other leading 'Rightists' and 'Leftists'.[293] Zinoviev testified that he had 'conducted negotiations

---

[289] RGASPI, f. 17, op. 2, d. 582, l. 40; RGASPI, f. 17, op. 2, d. 574, l. 33.
[290] Stalin and Kaganovich, at the December 1936 Central Committee Plenum, riddled Rykov with questions about that visit, with Kaganovich childishly stating 'they were searching for a four-legged companion not unlike themselves' and with Stalin questioning, to laughter in the hall, whether it was 'a good dog or a bad dog': RGASPI, f. 17, op. 2, d. 574, ll. 86–7.
[291] RGASPI, f. 17, op. 2, d. 579, ll. 110–12. According to Kaganovich's testimony at the December 1936 Central Committee Plenum, Sokolnikov made that confession before he knew Tomsky had killed himself: RGASPI, f. 17, op. 2, d. 574, ll. 78–80.
[292] Hedeler 2003, p. 37; Rogovin 1998, p. 5. At least according to one scholar, Stalin thought the confessions were genuine: van Ree 2002, p. 120.
[293] Another one of the defendants, Isaac Reingold, also implicated Tomsky: People's Commissariat of Justice of the U.S.S.R. 1936, p. 56. It has often been said their testimony was scripted. Elizabeth Wood calls that into question. She suggests the trials were more improvisational than that, with the defendants given 'only a skeleton version of their parts': Wood 2005 p. 195. What is clear is that Stalin oversaw their interrogations while Bukharin

with Tomsky', who 'expressed complete solidarity with us'.[294] Likewise, Kamenev testified that he had maintained relations with Tomsky in 1932, 1933, and 1934.[295] Kamenev said, 'we counted on the Rightist group of Rykov, Bukharin, and Tomsky', adding that Tomsky told him that Bukharin and Rykov 'think the same as I do' and sympathised with us.[296] These statements clearly signalled that the government intended to arrest Tomsky as well as Bukharin and Rykov. And indeed, at the end of the next day's session, on 21 August, Vyshinsky announced that he had given orders for the State Procurator's Office to open an investigation into the courtroom confessions regarding Tomsky, Bukharin, and Rykov, and 'in accordance with the results of this investigation, the office of the State Attorney will institute legal proceedings'.[297] This announcement that the 'Right Deviationists' had purportedly joined with the 'Left Oppositionists' in 'a treasonous network' came as a shock to many party members.[298]

On that very same day, elsewhere in Moscow, Tomsky was for the third straight day compelled to stand before another purge commission at OGIZ. Tomsky stood accused of not just being a 'double-dealer', but an 'enemy of the people', who had participated in the activities of the 'Trotskyist-Zinovievite counter-revolutionary terrorist band.' After he categorically denied participating in this so-call centre, the purge commission confronted Tomsky with a list of his 'counterrevolutionary conversations' with various 'oppositionists', including Kamenev in 1928, 1929, and 1932, Shlyapnikov in 1932, as well as numerous meetings with Zinoviev right up until recently.[299] While trying to downplay his role, Tomsky admitted to having met with them and having discussed creating

---

and Rykov were still in prison, with Kaganovich overseeing the actual trial: Rees 2012, p. 184; Slezkine 2017, p. 754.

294 People's Commissariat of Justice of the USSR 1936, p. 73.
295 Kamenev did not mention that he had to interact with Tomsky at OGIZ after he was appointed the director of one of the publishing houses in 1933, as noted above.
296 People's Commissariat of Justice of the USSR 1936, pp. 65, 68. If there is some truth in this, perhaps it was during Tomsky's and Kamenev's conversations at OGIZ. Similar statements, implicating the then deceased Tomsky, played a key role in the second Moscow show trial in January 1937. For example, Pyatakov testified that the Trotskyists relied on Tomsky because 'we had information that Tomsky had the most numerous and organised cadres and was best fitted to perform such illegal organisational work': People's Commissariat of Justice of the USSR 1937, p. 54.
297 *Pravda*, 2 August 1936; People's Commissariat of Justice of the USSR 1936, pp. 115–6; Goldman 2007, pp. 79–80.
298 Schapiro 1959, pp. 408–9. It should be noted that most Central Committee members were inclined to believe in the guilt of the accused: Thurston 1996, p. 31; Getty and Naumov 1999, p. 327.
299 Gorelov 1989, p. 71; *Pravda*, 23 August 1936; RGASPI, f. 17, op 2, d. 574, ll. 84–90.

a 'joint bloc' in 1929 and during the early 1930s, and that he had criticised party policies and complained about how he was being treated by the party. He also conceded that he had passed along conversations with Zinoviev and Kamenev to Bukharin and Rykov.[300] In addition, the OGIZ party cell charged Tomsky with various other meetings with 'Rightists', including with Smirnov and Uglanov, as well as with such other 'anti-party elements' as Shlyapnikov, who upon temporarily returning to Moscow from exile, despite their past differences, immediately went to OGIZ to meet with Tomsky in his office.[301] Sokolnikov, a prominent Zinovievite, had recently confessed that he met Tomsky in his OGIZ office in 1934 and 1935, but it is not clear whether the party cell raised this with Tomsky.[302] The OGIZ Party cell also planned to intensify the attacks the following day. According to his son's account, a worn-out Tomsky returned home late. He was clearly extremely upset and did not sleep at all that night.[303]

The 22 August morning edition of *Pravda* proved to be the proverbial last straw.[304] After his chauffeur arrived with the newspaper, Tomsky was stopped in his tracks in his yard when he saw the headline on the front page announcing the 'investigation of the ties of Tomsky-Bukharin-Rykov and Pyatakov-Radek with the Trotskyist-Zinovievite band'. In addition to publishing Vyshinsky's court pronouncement, *Pravda* also published an article on Tomsky's 'wretched double dealing' at the OGIZ purge meeting, where 'even now Tomsky is still hiding his ties with members of the [counterrevolutionary terrorist] bloc'.[305] Also, as part of an obviously orchestrated plan, *Pravda* as well as other newspapers published letters to the editor from workers, as well as a series of unanimous resolutions from offices and factories all over the country, demanding a full investigation of Tomsky and his links with his fellow 'despicable terrorists'.[306] Curiously, it was evidently widely suspected among

---

300 Davies et al. (eds) 2003, p. 334; Iakovlev (ed.) 1991, p. 244; Rogovin 1998, p. 70.
301 *Pravda*, 22 August 1936. Shlyapnikov, who also suffered from various illnesses, including 'shattered nerves' and growing deafness, might very well have shared with Tomsky his anger at his inability to refute accusations of 'anti-Soviet agitation and counterrevolutionary organisation' and his penal exile to the far north of the Soviet Union: Allen 2015, pp. 321, 328, 332, 335.
302 RGASPI, f. 17, op. 2, d. 574, ll. 78–88; RGASPI, f. 17, op. 2, d. 575, translated and reprinted in Getty and Naumov 1999, p. 307.
303 Yury had waited up for his father to discuss their planned, upcoming hunting trip: Gorelov and Shapovalova (eds) 2001, p. 150.
304 Throughout the trial *Pravda* printed a transcript of the trial proceedings.
305 *Pravda*, 22 August 1936.
306 *Pravda*, 22 August 1936; Medvedev 1980, p. 122; Conquest 1990, p. 102. A letter from a worker published in the trade-union newspaper referred to Tomsky as an 'enemy of the people':

foreign observers in Moscow at the time that it was Tomsky who had organised the assassination of Kirov.[307]

In the last hours of his life Tomsky went for a walk on the grounds of his dacha and decided to make a last-ditch phone call. The account of the walk comes from his then 15-year-old son Yury, who accompanied him. Yury recalled attentively listening to his father, who seemed to be his calm, usual self. After telling him, 'I am guilty of nothing, but I can't live without the party', he told Yury to run along.[308] Tomsky in desperation called Nikolai Yezhov, part of Stalin's innermost circle and now chair of the Party Control Commission, to complain about all 'the dirt and slander' being hurled at him. Tomsky asked, 'What do you want me to do? To resign? Clearly, the party has no further use for me'. To which Yezhov replied, 'Don't talk nonsense. All this is rubbish. Work. We trust you'.[309]

Tomsky was far from pacified by Yezhov's soothing words. Hopeless and despondent, he realised he would soon be arrested with no chance to prove his innocence. Determined to avoid further mistreatment and degradation, including providing any 'last service' to the party, and perhaps in an attempt to save his family, Tomsky grabbed one of his guns, and in the words of Bukharin's wife,

---

Trud, 22 August 1936. Ordinary Soviet citizens had no choice, of course, but to raise their hands in support of such resolutions at mass meetings. Although it is hard to know what ordinary people genuinely believed, the evidence suggests that terror against the party elite provoked either popular support or indifference: Davies 1997, pp. 123, 126, 131. For a contrary view see Walter Duranty, the *New York Times* correspondent, who wrote (in a book in which he apologised for his earlier reports denying the 1932–33 famine) that the people of the Soviet Union were 'distressed' by the trial and 'thought that it somehow smelt queer', which they said among themselves 'in private and under their breath': Duranty 1941, p. 47. Wendy Goldman identifies a wide variety of workers' responses to the trial: Goldman 2007, pp. 80–6.

307 According to a later account by a foreign correspondent, Nikolaus Basseches of the Vienna *Neue Freie Presse*: Basseches 1952, p. 275.
308 Gorelov and Shapovalova (eds) 2001, p. 150.
309 Gorelov 2000, p. 231. Tomsky's decision to turn to Yezhov is not as crazy as it might seem. Yezhov, before he became the 'Great Executioner', was well liked among 'Old Bolsheviks' and top officials commonly sought to bypass official channels to appeal to him directly. Yezhov had, for example, tried to help Shlyapnikov in 1934: Allen 2015, pp. 334, 344. Tomsky, in addition, might have thought that Yezhov would be sympathetic since this son of a factory worker had been like him a skilled worker in St. Petersburg (although not at the same time since Yezhov was 15 years younger than Tomsky): Getty and Naumov 2008, pp. 14–15, 128–9; Thurston 1993, pp. 159–60. Bukharin thought Yezhov was a 'good man' with 'a good soul' – an enormous improvement over Yagoda: Nosach and Zvereva 2007, p. 185; Larina 1993, pp. 268, 300.

Anna Larina, 'with his firm worker's hand put a bullet through his head'.[310] If he had not committed suicide, Tomsky undoubtedly would have been the third major defendant in the March 1938 show trial of Bukharin, Rykov, and 19 others, including Yagoda, in the case of the 'Anti-Soviet Bloc of Rightists and Trotskyites'. The report about his suicide in *Pravda* on 23 August stated as a proven fact that Tomsky had been linked with 'counter-revolutionary Trotskyite-Zinovievite terrorists'.[311]

There has been considerable confusion among historians about the basic facts of Tomsky's suicide. According to the Russian historian Roy Medvedev, Stalin visited Tomsky right before he killed himself. In this account, Stalin arrived at Tomsky's apartment in the Kremlin with a bottle of wine, and after a brief conversation in Tomsky's study, loud shouting could be heard as Tomsky denounced Stalin in the 'foulest language'. Tomsky demanded Stalin leave, screaming 'Get out! Get the hell out of here! You're a bastard, a real bastard'! Stalin left, shaking with anger. A few moments later, according to Medvedev, Tomsky fatally shot himself in his study.[312] Based on this account, Robert Tucker in his biography of Stalin speculated that Stalin went to Tomsky on the day of his suicide to offer reassurances so that Tomsky would not foil his purge-trial plans by committing suicide.[313] Other leading historians, such as Moshe Lewin, have repeated Medvedev's sensational account of Tomsky's suicide.[314]

Medvedev's account is simply not true. While Stalin's visit to Tomsky might well have happened, it must have been at some earlier time.[315] Tomsky's suicide did not come on the heels of a visit from Stalin, who in fact was some 800 miles away at his holiday resort in Sochi when Tomsky took his own life. Grigory Tokaev, in his 1956 account, stated 'that grand old man had hanged himself in his country cottage at Bolshevo near Moscow'.[316] While Tomsky did not hang himself, at least Tokaev got the location right. Why Medvedev did not seems

---

310 Larina 1993, p. 68. The court announced Tomsky's suicide at the end of the night session the day he shot himself, 22 August. Both Zinoviev and Kamenev were seen sobbing for the first time while Vyshinsky demanded that the 'mad dogs be shot': *New York Times*, 23 August 1936; People's Commissariat of Justice of the USSR 1936, p. 164.
311 *Pravda*, 23 August 1936.
312 Medvedev repeated this dramatic narrative, which he claimed was based on information from Tomsky's son Yury, in a number of his writings: Medvedev 1977, p. 213; Medvedev 1989, pp. 356–7; Medvedev 1980, p. 124; Medvedev 1979, p. 99. The Tomsky family moved out of the Kremlin in 1935.
313 Tucker 1990, pp. 374–5.
314 Lewin 1997, p. 117.
315 Fitzpatrick 2015, p. 55.
316 Tokaev 1956, p. 62.

odd, since the *Pravda* article announcing Tomsky's suicide clearly stated that he killed himself at his Bolshevo dacha.[317]

Why Tomsky killed himself rather than Stalin has attracted speculation. Tucker responded to Medvedev's account of his suicide by writing 'the history of Soviet Russia, and of Europe and the whole world would have changed in many ways, for the better, if Tomsky had shot the visitor instead of himself'.[318] If not on the eve of his suicide, Tomsky, who loved to go bear and wolf hunting with his Politburo colleagues, certainly had the means to do so earlier. His gun collection was unparalleled in party circles, and he was a good shot.[319] How much difference Stalin's assassination would have made is open to debate. But Molotov thought 'it would have been enough to kill Stalin, and two or three more leaders, for everything to collapse'.[320]

Trotsky wondered from abroad whether Tomsky wrote a suicide note. He assumed he did. 'I think it's inconceivable that he left the scene without attempting an explanation'.[321] Hidden away in the archives for 50 years, the fairly long letter finally came to light in 1996. Tomsky addressed it to 'Dear Comrade Stalin' and left it on his dacha desk. Given that he started it the day before, it is unclear whether, when Tomsky sat down to write this letter, he intended it to be a suicide note. Tomsky appealed to Stalin not only as the leader of the party but also as an old comrade-in-arms. As was true of other such letters, for example Bukharin's desperate letter to Stalin in December 1937, Tomsky felt the need to make one last attempt to convince Stalin of his innocence and loyalty. Perhaps he hoped that doing so would mitigate the consequences for his family and former colleagues. Tomsky categorically denied any participation in anti-party activity. 'I've never been anti-party, never in my life was I capable of any collaboration with enemies of the party'. But he conceded he was guilty of 'struggling against the Central Committee and its correct line … [and of] not understanding the tasks of the party and its leadership in this historical period'. While criticising himself for his 'harsh and rude attacks' on Stalin, Tomsky also

---

317   *Pravda*, 23 August 1936.
318   Tucker 1990, p. 374. Tucker recognised that using terrorism to bring about meaningful political change was contrary to Marxist theory and Bolshevik political culture. See also Berger 1971, p. 163.
319   Kun 2003, pp. 283–4; TsGAODM, f. 2870, op. 1, d. 296, reprinted in Karpachev and Minaeva (eds) 1992c, p. 112.
320   Molotov 1991, p. 300. Stephen Kotkin compellingly speculates that forced collectivisation would have been almost impossible if Stalin had died earlier: Kotkin 2014, p. 739. According to Khlevniuk, the Great Purges would not have occurred without Stalin: Khlevniuk 2009, p. xx.
321   Trotskii 1988, p. 230.

criticised himself for 'an exaggerated sense of self-worth'. In the letter Tomsky also repeatedly called upon Stalin to reject the slander of such 'frightened' leaders as Zinoviev and Kamenev. He insisted Zinoviev, in particular, was guilty of 'outrageous, insolent slander. I was never in any bloc with him; I never engaged in anti-party conversations with him. I deeply despise this vile gang'![322] Toward the end of the letter, Tomsky declared he was utterly exhausted and could no longer bear it after reading of Vyshinsky's decision to open legal proceedings. 'I'm too tired from such shocks. I am not able to live when I am put on a par with fascists'. Tomsky ended the letter by stating 'I'm leaving', but he hoped the party would enjoy 'great new victories'![323]

Tomsky added a surprising postscript that was perhaps written in the last moments before he killed himself. In the first part of it, Tomsky wrote 'don't take what I blurted out in our night time conversation in 1928 seriously – I have been deeply regretting that ever since. But I've never been able to change your mind, you have never believed me'. Here he was presumably referring to the conversation in 1928 noted in the previous chapter, when Tomsky had warned Stalin that workers would soon start shooting at him. In the most perplexing part of the postscript, Tomsky wrote that his wife would name those persons responsible for leading him down the path of the 'Right Opposition' in May 1928. It is hard to understand why he wanted to put his wife in that position. In any case, when the NKVD arrived at Tomsky's dacha, Maria Tomskaya refused to speak to Georgy Molchanov, a deputy of Yagoda. According to Tomsky's son, there was also a second letter addressed to the Central Committee, which has not come to light.

The NKVD forwarded Tomsky's note to Stalin in Sochi, who put Yezhov in charge of investigating the suicide. He was able to get Tomskaya to talk. Tomsky's widow stated that Tomsky was referring to Yagoda, the widely despised head of the NKVD, who she said had 'recruited' Tomsky and 'played an active role with the leading troika of the Rightists and regularly passed them materials on the situation in the Central Committee'.[324] The historian Stephen Kotkin thinks that was a clever way to implicate Yagoda.[325] Tomsky had reason to denounce Yagoda, who had tilted toward the 'Rightists' during the struggle with

---

322 Iakovlev (ed.) 1991, p. 244.
323 Reprinted in *Rodina* 1996, 2, pp. 92–3.
324 Getty and Naumov 2008, p. 195; Khlevniuk 2010, p. 264; Jansen and Petrov, 2002, p. 49. During the 1938 Moscow show trial, Yagoda testified that in 1928 he supplied the 'Rightists' with OGPU secret reports and provided protection for them: Tucker and Cohen (eds) 1965, p. 489.
325 Kotkin 2017, p. 332.

Stalin earlier, but had done Stalin's bidding by persecuting Tomsky and the other 'Rightists' during the 1930s.[326] Tomsky might also have been disgusted by Yagoda's corruption and high living, especially since he had arrested countless people for violating public morals. The inventory of personal possessions, when the NKVD arrested Yagoda in 1936, contained some tens of thousands of items, thousands of which were pornographic pictures and films.[327]

In Yezhov's unsolicited letter to Stalin, on which he laboured for over two weeks, he wrote, 'Is this Tomsky's counterrevolutionary kick from the grave or a real fact? I don't know. I personally think that Tomsky chose a peculiar way to revenge himself [on Yagoda], counting on the plausibility [of the view]: dead men don't lie'.[328] Although Yezhov suggested that Tomsky's charge was not credible, he went on to state 'so many deficiencies have been uncovered in the work of the NKVD that it is impossible to tolerate them any further'.[329] Yezhov skilfully planted enough doubts in Stalin's mind that a month later, he sent a telegram from Sochi replacing Yagoda with Yezhov.[330] Ironically, at least regarding Tomsky's suicide note, it was Yagoda's failure to concentrate on 'Rightist' conspiracies instead of his focus on policing campaigns against criminals, juvenile delinquents, and other marginalised groups, that led to Yagoda's March 1937 arrest.[331]

---

326 Cohen 1973, p. 288; Rees 2012, p. 141. The Hungarian historian Miklos Kun speculated that Tomsky had prearranged his denunciation of Yagoda with his wife in the hopes of saving his family: Kun 2003, p. 416. Bukharin shared Tomsky's contempt for Yagoda: Larina 1993, p. 69.
327 The inventory included almost everything imaginable from foreign refrigerators and ovens to 1,229 bottles of mostly foreign wines. For the inventory: Rayfield 2004, pp. 211–12; Kun 2003, p. 262. One former Chekist, Georges Agabekov, contemporaneously characterised Yagoda as 'a brutal, uncultivated, and gross individual [who] keeps his position through lickspittling and flattering the members of the Politburo and Central Committee, and because he is a past-master of intrigue': Agabekov 1931, p. 256.
328 Getty and Naumov 2008, p. 196; Khlevniuk 2010, p. 265. Stephen Kotkin has suggested that Tomsky cleverly achieved his desired revenge against Yagoda by having the 'secret' posthumously pried out of his wife, knowing this would feed Stalin's conspiratorial fears: Kotkin 2017, p. 332.
329 Koshelevoi et al. (eds) 2007c, p. 275.
330 Getty and Naumov explore, by examining the various deleted drafts of Yezhov's letters to Stalin, how subtly and tactfully Yezhov used Tomsky's suicide note to get Stalin to fire Yagoda and himself promoted; Getty and Naumov, 2008, pp. 195–204.
331 Shearer 2009, p. 293; Hagenloh 2009, pp. 147, 225, 230–1. Yagoda was found guilty of treasonous conspiracy with Bukharin and Rykov against the Soviet government and executed two days later. His entire family, including his wife, parents, brother-in-law, and father-in-law were either shot or sent to the camps: Montefiore 2004, p. 220.

Tomsky's success at carrying out the ultimate form of protest against the party's treatment of him enraged Stalin and those around him, who viewed suicide as 'a sharp weapon' against the party as well as tantamount to an admission of one's guilt.[332] Rather than feeling any sympathy or even pity for one of his fellow party leaders and earlier a friend, Stalin lashed out, attacking Tomsky as well as other party members who took their lives as engaging in acts of opposition blackmail. 'Here you see', Stalin stated, 'one of the ultimate and most cunning and easiest means by which one can spit at and deceive the party one last time'.[333] It was Tomsky's success in avoiding his impending arrest that especially infuriated Stalin. 'A person commits suicide', according to Stalin, 'because he is afraid that everything will come out in the open and he doesn't want to be a witness to his own universal disgrace'.[334] Other party leaders piled on. Voroshilov denounced Tomsky's suicide as a 'vile' attempt to proclaim his innocence.[335] Andreev asserted Tomsky committed suicide 'to avoid shame, public shame, and to evade the investigation'.[336] Not to be outdone, local party organisations sent telegrams to the Central Committee denouncing Tomsky's suicide as an attempt to cover up all traces of his and the other 'Rightist ringleaders' treasonous activity of aiming 'their guns at the heart of our party, the great Stalin'.[337] Tomsky's suicide also fed the Stalinists' belief in an 'omnipresent conspiracy'.[338] Molotov fumed, 'I cannot see in all this anything else but a typical example of underhanded scheming'. Fantastically, Molotov asserted that Tomsky's suicide was 'part of a plot, a premeditated act, in which Tomsky discussed committing suicide with not one, but with several people in order to inflict another blow against the Central Committee'.[339] Voroshilov asserted no mercy would be shown to Tomsky's 'collaborators'. 'Now that he has killed himself, 50 percent of their verdict is set, if not 75 percent'.[340]

---

332 Getty and Naumov 1999, pp. 90, 218. On suicide as a form of protest: Miller and Miller 1988, p. 313.
333 Earlier in the Bolsheviks' revolutionary tradition, as Sheila Fitzpatrick notes, suicide was considered 'an honorable way of registering a moral protest or exiting from an impossible situation; it had an honorable ring': Fitzpatrick 1999, p. 174.
334 Stalin speaking at the December 1936 plenum: RGASPI, f. 17. op. 2, d. 576, ll. 67–70, translated and reprinted in Getty and Naumov 1999, p. 322.
335 Getty and Naumov 1999, p. 375.
336 RGASPI, f. 17, op. 21, d. 2196, translated and reprinted in Getty and Naumov 1999, p. 338.
337 RGASPI, f. 17, op. 120, d. 271, l. 21, translated and reprinted in Getty and Naumov 1999, p. 257.
338 Rittersporn 1993, pp. 99–115.
339 Khlevniuk 1992, p. 201. In a more measured tone, Mikoyan lamented how Tomsky had undoubtedly carried to the grave many secrets about the 'Rightists' headquarters'; RGASPI, f. 17, op. 2, d. 579, l. 96.
340 RGASPI, f. 17, op. 2, d. 580, l. 96.

Émigré socialists responded quite differently when they learned the news of Tomsky's suicide. The obituary in the then Paris-based Menshevik newspaper *Sotsialisticheskii vestnik* painted an extremely positive portrait. The author, Mark Kefali, who knew Tomsky well as the former head of the Moscow Printers' Union, characterised Tomsky as the most colourful and remarkable figure among all the leaders of Bolshevism.[341] Even *Time* magazine, whose publisher Henry Luce was vehemently anti-communist, reported that his 'friends in Russia and abroad were numberless'.[342] The magazine later speculated that if Tomsky had been subjected to a show trial it would have 'split proletarian opinion irretrievably'.[343]

Tomsky's funeral was held on the grounds of his dacha, not far from where he shot himself. The attendance at the funeral by some former colleagues in the Central Committee and VTsSPS was evidence that some of his once widespread popularity remained. A large number of people bravely, if foolishly, even came inside the family dacha following the funeral.[344] A.S. Slavinsky, the chair of a department of the Union of Artists and a well-known personal friend of Tomsky, played on the piano Frédéric Chopin's funeral march and Tomsky's favourite piece of music, Mikhail Glinka's *Zhavoronok*.[345] It is worth noting that these friends and colleagues perhaps did not know the risk they were taking by attending. This is the summer of 1936 before the NKVD began arresting party members simply by virtue of their association with an 'enemy of the people'. Stalin ordered that Tomsky be buried in the Bolshevo cemetery, instead of the niche in the Kremlin wall that had been allotted to him.[346] In the following months, the NKVD exhumed his body and took it to an undisclosed location.[347]

Tomsky's suicide did win the admiration of many. The Trotskyist Victor Serge congratulated him for choosing 'a dignified end'.[348] Ante Ciliga noted that 'his mode of protest was hardly efficacious, but at least the whole world heard of

---

341 *Sotsialisticheskii vestnik*, 30 August 1936, p. 11; Liebich 1997, p. 90.
342 *Time*, 31 August 1936.
343 *Time*, 6 December 1937.
344 A significant number of former colleagues also, according to his son, paid their respects at their Moscow apartment: Gorelov and Shapovalova (eds) 2001, p. 156.
345 Getty and Naumov 1999, p. 316. The Union of Artists was in fact not a union but a professional association with a considerable number of coveted privileges: Komar and Melamid 1983, p. 168. Also, according to his son Yury, Tomsky was embalmed and a plaster death mask was made: Gorelov 2000, pp. 234–5, 268.
346 In doing so, Stalin was following the advice of Kaganovich, Yezhov, and Ordzhonikidze: Murin (ed.) 1996, p. 91. There had also been some consideration of burying him in the Novodevichy cemetery: Gorelov and Shapovalova (eds) 2001, p. 153.
347 Shelestov 1988, p. 27; Rayfield 2004, p. 278.
348 Serge 1937b, p. 226.

it'.³⁴⁹ Alexander Solzhenitsyn also complimented Tomsky for choosing suicide rather than waiting to be arrested. 'There was a choice! The most farsighted and determined of those who were doomed did not allow themselves to be arrested. They committed suicide first'.³⁵⁰ And, indeed, Tomsky was far from alone. There was a surge in suicides during the Great Purges including among top party and military officials.³⁵¹ But many wondered, as noted above, why Tomsky did not take others with him. Nadezhda Joffe, for example, asked, 'Why didn't he, when he had his gun in hand, kill a couple of the NKVD agents first? And then himself. Of course, they were grains of sand, they decided nothing, but at least they wouldn't have gone to arrest people as if they were going for a pleasurable stroll. They would have at least begun to fear arresting people'.³⁵²

Tomsky perhaps naively hoped that by taking only his own life he might be able to protect his family. In his suicide note he asked Stalin not to pursue his family, but 'to allow them to live in peace'. Yezhov assured Tomsky's son Yury that 'not one hair would fall from our heads and that he would try to be a father to us'.³⁵³ But during the Great Purges the family was to suffer the fate of other families of 'traitors'. The NKVD seized his dacha, divided it in two, and made it a safe house for agents who escaped back to the Soviet Union after being exposed in Europe.³⁵⁴ Further ostracised, Tomsky's grieving and already ill widow quickly became desperate. Tomskaya wrote to Yezhov a few months later, pleading, 'My dear Nikolai Ivanovich, please help me find a job. I cannot live without work. Sometimes I feel that I am going crazy. I can no longer go on living, cut off from life'. Presumably, after she had been fired from her job

---

349   Ciliga 1979, p. 186.
350   Solzhenitsyn 1973, p. 411.
351   Halfin 2003, p. 277. Party members began to kill themselves in increasing numbers by the end of 1936, cresting in a wave of suicides over the next two years: Schlogel 2012, pp. 168, 174. The leading members of the party who committed suicide include besides Tomsky, Yan Gamarnik, Panas Liubchenko, Nikolai Skrypnik, Vissarion (Besso) Lominadze, Agasi Khandzhian, V. Ia. Furer, and Grigory (Sergo) Ordzhonikidze, although Ordzhonikidze officially died from a heart attack and his funeral was given 'full state honours': Khlevniuk 1995, pp. 159–63.
352   Joffe 1995, p. 106. The daughter of the Bolshevik leader and Soviet diplomat Adolf Joffe, Nadezhda was a 'Left Oppositionist' in her own right, for which she was to spend years in the gulag.
353   Gorelov 2000, p. 232.
354   Marina Tsvetaeva, the celebrated Russian and Soviet poet, found herself living in Tomsky's former dacha for five months in 1939 because of her husband, the poet Sergei Efron. After serving as an officer in the White Army in the Civil War, Efron had fled to Europe to avoid retribution, where the NKVD eventually recruited him. During those five months both Tsvetaeva's daughter and husband were arrested: Karlinsky 1985, pp. 229, 290.

'for political motives', no one would hire her because of this notation on her record. But even if someone had offered her a job, it is not clear whether she was still able to do the sort of white-collar work she had done earlier. Tomskaya had quickly become a physical wreck, as she conceded. 'My eyes are hurting me now (the blood vessels in the pupils of both eyes have burst) and I can read and write for only short periods of time'.[355] In any case, her pleas to Yezhov went unanswered.

A year and half after Tomsky's suicide, on a freezing day in December 1937, NKVD men arrived at the Tomsky residence in the Arbat district, a lovely maze of crooked lanes and alleys, where Tomsky and his family had moved in April 1935.[356] It is not clear whether Tomsky and his family had been evicted from their apartment in the Kremlin or chose to move.[357] Their spacious apartment on Granovsky Street, a quietly stylish street just a couple blocks from the Kremlin's Trinity Gates, was in a five-story, U-shaped, nineteenth-century building. The ornate, French baroque residential complex, which had Art Nouveau touches and a grand entrance into a large inner courtyard, became the Fifth House of the Soviets after the Bolsheviks expropriated it after the revolution.[358] Besides the additional space, it must have been a relief, temporary though it proved to be, to move out of their unbelievably awkward situation in their Kremlin apartment, though this building was also full of party and governmental officials.[359] During the NKVD's 10-hour search, they confiscated virtually

---

355   RGASPI, f. 17, op. 120, d. 272, ll. 76–8, translated and reprinted in Getty and Naumov 1999, p. 297.
356   The Arbat, whose longstanding ties with the intelligentsia made it famous as Moscow's Greenwich Village, following the revolution was largely occupied by workers, who resided in the large houses the government had requisitioned from capitalists and members of the nobility and converted into communal apartments: Merridale 1990, p. 11; Bittner 2008, pp. 2, 22–3, 32–3.
357   RGASPI, f. 78, op. 1, d. 550, l. 9, reprinted in Kvashonkin et al. (eds) 1999, p. 306; RGASPI, f. 593, op. 1, d. 7, l. 1.
358   Mawdsley 1991, p. 150; Slezkine 2017, p. 187. Only the Kremlin was considered more prestigious for party officials: Colton 1995, p. 163. Count Sheremetev once owned the massive, red sandstone building. The street was named after Timofei Granovsky, a prominent history professor in the first half of the nineteenth century at nearby Moscow University, who tutored Alexander Herzen and others in liberal social thought: Eremina and Rodinskii (eds) 2000, p. 403. Arvo Tominen, a Finnish Comintern member, incorrectly remembered that Tomsky lived below him in the House of Government and that a large NKVD red seal was placed on the door of his residence in 1936: Tominen 1983, pp. 98–9.
359   When the up-and-coming Nikita Khrushchev moved into the building with his family, their spacious apartment had four bedrooms, two guest rooms, an office, a combination living room-dining room, as well as a kitchen and large bathroom: Taubman 2003, p. 143. After the war, many top officials preferred the Fifth House of Soviets to the House of Gov-

everything, including all of Tomsky's books, government and personal papers, photographs and cameras, as well as his large collection of guns, including those that had been gifts from Frunze, Ordzhonikidze, Stalin, and Dzerzhinsky.[360]

The family was doomed. A month before their arrest, Stalin declared at a Moscow banquet celebrating the twentieth anniversary of the revolution that family members were guilty by association with so-called enemies of the people: 'We will destroy each and every enemy even if he was an Old Bolshevik; we will destroy all his kin, his family'. Stalin ended with a toast: 'To the complete destruction of all enemies, themselves, and their kin'![361] Following the search, the NKVD arrested Maria Tomskaya and two of Tomsky's three sons as 'family members of a traitor of the motherland'. Thirty-three-year-old Mikhail, the oldest son, had moved in with his mother and his youngest brother Yury. Mikhail, no doubt traumatised during his youth as a son of revolutionary, including a year in Siberia, never achieved a higher education and worked in Moscow as a machinist. Perhaps unbeknownst to the family, the NKVD had arrested the other son, 29-year-old Victor in Leningrad, 10 months earlier on 10 February 1937 and then immediately transferred him to Moscow. Victor, who had followed in his father's footsteps, had worked as a technical director of lithography in OGIZ, which perhaps explains his earlier arrest. The two older sons were convicted of 'participating in an anti-Soviet subversive and terrorist organisation', although the NKVD arrested them of course simply because they were Tomsky's sons. Neither of them had become members of the party. The NKVD executed Mikhail on 19 March 1938 and Victor three days later on 21 March 1938 at Kommunarka, one of the two big, wooded execution sites outside Moscow, where nude bodies were tossed into ghastly pits and covered with shovelfuls of lime. Kommunarka was on the grounds of Yagoda's former dacha.[362] Both Yury, Tomsky's youngest son, who

---

ernment, including Molotov, Malenkov, Alexander Shcherbakov and Marshals Ivan Konev, Konstantin Rokossovsky, and Grigory Zhukov: Slezkine 2017, p. 925.

360   Gorelov 2000, p. 268. As noted in the Introduction, if they still exist, most of his papers presumably are in the Presidential or the former KGB archives. In any case, only a small amount is in Tomsky's *lichnyi fond* at RGASPI.

361   Quoted in Frierson and Vilensky 2010, p. 136. Arrests of family members had in fact begun before that proclamation. Baberowski speculates this can be traced back to Stalin's Georgian roots, where he argues a murderer had to kill all the relatives of his victim in order to be sure they could not avenge the killing: Baberowski 2016, p. 267.

362   NIPTs zherty online data base, cases 2656288 and 2741597; Khaustov (ed.) 2011, p. 411; Shelestov 1988, p. 27; Rogovin 1997, p. 146; Colton 1995, p. 286; Slezkine 2017, p. 862. Mikhail's and Victor's posthumous 'rehabilitation' occurred on 2 November 1957.

was deemed 'socially dangerous and capable of engaging in anti-Soviet activities', and Tomskaya, a longtime member of the party, received sentences of 10 years in separate labour camps, which they survived, followed by administrative exile in the western Siberian region of Krasnoyarsk, where they were able to reunite.[363] The Politburo had adopted on 5 July 1937 a NKVD proposal that all wives of 'Right-Trotskyite spy traitors' should be sent to special camps and 'to decide individually' the fate of children over 15 years of age.[364]

During the silent de-Stalinisation before Khrushchev's speech at the Twentieth Party Congress, Tomskaya was released in March 1954 as part of a mass amnesty. She requested to be 'rehabilitated' and allowed to return to Moscow. The commission established to review such cases reinstated her in the party and provided her with both a residency permit and an apartment in Moscow.[365] They even sent her to a sanatorium to help her recover from her nearly two decades in labour camps and exile. But when Tomsky's wife returned from the sanatorium to Moscow, Molotov personally blocked her 'rehabilitation' and ordered that she be returned to Siberian exile. When an outraged Nikita Khrushchev learned of this, he sent her a telegram reiterating the commission's decision, but it came too late. Molotov's order had proven fatal - Maria Tomskaya's heart could not withstand Molotov's brutal blow.[366] When Molotov was asked in his old age why the repression was extended to wives and children, he nonchalantly responded, 'they had to be isolated somehow. Otherwise they would have spread all kinds of complaints. And a certain amount of demoralisation'.[367] Hypocritically, that did not seem to bother him when he

---

363   Gorelov and Shapovalova (eds) 2001, p. 175.
364   Volkogonov 1994, p. 314; Radzinsky 1996, p. 419. Yezhov shortly afterward, on 15 August 1937, issued order No. 00486 to carry this operation out: Slezkine 2017, p. 801; Frierson and Vilensky 2010, p. 138; Barnes 2011, pp. 103–4. The official sentence was 'Member of the Family of an Enemy of the Revolution': Applebaum 2003, p. 102. Over 18,000 wives would be arrested: Jansen and Petrov 2002, p. 100. Tomskaya served time in Butyrka prison, where there was a whole full room of 'wives'. Yury also spent time there before being shipped off to a gulag: Gorelov 2000, pp. 248, 268–9; Fitzpatrick 1999, p. 199. That was the same prison where Tomsky spent two years, 1909–11 and Tomskaya was held for one month in 1912. Later in the Great Purges, wives could sometimes be brutally tortured or executed: Baberowski 2016, p. 266. Kamenev's first wife, Olga Kamaneva (Trotsky's sister) was executed in 1941, following the execution of their two sons in 1938 and 1939.
365   Formal 'rehabilitation' equalled being declared legally innocent and came with a better pension, healthcare, and living space for your family: Slezkine 2017, p. 936.
366   Rogovin 1997, pp. 145–6. Tomskaya died and was buried in the city of Kansk in Krasnoyarsk krai: Gorelov and Shapovalova (eds) 2001, p. 175n90.
367   Molotov 1991, p. 415; Gorelov 2000, p. 280.

pleaded with Khrushchev and Georgy Malenkov to 'Give me back my Polina'.[368] Molotov's wife, Polina Zhemchuzhina, who had been arrested in 1949 for having ties with 'Jewish bourgeois nationalists', was released and fully rehabilitated in May 1953.[369]

Tomsky's youngest son survived his years in the gulag and administrative exile and had some remarkable experiences later in life. Yury, who was released from the gulag in 1947, remained in administrative exile in Krasnoyarsk, working as a foreman at a textile factory in Kansk before he was rearrested in 1950. He was released again in 1954 and returned to Kansk before being 'rehabilitated' in 1956 and allowed to return to Moscow in 1957.[370] Incredibly, back in Moscow, where he enrolled as a student at the Moscow Textile Institute, Yury had a brief love affair with Stalin's daughter Svetlana. They had been in the Kremlin's Young Pioneers group in their youth and by chance ran into each other at the flat of one of their childhood friends shortly after Yury returned to Moscow. They went together to Koktebel' in the Crimea, where Svetlana had planned to take the released prisoner to the rest house favoured by the Writers' Union, but lacking the proper vacation passes [*putyovki*] was refused entrance. They were forced to spend the night in Svetlana's car, a *Pobeda*, on what was an empty beach, at least until rumours spread of their presence there.[371] The romance did not last long, at least partly because Yury felt humiliated when the fashionable Svetlana, embarrassed by his shabby clothes, took him to the top tailors in Moscow.[372] Moreover, he later recalled, 'after a while I did not see the sweet red-pigtailed little girl in her, but the pigheaded offspring of the Master'.[373] Less remarkably, but still surprising, Yury entered the party in 1966.[374] After he became seriously

---

368 Watson 2005, p. 101.
369 Dobson 2009, p. 51; Fitzpatrick 2015, p. 204.
370 RGASPI, f. 593, op. 1, d. 11, l. 4; Iakovlev (ed.) 1991, p. 622; Gorelov and Shapovalova (eds) 2001, p. 175n91. Yury claims that in pursuit of his rehabilitation and the right to live in Moscow, he illegally came to Moscow, where he met with Khrushchev's secretary, Grigory Shuisky. He saved a letter that seems to corroborate that: Gorelov 2000, pp. 280–1.
371 Runin 1995, p. 187; Kun 2003, pp. 416–17. The rugged *Pobeda*, which means Victory, was the first Soviet mass-produced car following the war. Although the hope was that someday in the future ordinary members of the middle class could buy one, only the relatively privileged could own a Pobeda in 1957: Siegelbaum 2008, pp. 63, 218. It was also rare for women to drive during the 1950s: Kuhr-Korolev 2011, p. 191.
372 A friend remembers that during the war, Svetlana came to classes at Moscow State University in her 'short squirrel coat, her dark English outfits, her brightly coloured silk blouses, and smart flat-heeled shoes': Voslensky 1984, p. 238.
373 Sullivan 2015, pp. 69, 218; Kun 2003, p. 416.
374 Tomsky, who had a career as an engineer, was not alone in joining the party. Other gulag returnees did so as well: Dobson 2009, p. 74.

ill, over the course of 1988 and 1989, he wrote a short memoir about his father and the Russian historian Oleg Gorelov conducted interviews with him.[375]

After Tomsky committed suicide, the NKVD swooped down on his former subordinates. One can imagine the fear that swept through OGIZ's offices. Almost immediately, the NKVD arrested Tomsky's personal secretaries and extracted confessions from them. For example, on 7 October 1936, Yezhov sent Stalin a protocol of the interrogation and testimony of M.Z. Stankin, who under pressure confessed that he was a member of a terrorist cabal of Rightists that included other former associates of Tomsky and was headed by Slavinsky, who had performed at Tomsky's funeral. According to Stankin's confession, this 'group of rightwing terrorists' planned to assassinate Stalin on 6 November 1936 in the Bolshoi Theatre during the celebration on the eve of the anniversary of the revolution. They were arrested shortly beforehand, at the end of October.[376] Yezhov also extracted testimony from another one of Tomsky's personal secretaries, the Old Bolshevik and historian Vladimir Nevsky, who implicated Bukharin and Rykov in the supposed plot.[377]

Just as virtually all of Tomsky's former colleagues in the trade-union leadership would perish in the Great Purges, as was noted above, so would seemingly every administrator under Tomsky at OGIZ.[378] On 5 November 1937, Lev Mekhlis, with Stalin's support, sent to the Central Committee a report that characterised the staff at OGIZ as 'a ragtag collection of spies, Trotskyists, politically ignorant people, crooks'.[379] The Central Committee responded by sending Pavel Yudin to OGIZ, a 'career hatchet man'.[380] Yudin almost immediately announced that OGIZ was 'contaminated to the utmost degree' with 'traitors and spies', beginning with two of Tomsky's former deputies, Saul Bron and N.A. Bykov. Yudin also denounced a certain Melman as a Tomsky lackey who was guilty of sending flowers to the grave of 'that son of a bitch Tomsky'.[381]

---

375 Gorelov and Shapovalova (eds) 2001, pp. 149–60; Gorelov 2000, pp. 266–82. Beginning in 1968, Yury served as the scientific secretary of the Soviet of senior power engineers. He died in Moscow at the age of 76 on 5 January 1997.
376 RGASPI f. 17, op 2 d. 574, l. 46; Iakovlev (ed.) 1991, p. 248; Rogovin 1998, pp. 92–3.
377 Gorelov 1989, p. 84; Getty and Naumov 1999, p. 303. Nevsky had previously been the director of the Lenin State Library.
378 Khaustov (ed.) 2011, pp. 121, 359, 410.
379 Khaustov (ed.) 2011, pp. 410–11.
380 That is how Edward Brown characterised Yudin: Brown 1971, pp. 218, 277n54. He had been Director of the Institute of Red Professors from 1932–34 and deputy head of the press department of the Central Committee.
381 Siegelbaum and Sokolov 2000, pp. 223–4.

Another employee, despite having already been expelled from the party, managed to work up the courage to try to convince Yudin that Tomsky and Bron had not been guilty of any sabotage.[382] Others more obligingly confessed to various 'crimes', especially that of having written positively about that 'enemy of the people', Tomsky.[383] The NKVD charged Bron, who would be interrogated for the first time later than month and categorised as a member of a 'Right-Trotskyist terrorist organisation,' with having discussed with Tomsky at the beginning of 1936 the use of terror to change the party leadership, including a plot to assassinate Stalin.[384] Bron under duress confessed to the 'poisoning' of OGIZ employees. The charges against Tomsky's former associates included 'serious political misprints' and the absurd charges of 'wrecking', including the publication of articles and books by such 'counterrevolutionaries' as Bukharin, Radek, and others.[385] Yudin demanded that 'all the scum and riffraff' kicked out of OGIZ 'be burned out with a red-hot iron'.[386] Over the course of six months, the NKVD arrested 130 top OGIZ officials, which they called the entire 'nest of enemies'.[387] Curiously, Tomsky's old nemesis Lozovsky would step into this void and become the director in 1937 of one of OGIZ's publishing houses, Goslitizdat, where he would survive the Great Purges.[388]

Tomsky's suicide shocked Bukharin and Rykov. A traumatised Bukharin, who became physically sick upon reading the press release of Tomsky's suicide, exclaimed that it was 'nonsense' that his 'dear friend and morally pure comrade' had killed himself because of 'ties to the counter-revolutionary Trotskyist-Zinovievist terrorists'.[389] Rykov would testify later that when he learned about Tomsky's suicide, he chalked it up to his nerves.[390] Both Bukharin and Rykov began to recognise their own situation was hopeless. They both became increasingly sullen and morose and rarely left their apartments.[391] Bukharin went

---

382 Siegelbaum and Sokolov 2000, p. 224.
383 Mackinnon 2005, p. 26.
384 Khaustov (ed.) 2011, pp. 13, 117, 426. Citrine had earlier spent a lot of time with Bron in 1929–31 when he was the head of the Soviet Trading Delegation in London: Citrine 1936, p. 133.
385 Khaustov (ed.) 2011, p. 410; Siegelbaum and Sokolov 2000, p. 225.
386 Siegelbaum and Sokolov 2000, p. 224.
387 Khaustov (ed.) 2011, p. 410; Siegelbaum and Sokolov 2000, p. 225.
388 Rubinstein and Naumov 2005, p. 178; Haupt and Marie (eds) 1974, p. 297.
389 Larina 1993, 288; Rogovin 1998, p. 99. Stalin responded to Bukharin that Tomsky was 'far from being pure': quoted in Slezkine 2017, p. 725.
390 RGASPI, f. 17, op. 2, d. 580, l. 46. Rykov believed that Tomsky's three-year-long nervous condition had played a role in his suicide: RGASPI, f. 17, op. 120, d. 574, ll. 37–8.
391 Shelestov 1990, p. 285; Medvedev 1980, p. 125; Getty and Naumov 1999, p. 324. Rykov had been removed from his post as chair of the commissariat of communications on

on a hunger strike.³⁹² Rykov became almost mute, while his wife Nina had a stroke and his daughter Natalia lost her job.³⁹³ Natalia recalled that Rykov 'aged a great deal, his hair thinned and was always disheveled looking, and his face was haggard with dark bluish circles under his eyes. I don't think he ever slept'.³⁹⁴ Bukharin wrote to Yezhov, 'I am ill, and my nerves are in very bad shape; for more than 10 days I have not gone to the editorial offices. I lie in bed, completely shattered'.³⁹⁵ Rykov whispered to Bukharin before their arrests, 'Tomsky proved to be the most farsighted among us ... [He] had will power. He understood it all back in August and he ended his own life while you and I, like fools, have gone on living'.³⁹⁶ But in fact they too had considered killing themselves. Family members forcibly took a gun out of Rykov's hand once, while Bukharin locked himself in his study on a number of occasions with the intention of committing suicide, but was never able to pull the trigger.³⁹⁷ Bukharin told the Central Committee Plenum in February 1937 that he was 'not able to shoot himself because it would then be said that I committed suicide in order to harm the party'. The delegates in response laughed and mocked him. They accused him of emotional blackmail.³⁹⁸

Bukharin and Rykov continued to try to refute the accusations. They wrote one desperate letter after another to Stalin and other members of the Politburo. Bukharin insisted in his letters that he had not talked with Tomsky or Rykov since 1933.³⁹⁹ Bukharin pleaded that it would be very easy to verify that by checking the logs of his driver and questioning his sentries and servants.⁴⁰⁰ In his letter to Voroshilov on 31 August 1936, written just over a week after Tomsky's suicide, Bukharin wrote: 'Poor Tomsky! Maybe he did "become

---

26 September 1936, while Bukharin officially remained chief editor of the leading government newspaper *Izvestiia*, a post he held from January 1934 until his arrest in February 1937. But Bukharin effectively lost any control of the editorship immediately after the Zinoviev-Kamenev trial.

392 RGASPI, f. 17, op. 2, d. 579, l. 100.
393 Slezkine 2017, p. 745.
394 Quoted in Slezkine 2017, p. 727.
395 Rogovin 1998, p. 99. Bukharin's loving wife, Anna Larina, described Bukharin as a 'solid, surprisingly strong man, a sportsman with the musculature of a prizefighter [who] literally wilted under severe nervous strain': Larina 1993, p. 127.
396 Larina 1993, p. 330; Solzhenitsyn 1973, p. 416.
397 Medvedev and Medvedev 2004, pp. 289–90. This was Stalin's former bedroom, where Nadezhda Alliluyeva had committed suicide. After her suicide, Stalin had asked to exchange apartments with Bukharin: Larina 1993, pp. 302–4.
398 RGASPI, f. 17, op. 2, d. 579, ll. 100–1; Schlogel 2012, pp. 183–4.
399 Bukharin 1993, p. 9; Shelestov 1990, pp. 292–3.
400 Zhuravlev et al. (eds) 1995, p. 164.

entangled [in criminal ties]", I don't know. I don't rule it out ... Maybe if I'd gone to see him he wouldn't have been so gloomy and wouldn't have got entangled'.[401]

Stalin, apparently shaken by the unexpected news of Tomsky's suicide, ordered proceedings against Bukharin and Rykov stopped for a lack of evidence, on 10 September 1936.[402] As a result, they remained free.[403] Bukharin, along with his wife Anna Larina, their son Yury, Bukharin's father Ivan Gavrilovich, and Bukharin's disabled first wife Nadezhda Lukina, continued to occupy Stalin's former apartment in the Kremlin until his arrest. Rykov's family, however, was instructed to move from the Kremlin to the House of Government at the end of 1936.[404] Stalin may have decided to pull back from his planned proceedings because other members of the Politburo were shocked at Tomsky's suicide and the executions of Zinoviev and Kamenev and the other prominent defendants after the show trial.[405] These were, after all, the first executions of Bolshevik leaders.[406]

The reprieve did not last long. After being hounded at the December 1936 and the February 1937 Central Committee plenums, during which Bukharin and Rykov both cast terrorist aspersions on Tomsky, the NKVD arrested them in late February 1937.[407] Bukharin, incredibly, wrote a total of 43 letters to Stalin after

---

401 Bukharin 1993, p. 15.
402 On 8 September 1836, Bukharin and Rykov were allowed to confront the arrested Sokolnikov at the Central Committee headquarters in the presence of a Politburo commission consisting of Kaganovich, Yezhov, and Vyshinsky. Kaganovich told Stalin that Sokolnikov admitted that he had no personal knowledge of Bukharin's or Rykov's guilt: Getty and Naumov 1999, p. 303; Gorelov 1989, pp. 71–2; Shelestov 1990, p. 293.
403 Instead, Stalin turned his attention to the arrested 'Trotskyists' – Pyatakov, Sokolnikov, and Radek – who would be the star defendants in the second Moscow show trial. Pyatakov, before his arrest, in a desperate attempt to save himself, told Stalin he would be willing to execute his former wife to demonstrate his loyalty: Baberowski 2016, p. 210; Kotkin 2017, p. 330.
404 Slezkine 2017, pp. 726, 734. The apartment had become vacant following Radek's arrest.
405 Ulam 1973, p. 416. By rule, Central Committee members still had to sanction the arrest of any of its full or candidate members: Medvedev and Medvedev 2004, p. 290.
406 The post-trial executions of Zinoviev and Kamenev broke the party taboo of killing 'Old Bolshevik' oppositionists: Fitzpatrick 2015, p. 118.
407 Rykov stated, under pressure at the December 1936 Central Committee plenum, that 'as far as I know, [Tomsky] had participated in this affair [Zinoviev-Trotsky terrorist organisation]. From all that has been said here, it seems to be absolutely beyond doubt'. While Rykov repeated his belief in Tomsky's guilt at the February 1937 Central Committee Plenum, he said he did not think so at the time of Tomsky's suicide, while Bukharin contradicted Molotov by stating 'I cannot say that [Tomsky] is guilty just because that person is dead': RGASPI, f. 17, op. 120, d. 271, l. 21; RGASPI f. 17, op. 2, d. 580, ll. 44, 46.

he was arrested, pleading for his forgiveness.[408] Bukharin and Rykov would be executed a little more than a year later, following their March 1938 show trial, during which they ludicrously testified that Tomsky had joined them in advocating for opening the front to Nazi Germany in the event of a war, and that it was Tomsky who had won Marshal Tukhachevsky's support for the plan.[409] All three would be finally rehabilitated on 21 June 1988, after twenty years of appeals, largely as the result of the persistent efforts of Bukharin's widow, Anna Larina, and Rykov's daughter, Natalia Rykova.[410]

In conclusion, coming back to the quote with which I began this chapter, at times Tomsky was indeed a lost and beaten man during the last seven years of his life. The unending and fabricated political attacks the Stalinist leadership hurled at him took a horrible toll on his precarious mental and physical health. Some of his breakdowns so incapacitated him that he received months of medical care in Germany. But that captures only part of his life during those years. Before succumbing to the pressure, he continued to meet in secret with other former party leaders worried about the direction in which Stalin was taking the country, and he handled the political attacks at party forums with more dignity than others. Tomsky also assumed a position of considerable responsibility as head of OGIZ, and if the devotion of his top deputies is any indication, performed extremely well in that capacity until, at age 56, he took his own life to avoid being swept up in the Great Purges and forced to perform at a show trial.

408 Radzinsky 1996, p. 376.
409 It was Rykov who was the most explicit on Tomsky's supposed role: Tucker and Cohen (eds) 1965, pp. 187–92, 389–96. Rykov's wife Nina Rykova and daughter Natalia Rykova spent 20 years in prison, the gulag, and exile. Bukharin's young wife Anna Larina and infant son Yury were separated when Larina was sent to a camp in Western Siberian. He was raised in an NKVD orphanage. Both survived. Larina lived until 1996.
410 Adler 2012, pp. 99–101; Gorelov 1989, p. 92. During the initial 'rehabilitations' following Stalin's death and Khrushchev's policy of de-Stalinisation, none of the members of the United Opposition or Right Opposition were rehabilitated, unlike the Stalinists who were executed during the Great Purges: Oppenheim 1967, pp. 102, 106.

Conclusion

Mikhail Tomsky was the embodiment of moderate Bolshevism. His moderate viewpoint was rooted in his working-class background and experiences during the first years after the Bolshevik seizure of power. Concerned with defending the interests of workers, in whose name the revolution had been carried out, Tomsky and fellow trade-union leaders were deeply opposed to such radical party proposals as Trotsky's programme to create 'labour armies' during the Civil War or Stalin's policy of forced collectivisation and breakneck industrialisation at the end of the 1920s. Trotsky attributed this moderation on Tomsky's part to the fact that he 'had to deal not only with the vanguard of the working class [namely party members] but with the larger backward strata as well'.[1] Indeed, although Tomsky most identified with those workers who strove to increase their skills, like he had as a youth, Tomsky worked hard to defend the interests and voice the grievances of his entire trade-union constituency. Tomsky had to balance that with the goal he shared with fellow members of the party Central Committee and Politburo of raising labour productivity, especially until the economy could recover from its almost complete collapse during the Civil War. While this has been a sympathetic account of Tomsky's role as an early Soviet leader, it is not an uncritical one. When he was on top, Tomsky engaged in the nasty political infighting against 'oppositionists' shared by all the Bolsheviks. He was anything but moderate in his intolerance of dissenting views, especially with oppositionists who attacked the moderate policies of NEP.

Tomsky, as we have seen, rose from an impoverished youth in a squalid industrial suburb of St. Petersburg, with no more than three years of elementary-school education, into the top ranks of the party leadership. He quickly demonstrated what proved to be a life-long eagerness to learn even though he entered the labour force at the tender age of 12. After enduring hardships in various menial industrial positions, and in the process becoming increasingly radicalised by the brutal labour policies and conditions in tsarist Russia, Tomsky took advantage of the opportunities Russia's booming late nineteenth-century urban economy afforded. By the time he was 21 years old, he had achieved the rank of master lithographer. Although Tomsky was only beginning to understand Marxist doctrine and the political goals of the Social-Democratic movement, he was among the first workers to be identified with Lenin's Bolshevik faction of the Social-Democratic Party. Blackballed as a res-

---

[1] Trotsky 1988, p. 233.

ult in St. Petersburg, Tomsky played a prominent role in the 1905 Revolution in Estonia, where he demonstrated his relative moderation by doing what he could to avoid bloodshed while organising worker protests. After the tsarist authorities regained the upper hand in January 1906, Tomsky in the following years would ultimately spend nine years in prison and Siberian exile. When healthy and not locked up, Tomsky became the relatively rare Bolshevik who early on focused much of his energies on trade unionism, which also attracted other relatively moderate members of the party determined to break the Mensheviks' then near total control of the trade-union movement. Tomsky awakened Lenin to the missed opportunities to organise workers this entailed. But while Lenin came to appreciate the value of trade unions in the revolutionary struggle, Tomsky long hated how many Bolsheviks, especially those from privileged backgrounds, were prone to view the trade unionists in the party as second-class Bolsheviks.

Uncommonly ambitious, Tomsky worked hard to rise within the party's ranks. He became a member in early 1907 of the St. Petersburg Committee, which rivalled in importance the émigré Bolshevik Central Committee, and became Petersburg's sole representative on the editorial board of the Bolsheviks' mouthpiece, *Proletarii*. It is no surprise then that Tomsky was chosen to attend party gatherings in Western Europe, where he attracted the attention of Lenin and other Bolshevik leaders. He did not shun the limelight. Tomsky eagerly threw himself into political debates at the party's highest level. His remarkable self-confidence distinguished him from fellow Bolsheviks from working-class backgrounds, who were afraid to go face-to-face with party intellectuals. Tomsky made a name for himself by attacking Social-Democratic luminaries just a couple years after joining the party. Gorky remembers Tomsky as one of the three most impressive speakers at the London congress in 1907. But this proclivity to zealously engage in party infighting was also an early sign of Tomsky's less moderate side.

Tomsky's confidence in his own political judgment continued to grow and he did not shy away from challenging party leaders. Following the collapse of the autocracy and the Provisional Government's sweeping amnesty of all political prisoners in early 1917, Tomsky arrived from Siberia in Petrograd, where he felt emboldened enough to spar with Lenin himself. Tomsky's conflicts with Lenin during 1917 reveal a man not content to be the party's favourite son from workers' ranks. Tomsky proved to be the voice of moderation in defending the notion of an independent newspaper for the Petersburg Bolsheviks and questioning calls for street demonstrations in June and July. Upon learning of the party's plans for an armed insurrection in October, Tomsky expressed his reservations because he thought the revolution's goal should be the creation of a coalition socialist government. But, like other party members, in the face of Lenin's unmatched determination, he ultimately pushed aside those reservations and helped the Bolshevik Party seize power in Moscow. Here too he did do what he could to limit bloodshed.

Tomsky moved quickly into positions of prominence and power after the October Revolution. Tomsky's responsibilities as a key member of the governmental leadership that was dealing with the collapse of the economy, and as the head of the institution responsible for protecting workers' interests, meant his career during the first years of the Soviet regime was inevitably a stormy as well as central one. Since the Bolsheviks came to power with no blueprints on how to address various major issues, holding these two positions simultaneously put Tomsky in the middle of the acrimonious debates that preoccupied early Soviet leaders over the function of trade unions in the 'workers' state'. Tomsky fought Trotsky's call to 'shake-up' the unions and militarise labour even though those policies enjoyed Lenin's support. Trotsky, who seemed to thoroughly enjoy provoking Tomsky, mocked Tomsky's views as those of an outmoded, old-fashioned trade unionist. This was the beginning of the deep antipathy Tomsky felt toward Trotsky. Tomsky succeeded in mobilising the trade-union leadership to deal Trotsky and Lenin an unprecedented, almost unanimous defeat in the March 1920 VTsSPS party caucus. But while fighting Trotsky's attempts to militarise labour, and ultimately persuading Lenin to take his side against Trotsky's proposals, Tomsky would abandon the goal of workers' control, or even maintaining a major role in enterprise management for trade unions, once it became clear in 1920 that he could not win the party leadership over to his side at the Ninth Party Congress.

Tomsky's willingness to compromise would ultimately outrage both members of the political leadership and militant trade unionists. Tomsky during the so-called trade-union debate, an extraordinary, unprecedented debate about the role of trade unions, and by extension, the relationship between workers, the state, and the party in the Soviet Union, proved surprisingly successful in working out a compromise that maintained the trade unions' autonomy from the government while accepting the party's oversight. But this put Tomsky in a difficult spot a couple months later at the Fourth Trade-Union Congress, where he was attacked by more radical trade unionists, namely Alexander Shlyapnikov and other leaders and supporters of the 'Workers' Opposition', as well as the idiosyncratic David Ryazanov. Tomsky's attempts to placate them outraged the Soviet leadership, which was determined to put the trade-union debate to rest once and for all and to crack down on all violations of party discipline. Lenin almost immediately stripped Tomsky of his position as chair of the VTsSPS.

The Politburo had no intention of having Tomsky languish in political disgrace. The party leadership instead entrusted him with what it considered a critical mission in Tashkent. In this role Tomsky proved to be the most moderate of Bolsheviks. Tomsky was sent to chair the leading governmental body in Central Asia, although Tomsky obviously knew little if anything about the Turko-Islamic world and shared the patronising view of virtually all Bolsheviks on the 'cultural backwardness' of the Indigenous population. It proved to be an extremely challenging assignment. Tomsky quickly found himself trying to rein in one of the party's most extreme and violent fanatics, Georgy Safarov. With Lenin's support, he favoured the forced confiscations of the land of Russian peasant settlers and the expulsion from the region of them and their entire families, to win the support of the Indigenous nomadic population whose grazing lands had been stolen. These experiences help explain why Tomsky would later so strongly oppose the Stalinists' plans for forced collectivisation and dekulakisation. The party leadership eventually took Tomsky's side, and brought him back to Moscow. Even more surprisingly, given his recent censure and banishment, the Central Committee elected Tomsky, over Lenin's objections, to become in 1922 one of the seven members on the Politburo, the highest policymaking body in the country. As a result, Tomsky and his family entered the world of material privileges that top party officials increasingly enjoyed. A world within which he would become increasingly comfortable despite whatever pangs of conscience he may have felt with its betrayals of the egalitarian ideals of the revolution.

Tomsky during the 1920s orchestrated one of the Soviet Union's few foreign policy achievements, linking British and Soviet trade unions together. Tomsky's brainchild, the Anglo-Russian Committee, was ratified in early 1925. He also made some headway toward unifying the wider European trade-union movement, despite fierce resistance by primarily German and French non-communist socialists. Tomsky achieved these successes by charming British trade unionists while holding his hard-line critics in Moscow at bay. Tomsky's prominent role in Soviet foreign policy has been obscured by historians' focus in these years on the intra-party combat between supporters and opponents of Trotsky's programme of 'permanent revolution' and Stalin's policy of 'socialism in one country'. But early foreign policy positions among the party leadership were far more diverse than that. Tomsky's more pragmatic and less ideological positions explain his success in England, where compromises and alliance rather than revolutionary agitation or strategic rigidity produced results. But the collapse of the British general strike in 1926, largely as a result of the British trade-union leaders' unforced capitulation, undermined his efforts. Opposition to Tomsky's ultimately unsuccessful efforts to work with leftist trade unionists in Europe brought Trotsky, Zinoviev, and Kamenev together against the Politburo's moderate majority. While Stalin, Rykov, and Bukharin came to Tomsky's defence, the collapse of the British general strike, and his attempts to rationalise their surrender, cost Tomsky politically.

Throughout the 1920s, Tomsky fought to increase the trade unions considerable autonomy while maintaining their position as one of the major pillars of the regime. He embraced the moderate economic policies of NEP as the best path to revive the economy after its collapse during seven years of war, revolution, and civil war. By 1927, if not earlier, economic output exceeded pre-war levels and workers enjoyed a standard of living higher than ever before. Tomsky represented all those workers who were more concerned with improving immediate conditions than with forsaking the present in pursuit of an economic programme to radically transform Soviet Russia overnight.

Tomsky also enthusiastically engaged in party politics in the 1920s. It is in this arena that the portrayal of Tomsky as a moderate becomes more complicated. Tomsky had always appeared to enjoy partisan wrangling, going back to how he first made a name for himself at the London Party Congress in 1907. A consistent opponent of the 'leftists' in the party, he supported Stalin, Bukharin, and Rykov against Trotsky and then also against Zinoviev and Kamenev. His commitment to maintaining the NEP status quo, both internationally and domestically, with the promise of gradually improving conditions for peasants as well as workers, was certainly a key factor behind his decision to align himself with Stalin. But Tomsky's personal dislike of the leadership's prima donnas, Trotsky and Zinoviev, also help explain his positions during the power struggle.

Tomsky was hardly a voice for pluralism and tolerance in this power struggle. He adopted positions that would ultimately help destroy his own political fortunes. At times, he could prove to be even more of a fanatic than his fellow party leaders, including Stalin, in how he attacked his political opponents when he perceived them to be a threat to the moderate policies of NEP. Tomsky not only argued that the oppositionists should be expelled from the party, during moments of extreme party infighting, he shockingly suggested they deserved to be arrested for such crimes as demoralising non-party workers or spreading ideas that encouraged them to conspire against the party. Tomsky would certainly come to deeply regret this and similar statements when he found himself on the outs. These harsh attacks by Tomsky against oppositionists, particularly those excoriating their tactics, would make it extremely difficult for him and his moderate associates, Bukharin and Rykov, to mount effective opposition against Stalin when he moved to abandon NEP. Perhaps most shamefully, both morally and politically, Tomsky exerted enormous influence in the unfounded attacks against the so-called bourgeois specialists that culminated in the 1928

Shakhty trial. Because of the trade unions' longstanding animosity toward the *spetsy* and his uncritical evaluation of the confessions the OGPU extracted from them, Tomsky unwittingly gave Stalin and his cohorts an opening to use against him after the Stalinists crushed the United Opposition.

Serious differences with Stalin over policy and its implementation would be at the heart of Tomsky's ouster from power at the end of the 1920s. Stalin's coercive implementation of the so-called extraordinary measures against the peasantry in early 1928 convinced Tomsky that Stalin posed an existential threat to the moderate, balanced economic policies of NEP. The friction between the Tomsky-led trade unions and advocates of a dramatic increase in the pace of industrialisation was also a central feature of NEP. In mid-1928, when Stalin was gaining the advantage over those he soon labelled Right Deviationists, Stalin considered the trade unions the major obstacle to his plans to push forward with forced collectivisation and breakneck industrialisation. The animosity between Tomsky and Stalin grew increasingly bitter. Tomsky angrily protested that a radical departure from NEP would exploit workers and peasants. He warned Stalin that workers would resist the inevitable deterioration in their standard of living. A drunken Tomsky even whispered in Stalin's ear at a family gathering in 1928 that workers would try to kill him, which Tomsky correctly knew Stalin would never forget.

The final showdown between the Stalinists and the trade-union leadership occurred during the Eighth Trade-Union Congress in December 1928. Tomsky enjoyed, for the most part, the delegates' continued enthusiastic support in the clashes on the congress floor against advocates for breakneck industrialisation and against critics from the Komsomol on the trade unions' treatment of young workers, but the decisive votes undermining Tomsky's leadership of the trade unions occurred behind closed doors, where the Stalinists prevailed by razor-thin margins in imposing Kaganovich and other Stalinists' on the VTsSPS Presidium over Tomsky's objections. A large number of his supporters at the congress continued to fight the Stalinist takeover of the unions even after Tomsky decided that further resistance was hopeless. These supporters, like Tomsky himself, would suffer for that later.

Historians have developed a range of compelling interpretations to explain Stalin's victory in the intra-party struggle.[2] The most widely accepted one is that Stalin owed his victory to his position as general secretary, which he used to pack the party with loyal political clients. But recent scholarship suggests that it was Stalin's skills as a political operator, rather than his ability to make appoint-

---

2 For a summary of six of these interpretative approaches: Ward 1999, pp. 18–31.

ments, that led to his success in the power struggle. While Stalin's exploitation of the position of general secretary certainly proved important, especially in the selection of delegates to national party congresses and conferences, in the words of James Harris, the Secretariat 'never became a source of paternalistic control of the party apparatus as is commonly assumed'.[3] In virtually all cases the Secretariat and Orgburo simply rubber-stamped staff recommendations.[4] Emphasis on Stalin's use of his position of general secretary also wrongly suggests Stalin's victory was all but inevitable.[5] This study of Tomsky's role in the power struggle demonstrated that Stalin had to fight hard in order to prevail. That he did so was primarily due to his embrace of moderate, popular policies, which stood in particularly sharp contrast with Trotsky's policies. Stalin achieved victory by playing the role of the advocate of the golden mean, of the sober-minded statesman, who impressed his colleagues with his calm and quiet manner.[6] Stalin's adroit support for moderate, pragmatic policies, and his apparent embrace of collective leadership, reassured Tomsky as well as Bukharin and Rykov. This apparent moderation enabled Stain to always be in the Politburo majority during the 1920s, but whether Stalin ever took those moderate policy positions seriously is open to question. In any case, it is important to remember when evaluating Tomsky's performance during the intraparty struggle, that the Stalin of the 1920s bore little relation to the Stalin of the 1930s. As Moshe Lewin argued, 'There was no Stalinism before the 1930s and even Stalin himself was not a "Stalinist" in the preceding decade'.[7] But when Stalin rallied other members of the Politburo to support his decisive break with NEP in 1928, Tomsky's political skills were no match for Stalin's unscrupulous cunning, including his use of blackmail. It certainly did not help that Tomsky was aligned with such an inept politician as Bukharin, who committed one naïve political blunder after another.[8] But Tomsky was hardly alone in being outmanoeuvred by Stalin. Nor was he alone in seriously underestimating Stalin. So did all the other Soviet leaders except Trotsky, until one-by-one their respective blinders finally came off, although in each case, as in Tomsky's, only after it was too late to stop Stalin.

---

3 Harris 2005, pp. 65, 79.
4 This was especially true after the Central Committee merged the Organisational (*Orgotdel*) and Record-Assignment (*Uchraspred*) Departments into the Department for Assignment (*Orgraspred*) in 1926. Orgraspred was headed by Ivan Moskvin, who was not close to Stalin and never became one of his lieutenants: Getty and Naumov 2008, pp. 71, 90–5, 102–3, 108.
5 Khlevniuk 2005, p. 109.
6 Cohen 1973, p. 329.
7 Quoted in Ward 1999, p. 31.
8 Kotkin aptly characterises Bukharin as a political amateur: Kotkin 2017, p. 16.

Tomsky's removal spelled doom for trade-union autonomy and for the promise of gradually rising real wages and consumption. Following the defeat of the 'Right Deviation', trade unions completely 'turned their faces to production' and stopped defending workers' interests. Management gained total control of the workplace as they struggled under pressure to meet Moscow's exorbitant production output norms. Although there were some enthusiasts, especially among the previously unemployed youth or peasants migrating to industrial sites from the collectivised villages, the majority of workers felt angry and completely powerless as their standard of living dramatically declined. Real wages for those who remained on the factory bench dropped by half between 1928 and 1932.

While Tomsky continued to hold a lame-duck seat on the Central Committee, as the regime embarked on Stalin's 'revolution from above', the leadership continued to value his skills as one of its best administrators. Tomsky, as a result, occupied positions of great responsibility during the 1930s, principally as the head of the huge Soviet publishing conglomerate, OGIZ. His tenure there, by all accounts, was an enormous success. But Stalinists, all the while, continually hounded him before purge commissions or Central Committee Plenums and Party Congresses. Initially Tomsky demonstrated considerable fortitude in the face of these attacks, tried to fight back, and continued to meet secretly with other former oppositionists, until he fully capitulated in 1934. The campaign vilifying him took a horrible toll on both his mental and physical health. Some of his breakdowns so incapacitated him that he received months of medical care in Germany.

In conclusion, the hardships and suffering that accompanied Stalinist economic policies, as well as the brutal purges that followed, might have been prevented if Tomsky and other relative moderates within the party leadership had been able to block Stalin's and his supporters' drive to power. But when Stalin began to intrigue against them behind the closed doors of the Politburo to further his radical agenda, Tomsky refused to tap the formidable political power of the nearly 100,000 trade-union administrators, strategically located in all industrial centres. Even though Tomsky and his fellow 'Right Deviationists' accurately predicted the Stalinists' plans for breakneck industrialisation and forced collectivisation would have catastrophic results, they continued to refuse to make their opposition public and appeal for support. Unlike in the case of 'Left Oppositions', the majority of lower-level party leaders might have supported the 'Right Opposition' against Stalin.[9] But Tomsky never wavered in

---

9 Gill 1990b, p. 10.

his belief in the necessity of preserving party unity. Tomsky was also acutely aware he had previously attacked 'left' oppositionists for doing exactly that, going public with their oppositional views. Tomsky's adherence to party discipline, as a result, tragically meant he was not able to mount effective resistance to the Stalinists, whose policies would so besmirch the revolutionary hopes that had motivated Tomsky throughout his life. Recognising before others that Stalin intended to physically as well as politically obliterate former oppositionists, Tomsky took his own life in August 1936. In his suicide's wake, as the Great Purges began to engulf the country, virtually everyone ever associated with Tomsky, including even his own family, would either be executed or sent to the gulag.

Bibliography

Archives Cited

British Trades Union Congress Archive (Modern Records Centre at the University of Warwick)
MSS 36   Russia and International Unity
MSS 229   The Minority Movement
MSS 292   International Trade-Union Unity

(GARF) Gosudarstvennyi arkhiv Rossiisskoi Federatsi (State Archive of the Russian Federation)
Fond 102   Department of Police
Fond 533   All-Union Society of Political Prisoners and Convict Exiles
Fond 5451   All-Russian Central Council of Trade Unions

(NIPTs) Nauchno-Informatsionnyi i Prosvetitel'skii Tsentr 'Memorial' ('Memorial' Scientific Information and Enlightenment Centre)
Fond 2   Kozelev, Boris, 1891–1937
Internet site   The Victims of Political Terror in the USSR

(RGASPI) Rossiiskii gosudarstvennyi arkhiv sotsial' no-politicheskkoi istorii (Russian State Archive of Social and Political History)
Fond 5   Secretariat of Lenin, Vladimir, 1870–1924
Fond 17   Central Committee of Russian/Soviet Communist Party
Fond 46   Tenth Party Congress
Fond 81   Kaganovich, Lazar, 1893–1991
Fond 122   Turkestan Commission
Fond 558   Stalin, Joseph, 1878–1953
Fond 593   Tomsky, Mikhail, 1880–1936

(TsA FSB) Tsentral'nyi arkhiv Federal'noi Sluzhby Besopasnosti (Central Archive of the Federal Security Service)
R27744   USSR Supreme Court Military Collegium
R33718   Workers Opposition, Moscow Group

(TsIAM) Tsentral'nyi istoricheskoi arkhiv Moskvy (Central Historical Archive of Moscow)
Fond 131   Butyrka prison

(TsGAODM) Tsentral'nyu gosudastvennyi arkhiv obshchestvennykh dvizhenii Moskvy (Central Government Archive of Social Movements of Moscow)

Fond 2870   Moscow Oblast's Commission for the Purging of the VKP(b)

Congresses, Conferences, Trials, Other Proceedings

Abrosimova, T.A. et al. (eds) 2003, *Peterburgskii komitet RSDRP(b) v 1917 godu: Protokoly i materialy zasedanii*, St. Petersburg: Bel'veder.

Adibekov, Zh. et al. (eds) 1990, 'Deiatel'nost' Tsentral'nogo Komiteta partii v dokumentakh, iiulia 1919 g.', *Izvestiia TsK KPSS*, 301, 2: 139–79.

Adibekov, G.M. et al. (eds) 2001, *Politbiuro TsK RKP(B) i Evropa: resheniia 'osoboi papki' 1923–1939*, Moscow: Rosspen.

Adibekov, G.M. (ed.) 2004, *Politburo TsK RKP(b)–VKP(b) i Komintern: 1919–1943 gg. Dokumenty*, Moscow: Rosspen.

Bramley, Fred (ed.) 1924, *Report of Proceedings at the 56th Annual Trades Union Congress (1924)*, London: Authority of Congress & General Council.

Citrine, Walter (ed.) 1925, Trades Union Congress, *Report of Proceedings at the 57th Annual Trades Union Congress (1925)*, London: Authority of Congress & General Council.

Citrine, Walter (ed.) 1927, Trades Union Congress, *Report of Proceedings at the 59th Annual Trades Union Congress (1927)*, London: Cooperative Printing Society Limited.

Istprof MGSPS 1927, *Moskovskoi sovet professional'nykh soiuza v 1917 godu: Protokoly 1927*, Moscow: Izdatel'stvo MGSPS, Trud i Kniga.

Khlevniuk, O.V. et al. (eds) 1995, *Stalinskoe Politbiuro v 30-e gody: Sbornik dokumentov*, Moscow: AIRO-XX.

Khlevniuk, O.V. et al. (eds) 2000, *Kak lomali NEP: Stenogrammy plenumov TsK VKP(b), 1928–1929 gg.*, vol. 5: Plenum TsK VKP(b) 10–17 noiabra 1929 g., Moscow: Materik.

Khordina, T. (ed.) 2000, *Politbiuro TsK RKP(b)-VKP(b): Povestki dnia zasedanii, 1919–1952*, vol. 1, *1919–1929*, Moscow: Rosspen.

Khordina, T. (ed.) 2001, *Politbiuro TsK RKP(b)-VKP(b): Povestki dnia zasedanii, 1919–1952*, vol. 2, *1930–1941*, Moscow: Rosspen.

Koshelevoi, L.P. et al. (eds) 1992, 'Materialy fevral'sko-martovskogo plenuma TsK VKP(b) 1937 goda', *Voprosy istorii*, 6–7: 3–29.

Koshelevoi, L.P. et al. (eds) 2007a, *Stenogrammy zasedanii Politbiuro TsK RKP(b), 1923–1938*, vol. 1: *1923–1926 gg.*, Moscow: Rosspen.

Koshelevoi, L.P. et al. (eds) 2007b, *Stenogrammy zasedanii Politbiuro TsK RKP(b), 1923–1938*, vol. 2: *1926–1927 gg.*, Moscow: Rosspen.

Koshelevoi, L.P. et al. (eds) 2007c, *Stenogrammy zasedanii Politbiuro TsK RKP(b), 1923– 1938*, vol. 3: *1928–1938 gg.*, Moscow: Rosspen.

Kudriatsev, I.I. (ed.) 2018, *Ob'edinennyi plenum TsK i TsKK VKP(b) 21–23 oktiabria 1927 g.: Dokumenty i materialy*, Moscow: Rosspen.

Kupcha, E. and S. Popov (eds) 1991a, 'Deiatel'nost' tsentral'nogo komiteta partii v dokumentakh, 17 iiulia-13 avgusta 1920 g., *Izvestiia TsK KPSS*, 2: 112–24.

Kupcha, E. and S. Popov (eds) 1991b, 'Deiatel'nost' tsentral'nogo komiteta partii v dokumentakh, 12–29 sentiabria 1920 g., *Izvestiia TsK KPSS*, 4: 147–57.

People's Commissariat of Justice of the USSR 1936, *Report of Court Proceedings: The Case of the Trotskyite-Zinovievite Terrorist Centre*, Moscow: Peoples Commissariat of Justice of the USSR, Moscow: People's Commissariat of Justice of the USSR.

People's Commissariat of Justice of the USSR 1937, *Report of the Court Proceedings in the Case of the Anti-Soviet Trotskyite Centre*, Moscow: Peoples Commissariat of Justice of the USSR.

People's Commissariat of Justice of the USSR 1938, *Report of Court Proceedings in the Case of the Anti-Soviet 'Bloc of Rights and Trotskyites'*, Moscow: Peoples Commissariat of Justice of the USSR.

RKP(b) 1926, *XIV s"ezd Vsesoiuznoi Kommunisticheskoi Partii (b), 18–31 dekabria 1925g.: Stenograficheskii otchet*, Moscow: Gosizdat.

RKP(b) 1927a, *Pervyi legal'nyi Peterburgskii komitet bol'shevikov b 1917 g.: Sbornik materialov i protokolov zasedanii Peterburgskogo Komiteta RSDRP(b) i ego Ispolnitel'noi komissiii za 1917 g. s rechami V I. Lenina*, edited by P.F. Kudelli, Moscow-Leningrad: Gosudarstvennoe izdatel'stvo.

RKP(b) 1927b, *Vtoraia i tret'ia Petrogradskie obshchegorodskie konferentsii bol'shevikov v iiule i otkiabre 1917 goda: Protokoly*, Moscow-Leningrad: Gosudarstvennoe izdatel'stvo.

RKP(b) 1927c, *Piatnadstataiia konferentsiia vsesoiuznoi kommunisticheskoi partii (b), 26 oktiabria-3 noiabria 1926 g.: stenograficheskii otchet*, Moscow: Gosudarstvennoe izdatelstvo.

RKP(b) 1928, *Piatnadstataiia s"ezd vsesoiuznoi kommunisticheskoi partii (b): Stenograficheskii otchet*, Moscow.

RKP(b) 1931, *XVI s"ezd vsesoiuznoi kommunisticheskoi partii (b): Stenograficheskii otchet*, second edition, Moscow: OGIZ Moskovskii rabochii.

RKP(b) 1933a, *Protokoly desiatogo s"ezda RKP(b), mart 1921*, Moscow.

RKP(b) 1933b, *Vos'moi s"ezd RKP(b), 19–23 marta 1919 g.: Protokoly*, Moscow.

RKP(b) 1934a, *Protokoly deviatogo s"ezda RKP(b), mart-aprel' 1920*, Moscow.

RKP(b) 1934b, *Protokoly soveshchaniia rasshirennoi redaktsii 'Proletariia', iiun' 1909 g.*, Moscow: Partizdat.

RKP(b) 1934c, *XVII s"ezd Vsesoiuznoi Kommunisticheskoi Partii (b)*, Moscow: Partizdat.

RKP(b) 1958, *Sed'maia (aprel'skaia) vserossiiskaia konferentsiia RSDRP (bol'shevikov)*.

Petrogradskaia obshchegorodskaia konferentsiia RSDRP *(bol'shevikov) aprel' 1917 goda: Protokoly*, Moscow: Gosudarstvennoe izdatel'stvo politicheskoi literatury.

RKP(b) 1961, *Odinadtsatyi s"ezd RKP(b), mart-aprel' 1922 goda: Stenograficheskii otchet*, Moscow: Politizdat.

RKP(b) 1963a, *Piatyi (Londonskii) s"ezd RSDRP: aprel'-mai 1907 goda*, Moscow: Gosudarstvennoe izdatel'stvo politicheskoi literatury.

RKP(b) 1963b, *Trinadtsatyi s"ezd RKP(b), mai 1924 goda: Stenograficheskii otchet*, Moscow: Gosudarstvennoe izdatel'stvo politicheskoi literatury.

Tomskii, M. 1924, *Itogi VI s"ezda professional'nykh soiuzov SSSR: 11–18 noiabria 1924 g.*, Moscow: Trud i kniga.

Tomskii, M. 1925a, *O novoi oppozitsii: Rech' na XIV s"ezde RKP(b)*, Moscow: Gosudarstvennoe izdatel'stvo.

Tomskii, M. 1926c, *Partiia i oppozitsiia: Rech' na XIV s"ezde RKP(b)*, Moscow: Gosudarstvennoe izdatel'stvo.

Tucker, Robert C. and Stephen F. Cohen (eds) 1965, *The Great Purge Trial*, New York: Gosset & Dunlap, Inc.

Vatlin, A. Iu. et al. (eds) 2000a, *Kak lomali NEP: Stenogrammy plenumov TsK VKP(b), 1928–1929 gg*, vol. 1: *Ob"edinennyi plenum TsK i TsKK VKP(b) 6–11 aprelia 1928g.*, Moscow: Izdatel'skaia firma 'Materik'.

Vatlin, A. Iu. et al. (eds) 2000b, *Kak lomali NEP: Stenogrammy plenumov TsK VKP(b), 1928–1929 gg.*, vol. 2: *Plenum TsK VKP(b) 4–12 iulia 1928 g.*, Moscow: Izdatel'skaia firma 'Materik'.

Vatlin, A. Iu. et al. (eds) 2000c, *Kak lomali NEP: Stenogrammy plenumov TsK VKP(b), 1928–1929 gg.*, vol. 3: *Plenum TsK VKP(b) 16–24 noiabra 1928g.*, Izdatel'skaia firma 'Materik'.

Vatlin, A. Iu. et al. (eds) 2000d, *Kak lomali NEP: Stenogrammy plenumov TsK VKP(b), 1928–1929 gg.*, vol. 4: *Ob"edinennyi plenum TsK i TsKK VKP(b) 16–23 aprelia 1929 g.*, Moscow: Izdatel'skaia firma 'Materik'.

Vatlin, A. Iu. et al. (eds) 2007, *Stenogrammy zasedanii Politbiuro TsK RKP(b)-VKP(b), 1923–1938*, vol. 1: 1923–1926 gg, Moscow: Rosspen.

VLKSM 1928, *VIII vsesoiuznyi s'ezd VLKSM, 5–6 maia 1928 goda: Stenograficheskii otchet*, Moscow: Molodaia gvardiia.

VTsSPS 1918, *Pervyi vserossiiskii s"ezd professional'nykh soiuzov, 7–14 ianvaria 1918 g.: Polnyi stenorgraficheskii otchet*, Moscow: Izdatel'stvo VTsSPS.

VTsSPS 1918, *Vtoroi vserossiiskii s"ezd professional'nykh soiuzov*, Moscow: Izdatel'stvo VTsSPS.

VTsSPS 1920, *Treti vserossiski s"ezd professional'nykh soiuzov: Stenograficheskii otchet*, Moscow: Izdatel'stvo VTsSPS.

VTsSPS 1921, *Chetvertyi vserossiiskii s"ezd professional'nykh soiuzov, 17–25 maia 1921 goda: Stenograficheskii otchet (Plenumy)*: Moscow: Izdatel'stvo VTsSPS.

BIBLIOGRAPHY 395

VTsSPS 1922, *Stenograficheksii otchet piatogo vserossiskogo s"ezd profesional'nykh soiuzov, 17–22 sentabria 1922 g*, Moscow: Izdatel'stvo VTsSPS.

VTsSPS 1923, *Vserossiiskaia konferentsiia profsoiuznal'nykh soiuzov, 4-ia, 1918: Protokoly i materialy sobrali i obrabotam dlia pechati*, Moscow: Izdatel'stvo VTsSPS.

VTsSPS 1925, *Shestoi s"ezd professional'nykh soiuzov s.s.s.r., 11–18 noiabria 1924 g.: Plenumy i sektsii: Polnyi stenograficheskii otchet*, Moscow: Izdatel'stvo VTsSPS.

VTsSPS 1927, *Sed'moi s"ezd professional'nykh soiuzov S.S.S.R, 6–18 dekabria 1926 g., Plenumy i sektsii: Polnyi stenograficheskii otchet*, Moscow: Izdatel'stvo VTsSPS.

VTsSPS 1929a, *Rezoliutsii i postanovlenia v plenuma VTsSPS, 25–29 oktiabr' 1928*, Moscow: Izdatel'stvo VTsSPS.

VTsSPS 1929b, *Vos'moi s'ezd professional'nykh soiuzov s.s.s.r., 10–14 dekabria 1928 g.: Plenumy i sektsii: Polnyi stenograficheskii otchet*, Moscow: Izdatel'stvo VTsSPS.

Primary Sources: Document Collections, Books, and Articles

Akademiia nauk Kazakhskoi SSR 1959, *Istoriia Kazakhskoi SSR*, vol. 2, third edition, Alma-Ata: Izdatel'stvo Akademii nauk Kazakhskoi SSR.

Alliluyeva, Svetlana 1967, *Twenty Letters to a Friend*, New York: Harper & Row.

Amanzholova, D.A. and O.I. Gorelov (eds) 2000, 'Peresmotrite delo s baranami: Pis'ma M.P. Tomskogo V.I. Leninu, 1921', *Istoricheskii arkhiv*, 4: 3–15.

Anfer'tev, I.A. (ed.) 2003: 'Dve besedy s professorom V.N. Slepkovym: Iz 'reabilitatsiodnogo dela: M.N. Riutina, 1932', *Istoricheskii arkhiv*, 5: 62–92.

Anfer'tev, I.A. (ed.) 2006, '"Delo M.N. Riutina" v sud'be G.E. Zinovieva i L.B. Kameneva, Oktiabr' 1932', *Istoricheskii arkhiv*, 1: 64–94.

Artizov, A.N. et al. (eds) 2004, *Reabilitatsiia – Kak eto bylo: dokumenty Prezidiuma TsK KPSS i drugie materialy*, vol. 3, Moscow: Mezhdunarodnyi fond 'Demokratiia'.

Bailey, Frederick 1946, *Mission to Tashkent*, London: J. Cape.

Balabanoff, Angelica 1964, *Impressions of Lenin*, translated by Isotta Cesari, Ann Arbor: University of Michigan Press.

Balabanoff, Angelica 1973 [1938], *My Life as a Rebel*, Bloomington: Indiana University Press.

Barmine, Alexander 1945, *One Who Survived: The Life Story of a Russian under the Soviets*, New York: G.P. Putnam's Sons.

Bazhanov, Boris 1980, *Vospominaniia byvshego sekretaria Stalina*, edited by Aleksandr Glezer, Paris: Tret'ia vol'na.

Bazhanov, Boris 1990, *Bazhanov and the Damnation of Stalin*, translated by David W. Doyle, Athens, OH: Ohio University Press.

Berkman, Alexander 1925, *The Bolshevik Myth: Diary, 1920–1922*, New York: Hutchinson.

Bonch-Bruevich, Vladimir 1931, *Na boevykh postakh fevral'skoi i oktiabr'skoi revoliutsii*, second edition, Moscow: Federatsiia.

Bramley, Fred 1925, *Relations with Russia: A Speech in Favour of International Trade Union Unity*, London: Trade Union Unity.

British Labour Delegation 1920, *British Labour Delegation to Russia, 1920: Report*, London: Trades Union Congress.

Bryant, Louise 1923, *Mirrors of Moscow*, New York: Thomas Seltzer.

Bourne, Kenneth and D. Cameron Watt (eds) 1986, *British Documents on Foreign Affairs: Reports and Papers from the Foreign Office Confidential Print*, Frederick, MD: University Publications of America.

Bukharin, Nikolai 1993, 'Vsiudu i vesde ia budu nastaivat' na svoei polnoi i absoliutnoi nevinovnosti: Pis'ma N.I. Bukharina poslednikh let (avgust-dekabr' 1936 g.)', *Istochnik*, 2: 4–18.

Citrine, Walter 1936, *I Search for Truth in Russia*, London: George Routledge & Sons.

Citrine, Walter 1964, *Men and Work: An Autobiography*, London: Hutchinson.

Davies, R.W. et al. (eds) 2003, *The Stalin-Kaganovich Correspondence, 1931–1936*, translated by Steven Shabad, New Haven: Yale University Press.

Degras, Jane 1956, *The Communist International, 1919–1943: Documents*, vol. 1: 1919–1922, London: Oxford University Press.

Degras, Jane 1960, *The Communist International, 1919–1943: Documents*, vol. 2: 1923–1928, London: Oxford University Press.

Dmitrievskii, Sergei V. 1932, *Sovetskie portrety*, Berlin: Izdatel'stvo Strela.

Donkov, I. et al. (eds) 1989, 'O dele tak nazyvaemogo "soiuza marksistov-lenintsev"', *Izvestiia TsK KPSS*, 292, 6: 103–15.

Duranty Walter 1941, *The Kremlin and the People*, New York: H. Hamilton.

Egorov, A.G. and K.M. Bogoliubov (eds.) 1983–84, *Kommunisticheskaia partiia Sovietskogo Soiuza v rezoliutsiiakh i resheniiax s"ezdov, konferentsii i plenumov TsK*, 15 volumes, ninth edition, Moscow: Izdatel'stvo politicheskoi literatury.

Eremina, L.S. and A.B. Rodinskii (eds) 2000, Rasstrel'nye spiski, Moskva, 1937–1941: 'Kommunarka', Butovo, kniga pamiati zhertv politicheskikh repressiii, Moscow: Izdatel'stvo Znenia.

Eudin, Xenia Joukoff and Robert C. North 1957a, *Soviet Russia and the East, 1920–1927: A Documentary Survey*, Stanford: Stanford University Press.

Eudin, Xenia Joukoff and Harold H. Fisher 1957b, *Soviet Russian and the West, 1920–1927: A Documentary Survey*, Stanford: Stanford University Press.

Fel'shtinskii, Iu. (ed.) 1988a, *Kommunisticheskaia oppozitsiia v SSSR iz arkhiva L'va Trotskogo*, vol. 3, Benson, VT: Chalidze Publications.

Fel'shtinskii, Iu. (ed.) 1988b, *Kommunisticheskaia oppozitsiia v SSSR iz arkhiva L'va Trotskogo*, vol. 4, Benson, VT: Chalidze Publications.

Feuchtwanger, Lion 1937, *Moscow, 1937: My Visit Described for My Friends*, translated by Irene Josephy, New York: Viking.

Fischer, Louis 1941, *Men and Politics: An Autobiography*, New York: Duell, Sloan and Pearce.
Garvy, P.A. 1958, *Professional'nye soiuzy v Rossii v pervye gody revoliutsii, 1917–1921*, edited by G. Ia. Aronson, New York: Rausen Bros.
Gorelov, O. and Iu. Tomskii 1988, 'Mikhail Tomskii – kakim on byl'? in *Reabilitirovan posmertno: Vypusk pervyi*, edited by F.A. Karmanov and S.A. Panov, Moscow: Izdatel'stvo Iuridicheskaia literature.
Gorelov, O.I. and L.D. Shapovalova (eds) 2000, 'Revoliutsiia ubita bogami bol'shevizma: Vospominaniia o M.P. Tomskom, 1936 g.', *Istoricheskii arkhiv*, 5: 210–14.
Gorelov, O.I. and L.D. Shapovalova (eds) 2001, *Mikhail Tomskii: Vospominaniia, Stat'i, Dokumenty*, Moscow: Rossiiskii gosudarstvennyi gumanitarnyi universitet.
Gorky, M. 1932, *Days with Lenin*, London: Martin Lawrence.
Gorky, Maksim 1997, *Maksim Gorky: Selected Letters*, edited and translated by Andrew Barratt and Barry P. Scherr, Oxford: Clarendon Press.
Great Britain Foreign Office 1984, *Documents on British Foreign Policy, 1919–1939*, first series, vol. 25, London: H.M. Stationery Office.
Gregor, Richard (ed.) 1974, *Resolutions and Decisions of the Communist Party of the Soviet Union*, vol. 2: *The Early Soviet Period, 1917–1929*, Toronto: University of Toronto Press.
Harrison, Marguerite E. 1921, *Marooned in Moscow: The Story of an American Woman Imprisoned in Russia*, New York: George H. Doran Company.
Iakovlev, A.N. (ed.) 1991, *Reabilitatsiia: Politicheskie protsessy 30–50-x godov*, Moscow: Politizdat.
International Labour Office 1927, *The Trade Union Movement in Soviet Russia*, Geneva: P.S. King & Son.
Joffe, Nadezha A. 1995, *Back in Time: My Life, My Fate, My Epoch: The Memoirs of Nadezha A. Joffe*, translated by Frederick S. Choate, Oak Park, MI: Labor Publications.
Kaganovich, Lazar' Moiseevich 1996, *Pamiatnye zapiski rabochego, kommunista-bol'shevika, profsoiuznogo, partiinogo i sovetsko-gosudarstvennogo rabotnika*, Moscow: Vagrius.
Kanatchikov, Semen 1986, *A Radical Worker in Tsarist Russia: The Autobiography of Semen Ivanovich Kanatchikov*, edited and translated by Reginald E. Zelnik, Stanford: Stanford University Press.
Karpachev, S.P. and M.E. Minaeva (eds.) 1992a, 'Pust' kazhdyi otvechaet za sebia: Materialy partiinoi chistki M.P. Tomskogo v 1933 g.', *Kentavr*, 4: 107–15.
Karpachev, S.P. and M.E. Minaeva (eds.) 1992b, 'Pust' kazhdyi otvechaet za sebia: Materialy partiinoi chistki M.P. Tomskogo v 1933 g.', *Kentavr*, 5: 100–18.
Karpachev, S.P. and M.E. Minaeva (eds.) 1992c, 'Pust' kazhdyi otvechaet za sebia: Materialy partiinoi chistki M.P. Tomskogo v 1933 g.', *Kentavr*, 6: 101–17.

Khordina, T. (ed.) 1999a, *Kronshtadtskaia tragediia 1921 goda: Dokumenty*, vol. 1, Moscow: Rosspen.

Khordina, T. (ed.) 1999b, *Kronshtadtskaia tragediia 1921 goda: Dokumenty*, vol. 2, Moscow: Rosspen.

Khrushchev, Nikita S. 1970, *Khrushchev Remembers*, translated and edited by Strobe Talbott, Boston: Little, Brown.

Koestler, Arthur 1941, *Darkness at Noon*, translated by Daphne Hardy, New York: Macmillan.

Kozelev, B.G. 1996, 'Nachalo razgroma profdvizheniia: Dnevnik B.G. Kozeleva, 1927–1930 gg.', *Istoricheskii arkhiv*, 5–6: 150–77.

Kozelev, B.G. 1997, 'Nachalo razgroma profdvizheniia: Dnevnik B.G. Kozeleva, 1927–1930 gg.', *Istoricheskii arkhiv*, 1: 115–51.

Krasil'nikov, S.A. (ed.) 2011, *Shakhtinskii protsess 1928 g.: podgotovka, provedenie, itogi*, vol. 1, Moscow: Rosspen.

Kravchenko, Victor 1946, *I Chose Freedom: The Personal and Political Life of a Soviet Official*, New York: Scribner's.

Krupskaya, N.K. 1959, *Reminiscences of Lenin*, Moscow: Foreign Languages Public House.

Kurilov, I. et al. (eds) 1990, 'Platforma Soiuza Marksistov-Lenintsev (Gruppa Riutina)', *Izvestiia TsK KPSS*, 308, 9: 105–83.

Kuusinen, Aino 1974, *Before and After Stalin: A Personal Account of Soviet Russia from the 1920s to the 1960s*, translated by Paul Stevenson, London: Michal Joseph.

Kvashonkin, A.V. et al. (eds) 1996, *Bol'shevistskoe rukovodstvo: Perepiska, 1912–1927*, Moscow: Rosspen.

Kvashonkin, A.P. et al. (eds) 1999, *Sovetskoe rukovodstvo: Perepiska, 1928–1941 gg.*, Moscow: Rosspen.

Larina, Anna 1993, *This I Cannot Forget: The Memoirs of Nikolai Bukharin's Widow*, translated by Gary Kern, New York: W.W. Norton.

Lee, Ivy 1928, *Present-Day Russia*, New York: Macmillan.

Lenin, V.I. 1941–50, *Sochineniia*, 35 volumes, fourth edition. Moscow: Gosudarstvennoe izdatel'stvo politicheskoi literatury.

Lenin, V.I. 1958–65, *Polnoe sobranie sochinenii*, 55 volumes, fifth edition, Moscow: Izdatel'stvo politicheskoi literatury (vols. 53 and 54 of the fifth edition appeared in 1970).

Lenin, V.I. 1960, *O Srednei Azii i Kazakhstane*, Tashkent: Uzbekistan.

Lenin, V.I. 1960–70, *Collected Works*, 45 volumes, fourth English edition, Moscow: Progress Publishers.

Lih, Lars T. et al. (eds) 1995, *Stalin's Letters to Molotov, 1925–1936*, New Haven: Yale University Press.

Lozovsky, A. 1926, *British and Russian Workers*, London: National Minority Movement.

Lyons, Eugene 1937, *Assignment in Utopia*, New York: Harcourt, Brace and Co.

Mandelstam, Nadezhda 1999, *Hope against Hope: A Memoir*, translated by Max Hayward, New York: The Modern Library.
Miliukov, Paul 1967, *Political Memoirs, 1905–1917*, edited by Arthur P. Mendel, translated by Carl Goldberg, Ann Arbor: University of Michigan Press.
Meijer, Jan M. 1964, *The Trotsky Papers, 1917–1922*, The Hague: Mouton.
Mikoian, Anastas 1999, *Tak bylo: Razmyshleniia o minuvshem*, Moscow: Vagrius.
Molotov, Vyacheslav Mikhailovich 1991, *Sto sorok besed s Molotovym: Iz dnevnika F. Chueva*, Moscow: Terra.
Molotov, Vyacheslav Mikhailovich 1993, *Molotov Remembers: Inside Kremlin Politics: Conversations with Felix Chuev*, edited by Albert Resis, Chicago: Ivan R. Dee.
Murin, Iurii (ed.) 1996, 'Samoubistvo ne opravdanie: Predsmertnoe pis'mo Tomskogo', *Rodina*, 2: 90–3.
Murphy, J.T. 1941, *New Horizons*, London: John Lane the Bodley Head.
Omerkhan, A. 1960, 'A History of the Establishment of Soviet Rule in Turkestan', *The East Turkic Review*, 2, 3: 3–22.
Plekhanov, A.A. and A.M. Plekhanov 2011, *Vserossiiskaia chrezychainaia komissiia SNK, 7 dekabria 1917–6 fevraliia 1922: kratkii spravochnik*, Moscow: Soiuz veteranov gosbezopasnosti.
Reed, John 1977 [1926], *Ten Days that Shook the World*, New York: Penguin Books.
Reswick, William 1952, *I Dreamt revolution*, Chicago: Henry Regnery Company.
Riddell, John (ed.) 1993, *To See the Dawn: Baku, 1920, First Congress of the Peoples of the East*, New York: Pathfinder.
Riutin, Martem'ian 1992, *No koleni ne vstanu*, edited by V.A. Starkov, Moscow: Izdatel'stvo politicheskoi literatury.
Safarov, G. 1985 [1922], *Kolonial'naia revoliutsiia: Opyt Turkestana*, Oxford: Society for Central Asian Studies.
Serge, Victor 1963 [1951], *Memoirs of a Revolutionary*, translated by Peter Sedgwick, London: Oxford University Press.
Shliapnikov, A. 1921, 'O zadachakh rabochikh soiuzov', in *Partiia i soiuza (k diskussii o roli i zadachakh profsoiuzov): sbornik statei i materialov*, edited by G. Zinoviev, Petrograd: Gosizdat.
Stalin, Joseph 1935, *Marxism and the National and Colonial Question*, New York: International Publishers.
Stalin, Joseph 1937, *The Moscow Trial, January 1937: Two Speeches*, London: Anglo-Russian Parliamentary Committee.
Stalin, I.V. 1946–51, *Sochineniia*, 13 volumes, Moscow: Gosudarstvennoe izdatel'stvo politicheskoi literatury.
Stalin, J.V. 1952–67, *Works*, 16 volumes, Moscow: Foreign Language Publishing House.
Stalin, J.V. 1995, *Stalin's Letters to Molotov, 1925–1936*, edited by Lars T. Lih, Oleg V. Naumov, and Oleg V. Khlevniuk, New Haven: Yale University Press.

Sukhanov, N.N. 1984 [1955], *The Russian Revolution, 1917: Personal Record*, edited, abridged, and translated by Joel Carmichael, Princeton: Princeton University Press.

Svanidze, Budu 1953, *My Uncle Joseph Stalin*, translated by Waverley Root, New York: G.P. Putnam's Sons.

Teptsov, N. 1992, 'Tainyi agent Iosifa Stalina: Dokumental'naia istoriia o donosakh i donoschike', *Neizvestnaia Rossiia xx vek*, edited by V.A. Kozlov, vol. 1: 56–128.

Tolstoy, Leo 2007, *War and Peace*, translated by Richard Pevear and Larissa Volokhonsky, New York: Alfred A. Knopf.

Tominen, Arvo 1983, *The Bells of the Kremlin: An Experience in Communism*, translated by Lily Leino, Hanover.

Tomsky, M. 1923, *The Russian Trade Unions in 1923*, Chicago: The Trade Union Educational League.

Tomsky, M. 1925b, *Printcipy organisationnogo stroitel'stva professional'nykh soiuzov*, Moscow: VTsSPS.

Tomsky, M. 1926a, *Getting Together: Speeches Delivered in Russia and England, 1924–1925*, translated by Comrade Rothstein, London: Labour Research Department.

Tomsky, M. 1926b, *Zadachi kommunistov v professional'nom dvizhenii*, Moscow: VTsSPS.

Tomsky, M. 1927a, *The Trade Unions, the Party and the State*, Moscow: Commission for Foreign Relations of the Central Council of the Trade Unions of the USSR.

Tomsky, M. 1927b, *Stat'i i rechi, 1917–1925*, vol. 3, Moscow: Knigoizdatel'stvo VTsSPS.

Tomsky, M. 1928a, *Izbrannye stat'i i rechi, 1917–1927*, edited by A.I. Dogadov, Moscow: Knigoizdatel'stvo VTsSPS.

Tomsky, M. 1928b, *Profsoiuzy SSSR i ikh otnoshenie k kompartii i sovetskomu gosudarstvu*, Moscow: Knigoizdatel'stvo VTsSPS.

Tomsky, M. 1928c, *Stat'i i rechi*, vol. 4, Moscow: Knigoizdatel'stvo VTsSPS.

Tomsky, M. 1928d, *Stat'i i rechi, 1918–1927*, vol. 6, Moscow: Knigoizdatel'stvo VTsSPS.

Tomsky, M. 1934, *XV let raboty OGIZa, 1919–1934*, Moscow: Gosizdat Sovetskoe zakonodatel'stvo.

Trotsky, Leon. 1921, 'Rol i zadachi professional'nykh soiuzov,' in *Parstiia i soiuz (k diskussi o roli i zadachakh profsoiuzov): Sbornik statei i materialov*, edited by G. Zinoviev, Petrograd: Gosizdat.

Trotsky, Leon. 1932a, *The History of the Russian Revolution*: Vol. 1: *The Overthrow of Tzarism*, translated by Max Eastman, New York: Simon & Schuster.

Trotsky, Leon. 1932b, *The History of the Russian Revolution*, Vol. 2, *The Attempted Counter-Revolution*, translated by Max Eastman, New York: Simon and Schuster.

Trotsky, Leon. 1932c, *The History of the Russian Revolution*, Vol. 3, *The Triumph of the Soviets*, translated by Max Eastman, New York: Simon and Schuster.

Trotsky, Leon. 1937, *The Stalin School of Falsification*, translated by John C. Wright, New York: Pioneer Publishers.

Trotsky, Leon. 1941, *Stalin: An Appraisal of the Man and His Influence*, edited and translated by Charles Malamuth, New York: Gosset & Dunlap.

Trotsky, Leon. 1961, *Terrorism and Communism: A Reply to Karl Kautsky*, Ann Arbor: University of Michigan Press.

Trotsky, Leon. 1970 [1930], *My Life: An Attempt at an Autobiography*, New York: Pathfinder Press.

Trotsky, Leon. 1973a, *Leon Trotsky on Britain*, New York: Pathfinder Press.

Trotsky, Leon. 1973b, *Writings of Leon Trotsky, 1930–31*, edited by George Breitman and Sarah Lovell, New York: Pathfinder Press.

Trotsky, Leon. 1975, *The Challenge of the Left Opposition, 1923–25*, edited by Naomi Allen, New York: Pathfinder Press.

Trotsky, Leon. 1979, *Writings of Leon Trotsky: Supplements, 1929–1933*, edited by George Breitman, New York: Pathfinder Press.

Trotsky, Leon. 1980, *The Challenge of the left Opposition, 1926–1927*, vol. 2, edited by Naomi Allen and George Saunders, New York: Pathfinder Press.

Trotsky, Leon. 1981, *The Challenge of the Left Opposition, 1928–29*, edited by Naomi Allen and George Sanders, New York: Pathfinder Press.

Trotsky, Leon. 1988, *Portrety revoliutsionerov*, compiled by Y. Felshtinsky, Benson, VT: Chalidze Publications.

TUC General Council 1925, *Russia: The Official Report of the British Trade Union Delegation to Russia and Caucasia, November and December 1924*, London: Trades Union Congress.

Vilkova, Valentina P. 1966, *The Struggle for Power, Russia in 1923: From the Secret Archives of the Former Soviet Union*, Amherst, NY: Prometheus Books.

Vilkova, Valentina P. (ed.) 2004, *RKP(b): Vnutripartiinaia bor'ba v dvatsatye gody: Dokumenty i materaly, 1923*, Moscow: Rosspen.

Viola, Lynne et al. (eds) 2005, *The War Against the Peasantry, 1927–1930: The Tragedy of the Soviet Countryside*, New Haven: Yale University Press.

Zhurablev, V.V. (ed.) 1995, *Vlast' i oppozitsiia: Rossiiskii politicheskii protsessy XX stoletiia*, Moscow: Rosspen.

Zinov'iev, Grigorii 1925, *God revoliutsii (fevral' 1917-mart 1918)*, Leningrad.

Secondary Sources: Books and Articles

Abramovitch, Raphael R. 1962, *The Soviet Revolution, 1917–1939*, New York: International Universities Press.

Abrosimova, T.A. 1998, 'The Composition of the Petersburg Committee of the RSDRP(b) in 1917,' translated by Steve Smith, *Revolutionary Russia*, 11, 1: 37–44.

Acton, Edward, Vladimir Iu. Cherniaev, and William G. Rosenberg (eds) 1997, *Critical*

Companion to the Russian Revolution, 1914–1921, Bloomington: Indiana University Press.

Agabekov, G.S. 1931, *OGPU: The Russian Secret Terror*, translated by Henry W. Bunn, New York: Brentano's.

Agabekov, G.S. 1996 [1930], *Sekretnyi terror: Zapiski pazvedchika*, Moscow: Terra.

Adler, Nanci 2012, *Keeping Faith with the Party: Communist Believers Return from the Gulag*, Bloomington: Indiana University Press.

Allen, Barbara C. 2002, 'The Evolution of Communist Party Control over Trade Unions: Alexander Shlyapnikov and the Trade Unions in May 1921', *Revolutionary Russia*, 15, 2: 72–105.

Allen, Barbara C. 2015, *Alexander Shlyapnikov, 1885–1937: Life of an Old Bolshevik*, Leiden: Brill.

Allen, Barbara C. 2019, 'The Workers' Opposition and the Specialists', *Canadian-American Slavic Studies*, 53, 1–2: 5–23.

Applebaum, Anne 2003, *Gulag: A History*, New York: Doubleday.

Argenbright, Robert 2011, 'Vanguard of 'Socialist Colonization'? The Krasnyi Vostok Expedition of 1920', *Central Asian Survey*, 30, 3–4: 437–54.

Ascher, Abraham 1972, *Pavel Axelrod and the Development of Menshevism*, Cambridge, MA: Harvard University Press.

Ascher, Abraham 1988, *The Revolution of 1905: Russia in Disarray*, Stanford: Stanford University Press.

Aves, Jonathan 1996, *Workers against Lenin: Labour Protest and the Bolshevik Dictatorship*, London: Tauris Academic Studies.

Avrich, Paul 1967, *The Russian Anarchists*, Princeton: Princeton University Press.

Avrich, Paul 1970, *Kronstadt, 1921*, Princeton: Princeton University Press.

Avtorkhanov, Abdurakhman 1959, *Stalin and the Soviet Communist Party: A Study in the Technology of Power*, New York: Frederick A. Praeger for the Institute for the Study of the USSR.

Azrael, Jeremy 1966, *Managerial Power and Soviet Politics*, Cambridge, MA: Harvard University Press.

Babcock, Sarah 2016, *A Prison without Walls? Eastern Siberian Exile in the Last Years of Tsarism*, Oxford: Oxford University Press.

Baberowski, Jorg 2016, *Scorched Earth: Stalin's Reign of Terror*, translated by Steven Gilbert, Ivo Komljen, and Samantha Jeanne Taber, New Haven: Yale University Press.

Bailes, Kendall E. 1978, *Technology and Society under Lenin and Stalin: Origins of the Soviet Technical Intelligentsia, 1917–1941*, Princeton: Princeton University Press.

Baker, Mark R. 2014, 'Did He Really Do It? Mirsaid Sultan-Galiev, Party Disloyalty, and the 1923 Affair', *Europe-Asia Studies*, 66, 4: 590–612.

Barber, John 1976, 'Stalin's Letter to the Editors of *Proletarskaya Revolyutsiya*', *Soviet Studies*, 28, 1: 21–41.

Barnes, Steven A. 2011, *Death and Redemption: The Gulag and the Shaping of Soviet Society*, Princeton: Princeton University Press.

Basseches, Nikolaus 1952, *Stalin*, translated by E.W. Dickes, New York: Staples Press.

Bater, James H. 1976, *St Petersburg: Industrialization and Change*, Montreal: McGill-Queen's University Press.

Bayerlein, Bernhard H. 2006, 'The Abortive "German October", 1923: New Light on the Revolutionary Plans of the Russian Communist Party, the Comintern and the German Communist Party', *Politics and Society under the Bolsheviks: Selected Papers from the Fifth World Congress of Central and East European Studies, Warsaw, 1995*, edited by Kevin McDermott, John Morison, New York: St. Martin's Press, 1999.

Beecher, Jonathan and Valerii N. Fomichev 2006, 'French Socialism in Lenin's and Stalin's Moscow: David Riazanov and the French Archive of the Marx-Engels Institute', *Journal of Modern History*, 78, 1: 119–43.

Beer, Daniel 2017, *The House of the Dead: Siberian Exile under the Tsars*, New York: Alfred A. Knopf.

Beerman, R. 1967, 'The Grain Problem and Anti-Speculation Laws', *Soviet Studies*, 19, 1: 127–9.

Beissinger, Mark R. 1988, *Scientific Management, Socialist Discipline, and Soviet Power*, Cambridge, MA: Harvard University Press.

Belykh, G. (ed.) 1969, *Lenin i Mosckovskie Bol'sheviki*, Moscow: Moscovskii rabochii.

Bennigsen, Alexandre and Chantal Lemercier-Quelquejay 1967, *Islam in the Soviet Union*, New York: Praeger.

Berger, Joseph 1971, *Shipwreck of a Generation: The Memoirs of Joseph Berger*, London: Harvil.

Berman, Jay 1987, 'The Perils of Historical Analogy: Leon Trotsky on the French Revolution', *Journal of the History of Ideas*, 48, 1: 73–98.

Bergson, Abram 1944, *The Structure of Soviet Wages: A Study in Socialist Economics*, Cambridge, MA: Harvard University Press.

Bettleheim, Charles 1978, *Class Struggles in the USSR: Second Period, 1923–1930*, translated by Brian Pearce, New York: Monthly Review Press.

Bittner, Stephen V. 2008, *The Many Lives of Khrushchev's Thaw: Experience and Memory in Moscow's Arbat*, Ithaca: Cornell University Press.

Black, Clayton 1994, 'Party Crisis and the Factory Shop Floor: Krasnyi Putilovets and the Leningrad Opposition, 1925–26', *Europe-Asia Studies*, 46, 1: 107–26.

Blank, Stephen 1987, 'The Contested Terrain: Muslim Political Participation in Soviet Turkestan, 1917–19', *Central Asian Survey*, 6, 4: 47–73.

Blank, Stephen 1994, *Stalin as Commissar of Nationalities, 1917–1924*, Westport, CT: Greenwood Press.

Bonnell, Victoria E. 1983a, *Roots of Rebellion: Workers' Politics and Organizations in St. Petersburg and Moscow, 1900–1914*, Berkeley: University of California Press.

Bonnell, Victoria E. (ed.) 1983b, *The Russian Worker: Life and Labor Under the Tsarist Regime*, Berkeley: University of California Press.

Borisova, L.V. 2006, *Trudovye otnosheniia v sovetskoi Rossii, 1918–1924 gg.*, Moscow: Sobranie.

Borkenau, F. 1938, *The Communist International*, London: Faber and Faber.

Braker, Hans 1994, 'Soviet Policy toward Islam', *Muslim Communities Reemerge: Historical Perspectives on Nationality, Politics, and Opposition in the Former Soviet Union and Yugoslavia*, edited by Edward Allworth, Durham: Duke University Press.

Brandenberger, David 2011, *Propaganda State in Crisis: Soviet Ideology, Indoctrination, and Terror under Stalin, 1927–1941*, New Haven: Yale University Press.

Brandenberger, David and Mikhail Zelenov (eds.) 2019, *Stalin's Master Narrative: A Critical Edition of the History of the Communist Party of the Soviet Union (Bolsheviks): Short Course*, New Haven: Yale University Press.

Brinton, Maurice 1970, *The Bolsheviks and Workers' Control, 1917–1921: The State and Counter-Revolution*, London: Solidarity.

Brooke, Caroline 2006, *Moscow: A Cultural History*, Oxford: Oxford University Press.

Broué, Pierre 1963, *Le Parti Bolshevique*, Paris: Les Editions de Minuit.

Broué, Pierre 1988, *Trotsky*, Paris: Fayard.

Broué, Pierre 1990, 'Party Opposition to Stalin (1930–1932) and the First Moscow Trial', in *Essays on Revolutionary Culture and Stalinism*, edited by John W. Strong, Columbus, OH: Slavica Publishers.

Brovkin, Vladimir N. 1998, *Russia after Lenin: Politics, Culture and Society, 1921–1929*, New York: Routledge.

Brower, Daniel 2003, *Turkestan and the Fate of the Russian Empire*, London: Routledge.

Brown, Edward J. 1971 [1950], *The Proletarian Episode in Russian Literature, 1928–1932*, New York: Octagon Books.

Brown, Edward J. 1982, *Russian Literature since the Revolution*, revised and enlarged edition, Cambridge, MA: Harvard University Press.

Broxup, Marie 1983, 'The Basmachi', *Central Asian Survey*, 2, 1: 57–81.

Broxup, Marie 1992, 'Comrade Muslims'! *Wilson Quarterly*, 16, 3: 39–47.

Bunyan, James 1967, *The Origin of Forced Labor in the Soviet State, 1917–1921: Documents and Materials*, Baltimore: Johns Hopkins University Press.

Burtsev, Vladimir 1927, 'Police Provocation in Russia: The Bolshevist Spy System', *Slavonic Review*, 6, 17: 247–67.

Buttino, Marco 1990, 'Study of the Economic Crisis and Depopulation in Turkestan, 1917–1920', *Central Asian Survey*, 9, 4: 59–74.

Buttino, Marco 1993, 'Politics and Social Conflict During a Famine: Turkestan Immediately After the Revolution', in *In a Collapsing Empire: Underdevelopment, Ethnic Conflict and Nationalism in the Soviet Union*, edited by Marco Buttino, Milan: Feltrinell Editore Milano.

Buttino, Marco 2007, *Revoliutsiia naoborot: Sredniaia Aziia mezhdy padeniem tsarskoi imperii i obrazovaniem SSSR*, Moscow: Zven'ia.

Buttino, Marco 2014, 'Central Asia (1916–20): A Kaleidoscope of Local Revolutions and the Building of the Bolshevik Order', in *The Empire and Nationalism at War*, edited by Eric Lohr, Vera Tolz, Alexander Semyonov, Mark von Hagen, Bloomington: Slavica.

Bykovtseva, L.P. and L.N. Iokar (eds) 1996, *A.M. Gork'kii i ego sovremenniki: Fotodokumenty, opisanie*, Moscow: Nasledie.

Calhoun, Daniel F. 1976, *The United Front: The TUC and the Russians, 1923–1928*, Cambridge: Cambridge University Press.

Calhoun, Daniel F. 1991, 'Trade Union Internationalism in the 1920s: Personalities, Purposes, Promises', in *Contact or Isolation? Soviet-Western Relations in the Interwar-Period*, edited by John Hiden and Aleksander Loit, Stockholm: The Center.

Callaghan, John 1990, *Socialism in Britain since 1884*, Oxford: Blackwell.

Cameron, Sarah 2018, *The Hungry Steppe: Famine, Violence, and the Making of Soviet Kazakhstan*, Ithaca: Cornell University Press.

Caroe, Olaf 1967, *Soviet Empire: The Turks of Central Asia and Stalinism*, second edition, New York: St. Martin's Press.

Carr, Edward Hallett 1950, *The Bolshevik Revolution, 1917–1923*, vol. 1, London: Macmillan.

Carr, Edward Hallett 1952, *The Bolshevik Revolution, 1917–1923*, vol. 2, London: Macmillan.

Carr, Edward Hallett 1953, *Bolshevik Revolution, 1917–1923*, vol. 3, London: Macmillan.

Carr, Edward Hallett 1954, *The Interregnum, 1923–1924*, New York: Macmillan.

Carr, Edward Hallett 1958, *Socialism in One County, 1924–1926*, vol. 1, New York: Macmillan.

Carr, Edward Hallett 1959, *Socialism in One Country, 1924–1926*, vol. 2, New York: Macmillan.

Carr, Edward Hallett 1964, *Socialism in One Country, 1924–1926*, vol. 3:1, New York: Macmillan.

Carr, Edward Hallett and R.W. Davies 1969a, *Foundations of a Planned Economy, 1926–1929*, vol. 1: 1, New York: Macmillan.

Carr, Edward Hallett and R.W. Davies 1969b, *Foundations of a Planned Economy, 1926–1929*, vol. 1: 2, New York: Macmillan.

Carr, Edward Hallett and R.W. Davies 1971, *Foundations of a Planned Economy, 1926–1929*, vol. 2, New York: Macmillan.

Carr, Edward Hallett and R.W. Davies 1976, *Foundations of a Planned Economy, 1926–1929*, vol. 3: 2, New York: Macmillan.

Carrère d'Encausse, Hélène 1967, 'Civil War and New Governments', in *Central Asia: A Century of Russian Rule*, edited by Edward Allworth, New York: Columbia University Press.

Carrère d'Encausse, Hélène 1982, *Lenin: Revolution and Power*, translated by Valence Ionescu, New York: Longman.

Carrère d'Encausse, Hélène 1992, *The Great Challenge: Nationalities and the Bolshevik State, 1917–1930*, translated by Nancy Festinger, New York: Holmes & Meier.

Carrère d'Encausse, Hélène 2009, *Islam and the Russian Empire: Reform and Revolution in Central Asia*, translated by Ouintin Hoare, London: I.B. Tauris.

Cassiday, Julie A. 2000, *The Enemy on Trial: Early Soviet Courts on Stage and Screen*, DeKalb: Northern Illinois University Press.

Chamberlin, William Henry 1935, *The Russian Revolution, 1917–1921: Volume Two 1918–1921: From the Civil War to the Consolidation of Power*, New York: Macmillan Company.

Chase, William 1986, 'The Dialectics of Production Meetings, 1923–29', *Russian History/Histoire Russe*, 13, 2–3: 149–86.

Chase, William 1987, *Workers, Society, and the Soviet State: Labor and Life in Moscow, 1918–1929*, Urbana: University of Illinois Press.

Chechevishnikov, A.L. 1990, 'Partiia i profsoiuzy: krisis otnoshenii', *Raborchii klass i sovremennyi*, 5.

Chokayev, Mustapha 1931, 'Turkestan and the Soviet Regime', *Journal of the Royal Central Asian Society*, 18: 403–20.

Ciliga, Ante 1979 [1940], *The Russian Enigma*, London: G. Routledge & Sons.

Clark, Katerina 1978, 'Little Heroes and Big Deeds: Literature Responds to the First Five-Year Plan' in *Cultural Revolution in Russia, 1928–1931*, edited by Sheila Fitzpatrick, Bloomington: Indiana University Press.

Clark, Katerina 1985, *The Soviet Novel: History as Ritual*, second edition, Chicago: University of Chicago Press.

Clark, Ronald W. 1988, *Lenin*, New York: Harper & Row.

Clark, William A. 2015, 'The Ryutin Affair and the "Terrorism" Narrative of the Purges', *Russian History*, 42, 4: 377–422.

Cliff, Tony 1987, *Revolution Besieged: Lenin, 1917–1923*, London: Bookmarks.

Cohen, Stephen F. 1973, *Bukharin and the Bolshevik Revolution: A Political Biography, 1888–1938*, New York: Alfred. A. Knopf.

Cohen, Stephen F. 1985, *Rethinking the Soviet Experience: Politics and History since 1917*, New York: Oxford University Press.

Colton, Timothy J. 1995, *Moscow: Governing the Socialist Metropolis*, Cambridge, MA: Harvard University Press.

Conquest, Robert 1985, *Inside Stalin's Secret Police: NKVD Politics, 1936–1939*, Stanford: Hoover Institution Press.

Conquest, Robert 1989, *Stalin and the Kirov Murder*, New York: Oxford University Press.

Conquest, Robert 1990, *The Great Terror: A Reassessment*, New York: Oxford University Press.

Conquest, Robert 1991, *Stalin: Breaker of Nations*, New York: Viking.

Cook, Lara 2013, 'Collegiality in the People's Commissariats, 1917–1920', *Revolutionary Russia*, 26, 1: 1–31.
Corney, Frederick C. (ed.) 2015, *Trotsky's Challenge: The 'Literary Discussion' of 1924 and the Fight for the Bolshevik Revolution*, Leiden: Brill.
Crews, Robert D. 2006, *For Prophet and Tsar: Islam and Empire in Russia and Central Asia*, Cambridge: Harvard University Press.
Crossman, Richard (ed.) 1949, *The God that Failed*, New York: Harper.
Crowl, James William 1982, *Angels in Stalin's Paradise*, Washington, D.C.: University Press of America.
Daniels, Robert Vincent 1960, *The Conscience of the Revolution: Communist Opposition in Soviet Russia*, Cambridge, MA: Harvard University Press.
Daniels, Robert Vincent 1991, *Trotsky, Stalin, and Socialism*, Boulder, CO: Westview Press.
Daniels, Robert Vincent 2007, *The Rise and Fall of Communism in Russia*, New Haven: Yale University Press.
David-Fox, Michael 1997, *Revolution of the Mind: Higher Learning among the Bolsheviks, 1918–1929*, Ithaca: Cornell University Press.
Davies, R.W. 1960, 'Soviet Economic Controllers: II', *Soviet Studies*, 11, 4: 373–92.
Davies, R.W. 1980, *The Socialist Offensive, The Collectivization of Soviet Agriculture, 1929–1930*, Cambridge, MA: Harvard University Press.
Davies, R.W. 1981, 'The Syrtsov-Lominadze Affair', *Soviet Studies*, 33, 1: 29–50.
Davies, R.W., Mark Harrison, S.G. Wheatcroft (eds.) 1994, *The Economic Transformation of the Soviet Union, 1913–1945*, New York: Cambridge University Press.
Davies, R.W., Melanie Ilic, and Oleg Khlevnyuk 2004, 'The Politburo and Economic Policy-Making', in *The Nature of Stalin's Dictatorship: The Politburo, 1924–1953*, edited by E.A. Rees, New York: Palgrave Macmillan.
Davies, Sarah 1997, *Popular Opinion in Stalin's Russia: Terror, Propaganda and Dissent, 1934–1941*, Cambridge: Cambridge University Press.
Davies, Sarah and James Harris 2014, *Stalin's World: Dictating the Soviet Order*, New Haven: Yale University Press.
Day, Richard B. 1973, *Leon Trotsky and the Politics of Economic Isolation*, Cambridge: Cambridge University Press.
De Jonge, Alex 1986, *Stalin and the Shaping of the Soviet Union*, New York: William Morrow & Co.
Demko, George J. 1969, *The Russian Colonization of Kazakhstan, 1896–1916*, Bloomington: Indiana University Press.
Deutscher, Isaac 1950, *Soviet Trade Unions: Their Place in Soviet Labour Policy*, London: Oxford University Press.
Deutscher, Isaac 1954, *The Prophet Armed: Trotsky, 1879–1921*, Oxford: Oxford University Press.

Deutscher, Isaac 1959, *The Prophet Unarmed, Trotsky, 1921–1929*, Oxford: Oxford University Press.

Deutscher, Isaac 1967 [1949], *Stalin: A Political Biography*, second edition, New York: Oxford University Press.

Dewar, Hugo 1976, *Communist Politics in Britain*, London: Pluto Press.

Dewar, Margaret 1979 [1956], *Labour Policy in the USSR*, New York: Octagon Books.

Dobson, Miriam 2009, *Khrushchev's Cold Summer: Gulag Returnees, Crime, and the Fate of Reform after Stalin*, Ithaca: Cornell University Press.

Drachkovitch, Milorad M. and Branko Lazitch 1966, 'The Communist International', in *The Revolutionary Internationals, 1864–1943*, edited by M. Drachkovitch, Stanford: Stanford University Press.

Dunaev, Boris 1926, *Tomskii: Kratkii biograficheskii ocherk*, Moscow: Trud i kniga.

Dunn, Robert W. 1928, *Soviet Trade Unions*, New York: Vanguard.

Eaden James and David Renton 2002, *The Communist Party of Great Britain since 1920*, New York: Palgrave.

Eastman, Max 1925, *Since Lenin Died*, New York: Bonie & Liveright.

Economakis, Evel G. 1998, *From Peasant to Petersburger*, New York: St. Martin's Press.

Edgar, Adrienne Lynn 2004, *Tribal Nation: The Making of Soviet Turkmenistan*, Princeton: Princeton University Press.

Ellman, Michael 2003, 'The Soviet 1937–1938 Provincial Show Trials Revisited', *Europe-Asia Studies*, 55, 8: 1305–21.

Engelstein, Laura 2018, *Russia in Flames: War, Revolution, and Civil War, 1914–1921*, Oxford: Oxford University Press.

Erlich, Alexander 1960, *The Soviet Industrialization Debate, 1924–1928*, Cambridge, MA: Harvard University Press.

Ermolaev, Herman 1997, *Censorship in Soviet Literature, 1917–1991*, Lanham, MD: Rowman & Little.

Farber, Samuel 1990, *Before Stalinism: The Rise and Fall of Soviet Democracy*, London: Verso.

Farbman, Michael 1924, *After Lenin: The New Phase in Russia*, London: Leonard Parsons.

Farman, Christopher 1972, *The General Strike, May 1926*, Frogmore: Panther.

Fel'shtinskii, Iu. G. 1993, *Razgovory c Bukharinym*, Moscow: Teleks.

Figes, Orlando 1996, *A People's Tragedy: A History of the Russian Revolution*, New York: Viking.

Filtzer, Donald 1986, *Soviet Workers and Stalinist Industrialization: The Formation of Modern Soviet Production Relations, 1928–1941*, Armonk, NY: M.E. Sharpe.

Finkel, Stuart 2007, *On the Ideological Front: The Russian Intelligentsia and the Making of the Soviet Public Sphere*, New Haven: Yale University Press.

Fischer, Louis 1930, *The Soviets in World Affairs: A History of Relations between the Soviet Union and the Rest of the World*, vol. 2, London: Jonathan Cape.

Fischer, Louis 1964, *The Life of Lenin*, New York: Harper & Row.

Fischer, Ruth 1948, *Stalin and German Communism: A Study in the Origins of the State Party*, Cambridge, MA: Harvard University Press.

Fitzpatrick, Sheila 1970, *The Commissariat of Enlightenment: Soviet Organization of Education and the Arts under Lunacharsky, October 1917–1921*, Cambridge: Cambridge University Press.

Fitzpatrick, Sheila 1976, 'Culture and Politics under Stalin: A Reappraisal', *Slavic Review*, 35, 2: 211–31.

Fitzpatrick, Sheila 1978, 'Cultural Revolution as Class War', in *Cultural Revolution in Russia, 1928–1931*, edited by Sheila Fitzpatrick, Bloomington: Indiana University Press.

Fitzpatrick, Sheila 1985, 'Ordzhonikidze's Takeover of Vesenkha: A Case Study in Soviet Bureaucratic Politics', *Soviet Studies*, 37, 2: 153–72.

Fitzpatrick, Sheila 1992, *The Cultural Front: Power and Culture in Revolutionary Russia*, Ithaca: Cornell University Press.

Fitzpatrick, Sheila 1993, 'The Great Departure: Rural-Urban Migration in the Soviet Union, 1929–33', in *Social Dimension of Soviet Industrialization*, edited by William G. Rosenberg and Lewis H. Siegelbaum, Bloomington: Indiana University Press.

Fitzpatrick, Sheila 1999, *Everyday Stalinism: Ordinary Life in Extraordinary Times: Soviet Russia in the 1930s*, New York: Oxford University Press.

Fitzpatrick, Sheila 2005, *Tear Off the Masks! Identity and Imposture in Twentieth-Century Russia*, Princeton: Princeton University Press.

Fitzpatrick, Sheila 2015, *On Stalin's Team: The Years of Living Dangerously in Soviet Politics*, Princeton: Princeton University Press.

Fraser, Glenda 1987, 'Basmachi–1', *Central Asian Survey*, 6, 1: 1–73.

Frierson, Cathy A. and Semyon S. Vilensky 2010, *Children of the Gulag*, New Haven: Yale University Press.

Furhmann, Joseph T. 1989, 'Lenin and Privilege', *The Historian*, 51, 3: 379–401.

Furr, Grover and Vladimir Bobrov 2007, 'Pervye priznatel'nye nokazaniia N.I. Bukharina na lubianke', *Klio*, 36, 1: 38–52.

Gaisinskii, M. 1932, *Bor'ba s uklonami ot general'noi linii partii: Istoricheskii ocherk vnutripartiinoi borb'by posleoktiabrs'kogo perioda*, Moscow: Moskovskii rabochii.

Gambarov, Iu. et al. (eds) 1989 [1927–29], *Deiateli SSSR i oktiabr'skoi revoliutsii: avtobiografi i biografi*, 3 parts, Moscow: Granat; reprinted Moscow: Kniga.

Garrard, John and Carol 1990, *Inside the Soviet Writers' Union*, New York: Free Press.

Genis, V.L. 1994, 'Raskazachivanie v Sovietskoi Rossii', *Voprosy istorii*, 1: 42–55.

Genis, V.L. 1998, 'Deportatsiia russkikh iz Turkestanta v 1921 godu: "Delo Safarova,"' *Voprosy istorii*, 1: 44–58.

Getty, J. Arch 1985, *Origins of the Great Purges: The Soviet Communist Party Reconsidered, 1933–1938*, Cambridge: Cambridge University Press.

Getty, J. Arch 1986, 'Trotsky in Exile: The Founding of the Fourth International', *Soviet Studies*, 38, 1: 24–35.

Getty, J. Arch 1991, 'State and Society Under Stalin: Constitutions and Elections in the 1930s', *Slavic Review*, 5, 1: 18–35.

Getty, J. Arch 1993, 'The Politics of Repression Revisited', in *Stalinist Terror: New Perspectives*, edited by J. Arch Getty and Roberta T. Manning, Cambridge: Cambridge University Press.

Getty, J. Arch 1998, 'Afraid of Their Shadows: The Bolshevik Recourse to Terror, 1932–1938', in *Stalinismus vor dem Zweiten Weltkrieg: neue Wege der Forschung*, edited by Manfred Hildermeier and Elisabeth Mueller-Luckner, Munich: Oldenbourg.

Getty, J. Arch 1999, 'Samokritika Rituals in the Stalinist Central Committee, 1933–38', *Russian Review*, 58, 1: 49–70.

Getty, J. Arch 2013, *Practicing Stalinism: Bolsheviks, Boyars, and the Persistence of Tradition*, New Haven: Yale University Press.

Getty, J. Arch and Oleg V. Naumov 1999, *The Road to Terror: Stalin and the Self-Destruction of the Bolsheviks, 1932–1939*, translated by Benjamin Sher, New Haven: Yale University Press.

Getty, J. Arch and Oleg V. Naumov 2008, *Yezhov: The Rise of Stalin's 'Iron Fist'*, New Haven: Yale University Press.

Getzler, Israel 1983, *Kronstadt, 1917–1921: The Fate of a Soviet Democracy*, Cambridge: Cambridge University Press.

Getzler, Israel 2002, 'The Communist Leaders' Role in the Kronstadt Tragedy of 1921 in the Light of Recently Published Archival Documents', *Revolutionary Russia*, 15, 1: 24–44.

Gill, Graeme 1988, *The Rules of the Communist Party of the Soviet Union*, Basingstoke: Macmillan.

Gill, Graeme 1990a, *The Origins of the Stalinist Political System*, Cambridge: Cambridge University Press.

Gill, Graeme 1990b, *Stalinism*, Atlantic Highlands, NJ: Humanities Press International.

Gill, Graeme 2018, *Collective Leadership in Soviet Politics*, Cham: Palgrave Macmillan.

Gimpel'son, E.G. 1998, *Sovetskie upravlentsy 1917–1920 gg.*, Moscow: Institut Rossiiskoi istorii RAN.

Gitlow, Benjamin 1940, *I Confess: The Truth about American Communism*, New York: E.P. Dutton.

Gitlow, Benjamin 1948, *The Whole of Their Lives*, New York: Charles Scribner & Sons.

Glotzer, Albert 1989, *Trotsky: Memoir and Critique*, Buffalo, NY: Prometheus Books.

Gluckstein, Donny 1994, *The Tragedy of Bukharin*, London: Pluto Press.

Goldman, Wendy Z. 1993, *Women, the State and Revolution: Soviet Family Policy and Social Life, 1917–1936*, Cambridge: Cambridge University Press.

Goldman, Wendy Z. 2002, *Women at the Gates: Gender and Industry in Stalin's Russia*, Cambridge: Cambridge University Press.

Goldman, Wendy Z. 2007, *Terror and Democracy in the Age of Stalin: The Social Dynamics of Repression*, New York: Cambridge University Press.

Golikov, G.N. (ed.) 1969, *Vospominaniia o Vladimire Il'iche Lenine*, vol. 3, Moscow: Politizdat.

Gordon, Manya 1941, *Workers before and after Lenin*, New York: D.P. Dutton.

Gorelov, O.I. 1989, *M.P. Tomskii: Stranitsy politicheskoi biografii*, Moscow: Znanie.

Gorelov, O.I. 2000, *Tsugtsvang Mikhaila Tomskogo: Shtrikhi k portretu*, Moscow: Rosspen.

Gorky, Maxim 1933, *Days with Lenin*, London: Martin Lawrence.

Gooderham, Peter 1982, 'The Komsomol and Worker Youth: The Inculcation of "Communist Values" in Leningrad during NEP', *Soviet Studies*, 34, 4: 506–28.

Gorodetsky, Gabriel, 1976, 'The Soviet Union and the General Strike of May 1926', *Cahiers du monde russe et sovietique*, 17, 2–3: 287–310.

Gorodetsky, Gabriel, 1977, *The Precarious Truce: Anglo-Soviet Relations, 1924-27*, Cambridge: Cambridge University Press.

Gorsuch, Anne E. 2000, *Youth in Revolutionary Russia: Enthusiasts, Bohemians, Delinquents*, Bloomington: Indiana University Press.

Graziosi, Andrea 1991, 'Building the First System of State Industry in History: Piatakov's VSNKh and the Crisis of the Nep, 1923–1926', *Cahiers du monde russe et sovietique*, 32: 4, 539–80.

Graziosi, Andrea 2000, *A New, Peculiar State: Explorations in Soviet History, 1917–1937*, Westport, CT: Praeger Publishers.

Gregory, Paul R. 2010, *Politics, Murder, and Love in Stalin's Kremlin: The Story of Nikolai Bukharin and Anna Larina*, Stanford: Hoover Institution Press.

Hagenloh, Paul 2009, *Stalin's Police: Public Order and Mass Repression in the USSR, 1926–1941*, Washington, D.C.: The Johns Hopkins University Press.

Halfin, Igal 2003, *Terror in My Soul: Communist Autobiographies on Trial*, Cambridge, MA: Harvard University Press.

Hammond, Thomas Taylor 1957, *Lenin on Trade Unions and Revolution, 1893–1917*, New York: Columbia University Press.

Harris, James R. 1999, *The Great Urals: Regionalism and the Evolution of the Soviet System*, Ithaca: Cornell University Press.

Harris, James R. 2005, 'Stalin as General Secretary: The Appointments Process and the Nature of Stalin's Power', in *Stalin: A New History*, edited by Sarah Davies and James Harris, Cambridge: Cambridge University Press.

Harris, James R. 2017, *The Great Fear: Stalin's Terror of the 1930s*, Oxford: Oxford University Press.

Haslam, Jonathan 1986, 'Political Opposition to Stalin and the Origins of the Terror in Russia, 1932–1936', *The Historical Journal*, 28, 2: 395–418.

Hatch, John 1994, 'Hangouts and Hangovers: State, Class, and Culture in Moscow's Workers' Club Movement, 1925–1928', *Russian Review*, 53, 1: 97–117.

Haupt Georges and Jean-Jacques Marie (eds.) 1974, *Makers of the Russian Revolution: Biographies of Bolshevik Leaders*, translated by C.I.P. Ferdinand, Ithaca: Cornell University Press.

Hedeler, Wladislaw 2003, 'Ezhov's Scenario for the Great Terror and the Falsified Record of the Third Moscow Show Trial', in *Stalin's Terror: High Politics and Mass Repression in the Soviet Union*, edited by Barry McLoughlin and Kevin McDermott, New York: Palgrave Macmillan.

Heinzen, James W. 2004, *Inventing a Soviet Countryside: State Power and the Transformation of Rural Russia, 1917–1929*, Pittsburgh: University of Pittsburgh Press.

Hellbeck, Jochen 2006, *Revolution on My Mind: Writing a Diary under Stalin*, Cambridge, MA: Harvard University Press.

Hincks, Darron 1992, 'Support for the Opposition in Moscow in the Party Discussion of 1923–1924', *Soviet Studies*, 1: 137–51.

Hingley, Ronald 1970, *The Russian Secret Police: Muscovite, Imperial Russian, and Soviet Political Security Operations*, New York: Simon and Schuster.

Hirsch, Francine 2005, *Empire of Nations: Ethnographic Knowledge and the Making of the Soviet Union*, Ithaca: Cornell University Press.

Hobson, Christopher and Ronald D. Tabor 1988, *Trotskyism and the Dilemma of Socialism*, New York: Greenwood Press.

Hoffman, David L. 2003, *Stalinist Values: The Cultural Norms of Soviet Modernity, 1917–1941*, Ithaca: Cornell University Press.

Hoffman, David L. 2018, *The Stalinist Era*, Cambridge: Cambridge University Press.

Holquist, Peter 1997, 'Conduct Merciless Mass Terror: Decossackization on the Don, 1919', *Cahiers du monde russe*, 38, 1–2: 127–62.

Holquist, Peter 2001, 'To Count, to Extract, and to Exterminate: Population Statistics and Population Politics in Late Imperial and Soviet Russia', in *A State of Nations: Empire and Nation Making in the Age of Lenin and Stalin*, edited by Ronald Grigor Suny and Terry Martin, Oxford: Oxford University Press.

Hopkirk, Peter 1984, *Setting the East Ablaze: Lenin's Dream of an Empire in Asia*, London: J. Murray.

Hosking, Geoffrey 2006, *Rulers and Victims: The Russians in the Soviet Union*, Cambridge, MA: Harvard University Press.

Hough, Jerry F. and Merle Fainsod 1979, *How the Soviet Union Is Governed*, Cambridge, MA: Harvard University Press.

Hudson, Hugh D. 2012a, *Peasants, Political Police, and the Early Soviet State: Surveillance and Accommodation under the New Economic Policy*, New York: Palgrave Macmillan.

Hudson, Hugh D. 2012b, 'The 1927 Soviet War Scare: The Foreign Affairs-Domestic Policy Nexus Revisited', *The Soviet and Post-Soviet Review*, 39, 2: 145–65.

Hughes, James 1991, *Stalin, Siberia and the Crisis of the New Economic Policy*, Cambridge: Cambridge University Press.

Hughes, Michael 1997, *Inside the Enigma: British Official in Russia, 1900–1934*, London: Hambledon Press.

Humbert-Droz, Jules 1971, *De Lenine a Staline: Dix ans au service de l'Internationale Communiste, 1921–1931*, Neuchâtel: la Baconnière.

Husband, William 1985, 'Workers' Control and Centralization in the Russian Revolution: The Textile Industry of the Central Industrial Region, 1917–1920', *The Carl Beck Papers in Russian and East European Studies*, 403: 1–52.

Husband, William 1990, *Revolution in the Factory: The Birth of the Soviet Textile Industry, 1917–1920*, Oxford: Oxford University Press.

Il'inskii, Mikhail 2002, *Narkom Iagoda*, Moscow: Veche.

Ivanova, Galina 1989, 'V izdatel'skom dele ia ne iskushen: M. Tomskii vo glave OGIZa', *Knizhnoe obozrenie*, 49: 6–7.

Ivanova, Galina 1992, 'Mikhail Pavlovich Tomskii v 1917 godu: Ocherk politicheskoi diatel'nosti', in *Otechestvennaia istoriiia; Problemy, poiski, suzhdendeniia*, edited by N.N. Vinogradov, Moscow: Luch.

Jacobson, Jon 1994, *When the Soviet Union Entered World Politics*, Berkeley: University of California Press.

Jansen, Marc 1982, *A Show Trial under Lenin: The Trial of the Socialist Revolutionaries, Moscow 1922*, translated by Jean Sanders, The Hague: Martinus Nijhoff Publishers.

Jansen, Marc and Nikita Petrov 2002, *Stalin's Loyal Executioner: People's Commissar Nikolai Ezhov, 1895–1940*, Stanford: Hoover Institution Press.

Jaryc, Marc 1935, *Press and Publishing in the Soviet Union*, London: School of Slavonic and East European Studies in the University of London.

Jo, Junbae 2006, 'Soviet Trade Unions and the Great Terror', in *Stalin's Terror Revisited*, edited by Melanie Ilic, New York: Palgrave McMillian.

Kamp, Marianne 2006, *The New Women in Uzbekistan: Islam, Modernity, and Unveiling under Communism*, Seattle: University of Washington Press.

Kaplan, Frederick I. 1968, *Bolshevik Ideology and the Ethics of Soviet Labor, 1917–1920: The Formative Years*, New York: Philosophical Library.

Kar'iakhiam, T., Ia. Krastyn, and A. Tila (eds.) 1981, *Revoliutsiia 1905–1907 godov v Pribaltike*, Tallin: Instituty istorii Akademii nauk Laviiskoi, Litovskoi i Estonskoi SSR.

Karcz, Jerzy F. 1967, 'Thoughts on the Grain Problem', *Soviet Studies*, 18, 4: 399–434.

Karlinsky, Simon 1985, *Marina Tsvetaeva: The Woman, Her World and Her Poetry*, Cambridge: Cambridge University Press.

Kassof, Brian 2015, 'Glavlit, Ideological Censorship, and Russian-Language Book Publishing', *The Russian Review*, 74, 1: 69–96.

Kassymbekova, Botakoz 2011, 'Helpless Imperialists: European State Workers in Soviet Central Asia in the 1920s and 1930s', *Central Asian Survey*, 30, 1: 21–37.

Katkov, George 1969, *The Trial of Bukharin*, New York: Stein and Day.

Katsunori, Nishiyama 2000, 'Russian Colonization in Central Asia: A Case of Semirechye, 1967–1922', in *Migration in Central Asia: Its History and Current Problems*, edited by Komatsu Hisao, Obiya Chika, Joshn S. Schoberlein, Osaka: Japan Center for Area Studies.

Keep, J.L.H. 1963, *The Rise of Social Democracy in Russia*, Oxford: Clarendon Press.

Keller, Shoshana 1992, 'Islam in Soviet Central Asia, 1917–1930: Soviet Policy and the Struggle for Control', *Central Asian Survey*, 11, 1: 25–50.

Keller, Shoshana 2001, *To Moscow, not Mecca: The Soviet Campaign against Islam in Central Asia, 1917–1941*, Westport, CT: Praeger Publishers.

Keller, Shoshana 2003, 'The Central Asian Bureau: An Essential Tool in Governing Soviet Turkestan', *Central Asian Survey*, 22, 2–3: 281–97.

Kemp-Welch, A. 1991, *Stalin and the Literary Intelligentsia, 1928–39*, Basingstoke: Macmillan.

Kenez, Peter 1985, *The Birth of the Propaganda State: Soviet Methods of Mass Mobilization, 1917–1929*, Cambridge: Cambridge University Press.

Khalid, Adeeb 1996, 'Tashkent in 1917: Muslim Politics in Revolutionary Turkestan', *Slavic Review*, 55, 2: 270–96.

Khalid, Adeeb 2001, 'Nationalizing the Revolution in Central Asia: The Transformation of Jadidism, 1917–1920', in *A State of Nations: Empire and Nation-Making in the Age of Lenin and Stalin*, edited by Ronald Grigor Suny and Terry Martin, Oxford: Oxford University Press.

Khalid, Adeeb 2005, 'Turkestan v 1917–1922 godakh: Bor'ba za vlast' na okraine Rossii', in *Tragediia velikoi derzhavy: Nasional'nyi vopros i raspad Sovetskogo Soiuza*, edited by G.N. Sevostianov, Moscow: Izdatel'stvo Sotsial'no-politicheskaia Mysl.

Khalid, Adeeb 2015, *Making Uzbekistan: Nation, Empire, and Revolution in the Early USSR*, Ithaca: Cornell University Press.

Kharkhordin, Oleg 1999, *The Collective and the Individual in Russia: A Study of Practices*, Berkeley: University of California Press.

Khaustov, V.N., V.P. Naumov, and N.S. Plotnikova (eds) 2003, *Lubianka: Stalin i VChK-OGPU-NKVD, ianvar' 1922-dekabr' 1936*, Moscow: Izdatel'stvo 'Materik'.

Khaustov, V.N., V.P. Naumov, and N.S. Plotnikova (eds) 2004, *Lubianka: Stalin i glavnoe upravlenie gosbezopasnosti NKVD: Arkhiv Stalina: Dokumenty vysshikh organov partiinoi i gosudarstvennoi vlasti, 1937–1938*, Moscow: Izdatel'stvo 'Materik'.

Khaustov, Vladimir and Lennart Samuel'son 2010, *Stalin, NKVD i repressii 1936–1938*, Moscow: Rosspen.

Khaustov, V.N. (ed.) 2011, *Lubianka: Sovetskaia elita na stalinskoi golgofe, 1937–1938*, Moscow: Mezhdunarodnyi fond 'Demokratiia'.

Khazanov, K. 1969, *V.I. Lenin i Turkbiuro TsK RKP(b)*, Tashkent: Uzbekistan.
Khlevniuk, O.V. 1992, *1937: Stalin, NKVD i sovetskoe obshchestvo*, Moscow: Izdatel'stvo Respublika.
Khlevniuk, Oleg V. 1995, *In Stalin's Shadow: The Career of 'Sergo' Ordzhonikidze*, edited by Donald J. Raleigh with Kathy S. Transchel, translated by David J. Nordlander, Armonk, NY: M.E. Sharpe.
Khlevniuk, Oleg V. 1996, *Politbiuro: Mekhanizmy poliiticheskoi vlasti v 30-e gody*, Moscow: Rosspen.
Khlevniuk, Oleg V. 2005, 'Stalin as Dictator: The Personalisation of Power', in *Stalin: A New History*, edited by Sarah Davies and James Harris, Cambridge: Cambridge University Press.
Khlevniuk, Oleg V. 2009, *Master of the House: Stalin and His Inner Circle*, translated by Nora Seligman Favorov, New Haven: Yale University Press.
Khlevniuk, Oleg V. 2010, *Khoziain: Stalin i utverzhdenie stalinskoi liktatury*, Moscow: Rosspen.
Khlevniuk, Oleg V. 2015, *Stalin: New Biography of a Dictator*, translated by Nora Seligman Favorov, New Haven: Yale University Press.
King, David 1997, *The Commissar Vanishes: The Falsification of Photographs and Art in Stalin's Russia*, New York: Henry Holt and Company.
Kislitsyn, S.A. 1993, *Shakhtinskoe delo: Nachalo stalinskikh repressii protiv nauchinotekhnicheskoi intelligentsia v SSSR*, Rostov-on-Don: Izdatel'stvo NMTS 'Logos'.
Kitaeff, Michael 1954, *Communist Party Officials: A Group of Portraits* (in Russian), New York: Research Program on the USSR.
Kivelson, Valerie A. and Ronald Grigor Suny 2017, *Russia's Empires*, New York: Oxford University Press.
Klugmann, James 1969, *History of the Communist Party of Great Britain:* vol. 2: *1925–1927: The General Strike*, London: Lawrence & Wishart.
Knight, Amy 1999, *Who Killed Kirov? The Kremlin's Greatest Mystery*, New York: Hill and Wang.
Koenker, Diane 1981, *Moscow Workers and the 1917 Revolution*, Princeton: Princeton University Press.
Koenker, Diane 2005, *Republic of Labor: Russian Printers and Soviet Socialism, 1919–1930*, Ithaca: Cornell University Press.
Kokosalakis, Yiannis 2015, '"Merciless War" against Trifles: The Leningrad Party Organizaton after the Fall of the Zinoviev Opposition', *Revolutionary Russia*. 28, 1: 48–68.
Komar, Vitaly and Alexander Melamid, Jamey Gambrell 1983, 'On the Experiment of Artistic Associations in Soviet Russia', *The Journal of Arts, Management and Law*, translated by Jamey Gambrell, 13, 1: 166–9.
Kotkin, Stephen 2014, *Stalin: Paradoxes of Power, 1878–1928*, New York: Penguin Press.
Kotkin, Stephen 2017, *Stalin: Waiting for Hitler, 1929–1941*, New York: Penguin Press.

Kozelev, B. 1927, *Mikhail Pavlovich Tomskii: Biograficheskii ocherk*, Moscow: Profizdat.

Kozlov, A.I. 1991, *Stalin: Borb'ba za vlast'*, Rostov-na-Donu: Izdatel'stvo Rostovskogo universiteta.

Krasil'nikov, S.A., A.I. Savin, S.N. Ushakov, 'Shakhinskii politicheskii protsessy 1928 goda: istochniki v kontekste epokhi', in Krasil'nikov (ed.) 2011: 10–70.

Krausz, Tamas 2015, *Reconstructing Lenin: An Intellectual Biography*, translated by Balint Bethlenfalvy, New York: Monthly Review Press.

Krylov, V.V. and E.V. Kichatova 2004, *Izdatel'stvo 'Academia': Liudi i knigi, 1921–1938–1991*, Moscow: Izdatel'stvo Academia.

Kudrova, Irma 2004, *The Last Days of Marina Tsvetaeva*, translated by Mary Ann Szporluk, Woodstock, NY: Overlook Duckworth.

Kuhr-Korolev, Corinna 2011, 'Women and Cars in Soviet and Russian Society', in *The Socialist Car: Automobility in the Eastern Bloc*, edited by Lewis H. Siegelbaum, Ithaca: Cornell University Press.

Kulikova, I.S. and B. Ia. Khazanov 1988, 'Mikhail Pavlovich Tomskii,' *Voprosy istorii*, 8: 64–83.

Kumanev, V.A. and I.S. Kulikova 1994, *Protivostoianie: Krupskaia – Stalin*, Moscow: Nauka.

Kun, Miklosh 1992, *Bukharin: Ego druz'ia i vragi*, Moscow: Respublika.

Kun, Miklosh 2003, *Stalin: An Unknown Portrait*, Budapest: Central European University Press.

Kuromiya, Hiroaki 1988, *Stalin's Industrial Revolution: Politics and Workers, 1928–1932*, Cambridge: Cambridge University Press.

Kuromiya, Hiroaki 1997, 'The Intelligentsia during the Soviet Regime: The Shakhty Affair', *South East European Monitor*, 4, 2: 41–64.

Kuromiya, Hiroaki 1998, *Freedom and Terror in the Donbas: A Ukrainian-Russian Borderland, 1870s–1990s*, Cambridge: Cambridge University Press.

Kuromiya, Hiroaki 2008, 'Stalin in the Light of the Politburo Transcripts', in *The Lost Politburo Transcripts: From Collective Rule to Stalin's Dictatorship*, edited by Paul R. Gregory and Norman Naimark, New Haven: Yale University Press.

Lampert, Nicholas 1979, *The Technical Intelligentsia and the Soviet State*, London: Macmillan Press.

Lane, David 1969, *The Roots of Russian Communism: A Social and Historical Study of Russian Social Democracy, 1898–1997*, Assen, Netherlands: Van Gorcum.

Laybourn, Keith 1992, *History of British Trade Unionism, c. 1770–1990*, Wolfeboro Falls, NH: A. Sutton.

Lazitch, Branko and Milorad M. Drachkovitch 1972, *Lenin and the Comintern*, vol. 1, Stanford: Hoover Institution Press.

Lazitch, Branko and Milorad M. Drachkovitch 1986, *Biographical Dictionary of the Comintern*, revised edition, Stanford: Hoover Institution Press.

Le Blanc, Paul 1990, *Lenin and the Revolutionary* Party, Atlantic Highlands, NJ: Humanities Press International.

Le Blanc, Paul 2015, *Leon Trotsky*, London: Reaktion Books.

Lee, Stephen J. 1996, *Aspects of British Political History, 1914–1995*, London: Routledge.

Leggett, George 1981, *The Cheka: Lenin's Political Police*, Oxford: Clarendon Press.

Lenoe, Matthew 2004, *Closer to the Masses: Stalinist Culture, Social Revolution, and Soviet Newspapers*, Cambridge, MA: Harvard University Press.

Lenoe, Matthew 2010, *The Kirov Murder and Soviet History*, New Haven: Yale University Press.

Levin, Dan 1965, *Stormy Petrel: The Life and Work of Maxim Gorky*, New York: Appleton-Century.

Levine, Isaac Don 1931, *Stalin*, New York: Cosmopolitan Book Corporation.

Lewin, Moshe 1968, *Russian Peasants and Soviet Power: A Study of Collectivization*, translated by Irene Nove, New York: George Allen & Unwin.

Lewin, Moshe 1985, *The Making of the Soviet System: Essays in the Social History of Interwar Russia*, New York: Pantheon.

Lewin, Moshe 1997, 'Stalin in the Mirror of the Other', in *Stalinism and Nazism: Dictatorships in Comparison*, edited by Ian Kershaw and Moshe Lewin, Cambridge: Cambridge University Press.

Liebich, Andre 1997, *From the Other Shore: Russian Social Democracy after 1921*, Cambridge, MA: Harvard University Press.

Lih, Lars T. 2011, 'The Ironic Triumph of Old Bolshevism: The Debates of April 1917 in Context,' *Russian History*, 38, 2: 199–242.

Lobok, D.V. 2006, 'Profsoiuzy sovetskoi rossii v usloviiakh novoi ekonomicheskoi politiki (1921–1928 gg.)', *Vesnik Sankt-Peterburgskogo universiteta*, 2, 4: 155–68.

Lobok, D.V. 2007, 'Profsoiuzy i sovetskoe gosudarstvo v usloviiakh stanovleniia komando-adminstrativnoi sistemy (1929–1930 gg.)', *Izvestiia Rossiiskogo gosudarstvennogo pedagogicheskogo universiteta im. A.I. Gertsena*, 2007: 165–77.

Lorenz, Richard 1994, 'Economic Bases of the Basmachi Movement in the Farghana Valley', *Muslim Communities Reemerge: Historical Perspectives on Nationality, Politics, and Opposition in the Former Soviet Union and Yugoslavia*, edited by Edward Allworth, Durham, NC: Duke University Press.

Lovell, Stephen 2003, *Summerfolk: A History of the Dacha, 1710–2000*, Ithaca: Cornell University Press.

Lunacharsky, Anatoly Vasilievich 1968, *Revolutionary Silhouettes*, translated by Michael Glenny, New York: Hill and Wang.

MacFarlane, L.J. 1966, *The British Communist Party: Its Origin and Development until 1929*, London: MacGibbon & Kee.

Mackinnon, Elaine 2005, 'Writing History for Stalin: Isaak Izrailevich Mints and the *Istoriia grazhdanskoi voiny*', *Kritika*, 6, 1: 5–54.

Malle, Sivana 1985, *The Economic Organization of War Communism, 1918–1921*, Cambridge: Cambridge University Press.
Mally, Lynn 2000, *Revolutionary Acts: Amateur Theater and the Soviet State, 1917–1938*, Ithaca: Cornell University Press.
Mandel, Bernard 1963, *Samuel Gompers: A Biography*, Yellow Springs, Ohio: Antioch Press.
Mandel, David 1984, *The Petrograd Workers and the Soviet Seizure of Power: From the July Days 1917 to July 1918*, London: Macmillan Press.
Manley, Rebecca 2009, *To the Tashkent Station: Evacuation and Survival in the Soviet Union at War*, Ithaca: Cornell University Press.
Manning, Roberta T. 2001, 'The Rise and Fall of "the Extraordinary Measures", January-June, 1928: Toward a Reexamination of the Onset of the Stalin Revolution', *The Carl Beck Papers in Russian & East European Studies*, No. 1504: 1–62.
Marshall, Alexander 2003, 'Turkfront: Frunze and the Development of Soviet Counter-Insurgency in Central Asia', *Central Asia: Aspects of Transition*, edited by Tom Everett-Heath, New York: Routledge.
Martin, Roderick 1969, *Communism and the British Trade Unions, 1924–1933: A Study of the National Minority Movement*, Oxford: Clarendon Press.
Massell, Gregory J. 1974, *The Surrogate Proletariat: Moslem Women and Revolutionary Strategies in Soviet Central Asia, 1919–1929*, Princeton: Princeton University Press.
Matthews, Mervyn 1978, *Privilege in the Soviet Union: A Study of Elite Life-Styles under Communism*, London: George Allen & Unwin.
Mawdsley, Evan 1991, *Blue Guide: Moscow and Leningrad*, second edition, New York: W.W. Norton.
Mawdsley, Evan 1987, *The Russian Civil War*, Boston: Allen & Unwin.
Mawdsley, Evan and Stephen White 2000, *The Soviet Elite from Lenin to Gorbachev: The Central Committee and It Members, 1917–1991*, Oxford: Oxford University Press.
Maynard, Sir John 1948, *Russia in Flux*, New York: Macmillan Co.
McAuley, Mary 1969, *Labour Disputes in Soviet Russia, 1957–1965*, Oxford: Clarendon Press.
McAuley, Mary 1991, *Bread and Justice: State and Society in Petrograd, 1917–1922*, Oxford: Clarendon Press.
McCormick, Anne O'Hare 1929, *The Hammer and the Scythe: Communist Russia Enters the Second Decade*, New York: A.A. Knopf.
McDermott, Kevin and Jeremy Agnew 1996, *The Comintern: A History of International Communism from Lenin to Stalin*, New York: St. Martin's Press.
McDermott, Kevin 2006, *Stalin: Revolutionary in an Era of War*, New York: Palgrave Macmillan.
McDonald, Geoffrey 1975, 'The Defeat of the General Strike', in *The Politics of Reappraisal, 1918–1939*, edited by Gillian Peele and Chris Cook, London: Macmillan.

McNeal, Robert H. 1972, *Bride of the Revolution: Krupskaya and Lenin*, Ann Arbor: University of Michigan Press.

McNeal, Robert H. 1975, *The Bolshevik Tradition: Lenin, Stalin, Khrushchev, Brezhnev*, Englewood Cliffs, NJ: Prentice-Hall.

McNeal, Robert H. 1988, *Stalin: Man and Ruler*, New York: New York University Press.

Medvedev, Roy 1977, 'New Pages from the Political Biography of Stalin' in *Stalinism, Essays in Historical Interpretation*, edited by Robert C. Tucker, New York: W.W. Norton.

Medvedev, Roy 1979, *On Stalin and Stalinism*, translated by Ellen de Kadt, Oxford: Oxford University Press.

Medvedev, Roy 1980, *Nikolai Bukharin: The Last Years*, translated by A.D.P. Briggs, New York: W.W. Norton.

Medvedev, Roy 1989, *Let History Judge: The Origins and Consequences of Stalinism*, revised edition, edited and translated by George Shriver, New York: Columbia University Press.

Medvedev, Roy and Zhores Medvedev 2004, *The Unknown Stalin: His Life, Death, and Legacy*, translated by Ellen Dahrendorf, New York: The Overlook Press.

Merridale, Catherine 1988, 'The Origins of the Stalinist State: Power and Politics in Moscow, 1928–32', in *Politics, Society and Stalinism in the USSR*, edited by John Channon, New York: St. Martin's Press.

Merridale, Catherine 1989, 'The Reluctant Opposition: The Right "Deviation" in Moscow, 1928', *Soviet Studies*, 41, 3: 382–400.

Merridale, Catherine 1990, *Moscow Politics and the Rise of Stalin: The Communist Party in the Capital, 1925–32*, New York: Palgrave Macmillan.

Merridale, Catherine 1995, 'The Making of a Moderate Bolshevik: An Introduction to L.B. Kamenev's Political Biography' in *Soviet History, 1917–53: Essays in Honour of R.W. Davies*, edited by Julian Cooper, Maureen Perie, and E.A. Rees, New York: St. Martin's Press.

Merridale, Catherine 2013, *Red Fortress: History and Illusion in the Kremlin*, New York: Metropolitan Books/Henry Holt and Company.

Merridale, Catherine 2017, *Lenin on the Train*, New York: Metropolitan Books/Henry Holt and Company.

Meyer, Alfred G. 1978, 'The War Scare of 1927', *Soviet Union/Union Sovietique*, 5, 1: 1–25.

Millar, James R. 1990, *The Soviet Economic Experiment*, edited by Susan J. Linz, Urbana: University of Illinois Press.

Miller, Martin A. and Ylana N. Miller 1988, 'Suicide and Suicidology in the Soviet Union', *Suicide and Life-Threating Behavior*, 12: 4: 303–21.

Montefiore, Simon Sebag 2004, *Stalin: The Court of the Red Tsar*, New York: Alfred A. Knopf.

Montefiore, Simon Sebag 2007, *Young Stalin*, New York: Alfred A. Knopf.

Morgan, Kevin 2013, *Bolshevism, Syndicalism and the General Strike: The Lost Internationalist World of A.A. Purcell*, London: Lawrence & Wishart.
Morris, Margaret 1976, *The General Strike*, Harmondsworth, Middlesex: Penguin Books.
Mowatt, Charles Loch 1955, *Britain between the Wars, 1918–1940*, Chicago: University of Chicago Press.
Morrison, Alexander 2015, 'Peasant Settlers and the 'Civilising Mission' in Russian Turkestan, 1865–1917', *The Journal of Imperial and Commonwealth History*, 43, 3: 387–413.
Murav'eva, L. and I. Sivolap-Kaftanova 1983, *Lenin in London: Memorial Places*, Moscow: Progress Publishers.
Murphy, Kevin 2001, 'Opposition at the Local Level: A Case Study of the Hammer and Sickle Factory', *Europe-Asia Studies*, 53: 2: 329–50.
Murphy, Kevin 2005, *Revolution and Counterrevolution: Class Struggle in a Moscow Metal Factory*, New York: Berghahn Books.
Naumov, Leonid 2010, *Stalin i NKVD*, Moscow: Novyi khronograf.
Nazarov, A.I. 1952, *Ocherki istorii sovetskogo knigoizdatel'stva*, Moscow: Iskusstvo.
Nettl, J.P. 1969, *Rosa Luxemburg*, abridged edition, Oxford: Oxford University Press.
Nicolaevsky, Boris I. 1965, *Power and the Soviet Elite: 'The Letter of an Old Bolshevik' and Other Essays*, edited by Janet D. Zagoria, New York: Praeger.
Northrop, Douglas 2004, *Veiled Empire: Gender and Power in Stalinist Central Asia*, Ithaca: Cornell University Press.
Nosach, V.I. 2001, *Professional'nye soiuzy Rossii (1905–1930)*, St. Petersburg: Sankt-Peterburgskii Gumanitarnyi Universitet Profsoiuzov.
Nosach, V.I. 2005, *Profsoiuznye lidery cherez tiur'my i ssylki: Istoriko-biograficheskie ocherki o vidneishikh deiateliakh professional'nogo dvizheniia Rossii*, second edition, Moscow: Nestor.
Nosach, V.I. and N.D. Zvereva 2007, *Rasstel'nye 30-e gody i profsoiuzy*, St. Petersburg: Izdatel'stvo Sankt-Peterburgskii Gumanitarnyi Universitet Profsoiuzov.
Nove, Alec 1992, *An Economic History of the USSR, 1917–1991*, third edition, New York: Penguin Press.
Olcott, Martha B. 1981, 'The Basmachi or Freemen's Revolt', *Soviet Studies*, 33:3, 352–69.
Olcott, Martha B. 1997, 'The Revolution in Central Asia', in *Critical Companion to the Russian Revolution, 1914–1921*, edited by Edward Acton, Vladimir Iu. Cherniaev, and William G. Rosenberg, Bloomington: Indiana University Press.
Oppenheim, Samuel A. 1967, 'Rehabilitation in the Post-Stalinist Soviet Union', *The Western Political Quarterly*, 20, 1: 97–113.
Oppenheim, Samuel A. 1977, 'The Making of a Right Communist: A.I. Rykov to 1917', *Slavic Review*, 36, 3: 420–40.
Oppenheim, Samuel A. 1979, *The Practical Bolshevik: A.I. Rykov and Russian Communism, 1881–1938*, Stanford: Hoover Institution Press.

Orlov, Alexander 1953, *The Secret History of Stalin's Crimes*, New York: Random House.
Pahlen, Konstantin 1964, *Mission to Tashkent*, translated by N.J. Couriss, London: J. Cape.
Pal'vadre, Ia. 1927, *1905 g. v Estonii v prilozhemno-dokumenty*, Leningrad: Rabochee izdatl'stvo 'Priboi'.
Pankratov A. Ia. 1972, Mezhdunarodnaia deiatel'nost' sovetskikh profsoiuzov, 1918–1941 gg., Gor'kii: Volgo-viatskoe knizhnoe izdatel'stvo.
Park, Alexander Garland 1957, *Bolshevism in Turkestan, 1917–1921*, New York: Columbia University Press.
Pavlov, I. 2001, *1920-e: revoliutsiia i biurokratiia: Zapiski oppozitsionera*, St. Petersburg: Peterburg – XXI vek.
Pelling, Henry 1987, *A History of British Trade Unionism*, fourth edition, London: Macmillan.
Peterson, Maya K. 2019, *Pipe Dreams: Water and Empire in Central Asia's Aral Sea Basin*, Cambridge: Cambridge University Press.
Phillips, Laura L. 2000, *Bolsheviks and the Bottle: Drink and Worker Culture in St. Petersburg, 1900–1929*, Dekalb: Northern Illinois University Press.
Pianciola, Niccolo 2001, 'The Collectivization Famine in Kazakhstan, 1931–1933', *Harvard Ukrainian Studies*, 25, 3–4: 237–51.
Pianciola, Niccolo and Paolo Sartori 2007, '*Waqf* in Turkestan: The Colonial Legacy and the Fate of an Islamic Institution in Early Soviet Central Asia, 1917–1924', *Central Asian Survey*, 26, 4: 475–98.
Pianciola, Niccolo and Elise Gaignebet 2008, 'Decoloniser l'Asie centrale? Bolcheviks et colons au Semirec'e (1920–1922)', *Cahiers du monde russe*, 49, 1: 101–43.
Pierce, Richard A. 1960, *Russian Central Asia, 1867–1917: A Study in Colonial Rule*, Berkeley: University of California Press.
Pinnow, Kenneth M. 2010, *Lost to the Collective: Suicide and the Promise of Soviet Socialism, 1921–1929*, Ithaca: Cornell University Press.
Pipes, Richard 1974, *The Formation of the Soviet Union: Communism and Nationalism, 1917–1923*, revised edition, New York: Athenuem.
Pipes, Richard 1990, *The Russian Revolution*, New York: Random House.
Pipes, Richard 1994, *Russia under the Bolshevik Regime*, New York: Random House.
Pipes, Richard 1995, *A Concise History of the Russian Revolution*, New York: Alfred A. Knopf.
Pirani, Simon 2008, *The Russian Revolution in Retreat, 1920–24: Soviet Workers and the New Communist Elite*, New York: Routledge.
Pisarenko, K.N. 2006, *Tridtsatiletniaia voina v Politbiuro, 1923–1953*, Moscow: Veche.
Plamper, Jan 2001, 'Abolishing Ambiguity: Soviet Censorship Practices in the 1930s', *The Russian Review*, 60, 4: 526–44.
Plekhanov, A.M. 2006, *VChK-OGPU v gody novoi ekonomicheskoi politiki, 1921–1928*, Moscow: Kuchkovo pole.

Pogorelskin, Alexis 2000, 'Kamenev and the Peasant Question: The Turn to Opposition, 1924–1925', *Russian History/Histoire Russe*, 27, 4: 381–95.

Pogorelskin, Alexis 2019, 'Under Seven Seals: New Perspectives on Lenin's Testament', *Canadian-American Slavic Studies*, 53: 90–106.

Pohl, J. Otto 1997, *The Stalinist Penal System: A Statistical History of Soviet Repression and Terror, 1930–1953*, Jefferson, NC: McFarland.

Polonsky, Rachel 2010, *Molotov's Magic Lantern: Travels in Russian History*, New York: Farrar, Straus, and Giroux.

Pospielovsky, Andrew 1997, 'Strikes during the NEP', *Revolutionary Russia*, 10, 1: 1–34.

Priestland, David 2007, *Stalinism and the Politics of Mobilization: Ideas, Power, and Terror in Inter-War Russia*, Oxford: Oxford University Press.

Rabinowitch, Alexander 1968, *Prelude to Revolution: The Petrograd Bolsheviks and the July 1917 Uprisings*, Bloomington: Indiana University Press.

Rabinowitch, Alexander 1976, *The Bolsheviks Come to Power: The Revolution in Petrograd*, New York: W.W. Norton.

Rabinowitch, Alexander 2007, *The Bolsheviks in Power: The First Year of Soviet Rule in Petrograd*, Bloomington: Indiana University Press.

Radkey, Oliver H. 1968 [1950], *Russia Goes to the Polls: The Election to the All-Russian Constituent Assembly, 1917*, Ithaca: Cornell University Press.

Radzinsky, Edvard 1996, *Stalin: The First In-Depth Biography Based on Explosive New Documents from Russia's Secret Archives*, translated by H.T. Willetts, New York: Doubleday.

Rappaport, Helen 1999, *Joseph Stalin: A Biographical Companion*, Santa Barbara: ABC-Clio.

Rappaport, Helen 2010, *Conspirator: Lenin in Exile*, New York: Basic Books.

Rayfield, Donald 2004, *Stalin and His Hangmen: The Tyrant and Those Who Killed for Him*, London: Viking.

Razumovsky, Maria 1994, *Tsvetayeva: A Critical Biography*, translated by Aleksey Gibson, New Castle upon Tyne: Bloodaxe Books.

Read, Christopher 1996, *From Tsar to Soviet: The Russian People and Their Revolution, 1917–21*, New York: Oxford University Press.

Read, Christopher 2005, *Lenin: A Revolutionary Life*, New York: Routledge.

Rees, E.A. 1987, *State Control in Soviet Russia: The Rise and Fall of the Workers and Peasants' Inspectorate, 1920–1934*, Basingstoke: Macmillan.

Rees, E.A. 1988, 'Stalinism: The Primacy of Politics', in *Politics, Society and Stalinism in the USSR*, edited by John Channon, New York: St. Martin's Press.

Rees, E.A. 2004, 'Stalin as Leader 1924–1937: From Oligarch to Dictator', in *The Nature of Stalin's Dictatorship: The Politburo, 1924–1953*, edited by E.A. Rees, New York: Palgrave Macmillan.

Rees, E.A. 2012, *Iron Lazar: A Political Biography of Lazar Kaganovich*, New York: Anthem Press.
Reiman, Michal 1987 [1979], *The Birth of Stalinism: The USSS on the Eve of the 'Second Revolution'*, translated by George Saunders, Bloomington: Indiana University Press.
Riddell, Neil 2000, 'Walter Citrine and the British Labour Movement, 1925–1935', *History*, 85: 285–306.
Rieber, Alfred J. 2001, 'Stalin: Man of the Borderlands', *The American Historical Review*, 106, 5: 1651–91.
Rigby, T.H. 1968, *Communist Party Membership in the USSR*, Princeton: Princeton University Press.
Rigby, T.H. 1979, *Lenin's Government: Sovnarkom, 1917–1922*, Cambridge: Cambridge University Press.
Rittersporn, Gabor T. 1993, 'The Omnipresent Conspiracy: On Soviet Imagery of Politics and Social Relations in the 1930s', in *Stalinist Terror*, edited by Getty and Manning, Cambridge: Cambridge University Press.
Robin, Regine 1992, *Socialist Realism: An Impossible Aesthetic*, translated by Catherine Porter, Stanford: Stanford University Press.
Rogovin, Vadim Z. 1993, *Vlast' i oppozitsii*, Moscow: Teatr.
Rogovin, Vadim Z. 1997, *Partiia rasstreliainykh*, Moscow: Moskva.
Rogovin, Vadim Z. 1998, *1937: Stalin's Year of Terror*, translated by Frederick S. Choate, Oak Park, MI: Mehring Books.
Rokitianskii, Iakov and Reinard Muller 1996, *Krasnyi dissident: Akademik Riazanov: Opponent Lenina, zhertva Stalina*, Moscow: Izdatel'stvo 'Academia'.
Rokitianskii, Ia. G. 2009, *Gumanist oktiabr'skoi epokhi: Akademik D.B. Riazanov: Sotsial-demokrat, pravozashchitnik, uchenii*, Moscow: Sobranie.
Rosenbaum, Kurt 1962, 'The German Involvement in the Shakhty Trial', *Russian Review*, 21, 3: 238–60.
Rosenberg, Arthur 1934, *A History of Bolshevism: From Marx to the First Five Year Plan*, translated from the German by Ian F.D. Morrow, London: Oxford University Press.
Rosenberg, William G. 1989, 'The Social Background to Tsektran', in *Party, State, and Society in the Russian Civil War*, edited by Diane P. Koenker, William G. Rosenberg, and Ronald Grigor Suny, Bloomington: Indiana University Press.
Rosmer, Alfred 1971, *Moscow under Lenin*, translated by Ian H. Berchall, New York: Monthly Review Press.
Rossman, Jeffrey J. 2002, 'A Workers' Strike in Stalin's Russia: The Vichuga Uprising of April 1932', in *Contending with Stalinism: Soviet Power and Popular Resistance in the 1930s*, edited by Lynne Viola, Ithaca: Cornell University Press.
Rossman, Jeffrey J. 2005, *Worker Resistance under Stalin: Class and Revolution on the Shop Floor*, Cambridge, MA: Harvard University Press.

Rousset, David 1982, *The Legacy of the Bolshevik Revolution*, translated by Alan Freeman, London: St. Martin's Press.
Rubinstein, Joshua 2011, *Leon Trotsky: A Revolutionary's Life*, New Haven: Yale University Press.
Rubinstein, Joshua 2016, *The Last Days of Stalin*, New Haven: Yale University Press.
Rubinstein, Joshua and Vladimir P. Naumov (eds) 2005, *Stalin's Secret Pogrom: The Postwar Inquisition of the Jewish Anti-Fascist Committee*, translated by Laura Esther Wolfson, abridged edition, New Haven: Yale University Press.
Ruble, Blair A. 1981, *Soviet Trade Unions: Their Development in the 1970s*, Cambridge: Cambridge University Press.
Ruder, Cynthia A. 1998, *Making History for Stalin: The Story of the Belomor Canal*, Gainesville: University Press of Florida.
Rudnev, D. 1989, 'Vozvrashchenie Mikhaila Tomskogo', *Kommunist Estonii*, 1: 96–103.
Runin, Boris Mikhailovich 1995, *Moe okruzhenie: Zapiska sluchaino utselevshego*, Moscow: Vosvrashchenie.
Rywkin, Michael 1990, *Moscow's Muslim Challenge: Soviet Central Asia*, revised edition, Armonk, NY: M.E. Sharpe.
Rywkin, Michael 1994, *Moscow's Lost Empire*, Armonk, NY: M.E. Sharp.
Sahadeo Jeff 2007, *Russian Colonial Society in Tashkent, 1865–1923*, Bloomington: Indiana University Press.
Sakharov, V.A. 2003, *'Politicheskoe zaveshchanie' Lenina: Real'nost' istorii i mify politiki*, Moscow: Izdatel'stvo Moskovskogo universiteta.
Sakwa, Richard 1988, *Soviet Communists in Power: A Study of Moscow during the Civil War, 1918–21*, New York: St. Martin's Press.
Sakwa, Richard 1995, 'The Soviet State, Civil Society and Moscow Politics: Stability and Order in Early NEP, 1921–24' in *Soviet History, 1917–53: Essays in Honour of R.W. Davies*, edited by Julian Cooper, Maureen Perrie, and E.A. Rees, New York: St. Martin's Press.
Sartori, Paolo 2010, 'What Went Wrong? The Failure of Soviet Policy on *Shari'a* Courts in Turkestan, 1917–1923', *Die Welt des Islams*, 50, 3–4: 397–434.
Schapiro, Leonard 1960, *The Communist Party of the Soviet Union*, New York: Random House.
Schapiro, Leonard 1977 [1955], *The Origin of the Communist Autocracy: Political Opposition in the Soviet State, First Phase, 1917–1922*, second edition, Cambridge, MA: Harvard University Press.
Schapiro, Leonard and Joseph Godson 1984, *The Soviet Worker: From Lenin to Andropov*, second edition, New York: Macmillan.
Schlogel, Karl 2012, *Moscow, 1937*, translated by Rodney Livingstone, Cambridge: Polity Press.
Schwarz, Solomon M. 1951, *Labor in the Soviet Union*, New York: Praeger.

Schweitzer, Viktoria 1992, *Tsvetaeva*, translated by Robert Chandler and H.T. Willets, London: Harvill.

Sebestyen, Victor 2017, *Lenin: The Man, the Dictator, and the Master of Terror*, New York, Pantheon Books.

Senin, A.S. 1993, *A.I. Rykov: Stranitsy zhizni*, Moscow: Izdatel'stvo Moskovskogo gosudarstvennogo otkrytogo universiteta.

Serge, Victor 1937a, *From Lenin to Stalin*, translated by Ralph Manheim, New York: Monad Press.

Serge, Victor 1937b, *Russia Twenty Years After*, translated by Max Shachtman, New York: Hillman-Curl.

Serge, Victor 1992 [1930], *Year One of the Russian Revolution*, New York: Writers and Readers.

Service, Robert 1985, *Lenin: A Political Life*: Vol. 1: *The Strengths of Contradiction*, Bloomington: Indiana University Press.

Service, Robert 1991, *Lenin: A Political Life*: Vol. 2: *Worlds in Collision*, Bloomington: Indiana University Press.

Service, Robert 1995, *Lenin: A Political Life*: Vol. 3: *The Iron Ring*, Bloomington: Indiana University Press.

Service, Robert 1999, *The Russian Revolution, 1920–1927*, third edition, New York: Palgrave.

Service, Robert 2004, *Stalin: A Biography*, Cambridge, MA: Harvard University Press.

Service, Robert 2009, *Trotsky: A Biography*, Cambridge, MA: Harvard University Press.

Shapovalova, L.D. 1988, 'Dokumenty TsGAOR SSSR o diatel'nosti M.P. Tomskogo', *Sovetskie arkhivy*, 6: 62–5.

Shapovalova, L.D. 1989, 'M.P. Tomskii: Materialy k biografii', *Istoriia SSSR*, 2: 82–96.

Shatunovskaia, Lidiia 1982, *Zhizn' v Kremle*, New York: Chalidze Publications.

Shearer, David R. 1996, *Industry, State, and Society in Stalin's Russia, 1926–1934*, Ithaca: Cornell University Press.

Shearer, David R. 2009, *Policing Stalin's Socialism: Repression and Social Order in the Soviet Union, 1924–1953*, New Haven: Yale University Press.

Shelestov, D.K. 1988, 'Do vystrela v Bolshevo', *Ogonek*, 31: 26–7.

Shelestov, D.K. 1990, *Vremia Alekseia Rykova*, Moscow: Progress.

Shelley, Louise 1982, 'Female Criminality in the 1920s: A Consequence of Inadvertent and Deliberate Change', *Russian History*, 9, 2–3: 265–84.

Shimotomai, Nobuo 1983, 'Defeat of the Right Opposition in the Moscow Party Organization, 1928', *Japanese Slavic and East European Studies*, 4: 15–34.

Shishkin, I.V. 1989, 'Delo Riutina', *Voprosy istorii*, 7: 33–52.

Shishkin, V.A. 2002, *Stanovlenie vneshnei politiki poslerevoliutsionnoi Rossii (1917–1930 gody) i kapitalisticheskii mir: Ot revoliutsionnogo 'zapadnichestva' k 'natsional-bol'shevizmy'*, St. Peterburg: Izdatel'stvo 'Dmitrii Bulanin'.

Shkliarevsky, Gennady 1993, *Labor in the Russian Revolution: Factory Committees and Trade Unions, 1917–1918*, New York: St. Martin's Press.

Shmelev, Gelii 1989, 'Pered povorotom', in *Surovaia drama naroda: Uchenye i publitsisty o prirode stalinizma*, edited by V.M. Podugol'nikov et al., Moscow: Politizdat.

Siegelbaum, Lewis H. 1992, *Soviet State and Society between Revolutions, 1918–1929*, Cambridge: Cambridge University Press.

Siegelbaum, Lewis H. 2008, *Cars for Comrades: The Life of the Soviet Automobile*, Ithaca: Cornell University Press.

Siegelbum, Lewis and Andrei Sokolov 2000, *Stalinism as a Way of Life: A Narrative in Documents*, New Haven: Yale University Press.

Sirianni, Carmen 1982, *Workers Control and Socialist Democracy: The Soviet Experience*, London: Verso.

Slezkine, Yuri 2017, *The House of Government: A Saga of the Russian Revolution*, Princeton: Princeton University Press.

Slonim, Marc 1977, *Soviet Russian Literature: Writers and Problems, 1917–1977*, second revised edition, New York: Oxford University Press.

Slusser, Robert M. 1987, *Stalin in October: The Man Who Missed the Revolution*, Baltimore: The Johns Hopkins University Press.

Smele, Jon 2015, *The 'Russian' Civil Wars, 1916–1926: Ten Years that Shook the World*, New York: Oxford University Press.

Smith, Jeremy 1999, *The Bolsheviks and the National Question, 1917–23*, New York: St. Martin's Press.

Smith, S.A. 1983, *Red Petrograd: Revolution in the Factories, 1917–1918*, Cambridge: Cambridge University Press.

Smith, S.A. 2017, *Russia in Revolution: An Empire in Crisis, 1890–1928*, Oxford: Oxford University Press.

Sochor, Zenovia A. 1988, *Revolution and Culture: The Bogdanov-Lenin Controversy*, Ithaca: Cornell University Press.

Solzhenitsyn, Aleksandr I. 1973, *The Gulag Archipelago, 1918–1956: An Experiment in Literary Investigation I–II*, translated by Thomas P. Whitney, New York: Harper & Row.

Sontag John P. 1975, 'The Soviet War Scare of 1926–27', *Russian Review*, 34, 1: 66–77.

Sorenson, Jay B. 1969, *The Life and Death of Soviet Trade Unionism, 1917–1928*, New York: Atherton Press.

Souvarine, Boris 1939, *Stalin: A Critical Survey of Bolshevism*, translated by C.L.R. James, New York: Longmans, Green & Co.

Spiridonova, L. 2013, *Nastoiashchii Gor'kii: Mify i real'nost'*, Moscow: IMLI RAN.

Starkov, Boris 1992, 'Trotsky and Ryutin: From the History of the Anti-Stalin Resistance in the 1930s', *The Trotsky Reappraisal*, edited by Terry Brotherstone and Paul Dukes, Edinburgh: Edinburgh University Press.

Startsev, V.I. 1989, Political Leaders of the Soviet State in 1922 and Early 1923, *Soviet Studies in History*, 28, 3: 5–40.

Steinberg, Mark D. 1982, *Moral Communities: The Culture of Class Relations in the Russian Printing Industry, 1867–1907*, Berkeley: University of California Press.

Steinberg, Mark D. 2017, *The Russian Revolution, 1905–1921*, New York: Oxford University Press.

Steinberg, Mark D. and Vladimir M. Khrustalev (eds) 1995, *The Fall of the Romanovs: Political Dreams and Personal Struggles in a Time of Revolution*, New Haven: Yale University Press.

Stites, Richard 1978, *The Women's Liberation Movement in Russia: Feminism, Nihilism, and Bolshevism, 1860–1930*, Princeton: Princeton University Press.

Stites, Richard 1989, *Revolutionary Dreams: Utopian Vision and Experimental Life in the Russian Revolution*, Oxford: Oxford University Press.

Stone, David R. 2000, *Hammer and Rifle: The Militarization of the Soviet Union, 1926–1933*, Lawrence: University of Kansas Press.

Stronski, Paul 2010, *Tashkent: Forging a Soviet City, 1930–1966*, Pittsburgh: University of Pittsburgh Press.

Sullivan, Rosemary 2015, *Stalin's Daughter: The Extraordinary and Tumultuous Life of Svetlana Alliluyeva*, New York: Harper.

Sunderland, William 2014, *The Baron's Cloak: A History of the Russian Empire in War and Revolution*, Ithaca: Cornell University Press.

Swain, Geoffrey 1983, *Russian Social Democracy and the Legal Labour Movement, 1906–14*, London: Macmillan Press.

Swain, Geoffrey 1987, 'Was the Profintern Really Necessary?' *European History Quarterly*, 17, 1: 57–77.

Swain, Geoffrey 2006, *Trotsky*, New York: Longman.

Swain, Geoffrey 2014, *Trotsky and the Russian Revolution*, London: Routledge.

Taniuchi, Yuzuru 1995, 'Decision-Making on the Ural-Siberian Method', in *Soviet History, 1917–53: Essays in Honour of R.W. Davies*, edited by Julian Cooper, Maureen Perrie, and E.A. Rees, New York: St. Martin's Press.

Taubman, William 2003, *Khrushchev: The Man and His Era*, New York: W.W. Norton.

Teichman, Christian 2018, 'Leviathan on the Oxus: Water and Soviet Power on the Lower Amu Darya, 1920s–1940s', *Eurasian Environments: Nature and Ecology in Imperial and Soviet History*, edited by Nicholas B. Breyfogle, Pittsburgh: University of Pittsburgh Press.

Teptsov, N. 1992, 'Tainyi agent Iosifa Stalina: Dokumental'naia istoriia o donosakh i donoschike', in *Neizvestnaia Rossiia XX vek*, edited by V.A. Kozlov, vol. 1, Moscow: Istoricheskoe nasledie.

Teshkin, Iu. A. (ed.) 1992, *Bolshevo: Literaturny istoriko-kraevedcheskii al'manakh*, second edition, Moscow: Pisatel'.

Thatcher, Ian D. 2003, *Trotsky*, London: Routledge.
Thompson John M. 1989, *Revolutionary Russia, 1917*, second edition, Long Grove, IL: Waveland Press.
Thorpe, Andrew 2000, *The British Communist Party and Moscow, 1920–1943*, Manchester: Manchester University Press.
Thurston, Robert 1993, 'The Stakhanovite Movement: Background to the Great Terror in the Factories, 1935–1938', in *Stalinist Terror: New Perspectives*, edited by J. Arch Getty and Roberta T. Manning, Cambridge: Cambridge University Press.
Thurston, Robert 1996, *Life and Terror in Stalin's Russia, 1934–1941*, New Haven: Yale University Press.
Tokaev, G.A. 1956, *Comrade X*, translated by Alec Brown, London: Harvill Press.
Toker, Leona 2008, 'Making the Unthinkable Thinkable: Language Microhistory of Politburo Meetings', in *The Lost Politburo Transcripts: From Collective Rule to Stalin's Dictatorship*, edited by Paul R. Gregory and Norman Naimark, New Haven: Yale University Press.
Tosstorff, Reiner 2003, 'Moscow versus Amsterdam', *Labor History Review*, 68, 1: 79–97.
Tosstorff, Reiner 2016, *The Red International of Labour Unions (RILU), 1920–1937*, translated by Ben Fowkes, Leiden: Brill.
Trukan, G.A. 1963, *Ian Rudzutak*, Moscow: Gosudarstvennoe izdatel'stvo politicheskoi literatury.
Tsuji, Yoshimasa 1989, 'The Debate on the Trade Unions, 1920–21', *Revolutionary Russia*, 2, 1: 31–100.
Tucker, Robert C. 1973, Stalin: *Stalin as Revolutionary, 1879–1929: A Study in History and Personality*, New York: W.W. Norton.
Tucker, Robert C. 1977, 'The Emergence of Stalin's Foreign Policy', *Slavic Review* 36, 4: 563–89.
Tucker, Robert C. 1990, *Stalin in Power: The Revolution from Above, 1928–1941*, New York: W.W. Norton.
Tumarkin, Nina 1983, *Lenin Lives! The Lenin Cult in Soviet Russia*, Cambridge, MA: Harvard University Press.
Turtan, Katy 2010, 'The Revolutionary, His Wife, the Party, and the Sympathizer: The Role of Family Members and Party Supporters in the Release of Revolutionary Prisoners', *The Russian Review*, 69, 1: 73–92.
Ulam, Adam B. 1965, *The Bolsheviks: The Intellectual and Political History of the Triumph of Communism in Russia*, Cambridge, MA: Harvard University Press.
Ulam, Adam B. 1968, *Expansion and Coexistence: The History of Soviet Foreign Policy*, New York: Praeger.
Ulam, Adam B. 1973, *Stalin: The Man and His Era*, Boston: Beacon Press.
Uldricks, Teddy J. 1979, 'Russia and Europe: Diplomacy, Revolution, and Economic Development in the 1920s', *The International History Review*, 1, 1: 55–83.

Uralov, Alexander 1953, *The Reign of Stalin*, translated by L.J. Smith, London: Bodley Head.
Vaidyanath, R. 1967, *The Formation of the Soviet Central Asian Republics: A Study in Soviet Nationalities Policy, 1917–1936*, New Delhi: People's Public House.
Vaganov, F.M. 1970, *Pravyi uklon v VKP(b) i ego razgrom, 1928–1930 gg.*, Moscow: Politizdat.
Vaksberg, Arkady 1991, *Stalin's Prosecutor: The Life of Andrei Vyshinsky*, translated by Jan Butler, New York: Grove Weidenfeld.
Van Goethem, Geert 2006, *Amsterdam International: The World of the International Federation of Trade Unions (IFTU), 1913–1945*, Burlington, VT: Ashgate.
van Ree, Erik 2002, *The Political Thought of Joseph Stalin: A Study in Twentieth-Century Revolutionary Patriotism*, London: Routledge Curzon.
Vasil'eva, Larisa 1996, *Deti kremlia*, Moscow: Atlantida.
Vatlin, Alexander 2008, '"Class Brothers Unite!" The British General Strike and the Formation of the "United Opposition"' in *The Lost Politburo Transcripts: From Collective Rule to Stalin's Dictatorship*, edited by Paul R. Gregory and Norman Naimark, New Haven: Yale University Press.
Vatlin, Alexander 2009, *Komintern: Idei, resheniia, sud'by*, Moscow: Rosspen.
Vaughan, James, C. 1973, *Soviet Socialist Realism: Origins and Theory*, London: Macmillan.
Viola, Lynne 1987, *The Best Sons of the Fatherland: Workers in the Vanguard of Soviet Collectivization*, New York: Oxford University Press.
Viola, Lynne 1996, *Peasant Rebels under Stalin: Collectivization and the Culture of Peasant Resistance*, Oxford: Oxford University Press.
Volkogonov, Dmitri 1991, *Stalin: Triumph and Tragedy*, translated by Harold Shukman, Rocklin, CA: Prima Publishing.
Volkogonov, Dmitri 1994, *Lenin: A New Biography*, translated by Harold Shukman, New York: The Free Press.
Volkogonov, Dmitri 1996, *Trotsky: The Eternal Revolutionary*, translated by Harold Shukman, New York: The Free Press.
Volobuev, P.V. (ed.) 1993, *Politicheskie diiateli Rossii 1917: Biograficheskii slovar'*, Moscow: Bol'shaia Rossiiskaia entsiklopediia.
Von Geldern, James and Richard Stites (eds.) 1995, *Mass Culture in Soviet Russia: Tales, Poems, Songs, Movies, Plays and Folklore, 1917–1953*, Bloomington: Indiana University Press.
von Hagen, Mark 1990, *Soldiers in the Proletarian Dictatorship: The Red Army and the Soviet Socialist State, 1917–1930*, Ithaca: Cornell University Press.
Voskresenskii, Iu. V. and D.T. Subbotin 1966, 'Uchastie sovetskikh profsoiuzov v bor'be Kommunisticheskoi partii s trotskistami v 1926–1927 gg.', *Voprosy istorii KPSS*, 7: 113–19.

Voslensky, Michael 1984, *Nomenklatura: The Soviet Ruling Class*, translated by Eric Mosbacher, Garden City, NY: Doubleday.

Walker, Gregory P.M. 1991 'Soviet Publishing since the October Revolution', in *Books in Russia and the Soviet Union: Past and Present*, edited by Miranda Beaven Remnek, Wiesbaden: Harrassowitz.

Ward, Chris 1999, *Stalin's Russia*, second edition, London: Arnold.

Warth, Robert D. 1958, 'The Arcos Raid and the Anglo-Soviet "Cold War" of the 1920s', *World Affairs Quarterly*, 29, 2: 115–51.

Warth, Robert D. 1977, *Leon Trotsky*, Boston: Twayne Publishers.

Watson, Derek 2005, *Molotov: A Biography*, Houndmills: Palgrave Macmillan.

Weissman, Benjamin M. 1974, *Herbert Hoover and Famine Relief to Soviet Russia, 1921–1923*, Stanford: Hoover Institution Press.

Wheatcroft, Stephen G. 2004, 'From Team-Stalin to Degenerate Tyranny', in *The Nature of Stalin's Dictatorship: The Politburo, 1924–1953*, edited by E.A. Rees, New York: Palgrave Macmillan.

White, Stephen 1994, 'British Labour in Soviet Russia, 1920', *The English Historical Review*, 109, 432: 621–40.

Whitewood, Peter 2015, *The Red Army and the Great Terror: Stalin's Purge of the Soviet Military*, Lawrence: University of Kansas Press.

Wildman, Allan K. 1967, *The Making of a Workers' Revolution: Russian Social Democracy, 1891–1903*, Chicago: University of Chicago Press.

Williams, Andrew J. 1989, *Labour and Government: The Attitude of the Labour Party to the USSR, 1924–34*, Manchester: Manchester University Press.

Williams, Robert C. 1986, *The Other Bolsheviks: Lenin and His Critics, 1904–1914*, Bloomington: Indiana University Press.

Wolfe, Bertram B. 1957, *Khrushchev and Stalin's Ghost: Text, Background and Meaning of Khrushchev's Secret Report to the Twentieth Congress on the Night of February 24–25, 1956*, New York: Praeger.

Wolfe, Bertram B. 1970 'Dress Rehearsals for the Great Terror', *Studies in Comparative History*, 3, 2: 1–24.

Wood, Elizabeth A. 1997, *The Baba and the Comrade: Gender and Politics in Revolutionary Russia*, Bloomington: Indiana University Press.

Wood, Elizabeth A. 2005, *Performing Justice: Agitation Trials in Early Soviet Russia*, Ithaca: Cornell University Press.

Woods, Alan 1999, *Bolshevism: The Road to Revolution*, London: Wellred Publications.

Worley, Christopher 2002, *Class against Class: The Communist Party in Britain between the Wars*, London: I.B. Tauris.

Wynn, Charters 1992, *Workers, Strikes, and Pogroms: The Donbass-Dnepr Bend in Late Imperial Russia, 1870–1905*, Princeton: Princeton University Press.

Yedlin, Tova 1999, *Maxim Gorky: A Political Biography*, Westport, CT: Praeger.

Yemelianova, Galina M. 2002, *Russia and Islam: A Historical Survey*, New York: Palgrave Macmillan.

Zagorsky, S. 1930, *Wages and Regulation of Conditions of Labour in the USSR*, Geneva: P.S. King & Sons.

Zaleski, Eugene 1971 [1962], *Planning for Economic Growth in the Soviet Union, 1918–1931*, translated and edited by Marie-Christine MacAndrew and G. Warren Nutter, Chapel Hill: University of North Carolina Press.

Zalesskii, K.A. 2000, *Imperiia Stalina: Biograficheskii entsiklopedicheskii slovar'*, Moscow: Veche.

Zelnik, Reginald E. 1976a, 'Russian Bebels: An Introduction to the Memoirs of the Russian Workers Semen Kanatchikov and Matvei Fisher', *The Russian Review*, part one, 35, 3: 249–89.

Zelnik, Reginald E. 1976b, 'Russian Bebels: An Introduction to the Memoirs of the Russian Workers Semen Kanatchikov and Matvei Fisher', *The Russian Review*, part two, 35, 4: 417–47.

Zelnik, Reginald E. 1995, 'The Fate of a Russian Bebel: Semen Ivanovich Kanatchikov, 1905–1940', *The Carl Beck Papers in Russian and East European Studies*, 1105, Pittsburgh: REEES: 1–43.

Zenkovsky, Serge A. 1960, *Pan-Turkism and Islam in Russia*, Cambridge, MA: Harvard University Press.

Zhuravlev, V.V. et al. (eds) 1995, *Vlast i oppozitsiia: Rossiiskii politicheskii protsessy XX stoletiia*, Moscow: Rosspen.

Zinov'iev, Grigorii 1925, *God revoliutsii (fevral' 1917-mart 1918)*, Leningrad.

Dissertations and Unpublished Works

Black, T. Clayton 1996, 'Manufacturing Communists: Krasnyi Putilovets and the Politics of Soviet Industrialization, 1923–1932', PhD dissertation: Indiana University.

Bowman, B'Ann 1973, 'The Moscow Bolsheviks, February-November 1917', PhD dissertation: Indiana University.

Clement, Peter Albert 1987, 'Stalin and the Seventeenth Congress of the Communist Party in the Soviet Union: The Party in Conflict', PhD dissertation, Michigan State University.

Guillory, Sean 2009, 'We Shall Refashion Life on Earth! The Political Culture of the Young Communist League, 1918–1928', PhD dissertation: University of California, Los Angeles.

Hagenloh, Paul M. 1994, 'The Komsomol, 1927–28', MA thesis, University of Texas at Austin.

Hatch, John Brinley 1985, 'Labor and Politics in NEP Russia: Workers, Trade Unions and the Communist Party in Moscow, 1921–1926', PhD dissertation, University of California, Irvine.

Jo, Junbae 2007, 'Soviet Trade Unions during the Stalinist Industrialisation, 1928–1937', PhD dissertation, University of Birmingham.

Kassof Brian Evan 2000, 'The Knowledge Front: Politics, Ideology, and Economics in the Soviet Book Publishing Industry, 1925–1935', PhD dissertation, University of California, Berkeley.

Kocho-Williams, Alistair 2008, 'The Soviet Union and the British General Strike, 1926', BIHG Annual Conference, University of Ulster.

Langsam, David E. 1973, 'Pressure Group Politics in NEP Russia: The Case of the Trade Unions', PhD dissertation, Princeton University.

Morrell, Edwin Blackhurst 1965, 'Communist Unionism: Organized Labor and the Soviet State', PhD dissertation, Harvard University.

Oppenheim, S.A. 1972, 'Aleksei Ivanovich Rykov (1881–1938): A Political Biography', PhD dissertation, Indiana University.

Schrand, Thomas Gregory, 'Industrialization and the Stalinist Gender System: Women Workers in the Soviet Economy', PhD dissertation, University of Michigan.

Straus, Kenneth 1990, 'The Transformation of the Soviet Working Class, 1929–1935: The Regime in Search of a New Social Stability', PhD dissertation, University of Pennsylvania.

Index

Academy of Science 329, 329n95
agitational politics
   against Bolshevik Party 341n164, 363n301
   in Bolshevik Party 16, 30, 136, 136n120, 170–171, 384
alliance *see smychka*
Alliluyeva, Nadezhda 237–238, 238nn116–118, 342
All-Russian Central Council of Trade Unions (VTsSPS) 76n93, 93nn183–184, 99, 107n282, 167n167
   with Amsterdam and British unions 173
   on Anglo-Russian Committee 185, 188, 202–203, 203n190, 205
   on British general strike 197, 197n152
   British trade unions and 187–188, 187n98, 205, 211
   Central Committee on 74, 106–107
   Civil War and 71, 95–96
   establishment of 45, 45n206, 59n1
   European unions attending meetings of 175, 175n30
   on food and factory committees 75
   international trade visitors and 190, 190n116, 195
   Komsomol tensions with 283–284
   Lenin and 83–84, 87, 112
   Lozovsky and 99, 100n230
   Mensheviks in 68n46
   Narkomtrud and 72
   office space and 68–69, 68n49, 69nn51–53
   Politburo and 296–297
   productivity norms by 70–71
   Purcell on 203n192
   Right Opposition power in 281
   Rudzutak and 144n167
   Ryazanov and 108–110
   Shlyapnikov and 78n107, 99, 110
   Stalinists pressure on 318–319
   on statification of trade unions 66
   Tomsky and 45, 59–60, 66, 66n35, 68, 74, 76–77, 78n106–107, 85, 102, 113–114, 157–158, 169, 186–187, 202, 216, 216n2
   Tomsky and collegiality with 85, 89, 92
   on Tomsky and one-man management 86
   Tomsky resignation from 311–312
   on trade union independence 73–74, 73n76, 74n79–81, 78, 218
   on trade union sacrifices 283
   on Trotsky 97, 99–100
   Tsektran support in 97n208
   TUC on 210
   United Opposition and 257, 257n215, 258n218
   on wages 249, 249n170
All-Russian Central Executive Committee (VTsIK) 77, 81, 81n117, 130–131, 216
Anarchist mass demonstrations 49–50, 50n224, 50n230
Andreev, Andrei
   Anglo-Russian Committee and 204–205, 204n202, 206, 206n212, 208n229
   in Central Committee 93n184
   children of 163n274
   in Moscow Secretariat 62n12
   Stalin and 204n202, 266n265, 275, 279, 289
   Tomsky and 102, 113, 157, 157n242, 204–205, 205n204, 206n215, 220n20, 225n46, 349–350, 369
Anglo-Russian Committee
   Andreev and 204–205, 204n202, 206, 206n212, 208n229
   as British and Soviet trade unions 1, 185–186, 187n100, 206n211, 208, 210–211
   British general strike and 195–196, 204
   collapse of 211–213
   Fourteenth Party Conference on 188, 195
   IFTU on 193
   Lozovsky for 186, 208–209
   Murphy, J., on 202n181
   pinnacle of 190–191
   Politburo on 201–202
   Profintern on 188
   starting of 170, 187
   Tomsky and 170, 183, 183n71, 194–195, 204n199, 205, 205n206, 206–207, 208n229, 213, 253, 384
   Trotsky on 209

TUC on   203, 206–208, 208n230, 211–212, 211n249
United Opposition on   207–208
VTsSPS and   185, 188, 202–203, 203n190, 205
Zinoviev on   186–187, 200–201
Anti-Soviet Bloc of Rightists and Trotskyites   361–365, 363n304, 363n306, 365n310
April Theses   42, 42nn184–186, 63n17
Artamonov, Alexander Fedor   *see* Tomsky, Mikhail
Assessment and Conflict Commission (RKK)   250, 250n175
Association of State Publishing Houses (OGIZ)   323n58, 325nn71–73
  Gorky and   322–323, 324n65
  Great Purges and Tomsky staff of   354n259, 356n271
  Kamenev and   329–331, 330nn97–98
  Kanatchikov at   325–326, 325n74, 326nn75–76, 330
  Khalatov chairing   323n56, 325, 355, 355n261
  Lozovsky at   377
  on popular books   333–335, 334n125
  textbooks by   331–332, 332nn112–113, 332nn115–116, 333–334
  on Tomsky   354–355, 355n260
  Tomsky chairing   322–328, 322nn54–55, 323nn56–57, 327n82, 327n85, 331–335, 359

Barmine, Alexander   120–121, 120n19, 121nn22–23
Basmachi guerrillas
  as anti-Soviet   126, 130
  fighting and   116n1, 133, 133n102, 262, 263n245
  negotiations with   131
  Soviets on   127, 131
  on Tomsky   133, 133n102
Bogdanov, Alexander   23–24, 31, 31n118
Bolshevik Centre   31, 31n117
Bolshevik Party
  agitational role and   16, 30, 136, 136n120, 170–171, 341n164, 363n301, 384
  Bukharin and   10n3
  Civil War and survival of   74
  on economic problems   60–62, 62n13

Europe emigration and   21, 21n63
expropriations and   24, 24n82, 27n99
Goloshchekin   142n156
Great Purges of   1, 353
Kremlin captured by   56–57
Lenin on split and   101, 101n238, 102n241, 105
on mass demonstrations   45–50, 47n209
membership in   32n123, 43, 43n189
Mensheviks and   22, 22n70, 23, 24n77, 25n84, 26, 43
moderation in   6, 6n26, 42
newspaper of   51
Right Deviationists purged by   319, 319n28
RSDRP as   23, 23n74
Second Congress of Trade Unions and   76n93
Stalin on   273–274
on strikes and unions   67
Tomsky as right wing of   45
Tomsky career in   17, 17n32, 23, 26–28, 32, 43–45, 49, 49nn216–217, 382
Tomsky on opposition and   317–318, 317n20
on trade-union debate   114
on trade unions   21–22, 25n83, 27, 27n95, 61, 79–80
after tsarist abdication   42–43, 43n190
workers and   27, 61
Bonch-Burevich, Vladimir   159, 159n257
books   20n59
  Central Committee on class-enemy   331–332, 331n108, 331n110, 332n116
  Khrushchev and   16n29
  OGIZ on popular   333–335, 334n125
  OGIZ textbooks and   331–332, 332nn112–113, 332nn115–116, 333–334
  on Trotsky   314n3
Bramley, Fred   178, 185, 188, 192, 192n125
Britain
  IFTU controlled by   175n28, 177–179
  on Soviet state   191n121, 192
  on sympathy strikes   210n241
  on Tomsky   206–207, 206n216
  war scare and   252–254, 252n192
British Communist Party   187, 203, 203nn194–195
  members of   204–206, 205n208

Murphy, J., leading   172, 201–202
  Tomsky on   208
British general strike
  Anglo-Russian Committee and   195–196, 204
  failure of   171, 195–196, 203
  Politburo on   197, 197n151
  Soviet state on   196–197, 212, 296n149
  surrender reactions on   198–199, 199n162
  Tomsky on   199–200, 209, 212
  VTsSPS on   197, 197n152
British Trades Union Congress (TUC)   171, 208n228
  on Anglo-Russian Committee   203, 206–208, 208n230, 211–212, 211n249
  Bramley of   178, 185, 188, 192, 192n125
  Citrine of   183, 190, 192, 192nn126–127, 205, 211n246
  general strike surrender reactions on   198–199, 199n162
  Labour Government and   176
  Purcell heading   176–177, 188, 194, 199, 199n164, 210–211
  on Soviet assistance offer   197–198, 198n156
  Tomsky and   175–176, 176n31, 183, 183n76, 194, 194n136, 206–207, 207n218, 208–210, 212
  Tomsky on London raid and   253n195
  Trotsky, Zinoviev, Kamenev on   200
  on VTsSPS   210
  on war threat   190
British trade unions
  on IFTU and VTsSPS   187–188, 187n98, 205, 211
  on Lozovsky   182
  Sixth Trade-Union Congress and   184–185, 184n83, 185nn88–89, 186
  Stalin on   188, 188nn106–107, 200–201, 201n175
  Tomsky charming   170, 170n3, 176–177, 177n36, 177n38, 178, 178n42, 178n44, 180, 184, 186n92, 190, 205n208, 235
  Trotsky on   188, 188nn106–107
Bubnov, Andrei   332, 332n113
Bukharin, Nikolai   1, 2n7, 215, 242n138, 352n244, 387n8
  adherents of   355–356
  Bolshevism and   10n3

  communist caucus leader as   74
  execution of   380
  image of   217, 230, 241
  Kamenev and   287, 287n46
  Krupskaya and   344n181
  on Kuibyshev   290, 290n70
  on labour militarization   86, 86n149
  moderation by   236–237, 237n107
  Molotov on   278, 286
  NEP and   2, 287, 287n43
  1929 Central Committee and   309–310, 310n188
  on peasantry   241–242
  popularity of   4nn13–14
  removal of   315n8, 316n13
  resignation by   293–294, 294n95
  Right Deviationism and   5
  Right Opposition as   310–311, 344, 344n182, 350
  on Sokolnikov   379n402
  on Stalin   265–267, 286, 290–291, 290n70, 319, 379–380
  Stalinists on   310–311
  Stalin on   242n137, 310, 319
  on suicide   378
  Tomsky and   5, 7, 358–359
  on Tomsky and British trade unions   188, 188nn106–107
  on Tomsky suicide   377–378, 377n389, 378n397
  United Opposition and   55n257, 208
  wife of   378n395
  worker radical literature and   16, 16nn29–30
  on Yagoda   364n309

CCC   see Central Control Commission
Central Asia   see Turkestan
Central Committee   113n321
  Andreev in   93n184
  on class-enemy books and schoolbooks   331–332, 331n108, 331n110, 332n116
  on extraordinary measures   279, 287
  on guilt   362n298
  on IFTU   193
  on Kamenev   261–262, 261n234, 261n236, 261n238
  for Lenin   87
  members of   93n183

on one-man management 94n189
Party Unity resolution and 105, 114, 114n323
Politburo and 97n210
relations in 286
Ryazanov and 108–110, 108n291, 109n293, 112–113, 112n314
Shlyapnikov and 88n159, 113n317, 114n323
on specialists 98
for Stalin 294
Stalin on delegates and 111, 111n301
Tomsky, Bukharin, Rykov and 1929 309–310, 310n188
on Tomsky 91, 97n211, 108, 111–113, 111n305, 187, 319
Tomsky and 59, 357
on Tomsky and Central Asia 114–115
Tomsky criticizing 151, 151n211
Tomsky on 81, 81n116, 89, 93, 103, 114, 388
on Tomsky suicide 379
on trade unions 98–99, 190, 190n119
on Trotsky 256n208, 258–259, 258n223, 261–262, 261n234, 261n236, 261n238
Trotsky and labour armies to 81–83
after Twelfth Party Congress 229n71
on VTsSPS 74, 106–107
on Zinoviev 259, 261–262, 261n234, 261n236, 261n238
see also Pravda
Central Committee Plenum (April 1928) 273–275, 275n331, 278n347
Central Committee Plenum (December 1936) 360–361, 361nn290–291
Central Committee Plenum (January 1933) 350–353, 352n244, 352n248
Central Committee Plenum (July 1928) 278–279
Central Committee Plenums 359, 388
Central Control Commission (CCC)
  function of 343n179
  interrogation by 346, 346n193
  Kaganovich bypassing 353n253
  on oppositionists 343–345, 343n179
  purge by 352n248, 353, 353n253
  on Tomsky 343–350, 352
Central Purge Commission 356, 361n292
Chamberlain, Austin 253–254, 253n198

Citrine, Walter 191, 197–198, 203–204, 331n106
Tomsky and 190n119, 203n193, 208–210, 322n53, 334n126, 358, 358n281
of TUC 183, 190, 192, 192nn126–127, 205, 211n246
Civil War
  Bolshevik survival and 74
  Club of the Nobility during 68–69
  economic crisis after 72, 94, 102–103
  epidemics and food in 70, 75–76, 75n89
  Kanatchikov after 115, 115n326
  Koshchi during 145–146, 145n174, 152n216
  Samara-Orenburg-Tashkent railroad line in 126, 126n56
  Tomsky during 60, 72, 76
  trade unions during 74–75, 80
  VTsSPS and 71, 95–96
  White Armies and foreign intervention in 74, 79n110
class consciousness
  Safarov on 145, 145n173
  trade unions with 21, 21n65
collective leadership 245, 265, 341n163, 387
collectivisation
  avoidance of 280, 288
  health under 337–338, 338n139
  kulaks and 3, 139, 155n236, 169
  party expelling over 342
  peasantry on 317n15
  Politburo on 338–339, 338n147
  problems with 337–339
  Sixteenth Party Congress during 315
  Stalin and 264, 264n251, 287n42, 317n16, 337–338, 344–345, 365n320, 388
collegial management
  Lenin on 86, 86n150, 91
  Tomsky for 85, 89, 92
  trade unions for 84n133, 85, 89, 92n178
Comintern see Communist International
Commissariat of Labour see Narkomtrud
Communist International (Comintern) 180
  Fifth Congress of 179, 179n50
  forged trade union 'letter' and 191–192, 192n123
  Tomsky and 172, 172n12, 173n21, 212–213, 216
  united front strategy by 175, 175n25, 212

INDEX 437

Communist Party Central Control Commission (CCC) *see* Central Control Commission
Communist Party Politburo *see* Politburo
Congresses
   of trade unions 62–65, 62n14, 63nn19–20, 65n25
   trade unions on 312n203
Constituent Assembly 53, 57, 57n276, 62–63, 63nn17–18
cotton
   Frunze on 134n111
   Russian peasants on 135n113
   Tomsky on 135, 144, 150
   in Turkestan 122–123, 126, 126n57, 129, 134n111, 135–136, 135n113, 135n118, 139n135

dachas
   NKVD on Tomsky 167n304, 371
   for Tomsky 166–168, 166nn304–305, 167n304, 336–337, 337nn134–135, 339
   for top party leaders 166–167, 166n302
'Declaration of the 46' 232–233, 232nn84–86
democracy
   Trotsky on 232, 232n80
   Workers' Opposition for 96, 101
Democratic Centralists 84n134, 87n156, 92, 101n236, 103
de-Stalinisation 358n278, 359n285, 374–375, 380n410
Dogadov, Alexander 318–319, 319n27
Dzerzhinsky, Felix
   death of 221n22, 285n33
   image of 217
   Lenin on 159, 159n256
   Politburo and 229n71
   as political police head 230, 285n33
   as right wing 255n202
   on Tomsky 112

economy
   Bolshevik takeover and 60–62, 62n13
   Civil War crisis in 72, 94, 102–103
   Eleventh Party Congress on 221, 221n23
   industrial production in 84n136, 219, 224, 239
   Kalinin on 155n234

   kulak agriculture surplus on 240, 242n136
   Mensheviks on 103
   peasants on prices and 264, 264n256, 286, 286nn39–40
   Petrograd demonstrations on 103
   'scissors crisis' on 232, 232n81
   Stalinists on 388
   Tomsky on unions and 67, 70–72, 225–226, 226n48
   tsarist regime and 61n10
   War Communism on 219, 221–222, 250, 266, 325n72
   worker demonstrations on 103, 103n252, 103n254, 103n256
   Workers' Opposition on 87–88, 101
   see also collectivisation; New Economic Policy; Supreme Council of the Economy
Efremov, Mikhail Pavlovich *see* Tomsky, Mikhail
Eighth Congress of Komsomol of Leningrad 283–284
Eighth Party Congress 79–81, 106n274, 119, 129n83
Eighth Trade-Union Congress 301n141
   on Kaganovich 306–307, 312–313
   Kuibyshev on Five-Year Plan at 285, 297
   Molotov at 306–308
   NEP and 280, 312–313
   Stalinist showdown and trade unions at 282, 295, 309, 386
   Tomsky and 52, 215, 297, 297n117
   Tomsky defeat at 214, 249, 282, 304–305, 304n157, 305n159, 309, 386
Eismont, Nikolai 342–343, 345, 349–350, 355
Eleventh Party Congress 332n113
   on specialists and economy 221, 221n23
   Tomsky and 158–159, 158n249, 220–222, 225–226, 226n48, 227n56
entrapment 330, 330nn102–103, 341n161
Europe
   Bolshevik emigration and 21, 21n63
   on Tomsky moderate inclinations toward 31
   Tomsky on revolution and 73
   VTsSPS with unions of 175, 175n30

expropriations 24, 24n82, 27n99
'extraordinary measures' 279
    Stalin on peasants and 215, 278, 287n42
    Tomsky on 278n345, 310

factory committees 44–45, 67–68, 67n42, 68n44
factory elders 18n41
famine
    Civil War and 70, 75–76, 75n89
    of First Five-Year Plan 313
    Lenin on 141n150
    of 1932–1933 344n183
    in Russia 133–134, 134n107, 144, 149n197, 224
    Stalinists and grain in 266nn265–266
    Stalin on 344, 344n184
    in Turkestan 125–126, 126n57, 149n197
    VTsSPS on factory committees and 75
Fifteenth Party Conference 207, 247–248, 261n239, 282
    five-year plan by 263
    on United Opposition 261–262, 274
Fifth Congress of the Comintern 179, 179n50
Fifth Party Congress 28–29, 215
Fifth Trade-Union Congress 95, 157n243, 219n14, 226
First Congress of the Writers' Union (1934) 327n81
First Five-Year Plan
    falling wages in 283n16, 283n19
    hardships and famine of 313
    Kuibyshev drafting 285, 297
    Tomsky on 281, 298, 351
First Trade-Union Congress 59, 59n1, 60, 78n93
    on strikes 67
    Tomsky and 63, 77, 101, 171
forced collectivisation see collectivisation
foreign intervention 74, 79n110
foreign policy
    of Soviet regime 170n2
    Tomsky and 170, 384
    see also Anglo-Russian Committee
Fourteenth Party Conference
    on Anglo-Russian Committee 188, 195
    Krupskaya at 244
    Stalin and 243n141

Tomsky at 240, 240n134, 243n143, 246n159
Fourth Trade-Union Conference 73, 328
    Tenth Party Conference and 106, 113
    Tomsky and 68, 72, 113, 116, 157, 169, 204–205, 262, 347, 383
French Communist Party 187n96, 195n145
Frunze, Mikhail 127n67
    on cotton access 134n111
    image of 217
    on Indigenous population 124, 127–128
    influence of 159n255
    as Old Bolshevik 159n253
    as Politburo candidate member 229n71
    Red Army and 116n1, 124, 134n111, 153n221
    Tomsky and 111–112, 116n1, 158–159, 166, 373
    on Trotsky 159, 159n253

German trade unions 174–175, 175n24
Goloshchekin, Filipp 127, 142n156
Gompers, Samuel 85, 85n142, 177n39, 220n21
Gorky, Maksim
    on Lenin 31, 31n118
    on Lenin and Bogdanov feud 31, 31n118
    Moscow return by 324n62
    OGIZ and 322–323, 324n65
    on Socialist Realism 326n78, 327
    on Tashkent scientists and scholars 132, 132nn98–99
    Tomsky and 26, 290, 291, 332n115, 351
    on Tomsky and OGIZ 322–324, 324n64, 329n96
Great Purges
    by CCC 352n248, 353, 353n253
    on dissenting voters 309, 309n186
    executions of 317, 317n18
    Great Terror as 314n2
    on Old Bolsheviks 1, 353
    on publications 334
    on Shlyapnikov 352n248, 355n260, 362–363
    Stalin and 320, 366n320, 388
    suicides in 371, 371n351
    Tomsky OGIZ staff and 354n259, 356n271

INDEX

Tomsky on 9
on Tomsky staff 354n259, 376–377, 376n380
Tomsky suicide in 1, 3, 56n265, 167n304, 168, 334, 358, 360n288, 364–372, 376–377, 379, 389
on United Opposition and Right Deviation 314
Great Terror 314n2

Hall of Columns
congresses in 74, 184, 186, 297, 327n81
former Club of the Nobility with 68–69
Lenin body in 233–234
Shakhty trial in 276
for speeches 258
hereditary workers 11, 11n6
hunting
Tomsky and 16, 38, 166–167, 239, 316n14, 347–348, 359, 363n303, 366
by top party leaders 166n299

IFTU see International Federation of Trade Unions
imprisonment 34n134
avoidance of 21, 30n114, 33
of Kanatchikov 20, 33–35, 33n129, 35n146, 40n171
of Krupskaya 371
Russian Criminal Code and 36n148
in Siberia 6, 10, 16, 20–21, 33–40, 37nn155–156, 43
of Tomskaya 33, 36
of Tomsky 6, 10, 20–23, 29, 30n114, 31, 33–37, 34n133, 37n154, 39–41
Indigenous population
activities by 122, 122n32
Frunze on 124, 127–128
land requests from 139n134
Russia settlers on 139
Tashkent Soviet on 122–126, 123n38, 124nn41–42, 125n49, 125n51
Tomsky and 127, 168
tsarist regime on 124, 124n46
in Turkestan 116
industrialisation
economy production in 84n136, 219, 224, 239

Kaganovich supporting 303–304
Kuibyshev on 286, 290, 290n70, 292, 292n80, 297
Sixteenth Party Congress during 315
Tomsky and 282–283, 310, 321, 321nn40–41, 388
industrial managers 220–221, 220n18, 221n23
International Federation of Trade Unions (IFTU)
as Amsterdam International 171, 171n6
on Anglo-Russian Committee 193
British control of 175n28, 177–179
British trade unions on 187–188, 187n98, 205, 211
Central Committee on 193
international members of 172n10
Lozovsky and 179–180, 194
Politburo and negotiations with 181, 181n60, 183
Purcell heading 178, 178n44, 185, 193, 210–211, 211n246
on Russian trade unions 184–185
Thomas of 178, 192, 198–199, 198n158, 198n160, 203n190, 329n92
on Tomsky 185n86, 212
Tomsky on 171–172, 177–178, 177n39, 193–195, 193n132
International Trade-Union Council (ITUC) 172–173
international trade-union issues 171–172, 171n7
international trade-union visitors 190, 190n116, 195
ITUC see International Trade-Union Council
Ivanovna see Tomskaya, Maria

Joffe, Adolf 147–148, 147n187, 148n191
Joint Central Transport Committee (Tsektran)
for military discipline in unions 94–95, 94n193, 95n199
Platform of the Ten on 99–100, 99n225, 102n248, 104
Trotsky for 96
VTsSPS support of 97n208

Kaganovich, Lazar
  CCC bypassed by   353n253
  Eighth Trade-Union Congress on   306–307, 312–313
  from exile   120, 304n152
  Molotov on   304
  at 1936 Central Committee Plenum   361n291
  Purge Commission chaired by   353n253
  for rapid industrialisation   303–304
  show trials by   361n293
  Stalin and   204, 267, 295, 303
  on Tomsky   4, 304n151
  on Tomsky purge commission   366–367
  trade union purge by   312, 312n212
  Turkestan Commission and   127
  Turkestan trip by   120n19
  on VTsSPS Presidium   302
Kalinin, Mikhail   2n6, 23–24, 245, 319, 333
  on economy importance   155n234
  image of   90, 217, 234, 247, 335
  on Lenin death   234
  moderate politics of   248, 261, 311, 311n198
  on Rightists   311, 311n198
  Stalin and   280n3, 288, 288n54
  as Stalinist   248, 288, 288n51
  wife of   164n281
Kamenev, Lev
  biography on   1n4
  Bukharin and   287, 287n46
  Central Committee on   261–262, 261n234, 261n236, 261n238
  execution of   379, 379n406
  hard labour and death of   331
  image of   217, 254
  1926 purge and   246
  as not erased   56n269
  OGIZ and   329–330, 330nn97–98
  Politburo and   252, 252n189
  at Seventeenth Party Congress   346n195
  show trial on   361–362, 362nn295–296
  on Stalin   159n258, 244–245, 245n155, 279
  Tomsky and   200, 215, 243n143, 244, 262–263, 279, 367
  troika including   227–228, 228n57

on Trotsky   233
  as United Opposition leader   200, 251–252, 251n184
  wife of   164n281
Kanatchikov, Semen
  anti-drunkenness congress and   31n116
  autobiography by   3n11, 11, 115, 326, 326n76
  after Civil War   115, 115n326
  factory labor by   13–14, 14n19, 15, 15n25, 23
  imprisonment of   20, 33–35, 33n129, 35n146, 40n171
  newspaper of   40
  1905 Revolution and   18
  1926 purge and   24–248
  at OGIZ   325–326, 325n74, 326nn75–76, 330
  on public speaking   27–28, 28n103, 58
  reading by   20n59
  in Siberia   40, 40n173
  Tomsky and   11–12
  on Trotsky   229
  on worker radical literature   16, 16nn29–30
Khalatov, Artashes   323n56, 325, 355, 355n261
Khrushchev, Nikita
  banned books and   16n29
  de-Stalinisation and   358n278, 359n285, 374–375, 380n410
  home of   372n359
  on Tomskaya   374
  on Tomsky   56n269
Kirensk, Siberia   37–41, 41n180
Kolpino industrial complex   11n5
Komsomol
  Komsomolskaia Pravda of   284–285, 296, 298, 302
  leadership of   243, 243n145
  of Leningrad   298n121
  party leaders on   246
  Stalin and   244, 283–284
  Tomsky and   243–244, 275n327, 285, 298–301
  trade unions on   284–285
  VTsSPS tensions with   283–284
Komsomolskaia Pravda   284–285, 284n23, 296, 298, 302

INDEX

Koshchi (peasants) 145–146, 145n174, 152n216
Kosior, Stanislav 284, 284n27
Kozelev, Boris
  diary and execution of 312n204
  on Moscow Committee 55n264, 65n27, 66n30
  as Tomsky friend 205n204, 284, 301–302, 312
Kremlin
  Bolshevik Party capturing 56–57
  cafeteria of 164, 164n286
  capture with destruction 57, 57n274
  life in 160–165, 163n274, 163n277, 163n280, 164nn285–286, 165nn289–290
  1928 party regime at 281
  Ninth Party Congress on 161, 161n267
  Tomsky on capture of 56–58, 56nn265–267, 57n273, 57n276
Kronstadt Revolt 49, 103–105, 103n254, 104n258, 107, 338
Krupskaya, Nadezhda
  Bukharin and 344n181
  at Fourteenth Party Conference 244
  image of 234
  imprisonment of 371
  as Lenin wife 24n82, 136, 136n123, 161n270, 164n281, 297n116
  opposition by 242, 316n13
  Testament and 235nn98–99, 236
  Tomsky and 244, 244n148, 244n150, 316n13, 323n56, 337n138
Kuibyshev, Valerian 229n71, 248n168, 296n113
  Bukharin on 290, 290n70
  First Five-Year Plan and 285, 297
  on industrialisation 286, 290, 290n70, 292, 292n80, 297
  on military affairs 127
  in Politburo 267
  Tomsky and 108, 221, 285–286, 289, 297–298, 303–304, 347–349
  on Trotsky 263n249
  VSNKh and 269n285, 285n33
kulaks
  agriculture surplus by 240, 242n136
  definition of 140n149, 240
  forced collectivisation and 3, 139, 155n236, 169

image of 141
Lenin on 141n150, 147, 149
Molotov on 266n267
OGPU on 265–266, 266n269
Platform of the Four on 242–243, 243n142
Politburo on 140, 140n141, 140n149, 143–144
Safarov on 137, 137n124, 140–142, 147–148, 155n229
Soviet regime on 144, 240, 266
Stalin on 265–266, 266n266, 337
stealing from 75
Tomsky on 2, 145, 168

labour militarization 95n196
  Bukharin on 86, 86n149
  Central Committee with Trotsky on 81–83
  Lenin on 81–83, 83n123, 88n158, 97–98, 100–101
  Rudzutak on 97
  Tomsky on 93–96, 100–101
  Trotsky for 27, 81–83, 83n126, 89n161, 94–95, 97–98, 100, 114, 175, 232–233, 381
  workers in 27, 81–83, 83n123, 83n126, 83n129, 86, 97, 105, 114, 232–233, 381
labour unions *see* trade unions
land reform
  Joffe on Turkestan 147–148, 148n191
  results in Turkestan 148–149, 149n197, 155
  Safarov on 139–143, 145, 155n229
  Stalin and 155n236
  Turkestan and 139–142, 142nn153–154, 148–149, 149n197, 155
'last service' 1, 1n2, 364
Lenin, Vladimir
  on Bolshevik Party split 101, 101n238, 102n241, 105
  brutality of 149–150, 149n202
  Central Committee for 87
  on collegial management 86, 86n150, 91
  on Constituent Assembly 63n17
  death of 233–234, 233n88–89, 233n91–92, 234nn93–95
  on Dzerzhinsky 159, 159n256
  Eighth Party Congress and 129n83
  on food shortages 141n150

Gorky on 31, 31n118
health of 120, 120n18, 146, 146n180, 155, 158, 229n68, 229n70
image of 80, 90, 217
indecision by 50, 50n226
Kalinin on death and 234
on Kronstadt revolt 103, 103n254
on kulaks 141n150, 147, 149
on labour militarization 81–83, 83n123, 88n158, 97–98, 100–101
on mass demonstrations 45, 47–48, 47n209
Mensheviks and 23
on Muslims 129n83, 150, 150n209
newspaper of 32
at Ninth Party Congress 90–91, 91n174
as Old Bolshevik 5n14
on one-man management 83–84, 83n131, 84n133
on party newspaper 44, 44n197
return of 41–42
on Rudzutak 173–174, 174n23
Rudzutak on death of 233n91, 234
on Russian chauvinism 128–129, 128n76, 147, 150–151, 150n210
on Ryazanov 110–111, 111n300
on Safarov and Tomsky 146, 146n183, 154–155
on self-determination 119–120
sister as Ulyanova 311
Sokolnikov and 153n222
on Stalin 235–236, 235n99
for statification of trade unions 77–78, 111
on Tashkent and food 133–134, 134nn110–111
Testament of 235–236, 235nn97–98, 236n101
title by 30, 30n112
on Tomsky 97, 101–102, 111–114, 116, 159, 159n258, 169, 173–174, 174n23
Tomsky opposing 5, 31–32, 41, 49, 58, 85–86, 158, 158n250, 382
Tomsky role after death of 233–234
Tomsky supporting 2, 4, 25–26, 28n104, 60, 114n324, 351
on trade unions 22–23, 29, 61
Trotsky after death of 233, 233n88, 233n92
Trotsky and 227, 227n56
on Turkestan 126–127, 133–134
VTsSPS and 83–84, 87, 112
wife of 24n82, 136, 136n123, 161n270, 164n281, 297n116
on Zinoviev 50, 236
Lomov, Grigory 156, 156n237
lower-class culture 11–12
Lozovsky, Alexander 172n14
  Anglo-Russian Committee and 186, 208–209
  on Constituent Assembly closing 63n18
  description of 173, 179n49, 179n52, 181–182
  on IFTU invitation 179–180, 194
  image of 174
  ITUC headed by 173
  on languages 172, 172n13
  Molotov and 295n101
  at OGIZ 377
  on Platform of the Ten 102n248
  as Profintern general secretary 172–173, 173n19, 179–180
  Tomsky and 172–173, 179–181, 184, 188, 213, 213n254, 307–308, 308n177
  VTsSPS majority and 99, 100n230
Luppol, Ivan 328, 328nn88–89, 330n97, 354n254

mass demonstrations
  as armed 50, 50n229
  Bolshevik Party on 45–48, 47n209
  Lenin on 45, 47–48, 47n209
  in Petrograd 45–49
  Soviet state on 51–52
  Tomsky on 45–52, 50n226, 52n238, 56n269, 56nn265–267
Medvedev, Roy 277, 277n340, 286n40, 365–366, 365n312
Medvedev, Sergei 220
Mensheviks 108n288
  Bolsheviks and 22, 22n70, 23, 24n77, 25n84, 26, 43
  for economic demonstrations 103
  at Fourth Trade-Union Conference 73
  Lenin and 23
  newspaper of 5
  as passive 17
  in Revel, Estonia 18

INDEX 443

on Tomsky 370
Tomsky on 44–45, 75–76, 293n85
trade unions and 21–22, 26n93, 76
in VTsSPS 68n46
moderation
 Bolshevik Party and 6, 6n26, 42
 by Bukharin 236–237, 237n107
 expectations on 280
 Kalinin politics of 248, 261, 311, 311n198
 Nogin and Right wing 45, 53–54, 54n255, 55
 by Rykov 236–237
 Stalin on 255, 267, 279, 387
 Stalin ousting rumors and 254–255, 255n202
 Tomsky on demonstration of 50–51, 55–56, 56nn265–267
 Tomsky on lack of 77, 77n100
 Tomsky on rapid industrialisation and 282–283
 Tomsky on Stalin and 236–237
 Tomsky politics with 6–8, 10, 22, 41–42, 87, 104, 171, 201, 213–215, 226, 237, 292, 381
Molotov, Vyacheslav 110n294
 on Bukharin 278, 286
 children of 163n274
 at Eighth Trade-Union Congress 306–308
 on Kaganovich 304
 Komsomol of Leningrad and 296
 on kulaks 266n267
 Lozovsky and 295n101
 Orgburo and 157n246
 on Politburo commission 106
 on Right Deviationists 278
 on Rightist families 374–375
 on Rudzutak 117n5
 on Rykov 278, 286
 Stalin and 248, 267, 278, 366
 as Stalin devotee 248, 267, 278
 on Stalin potential assassination 366
 at Tenth Party Conference 113
 on Tomsky 4–5, 18, 52, 278, 286, 307, 349, 369
 on top government privileges 167
Moscow
 Bolsheviks on Kremlin and 56–57
 economic demonstrations in 103

Gorky return to 324n62
Government moved to 160n263
newspapers in 58n278
1928 trade-union regime at 281
Tashkent and 117n3
Tomsky to 52, 152, 156
trade unions and Soviet of 62, 68n49
Uglanov as party boss and 282, 340n158
workers in 55
Moscow Committee 55n264, 65n27, 66n30
Moscow Secretariat 62n12
Murphy, John 172, 201–202, 202n181, 232n86
Murphy, Kevin 250
Muslims
 on class tensions 145n173
 land holdings by 139n135
 Lenin on 129n83, 150, 150n209
 on pan-Islamism 128, 128n70
 on Soviet state 128
 Soviet state on religion and 129–131, 129nn84–85, 130n88
 of Tashkent 119, 121–130, 132, 136, 139, 141–142, 145–147, 149–151, 153, 155, 168
 Tomsky on religion and 129–130, 129n84, 130
 veiling and 130–131, 130n88, 130n90, 131n93
 women and 130–131, 131nn92–93
mutual aid societies 29, 29nn109–110, 39

Narkomtrud (Commissariat of Labour) 66, 70, 72–73, 78, 249, 293n83
 for workers 222–224, 223n35
nationalizations 70n58
national self-determination 119–120, 136–137, 168
Nevsky, Vladimir 376
New Economic Policy (NEP)
 for agriculture development 219
 Bukharin and 2, 287, 287n43
 for cost-accounting procedures 219, 219n11
 for economic development 219
 Eighth Trade-Union Congress and 280, 312–313
 industrial managers during 221n23
 peasantry during 240

Stalin abandoning   267, 279, 281
Stalin and   267, 279, 280–281, 317
Stalin on   267, 317
Tomsky on inequality and   168
Tomsky on preserving   281, 286–287, 289, 316n14, 357, 385
Tomsky on Tashkent and   129, 144, 151, 155
Tomsky roles during   214–215
trade unions during   216, 220–221, 220n21, 223, 282
unemployment under   224–225, 225n42, 225nn44–45
wage levels under   248n168, 251
newspapers
  of Bolsheviks   51
  of Gorky   54
  of Kanatchikov   40
  of Lenin   32
  Lenin on party   44, 44n197
  of Menshevik   5
  in Moscow   58n278
  Purcell and British   189n113
  of RSDRP   23, 23n74
  on Shakhty Affair   267–277, 277n336, 277n339
  Tomsky and   17–18, 23, 41, 43–44, 58
  for workers   43–44, 43n195
the Revolution of 1905   17–18
  Tomsky and   10, 19, 19n42, 20–21, 33, 55, 381–383
  on tsarist government during   196n149
Ninth Party Congress
  on Kremlin living conditions   161, 161n267
  Lenin at   90–91, 91n174
  Tomsky at   88–93, 93n183, 383
  trade-union debate at   95n202
  worker management resolution by   92, 92n182, 95n202
NKVD   see political police
Nogin, Victor   45, 53–54, 54n255, 55, 57n276, 63n18

OGIZ   see Association of State Publishing Houses
OGIZ Purge Commission   332, 352
  on criticism lack   355
  on Tomsky   353–354, 354n254, 356

Tomsky popularity at   354–355
Tomsky response at   354–356, 355n265, 362–363
OGPU   see political police
Old Bolsheviks
  child adoptions by   161n271
  executions of   379n406
  Frunze as   159n253
  Goloshchekin as   142n156
  Great Purges on   1, 353
  last service by   1, 1n2, 364
  Lenin as   5n14
  Nevsky as   376
  Pravdin as   150n210
  relations among   163n277, 239
  Ryutin Platform of   340
  Safarov as   136, 136n122
  Smilga as   256
  Sokolnikov as   153n22
  on Stalin   336n30
  Stalin as   5n14
  Stalin on   236, 274, 297, 373
  Tomsky as   5n14, 6, 314, 335
  Trilisser as   339n153
  Trotsky as   3n11
  on United Opposition   251n184
  on Yezhov   364, 364n309
one-man management
  Central Committee on   94n189
  introduction of   93, 93n187
  Lenin on   83–84, 83n131, 84n133
  Stalin on collective leadership and   245, 265, 341n163, 387
  Tomsky on   84–85, 89, 221
  trade unions on   83–84, 83n131, 84n133, 84n135
  Trotsky on   89, 94
opposition
  CCC on   343–345, 343n179
  by Krupskaya   242, 316n13
  Murphy, J., on   232n86
  Trotsky on   231–232, 232n82
  see also Right Deviationists; Right Opposition; United Opposition; Workers' Opposition; Zinovievite Opposition
Organisational Bureau (Orgburo)   160n261, 216n5
  Molotov and   157n246

post appointments by 231, 231n77, 231n79
power in 93nn185–186, 157–158, 158n247
Stalin controlling 157n246
Tomsky and 93, 104
Tomsky as full member of 117, 157, 157n245, 216, 226, 226n53
Osinsky, N 61, 61n5
output norms 239–240, 388

'palace coup' 288, 288n55, 339–340, 339nn152–156, 358n278
Party Unity resolution 105, 114, 114n323
peasantry
    Bukharin on 241–242
    on economy and prices 264, 264n256, 286, 286nn39–40
    on forced collectivisation 317n15
    Kalinin on 248
    mid-1920s concerns on 240
    purge order on 352–353, 352n248
    Rykov on 241n135
    smychka toward 351, 351n235
    Stalin on 286, 286n39
    Stalin on agriculture and 263–264, 264n254
    Stalin on extraordinary measures and 215, 278, 287n42
    Tomsky on middle 240, 278, 286
    on war possibility 254, 264, 264n251
    see also kulaks
Petrograd 45–49, 103
Platform of the Four 242–243, 243n142
Platform of the Ten 99–100, 99n225, 102n248, 104
Poletaev, Nikolai 28n104
Politburo 179n51, 216nn3–5
    accurate information for 147n186
    on Anglo-Russian Committee 201–202
    anti-Stalinists in 280, 280n3
    on British general strike 197, 197n151
    Central Committee and 97n210
    on collectivisation 338–339, 338n147
    on 'Declaration of the 46' 232–233, 232nn84–86
    Dzerzhinsky and 229n71
    Frunze and 229n71
    health benefits of 164–165, 165n289, 165n297
    on IFTU negotiations 181, 181n60, 183
    Kamenev and 252, 252n189
    Kuibyshev in 267
    on kulaks 140, 140n141, 140n149, 143–144
    on London raid 253n195
    Molotov on 106
    1933 Central Committee Plenum on purge order by 352–353, 352n248
    purge order by 352–353, 352n248
    relations in 286, 286n38, 291
    on resignations 294
    Rykov to 159n255, 228, 319n30
    on Second Congress of Trade Unions 74
    on Shakhty Affair 269
    Stalin and 342, 342n172
    Stalinists and 295–296, 302
    on Tomsky 108, 114, 301–302, 319–322
    Tomsky and Turkestan at 153
    Tomsky as full member of 117, 155, 169, 216, 223, 226, 384
    Tomsky on 352
    Tomsky warned by 35n8, 35n10
    Trade-union commission of 301–302, 301n141
    for trade unions 285
    Trotsky and 228–229, 228n58, 248n163, 252
    VTsSPS and 296–297
    Zinoviev and 252
political police (NKVD)
    at show trials 361
    on Tomskaya 367
    on Tomsky associates 376–377, 379
    on Tomsky dacha 167n304, 371
    on Tomsky dead body 370
    on Tomsky family 373
    on Tomsky papers 372
    on Tomsky sons 373
    on wives and Right-Trotskyite spy traitors 374, 380n409
    Yagoda heading 367–368
    Yezhov on 368
political police (OGPU)
    Dzerzhinsky heading 230, 285n33
    on enemy agents 253n196
    on kulaks 265–266, 266n269
    as NKVD 143n157
    on Ryutin Platform 341, 341n165

on Shakhty Affair 267–274, 267n278, 268n284, 271n299, 277n336, 277n340
Stalin sent agent 256
Tomsky on 231, 273, 273n314
Yagoda heading 290, 329n96, 339
Yevdokimov of 268, 268n281, 277n342
Pospelov, Peter 359n285
Pravda (Central Committee newspaper)
on engineers 269
false congress summation by 309
Testament and 236
on Tomsky 56n265, 294, 294n95, 363, 363n306, 365–366
Tomsky on 43–44, 49
Tomsky suicide and 363–364, 363n306
tsarist troops on 51
Pravdin, Alexander 150n210
Profintern *see* Red International of Labor Unions
public speaking
Kanatchikov and 27–28, 28n103, 58
by Tomsky 1, 4, 18, 58, 81n118, 186, 263, 348–349, 351, 354
Purcell, Alf
British press on 189n113
on British socialist revolution 193n130
IFTU headed by 178, 178n44, 185, 193, 210–211, 211n246
image of 189
Russian trade unions on 185, 185n89, 257
Tomsky and 187
TUC headed by 176–177, 188, 194, 199, 199n164, 210–211
on VTsSPS 203n192
Purge Commission 305n161, 332, 352–356, 353n253, 362
purges
Kaganovich and trade union 312, 312n212
of 1926 246
on peasantry 352–353, 352n248
Politburo ordering 352–353, 352n248

Radek, Karl 158n249
on compulsory labour 95n196
investigations on 363, 377, 379n403
on Party Unity resolution 105
VTsSPS Presidium and 86, 108, 303n150

Rakovsky, Christian 176n32, 177n36, 217
Red Army
Frunze and 116n1, 124, 134n111, 153n221
Tomsky on 133, 133nn103–105
trade unions and 70, 74–75, 75nn85–86
tsarist officers in 86n152
Red International of Labor Unions (Profintern)
on Anglo-Russian Committee 188
ITUC preceding 172
Lozovsky and 172–173, 173n19, 179–180
Tomsky and 173, 180, 183–184, 193–194, 218n7
rehabilitation 1n3, 373n362, 374–375, 375n370, 380, 380n410
Rei, August 20, 20n55
Revel, Estonia 17–19, 19n42
Right Deviationists
Bolshevik Party purging of 319, 319n28
Bukharin and 5
deaths of 314
Great Purges on 314
Kalinin on 311, 311n198
Molotov on 278
popularity of 4n13
Rykov and 1
Stalin and 282n15, 293–294, 310n194, 316–317, 358
Stalinists and 280, 280n1, 310, 358n279
Tomsky linked to 1, 1n3, 293n87, 388
see also Right Opposition
Right Opposition 310n188, 310n194
as Bukharin 310–311, 344, 344n182, 350
for internal opposition 356, 356n268
meetings of 290
Molotov on families and 374–375
'palace coup' and 288n55, 339–340, 358n278
Seventeenth Party Congress capitulation by 357n276
Shmidt as 294
Sixteenth Party Congress on 311
Tomsky and 1, 1n3, 310–311, 318n24
VTsSPS in 281
Yagoda on 339, 367n324
see also Right Deviationists

right to strike
    First Trade-Union Congress on   67
    Tomsky and Second Trade-Union Congress on   74, 78–79, 79n111
    Tomsky on   225–226, 225n46
Rodchenko, Alexander   334–335, 335n128
Rosenberg, Arthur   6–7
RSDRP   see Russian Social Democratic Labour Party
Rudzutak, Yan   25n85, 112
    execution of   143n157, 352n245
    Fifth Trade-Union Congress and   157n243
    food requisitions by   143n157
    illness of   144n169
    image and description of   117–118, 117n5
    on labour armies   97
    on Lenin death   233n91, 234
    Lenin on   173–174, 174n23
    Molotov on   117n5
    1905 Revolution and   117n4
    on Safarov   142–146
    for Stalin   288
    at Tenth Party Congress   117n4
    Tomsky and   117, 117n4, 119, 144, 157n241
    as Turkestan Bureau head   117, 127
    VTsSPS and   144n167
Russia
    famine in   133–134, 134n107, 144, 149n197, 224
    informal first person in   270n296
    peasants on cotton   135n113
    settlers on Indigenous   139
    specialists for   89–90, 90n167
    Tashkent with enclave and   121, 121nn26–27
    Tomsky in post-tsarist   41–42
    Turkestan and   122–123, 122nn29–30, 124, 124n46, 125–126, 125n51
    Turkestan settlers from   138–140, 138nn130–132, 140n141
    vodka and   349n222
Russian chauvinism   155, 169
    Lenin on   128–129, 128n76, 147, 150–151, 150n210
Russian Social Democratic Labour Party (RSDRP)
    newspaper of   23, 23n74
    Tomskaya in   32, 37
    Tomsky and Congress of   24–25, 24n79, 28
    Turkestan Commission and   117n3
    Unity Congress by   22–23, 22n71
Ryazanov, David
    Central Committee on   108–110, 108n291, 109n293, 112–113, 112n314
    on Constituent Assembly   63n18
    Fourth Trade-Union Conference and   328
    image of   109
    Lenin on   110–111, 111n300
    as Marxist scholar   113n315, 329nn92–93
    Tomsky and   110, 328–329
    for trade unions   60, 65–66, 68, 71n65, 78
    VTsSPS and   108–110
Rykov, Alexei   32, 83n128, 215, 352n244
    on Bogdanov   31
    on British war scare   252–254, 252n192
    on compulsory labour   95n196
    execution of   380
    image of   90, 217, 230, 249
    on Lenin   31, 42n185, 98, 99n225
    moderation by   57, 57n275, 236–237
    Molotov on   278, 286
    1929 Central Committee and   309–310, 310n188
    1936 Central Committee Plenum on   360–361, 361n290
    as not erased   56n269
    on peasantry   241n135
    Politburo and   159n255, 228, 319n30
    popularity of   4n13
    resignation by   63n18, 293–294
    Right Deviationists and   1
    on Shakhty Affair   269–270, 269n285, 273–274
    Sixteenth Party Congress on   316
    on Sokolnikov   379n402
    on Stalin   58, 245, 255n203, 265–267, 286, 292
    Stalinists on   310–311
    Stalin on   310
    Tomsky and   7, 13n13, 358n282
    on Tomsky suicide   377–379, 377nn390–391, 379n407, 380n409
    on trade unions   104
    on Trotsky   255n203

Trotsky on 228n62
university and 36n151
as VSNKh head 84, 91–92
warnings to 35n10, 315n8
on worker management 91–92, 92n178
Yagoda and 339n153
on Zinoviev and Kamenev 54n255
Ryskulov, Turar 128, 128n74
Ryutin, Martemian
on Stalin 340–341, 340n160, 341n161, 341n164
on United Opposition 340nn158–159
Ryutin Platform 339n156, 341n164, 341n166
OGPU on 341, 341n165
Stalinists on 340–341, 343, 345–346, 345n191, 346n193, 350
on Stalin removal 341–342
Tomsky and 339–341, 344n182, 346n194, 347–348

Safarov, Georgy
Bolshevik history of 136, 136n122
on class tensions 145, 145n173
image of 137
Joffe on land reform and 147–148, 148n191
on kulaks 137, 137n124, 140–142, 147–148, 155n229
on land reform 139–143, 145, 155n229
Lenin on 146, 146n183, 154–155
as ruthless 137–140, 142–143, 142n156, 148, 266
on self-determination 136–137
Sokolnikov on 154
Stalin on 147
on Tashkent 124, 127, 137n124, 142
Tomsky on 116, 136–138, 144–146, 158
War Communism and 148
Saltykov-Shchedrin, Mikhail 167, 167n308
Second Congress of Trade Unions 74, 76n93, 78–79, 79n111
self-criticism campaign
by Stalin 274, 284n27
against Tomsky 274, 284–285, 284n27, 346–350, 355, 357, 366–367
Seventeenth Party Congress 343n179, 346n195, 357, 357n276, 358n278
Seventh Trade-Union Congress 240, 248

Shakhty Affair 156n237
Germans in 277n338
interrogations in 268, 268n280, 268nn283–284
investigation in 269–271, 270n292, 270n294, 272n308, 272n311
newspapers on 267–277, 277n336, 277n339
OGPU on 267–274, 267n278, 268n284, 271n299, 277n336, 277n340
Pravda on engineers and 269
Rykov on 269–270, 269n285, 273–274
as Stalinist show trial 276–278
Tomsky and 215, 267, 270–273, 271n304, 272n311, 273n314, 275, 275n327, 276n335, 386
town of 267n277
trade unions and specialists in 222
trial on 273, 275–277, 275n331
Vyshinsky as judge and 277, 277n338, 277n340
see also specialists
Shelekhes, Yakov 156, 156n240
Shlyapnikov, Alexander 24n77
on arbitration or strikes 226n50
biography on 3n12
on Central Committee 88n159
Central Committee on 113n317, 114n323
Europe emigration by 21n63, 33
Great Purge on 352n248, 355n260, 362–363
image of 82
nepotism and 78n105
on Tomsky 104–105, 111, 111n306, 113–115
Tomsky and 85n139, 96n207, 99n224, 113, 220, 227n50, 261n236, 363, 363n301, 383
Tomsky on 85n139, 87–88, 110
trade unions and 65–66, 71, 78, 78n106, 83n129, 84–85, 87, 114
on Trotsky 229n64
VTsSPS and 78n107, 99, 110
'Workers' Opposition' head as 5, 10n2, 59, 62, 87–88, 88n159, 102, 104–105, 107, 111, 220
Yezhov and 364n309

INDEX 449

Shmidt, Vasily
   accusations on   343, 347–348, 352
   as Commissar of Labour   42, 78, 223n35, 281–282, 293, 339n156
   rightist support by   294
   Stalinists on   293, 293n83
   Tomsky replaced by   111
   trade unions and   42, 78, 223n35, 281–282, 293, 339n156
show trials
   of Anti-Soviet Bloc of Rightists and Trotskyites   361–365, 363n304, 363n306, 365n310
   as first major   276n333, 361
   by Kaganovich   361n293
   on Kamenev   361–362, 362nn295–296
   new Soviet Constitution before   361
   on 'palace coup' and Tomsky   288n55, 339–340, 339nn152–156, 358n278
   Shakhty trial as   276–278
   Sokolnikov and   361, 361n291, 363, 379nn402–403
   of Tomsky deceased   361–362, 362nn295–296
   Tomsky without   314
   Trotskyists in second   379n403
   on Zinoviev   361–362, 361n293
Siberia exile
   as criminal   40–41
   distrust in   39, 39n168
   imprisonment in   6, 10, 16, 20–21, 33–40, 37nn155–156, 43
   Kanatchikov in   40, 40n173
   in Kirensk   37–41, 41n180
   location choice in   36, 36n151
   as political   38, 38n161, 39–41, 39n166
   spouses joining   36–38, 37nn159–160, 38n164
   Tomsky to   20–21, 20nn57–58, 36–40
Sixteenth Party Congress
   Bubnov at   332n113
   demoralization at   318, 340
   during forced collectivisation   315
   during industrialisation   315
   on Rightists   311
   Tomsky after   319–321, 354
   Tomsky humiliation at   315–316, 329, 337
   on trade unions   304n151, 316n11

Sixth Trade-Union Congress   184–185, 184n83, 185nn88–89, 186, 239
Smilga, Ivar   256, 256n206, 258, 329n96
Smirnov, Alexander (Foma)   290, 339
Smirnov, Vasily
   purging of   356n267
   Stalinists on   342–345, 347–348, 363
   on Tomsky   42n185
   Tomsky defending   351, 356, 356n266, 363
Smirnov-Eismont-Tolmachev group   342, 345, 349–350, 355
smychka (alliance)   279, 285n33, 286, 310, 351, 351n235
Socialist Realism   326n78, 327
Sokolnikov, Grigory
   Bukharin and Rykov on   379n402
   Lenin and   153n222
   1926 purge of   246
   as Old Bolshevik   153n222
   on Safarov   154
   show trial and   361, 361n291, 363, 379nn402–403
   Stalin and   242, 242n139, 246, 287n45
   Tomsky and   363
   Turkestan Commission and   117n3, 153–154, 153n218, 153n221
Solzhenitsyn, Alexander   371
Soviet state
   on Basmachi guerrillas   127, 131
   Basmachi guerrillas as anti-   126, 130
   on British general strike   196–197, 212, 296n149
   British Labour government on   176
   British on   191n121, 192
   factory nationalizations by   70n58
   foreign policy of   170n2
   on kulaks   144, 240, 266
   on mass demonstrations   51–52
   Muslim opinions on   128
   on Muslim religion   129–131, 129nn84–85, 130n88
   new Constitution of   361
   on Orthodox Church   129n84
   on Russian settlers   140, 140n141, 140n149, 143–144
   on Stalin   255n204
   of Tashkent   122–123, 126, 126n61, 126n63
   Tomsky and   1–2, 2n6, 59

specialists   214–215, 233, 269, 385
    Central Committee on   98
    Central Committee Plenum on   275, 275n331
    Eleventh Party Congress on   221, 221n23
    informal first person used by   270n296
    Lenin on   90–91
    Russia need of   89–90, 90n167
    Rykov on   91–92, 92n178
    Stalin on   273, 275n330
    Tomsky on   86, 89–90, 222, 270, 274–275, 386–387
    wage disparities for   223
    workers on   72, 84, 221–222, 267–268, 270–271, 271n299, 271n303
    as 'wreckers'   273–274
    see also Shakhty Affair
Stalin, Joseph
    Alliluyeva as wife and   237–238, 238nn116–118, 342, 342n169
    Andreev and   204n202, 266n265, 275, 279, 289
    on British trade unions   188, 188nn106–107, 200–201, 201n175
    on British war scare   252–254, 252n192
    on Bukharin   242n137, 310, 319
    Bukharin on   265–267, 286, 290–291, 290n70, 319, 379–380
    on Central Committee delegates   111, 111n301
    Central Committee for   294
    at Central Committee plenum, April 1928   273–274
    on Chamberlain   253–254, 253n198
    on collective leadership   245, 265, 341n163, 387
    on collectivisation   264, 264n251, 287n42, 317n16, 337–338, 344–345, 365n320, 388
    on confessions   361n292
    dark side of   237–239, 238n114, 239n122, 265, 387
    on famine   344, 344n184
    Fourteenth Party Conference and   243n141
    as General Secretary   159, 159n258
    as 'high-functioning psychopath'   345n190
    images of   80, 217, 230, 247

Kaganovich and   204, 267, 295, 303
Kalinin and   280n3, 288, 288n54
Kamenev on   159n258, 244–245, 245n155, 279
Komsomol of Leningrad and   244, 283–284
    on Komsomolskaia Pravda   284–285, 284n23, 296, 302
on kulaks   265–266, 266n266, 337
land reform and   155n236
Lenin on   235–236, 235n99
on Lenin Testament   236, 236n101
on moderates   255, 267, 279, 387
moderates on   254–255, 255n202
on Muslim religion   130n88
NEP and   267, 279, 280–281, 317
on non-party writing   328, 328n87
office space and   68n48
Old Bolsheviks and   5n14, 236, 273–274, 297, 336n130, 373
opposition to   335–337, 335n129, 336n130, 338n147, 340n157
on Orgburo   157n246
'palace coup' against   288, 288n55, 339–340, 358n278
on pan-Islamism   128n70
on peasantry   286, 286n39
on peasants and agriculture   263–264, 264n254
on peasants and extraordinary measures   215, 278, 287n42
Politburo and   342, 342n172
political skills of   386–387
Pospelov on   359n285
purges of   320, 366n320, 388
radical positions of   264–265
on Right Deviationists   282n15, 293–294, 310n194, 316–317, 358
Rudzutak for   288
Rykov and   58, 245, 255n203, 265–267, 286, 292, 310
Ryutin on   340–341, 340n160, 341n161, 341n164
Ryutin Platform on   341–342
on Safarov   147
seamstress mother of   12, 12n11
self-criticism campaign by   274, 284n27
on Socialist Realism   326n78
Soviet party leaders on   255n204

INDEX 451

Stalinists removed by 294n92
Thirteenth Party Congress and 312, 312n205
Tomskaya and 237–239
against Tomsky 255n201, 274–275, 283–284, 286, 288–289, 288n50, 294, 294n93, 310–311, 315, 315n5, 386
Tomsky and 3, 8, 32n126, 58, 215, 236–239, 245, 245n156, 279
Tomsky and potential assassination of 366, 366n318
as Tomsky friend, former ally 1, 237–239, 283, 333n123, 367
Tomsky on 253–255, 265–266, 279, 289nn62–63, 292, 335n129, 358, 380
on Tomsky suicide 369, 369n333, 379
on trade unions 282, 294
troika including 227–228, 228n57
on Trotsky 237
Trotsky on 252n189, 255n204
at Twelfth Party Congress 155
on United Opposition 256, 256n212
United Oppositionists on 253n197
Voroshilov for 248, 288
War Communism copied by 265–266
Yaroslavsky for 259
Stalin, Svetlana (daughter) 165, 238, 342n169, 375, 375n372
Stalinists
on Bukharin 310–311
economics by 388
at Eighth Trade-Union Congress 282, 295, 309, 386
entrapment by 330, 330nn102–103, 341n161
on families 374, 374n364
fear by 343, 345
grain hunting by 266nn265–266
group against 280, 280n3
at January 1933 Central Committee plenum 350–351
Kalinin as 248, 288, 288n51
over Rightists 280, 280n1
on 'palace coup' 288n55, 339–340, 339nn152–156, 358n278
Politburo for 295–296, 302
Politburo with anti- 280, 280n3
on Right Deviationists 280, 280n1, 310, 358n279

on Rykov 310–311
on Ryutin Platform 340–341, 343, 345–346, 345n191, 346n193, 350
on Shmidt 293, 293n83
on Smirnov, V 342–345, 347–348, 363
Stalin removing 294n92
on Tomsky 263, 263n248, 279, 291–292, 307, 310–311, 348–349
Tomsky on 351
on Tomsky suicide 369, 369n333
on trade unions 297n118, 312–313
trade unions on 311n199
on VTsSPS 318–319
on VTsSPS Presidium 302, 302nn147–148
Stalinist show trial see show trial
State Depository of Precious Metals and Precious Stones 156, 156n238, 156n240
statification of trade unions 64–66, 66n31, 66n34, 96
Lenin for 77–78, 111
Platform of the Ten on 99, 104
Stepanova, Varvara 334–335, 335n128
St. Petersburg Committee 31n118, 43
St. Petersburg industrial complex 11n6, 22, 22n70
strikes
Britain on sympathy 210n241
Citrine on 197–198, 203–204
First Trade-Union Congress on 67
German trade unions failure by 174–175, 175n24
of 1926 249–250, 250n173
Shlyapnikov on 226n50
trade unions and 14, 14nn17–18, 78–79
see also British general strike; right to strike
Subotsky, Lev 331–332, 332n104
suicide
by Alliluyeva 342
Bukharin on 378
Great Purges and 371, 371n351
by Tomsky 1, 3, 56n265, 167n304, 168, 334, 358, 360n288, 364–372, 376–377, 379–380, 389
Supreme Council of the Economy (VSNKh) 68n48, 269n285, 285n33, 286
production and 72, 72nn72–73
Tomsky on 321
syndicalism 26n93, 80n114

Tashkent
- Barmine and 120–121, 120n19, 121nn22–23
- food from 133–134, 133nn107–108, 133nn110–111
- irrigation structures in 135–136, 135n119
- Lenin on 133–134, 134nn110–111
- Moscow and 117n3
- Muslims of 119, 121–130, 132, 136, 139, 141–142, 145–147, 149–151, 153, 155, 168
- population of 123n35
- with Russian enclave 121, 121nn26–27
- Safarov on 124, 127, 137n124, 142
- scientists and scholars of 132, 132nn98–99
- Soviet of 122–123, 126, 126n61, 126n63
- Soviet on Indigenous population 122–126, 123n38, 124nn41–42, 125n49, 125n51
- Tomsky on military and 133
- Tomsky on NEP and 129, 129n80
- Tomsky Russian chauvinism on 119, 130
- Tomsky sent to 117, 120–122, 384
- on trade unions 120n21
- Turkestan and 121
- weather in 122, 122n28
- *see also* Indigenous population

Tenth Party Congress 110n294, 157
- Fourth Trade-Union Conference and 106, 113
- Kronstadt and 103
- on lifestyles 161n267
- Molotov at 113
- Rudzutak at 117n4
- Tomsky and 104, 107n286
- trade-union debate at 100, 104, 113
- on Workers' Opposition 105–106, 106n274

Testament
- Krupskaya and 235nn98–99, 236
- of Lenin 235–236, 235nn97–98
- *Pravda* and 236
- Stalin on Lenin 236, 236n101
- Tomsky on 235, 310
- Trotsky on 236n104, 236n106

Third Congress of the Profintern 179–181

Thirteenth Party Congress 114n323
- Lenin Testament and 236, 236n102
- Stalin and 312, 312n205
- Tomsky and 240n133

Thomas, Jimmy 178, 192, 198–199, 203n190, 329n92
- of IFTU 198n158, 198n160

Tolmachev, Vladimir 342–343, 345, 349–350, 355

Tomskaya, Maria Ivanovna
- death of 374n366
- description of 35–36
- exile joined by 37–38, 37n159
- on illegitimate child 189, 189n112
- imprisonment of 33, 36
- Khrushchev on 374
- necklace for 168, 188–189
- NKVD on 367
- as RSDRP member 32, 37
- Stalin and 237–239
- on Tomsky imprisonment 35
- Tomsky marriage with 15, 20, 162
- on Tomsky suicide 367
- work by 163–164
- Yagoda implicated by 367, 368n326, 368n328
- Yezhov and 367, 372, 374n364

Tomsky, Mikhail
- Artamonov, alias of 29n107
- biography of 117, 117n2
- capitulation and death of 315
- charisma of 4–5, 58
- descriptions of 34–35, 37, 120–121, 165, 165n295, 173, 183, 186, 188
- family of 1, 3, 21, 121–122, 158–162, 161nn269–271, 162n272, 238, 373–376, 373n362, 375n370
- funeral and burial of 370, 370nn344–346
- health of 52–53, 69, 69n57, 195, 304–305, 304n157, 305n159, 321–322, 321n43, 322n52, 322nn48–49, 324–325, 324n67, 325n68, 333, 349n221, 358, 358n282, 380
- images of 46, 64, 80, 88, 90, 152, 162, 182, 189, 217, 247, 249, 260, 335, 360
- personal archive of 3–4, 3n12
- public speaking by 1, 4, 18, 58, 81n118, 186, 263, 348–349, 351, 354
- residence of 372, 372n356, 372nn358–359
- temperament of 5–6, 16, 16n28
- youth of 10–14, 20n50, 381–382
- *see also specific subjects*

INDEX 453

Tomsky, Yury 364, 375–376, 376n375
Trade-Union Commission 98–99, 99n221, 176n33
trade-union debate
  Bolshevik Party on 114
  at Ninth Party Congress 95n202
  at Tenth Party Congress 100, 104, 113
  Tomsky in 59–60, 383
trade unions 222
  Anglo-Russian Committee on British and Soviet 1, 185–186, 187n100, 206n211, 208, 210–211
  bargaining by 220, 220n17
  benefits for 250–251, 250n177
  Bolshevik Party and 21–22, 25n83, 27, 27n95, 61, 79–80
  Central Committee on 98–99, 190, 190n119
  during Civil War 74–75, 80
  with class solidarity and class consciousness 21, 21n65
  collegiality and 84n133, 85, 92n178
  Comintern and forged 'letter' of 191–192, 192n123
  comradely courts of 71–72, 71n68
  Congresses, lack of 312n203
  congresses of 62–65, 62n14, 63nn19–20, 65n25
  cost accounting and 219–220
  at Eighth Trade-Union Congress 282
  factory committees and 44–45, 67–68, 67n42, 68n44
  IFTU on Russian 184–185
  independence of 73–74, 73n76, 74n79–81, 158, 217–218
  Kanatchikov and 21
  on Komsomol of Leningrad 284–285
  legalization and creation of 21–22, 21n64
  membership in 30nn113–114, 70n60
  Mensheviks in 21–22, 26n93, 76
  Moscow Soviet of 62, 68n49
  negotiations for 223, 223nn31–33
  during NEP 216, 220–221, 220n21, 223, 282
  1928 autonomy and power for 281
  office space and 69n50
  on one-man management 83–84, 83n131, 84n133, 84n135

  on output norms 239–240, 388
  of Politburo 301–302, 301n141
  Politburo for 285
  Purcell on Russian 185, 185n89, 257
  Red Army recruits by 70, 74–75, 75nn85–86
  Ryazanov for 60, 65–66, 68, 71n65, 78
  Shlyapnikov and 65–66, 71, 78, 78n106, 83n129, 84–85, 87, 114
  Shmidt and 42, 78, 223n35, 281–282, 293, 339n156
  Sixteenth Party Congress on 304n151, 316n11
  skilled and unskilled workers of 14–15
  on Stalinists 311n199
  Stalinists on 297n118, 312–313
  Stalin on 282, 294
  statification of 64–66, 66n31, 66n34, 77–78, 96, 99, 111
  St. Petersburg industrial complex and 22, 22n70
  strikes and 14, 14n17, 78–79
  subsidies and 219n12
  Tashkent on 120n21
  Tomsky and publishing 8–9, 14, 14n20, 14n22, 15–16
  Tomsky and strike by 14, 14n18
  Tomsky heading 1–3, 4n15, 7, 20, 20n49, 21–22, 68, 71n66, 72–73, 106, 117, 216, 226, 259, 259n226, 281–282, 388
  Tomsky missed by 338
  Tomsky on 30, 63–66, 65n25, 67n38, 67n40, 70, 87–88, 91–94, 114, 161, 385
  Tomsky resignation of 293–294
  Trotsky on 60, 62n11, 81–83, 94, 175, 228nn60–61
  Tsektran on 94–95, 94n193, 95n199
  TUC on assistance and 197–198, 198n156
  United Opposition and support within 257
  on VSNKh 286
  VTsSPS 283
  VTsSPS on independence and 73–74, 73n76, 74n79–81, 78, 218
  wages and 223–224, 224n36, 224n39, 240n130
  workday reductions for 259–260, 259n226, 260n232
  workers and 70, 164n283, 214

Yaroslavsky on   307–308, 308n181
Zinoviev on   51n234, 63–64, 66n36, 68
transliteration   9
Trilisser, Meer   339n153
troika
  of Stalin, Zinoviev, and Kamenev   227–228, 228n57
  Tomsky joining   228–229
  on Trotsky   228, 228n58, 229n71, 230–232, 230nn72–73
  Trotsky on   231, 231n76
Trotsky, Leon
  on Anglo-Russian Committee   209
  on anti-Stalinists   280–281
  autobiography by   3n11
  books on   314n3
  on British trade unions   188, 188nn106–107
  Central Committee on   256n208, 258–259, 258n223, 261–262, 261n234, 261n236, 261n238
  clothes of   165n295
  'Declaration of the 46' for   232–233, 232nn84–86
  on democracy   232, 232n80
  Frunze on   159, 159n253
  image of   88, 217, 227, 254
  Kamenev on   233
  Kanatchikov on   229
  Kuibyshev on   263n249
  for labour militarization   27, 81–83, 83n126, 89n161, 94–95, 97–98, 100, 114, 175, 232–233, 381
  on labour militarization and Central Committee   81–83
  Lenin and   227, 227n56
  after Lenin death   233, 233n88, 233n92
  on 'nominating from above' and 'trade-union debate'   231–232
  as Old Bolshevik   3n11
  on one-man management   89, 94
  oppositional letters by   231–232, 232n82
  on Platform of the Four   242–243, 243n142
  Politburo and   228–229, 228n58, 248n163, 252
  on railways   94
  Rykov and   228n62, 255n203
  on 'scissors crisis'   232, 232n81
  second show trial and   379n403
  Shlyapnikov on   229n64
  on Stalin   252n189, 255n204
  Stalin on   237
  on Testament   236n104, 236n106
  on Tomsky   5, 10, 18, 51, 96, 97n211, 100, 102, 104–105, 114, 210, 318, 318n25, 383
  Tomsky opposition to   7–8, 60, 85, 94, 96, 96n207, 97, 100, 159, 214–215, 263n249
  on Tomsky suicide note   366
  on trade unions   60, 62n11, 81–83, 94, 175, 228nn60–61
  on troika   231, 231n76
  troika on   228, 228n58, 229n71, 230–232, 230nn72–73
  for Tsektran expansion   96
  at Twelfth Party Congress   228, 230n72
  as United Opposition leader   200, 251–252, 251n184
  VTsSPS on   97, 99–100
  for War Communism   96, 96n206
  wife of   164n281
  workers on   103
  Yaroslavsky on   259
  for Zinoviev   202n182, 233
  Zinovievite Opposition and   362–363, 365
tsarist regime
  abdication of   40, 40n172
  Academy of Science from   329, 329n95
  Bolshevik Party after   42–43, 43n190
  on child labor   13n14
  economic decline in   61n10
  1905 Revolution on   196n149
  political trials of   34, 34n138
  on *Pravda*   51
  Red Army and   86n152
  on Social-Democratic movement   16–17
  Tomsky and political police of   10, 20, 29, 29nn107–108, 382
  on Turkestan Indigenous population   124, 124n46
  on worker discontents   18n41
  see also imprisonment
Tsektran   *see* Joint Central Transport Committee
Tsvetaeva, Marina   167n304, 371n354
TUC   *see* British Trades Union Congress

INDEX 455

Turkestan
  cotton in 122–123, 126, 126n57, 129, 134n111, 135–136, 135n113, 135n118, 139n135
  famine in 125–126, 126n57, 149n197
  Kaganovich to 120n19
  land reform results in 139–142, 142nn153–154, 148–149, 149n197, 155
  Lenin on 126–127, 133–134
  as place of exile 119n8
  recall from 117
  RSDRP and Commission on 117n3
  Rudzutak as Bureau head and 117, 127
  Russia and 122–123, 122nn29–30, 124, 124n46, 125–126, 125n51
  Russian chauvinism on 128, 150, 155, 169
  Russia settlers to 138–140, 138nn130–132, 140n141
  Tashkent and 121
  Tomsky sent to 114–116, 116n1, 118–120, 153
  trips to 120, 120n19
  see also Tashkent
Turkestan Commission
  on bride price 131
  on cotton 135
  creation of 127, 127n66, 128
  Kaganovich and 127
  on requisitioning 129, 132
  Sokolnikov and 117n3, 153–154, 153n218, 153n221
  Tomsky chairing 117, 117n3
Twelfth Party Congress 229n71, 231n74
  Stalin at 155
  Tomsky and 231, 240n133
  Trotsky at 228, 230n72

Udalov, A.I 332, 354–355
Uglanov, Nikolai 278, 363
  expelling and execution of 293n81, 346, 346nn194–195
  as Moscow party boss 282, 340n158
  undermining of 292–293, 292n80, 293n83
Ulyanova, Maria 311
unemployment 248, 248n167
  under NEP 224–225, 225n42, 225nn44–45
  of youth 298–299, 298nn125–126

United Opposition
  on Anglo-Russian Committee 207–208
  Bukharin and 55n257, 208
  as crushed 215, 260–261, 292
  Fifteenth Party Conference on 261–262, 274
  Great Purges on 314
  as Left 389
  Old Bolsheviks on 251n184
  Right Deviationists and 362
  Ryutin on 340nn158–159
  Seventeenth Party Congress capitulation by 357n276
  on Stalin 253n197
  Stalin on 256, 256n212
  Tomsky and 207–208, 215, 251–252, 255–256, 255n205, 257–258, 279, 385
  on trade-union support 257
  as Trotsky, Zinoviev, and Kamenev 200, 251–252, 251n184
  VTsSPS and 257, 257n215, 258n218

Voinov, N.I 358–359, 359n283
Voroshilov, Kliment 25n88, 248, 288, 351–352, 352n242
VSNKh see Supreme Council of the Economy
VTsIK see All-Russian Central Executive Committee
VTsSPS see All-Russian Central Council of Trade Unions
VTsSPS Presidium
  Kaganovich on 302
  Radek and 86, 108, 303n150
  Stalinists on 302, 302nn147–148
Vyshinsky, Andrei 277, 277n338, 277n340

wages
  First Five-Year Plan with falling 283n16, 283n19
  levels of 248n168, 251
  Seventh Trade-Union Congress on 248
  for specialists 223
  Tomsky on 240
  trade unions negotiation of 223–224, 224n36, 224n39, 240n130
  VTsSPS on 249, 249n170

War Communism
  on production and workers 219, 221–222, 250, 266, 325n72
  Safarov and 148
  Stalin copying 265–266
  Tomsky against 129, 225–226
  Trotsky for 96, 96n206
war scare
  on British 252–254, 252n192
  peasantry on 254, 264, 264n251
White Armies 74, 79n110, 346
workdays 259–260, 259n226, 260n232
Worker-Peasant Theatre Administration 163–164, 164n281
workers
  Bolshevik Party and 27, 61
  as compulsory 95n196
  economic demonstrations by 103, 103n252, 103n254, 103n256
  education for 23, 23n73
  Eighth Party Congress and control by 79
  as industrial managers 220, 220n18
  Kanatchikov, Bukharin, Tomsky on 16, 16nn29–30
  Kanatchikov as 13–14, 14n19, 15, 15n25, 23
  in labour armies 27, 81–83, 83n123, 83n126, 83n129, 86, 97, 105, 114, 232–233, 381
  in Moscow 55
  Murphy, J., on 232n86
  Narkomtrud for 222–224, 223n35
  Ninth Party Congress resolution on 92, 92n182, 95n202
  one-man management and 83–84, 83n131, 84n133, 84n135
  on output norms 239–240, 388
  party newspaper for 43–44, 43n195
  RKK on 250, 250n175
  Rykov on management and 91–92, 92n178
  Tomsky for 279
  trade unions and 70, 164n283, 214
  tsarist regime on 18n41
  War Communism on 219, 221–222, 250, 266, 325n72
  on youth 299–300, 299nn130–131
  Zinoviev on 51n234, 63–64, 66n36, 68
  see also specialists

Workers' Opposition
  for democratization and trade unions 96, 101
  on economy management 87–88, 101
  on Point Five at Eighth Party Congress 79–80
  Shlyapnikov heading 5, 10n2, 59, 62, 87–88, 88n159, 102, 104–105, 107, 111, 220
  Tenth Party Congress on 105–106, 106n274
  Tomsky and 220, 220n20

Yagoda, Genrikh
  arrest and execution of 368, 368n327, 368n331
  Bukharin on 364n309
  image of 291
  OGPU and NKVD headed by 290, 329n96, 339, 367–368
  on Rightists 339, 367n324
  Rykov and 339n153
  show trial on 365
  Tomskaya implicating 367, 368n326, 368n328
  Tomsky implicated by 337n134, 339, 367–368
  Yezhov on 368, 368n330
Yaroslavsky, Emelyan 259, 304, 307–308, 308n181, 346
Yevdokimov, Yefim 268, 268n281, 277n342
Yezhov, Nikolai
  depositions by 359n285
  Old Bolsheviks on 364, 364n309
  on 'palace coup' 339n155
  Shlyapnikov and 364n309
  Tomskaya and 367, 372, 374n364
  on Tomsky 368, 370n346, 371, 376
  Tomsky suicide and 364, 364n309
  on Yagoda 368, 368n330

Zinoviev, Grigory
  on Anglo-Russian Committee 186–187, 200–201
  biography on 11n4
  Central Committee on 259, 261–262, 261n234, 261n236, 261n238
  as Comintern president 180
  execution of 379, 379n406

forged trade union 'letter' of   191–192, 192n123
image of   217, 230, 254
on Lenin   50, 236
1926 purge and   246
as not erased   56n269
Politburo and   252
popularity lack by   4n13, 180, 180n57
at Seventeenth Party Congress   346n195
show trial on   361–362, 361n293
on Stalin   159n258
St. Petersburg and   24n77
on Tomsky   22, 180, 200–201
Tomsky and   359, 359n284, 361–363, 365, 367
Tomsky on   63–66, 181, 215, 243n143, 367
as Trade-Union Commission chair   98–99, 99n221, 176n33
troika including   227–228, 228n57
Trotsky and   202n182, 233
on unions and workers   51n234, 63–64, 66n36, 68
as United Opposition leader   200, 251–252, 251n184
Zinovievite Opposition   7, 155n229, 194, 243, 246
Trotsky and   362–363, 365

www.ingramcontent.com/pod-product-compliance
Lightning Source LLC
Chambersburg PA
CBHW071226070526
44583CB00017B/2073